A COLONIAL COMPLEX

A Colonial Complex

SOUTH CAROLINA'S
FRONTIERS IN THE ERA
OF THE YAMASEE WAR,
1680–1730

Steven J. Oatis

University of Nebraska Press
Lincoln and London

∞

Portions of chapters 2 and 4 were previously
published in " 'To Eat Up a Village of White
Men': Anglo-Indian Designs on Mobile and
Pensacola," in *The Gulf South Historical
Review* 14, no. 1 (Fall 1998), 104–19, and are
reprinted with permission.

Library of Congress Cataloging-in-
Publication Data
Oatis, Steven J. 1970–
A colonial complex: South Carolina's
frontiers in the era of the Yamasee War,
1680–1730 / Steven J. Oatis.
p.   cm.
Includes bibliographical references and index.
ISBN 0-8032-3575-5 (cl.: alk. paper)
1. Yamassee Indians—Wars.   2. South Carolina—
History—Colonial period, ca. 1600–1775.
3. South Carolina—Historical geography.   I. Title.
F272.O18   2004
975.7'02—dc22
2004010596

For Amy, Lilly, and Dad

Contents

Acknowledgments

In researching, planning, and writing this book, I have benefited from the advice, inspiration, and comfort of a number of individuals and organizations. My interest in the Yamasee War was first piqued in a graduate seminar at Emory taught by John Juricek. From that point on, he offered expert guidance as I worked a seminar paper into a dissertation. I could not have asked for a better advisor, not only for his vast knowledge on the colonial Southeast, but also for his patience with the wild and crazy ideas that I would come up with from time to time. Other scholars were also generous in sharing their advice at various stages of the project, particularly Greg Nobles, Michael Bellesiles, Steve Hahn, Elizabeth Fox-Genovese, Eugene Genovese, Lara Smith, Nick Proctor, Margaret Storey, Bobby Donaldson, Hyman Rubin, James Merrell, David Rayson, William Ramsey, and John Worth. I would also like to thank the staffs of the South Carolina Department of Archives and History and the P. K. Young Library of Florida History at the University of Florida in Gainesville for their valuable assistance in making sense of some important documents. Financial support from the American Historical Association's Michael Kraus Grant and Emory University's Mellon Fellowship in Southern Studies also proved to be of great assistance. More recently I have benefited from the unparalleled environment of the University of the Ozarks, where colleagues and students alike continue to stoke my passion for history and my enthusiasm for being part of a place with so many sharp minds and warm hearts. Stuart Stelzer, the university librarian, was especially helpful with all my interlibrary loan requests. I am grateful to the University of Nebraska Press for introducing me to the world of academic publishing. And finally I have always drawn and will continue to draw on the love and support of family. I never cease to hope that my mother, stepfather, stepmother, brother, grandparents, and in-laws (and cats!) know how much they mean to me. The same goes thousandfold for my wife, Amy. This whole book is for her and also for my baby daughter, Lillian, who is nestled in my arms as I write this. This book is also dedicated to the memory of my father, who certainly would have liked reading it.

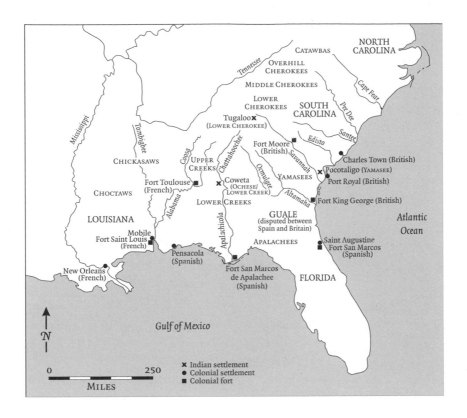

The North American Southeast in the Era of the Yamasee War

A COLONIAL COMPLEX

Introduction

THE SOUTHEASTERN
FRONTIER COMPLEX

When Thomas Nairne went to sleep on the eve of Good Friday, 1715, he had no idea that he would wake to star in his own passion play. Nairne, one of the most prominent and influential residents of the British colony of South Carolina, spent the night in the Yamasee Indian village of Pocotaligo, a few miles inland from Port Royal Sound. Though South Carolinians had begun to hear disturbing rumors of Indian discontent, Nairne considered the Yamasees to be old friends and loyal allies and felt entirely capable of appeasing them in the name of the provincial government. Nairne's small circle of fellow ambassadors put great stock in his abilities; in their eyes he was a highly respected soldier, trader, scholar, planter, and gentleman who knew more about the Indians than did any white man in South Carolina. Most of the Yamasees, however, had gradually come to see Nairne as a leader of an irredeemable collection of bullies, trespassers, and slave mongers. On the morning after the South Carolinians' latest assurances of friendship, a parcel of Yamasee warriors burst into Nairne's lodgings and dragged him to Pocotaligo's town square, where they tied him to a post and pierced his body with burning splinters of wood. While most of his colleagues died quickly in their bedrolls, it probably took Nairne several agonizing hours—and perhaps days—to meet his end.

The murders at Pocotaligo quickly mushroomed into one of the most disruptive and unsettling conflicts in the history of colonial North America. Before the alarm could spread, the Yamasees killed most of the British traders among them and raided several of South Carolina's most prosperous coastal parishes, sacking plantations and killing more than a hundred colonists and slaves. Within weeks they were joined by a number of other disgruntled Indian societies that appeared intent on driving the remaining South Carolinians into the sea. Despite swift and successful countermeasures from the South Carolina militia, by late summer the colony's prospects seemed grim. Terrified sentries faced the threat of renewed Indian invasion from nearly every direction, women and children began to starve in the streets of a fortified Charles Town, and help proved slow to arrive from the homeland and other British colonies. Only after a timely alliance with the powerful Cherokee Indians in early 1716 did most South Carolinians allow themselves to breathe a little easier. By the time the last of the colony's major Indian foes withdrew from the conflict in the fall of 1717, the South Carolinians had already embarked on the slow and uncertain process of repairing their severely shaken economy, diplomacy, and sense of security.

Most Americans have probably never heard of the Yamasee War, but it has rarely failed to spark at least some interest among those who have. The war not only constituted one of the American Indians' most serious challenges to the dominance of European colonists, but it also stands as one of the most significant episodes in the colonial history of the North American Southeast. While inherently intriguing to anyone with an interest in the histories of early America and European-Indian relations, the Yamasee War also contains epic doses of heroism, scandal, treachery, and revenge. Not surprisingly the Yamasee War has provided inspiration for dramatists as well as historians.

In the mid-1830s one young and ambitious author chose to approach the Yamasee War from both a historical and a literary perspective. *The Yemassee: A Romance of Carolina* (1835) was William Gilmore Simms's attempt to glorify his home state in the popular style of Sir Walter Scott and James Fenimore Cooper. As Simms saw it, the Yamasee War boiled down to a noisy and dramatic collision between two incompatible worlds. Simms instilled his Indians with a bit more complexity than the noble savages of Cooper, but he had no trouble concluding that their way of life had to give way before the advance of the South Carolinians, who—led by a core of chivalrous, highborn characters— managed to triumph over the impediments laid down by crude traders, Spanish spies, and other base-hearted colonists. According to Simms, the triumph of a gentrified English civilization over barbarism marked the defining event of South Carolina's history and even the history of the entire South as a region.[1]

Simms continues to draw praise as one of the United States' most significant writers of the Romantic era, but his reputation as a historian of the early South has withered over the years. Since Simms's day, however, there have been remarkably few attempts to understand the Yamasee War and its role in shaping the early development of South Carolina. When American history textbooks mention the Yamasee War at all, they afford it little more than a few lines, and even more specialized works tend to gloss over it. Synopses and broad generalizations about the Yamasee War are no longer difficult to find, but anyone looking to swim in deeper waters is bound to find them murky at best. Nearly thirty years ago one of the foremost scholars of colonial South Carolina lamented that the history of the Yamasee War "has never been adequately pieced together."[2] Despite some valuable contributions to the historiography over the last several decades, this judgment still rings true, and those in search of the war's deeper ramifications have to look to scattered and less accessible sources.

Though often difficult to interpret and analyze, these sources indicate quite clearly that the Yamasee War did not simply amount to Indians and colonists offending each other, betraying each other, and killing each other. The carnage of the colonial Southeast's most violent Indian war was merely one, short-lived form of expression of the numerous, long-standing ties that connected the region's distinct and contesting groups of people. Greater appreciation of the causes and consequences of this intense conflict requires a long, hard look at a lengthy period.

During the era of the Yamasee War, three European empires and dozens of Native American societies attempted to assert their own ideas and interests within the vaguely defined areas where they impinged on one another. Such intermediary zones necessarily gave rise to interaction between different peoples and cultures. Here at first there were no rules or rulers acknowledged by all concerned: no universal standards, no established laws, no ultimate appeal, no official truth, no single hierarchy of anything. Stability, when it came at all, was usually fleeting and often came at tremendous cost to one group or another. Within these zones all was in flux and all were at risk, no more so than in the half-century after 1680. Careful study of these fluctuations—some gradual, some dramatic—is essential to understanding the Yamasee War in its proper historical context.

The idea of linking the Yamasee War to these kinds of changes is not a new one. More than seventy-five years ago, historian Verner Crane wrote what is widely considered the most authoritative treatment of the Yamasee War as a twenty-five page chapter of The Southern Frontier, 1670–1732 (1928). Crane's eloquent prose, thorough research, and path-breaking scope have established his work as a classic in American historiography, giving it great influence in the study of Indian-white relations in the early colonial Southeast. For all its obvious merits, however, Crane's book is neither infallible nor exhaustive. While it remains a compelling treatment of Britain's imperial strategy in the North

American Southeast, it leaves many key aspects of the "southern frontier" unexplained.

Any critique of this important work would have to begin with Crane's understanding of the "frontier," a concept that seemed deceptively simple, even intuitive, to most of his generation. Crane's take on frontiers was based firmly on that of Frederick Jackson Turner, the man who had helped train him as a historian during the early years of the twentieth century. Turner's brief, eloquent, and phenomenally influential treatise on "The Frontier in American History" (1893) essentially defined the concept as the outer edge of a "wave" of European American settlement making its way through a hostile, character-building wilderness. Turner argued that the patterned phases of westward expansion—from trapper, to trader, to farmer, to merchant, and so on—had molded a uniquely American quality of progress, persistence, and democratic individualism.[3] While Turner and his generations of disciples never completely ignored the importance of the peoples on the other side of the advancing frontier, they clearly afforded these peoples much less attention and consideration than they deserve. When Crane concisely depicted his southern frontier as a zone of European influence "merging into the wilderness," he showed little appreciation for the complex and diverse Indian societies that had inhabited the region for centuries. Crane acknowledged that the Indians—or rather, "a sphere of influence over the Indian tribes"—formed an important part of the frontier, but he held that as this frontier expanded, it did so in only one direction.[4]

For the last forty or so years, Turner's frontier thesis has taken its lumps, especially from a generation of critics more attuned to its obvious ethnocentrism. Though Crane remains less well known than Turner, his epic work on the early colonial Southeast is subject to similar attacks. But over the years the best critics of the Turner school of frontier historiography have done more than simply wave the banner of cultural relativism. More significantly these revisionists have worked toward alternative models to help students wrestle with questions and themes similar to those that occupied the Turner school: the dynamics of migration and settlement, intercultural contact, cultural ecology, and cultural change. In building a more nuanced and sophisticated understanding of frontiers, a recent generation of scholarship has cast a new light on important topics that once seemed so cut-and-dried.

The most forceful challenge to the Turner thesis has developed in the past twenty or so years among historians working with the North American West, a section of the continent more steeped than any other in frontier myths and legends. For Patricia Nelson Limerick, Donald Worster, William Cronon, and other "New Western historians," the Turnerian view of an advancing frontier line is too static, predictable, and triumphal to do justice to a history that they see as a patchwork of racial, class, and ecological conflicts, many of which remain relevant to the North American West to this day. The New Western historians share an aversion to the very word "frontier," believing that more than a century of misuse and oversimplification has rendered it all but meaningless. Instead, they choose to work within the conceptual framework of "region," staking out a broad geographic space and observing the salient conflicts and innovations that have taken place within it. By highlighting such topics as labor activism, ethnic identity, water usage, and immigration quotas, these historians have helped depict a West far more diverse, dynamic, and contentious than the one defined by dime novels, John Wayne movies, and older frontier histories.[5]

Significantly the "regional" methodology of the New Western historians can also be applied to regions outside the West. In *The Indian Slave Trade: The Rise of the English Empire in the American South, 1670–1717* (2002), the first comprehensive study of the Southeast in the late seventeenth and early eighteenth centuries since Crane's *Southern Frontier*, historian Alan Gallay tackles the interaction between diverse groups of European colonists, Native Americans, and African slaves and discerns a regionwide pattern of social and economic exploitation driven by the English South Carolinians through their successful trade, diplomatic aggression, and enslavement of racial "others." Gallay, like Crane, includes a section on the Yamasee War as part of his narrative. Unlike Crane, however, Gallay treats the Yamasee War less as an outgrowth of an advancing South Carolina frontier than as a milepost on the way to the racially cast, plantation-based society that would serve as the basis for the more familiar "Old South" of the nineteenth century.[6]

Gallay and other New Western historians who would study the Yamasee War as an episode in "region making" tend to distance themselves from the Turnerian view that intercultural contact and conflict can be consigned to any single, overarching model. Their cautionary points about the potential pitfalls of frontier studies are well taken, but their outright rejection of the Turner thesis is excessive. In their eagerness to debunk the myths of the "frontier," these revisionists turn away from a concept that, if qualified properly, remains the best and most concise way to express a historical process of profound importance to early America in general and to the early colonial Southeast in particular.

Unlike the New Western historians, "New Indian historians" such as James

Axtell, James Merrell, Daniel Usner, and Daniel Richter have immersed themselves in the study of frontier relationships. In the past thirty or so years, these and other like-minded scholars have demonstrated that the concept of the frontier popularized by Turner and Crane—while undeniably rigid and ethnocentric—is valuable in its ability to evoke both process and place. Turner and Crane correctly contended that wherever European Americans moved up against unfamiliar cultural and ecological environments, they changed, and were in turn changed by, these environments. What Turner and Crane failed to grasp adequately was the complexity of this process, not only insofar as it shaped the character of Europeans, but also as it challenged and changed human cultures that had some very different needs and priorities from those of Europeans. In contrast the New Indian historians have looked to a wide range of archival and anthropological sources in order to analyze the meaning of intercultural contact, interaction, and conflict for all groups involved. Their efforts have resulted in a far more nuanced and satisfying usage of "frontier" than the usage of old, defining the concept not as an advancing line of civilization against emptiness or savagery but as a broader geographic zone in which various groups of people traded with, lived with, fought with, and ultimately changed one another.[7]

In this book I embrace the definition of "frontier" that has been reshaped by the New Indian history. I find the term to be the most concise and historically grounded way to evoke the interaction of distinct cultures in a context of undefined power relations; such alternative terms as "human ecotone" and "zone of interpenetration" not only are cumbersome but also are absent from primary historical sources.[8] Like Verner Crane I believe that the process of frontier interaction is the key to understanding the Yamasee War and its historical importance. I also share Crane's conclusion that the English colonists of South Carolina acted as the most forceful catalysts for many of the Southeast's frontier relationships. Unlike Crane, however, I emphasize that the frontier history of South Carolina and its surrounding region always depended on various forms of "exchange" between more than one culture. Though one culture in a frontier relationship could always pick and choose the traits that it wanted to adopt from another, extensive contact and interaction could often bring about unwanted or unintended cultural transformations, a phenomenon that James Axtell has described as "reactive change."[9] Such transformations tended to appear in situations where one culture began to overpower the other and tended to be most visible within the culture that faced the most outside pressure. But as long as there remained at least some possibility for effective resistance or confrontation, the process of reactive change could continue to cut both ways. The importance of each competing culture in a frontier relationship therefore compels frontier scholars to study the outlooks and motivations of each side as thoroughly as possible.

While frontier studies in the mold of Turner and Crane fall notably short of the mark in this respect, they are open to criticism on another front as well: their tendency to minimize the variety of the "frontier experience." Since no one in the early colonial period could precisely define the borders of South Carolina, provincial officials actually claimed authority over most of the territory south of Virginia and east of the Mississippi River. As a result of their territorial ambitions and their demands for creating profitable enterprises, the new South Carolinians were forced into relationships with racial and ethnic groups that many of them would rather have avoided. The demands of mercantilism and imperial rivalry locked them into competition with different groups of fellow Europeans: the Spanish in Florida, the French in the Lower Mississippi Valley, the Scots around Port Royal, and even the English in Virginia. To cultivate the crops on their plantations, South Carolinians imported a growing number of black slaves from Africa and the West Indies. Above all, their colony's very expansion into the terra incognita of the southeastern interior depended in large part on the aid and cooperation of the Muskogean, Iroquoian, and Siouan cultural groups that had inhabited and shaped this territory long before the arrival of Old World peoples. Some of these different groups shared certain characteristics that allowed South Carolinians to confront them more easily, but for the most part each group remained distinct enough to demand its own brand of give-and-take. The further South Carolinians' economic and political influence expanded during the early eighteenth century, the more unrealistic it became for them to lump all their various allies and adversaries into a single frontier relationship.

South Carolinians in the era of the Yamasee War engaged different cultures not along a single "southern frontier" but within what historian Jack Forbes has called a "frontier complex." This term he defines as "a multiplicity of frontiers in dynamic interaction."[10] Forbes' concept, unlike Turner's, invites attention to the cultural diversity that characterized the Southeast in the late seventeenth and the early eighteenth century. Moreover, it offers a convenient way to combine the cultural dynamics of "frontier" with the broader geographic implications of "region," thereby serving as a kind of link between the New Western and the New Indian histories. Finally the notion of a frontier complex also encourages a more careful focus on frontier relationships in which the

English colonists of South Carolina did not play direct roles. As important and dominant as the English eventually became, they could not begin to control or apprise themselves of all that transpired in the region. As a result historians guided by Anglocentric impulses run the risk of missing as much as did the English colonists themselves.

The concept of the southeastern frontier complex therefore allows for a more complete and balanced picture of South Carolina's various frontier relationships. Even so it presents some significant challenges. From the comfort of modern desks and chairs, it is often easy to underestimate both the vastness and the fluidity of the early colonial Southeast. Few of the region's Indian and colonial societies lived in close proximity to one another, and the forces that bound them together often had to cut across several hundred miles of difficult terrain. Today a traveler can go overland from Charleston, South Carolina, to the Lower Chattahoochee River in less than seven hours; in 1700 the same trip often took two or three weeks.

Despite these distances, however, the Indians and the Europeans of the early colonial Southeast often went to great lengths to keep in touch with the groups around them. Just as no southeastern society remained entirely isolated from the outside world, no southeastern frontier was allowed to develop or evolve in a vacuum. In exploring the nuances of a particular frontier, it is important to keep sight of its connections to other frontiers in the region. Even as this book branches out into different, far-flung directions, its overall task remains a synthetic one: to integrate insights about numerous intercultural relationships into a general interpretation of the lengthy power struggle that resulted from South Carolina's incursions into the Southeast.

The frontier transformations of the early colonial Southeast unfolded simultaneously on a number of levels, from the deeply personal to the utterly mysterious. Events that altered the map of the Southeast often had their roots in intimate relations between small groups of people, where basic human emotions like love, trust, jealousy, and fear could have deep and rippling effects on one society's connections to another. The wide-sweeping themes associated with frontier exchange and imperial rivalry had profound and often tragic impacts on human beings who were every bit as real and imperfect as we are. At the same time, however, these themes also involved forces, patterns, and customs that operated far beyond the control of any single person. Whenever individuals and cultures interacted with one another, they opened doors—both voluntarily and involuntarily—to the exchange of everything from biological substances to manufactured goods to revolutionary ideas.

In recent years frontier historians have focused on a wide variety of topics, thereby depicting frontier exchange as a multifaceted process involving all kinds of actors and motives.[11] But in a study examining frontier exchange as a protracted power struggle that changed the shape and extent of entire societies, certain aspects of the exchange process warrant more emphasis than others. Generally speaking, the interaction between Indian and colonial polities in the early Southeast most often hinged on the three closely related themes of trade, combat, and diplomacy. While diplomatic history can occasionally come across as a rigidly Eurocentric discipline, it is perfectly possible to discuss trade, combat, and diplomacy in a way that remains sensitive to the different perspectives and passions of different groups. Indeed, this kind of sensitivity is essential in the study of diplomatic relations between peoples who often espoused markedly different views of the world.

For example, colonial North America was home to two dramatically opposing visions of European-Indian warfare. In the late seventeenth and early eighteenth centuries, Europeans and Indians both viewed warfare as an important part of life and a potent expression of deeply ingrained values. Although the process of frontier exchange inspired Europeans and Indians to borrow a great deal from each other in terms of weapons and tactics, the two groups always clung to some distinct ideas about how war should work. For the most part European governments of the day had developed a highly linear view of warfare. In their eyes wars were *exceptional* situations: no matter how intense or costly, they always came to an end sooner or later. Ordinarily European governments waged war with definite territorial, diplomatic, or commercial goals in mind and ended their conflicts through written and officially recognized treaties. For most southeastern Indian societies, however, war was a permanent part of a dualistic worldview: a "red" state of violence that always coexisted with a "white" state of peace. Most societies had designated towns and leaders who had the more or less permanent job of waging war against enemies. Though a certain group of Indians might not always decide to fight exactly the same enemies from year to year, it was almost certain that they would be fighting *someone* every year, usually during the summer. Warfare was a cyclical, ever-present part of Indian life, as essential to a community's existence as an annual harvest. Not surprisingly southeastern Indian warriors did not always conform to the expectations of colonial governments.

Because colonists found it so difficult to understand these foreign cultures, they were often prone to oversimplification or exaggeration when attempting to analyze Indian behavior. As a result historians who have relied too much on the colonists' perceptions of the Indians have done little more than give new life to old misconceptions. This mistake is especially apparent in what has long been the conventional wisdom about the outbreak of the Yamasee War. By parroting early South Carolinian rhetoric of a universal Indian "conspiracy," scholars have misrepresented both the nature and the extent of the province's wartime opposition. The notion of a regionwide conspiracy not only attributes too much foresight and cohesion to the various groups of Indians that turned against South Carolina in the spring of 1715, but it also blurs the identity of these Indian combatants. Some of the Southeast's Indian societies proved far more active than others in fueling the Yamasee War and had far more at stake in its outcome. Some fought the South Carolinians to the bitter end; some fought only briefly, belatedly, or half-heartedly; some switched sides in midcourse; some tried to stay out of the maelstrom altogether. Though many of the confused, frightened, and desperate South Carolinians were initially inclined to see all the region's Indians as traitors and conspirators, historians interested in a more accurate picture of the Yamasee War must account for the diversity and complexity of Indian cultures in the early colonial Southeast.

The necessity of drawing more accurate distinctions among the combatants and noncombatants of the Yamasee War requires a general overview of the ethnicity and political organization of the southeastern Indians. Most historical treatments of South Carolina's early frontiers have tended to gloss over internal differences and transformations within Indian societies by lumping these groups into static, easily discernible "tribes." The main problem for those scholars who seek to move beyond such vague and unsatisfying labels is that ethnohistorical evidence for the Indians' cultural and political connections often proves scanty and ambiguous. Though I have had some success in distinguishing certain Indian groups from others, this study occasionally makes use of conventional labels that probably homogenize groups that were actually distinct.

The most serious pitfall here is the potential for describing situations and affiliations that had yet to emerge. This type of counterhistorical mistake is most frequently made in regard to the "Creeks," an influential but extremely malleable group whose origins are only beginning to be pieced together by historians and archaeologists. While it begins to make sense to speak of a Lower Creek or Upper Creek confederacy for the 1720s and 1730s, such terminology simply does not hold up for the 1680s and 1690s, a time when many of the Creeks' forebears were scattered across different parts of the Southeast and living under markedly different circumstances. Consequently, I make a conscious effort to avoid referring to these Indians as "Creeks" until I reach a point in time when the concept of a Creek nation is more justifiable. In the first several chapters, readers will see these proto-Creeks described either as "Muskogeans" to denote their ethnic/linguistic background or as any number of other names (e.g., Ocheses, Tallapoosas, Abeikas, and Apalachicolas) to denote their localized political affiliations. My use of different names and descriptors throughout this book is intended not to blur an already complicated picture but to underscore the point that the Southeast's Indian polities changed a great deal during the late seventeenth and early eighteenth centuries as a result of their interaction with other groups. Such interaction was most intense and such change most extensive during the Yamasee War.

On the whole the nomenclature seems far more straightforward in respect to the various European societies of the early colonial Southeast. When examining the region's rival colonial "empires," however, it is important to remember that they, like the Indians, were also subject to important transformations and internal divisions. In many ways the English—the "British" following the 1707 Act of Union between England and Scotland—remained the most factious of the Southeast's three colonial powers. While disputes and discrepancies frequently strained the relations between different English provinces, they also arose between subjects of the same province. Until 1729 North and South Carolina officially comprised a single colony owned by a small group of aristocratic proprietors based in England. Nevertheless, the residents of the northern and southern sections of Carolina were effectively divided in origin, ambition, and orientation throughout the entire colonial period. From the day they laid out the first crude streets of Charles Town in 1670, there was something distinct about the colonists who gradually expanded this small enclave and forged a common identity as South Carolinians.

The growing commonality between these colonists depended in large part on their ability to fend off the real or imagined challenges of groups they deemed threatening. South Carolina covered a huge section of European maps of the Southeast, but only a small percentage of its residents were seen as "South Carolinians." As South Carolinian merchants, traders, planters, soldiers, and officials sought to expand their influence over the unsettled areas of their perceived domain, they had to confront numerous Indian, African, and European "outsiders" who had their own views on South Carolina's boundaries. Though rarely acknowledged by British cartographers, these views were essential to the *real* map of an expanding South Carolina. It is to the task of redrawing and interpreting this map that this book turns its attention.

1. Builders and Borrowers

SOUTH CAROLINA'S EARLY

FRONTIER EXPANSION

Well before its first colonists stepped ashore, Carolina existed as a name on English maps. As early as 1629, the term was used to identify a vast portion of the North American Southeast that stretched south from Virginia to the Florida peninsula and west from the Atlantic Ocean to the Pacific. Though the English Civil War temporarily prevented the settlement of this province, the restoration of the monarchy in 1660 allowed the country's wealthiest and most powerful men to return their attention to the business of colonization. In 1663 King Charles II issued a new royal charter that confirmed Carolina's extensive boundaries and granted control of the province to eight of his closest friends and supporters. These Lords Proprietors of Carolina soon authorized several voyages of exploration to ascertain the best ways to start settling, subduing, and exploiting their new colonial possession.[1]

Even after the English began to learn more about the most promising portion of Carolina, there remained far more to the province than met the eye. What the English initially saw as virgin, untapped territory was actually a region that had housed a multitude of large, distinct, and well-developed cultures for hundreds of years. Many of these powerful and rapidly changing Indian societies had developed strong connections to the Spanish, who had enjoyed an extensive colonial regime in the region since the mid-sixteenth century. As the first English residents of South Carolina studied and revised their maps, few of them bothered to notice that their province had already given rise to an elaborate frontier complex.

Soon, however, the South Carolinians began to appreciate the extensiveness and importance of the Southeast's preexisting frontiers. As the South Carolinian fortune seekers of the late seventeenth century set their sights further and further afield, they realized that they would not have to delve into completely uncharted territory. South Carolina's early frontiersmen encountered, not groups of ignorant savages in an unspoiled state of nature, but groups of indigenous people who had—to varying degrees—already been shaped, damaged, and inspired by extended intercultural contact. Though the South Carolinians initially stood out as neophytes in the region, it did not take long for them to start constructing a commercial and military network that both reflected and fueled their drive for more wealth and power. Once the South Carolinians discovered that they could follow lines that were already in place, they began to plunge along a course that promised to intensify the process of frontier exchange within the vast expanse of territory that they claimed for their own.

The Making and Breaking of the Spanish Monopoly

Prior to the onset of colonization in the early sixteenth century, the Southeast was dominated by the Mississippian cultural complex, a collection of Native American civilizations that at various times extended from the Mississippi River Valley through much of present-day Alabama, Georgia, South Carolina, and Florida. Mississippian societies flourished in the Southeast for nearly a thousand years and developed into the largest and most institutionally sophisticated cultures in eastern North America. The ability to supplement hunting and gathering techniques with the cultivation of corn, beans, squash, and other vegetables allowed Mississippian settlements to sustain relatively dense populations, occasionally reaching totals that numbered in the tens of thousands. The political organization of the Mississippians tended to be more centralized than elsewhere in Native North America and often had close associations with their prevailing religious beliefs. Most of their individual settlements were protected by palisades and could act with some autonomy, but they were usually grouped along with neighboring settlements into chiefdoms presided over by hereditary lines of powerful ruler-priests. Though all Mississippian chiefdoms were characterized by centers of social, military, economic, and political coordination, even the strongest of polities remained subject to significant change over time, often undergoing cycles of consolidation and fragmentation.[2]

By the early sixteenth century, most Mississippian cultures of the Southeast had already declined from the pinnacles of population and political cohesiveness that they had reached several centuries earlier. Nevertheless, the Indian societies of the late Mississippian period remained large and powerful enough to impress some newcomers to the region. Much of what is known about these indigenous cultures comes from the Spanish explorers who marched through the Southeast in search of golden empires to rival those of Mexico and Peru.

While they preserved important records of Mississippian culture for posterity, the Spanish settlements and *entradas* of the sixteenth century likely hastened the downfall and dispersal of most of the region's chiefdoms. Many of these polities sustained devastating losses in battles against Hernando de Soto's well-armed, six-hundred-man expedition through the Southeast between 1539 and 1543. One noted scholar of the Mississippian Southeast has estimated that the Gulf Coast chiefdom of Mabila lost between twenty-five hundred and five thousand people in a single disastrous encounter.[3]

The Spanish explorers failed in their attempts to conquer the Mississippian chiefdoms by force of arms, but they ultimately proved much more destructive by bringing European diseases to the region. The expeditions of de Soto, Narváez, de Luna, and Pardo, along with Lucas Vázquez de Ayllón's short-lived colony on the Carolina coast, all spread Old World pathogens like measles, typhus, mumps, and influenza among "virgin soil" populations that had built no natural immunities to these diseases. Once introduced to the Indians, the diseases could extend rapidly over great distances, lying dormant for some time and periodically erupting into devastating epidemics that, in some cases, wiped out entire villages.[4] Unfortunately death by alien disease was not a fleeting trend in the Southeast; by the mid-sixteenth century, it had settled in for an extended stay and would only worsen with the increase of trade and intercultural contact over the next two hundred years.[5] The growth of new colonial enclaves, such as the Spanish settlement founded at Saint Augustine in 1565, replenished the pipeline of deadly microbes and ensured that even groups that went temporarily unaffected would eventually have to come to grips with new, invisible killers.

Even without precise mortality statistics, it is clear that these epidemics constituted a crisis of apocalyptic proportions and became a major catalyst for the great cultural changes that swept through most southeastern societies in the sixteenth and seventeenth centuries.[6] Disease had a drastic impact on the populations of most Indian polities, and the sharp decline in population density forced most societies to work out new ways of delegating political and social authority. As the fairly large and cohesive chiefdoms of the Mississippian period gave way to smaller and more dispersed polities commonly referred to as "towns," leaders lost the ability to coerce residents of their own and other settlements and instead sought to rule by persuading all politically active residents to reach a consensus. These newly fashioned societies, while lacking the centralized trappings of Mississippian chiefdoms, maintained a sociopolitical structure that could be quite rigid in its own way. Nearly all the smaller Indian societies that began to coalesce throughout the seventeenth-century Southeast divided themselves into a number of distinct clans, extended kinship networks that rooted their identity in a common animal or natural force. The wind, bear, raccoon, and mountain lion clans were among the most common southeastern clans and existed in various towns throughout the region. Individual Indians paid strict homage to the rules and social mores of their clans, which probably provided them with the degree of social cohesiveness that was necessary for building new societies out of the ashes of old ones.[7]

More than 150 years after their first disastrous contacts with Europeans, most of the Southeast's fractured Indian societies were gradually stabilizing and regrouping into enclaves based loosely on ethnicity or shared cultural fragments held over from the Mississippian period. As archeologist Marvin T. Smith has demonstrated in a study detailing the collapse of the Coosa chiefdom into smaller and more loosely affiliated towns, the seventeenth century was a period of especially significant migration.[8] In the fertile valleys of the Coosa, Tallapoosa, and Chattahoochee rivers, the towns of Coweta, Cussita, Tuckabatchee, and Abeika found themselves jostling for territory with Oconee, Ocmulgee, Apalachicola, and other towns of Hitichi stock. The people of these towns, like the vast majority of Indian societies in the early colonial Southeast, were part of the Muskogean language group. Hitichi speakers belonged to the southern division of the Muskogean branch, while Coweta, Cussita, Tuckabatchee, and Abeika spoke a language that corresponded to the northern division of the Muskogean branch. Though the various dialects from these two divisions shared some distant connections, they were not closely related.[9] By the late seventeenth century, the towns in the Coosa, Tallapoosa, and Chattahoochee basins were being joined by groups that traveled even greater distances and spoke even stranger languages: the Alabamas, forced east by the powerful and aggressive Choctaws; the Koasatis, forced south by the Cherokees and a gun-toting group of raiders known as the Westoes; and the Yuchis, whose tongue and origins were nearly indecipherable to most of the other Indians.[10]

The interaction between different Indian groups was becoming increasingly complex throughout the seventeenth century, but the direction taken by these protean societies was also strongly affected by European newcomers. While European weapons and diseases had sparked many of the Indians' cultural and political transformations, the continued presence of European colonists along the fringes of the region foreshadowed further interaction with the natives of the Southeast. Though many Indians would go a long time without seeing a white face, most would feel the direct or indirect effects of a colonial regime even before the most aggressive colonists—the English—set foot in the region.

Before 1670 the Spanish were the only Europeans to establish a durable presence in the Southeast. Following the expeditions and failed settlements of the early and mid-sixteenth century, the Spanish managed to crush some tentative French outposts in the 1560s and establish more tenable enclaves of their own, most notably at Saint Augustine on the Atlantic coast. Their new colony of Florida, which appeared to possess few exploitable resources, seemed destined to play the role of poor sibling to Spain's other, more profitable American possessions. In 1565 King Philip II acknowledged that Florida's only value to the empire would lie in protecting Caribbean shipping lanes from Dutch, French, and English pirates. [11] Though their colony was practically worthless from an economic standpoint, officials in Saint Augustine soon discovered that they would have ample opportunity to fulfill another part of Spain's professed imperial agenda: the propagation of the Catholic faith.

The southeastern Indians had proved resistant to military coercion, but optimistic officials hoped to integrate them into the empire by more peaceful means. Despite suffering from various epidemics, the Southeast's indigenous population compared favorably to that of some other parts of the Spanish empire, where reduction had been even more drastic. In seeking to bring the trappings of their faith and culture to the Indians of Florida, the Spanish could draw on a model that had achieved considerable success in Mexico. They decided to construct a series of missions near or within existing Indian villages and staff them with a number of resident and itinerant priests. After a few years of experimentation with Jesuit priests, Florida's governor sent out a call to the enthusiastic Franciscans, who in the early 1570s set to work constructing and supervising dozens of missions that extended further and further from Spain's coastal enclaves. [12]

For the next hundred years, the Franciscan missions remained the dominant colonial regime in the Southeast. By the mid-seventeenth century, they had penetrated hundreds of miles into the interior of Florida and had attained a degree of prosperity that some scholars have likened to a "golden age." [13] Accompanied by only a handful of widely dispersed soldiers, the missionaries claimed to have successfully brought thousands of Indians into the fold of the Spanish Empire and the Catholic Church. A formal inspection of the missions conducted in 1674 by Gabriel Diaz Vara Calderón, the bishop of Cuba, seemed to substantiate these claims. Though the number of active missionaries had dropped from seventy to forty in the previous twenty years, the missions ranged over a larger territory than ever before, which Spanish officials had divided into three different administrative "provinces." Calderón counted thirteen missions in the province of Apalachee (present-day northwestern Florida), eleven in Timucua (between Saint Augustine and Apalachee), and six in Guale (present-day Georgia).[14]

To Calderón and other Spanish observers, Apalachee and Timucua appeared to be the most successful of the mission provinces. Both regions were home to large, well-integrated Native chiefdoms whose experience with Europeans dated back to the days of de Soto. The agricultural economies and sedentary populations of Apalachee and Timucua made them ideal proving grounds for missionaries, who favored dependable food supplies and accessible flocks. By the 1670s Apalachee was by far the larger, wealthier, and more promising of the two western provinces. Bishop Calderón claimed that the Apalachees constituted more than three-fourths of the 13,152 Indians living under the supervision of the missions and was confident that they "attended mass with regularity" and "embraced with devotion the mysteries of [the Spaniards'] holy faith."[15] Though Calderón might have embellished his report to please his superiors, he probably had good reason to approve of many of the Indians he encountered in Florida's missions. The Franciscans worked long and hard to teach the articles of faith, commandments, sacraments, and corporal works of Catholicism to their Indian charges and regularly used ornate rituals and Native dialects as a means to transmit their messages more effectively.[16] Nevertheless, there were certainly limits to the religious transformations undergone by the mission Indians, for "conversion" was and still remains a highly ambiguous concept. Not only could mission Indians be selective about the particular rituals and/or beliefs that they wished to integrate into their traditional religious worldviews, but it was also possible for the Indians—especially Indian leaders—to simply go through the expected motions of Catholic devotion to get what they could out of the missionaries.[17]

Regardless of the depth of the Indians' devotion to Catholicism, the missions of Florida displayed many signs of Spanish influence, from the bells rung at mass to the silk tapestries and silver chalices that adorned several of the mission chapels. At the same time the missions were also part of a secular administrative system, one whose leaders placed a strong emphasis on military order and smooth chains of command. Florida's government was a government of soldiers: not only the hidalgos who served as governors, but also the lieutenants, sergeants, and troops who served under their command. In numeric terms the Spanish military presence in Florida never grew daunting; the royal allotment from Madrid never allowed for more than 355 positions, many of which were staffed by men unfit for active duty. Still, Florida's governors made good use of what they had, especially as improvements in communication and transportation made it easier to place troops in strategic locations. By the mid-seventeenth century, each of the mission provinces housed Spanish garrisons commanded by a resident lieutenant. While the actual deployment of Spanish troops fluctuated from province to province and year to year, their presence in the hinterland helped integrate the economy and administration of Florida's far-flung domains. Corn, wheat, and other essential crops grown in the fertile fields of Apalachee were either loaded onto ships at the Gulf Coast port of San Marcos or carried overland along the *camino real*. This major east-west thoroughfare also served as the route for the growing numbers of Indian men who were drafted in the mission provinces to assist with public works projects in Saint Augustine.[18] In the eyes of Florida officials, the Apalachees and other mission Indians had become vital components of the colony and appeared more or less reconciled to the embrace of the Spanish Empire.[19]

The subjection of these "civilized" Indians was not nearly as complete as it might have seemed, however. Only a fraction of the Indians living in the mission provinces chose to convert to Christianity, and these converts did not have to make as many serious cultural adjustments as one might expect. In exchange for moderate tributes to the governor, Indian leaders were allowed to maintain—or even augment—their influence and authority within an extensive "republic of Indians."[20] These leaders were often the only Indians who permanently resided in the missions. In the surrounding villages and outlying provinces, Indians continued to build, plant, hunt, and fish in traditional ways, even after receiving European tools from the missions.[21] Within the missions themselves—even those that housed Spanish garrisons—evidence suggests that European and Native cultures could coexist in relative harmony without making too many impositions on each other.[22]

Other evidence, however, suggests that inexperienced, impatient, or abrasive soldiers and missionaries ran the risk of stepping out of line. When pushed too far, Native leaders could push back, occasionally with explosive consequences. In 1647 a group of non-Christian Apalachee chiefs sparked a rebellion that claimed the lives of three Franciscans, along with those of the lieutenant governor and his family. Eight years later Timucuan leaders lashed out in response to an official order calling them into militia service. In both instances the Spanish—with the invaluable assistance of Indian militia contingents—responded quickly and ruthlessly, hanging the suspected ringleaders and forcing numerous other insurgents into several years of hard labor.[23] The calm that prevailed in the ensuing twenty years could not obscure the reality that Apalachee and Timucua were, for all intents and purposes, conquered provinces. While Florida's secular and spiritual conquerors did little to substantiate the "black legend" associated with the conquistadors of Mexico and South America, they did take a toll on the Indians of the mission provinces. Between 1635 and 1675 the combination of disease, rebellion, and flight helped reduce the number of mission Indians from an estimated thirty thousand to an estimated thirteen thousand.[24]

After a century of colonial rule, the Spanish had clearly established themselves as the most powerful and disruptive force in Florida. Beyond the coastal settlement at Saint Augustine, their presence took the form of a widespread system that combined the forces of religious and military discipline. Nevertheless, it would be wrong to assume that the viability of the mission provinces depended exclusively on indoctrination and subjugation. The Spanish clearly had the upper hand in most of the missions, but at the same time their relationship with the various Native peoples of Greater Florida was far more reciprocal than dictatorial.

While it is commonly assumed that the Spanish principally relied on the cross and the sword to carve out influence among the American Indians, their mission system in the Southeast could never have lasted as long as it did had they not established a successful trade with the region's Indians. Though they favored the Christianized and more sedentary Indians, Spanish religious and imperial officials acknowledged the economic importance of the Southeast's thousands of "infidel" Indians, usually after establishing contact with them through the missions. Many Indian societies of the southeastern interior developed a strong taste for certain European goods and discovered ways to acquire them—either directly or indirectly—from the Spanish. Though both direct and indirect trade prevailed in all the mission provinces, they were heaviest in Apalachee, which received a steady flow of European goods used by the friars, soldiers, and Indians.[25] The various Indian societies that were taking shape to the northwest of Apalachee, especially the Muskogean and Hitichi towns of the Lower Chattahoochee Valley, quickly learned about the brass and iron hoes, knives, and armbands circulating through the Apalachee villages and soon came to desire these goods for ornamental and utilitarian purposes. By virtue of indigenous trade links that had existed before the arrival of the Spanish, the mission Indians were often in a position to serve as intermediaries between the Spanish and other Indian groups. The Apalachees were soon distributing

Spanish goods to their "infidel" neighbors in exchange for deerskins, which they could trade back to the Spanish for more European goods. [26]

By the late seventeenth century, the Spanish were also engaged in an increasingly profitable direct trade with various Indian societies. Some of this trade occurred in Saint Augustine, Florida's only colonial settlement of any note. Jonathan Dickinson, an Englishman shipwrecked on the coast of Florida in the early 1690s, learned that one of his Indian captors had visited the town and had been thrilled to receive a mirror, an axe, two knives, and six pounds of tobacco in exchange for five pounds of ambergris. [27] Most of the direct trade, however, transpired along the Gulf Coast near present-day Apalachicola, where Spanish smugglers from Havana, seeking to avoid cumbersome customs duties, established a clandestine trade with the Indians beginning about 1640. This trade outlet was probably the most attractive to Indians living beyond the pale of the missions and was likely an important factor in the movement of groups like the Yuchis and the Savannahs (Shawnees) into the Southeast during this period. Groups that could not move closer to the Spanish regularly sent trading parties as far as three hundred miles to acquire European goods. [28]

It is unlikely that the goods obtained from the Spanish at this stage in the trading process had any revolutionary impact on the culture of the Indians. Metal hoes, knives, hatchets, cooking pots, and ornaments caused Indians not to abandon traditional activities but to practice them with greater ease and convenience. Most of the southeastern groups that traded with the Spanish lived far enough from areas of colonial settlement that they did not have to worry about intruders foisting undesired objects on them. They could afford to be selective, and the things they picked out and brought back home with them were usually things they could use. Nevertheless, trade with Europeans was becoming increasingly important to the Southeast's Indian societies, many of which began to go to greater and greater lengths to increase their shares.

In the mid-1670s two Indian towns along the Lower Chattahoochee invited Spanish authorities to establish missions among them. Most of the residents of these towns probably had no real desire to convert to Christianity but had learned from their visits to Apalachee that the villages with missions had better access to trade goods. The Indians' real motives meant less to the Spanish than the exciting possibility of extending Spanish authority to a fourth province, that of Apalachicola. [29] By this time Spanish officials had come to realize that the strength and security of the colony depended on the assistance and cooperation of the Indians. Though they had not grown as powerful as they might have hoped, the Spanish in Florida had helped initiate a number of important and expanding frontiers within the region. The seventeenth century is generally perceived as a period of decline in the Spanish Empire, but three-fourths of the way through that century, Spain's influence in southeastern North America had never been stronger. Imperial officials thought that they could look forward to a period of increasingly profitable relations within an expanding dominion. Still, nagging doubts about the security of their colony persisted, especially in light of England's growing interest in the region.

Spain's disputes with England over the Southeast began even before the arrival of the first English colonists. In drawing up a revised royal charter for Carolina in 1665, Charles II gave England access to territory that the Spanish, with some justification, claimed for their own. At twenty-nine degrees latitude, the southern boundary of the 1665 sea-to-sea Carolina charter was well below Saint Augustine, a site the Spanish had occupied for nearly a hundred years. Having regarded the English as Protestant heretics and bitter enemies since the days of Queen Elizabeth and the Spanish Armada, the Spanish Floridians were not likely to extend a generous welcome to the English ships that began mooring at the junction of the Ashley and Cooper rivers in 1670. Though a treaty signed that year in Madrid seemed to alleviate the most glaring aspects of the border controversy, the presence of a traditional foe within a mere five hundred miles of Florida's capital appeared to foretell the continuation of an imperial conflict that had raged in the Caribbean, among other places, for the previous century.[30]

As much as they disliked each other, the English and the Spanish colonists would wait many years before meeting face to face in combat. Their earliest clashes were indirect and took place between Native groups courted and supplied by the Europeans. The Spanish knew that Indians of strange origins—the Westoes, or "Chichimecos"—had been harrying familiar southeastern Indians for some time. Having been provided with English guns to help them capture slaves for Virginia plantations, the Westoes soon made the acquaintance of the newly arrived South Carolinians, who had become apprised of the West- oes' fierce reputations when other, terrified groups of Indians began seeking English protection. Rather than engaging the Westoes in battle, however, the South Carolinians enticed them away from Virginia and put them to work for their own purposes.[31]

A mutually beneficial relationship quickly developed: the Westoes found a better source for trade goods and weapons, and the South Carolinians could use the Westoes to exert their own influence in the region. Throughout the 1670s the Westoes served as key intermediaries in South Carolina's nascent

Indian trade, which at this time focused mainly on the acquisition of slaves for local plantations and for export to other English colonies. In 1675 a Yuchi woman captured by the Westoes managed to escape from a South Carolina plantation after being traded to an English colonist for a musket. Her harrowing tale confirmed to the governor of Florida that the English and their Westo allies were intent on "making war upon the natives now converted to the Catholic religion."[32]

Indian war parties supplied and encouraged by the South Carolinians soon discovered that the Spanish missions made easier targets than the towns of unconverted Indians. The Spanish had strung their Guale missions along the Atlantic coast to remove them from the marauding Indians of the interior, but this strategy soon set them up for assaults from both land and sea. In 1680 Santa Catalina de Guale, complete with a recently constructed stone fortress, became the first coastal mission to fall when its defensive force of six Spanish soldiers and forty Christian Indians failed to hold back a party of some three hundred enemy Indians. The invading force included not only Westoes but also some Indians hailing from the unconverted Indian settlements on the northern and western edges of Guale.[33] After the fall of Santa Catalina, other nearby missions toppled in quick succession and with surprisingly little resistance, mainly because most of the resident Indians—well acquainted with the reputations of the raiders—fled in terror. In 1683 an especially violent sacking of a mission by the French Huguenot pirate Grammont added more fuel to the fire. By 1684 all six of the Guale missions had been abandoned, and the Indians who chose to remain with the Spanish were relocated to two new missions south of the present-day Georgia-Florida border.[34]

The collapse of the Guale missions has been called the most significant episode in the seventeenth-century conflicts between South Carolina and Florida, the one that launched the "long process of dissolution of Spanish authority" in the Southeast.[35] This episode was probably even more significant in demonstrating some of the new relationships that had begun to form within the region. The South Carolinians, active in the Southeast for only a little more than ten years, had managed to court, attract, and influence the behavior of several important Indian societies with which the Spanish, after 150 years, had only recently experienced some breakthroughs. The Spanish had patiently been learning the rules of the game for decades, but the relatively inexperienced English—with the help of a larger and less expensive supply of European trade goods—already seemed to be winning it. The gap would only appear to widen throughout the 1680s, as the South Carolinians pursued relations with more Indian groups in areas where the Spanish had already established themselves.

What looked from a European perspective like the steady advance of South Carolina's sphere of influence was actually the extension of a complex relationship that different Indian societies willingly joined for a number of different reasons. As it had been with the Spanish, trade became the foremost factor in the burgeoning attraction between the Indians and the English. The English traders, who were able to visit the important Indian towns of the southeastern interior with such apparent ease, owed much of their success to patterns that had already been established between the Indians and the Spanish.[36] The picaresque Henry Woodward, South Carolina's most accomplished and effective ambassador among the Indians during the 1670s and 1680s, had actually cut his teeth as a trader-diplomat while spending five years as a well-treated "prisoner" of the Spanish during the 1660s.[37] Woodward and a few other adventurers working out of Charles Town started circulating among the wealthy and influential towns along the Chattahoochee River by the mid-1670s but did not begin bringing significant quantities of coveted trade goods with them until the early 1680s. Trade with these interior groups technically fell under a monopoly held by South Carolina's Lords Proprietors, but Carolina planters, tired of trading with the poorer coastal groups, were anxious to cut in. The planters helped organize a campaign to exterminate the Westoes, the group of "middlemen" who stood in the way. With the invaluable aid of the Savannahs, erstwhile trading partners of the Spanish, the South Carolinians killed or enslaved most of the Westoes and put the rest to flight, clearing the way for direct access to the enticing markets of the Chattahoochee basin.[38]

Within a few years Woodward and a dozen other South Carolina traders had gained access to Coweta and Cussita, widely recognized as the most important Muskogean towns along the Chattahoochee. The Indians seemed most impressed with the several dozen packhorses laden with colorful cloth, glass beads, metal tools and trinkets, and guns and ammunition. The Spanish, who had already been providing these goods to the Indians, were deeply troubled by the warm welcome extended to the English by the Indians of "Apalachicola province." Two Franciscans had been forced out of the province a few years earlier, and there no longer appeared to be any chance of establishing missions among these influential Indians. In retrospect there are several likely reasons for the Indians' preference for the English traders. The groups of the southeastern interior had grown used to acquiring European goods without having to tolerate extended meddling from European authorities. The itinerant English peddlers were offering a continuation of this arrangement—and sweetening the deal by bringing the goods directly to the Indians—at the same time the Spanish were becoming a little too assertive.[39]

The Spanish could not help noticing a marked decline in the number of Indian visits to Apalachee and Apalachicola. Evidently the Indians had begun to spread the word that the rewards were no longer worth the trip. On a voyage through some of the towns in the Upper Coosa and Tallapoosa valleys, Spanish officer Marcus Delgado was politely informed by a Koasati Indian that the Indians along the Lower Chattahoochee had been saying that the "friendship of the Spaniards and Christians was not good." Apparently "the presents of the English were better," because "in trading they gave more powder, balls, and muskets."[40] A puzzled Delgado asked the Koasatis how they could embrace the very people whose weapons, in the hands of the Westoes, had caused them so much grief and suffering. The Koasatis, along with several other groups of the region, could easily shrug off this kind of European logic. With more guns of their own, they would be able to provide better protection for themselves than the well-intentioned but poor and remote Spanish ever could. Clearly the need for protection played a significant role in their receptiveness toward the South Carolina traders. Having contributed to the feelings of fear and uneasiness among many of the Southeast's Indian societies, the English were increasingly able to profit from the Indians' insecurity.[41]

The Origins of the Yamasee–South Carolina Alliance

Nowhere did the South Carolinians reap more benefits from Indian warfare than in the collapsing province of Guale. For nearly a hundred years, the coastal Guales, a chiefdom of Mississippian ancestry, had comprised the most tenuous and volatile of Florida's mission provinces. Though conquered by the Spanish in the 1580s, the Guales had enjoyed a clandestine trade with French privateers through the early seventeenth century and had generally proven more inclined than the Apalachees and the Timucuans to resist Spanish authority. Major revolts in 1597 and 1645 nearly succeeded in destroying the Guale missions from within, resulting in some stringent Spanish reprisals.[42] Guale was the least stable of the mission provinces even before the English arrived in Carolina, but the devastating English-sponsored raids of the early 1680s made the province even less hospitable, not only for the Spanish and the native Guales, but also for the many non-Christian Indians who had, ironically, begun to settle near the missions in search of Spanish protection.

Most of these Indian refugees hailed from La Tama, the Spanish name for an Indian province located in present-day north-central Georgia. In the late sixteenth century, Spanish explorers had hoped that La Tama might contain deposits of gold and other precious metals but had eventually given up hopes of settling and subduing the province.[43] Despite a lack of direct Spanish contact, however, the Indians of La Tama remained aware of the transformations that had begun to shape the surrounding region. By the mid-seventeenth century, they had acquired indirect access to Spanish trade goods through other Indians of the Southeast, possibly the Apalachees and the Timucuans, but most likely the Guales.[44] The lure of more European trade goods inspired some Tama Indians to migrate toward the missions, but most of them did not feel a pressing need to move closer to the Spanish until the early 1660s, when the first waves of Westo slave raiders began crashing down from the Appalachian Mountains.[45]

Over the next two decades, the Indians of La Tama dispersed in several different directions. Some of them probably sought refuge within some of the towns along the Lower Chattahoochee, where many Indians spoke a language intelligible with La Tama's Hitichi dialect.[46] Most of these refugees, however, headed toward the Spanish missions. In 1675 the commander of the Spanish garrison in Apalachee remarked that several of the province's missions had begun to swell with newcomers from the north. His report on these refugees contains one of the first known references to the "Yamasees," a group he described as "all of one nation with the people of La Tama."[47] By this time most of the Yamasees had begun to flee closer to Guale. While some of them moved into the Guale missions to mix with the local population and experiment with Christianity, others continued to lurk around the periphery, hoping to pick up material support from the Spanish without having to make any drastic submissions to Spanish authority.[48]

When the Guale missions began to crumble under pressure from Indian raiders and European buccaneers, the entire region quickly emptied of almost all settlement. Florida authorities were alarmed to see that most of the Indians who had crowded into and around the Guale missions now wanted nothing to do with the Spanish. The demands of the *repartmiento* labor draft and the abusive behavior of a few Spanish officers probably contributed in some way to the massive Indian "defections" of the early 1680s, but most of the flight was due to the Florida government's inability to adequately defend or arm their Indian "subjects."[49] In 1685 Governor Diego Leturiondo perceived considerable exasperation among the Indians, even those who remained most loyal to the Spanish. On an official visit to one of the Guale missions that had been relocated closer to Saint Augustine, Leturiondo found that the Indians did not "have powder or balls, nor [did] they find themselves in a position to buy them, although they would [have] liked to." When told that they could be supplied when an emergency warranted, the Indians disgustedly replied that this answer was "the same as nothing."[50]

While most of Guale's Christian and non-Christian Indians had left for Apalachee and Apalachicola by 1684, a small group of Yamasees led by a chief named Altamaha moved in the opposite direction and took up residence near the mouth of the Savannah River.[51] Though temporarily cut off from the flow of European trade goods, Altamaha and his people did not take long to find a new source for security and prosperity. Charles Town remained too distant to serve as an option, but in 1684 Carolina's Lords Proprietors allowed Lord Henry Cardross to set up the Scottish colony of Stuart's Town on Port Royal Sound, a site with an excellent harbor and river system that had supported short-lived French and Spanish settlements in the late sixteenth century. Taking a cue from the English and the Huguenots of the Charles Town area, Cardross and his followers jumped headlong into the Indian trade and planned to use the nearby Savannah River as a shortcut to the enticing Indian markets of the interior. Before the Scots could launch their excursions toward the Chattahoochee, however, they found themselves wrapped up in a budding relationship with the Indians closer to home.

In late 1684 the Scots at Stuart's Town entered into an arrangement with the man they referred to as "King Altamaha." After receiving an advance of twenty-three muskets and ammunition, Altamaha set out with about fifty Yamasee warriors for Timucua, a province that Carolina-sponsored Indians had not yet been able to penetrate. Altamaha's band devastated the mission of Santa Catalina de Afuyca, killing eighteen Timucuans and returning with twenty-two prisoners, whom they "delivered to the Scots as slaves."[52] Following a clandestine pattern that had already been established between the English and several other southeastern Indian societies, Altamaha and his people had found a way to profit from their familiarity with Spanish Florida.

Though pleased with the results of Altamaha's raid, the Scots soon saw their satisfaction give way to astonishment as other groups of Indians hailing from similar circumstances soon began to decide that they, too, would be better served by moving closer to the South Carolinians. One trader estimated (and almost certainly exaggerated) in February 1685 that "a thousand or more" Indians were approaching Port Royal every day.[53] Cardross informed the proprietors that he had "consented to them [the Indians] that they remain [there] during their good behaviour," but admitted that the refugees were "so considerable and warlike that [the proprietors] would not do otherwayes." [54] Once they learned that they could stay, some Indians made several trips to and from the Scottish enclave, returning to Port Royal with more Indian migrants from different parts of the Southeast. The general impression was one of a reunion of Yamasee relatives who had temporarily been forced to live apart as refugees. The Indians claimed to be coming not only from the ravaged province of Guale but also from as far to the west as the Chattahoochee towns of Coweta and Cussita. [55]

It is likely, however, that this first wave of Yamasee migration toward Carolina was not simply a case of the chiefdom of La Tama finding new life on new soil. The group of Indians that took shape around Port Royal in the mid-1680s was, in many ways, a new Indian society. Though many of these Indians shared a common language (Hitichi, a branch of Muskogean) and lineage, they had absorbed varying degrees of Spanish and other Indian cultures over the several preceding decades. The newly coalescing group included mostly pagans but some Christians; mostly descendants from the old chiefdoms near La Tama, but quite a few from Guale, Muskogean, and other Indian backgrounds. The Yamasees whom the South Carolinians would come to know were never a cohesive nation composed of a pure ethnic stock. Instead, they comprised a classic example of how the continually evolving Indian societies of the colonial period could experience frequent "rebirths" in various guises.

In their new incarnation, the Yamasees had closer ties to colonial institutions and agendas than did most contemporary Indian societies of the Southeast. Once they got over an initial sense of alarm, the Port Royal traders began to see their new Yamasee neighbors as a potentially rewarding windfall. Settled initially on easily accessible Saint Helena and Hilton Head Islands and soon spilling over to the nearby mainland, the Yamasees were proving themselves valuable and enthusiastic trading partners. They not only offered the Scots indirect access to a supposedly wealthy mission province but also could serve as a possible defensive "out guard" in case of an attack from the south.

Although the Yamasees' presence pleased and comforted many South Carolinians, it also heightened tension between the colony's English and Scottish enclaves. The English traders, having begun to gain the upper hand on the Spanish, justifiably feared that the Scots might do much the same thing to them. With the tacit blessing of the Lords Proprietors, who were growing tired of the recalcitrance of Charles Town traders, the Scots jealously guarded their access to the Yamasees. [56] English trader John Edenburgh traveled to Port Royal to try his luck, only to be apprehended and forced home with a nasty parting shot from Cardross, who told him that if he caught the troublesome ringleader Henry Woodward, "he would put him in prison."[57] Stuart's Town experienced more than its fair share of problems during its two-year existence, but it still managed to stand, however briefly, as a formidable trade rival to Charles Town along a kind of English-Scottish frontier.[58]

Though this rivalry pointed to important internal differences within South Carolina, the Spanish were inclined to view the English and the Scots in much the same light. England and Spain had been at peace for years, but the Spanish in Florida felt that they were actually living in a state of undeclared warfare. Despite their stingy budget, they had begun to do what they could to improve their colony's defenses. Fears of encroaching English pirates and colonists inspired the Spanish to start work on the Castillo de San Marcos, an impressive stone fortress on Saint Augustine Harbor whose construction dragged on into the late 1680s. Even before the fort was finished, however, the Spanish premium on defense was joined by a new strategy based on offense. The accumulation of suffering in Guale, the beginnings of a similar situation in Timucua, and the well-founded suspicions that the South Carolinians were harboring pirates finally pushed Florida's notoriously short-tempered Governor Juan Cabrera into action.

Cabrera's closest and most convenient target was Stuart's Town, which fell under attack from a contingent of three small ships and a hundred Spanish soldiers in August 1686. Stuart's Town had been suffering from a debilitating outbreak of disease as well as the defection of several traders to Charles Town. Those few who remained received a timely warning of the invasion from the neighboring Yamasees and were able to evacuate, leaving behind only a mentally retarded Scottish boy to greet the invaders. After putting Stuart's Town to the torch, the Spanish moved further up the coast to Edisto Island, where they sacked the plantations of the governor and the secretary of South Carolina. After taking eleven slaves and two indentured servants as prisoners, they tried to move on to Charles Town but were turned back by a sudden hurricane. They returned to Saint Augustine without one of their ships, but with the satisfaction of having put an end to the intrigues of the Cardross colony.[59]

Nor had the Spanish forgotten the intrigues of another enemy: the Indians who had left their fold and begun tormenting their missions. Turning the tables on the South Carolinians, the Spanish assembled a series of attack forces led by Spanish officers and composed mainly of Christianized Guale, Timucuan, and Apalachee Indians who looked forward to plundering their enemies.[60] Some Yamasees living near Carolina had begun to spread down the coast and cross the Savannah River, but an attack launched by three hundred Spanish-supplied Indians in late 1686 forced them to flee this area. Other attacks directed against the immediate vicinity of Port Royal in early 1687 temporarily forced the Yamasees even further into Carolina, as far north as the land between the Ashepoo and Combahee rivers. Though the Yamasees soon returned to the Port Royal region, they would not return to the old province of Guale for another twenty years. From the Spanish perspective, the retaliatory raids of 1686–87 had seemingly served their purpose. The Yamasees continued to travel through Guale to hunt and trade, but for the time being they seemed reluctant to confront the Spanish and their Indian allies again. When Jonathan Dickinson and his Spanish escort—on their way from Saint Augustine to Charles Town a few years after the raids on Port Royal—encountered some Yamasees in canoes, the Indians paddled away in fear.[61]

English South Carolinians expressed alarm and outrage over the Spanish "invasion" of Port Royal but soon came to realize the futility of their complaints. Though the English parliament allowed the South Carolinians to outfit privateers for preventing further Spanish attacks, the proprietors showed surprisingly little sympathy. Claiming that the Scots' "unjustifiable" encouragement of Yamasee raids had provoked a justifiable response from Florida, the proprietors warned the English colonists that they could "not expect the Spaniards to live peaceably by [them] if they [were] thus provoked." [62] Many South Carolinians resented the proprietors for allowing the "barberous" actions of the Spanish to be "buryed in silence," but few of the growing number of planters and government officials involved in the Indian trade were likely to complain too loudly. Removal of the stubborn Cardross gave them free access to the Yamasees, who were now more willing than ever to cling to the security offered by the English. The surviving South Carolina traders had no reason to mourn the passing of the Scottish colony, especially at a time when their situation along other frontiers appeared so promising.[63]

Indian Resistance in Apalachicola

As Guale became a lost cause, Spanish authorities shifted much of their concern to Florida's remaining provinces, where the possibility of foreign incursions seemed to pose an even greater threat to Spanish interests. Their concern for Apalachee and the territory to the northwest of the mission provinces actually predated the beginnings of the Guale collapse. By the mid-1670s the establishment of Carolina and rumors of French designs in the Mississippi Valley had brought the governor of Florida to request colonists from Cuba and the Canary Islands to strengthen the fertile territory around the missions.[64] The fear of French and English designs on Apalachee also brought Florida authorities to militarize the westernmost mission province. Spanish officers distributed more firearms to mission Indians, and more of Florida's allotment of 355 soldiers began to head west from Saint Augustine. In 1682 the small Apalachee fort at San Luis de Talimali held an unprecedented force of forty-five Spanish troops.[65]

Though the Spanish initially focused on the French, they soon realized that the English were the more dangerous imperial rival. As they mobilized to meet the English threat in the west, Florida officials began to make what turned out to be their greatest mistake: they overestimated both the influence they had built among the region's nonmission Indians and the threats that the English posed to Spanish interests among these Native groups. Though Spanish efforts to establish missionaries in the region annoyed some of the Muskogeans and their newly arrived Indian neighbors, relations between these Indians and the Spanish had always been more cooperative than confrontational. When the arrival of English traders began to place some strain on these relations, the Spanish—however understandably—overreacted. They began to misinterpret the attitudes of the Indians along Florida's northwestern frontiers, and from there it did not take long for them to see these Indians as enemies, treat them as enemies, and eventually help turn some of them into real enemies.

The Indians of "Apalachicola province" probably knew that the Spanish would not react kindly to the expulsion of their missionaries in the late 1670s, but it is also likely that the Indians did not expect their receptiveness toward English traders to cause as great an uproar as it did. Most of the Native groups in this area had long acquired their trade goods from multiple sources: the Apalachee missions, the Spanish smugglers on the Gulf Coast, and the conveniently situated towns along the Lower Chattahoochee. For many of these Indians, the English traders became just another source, albeit a more convenient one with cheaper and better quality goods. The English were somewhat less intrusive than Spanish soldiers and missionaries, but most Indians of the region would have been reluctant to throw themselves at the feet of a group they still did not know well. Though there was a growing disillusionment with the Spanish and their goods during the mid-1680s, many Indians were probably hesitant to sever all ties with the Spanish and give up on a long-standing relationship that had actually been strengthening for decades.[66] Even the sullen Indians who told Delgado that "the friendship of the Spanish was not good" quickly brightened when the officer promised them a larger and better supply of goods in Apalachee. [67] Had the Spanish been able to follow up on Delgado's promise, most of the region's Indians probably would have been content to deal simultaneously with both groups of Europeans for as long as possible.

For the Spanish the easiest way to restore the Indian trade to former levels was not to supply more goods at cheaper rates, but to eliminate the competition with a display of force. In so doing they proved unable to heed the lessons of the previous fifty years: that it was far more rewarding to trade with the southeastern Indians than to intimidate them. Though the Indians of Apalachicola differed in many important ways from the Indians who were besieging Guale, the Spanish conflated the two contexts and soon began to see all nonmission Indians as potential raiders for the enemy English. Spanish military officials in Apalachee were especially wary, having been on guard against possible enemy incursions for several years. On first word of a visit to the Chattahoochee by Henry Woodward and several other South Carolina traders in 1685, Lieutenant Governor Antonio Matheos departed from the mission of San Luis with six Spanish soldiers and as many as two hundred gun-wielding Apalachee Indians. [68]

Word of Matheos's force spread quickly through the towns along the Lower Chattahoochee. For those Indians who had not expected to upset the Spanish by receiving the English, it was now obvious that they had done just that. By the time the Spanish expedition passed through the major towns of Apalachicola province, many of the Indians and all of the English traders had gone into hiding. Matheos saw plenty of evidence to confirm his worst suspicions about the English. He was enraged by the presence of a half-constructed warehouse and seethed at a note from Woodward with a hastily scrawled postscript: "I trust in God that I shall meet you gentlemen later when I have a larger following." [69] Matheos went back to Apalachee in frustration, only to return the following year with an even larger force after hearing that the English had resurfaced. He arrived to find that Woodward and the others had returned to Charles Town and was left with no outlet for his rage other than the Indians, who were clearly put off by the presence of his small army. Matheos's force proceeded to march from town to town, confiscating scores of guns and hundreds of treated furs and deerskins. [70] Though convinced by now that many of the Indians in Apalachicola were up to no good, Matheos was under orders to offer them another chance to render obedience to the Spanish Crown.

If the Indians had previously misunderstood Spanish concepts of obedience, they now got the message loud and clear. Eight of the Apalachicola towns intimidated by Matheos's force agreed to give him what he wanted, but four refused. Among the recalcitrant towns of Tuskegee, Coolamee, Coweta, and Cussita, the latter two most likely were the ringleaders; leaders from Tuskegee and Coolamee later told Spanish spies that "the ones fully responsible were the caciques of Casisto and Cabeta, who had deceived and entangled all the rest in bringing the Englishmen and forcing them to receive them."[71] Coweta and Cussita were the towns most frequently visited by the English traders and stood to lose the most by renouncing them. At the same time Indians of these towns had seen the Spanish take their most valuable possessions and dismiss their petition for redress, and they therefore had compelling reasons to deny the Spanish the satisfaction of the obedience ritual. Matheos would not take no for an answer and decided on his own authority to make examples of the four towns by burning them to the ground. This act of war alarmed even the governor in Saint Augustine, who claimed that "it was a great providence of God that in revenge of their grievance they did not unite with the enemy from San Jorge [South Carolina] and devastate [their] country, as the Yamasee Nation [had] done."[72] It also prompted fear and outrage among the Indians of the four towns, who sent an emissary to Apalachee to pledge obedience but did not easily forget the Spanish act of brute force.

Not only did these Indians express their disapproval to Matheos, but more importantly they also continued to welcome the English traders, minus Woodward, who had died back in Charles Town.[73] After two more of the now-annual expeditions failed to turn up the South Carolinians, the Spanish decided to keep watch over Apalachicola province and its most troublesome towns by constructing a four-towered fort with a garrison of twenty Spaniards and twenty Apalachees near Coweta in late 1689. Flying the royal standard over this fort for the next year briefly made Spanish authorities more confident but soon proved to be a hollow victory.[74]

While the Spanish were building their fort in Apalachicola province, South Carolina trader George Smith was having an exceptionally busy and productive year right under their noses. After making his way through the Muskogean towns along the Chattahoochee and coming "within 3 or 4 days Jurnay of the bay of Apalatier [Gulf of Mexico]," Smith and his assistants returned to Charles Town. They brought with them not only an enormously profitable cargo of twenty-eight hundred deerskins but also several headmen from the towns of Coweta and Cussita. After meeting with government officials in the

South Carolina capital, the Indian leaders returned "loaded with presents" to their new home along the Ocmulgee River, "10 days Jurnay nearer" the English settlements.[75] Coweta, Cussita, and nine other Muskogean towns—along with the nearly twenty-five hundred warriors they could muster—were seen as an immensely valuable prize by South Carolina authorities.

Many South Carolinians flattered themselves that they had brought these valuable Indians closer to them by virtue of the superior trade and "protection" they could provide.[76] The allure of the English trade and English provisions undoubtedly played a part in this important Indian migration; the towns of Coweta and Cussita had proven especially devoted to the South Carolina traders, and the presence of the new Spanish fort had made it harder to continue receiving them. Many of these Indians, however, were probably as repelled by the Spanish as much as they were enticed by the English. The burning of four towns, along with other unsettling displays of force, had left many Muskogeans with an enduring distrust of the Spanish. Nearly thirty years after the great Muskogean migration to the Ocmulgee, a Spanish officer on a dangerous mission to Coweta and Cussita would lament that "little confidence can be placed in their friendship, and that they remember the extortions upon them made by the Spaniards and to have seen them burn their villages, with some killed." "This," concluded the officer, "is the reason why they rebelled and maintained the war against us for so much time."[77] Within the space of ten years, the Spanish in Florida had gone from reliable partners to minor annoyances to bitter foes.

Fugitives to Florida

The destruction of the Guale missions and the removal of several important Muskogean towns were damaging blows to Spanish interests in the Southeast, but the Florida government still managed to find some cause for satisfaction in its rivalry with the English during this period. Among the key players in this Spanish retribution were black slaves, a group that had been present in South Carolina since the arrival of the first English colonists. Slaves brought over from Barbados and other West Indian colonies soon began to play important roles on the province's expanding frontiers, working as scouts, trade assistants, or cowboys on the cattle ranches that were beginning to appear on the southern fringes of the English settlements.[78] Almost all of them, however, were slaves and as such were considered among the colonists' most valuable forms of property. When an alarming number of slaves began to disappear from South Carolina plantations in the 1680s, many English slave owners were quick to place the blame on the Spanish.

Though they found it troubling enough that the Spanish raids of 1686 had taken eleven of their governor's slaves, South Carolina planters were even more alarmed to find that more of their slaves were winding up in Florida on their own initiative. In September 1687 a group of eleven African slaves made their way into Saint Augustine after escaping from South Carolina in a small boat. When presented to the governor, they claimed to be seeking instruction in the Catholic faith.[79] Unwilling to return them to the English heretics, the governor marshaled all his diplomatic skill and charm to stymie an English delegation sent to protest the Spanish reception of slaves who were "dayly" taking flight from South Carolina.[80] Five years later Spanish colonial officials were backed by a royal proclamation that officially emancipated all fugitive slaves seeking religious asylum in Florida. By establishing his colony as a beacon for South Carolina's fugitive slaves, King Carlos II not only won praise as a champion of the Holy Faith but also found a way to strike a satisfying blow at Florida's English tormentors.

Though it did not topple South Carolina from within, Spanish policy on runaway slaves did cause rising concern among the province's white population throughout the last decade of the seventeenth century. In South Carolina's earliest years, African slaves had not posed much of a problem to the colonists. Most of South Carolina's slaves had come over from Barbados with their owners, and its black population had remained relatively low. Prompted by the influx of more West Indian colonists, as well as the first successes with staple agriculture, South Carolina's black slave population increased nearly sixfold between 1685 and 1700, from about five hundred to about thirty-eight hundred. Meanwhile, South Carolina's white population rose only from about fourteen hundred to about thirty-eight hundred in the same period.[81] As population ratios grew more unsettling to white South Carolinians, the potential for Spanish malfeasance seemed even more acute. Florida's reputation as a depot for "incorrigible" slaves from Cuba, along with the memory of black and mulatto soldiers who had participated in the 1686 raid on Port Royal, did little to ease the minds of South Carolina slave owners.[82]

Anxieties over the rising slave population and the perceived instability of the southern borderlands helped lead to a tighter clampdown on African slaves in South Carolina, as instituted in the colony's 1696 slave code. Copied almost verbatim from the brutal laws of Barbados, the code insisted that blacks possessed "barbarous, wild, and savage natures" and had to be forcefully restrained from committing the atrocities "to which they [were] naturally prone and inclined."[83] To this way of thinking, a frightened slave on the run was tantamount to a bloodthirsty insurrectionary. The threats and vigilance of slave owners were usually enough to keep slaves from absconding, and the well-publicized castration of three would-be escapees in 1697 undoubtedly provided another compelling deterrent.[84] The small number of successful fugitives, however, did not diminish the extent to which slaves had made themselves an important security issue linked to South Carolina's frontier concerns. This issue would remain in place throughout much of the colonial period, becoming especially conspicuous during times of imperial crisis.

South Carolina's Frontier Offensives

The South Carolinians responsible for their province's late seventeenth-century slave policy came from the same group of men who helped expand the province's profitable and aggressive Indian trade. These colonists, many of whom arrived in South Carolina after stays in the West Indies, were called "Goose Creek men" after the small stream about ten miles west of Charles Town where many of them settled. Though they did not compose a true political party, they all shared a driving will to amass personal fortunes and a contempt for anyone who stood in their way.[85] After several years of struggling to build plantations and find profitable staple crops, the Goose Creek men realized that the way to the top of South Carolina's socioeconomic ladder went through the Indian trade.[86] Though the proprietors claimed a monopoly over trade with the larger and wealthier Indian societies of the interior, South Carolina planters could easily circumvent it, especially after their successful reduction of the Westoes. The proprietors soon grew incensed with the rising political and economic influence of Goose Creek men like Maurice Matthews, Arthur Middleton, and James Moore, clandestine "dealers in Indians" who allegedly boasted that they could bribe their way to greater power within the province.[87]

By the early 1690s many of the Goose Creek men were important office holders, serving in the Carolina Commons House of Assembly or on the governor's council. Even in cases where they could not use their political clout to sanction the more nefarious aspects of their trade with the Indians, they found it easy enough to break the laws. In 1690 Matthews and Moore, flying in the face of a direct order from the governor, led an expedition into the Appalachian Mountains and enslaved several dozen Cherokee Indians. The following year accusations surfaced that Governor Seth Sothel was engaged in an illegal attempt to "Ingrosse the Indians trade to himself."[88] By then, however, there was no reason to believe that colonists' access to the Indian trade would be unduly restricted. The trade had blown wide open and offered enticing profits for any planter with capital to invest in a supply of trade goods and a few assistants.[89]

Over the next decade Indian groups ranging from South Carolina's coastal settlements all the way to the Mississippi River experienced more interaction with South Carolina traders. Contact was most sustained among small low-country groups like the Cussaboes and the Seewees, but it was also becoming more frequent and intense among the larger, strategically situated groups with "favored nation" trading status, most notably the Savannahs and the Yamasees. These Indians continued to trade for increasing quantities of guns and cloth, goods that had attracted them to the English in the first place. They provided such a convenient and alluring market for South Carolina traders that it was not long before the frequency and irregularity of the visits had thrown the Indian trade into what the governor called a "very great Disorder."[90]

Though traders viewed them as an insatiable market, some Indians were apparently getting too much of certain goods that the proprietors and the governor had sought to outlaw. The abuse of alcohol quickly emerged as an especially serious problem on all of South Carolina's frontiers, especially in light of the Indians' apparently limitless thirst for strong drink. Because of its ability to provide release from strict social codes, alcohol could fill an important cultural need for Indians as well as whites. In his early eighteenth-century account of the southeastern Indians, Robert Beverly wrote that Indians tended to avoid alcohol "unless they [could] get enough to make them quite drunk, and then they [went] as solemnly about it, as if it were part of their Religion."[91] John Lawson, traveling among the Indians of the Carolina Piedmont in 1700, learned that South Carolina's attempt to ban the trading of alcohol in 1691 "was never strictly observed, and besides, the young Indians were so disgusted at that Article, that they threatened to kill the Indians that made it, unless it was laid aside." When under the influence of alcohol, the Indians, according to Lawson, became "the [most] impatient creatures living, 'till they [had] enough to make them quite drunk, and the most miserable spectacles when they [were] so." Though Indians held each other strictly responsible for their behavior when sober, "they never call[ed] any Man to account for what he did, when he was drunk; but [said], it was the Drink that caused his misbehaviour, therefore he ought to be forgiven."[92] But not all Indians were as comfortable with the disorienting effects of alcohol, especially in the early days of the trade. In 1692 several Savannah headmen complained that the rum supplied to them by the traders was making their people behave in strange and shameful ways.[93] No amount of sympathy and concern from the governor could staunch the flow of "firewater," and within a year Savannah and South Carolina leaders were forced to deal with the murders of several Indians and traders, crimes in which alcohol almost certainly played a role.[94]

The Yamasees had to confront not only the increasing chaos associated with alcohol and other aspects of the trade but also several problems that arose from their proximity to expanding colonial settlements. After the destruction of Cardross's colony, Colleton County in the Port Royal area gained a reputation as an ideal location for newly arrived English and Huguenot colonists. By the late 1680s they had already begun to carve out plantations and cattle ranches that stretched closer and closer to the Yamasee settlements. Some colonists decided that the Yamasees' skill at growing watermelons, corn, beans, and other crops would make them ideal workers on English plantations. One Sea Island resident made arrangements with Altamaha to hire three hundred Yamasees to help him with cotton and silk production and complained bitterly when the governor coopted his plan.[95] Most Yamasees, however, continued to hunt and work in their own fields, and the English planters seemed content to rely on the help of Indian and African slaves.

The movement of more slaves into Colleton County presented the Yamasees with another opportunity to work for the colonists. They found that they could supplement their incomes by capturing fugitives en route from South Carolina to Florida and soon acquired a glowing reputation for their slave-hunting skills.[96] The Yamasees' connections to South Carolina's growing system of slavery, however, also left room for disputes and controversy. Some myopic or especially unscrupulous plantation owners had a hard time distinguishing between the Yamasees and other, more "enslaveable" Indians. On one occasion South Carolina authorities were horrified to learn that a son of Altamaha himself had been seized and put to work by an English planter, and they quickly had the boy returned to his father.[97] The Yamasees, for their part, could also be less than cooperative. Of the Indian slaves who made it back to Florida, some of them likely did so with the aid or consent of the Yamasees, who occasionally adopted fugitives into their own towns, much to the displeasure of South Carolina authorities.[98]

For the men in charge of defending South Carolina's imperial interests, the burgeoning Indian trade was important not only for economic reasons. Just as certain Indian groups saw trade as a means to acquire English protection from their enemies, South Carolinians began to seek similar fringe benefits from the Indians. While the governor of South Carolina could tell the Spanish that the Yamasees were "people who live within [South Carolina's] bounds after their own manner taking no notice of [the colony's] Government," English officials actually sought to play an active role in Yamasee diplomacy, to the point of intervening in the Yamasees' relations with other Indian groups.[99] Despite the violence and dislocations of the previous decade, many Yamasees maintained connections with Indians in Florida's mission provinces. In 1693 they were prepared to allow the "Spanish Indians" to come up to Port Royal to trade for corn and peas but were forbidden by a Commons House fearful of letting potential Spanish "spies" into the colony. The same year the Muskogean towns of Tuskegee, Coweta, and Cussita, prospering from a steady flow of trade, offered to provide refuge for a beleaguered remnant of the Westoes. The House also rejected this idea out of hand, claiming that the Westoes would merely seek revenge against the colony by trying to stir up South Carolina's loyal Indian allies.[100] Though the Yamasees and the Muskogeans did not heed these decisions as closely as the colonial government might have wished (the Yamasees continued to trade in Florida, and the Muskogeans welcomed at least a few Westo refugees), they did comply enough to give the impression that they were taking part in the formation of a protective buffer zone around the province.[101]

Efforts to secure and solidify this buffer zone caused some South Carolina officials to worry even more about the detrimental effects that the Indian trade could have on their real and imagined allies. From their estates and offices in England, the proprietors found it easy to keep the "big picture" of South Carolina's imperial relations in mind. By the early 1690s the proprietors had been joined by several important local authorities, including Governor Sothel, who began the first—and eventually unsuccessful—efforts to reform and regulate the Indian trade in 1691–92.[102] The greatest concern of Sothel and the proprietors was the capture and sale of Indian slaves. Though already considered inferior to Africans for work on South Carolina plantations, Indian slaves remained an important alternative and a valuable export. Despite orders from the proprietors and the governor's council forbidding the capture of Indian slaves within a four-hundred-mile radius from Charles Town, enslavement continued unabated.[103] Slaves were occasionally taken from among South Carolina's most valuable Indian allies, but more came from less familiar trading partners like the Congarees and the Cherokees.[104] Moore's 1690 expedition showed that colonists were directly responsible for some of this traffic, but most of it followed channels that were hidden from the view of most white men.

Indians continued to interact with one another in ways that colonial traders only vaguely understood. Southeastern Indian societies had fought one another long before the arrival of Europeans, and the taking of captives had long played a part in Indian military strategies.[105] With South Carolina traders helping to make such raids more possible and profitable, it was becoming easier for cyclical violence to break out and continue between groups of Indians that did not necessarily know or care that they were—from the proprietors' perspective—supposed to be getting along with one another. Before long most South Carolinians began to realize that they could not wield total control over the levels of violence between different Indian societies. In 1692 a party of Savannah warriors attacked a small and defenseless Cherokee village, taking nearly all its women and children as slaves to sell to the English traders. Informed of this outrage, the Commons House essentially shrugged its collective shoulders, claiming that there was no way to prevent the Savannahs from enslaving "their Long before enemies."[106] A few years later Governor John Archdale tried to mollify a frustrated petitioner by explaining "how hard a matter it [was] to keep them [the Indians] from taking Revenge for any Injuries received, to the third or fourth Generation; making personal Murders oftentimes National Quarrels."[107] To the delight of English slave traders and the concern of farsighted imperial officials, the Indians of the Southeast often proved eager enough to take up arms against one another even without too much prodding from the colonists.

As badly as some of South Carolina's allies were beginning to fare in these "national quarrels," their situation compared favorably to that of the Florida Indians. The increasing violence between South Carolina's Indian trading partners coincided with a brief respite for the Florida mission provinces, one that had probably been gained by the Spanish reprisals of the mid to late 1680s. Having been warned by the proprietors not to give any trouble "to that Crowne that [was] in league with [them]," South Carolina traders and officials were not likely to go on record encouraging the Indians to channel their raids into Spanish territory.[108] But despite England's need of Spain's assistance in its first great colonial war with France (King William's), Indians living under the nominal and actual protection of the Spanish were soon suffering from attacks by Indian groups armed and outfitted by South Carolina traders. Even Indians south of Saint Augustine felt the sting of these slave raids. Jonathan Dickinson, shipwrecked on the Florida coast, was startled to hear one headman use the expression "English son of a bitch," and slave raids had instilled other Indians with such a hatred of the English that Dickinson and his stranded shipmates were only able to survive by pretending to be Spanish. [109] While Dickinson's eventual safe escort to South Carolina proved that there was not yet any great danger of the Spanish and the English killing each other directly, South Carolina and Florida officials did not extend this courtesy to the region's Indians. Angered out of his usual stupor by the covert actions of the South Carolinians, Spain's King Carlos II ordered the governor of Florida in 1693 to "take reprisals" against South Carolina "and retain as many of their subjects as the Indians [whom] they took away from [the Spanish]." [110]

By the mid-1690s the Muskogeans had begun to replace the Savannahs as the most prolific slave raiders contracted to the South Carolina traders. Raiding parties from the Ocmulgee were now almost centrally located between Florida's inviting mission provinces, and soon their warriors were circulating within Apalachee and Timucua to pick off small and vulnerable groups of Indians. In August 1694 the Muskogeans went a step further by sacking the mission of San Carlos and capturing forty-two Chatot Indians, a largely Christianized group related to the neighboring Apalachees. When Spanish reprisals failed to cow the Muskogeans into submission, Muskogean raids on Florida continued to the point that Governor Torres y Ayala even began to worry that the Guale, Apalachee, and Timucua Indians in the remaining missions might decide to "rise up with the influence and the aid of the English." [111] Having enjoyed over a hundred years as the Southeast's sole colonial power, the Spanish at the end of the seventeenth century had already entered a desperate struggle to remain in the region.

The myriad problems that confronted the Spanish reflected a larger pattern that had been spreading throughout the Southeast since the establishment of South Carolina. Overall the region witnessed more change in the last twenty years of the seventeenth century than it had in the previous eighty. [112] Many of the English, Scottish, and Huguenot colonists who came to South Carolina from Europe and the West Indies were in a great hurry to make something of themselves and leave their mark on the world. They were not the only Europeans to come to the region with grand ambitions, but unlike most of their predecessors, the South Carolinians had the energy and financial backing to make their ambitions seem practical. The early success of the South Carolina Indian traders makes it easy to see the South Carolinians as the primary "givers" in the process of intercultural exchange. While they undoubtedly did a lot of giving—everything from trade goods to trouble—they also did a lot of taking from the groups they befriended and confronted. The South Carolinians not only took large quantities of deerskins and slaves but also proved quite adept at using preexisting trade routes and rivalries to their own advantage. The South Carolinians' growing success in these areas was due in part to their own initiative and perceptiveness but also depended on the actions and decisions of the Spanish and many of the Southeast's influential Indian societies.

The deepest impact of South Carolina's initial expansion into the southeastern interior was in exacerbating a complex process of cultural interaction that had been transpiring within the Southeast from time immemorial. The influence of the South Carolinians became heaviest where exchange patterns had already been growing more elaborate and intensive, and South Carolinians' ties were definitely closest with Spanish-influenced groups like the Yamasees, the Savannahs, and the Muskogeans. At the same time, however, the English colonists were also beginning to exert influence on Indian societies that had previously endured fewer contacts with outsiders. The small Siouan groups of the Carolina Piedmont, the numerous but isolated Cherokees of the Appalachians, and even the far-off Chickasaws near the Mississippi River were all, to varying degrees, entering into economic and political relationships with South Carolina. In addition the settlement and expansion of South Carolina led to the establishment of new kinds of frontiers that the Southeast had never experienced to any significant extent: those between European rivals and those surrounding a growing black slave society.

A mere thirty years after South Carolinians began arriving in the region, they had already laid the foundations for many of the frontiers that would remain influential throughout the colonial period. It would be safe to say that no society in the Southeast had ever accomplished so much in such a brief length of time. In the first decade of the eighteenth century, South Carolina seemed to continue along its upward trajectory. Its planters, traders, and government officials began to reveal plans and outlooks even more nakedly ambitious than those of previous years. A budding quest to bring all the Southeast's peoples and resources into the province's grip further intensified interaction along existing frontiers and even led to the creation of a few new ones.

2. Contested Empires

For all their apparent greed, many of the colonists who improved their fortunes on the plantations and frontiers of South Carolina were driven by a desire to serve something greater than themselves. They were imperialists: men who believed in the superiority of their own culture and the need to impose their economic and political authority on inferior parts of the world. South Carolina's traders and officials expected to face competition in their drive to amass wealth and influence in the Southeast, but they considered only certain groups to possess the stuff of true rivals. Though many of the Southeast's Indian societies had proven themselves actual or potential obstacles to South Carolina's expansion, they were perceived as serious threats only if they fell under the corrupting influence of another European power. From a colonist's perspective, leadership in this important power struggle almost invariably belonged to men of European origin.

By the time the English arrived to contest the Spanish "monopoly" in the late seventeenth century, several other parts of North America had already been shaped by decades of imperial competition. The rivals in the Southeast, however, quickly made up for lost time. As the end of the century approached, an already tense situation in the region grew even more precarious when an experienced group of French-Canadian soldiers and traders took up residence on the Gulf Coast, ominously close to the all-important mouth of the Mississippi. The establishment of a durable French colony at Mobile added a new dimension to imperial rivalry in the Southeast, making it the only region in North America to pit three imperial powers against one another.

At the turn of the eighteenth century, the French, the Spanish, and the English shared a mutual wariness and suspicion. In a complex, ever-changing web of disputes and alliances, a bitter enemy in one conflict could become a necessary partner in the next. In 1701, after France's Louis XIV attempted to gain untold power for the House of Bourbon by replacing Spain's deceased Carlos II with his own nephew, England headed a coalition against France and Spain in the resulting War of Spanish Succession. In North America the dispute over Spain took the name of Queen Anne's War and for nearly a decade brought even more bloodshed to a continent that had already grown familiar with it. In the Northeast this conflict continued a bitter struggle between French Canada and the New England colonies. In the Southeast it pushed English colonists into their first official war with their imperial rivals. The Spanish, nominal allies of the English during the 1690s, were now mortal enemies reinforced by the French. While Queen Anne's War engulfed the Southeast between 1702 and 1713, South Carolinians stepped up as the sole champions of the English Empire and for the first time saw their imperial ambitions in the region put to a serious test.

South Carolinians did not plan to face this challenge on their own, however. They hoped that many—if not most—of the war's burdens could be shouldered by their recently acquired Indian allies. With the Southeast's European settlements still confined to a few coastal enclaves, influence in the vast and strategic interior could make or break a colony in times of crisis. Despite the apparent extent of the colonists' influence at the beginning of the eighteenth century, getting allied Indians to act as loyal, cooperative, and productive servants provided South Carolina's imperialists with a daunting task. Throughout Queen Anne's War, they would find this kind of alliance easier to establish with some Native groups than with others.

Most Indian societies remained too powerful for the colonists to coerce into action and autonomous enough to provide assistance only when it suited their own interests as well as those of the English. Still, there were limits to Indian autonomy, even at this early stage in the colonial period. For several decades different southeastern Indian societies had been drawing closer to colonial regimes, acquiring European weapons, feeling the pull of European markets, and facing overtures from different European emissaries. All over the Southeast, the open warfare of the early 1700s added weight to these mitigating factors, presenting the Indians with more trade, more violence, and increasingly blatant invitations and affronts from colonial powers. The cumulative effect of Queen Anne's War on any given Indian society, however, also depended on factors such as that society's geographic situation, the intensity of its prewar contact with Europeans, and its traditional connections to other Indian groups. South Carolina's prewar frontiers had already displayed a great deal of diversity, and as a result the war ostensibly directed by colonial rivals had different effects on different parts of the Southeast. Like most wars in most parts of the world, Queen Anne's War in the Southeast was a conflict with several distinct but interconnected theaters.

The Florida Theater

The theater that figured most prominently in the early stages of the war encompassed the various "provinces" of Spanish Florida, frontier regions that had already developed a high degree of animosity between competing groups. Even before the dynastic quandary in Spain, these areas had become war zones. Despite the South Carolinians' contentions that they had nothing to do with the harassment of the Florida missions, one Spanish official remarked that peace with the English existed "no more than in name," and that the South Carolinians were "enemies going along seizing control of the lands of Florida under the cover of friendship."[1] In addition to the English guns wielded by Muskogean and Yamasee slave raiders, the Spanish perceived other evidence of the South Carolinians' dangerous intentions. Emissaries to Charles Town confirmed that the English were devising expeditions to settle the Gulf Coast and possibly the province of Apalachee. In 1698 Governor Joseph Blake coolly informed a Spanish officer that he planned to have an English settlement on Pensacola Bay within a year.[2] The Spanish soon began to believe that if the English could dare to show such effrontery "in a time of friendship," they would "seize control of everything in time of war, if they [were] not confronted with a strong defense and resistance."[3]

But as war appeared more imminent, South Carolina's imperial adversaries expressed doubts about their abilities to stop English encroachments into Florida. Pierre Le Moyne, sieur d'Iberville, the leader of France's fledgling colony in Louisiana, had orders to carefully evaluate Florida's prospects as a bulwark against the English. Having given the English fits as a naval commander in Canada, Iberville claimed to know his enemies well and expressed a grudging admiration for their "esprit de colonie." South Carolina, he warned, was growing "at such a rate that in less than a hundred years it [would] be strong enough to take all of America and force out all the other nations."[4] In his opinion the Spanish could never hold back the English without help from the French. The newly constructed Spanish bastion in Pensacola was "more like a horse corral than a fort," and the soldiers who staffed it did "not know the interior of the country very well." Within this interior the Spanish seemed to rely too much on the assistance of the Apalachees, a weakening group that would never be able to withstand a full-scale assault from the more aggressive "Apalachicolys," a blanket term that the French applied to the various Hitichi- and Muskogean-speaking towns along the Chattahoochee and the Ocmulgee.[5] Though their situation was not as bleak as Iberville depicted it, the Spanish in Florida were certainly on their heels even before the war against South Carolina began in earnest.

Nevertheless, South Carolinians showed some concern about the task that lay ahead of them. While they generally regarded the Spanish with contempt, the recently arrived French were another matter.[6] The French were perhaps the greatest military power in Europe, and their presence in Louisiana caused immediate panic throughout England's seaboard colonies, driving English authorities to contemplate the prospects of French "encirclement."[7] The French seemed even more dangerous because of their reputation as masters of Indian diplomacy in Canada. James Moore, the ambitious Goose Creek slave trader and recently appointed governor of Carolina, feared that the French had already begun trading among all Indian groups south of the Savannah River, and that many of the Indians were already being won over by the "liberality and conversation" of South Carolina's Gallic enemies.[8] Since trade was clearly the most crucial component of the colony's Indian alliances, it compelled South Carolinians to defend their trade networks with great vigilance. In true imperialist fashion, Moore announced that it was unthinkable for South Carolina's Indian allies and trading partners to entertain the French or to act as "friends to them and to [the South Carolinians] at the same time."[9]

This attitude bore striking similarities to that displayed by certain Spanish officials fifteen years earlier. Unlike Matheos and the other officers in Apalachee, however, the South Carolinians soon discovered that fears of enemy activity among their allies were largely unfounded. Iberville had begun some tentative efforts to court the "Apalachicolys" but had not managed to get very far.[10] South Carolinians continued to harbor fears about French and Spanish "spies," but it was fairly obvious that many of the problems in their Indian relations were of the South Carolinians' own making. Some of these problems emerged among the Savannahs and the Coosa, Tallapoosa, and Ocmulgee Muskogeans, groups prized by South Carolinians as "the only people by whom [they might] expect advice of an Inland Invasion."[11] These groups were not only suffering the ravages of a smallpox epidemic brought by European traders in 1698, but they were also beginning to pile up some hefty trade debts, a source of anxiety for Indian and white traders alike.[12]

As concerned as South Carolina authorities were about these groups, they urged "that there be a particular care taken of the Yamasees."[13] Residing closer to the expanding colonial settlements, the Yamasees had ties to South Carolinians that were even more intensive and potentially problematic. In the shadow of expanding ranches and plantations, the Yamasees were forced to raise an increasing number of complaints about the behavior of the traders operating near Port Royal, a group that seemed more inclined than most to take out their frustrations on the Indians.[14] Reports of beatings, robberies, and blatant fraud had a disturbing effect through the corridors of power in Charles Town, where even a scoundrel like Governor Moore could see that "heathenous, immoral, and unjust" behavior was no way to endear South Carolinians to their most valuable Indian allies.[15]

One result of this growing sense of urgency was another campaign by government officials to reform South Carolina's Indian trade. Unlike previous efforts in 1691 and 1697, the drive for trade reform between 1700 and 1702 promised to have more than a rhetorical impact. The Commons House began by forming a committee to summon and interrogate all available traders about the existing abuses in the Indian trade. Though unwilling to incriminate themselves, some traders proved eager to talk about the wrongdoing of others, helping the House begin prosecution of seven traders working among the Yamasees.[16] At the same time officials showed evidence that they were willing to get at the roots, as well as the symptoms, of trade abuse. They proposed one bill to appoint "a Judicious man" to supervise trade in the various Indian towns and another to ensure "that there be some convenient time given the Traders to gett in their Debts without oppression to the Natives."[17] Though most of the South Carolina officials agreed about the need to mollify Indians who could fight the French and the Spanish, they had difficulty reaching a consensus about the proper means for these ends. As a result the issue of a comprehensive code for reforming the Indian trade would remain up in the air for the next several years, acting as a political volleyball between South Carolina's rival government factions.[18]

The push for trade reform soon took a backseat to an emphasis on military preparedness among the Indians. Colonial emissaries began traveling from Charles Town to the villages of South Carolina's Indian allies, going as far west as the Coosa and Tallapoosa basins.[19] In August 1701 James Stanyarne was sent to visit the Yamasees "to Give them An Assurance of [South Carolina's] frindshipp, the more to Engage them to [the colony's] Interest." He brought with him a "present" of a hundred pounds of gunpowder, 150 pounds of shot, five hundred gunflints, one "great gun," and 288 knives: the kinds of military accessories that were often in greatest demand among the Indians.[20] Gifts like this one were expected not only to earn the gratitude of the Indians but also to indicate how groups like the Yamasees fit into South Carolina's immediate plans.

The most pressing item on South Carolina's wartime agenda was the conquest of Florida, an action that would expel the Spanish from the region and render the French more vulnerable. Because of Florida's strategic value and proximity to South Carolina, the Florida campaigns of Queen Anne's War were those in which the South Carolinians played their most direct role. Nevertheless, the South Carolina volunteers—like those New England colonists fighting the French in Canada—relied heavily on the assistance of various Indian groups.[21] Though ostensibly under the command of English officers, Indian warriors had a great deal of influence on the ways in which most of the battles and skirmishes unfolded. Queen Anne's War marked the first time South Carolinians and the southeastern Indians fought alongside each other in large-scale military operations, thereby greatly expanding opportunities for intercultural exchange.

As the commander of South Carolina's militia, Governor Moore felt a need to take Florida's main stronghold of Saint Augustine "before it [could] be strengthened with French forces."[22] In August 1702 he assembled a force of nearly 500 whites and 370 Indians, mostly Yamasees, which headed south from Port Royal in fourteen boats. In its early stages Moore's expedition followed patterns that had been established by more than two decades of Indian slave raids. One group of Indians, accompanied by several colonists and Deputy Governor Robert Daniel, demolished the two coastal missions that had retreated southward after the Guale raids of the 1680s. Many of the missions' occupants, Christianized Guale and Yoa Indians, fled to the Port Royal region, where they became a new and welcome addition to the Yamasee mosaic.[23] Following the successful raids on these missions, another splinter from the South Carolina expedition, thirty-three Yamasee warriors and South Carolina officer Thomas Nairne, moved inland along the Saint Johns River to prey on the Timucuans.[24]

Once Moore's and Daniel's forces converged in Saint Augustine, Indian warriors were relegated to the background.[25] The vulnerable town, evacuated upon word of the impending invasion, provided an easy prize for the South Carolinians. After razing scores of Spanish buildings and digging siege trenches, however, Moore's army hit its first major obstacle: four walls of sturdy coquina stone. While the Indians were judged incapable of investing the Castillo de

San Marcos, the swaggering South Carolinians proved just as ineffective, having thoroughly underestimated one of the most powerful fortresses in North America. Forced to care for fifteen hundred hungry civilians and fight off the invaders with fewer than seventy able-bodied soldiers, Governor Joseph de Zúñiga y Zérda displayed the abilities that would soon get him promoted out of Spain's colonial backwater. [26] Outclassed by Zúñiga at every turn, a frustrated Moore finally turned to his Indian allies, hoping that a Spanish-speaking Yamasee might be able to trick his way into the fort and incite a rebellion of the Indian refugees within. [27] Once inside, this daring "spy" was seized by the Indians and turned over to the Spanish, who were eventually relieved by a flotilla from Havana that sent the invaders packing. Though the South Carolinians' Trojan horse ruse failed, it demonstrated their recognition that preexisting connections between Indian groups could be useful to their province's war effort.

The Spanish were much less effective beyond the walls of their fort. In the provinces of Apalachee and Timucua, the Spanish missions proved wholly inadequate for the purpose of imperial defense. Indeed, the rapid collapse of the Guale missions had convinced most Florida officials of the missions' shortcomings as "frontier institutions" even before the start of Queen Anne's War. Any hopes that the Apalachee or Timucuan missions might be able to stand firm gradually diminished as the mission Indians suffered an array of internal and external pressures. [28]

Many Indians were clearly growing disillusioned with Christianity and Spanish authority. Fewer Apalachees were choosing to convert, "saying that, on their becoming Christians, the Spaniards treat[ed] them as slaves." [29] The demands of the *repartmiento* labor draft, along with the potential for abusive on-the-job treatment, undoubtedly increased as desperate authorities struggled to shore up the defenses of Saint Augustine and Pensacola. [30] For all the Indians' complaints about abusive soldiers and officers, however, just as many indictments of the friars found their way to Madrid. [31] Moreover, the turn of the eighteenth century saw a small but increasingly aggressive group of Spanish colonists impose on the Apalachee missions by pushing their way into the Indians' livestock trade and abusing any Indians who dared to challenge them. [32] Within a relatively short time, the Indians had begun to lose many of the freedoms that the missions had previously allowed them.

The deteriorating situation within the missions was exacerbated by the continued visits of "outsiders" to the mission provinces. The Apalachees shared some cultural commonalties with other Muskogean speakers in the Southeast, and the imperial rivalry of the previous thirty years was not enough to completely sever their centuries-old ties to these Indians. Traditional trade networks were in some ways strengthened by the distribution of European goods: the Ocmulgee Muskogeans, for example, actively sought out Apalachee horses, which they traded to the South Carolinians for guns.[33] The Apalachees were also gaining direct access to some of the more daring South Carolina traders and were beginning to hunt for the market with an intensity that placed the province's deer supply in jeopardy.[34] Such connections suggested to some Apalachees that life might be better beyond the pale of the missions. Increasing numbers of mission Indians began to leave Florida, with most of them moving north to settle among the Yamasees and the Ocmulgee Muskogeans.[35] Despite their best efforts to impose order on their remaining missions, Florida authorities could not prevent a strong anti-Spanish element from emerging, convincing one frustrated officer that the missions held "hidden and concealed enemies, thieves within the house in whom one [could] not trust."[36]

Enemies from within became all the more disturbing when combined with the continued depredations of external enemies. While some Muskogeans and Yamasees continued to go to Florida to trade with the Apalachees and the Timucuans, others continued to take the same paths to kill, plunder, or enslave them. By the first years of the eighteenth century, the one thing an Indian in a Florida mission could depend on was the growing likelihood of meeting a violent end. For all their grievances against Spanish abuses, the Apalachees and the Timucuans complained loudest about the inadequate protection provided by the missions.

Several months before the English assault on Saint Augustine, some of the Christian Apalachees approached Governor Zúñiga and requested military support for a massive retaliation against the Muskogean raiders they knew as the "Apalachicolas." The Christian Indians had suffered not only three more devastating raids in the past year but also, perhaps more seriously, the torture and murder of three Apalachee emissaries in an "Apalachicola" village.[37] Zúñiga agreed to support them, and the resulting punitive expedition was much larger than those of the 1680s and 1690s. In addition to Captain Francisco Romo de Uriza and several Spanish troops, it included more than eight hundred Apalachee warriors. Word of the invasion somehow reached the "infidel" towns, where several South Carolina traders took part in the councils that were assembled to plan a defense. Trader Anthony Dodsworth joined five hundred warriors from towns on the Ocmulgee and the Chattahoochee in hastening to a spot by the Flint River, where they arranged a clever ambush of the Spanish-Apalachee force. With advantages of surprise and firepower, the smaller Muskogean force was able to rout the Apalachees, five hundred to six hundred of whom were killed, enslaved, or subsequently adopted into Muskogean towns. The others returned to the missions thoroughly demoralized, spreading their hopelessness like a disease and leaving their province in an even weaker state.[38]

The Spanish and the Christian Indians now faced a lost cause in the mission provinces. They were critically wounded and critically divided, and their tormentors from the north knew it. In 1703 Muskogean raids destroyed three more missions and carried off some five hundred more Florida Indians. The ease and success of these forays soon convinced other groups to try some of their own, giving ambitious South Carolinians an opportunity to adopt tried and true Indian strategies as a means to further their imperial and personal agendas.

Since the expensive failure of his Saint Augustine expedition, James Moore had seen himself removed from the governor's office, accused of drunkenness and incompetence, and embroiled in shouting matches and fistfights to defend his honor.[39] The vulnerability of Apalachee gave him the perfect chance to recoup the losses to his fortune and reputation. In his excitement Moore could come up with a dozen reasons for the South Carolina government to support an offensive against the missions.[40] Some of these reasons, such as the need to protect South Carolina's Indian allies from the Apalachees, rang fairly hollow. Other motives—such as the further humiliation of the Spanish, better access to Pensacola, and the prospect of new Indian allies and trading partners—were more compelling. The Commons House granted Moore permission "to gain by all peaceable means possible the Apalachees to [their] interest," but refused to give him a penny for it, forcing the tough old soldier to recruit his own private army.[41] The force of fifty white Carolinians and one thousand Muskogeans that he assembled in 1703—largely with promises of plunder—was bound to be anything but "peaceable" in its march through Apalachee.

Moore's army was indicative of the trend toward larger Indian fighting forces during Queen Anne's War. Though Indian groups like the Muskogeans were capable of organizing sizable war parties on their own, the process was undoubtedly facilitated by the colonists' ability—through trade goods and other incentives—to attract warriors from different towns.[42] In any event Moore's expedition showed that Indian warriors recruited by colonists were not necessarily subordinate to colonial officers out in the field. In January 1704, when the expedition set upon its first Apalachee target, the mission of Ayubale, the Muskogean warriors went off to raid the surrounding "plantations" while the South Carolinians took nine hard-fought hours to remove a friar and a stubborn group of Christian Apalachees from the village chapel. The Muskogeans returned in time to help defeat a Spanish-Apalachee relief force of some four hundred men, killing nearly half of them and saving about forty prisoners for an even worse fate.[43] The Muskogeans' treatment of their captives gave some indication of the enmity they had built for the Spanish and their Indian allies; like most North American Indian cultures, they reserved torture for their most bitter enemies. In Apalachee they left behind a gruesome sight: rows of "bound and burned" corpses with eyes, ears, and tongues cut from their heads. When a priest complained about the atrocities outside Ayubale, Moore simply said that he and the other whites "could not prevent it" even if they tried.[44] His response gave the impression that the South Carolinians were not directing a Muskogean war party but hitching a ride with one.

By the time they left Apalachee that spring, the South Carolinians and the Muskogeans had destroyed four more missions and spared another for a ransom of church silver and Spanish trade goods. They returned north with a hefty supply of plunder and slaves, but not quite enough to suit Moore.[45] Under government orders to provide safe escort for all Indians who desired it, Moore grudgingly brought thirteen hundred free Apalachees—those who had surrendered voluntarily—to the Savannah River basin, where most of them took up residence as a valuable addition to South Carolina's defensive perimeter, and from whence some of them continued on to the Yamasee towns around Port Royal or the Muskogean towns along the Ocmulgee.[46] More Apalachees joined this exodus throughout the remainder of the year, for reasons that were clear enough. As several Apalachees explained to Deputy Governor Manuel Solana that summer, "they were weary of waiting for aid from the Spaniards," and they knew "with certainty" that more damaging raids from the "pagans" would be on the way.[47] Those who did not head north had to deal with another wave of raids in July, this time conducted solely by the Muskogeans, who had grown quite adept at terrorizing the Spanish on their own.[48] Realizing the futility of further resistance, the Spanish burned the San Luis blockhouse and retreated to Pensacola and Saint Augustine. Most of the remaining Indian converts followed suit, with some of them forsaking the Spanish and settling near the French enclave at Mobile, where they expected to find better trade goods and protection.[49]

Through the end of 1705, the war in the Southeast seemed to be going very well for the English. South Carolinians and their Indian allies had remained almost exclusively on the offensive but at the same time had not ignored the need to maintain a sound defense. Most of the essential preparations for this defense fell under the direction of newly appointed Governor Nathaniel Johnson, a wealthy Goose Creek planter with considerable military experience, "haveing been bredd abroad a Soldier from his Youth."[50] Johnson oversaw the revamping of the capital's walls and bastions, as well as the construction of the fort on Charles Town Harbor that would bear his name for the next two centuries. The governor also devised the 1703–4 acts that restructured South Carolina's militia system, grouping planters, laborers, servants, and even some "trustworthy" slaves into a reasonably effective fighting force.[51] The colonists themselves did not lack confidence in their martial skills: one of them asserted that every South Carolinian "from the Governour to the meanest Servant" was "dextrous and expert in the use of Fire-Arms," and "a better Soldier, upon Occasion, than a company of raw Fellows raised in England."[52]

South Carolinians' confidence in their home guard was seemingly justified in August 1706, when it passed its only real test of Queen Anne's War. Governor Zúñiga, convinced that any group that let Indians do its fighting would be "very easy" to overrun, had worked with Iberville to persuade the French and Spanish governments to support a seaborne invasion of South Carolina.[53] A force of five French privateers and several hundred troops from Saint Augustine and Havana struck—much as the Spanish had done in 1686—while the colony was suffering from an outbreak of yellow fever. This "second Spanish Armada," as the South Carolinians called it, met with about as much success as the first Spanish Armada had 118 years earlier. The French ships were driven off by a makeshift South Carolinian fleet, and those Spanish troops who made landfall suffered dozens of casualties and lost over two hundred prisoners.[54]

The South Carolina militia had risen to the challenge, but not all the glory belonged to the white citizen-soldiers. A black slave had spotted and raised the first alarm about the invasion, and the most heroic troops during the skirmishes had been a company of some one hundred Indians from a low-country group known as the Santees. The Indians connected to South Carolina had clearly proven themselves capable of playing a defensive as well as an offensive role during time of war. At the same time, however, the failed Franco-Spanish invasion underscored what many South Carolinians had known for some time: that if a more formidable invasion struck, they would have to rely on the help of Indian groups much larger and more powerful than the Santees.

The Indian trade still provided the key to incorporating these groups into the colony's defensive network. Keeping the trade running as smoothly as possible had been a priority at the beginning of Queen Anne's War, and it took on even greater importance several years into the conflict. The South Carolina government continued to grant important Indian groups occasional supplies of weapons and powder as gifts or bribes but usually required the Indians to pay for the implements, which were growing more and more essential to their ability to hunt and fight effectively.[55] Export and population statistics suggest that the Indians' acquisition of deerskins and slaves reached a peak roughly midway through Queen Anne's War.[56] As always the traffic in slaves remained the most lucrative and problematic aspect of the Indian trade. Queen Anne's War made the Southeast an even more violent place, making it easier for some traders to practice "the trick of setting them [the Indians] to surprise one another's towns" with little regard for the possible consequences.[57] Less than two years after their arrival on the Savannah River, thirty-five of the Apalachee refugees from Florida were seized and enslaved under orders from trader John Musgrove. In 1703 and again in 1706, Cherokee raiding parties sponsored by trader James Child took more than 160 slaves from the Coosa and Tallapoosa Muskogeans, groups considered vital to South Carolina's security. It did not take a political genius to realize that acts like these could alienate South Carolina's allies and prove "very prejudicial" to the safety of the province.[58]

Still, there was no effective way to legally prevent these transgressions. Despite nearly fifteen years of intermittent effort, South Carolina's Indian trade remained unregulated and unreformed. Debate over the trade had been overshadowed for several years by the province's military campaigns and a bitter religious controversy between Anglicans and Dissenters but soon returned to the forefront of a factious political climate.[59] During the first part of Queen Anne's War, the overwhelmingly Anglican and conservative Goose Creek faction held most positions of power. Since they controlled both the governor's seat and the council, they shaped most official decisions regarding the Indian trade. Moreover, they had "a vested interest in the status quo."[60] The governor and the council grew wealthy from the various "gifts" and tributes they acquired from South Carolina's Indian trading partners and probably received substantial kickbacks from the several traders who enriched themselves through illegal slave raids. Governors Moore and Johnson were the subjects of a great deal of bitter, and probably well-founded, rumors about their involvement in the slave trade. As an ally of the Lords Proprietors, Daniel Defoe accused Moore of "having already almost utterly ruined the Trade for Skins and Furs and turned it into a Trade of Indian or Slave-making, whereby the Indians to the South and West of [South Carolina were] already involved in Blood and Confusion, a Trade so odious and abominable, that every other colony in America (altho' they [had] equal temptation) abhor to follow."[61]

Those who pushed most adamantly for changes to the existing system came largely from the growing ranks of the Goose Creek faction's enemies. They included not only Quakers, Huguenots, and Scottish Presbyterians, who had faced religious persecution from the Anglicans, but also a bloc from the colony's expanding southwestern settlements that had legitimate concerns for their own security.[62] They believed that the Yamasees, the Ocmulgee Muskogeans, the Apalachees, and other Indians necessary for the colonists' protection could be induced to play this role only through trade reform. As one member of the Commons House noted, "Want of Watches, forts, loss of duties, etc. is not to be Named in Comparison with it, & if it be Our unhappy fate to Live in Such a time when Our Country is Doomed to be ruined, we are not sollicitous to provide a defence for Our breasts when we may at the same time receive a mortall stabb thro Our Backs."[63]

Frustrated by Governor Johnson's recurring vetoes of their trade bills, the reform faction alternately flattered, cajoled, and threatened him. In the end they overcame his opposition only by winning thirty new seats in the 1707 elections and agreeing to pay the governor an annual stipend to substitute for his lost tributes from the Indians. The reform faction also had valuable support from the increasingly influential Charles Town merchants, who saw trade regulation as a good way to cut down on the cheating by the Indian traders they employed.[64]

South Carolina's "Act for Regulating the Indian Trade and Making it Safe to the Publick" was ratified on July 18, 1707, and entered the province's books on the following day. It clearly aimed at overseeing the province's trade with strategically important Indian societies and explicitly exempted small and beleaguered low-country groups like the Santees, the Ittawans, the Seewees, the Kiawas, the Edistoes, and the Stonoes. All trade carried out beyond the colonial settlements was to fall under the supervision of a new government agency, the Board of Commissioners for the Indian Trade. Selected mainly from the Upper and Lower Houses of Assembly, the board's nine rotating members were empowered to levy fines for such crimes as selling liquor to the Indians, selling free Indians into slavery, or extorting goods from the Indians "under the notion of presents for the Governours." For the first time colonial traders were required to purchase licenses granted and renewed at the discretion of the commissioners, who were legally forbidden from being "directly or indirectly concerned in the Indian trade." The nine commissioners and their secretary expected to be kept apprised of all of South Carolina's traders in the Southeast through the herculean efforts of the regulatory body's most important official: the Indian agent. In exchange for a substantial salary, the Indian agent was required to spend ten months per year in "the principal towns among the Indians in amity with [the] Province," inquiring into their needs and complaints and reporting on the behavior of the various traders.[65]

Thomas Nairne, the principal author of the 1707 Indian act, devised the position of Indian agent with himself in mind. A "Carolina Whig" who owned a plantation in the southernmost reaches of Colleton County, Nairne was an intelligent and energetic man who brimmed with ideas and contradictions.[66] Nairne had experience as a trader among the Yamasees and also was an avowed imperialist who had taken part in slave raids during Moore's 1702–4 Florida campaigns. At the same time he probably knew more about the Southeast's various Indian societies than any other South Carolinian of his day and was honestly disturbed by some of the abuses they suffered at the hands of the whites. With Nairne installed at the head of South Carolina's regulatory efforts, the colonial government had taken a significant step toward addressing some of the problems on the province's most important frontiers.

This most recent attempt to regulate the Indian trade reflected a general trend toward a more "hands-on" approach to South Carolina's Indian allies. Colonial authorities had long sought to monitor strategically important Indian groups, but the imperial struggle and steadily expanding trade associated with Queen Anne's War made it even more crucial for them to engage in Indian diplomacy. To accomplish this goal, they would have to venture into Indian villages and council houses, where politics and diplomacy tended to bear little resemblance to European models. When negotiating with fellow Europeans, English diplomats usually dealt with leaders and ambassadors who could confidently claim the authority to speak on behalf of their nations. Though guided by strict codes of decorum, Indian councils lacked the kind of authoritarian ambiance that many Europeans held dear. Indian leadership usually displayed so much dissension and so little hierarchy that colonial observers like Nairne were often at a loss for words to describe it. During his first tour of duty as South Carolina's Indian agent, Nairne noted of Tallapoosa leaders, "[They] seldom ever use any Coercion, only harrangue[;] if by that they can persuade it's well, if not they rarely enforce their orders by sanctions." Techniques such as these were foreign to Nairne's own political experience, but like all intercultural mediators on the Southeast's early frontiers, he tried to understand Indian politics through a somewhat ethnocentric lens. Even then he realized that he could not provide an accurate analogy for what he saw; the best he could do was claim that "Plato nor no other writter of Politicks even of the most republican principles, could never contrive a Government where the equallity of mankind is more Justly observed than [there] among the savages."[67]

Indian politics appealed to the more idealistic impulses of some colonists but invariably proved confusing for those who tried to intervene in them. The frustration of colonial emissaries only increased when they attempted to move beyond the village level, for even those settlements that shared linguistic, ethnic, or cultural traits usually found it difficult to unite on any single course of action. Nowhere was this tendency toward disunity more apparent than among the Muskogeans, and nowhere did South Carolina officials feel a more pressing need to modify it. Eventually South Carolinians—along with future generations of historians—would settle on a convenient shorthand for the Muskogeans and their adopted fringe groups and lump them into a single "Creek confederacy" composed of upper and lower divisions. By the time of Queen Anne's War, however, South Carolinians attempting to consolidate the Muskogeans into a more manageable polity had not managed to get very far. The term "Creek" was used only sparingly, and only in reference to those Indians of the eleven towns in the area of Ochese Creek, a principal tributary of the Ocmulgee. [68] These Indians were more frequently referred to as the Ocheses and generally seen by the South Carolinians as an entire nation in and of themselves. Similarly colonial officials began to speak of distinct nations situated in other Muskogean regions: the Tallapoosas in the Coosa-Tallapoosa basins, the Abeikas further to the north, and the Alabamas further to the west.

Like the Ochese Creek Indians, most of the other Muskogean "nations" were known among the Europeans by more than one name. The English ("Creeks"), the Spanish ("Apalachicolas"), and the French ("Alibamons") occasionally used blanket terms for the southeastern Muskogeans, but for most of the early eighteenth century, they all recognized distinct divisions among these Indians. The Spanish broke them down into seven groups: the Apalachicolas (on the Chattahoochee), the Uchises (on the Ocmulgee), the Tasquiques, the Talapuses, the Alibamos, the Tequipaches, and the Apiscas. The French tended to recognize four divisions: the Caouitas (on the Ocmulgee), the Talapouches, the Abihkas, and the Alabamons. These bore close resemblance to the four divisions recognized by the English: the Ocheses, the Abeikas, the Tallapoosas, and the Alabamas. The rough correlation between the Spanish, the French, and the English nomenclature suggests that the different colonial powers were making largely independent evaluations of Indian political organization, and that these "national identities" were—at least to some extent—being recognized by the Indians themselves.[69]

Despite the many mistakes and inconsistencies they made along the way, South Carolinians and other Europeans were not completely misguided in their attempts to group individual Muskogean settlements into larger polities. The town, or talwa, continued to operate as the fundamental governing unit among the Muskogeans, but various towns had been sharing and building certain connections to one another even before the establishment of South Carolina.[70] The regional polities or "provinces" that began taking shape in the Tallapoosa, Chattahoochee, and Apalachicola basins during the seventeenth century drew not only from extensive, intervillage clan networks but also from an emerging village hierarchy in which older towns like Coweta, Cussita, Tuckabatchee, and Oakfuskee served as a kind of central core for smaller and more recently established towns.[71] Even before the beginning of extensive contact with Europeans, certain Muskogean leaders from the prestigious founding towns were able to wield some influence beyond their own settlements. The first European traders and officials to circulate among the Muskogeans did not hesitate to seek out these leaders, or anything remotely suggestive of centralized authority, to help them gain influence over the Indians. By relying on the most prominent Muskogean towns as trade depots or command centers, colonists helped reinforce the status of these towns and their leaders in the outlying areas. After several decades of sustained interaction with Europeans, it appeared that the Muskogeans were well on their way to adopting various national identities to go along with the more traditional identities rooted in the clans and towns.[72]

While they did not thrust these national identities on the Muskogeans, the South Carolinians did try to make a little too much of them, especially when faced with the pressures of Queen Anne's War. In their struggle against the French and the Spanish, they wanted to be able to count on the aid of well-coordinated nations instead of loose conglomerates of indecisive towns. The most fantastic example of wishful thinking on the part of the South Carolinians came with a treaty signed at the "Court" of Coweta in August 1705, in which sundry "Kings," "Princes," "Generals," and "War Captains" representing the towns of five different Muskogean "Nations" pledged their "Hearty Alliance" and "Subjection" to the "High and Mighty Ann, Queen of the English, and to all her Majesties Governours of Carolina."[73] The five "Nations" listed in the treaty were the Ocheses, the Tallapoosas, the Alabamas, the Abeikas, and the "Haritaumau," which one historian has deciphered as the "Altamaha." The inclusion of this last nation suggests that the Yamasees might have participated in the treaty, which would constitute further evidence of cultural-political connections between the Yamasees and the Muskogean-Hitichi groups of the interior. [74] This treaty did not make everything fall into place for the South Carolinians, and for the duration of the war, they were forced to continue their efforts to consolidate their Muskogean allies. In 1708 Thomas Nairne attended a "corronation" ceremony for a respected headman in the town of Oakfuskee and saw it as an ideal opportunity to invest the respected leader with a governor's commission to be "head of all the Tallapoosies settlement[s]." [75] Such stratagems helped add new elements to Muskogean political culture but hardly led to the implementation of an English-style bureaucracy or military chain of command. The Muskogeans would continue to impress the South Carolinians as "great hunters and warriors" with a healthy appetite for English goods, but they remained far too remote, powerful, and dynamic to be considered anything like the "subjects" the South Carolina authorities wanted them to be. [76]

On some of their other frontiers, however, South Carolinians were able to wield a more direct and thorough influence over their Indian allies. In terms of size, strength, and military prowess, the Yamasees were nearly on par with the Ocheses, the Tallapoosas, and other Muskogean nations. At the same time they faced the disadvantage of residing much closer to South Carolina's expanding colonial settlements. In the eyes of colonial authorities, this made the Yamasees the most important and delicate cog in South Carolina's defensive network. Government officials had taken extra steps to mollify the Yamasees even before the outbreak of Queen Anne's War, and several years into the conflict, such efforts appeared even more necessary. For committed imperialists, however, these efforts were more rewarding than burdensome; the more the Yamasees came to depend on the government's protection, the more susceptible they became to government manipulation.

The regulation of the Indian trade was not the only government act of 1707 designed to increase South Carolina's influence over the Yamasees. The previous year the South Carolina Commons House had received several complaints from Yamasees about colonists encroaching on their lands and coming "so near their Settlements that the Stock put thereon [ate] up and destroy[ed] their provisions." [77] Concerned that further encroachments would "occasion the Indians to leave [them]," the Commons House drew up a bill "to Limitt the bounds of the Yamasees and prevent people from running out land amongst them." [78] When ratified in November 1707, this act carved out a tract of land bounded on the northeast by the Combahee River, on the southeast by the marshes of the Port Royal River, on the southwest by the Savannah River, and on the northwest by a line running between the headwaters of the Combahee and the Savannah. All colonists holding tracts or livestock in this area were required to remove them, with all future encroachments punishable by a fine of one hundred pounds Carolina money. It appeared that the Yamasees would be able to live, hunt, and farm without disturbance on South Carolina's first official Indian reservation.[79]

Not surprisingly this offer of security came with several strings attached. First of all, the new layout of the Yamasee settlements followed designs that were more English than Indian in origin. Within the "Indian land," South Carolina authorities hoped to complete the "nationalization" of a diverse group of Tamas, Guales, Yoas, and Muskogeans.[80] Formerly widespread and highly transient, the settlements of these Indians were now to be centered around ten towns: the "upper" towns of Pocotaligo, Huspah, Saupaulau, Pocosabo, and Tomatley, and the "lower" towns of Altamaha, Oketee, Chechesee, and Yoa.[81] The northernmost of these towns, Pocotaligo, quickly achieved the status of head town, not because the Yamasees recognized it as such, but because it was most convenient for South Carolina traders and officials.[82] Overall, the entire reservation was designed to serve colonial interests, for it positioned the Yamasees in an ideal location: directly between Charles Town and Saint Augustine. This area not only served as a strategic buffer but also sat comfortably away from the Port Royal marshes that had begun to produce bountiful crops of rice.[83] The Yamasees' tract between the Combahee and Savannah rivers had not yet shown this kind of agricultural promise, but if it ever did, colonists were promised that they would be able to occupy it "in case the Yamasees remove[d] from the aforesaid limits on their own, or by order of the Government."[84] With this clause South Carolina authorities expressed great confidence in their ability to keep the Yamasees safely under control.

Even if the Yamasees had wanted to leave their reservation, the South Carolina government would not have allowed them to do so. In 1707–8 the fate of several hundred Savannah Indians provided a vivid example of the lengths South Carolinians would go to in order to preserve their Indian defense network. Situated about 150 miles west of Charles Town on the river named after them, the Savannahs had experienced the advantages and disadvantages of more than twenty-five years of intensive trading with the South Carolinians. Frustrated with the traders and increasingly overshadowed by the neighboring Yamasees, Apalachees, and Muskogeans, more than half of them decided to try their luck elsewhere, beginning a long and gradual migration to the north in the spring of 1707.[85] Convinced that "some wrong hath heretofore been done to these people which forced them into the measures of deserting," the Commons House initially suggested that "gentle means" be used to return them to their old towns. When they failed to persuade the "deserters," the House joined the governor in authorizing the use of force to "reduce" them.[86] For the next year, before they could make their way to the relative safety of Maryland and Pennsylvania, the Savannah refugees were crippled by various attacks from the Ocheses, the Catawbas, and even a small party of South Carolinians led by James Moore Jr., son of the former governor.[87] Though the Savannahs had at one time been among the most active and effective of South Carolina's allies, many of them were treated as enemies or runaway slaves once they decided to alter the blueprints designed by the colonial government.

For the time being, however, the Savannahs remained the only group to give the South Carolinians any trouble along their southern frontiers. Authorities generally expressed great pleasure with the conduct of other Native groups, especially the Muskogeans and the Yamasees, who were continuing to inflict misery on the Spanish and their dwindling Indian allies. The prominence of Indian warriors in the Florida theater of Queen Anne's War did not end with the devastation of Apalachee. As the Ocheses and other Muskogean groups began to turn their attention to the Pensacola region and points further west, the Yamasees assumed the role of primary raiders on the Florida peninsula. By 1706 Yamasee warriors and slave raiders had "wholly laid waste" to the Timucuan missions along the road from Saint Augustine to Apalachee.[88] Soon they were compelled to roam as far south as the Florida Keys in search of slaves to bring back to South Carolina. In a 1710 promotional pamphlet, Thomas Nairne boasted that there remained not "so much as one Village with ten Houses in it, in all Florida, which [was] continually infested by the perpetual Incursions of the Indians subject to this Province."[89] Though Nairne was wont to some exaggeration, Florida authorities readily admitted to the sorry state of their influence within the region. They scoffed at royal orders for another invasion of South Carolina and insisted that only their fort in Saint Augustine prevented them from being driven from Florida altogether.[90] In 1711 a census of the remaining missions huddled in the immediate vicinity of Saint Augustine counted only 401 Indians in seven settlements, all of them located within a "pistol shot" of the fortress. This total was a far cry from the tens of thousands considered under Spanish jurisdiction only a few decades earlier.[91]

Though the Spanish managed to preserve a tenuous toehold in Florida, their rapid and dramatic collapse during Queen Anne's War reflected some monumental changes that were occurring along several of the Southeast's most prominent frontiers. All the Indian societies that took part in the Florida campaigns of the war had at one time maintained important relationships with two different kinds of colonial regimes. Before Queen Anne's War even those groups that had already turned toward the South Carolinians were not all that far removed from the influence of the Spanish. After several years of hard raiding and fighting, however, even most of the Apalachees could see that the Spanish were no longer a viable source for the kind of assistance necessary for prosperity and survival. The South Carolina imperialists had thrust their way into the old provinces of Florida, following the tracks that the Ocheses, the Yamasees, the Savannahs, and the Apalachees had laid down in their relationships with the Spanish and with one another. Along South Carolina's southern frontiers, the confidence and influence of the South Carolinians seemed to be growing almost exponentially.

The Western Theater

In the broad region between the Alabama and Mississippi rivers, an area beyond the reach of the old provinces of Florida, Indian societies with strong Mississippian foundations cooperated and competed in a context where European influence was slower to emerge. Neither those groups closer to the Gulf Coast, like the Mobilians, the Tohomes, and the Pascagoulas, nor those further to the north, like the Choctaws, the Chickasaws, and the Yazoos, encountered more than a handful of whites between the de Soto expedition and the end of the seventeenth century. When the first European colonists and traders finally began to filter into the region, however, they noticed that its Native peoples were not completely isolated from the outside world. Piles of blanched human skeletons attested to the work of deadly epidemics, and the requests and demands of Native warriors suggested that the reputation of certain European goods had preceded the Europeans themselves.[92] Many of these western groups seemed to embrace European trade and diplomacy with an enthusiasm that encouraged colonial imperialists, even those in far-off South Carolina. Within little more than a decade, South Carolina's western frontiers were transformed from virtually unknown lands into violent and important fronts in the province's imperial struggle.

The first South Carolinians arrived along these western frontiers only a few years ahead of Queen Anne's War. Just as they had done among the Yamasees, the Savannahs, the Apalachees, and the Muskogeans, South Carolina traders took advantage of preexisting connections in their quest to branch into new territory. When Henry Woodward and his colleagues made their first profitable trips to the Chattahoochee in the mid-1680s, they came across several Chickasaw Indians who had married Muskogean women and—fitting with the norms of the Southeast's matrilocal societies—moved into the towns and homes of their wives. The relatively strong connections between the Chickasaws and the Muskogeans not only helped South Carolina traders discover a new western market but also helped familiarize them with the rudiments of Chickasaw language and culture.[93] By the early 1690s the most adventurous traders felt confident enough to visit the Chickasaw towns scattered throughout present-day northern Mississippi and western Tennessee, a distance of over nine hundred miles from the colonial settlements of South Carolina.[94]

Over the next several years, South Carolina traders entered into relationships with various Native groups as far west as the areas of the Tombigbee, Pearl, and Yazoo rivers. In 1698 Thomas Welch, a neighbor and friend of Thomas Nairne, went as far as the west bank of the Mississippi to establish a trading post among the Quapaw Indians. Overall, however, the South Carolinians devoted most of their attention to the Chickasaws. Composed of roughly five thousand people in several dozen loosely associated, agriculturally based towns, the Chickasaws were a highly militaristic group, whose warriors had a reputation as the deadliest in the region. Their skills in hunting and fighting—and the needs that these skills engendered—made them ideal partners for the South Carolina trader-imperialists. But while the Indian trade conducted closer to South Carolina mainly involved deerskins, trade on South Carolina's western frontiers revolved almost exclusively around the capture of slaves, the easiest and most cost-effective cargo to transport over long distances. The Chickasaws had long been accustomed to taking slaves from their enemies for purposes such as blood revenge and status enhancement, but when South Carolinians began to offer highly prized firearms in exchange for these prisoners, they presented the Chickasaws with the motivation to step up the frequency and intensity of their raids.[95]

By the time Iberville established his Louisiana colony in 1699, the Chickasaws had already become the scourge of the entire region. When Henri de Tonti, an experienced trader and officer from Canada, led the first major French reconnaissance mission into interior Louisiana in 1702, he got a close look at the devastation wrought not only on the small and most vulnerable Indian groups but also on nations as apparently large and stable as the Choctaws. Distantly related to their Chickasaw neighbors, the Choctaws were probably the largest Indian society in the Southeast, a conglomeration of forty to fifty towns rooted in a solid agricultural foundation.[96] Tonti discovered that several Choctaw villages were nearly paralyzed with fear of their longtime enemies, and that the threat of well-armed Chickasaw raids even prevented one village from harvesting its crops.[97]

Though the Chickasaws and other Indians of the Lower Mississippi Valley maintained considerable strength and leverage, they quickly began to feel the pull of the competing colonial powers. By the turn of the eighteenth century, English colonial promoters like Dr. Daniel Coxe had begun to insist that the fertile Mississippi country could eventually house colonies richer and more powerful than those on the Atlantic seaboard.[98] For the time being, however, the English goal was to prevent Louisiana from linking up with the French colonies in Canada and the Upper Mississippi Valley. The Chickasaws, situated almost due north of the new Louisiana settlements, therefore increased their considerable value in the eyes of South Carolina imperialists.[99] The Chickasaws' numerous Indian enemies were left out to dry and understandably showed great enthusiasm when a newly arrived group of whites professed their undying hatred of the English. The French quickly recognized their good fortune; in addition to promising extensive trade with the Choctaws, they began the process of arming nearby groups like the Mobilians.[100] Shortly after their arrival in Louisiana, the French seemed to have an extensive Indian alliance network thrown at their feet.

At the same time the French realized that this network would do them little good unless they could manage to gain some influence over the groups that were tormenting their new Indian allies. This need compelled them to reach out not only to the Chickasaws but also to groups like the Alabamas, who had begun to terrorize some of the smaller Indian societies in the vicinity of Pensacola and Mobile.[101] In the early stages of Queen Anne's War, the French imperial strategies toward these Indian groups differed markedly from the approaches of the English. Knowing that South Carolinians saw intertribal warfare as a means to exert their own imperial influence, Iberville attempted to establish peace between the region's major Indian societies. In February 1702 he convinced four Choctaw and seven Chickasaw headmen to attend a conference in Mobile, in which he promised that the South Carolinians would weaken both the Choctaws and the Chickasaws and then would "come with other nations from the east and carry off what few people remain[ed]" to be sold as slaves in "far-off lands."[102] When the apparent success of this Chickasaw-Choctaw "treaty" was repeated several months later with a delegation of eight Alabama headmen, French officials brimmed with confidence in their ability to reconcile the Indians and frustrate English designs.[103]

The French soon realized that it would take more than a few treaties to accomplish their agenda among the Louisiana Indians. Like the South Carolinians, they had trouble getting Indian societies to behave like disciplined, well-ordered nations. The various headmen who visited Mobile represented, at most, the positions of their town councils. They could not really speak for the other towns in their respective nations or, for that matter, for many of the Indians within their own towns. In 1703 five French traders were invited among the Alabamas, who proceeded to kill four of them and steal all their goods. To the French this ambush was nothing less than treachery and grounds for a French-Alabama war that lasted for the next nine years.[104] More likely the Alabamas who supported the French were simply cajoled or overwhelmed by a larger group of Alabamas who had never relinquished their attachment to the English or their traditional hatred of France's Choctaw and Mobilian allies. Their attack on the French also could have had something to do with the South Carolina emissaries present in several Alabama villages, who used reports of their military success in Florida to persuade some of the western Muskogean nations to back the winning side.[105] Whatever its causes, this outbreak of violence put a sudden stop to Iberville's peace plan. Louisiana officials began to offer bounties for the scalps of Alabamas, Abeikas, or any other "English Indians" and finally began to provide firearms for the beleaguered Choctaws. The battle lines for the western theater of Queen Anne's War had been drawn.[106]

The first decade of the eighteenth century marked a tumultuous period for all the Native groups of Louisiana. The combination of slave raids, battles, and newly introduced diseases caused an astounding demographic decline: the French estimated the wartime casualties of the Chickasaws and the Choctaws alone at over three thousand people.[107] Heavy slave raids destroyed crops and caused famine among the Choctaws, and the rising death rate forced the Chickasaws "to break up their Townships and unite them for want of inhabitants."[108] Queen Anne's War affected Indian polities in other ways as well. For many of the Chickasaws, warfare and slave raiding were transformed from favorite pastimes to near obsessions, and the most skillful Chickasaw warriors began to challenge and override the prestige of the village headmen. One well-respected Chickasaw "peace chief," whose position had long held him aloof from military concerns, broke with tradition when he discovered that "slave catching was much more profitable than formall harranguing." During a stay among the Chickasaws in 1708, Thomas Nairne observed, "No imployment pleases the Chicasaws so well as slave catching. A lucky hitt at that besides the Honor procures them a whole Estate at once . . . which would not be procured without much tedious toil a hunting." [109] Like those Native groups to the east, the Indians on South Carolina's western frontiers found that war involved them in closer relationships with European traders, the men who provided them with the guns, bullets, and other goods that were growing more essential by the day.

Despite such substantial "reactive changes," some groups in the western theater of Queen Anne's War were able to maintain a degree of autonomy that kept them from becoming pawns in the imperial struggle between France and England. Societies as large, powerful, and relatively remote as the Choctaws and the Chickasaws were generally able to insist on their own terms when entering economic and political arrangements with different colonial powers. [110] Because these Indians were not totally dependent on them, the French and the English could never be completely assured of the "loyalty" of their most important allies. The individual towns of these nations took great pride in their ability "to manage their affairs as best please[d] themselves," and it occasionally pleased a Choctaw town to welcome some South Carolina traders. By the same token Chickasaw delegations continued to seek out the French when the mood struck them. [111] In spite of the considerable suffering they had to endure, the Choctaws and the Chickasaws in many ways faced the advantages of a "buyer's market," for the English and the French at times seemed to need them more than they needed the Europeans. [112]

In contrast to their convincing victories in Florida, South Carolina imperialists could not deny that, so far, their advantage in Louisiana seemed less secure. New kinds of obstacles required them to act with a bit more stealth and finesse than heretofore. In an area that was inaccessible to large numbers of South Carolina troops and officials, the province's future was placed in the hands of a select group of emissaries who had to figure out the best way of getting through to those Indians whose assistance they coveted.

For the English the most successful cultural intermediaries were the traders who lived and worked in close contact with the Indians. [113] Thomas Nairne and Thomas Welch, two of the most experienced and perceptive of these traders, hatched a plan to bring important groups like the Choctaws and the Chickasaws closer to South Carolina's imperial agenda. On an official expedition to the western theater in the spring of 1708, Nairne and Welch were armed with the knowledge that the English "cause"—the defeat of popery and royal absolutism—would mean nothing to the Indians. Instead, they took the position that "nothing but a much better trade and the reputation of far greater Courage than the French" would win the western Indians over to the English side.[114] In his extensive travels Nairne had observed that most Indians tended to value strength and courage in themselves and show respect to those outsiders who possessed such traits. Nairne and Welch therefore made an extra effort to act courageously, gambling with their lives by traveling largely unescorted through the towns of the Yazoos, the Taensas, and the Choctaws.

Even more important than courage, according to Nairne, was the ability to appeal to the Indians' sense of self-interest. The two South Carolina emissaries followed each of their addresses to the Indians by distributing various presents and confidently promising that the English would always give them cheaper and better goods than the French could ever provide. One of Nairne's Chickasaw friends assured him that this was the best way to appeal to his people: not only "every one of the officers and military men," but also the Chickasaw women, who were "so pleased to look sparkling in the dances, with the Cloaths bought from the English," that they would never stand for being "reduced to their old wear of painted Buffaloe calf skins."[115] By the time Nairne returned to Charles Town after a brief but action-packed stay in the west, he appeared fully convinced that the Indians were a highly acquisitive and materialistic people willing to sell their services to the highest bidder.[116]

But even in the midst of self-congratulation, Nairne had to concede that "the savages, especially those so remote, ha[d] not a right notion of Alegiance and its being indefeasible."[117] If the Indians had room for the English, they could make room for the French as well, especially since Louisiana had its own share of emissaries willing to work just as hard as Nairne and his colleagues. Far less numerous or wealthy than the South Carolinians, the French in Louisiana depended on the cooperation and assistance of their Indian neighbors to an even greater extent. About 1700 Louisiana's white population of less than two hundred was only a fraction of South Carolina's, estimated at around seventy-five hundred.[118] Though Louisiana's small size put it at many disadvantages, it did help somewhat in implementing an effective system of Indian relations. The ability to pursue a highly personalized Indian policy under the direction of a small circle of experienced and skillful officials helped the French hold their own for a significant portion of Queen Anne's War.[119]

The officials in charge of Louisiana's early Indian relations had acquired years of valuable experience in French North America, a regime that placed a premium on the economic and military assistance of the natives. Along the Saint Lawrence, the Great Lakes, and the Upper Mississippi, the French had spent nearly a hundred years learning how to interact with the Indians and frustrate the imperial ambitions of wealthier English colonies. The relative success of the Canadians depended on an effective commerce backed up by traders, missionaries, and secular officials who were often willing to make important concessions to Indian culture. In Louisiana, Iberville and his younger brother, Jean Baptiste Le Moyne, sieur de Bienville, initially hoped to replicate the Canadian system. The region contained many convenient north-south waterways and a number of Native societies clamoring for French trade goods. Like the South Carolinians, the Le Moyne brothers realized that they would "inevitably be obliged to give presents to all these nations in order to constrain them to attach themselves to [them]." [120] Soon, however, the French in Louisiana discovered the limitations of this strategy, as they watched their already small budget decrease by the year. Canada was poor enough, but Louisiana—with few colonists, little agriculture, and no industry whatsoever—seemed destined to be even poorer. Like several of the Florida governors, the Le Moyne brothers had many of their best ideas dismissed as *trop cher* by the royal court: not only a proposal to send Choctaw and Chickasaw leaders to Versailles but also requests for more firearms to arm potential Indian allies. [121]

The French in Louisiana were therefore forced to slog through Queen Anne's War by making the best of a bad situation, one that only grew worse when Iberville died of yellow fever during a visit to Havana in 1706. The colony's imperial policy now fell squarely on the shoulders of the twenty-six-year-old Bienville. Knowing that he could not cater to many of the Indians' material interests, he worked hard to earn their trust and respect. Not only did Bienville continue a Canadian strategy by sending young French boys to be raised in several Choctaw and Chickasaw towns; he also taught himself the Mobilian language, a kind of lingua franca that later made it easier for him to converse in several other Indian tongues. [122] Many Indian leaders were pleasantly surprised to find a colonial governor who would speak with them directly and participate in many of their ceremonial rites; in one village Bienville even joined in a war dance and had a large snake tattooed on his chest. [123] When Chickasaw leaders visited Charles Town, they were insulated from the governor and other important officials by a layer of interpreters and formal parliamentary protocol. [124] When they visited Mobile, they sat with the governor at his own dinner table and drank from his own private liquor stock. One Louisiana official claimed that these Indians "delighted to see a French chief caress them and have them eat with him" and "would return home with a few little presents that M. De Bienville would give them and would assure their people that the French nation was the best nation in the world."[125] For many Louisiana Indians, Bienville was as much a friend as a representative of a foreign power. They did not hesitate to stop by his house at all hours of the day to trade with him or request his help in settling some kind of dispute.[126]

For all of Bienville's undeniable skill in Indian diplomacy, his behavior toward the Indians was inspired more by necessity than by any genuine fondness for Indian culture.[127] At times he was capable of dealing with Indians in an intrusive and even ruthless manner. In his opinion governing "despotically" was often the best way to earn the Indians' respect and assistance. Indians who protested Bienville's judgments often found themselves rudely dismissed or clamped in chains, and anyone who dared to harm a French colonist or one of his Indian allies literally had a price put on his head. Bienville was occasionally known to persuade one small Indian nation to attack another, after which he would buy prisoners from them and set the prisoners free "to show them that the French nation was a friend of theirs and that he himself was glad to protect them as far as it was in his power to do so."[128] For Bienville and his protégés, Indian diplomacy boiled down to an intricate process of manipulation. He believed that once he learned the rudiments of their culture and entered their good graces, the Indians "could hide nothing from [him] since there [were] among them only very limited intellects."[129]

Even accounting for Bienville's tendency to sing his own praises, there probably was some truth behind his oft-repeated claims that the Indians "naturally liked" the French and merely tolerated the English.[130] The Chickasaws seemed to provide a case in point; despite the constant ministrations of Thomas Nairne and other South Carolina trader-imperialists, many of these Indians refused to renounce the French even though Bienville was hard pressed to "give them any presents at all."[131] Bienville did, however, go a little too far in attributing the loyalty of these Indians to his own diplomatic skills. Instead, most of the Indians in the western theater expressed a fondness for Bienville and his subordinates because they realized that the French were the only viable alternative to the English. Midway through Queen Anne's War, it had become impossible for the French and the English to form clear impressions of Choctaw and Chickasaw "allegiance." For every Indian who steadfastly supported one side or the other throughout the entire war, more Indians chose to experiment with both colonial rivals. It was relatively common for a group of Indians to contritely tell a colonial official that they had dabbled with the other side but now saw the error of their ways. They would not, however, agree to surrender the presents or bounties that the "enemy" had given them.[132]

The presence of the French could become helpful even for those Indians who did not necessarily need French weapons or protection. Some of the Chickasaws, for example, began to express concerns over the acceleration of the slave trade and were comforted by Louisiana's willingness to purchase deerskins. The English generally offered better bargains, but their aggressiveness could be unsettling, as it was for one Chickasaw headman who derisively dismissed a South Carolina trader with the insult "that the French only had one mouth and that he [the Englishman] had two."[133] During his stay among the Chickasaws, Nairne learned of several headmen and other Indians who were continuing to visit the French. Though he tried to write them off as a "few refugee people who can neither hunt nor take slaves," the divided loyalties of the western Indians continued to concern the South Carolina government.[134]

The Chickasaws' elusiveness in some ways made them even more attractive to South Carolina's trader-imperialists. Thomas Nairne shared the high opinion that these Indians had of themselves, describing them as "much more brisk, airy, and full of life" than groups like the Tallapoosas, "as men of Quality among [the South Carolinians were] to the peasants."[135] While the Chickasaws had the potential to be ideal allies, they were neither numerous nor reliable enough to carry out all of South Carolina's ambitions in the western theater of Queen Anne's War. At the beginning of the war, the English had initially worried that the Muskogean nations closest to Louisiana might fall under the spell of the French. Despite a temporary understanding between the French and a small group of Alabamas, there was never any real possibility that those Indians would bend to French wishes for a significant length of time. Too many Alabamas harbored a lingering hatred of the Choctaws and the Mobilians, groups that had forced them eastward during the mid to late seventeenth century. Likewise, the Abeikas, the Tallapoosas, and the Ocheses—bolstered by a number of Chickasaws who had moved among them—had bones to pick with the Choctaws. These Muskogean nations needed little motivation to attack the nations that had begun to line up with the French, but the South Carolina traders were willing to provide an extra push. By 1704 the major towns of the Alabamas, the Abeikas, and the Tallapoosas were being supplied with all the firearms and ammunition that they could afford to purchase.[136] Within a year they were joined by large numbers of Ochese warriors, many of them fresh from their rampages in Apalachee. In the fall of 1705, a wave of perhaps three thousand Muskogean warriors accompanied by a handful of South Carolina traders fell upon the towns of the Choctaws, seizing several hundred slaves but suffering numerous casualties of their own.[137] For the remainder of Queen

Anne's War, the Muskogeans would have a hand in most of the carnage inflicted on the western theater.

Despite their use of English weapons and apparent willingness to follow the lead of South Carolina officers, the Muskogeans actually paid little attention to English military etiquette during their attacks on other Indian nations. Theophilus Hastings, the trader charged with leading a force of thirteen hundred assorted Muskogeans against the Choctaws in 1711, remarked that the expedition would have gone much better had the Indians been more "governable" and less enthusiastic to "run upon the Enemies at first without command."[138] Most Muskogeans viewed such campaigns not as blows for the glory of South Carolina and the British Empire but as slave raids and grudge matches that promised them wealth, prestige, and an important expression of their militaristic values. When some South Carolinians suggested the possibility of a peace with the Choctaws, others warned that it would never work without "the Consent of the Creek and Talabushees Indians."[139] For all their talk of harnessing the Muskogeans into a disciplined auxiliary army, South Carolina officials realized that the war against the French-influenced Indians was being run by the Muskogeans themselves.

Though Indians wound up doing most of the fighting, Queen Anne's War in many ways remained a European conflict. The French and the Spanish continued to be the focus of South Carolina's military strategies, and after the sobering invasion of 1706, South Carolina officials increased their efforts to destroy their enemies' seats of power. Instead of making another run at redoubtable Saint Augustine, they figured to have better luck with the smaller outposts of Mobile and Pensacola, the Spanish enclave that was entirely dependent on charity from Mobile and Mexico. With fears of another Franco-Spanish invasion keeping most of South Carolina's white troops close to home, the assaults on far-off Mobile and Pensacola would have to rely mostly on Indian manpower. Plans for a campaign against Mobile in 1707 called for fifteen hundred Muskogean warriors and only fifty white traders. Though this invasion was nipped in the bud by a number of untimely political controversies, it indicated a newfound confidence in the Indians' ability to fight against Europeans.[140] Having relegated their Yamasee allies to a secondary role in the 1702 siege of Saint Augustine, South Carolinians now expected Indians to bear the brunt of attacks on enemy outposts.

In the summer and fall of 1707, several hundred Tallapoosas and a few South Carolina traders launched two separate offensives against Pensacola.[141] These Indian warriors were essentially acting as mercenaries of the South Carolinians, and their performance in these engagements left a big impression on their colonial employers. Their first assault took the Spanish completely by surprise, and the Indians razed the small town and even managed to briefly invest the fort before being repelled. Several months later a second attack fared worse against a more alert Spanish garrison, and after a disorganized siege of less than a month, the Indians returned home in frustration. Though a small "expeditionary" force made one more halfhearted attempt against the fort in 1711, and Muskogean war parties continued to terrorize the area just beyond the fort's walls, South Carolina essentially abandoned the idea of sending Indians against European outposts.[142] For most Indians it was easier and more rewarding to fight against other Indians. Bienville was alarmed by a rumor in 1709 that the South Carolinians were delivering three cast-iron cannons to the Alabamas, but he and other French and Spanish officials remained confident that sturdy walls and well-trained troops would provide sufficient protection against South Carolina's Indian allies.[143]

Nevertheless, the constant pressure supplied by the Muskogeans took a toll on South Carolina's imperial enemies. The Spanish remained confined to their two forts, and the French began to lose much of their frontier influence. With Mobile running low on food and supplies, those soldiers who did not desert to South Carolina were compelled to dress in animal skins and find their subsistence among the Indians, a development that gave a "sad impression of French power."[144] In 1711 the French moved Mobile closer to the seacoast, a decision that discredited them in the eyes of those Indians who had been promised a new French fort and trading post far up the Tombigbee River.[145] Increasing expenditures on the Mobile garrison helped decimate the budget set aside for Indian relations; Bienville admitted that he could now spare less than 3 percent of what the South Carolinians were spending on gifts and trade goods.[146] This obvious decline proved too much even for some of Louisiana's staunchest Chickasaw supporters, who apologetically informed Bienville that "not being able to obtain from [the French] their needs which ha[d] become indispensable to them, they [found] themselves obliged to take them from the English."[147] With their Choctaw and Mobilian allies facing renewed pressure from the Chickasaws and the Muskogeans, Mobile—and by extension Pensacola—appeared vulnerable to the massive two-pronged assault that the English were planning for 1712. After nearly ten years of fighting in the western theater, the South Carolinians appeared ready for a victory nearly as convincing as the one they had achieved on the Florida peninsula.

But such a victory eluded them. News of a cease-fire in Europe prevented the invasion of Mobile from going forth, and the French proved more resilient than they had appeared at first glance. Once again they were saved by a seemingly uncanny knack for Indian relations, which in 1712 allowed them to enter into a timely peace with the Alabamas, the Abeikas, and the Tallapoosas. Though Bienville sought out these Indians in desperation, the decision for peace was implemented more by the Indians than the French. Despite the increasing flow of European goods into their towns, some of South Carolina's allies had suffered a great deal during Queen Anne's War, sustaining many casualties and putting up with the often intrusive behavior of South Carolina traders and officials. Much like the Chickasaws at the height of Queen Anne's War, some of the western Muskogeans were coming to the conclusion that the French—as unimpressive as they often seemed—comprised a valuable alternative to the English. By consenting to a truce with the French and their Native allies, they acquired an opportunity to heal their wounds while dealing with two different groups of colonial traders.

The Indian participants in the western theater were able to pursue the kinds of options that were denied to many of the Native groups encompassed by the Florida theater. Not only did the French comprise a better alternative than the Spanish, but the Chickasaws and the western Muskogean nations were far enough removed from South Carolina's authority as well. South Carolinians could not treat the Alabama "deserters" in the same way they treated the Savannahs; they could only sit back and hope that the Alabamas would still consent to receive them and trade with them. As a result the war in the western theater differed significantly from the conflict that played out in Florida. Not only did the South Carolinians face a different kind of enemy in the French; they also dealt with different kinds of allies.

The Northern Theater

The imperial war that unfolded in the Southeast was far more complex than it must have appeared to far-off officials in London, Paris, and Madrid. Those who only concerned themselves with enemy outposts and large-scale campaigns were bound to overlook one of the less spectacular theaters of Queen Anne's War. Stretching roughly from the Peedee to the Little Tennessee River and encompassing a significant portion of the Appalachian Mountains and foothills, this northern theater differed markedly from the war zones of Louisiana and Florida. The French and the Spanish—who clung to their coastal enclaves hundreds of miles away—had a negligible influence on this region throughout the war. The South Carolinians began Queen Anne's War with a free run of this area, but they had done relatively little to press their advantage. As James Merrell has contended, they "probably knew as much about the Indians on the Mississippi River as about those beyond the Santee."[148] The Native societies to the north and northwest of the South Carolina settlements had experienced relatively little contact with Europeans and knew almost nothing of imperial rivalry.

By 1700 or so the Catawba, Wateree, and Santee basins were home to at least fourteen distinguishable groups of widely diverse origins.[149] Some of these were probably remnants of Cofitachique, a nearby Mississippian polity that had met an uncertain end some time during the late seventeenth century. Other groups were relatively new to the Piedmont, having migrated from low-country areas where the pressures from colonists had already become too much to bear. Though they settled in the same general area, these various groups—none of them larger than five hundred people—did not immediately band together in any kind of unified polity.[150] John Lawson, an English naturalist who visited the Carolina Piedmont in 1700–1701, was astonished to find that nations residing within thirty miles of each other could have very different languages, governments, and material cultures.[151] Other outsiders, however, were less likely than Lawson to take account of this cultural diversity among the Piedmont Indians. Their Iroquoian enemies tended to lump them together as "Flatheads," and South Carolinians usually referred to them collectively as the "Northern Indians." By the turn of the eighteenth century, both kinds of outsiders were beginning to look on the Piedmont Indians with greater interest.

A handful of English traders had been circulating among these Indians since the 1670s, but the South Carolina government had, for the most part, looked on them with indifference. Like the Cherokees, the Piedmont Indians rarely appeared in the government records of the 1680s and 1690s except as victims of the Savannahs and other prominent South Carolina allies. Among groups like the Savannahs and the Yamasees, colonial traders had become fairly common sights and had generally grown comfortable in dealing with the Indians. The traders who visited the towns along the Santee, Wateree, Peedee, and Catawba rivers were in many ways paddling in uncharted waters. They often proceeded with a good deal of wariness, uncertain whether the Piedmont groups followed the same rules of exchange as other southeastern Indian societies.[152] One of John Lawson's traveling companions appeared to seduce an Indian girl with a gift of cloth and beads, only to wake up the next morning without his mistress, his shoes, or any of his trade goods. When the Indians in the village "laughed their Sides sore" at the pathetic Englishman, who "in less than 12 Hours, was Batchelor, Husband, and Widdower," they showed which side had the upper hand in the exchange process.[153]

Among many of the Piedmont groups, however, a shift was already in the works. Diseases such as smallpox and dysentery had begun to take a harsh toll on every village visited by English traders, making it harder for the Indians to resist the incursions of outsiders. Lawson reported that officials in Charles Town, led by staunch imperialist James Moore, were hoping to make the up-country groups as "tractable" as low-country groups like the Santees.[154] A few years earlier a prominent young South Carolinian had been murdered on his way up to Virginia, and an upcountry group known as the Esaws had refused to cooperate in the government's investigation.[155] With South Carolina on the verge of war with the French and the Spanish, officials felt the need to bring such troublesome groups to heel and realized that they could only accomplish this by making the Piedmont Indians "more dependent" on the South Carolina government.[156] By the turn of the century, South Carolina traders began to make more frequent and unpredictable trips to the upcountry, entering villages without the invitations that they formerly had awaited.[157] South Carolina's Indian trade had worked so well on the province's other frontiers that authorities expected similar results in the Piedmont. Soon, however, South Carolina's trader-imperialists found themselves frustrated by serious competition from an unexpected source.

In the northern theater of Queen Anne's War, South Carolinians' most bitter rivals were not the French or the Spanish, but fellow English subjects from the province of Virginia. They spoke the same language, obeyed the same sovereign, and shared similar concerns about French encroachments from the Mississippi Valley, but South Carolina and Virginia authorities still found many grounds for disagreement. Established at different times, in different ecosystems, and by different groups of people, England's North American colonies often stressed their differences over their commonalties. Virginians tended to look on the struggling settlements of North Carolina—or "Lubberland"— with a combination of disdain and wry amusement, and they did not take long to realize that the upstart South Carolinians would be the ones to watch on their southern frontiers.[158] The rapid growth of South Carolina's population and staple agriculture during the 1690s incited a good deal of alarm, envy, and snobbery within the Old Dominion. By 1700 the two provinces were locked in an acrimonious contest for prospective settlers.[159] Despite the growing agricultural concerns of South Carolina and Virginia, however, the most intense competition between the two colonies occurred over the uncultivated backcountry and its Indian inhabitants.

As they liked to remind everyone, Virginians had been trading with the Indians of the Piedmont and mountains "before the name of Carolina was known."[160] The first Virginia traders came to this region as early as the 1650s, shortly after their government's final victory over the Powhatan Confederacy.[161] Some of these men, such as the first William Byrd, used their profits from the Indian trade to establish plantation dynasties. In this respect the Virginians provided a model for the first South Carolina traders, just as they did through their purchase of Indian slaves.[162] The Virginia traders had lost their slave-raiding Westo allies to the South Carolinians in the 1670s but had never completely relinquished their ambitions in the backcountry. In 1699 the House of Burgesses' motion to "encourage a trade with the Western Indians that [lay] behind Virginia and Carolina" revealed their hopes for a resurgent Indian trade.[163] It did not seem to bother them that their old stomping grounds fell within the territory circumscribed by Carolina's charter.

It certainly bothered the South Carolinians. As far as they were concerned, any Virginian who traded south of the thirty-sixth parallel was a trespasser. Queen Anne's War stirred imperialistic sentiment among South Carolinians, but it did not allay their deeply ingrained suspicion of outsiders, even those from another English colony. In 1704 Deputy Governor Robert Daniel leveled complaints against the conduct of two free black traders from Virginia, "particularly their stirring up the Indians called the Windaws to cutt off and carry away diverse of the Indians called Wawees living under the Government of South Carolina."[164] Though Virginia authorities rose to the defense of these traders, Daniel had reasons to remain apprehensive. Government authorities used traders as military agents on many of South Carolina's frontiers, but their ongoing efforts to reform the Indian trade showed that they did not always trust these men to act in the province's best interest. If they found it difficult to trust some of their own traders, they found it nearly impossible to trust traders from another government, even one with English roots.[165]

The relatively experienced and well-supplied Virginia traders also impinged on South Carolina's potential profits in the northern theater, which made them an even greater concern for the South Carolina government. Not surprisingly the Virginians became a substantial issue in the campaigns to reform the Indian trade during the first years of the eighteenth century. As part of the abortive effort to reform the trade in 1701, the Carolina Commons House resolved that the Virginians "be forbid to trade among any Indians inhabiting in [that] Province, and after notice given to Confiscate Goods."[166] Two years later the South Carolina assembly passed an act that required traders from Virginia or any other colony to pay duties on any trade goods brought into Carolina territory.[167] When the Virginians refused to comply, the South Carolina authorities decided to take action. In early 1708 they confiscated several hundred deerskins belonging to Robert Hix, David Crawley, and several other Virginians who were working among the Piedmont Indians. Hix proceeded to Charles Town to reclaim his property, only to have Governor Johnson refuse his petition with a stern warning "never to cross the Santee River again."[168] The South Carolinians had drawn their line in the sand.

Surprised and offended by the unyielding stance of the South Carolina government, Virginia authorities decided to plead their case in London, where they were prepared to cite several "royall instructions" that gave them "a free trade . . . with all Indians whatsoever."[169] But the South Carolinians were quick to reply that Virginia's incursions compromised British imperial interests.[170] With the Iroquois and the Ohio Valley Indians remaining effectively neutral in Queen Anne's War, Virginia's financial and military contributions to the imperial struggle were minuscule at best. North Carolina, it was commonly assumed, could not "get 60 men together in 10 or 15 days' time for their defense."[171] In the eyes of Charles Town officials, South Carolina *was* the British Empire, at least in the Southeast.

Back in London, however, officials tended to espouse a different view of the empire. When compared to the invasion of Spain, the new union with Scotland, or even the wartime suffering of the New England colonies, the South Carolina–Virginia dispute struck royal officials as little more than an annoying distraction. Colonies were supposed to cooperate, not wrestle with each other. When the Virginians argued that a South Carolina monopoly would raise prices, alienate the Indians, and sacrifice Britain's imperial influence to "the Avarice of a few private men," the Board of Trade was inclined to agree.[172] Virginia was a royal colony whose governor and council had maintained direct ties to the Crown's imperial bureaucracy for nearly a hundred years. As a proprietary colony, South Carolina was under the nominal control of a select group of noblemen who were the source of much frustration and contempt in Whitehall. While Virginians imported most of their Indian trade goods directly from Great Britain, South Carolinians acquired many of their goods from Caribbean smugglers.[173] In spite of the imperial rhetoric they often employed in times of crisis, South Carolinians had proven something of an obstacle to the imperial designs hammered out in London.

Though disappointed by the Board of Trade's intervention on behalf of Virginia, South Carolina authorities continued their efforts to bring the Piedmont Indians under their control. Governor Johnson took a special interest in these groups and helped lead a promotional campaign to send more traders among them. [174] As they grew more familiar with these Indians, South Carolinians began to perceive them in a new light, lumping all of them under the name of the Piedmont's largest and most influential group: the Catawbas. [175] This kind of catchall terminology made it easier for them to get a handle on these Indians and perceive them as a new addition to South Carolina's defensive perimeter. [176] The Catawbas' war against the Savannah "deserters" in 1708 showed them to be practiced, skillful, and enthusiastic warriors who could provide valuable military assistance to South Carolina. In 1709 the Commons House felt confident enough about the Catawbas' loyalty to summon one hundred of their warriors to Charles Town, "to be placed where the Governor [should] think fitt." [177]

On the whole, however, most of the Catawbas were not subject to this kind of manipulation. When they did take up arms, it was not necessarily because the South Carolinians told them to do so. In many ways the culture of the slowly coalescing Piedmont groups was shaped around warfare. Success in battle was essential not only to a Catawba warrior's sense of self-worth but also to the survival of his people. As inhabitants of an ecologically rich zone located on the fringes of larger and aggressive Indian societies, the Catawbas had long faced an almost constant barrage of enemy raids. [178] Though incursions from the Cherokees, the Tuscaroras, and the Savannahs had begun to diminish by the early eighteenth century, the "mourning wars" of the Iroquois Five Nations brought a new wave of devastation to the Carolina Piedmont. [179] The Catawbas were compelled to do a great deal of fighting during Queen Anne's War, but most of it had little or nothing to do with South Carolina's imperial struggle.

To be sure, the South Carolina trader-imperialists exerted at least some influence on the Catawbas' military activities. Since these Indians needed a steady supply of firearms and ammunition to fend off their enemies, they were bound to pay at least some attention to their suppliers. By the same token, however, the Catawbas' subservience to Charles Town was likely to be less than complete as long as they could meet their needs through an alternative source. The South Carolinians of Queen Anne's War "understood nullification in practice, if not yet in theory": despite the unfavorable verdict from the Board of Trade, they continued their efforts to harass the Virginia traders. [180] Nevertheless, the Virginians seemed undeterred and acquired more deerskins from the Catawbas in the five years after 1708 than they had in the five previous years. [181]

The staying power of the Virginians resulted from a combination of different factors. Unlike the Spanish or the French, they were relatively well supplied and could afford to undercut South Carolina's prices if the need arose. [182] Though less numerous than the South Carolinians, the Virginia traders could often draw on longer experience among the Catawbas. Moreover, they benefited from a situation similar to the one that was keeping the French afloat in Louisiana. Like the Chickasaws and the Alabamas, many Catawbas were willing to take full advantage of any viable alternative to the South Carolinians. When the pressure from Charles Town grew too heavy, the Catawbas could seek out another breed of Englishmen who tended to be somewhat less demanding. [183] Through the end of Queen Anne's War, most of the Catawbas were able to stay on the tightrope of independence, pulling off a balancing act that frustrated South Carolina's most committed imperialists.

Further to the west, the power of the South Carolinians was even more circumscribed. There, nestled in the narrow valleys of the Appalachian Mountains, lived the Cherokee Indians, a large group of loosely affiliated Iroquoian speakers. Having migrated from the north some time prior to the de Soto expedition, the Cherokees were forced to fight with their new neighbors to secure a suitable resource base in the Southeast. Their strength and numbers helped them fend off enemy attacks and expand into territory that had previously been occupied by the Muskogeans. [184] Warfare remained an important part of Cherokee culture, but that did not prevent these Indians from forging more peaceful connections with their neighbors. The Cherokees soon became an important source for trade goods, particularly the steatite stone that many southeastern groups used in making their ceremonial pipes. [185] Trade with their southern and eastern neighbors allowed the Cherokees to acquire new goods of their own, including a surprising number of guns from Florida and Virginia. [186] By the time the first adventurous white men reached their towns in the 1670s and 1680s, the Cherokees already had a vague idea about what to expect from them.

For several more decades, however, the Cherokees' interaction with whites remained fairly limited and uneven. Though their population declined sharply as a result of disease and enemy raids during the late seventeenth and early eighteenth centuries, they remained one of the largest Indian societies in the Southeast. [187] Taken as a whole, the Cherokees seemed imposing, and South Carolinians were gradually coming to appreciate their potential as allies. A strong relationship with these Indians would not only improve South Carolina's access to the Tennessee and Mississippi valleys but also cut off a potential escape route for fugitive slaves. [188] With the French and the Spanish effectively pinned down, the Cherokees appeared immanently vulnerable to South Carolina's most optimistic imperialists. In a 1708 letter to London, Thomas Nairne extolled the virtues of the Cherokees and confidently described them as "entirely Subject to [South Carolina]." [189]

If Nairne had known the Cherokees even half as well as he knew the Yamasees, the Tallapoosas, and the Chickasaws, his comments about them probably would have been more circumspect. In a letter written just two months after Nairne's, Governor Johnson called the Cherokees "a numerous people but very lazy" and described South Carolina's trade with them as "inconsiderable." [190] Like Nairne, Johnson was guilty of overgeneralization. The Cherokees were actually a diverse group whose sixty or so towns encompassed several distinct dialects and regions. In the so-called lower towns on the far fringes of the Piedmont, South Carolina traders were fairly successful in peddling their wares, especially the firearms that the Cherokees needed for protection against their Muskogean, Yuchi, and Iroquoian enemies. By the end of Queen Anne's War, Lower Cherokee towns like Tugaloo were providing an increasing number of skins and slaves and had even taken a place in South Carolina's defensive perimeter. [191]

Further into the mountains, however, the situation was quite different. Fewer white traders were able to reach the middle towns along the Little Tennessee and the upper (or "overhill") towns along the headwaters of the same river. One of the rare British visitors to these Cherokees claimed that they hardly ever saw or dealt with white men and thereby managed to keep up their precontact rituals and traditions more successfully than other Indian societies. [192] Since many of the Cherokees' traditions were as militaristic as those of most southeastern Indian groups, Governor Johnson's claim that the Cherokees were "but ordinary hunters and less warriors" should not be taken at face value. [193] Instead, this comment merely indicates that many Cherokees were failing to harness their hunting and war-making skills to the agenda of South Carolina imperialists.

As long as the South Carolinians continued to perceive the Cherokees as a more or less unified nation, they were bound to be disappointed in them. The Cherokees remained relatively aloof from the vicissitudes of Queen Anne's War, possibly because most of South Carolina's traders and officials simply cared less about the Cherokees than about the more conveniently and strategically located groups in the Florida and Louisiana theaters. For some traders, however, the Cherokees were important enough to warrant long trips over difficult terrain. These men were not inclined to welcome any undue obstacles, especially competitors from a rival colony. Throughout most of Queen Anne's War, Virginia's stake in the Cherokee trade was even smaller than South Carolina's, and the presence of a few Virginia traders probably had little effect on the profits of the South Carolinians. By 1710, however, an ambitious new governor named Alexander Spotswood was heading a campaign to improve Virginia's access to the Overhill Cherokee towns.[194] When added to the more intense competition that was taking place among the Catawbas, Virginia's initiatives in the mountains provided South Carolinians with a scapegoat for their own frustrations along their northern frontiers.

In a sense the northern theater was becoming the "soft underbelly" of the South Carolina imperialists. In 1711, the same year that witnessed large-scale offensives against Louisiana and Florida, the South Carolina government passed an act that clearly reflected the anxieties and frustrations caused by their rivalry with Virginia.[195] Once again the South Carolinians decided to enforce their duties on the Virginians' trade goods, through search and seizure if necessary. In addition their act required "those traders that [came] from Virginia and other neighbouring colonies" to purchase licenses in Charles Town and subject themselves to the same laws and restrictions that ostensibly guided the South Carolina traders. Though they frankly admitted to keeping a jealous eye on their profits, the South Carolina authorities displayed an even greater concern for other aspects of their Indian trade. On the one hand, any interlopers who were not subject to the 1707 act could "without any restraint commit all those evil practices among the Indians which [might] be of the most destructive consequence to [the] Province."[196] On the other hand, traders who operated under different rules and advantages simply made it too difficult for South Carolinians to "reduce" recalcitrant Indians to obedience "by stopping them from being supplied with goods for their necessary occasions, and especially from arms and ammunition."[197] These arguments showed, in a nutshell, the hallmarks of South Carolina imperialism: a nagging uncertainty and reasonable paranoia combined with a driving ambition for dominance and control.

It was also significant that one of the best defenses and expressions of their imperialistic values was the 1711 Indian Trade Act, a measure that showed a glaring disregard for the earlier pronouncements of the Board of Trade, the Privy Council, and even Queen Anne herself. But in posing this challenge to royal authority, South Carolinians did not intend to divorce themselves from the British Empire. Like political allegiance and nationalism, imperialism could operate on a number of different levels at the same time. For an over-whelming majority of South Carolinians, loyalty to the British Crown was never really at issue. Rather, most of the confusion and controversy over the 1711 Indian Trade Act centered around the *expression* of this loyalty: what was necessary to uphold one's duties to the empire. This question would eventually lie at the heart of the American Revolution, but in many ways it was even more difficult to answer during the early eighteenth century, a period when London's imperial authority was much less pronounced. [198] Carrying on the tradition of the first Goose Creek men, South Carolina's colonists, traders, and officials lived through Queen Anne's War thoroughly convinced that they knew what was best for their own prosperity and security. For over a decade they had waged a successful war against two foreign powers with little assistance from Britain or any other British colonies, extending and consolidating their influence within a widespread frontier complex. This success only served to increase their sense of insularity and self-confidence; by the later stages of the war, they practically considered themselves an empire within an empire.

When the Treaty of Utrecht put an official end to the War of Spanish Succession in April 1713, no clear victor had emerged. The Bourbon alliance had kept Philip V in power, but only after considerable losses in manpower and territory. Great Britain and its New England colonies had likewise found the war to be financially and humanly exhausting. Despite some setbacks of their own, the South Carolinians had probably weathered the military storm better than any other European combatants. [199] New allies, crippled enemies, and a steadily improving balance of trade left many South Carolinians with feelings of triumph and confidence. Few of them, however, would have been so bold as to venture that their struggle had ended. Even after hearing rumors of a truce throughout 1712 and confirmations of the treaty a year later, they could see that nothing in the Southeast had truly been settled. After all, there were still Frenchmen in Mobile, Spaniards in Pensacola and Saint Augustine, and pesky Virginia traders in the Piedmont and mountains. Though obliged to behave less aggressively, the South Carolina imperialists felt compelled to carry on.

The unwritten rules of imperialism dictated constant pressure. Men who pored over maps, strategies, and lines of defense firmly believed that what belonged to them on one map could belong to someone else on the next revision. Relative advantages merely whetted their appetite for complete control of the Southeast.

At the same time those who had amassed experience on the front lines of Queen Anne's War had begun to appreciate the difficulties of achieving this kind of control. True, the war had allowed South Carolinians to extend their influence over the Southeast and its Native inhabitants. For some groups, like the Santees, the Yamasees, and the Apalachees, the war brought closer ties to South Carolina's government and burgeoning settlements. For other groups, such as the Catawbas and the Lower Cherokees, it meant new exposure to South Carolina traders and ambassadors. For all groups, even those as powerful as the Ocheses or as distant as the Chickasaws, it meant a growing fondness for English textiles and a growing reliance on English firearms. But while South Carolina's influence existed to varying degrees in almost every southeastern Indian town, this influence still remained open to different interpretations. These differences grew more evident and more important as the bills for imperialistic expansion gradually came due in the years surrounding the uncertain end of Queen Anne's War.

3. Beneath the Buffer Zone

STRAINS ON SOUTH CAROLINA'S
INDIAN ALLIANCE NETWORK

Despite its wartime success, South Carolina retained a rather unsavory reputation in some circles. If a British farmer, craftsman, laborer, or merchant were to consider trying his luck across the Atlantic, he was likely to hear at least something about the insects, humidity, and diseases that prevailed in the Southeast, as well as some disturbing rumors about the ferocity of the region's Indians. During a visit to England in 1710, Thomas Nairne took up the task of polishing South Carolina's image by writing *A Letter from South Carolina*, a promotional tract published by the Lords Proprietors. Though this work depicted South Carolina as an ecological paradise and bastion of Whiggish liberty, it made its most far-reaching claims when describing the situation along the province's frontiers. According to Nairne, the Indians of the Southeast were not objects of fear and loathing, but "a very considerable Part of [South Carolina's] Strength." South Carolina's "thousands" of Indian allies were all "hardy, active, and good marksmen," who for "little or no Charge" had "added very much to [the colony's] Strength and Safety . . . by drawing over to [their] side, or destroying, all the Indians within 700 miles of Charlestown."[1] As one of the principal architects of South Carolina's imperial policy, Nairne undoubtedly took considerable pride in what appeared to be one of his province's greatest imperial triumphs: the construction of a solid Indian buffer zone.

Nevertheless, Nairne must have realized that he could not do justice to this frontier defense network in a few short paragraphs. South Carolina's settlements appeared safe from enemy invasion, but its Indian neighbors did not always behave like the devoted servants described in Nairne's pamphlet. By the end of Queen Anne's War, every imperialist in South Carolina was familiar with the difficulties of dealing with groups like the Catawbas and the Alabamas. If promoters of the province could gloss over these frustrations, it was even easier for them to avoid taking a close look at the frontiers that seemed more stable.

While the South Carolinians' influence was unquestionably on the rise, their control over the Indians' lives was nowhere near complete. For those who were willing to look hard enough, South Carolina's armor revealed numerous chinks, even in the places where it appeared strongest. During their war against the French and the Spanish, moments of apparent triumph had often masked evidence of potential weaknesses. This trend was revealed even more starkly as South Carolina's traders and officials abandoned Queen Anne's War for a different range of conflicts, taking their quest for wealth and power to a new level.

South Carolinians in the Tuscarora War

While South Carolinians spent the early part of 1711 planning invasions of Florida and Louisiana, their neighbors in North Carolina were engaged in some struggles of their own. By this time North and South Carolina, though officially part of the same proprietary province, were administered by different colonial governments and had long been developing in different directions. North Carolina housed far fewer European colonists and African slaves, but these newcomers nevertheless had begun intensive contact and exchange with Native Americans, especially the smaller Algonquian and Iroquoian tribes that lived along Pamlico Sound and up the Pamlico and Neuse rivers.

Tensions between whites and Indians in the North Carolina tidewater grew more acute after about 1700. Though not as extensive as it was in South Carolina, the Indian slave trade claimed a growing number of victims among North Carolina Indians: not only those seized by South Carolina–sponsored groups like the Catawbas, but also those kidnapped by English colonists and traders along the Neuse. The smaller North Carolina tribes also lodged some official complaints about colonists' fraudulent purchases of Indian land. Colonists, for their part, made their own complaints about the local Indians, accusing them of everything from cattle rustling to physical assault. Not surprisingly North Carolina officials usually sided with the colonists and tended to view the Indians as public nuisances at best and mortal enemies at worst. In 1703 the North Carolina government even went so far as to make war on the Corees and the Nynees, chasing them from their villages and forcing them to the west, where they sought refuge near one of the main towns of the Tuscarora Indians.[2]

The Tuscaroras, though larger, stronger, and more remote than the beleaguered Indians of the tidewater, had already begun to develop their own wariness of the North Carolinians. An aggregate of some twenty-five hundred Iroquoian speakers, the Tuscaroras had formerly enjoyed a profitable position as middlemen in Virginia's Indian trade. For several decades, however, they had been suffering from an increasing number of enemy slave raids as well as a rapidly shrinking resource base. Because of the increased pressure of the deerskin trade, hunting was becoming especially difficult; the Catawbas and the Cherokees were taking over the hunting grounds to the west, forcing Tuscarora hunters to forage closer and closer to the expanding North Carolina settlements. In addition to experiencing some run-ins with colonists along the Pamlico, the Tuscaroras also fueled their resentment of the North Carolinians through their close ties to the smaller, down-river tribes. Even before the developments that would bring the crisis to a head in 1711, an anti-English faction of Tuscaroras under the leadership of "King Hancock," the principal headman of Catechna town, had already begun planning for a major preemptive attack on the North Carolina settlements.[3]

One of the short-term catalysts for war between the Tuscaroras and the North Carolinians was Cary's Rebellion, a bitter political conflict between the supporters of former governor Thomas Cary and those of newly appointed governor Edward Hyde. Disgruntled Indians did not take long to realize that this civil disturbance had left North Carolina, already weak to begin with, less capable of raising a defense against an external enemy. But even as the province was at its most vulnerable, it remained as capable as ever of provoking its Indian neighbors. The year 1711 saw the arrival of more than four hundred new colonists, most of them Swiss and German Palatine settlers under the leadership of Cristophe de Graffenreid. Construction of a new Swiss-Palatine settlement at New Bern alarmed and angered Hancock and his followers, especially in light of the newcomers' clear intention to move further inland.

In early September Graffenreid set out with the Carolina naturalist-frontiersman John Lawson on an expedition to survey land up the Neuse River. Three days into their journey, the men were seized by Tuscarora warriors and brought before a council of Tuscarora, Coree, Pamlico, and Neuse leaders that had assembled in Hancock's town of Catechna. After two days of interrogation and deliberation, the council decided to put Lawson to death and carry out plans for an attack on the colonial settlements along the Neuse and the Pamlico.

Graffenreid, his life spared by his Indian captors, watched helplessly as a party of about five hundred warriors—about half of them Tuscaroras—made its final preparations. After setting out in the early morning of September 22, the warriors split into small groups and easily overwhelmed the homesteads, plantations, and villages that lay in their path. In a matter of hours, the Indians had killed over sixty English and sixty Swiss and Palatine colonists and had taken several dozen captives. Panic-stricken survivors of the first assaults fled to makeshift garrisons in New Bern and Bath without even bothering to bury their loved ones. In October an attempt at a counterattack by the North Carolina militia failed miserably, leaving the numbed and poorly provisioned North Carolinians with no choice but to send out a desperate call for outside assistance.[4]

Their deliverance was hardly a foregone conclusion. Self-interest and intercolonial jealousies were not easily overcome, even in times of obvious crisis.[5] Nevertheless, a few farsighted advocates of a more united British Empire attempted to swim against the stream. One such man was Virginia governor Alexander Spotswood, who realized that his province, by virtue of its long-standing connections to the Tuscaroras, was in an ideal position to help North Carolina.[6] Other Virginia officials, however, proved much less enthusiastic. The wealthy, Oxford-educated William Byrd II ignored a summons to an emergency meeting of the governor's council, feeling that his dinner guests were a more pressing concern.[7] The House of Burgesses initially seemed receptive to Spotswood's plans to assist North Carolina but soon found that the required funds "were not easily raised without laying heavy taxes upon themselves." Ignoring Spotswood's warnings that they risked exposing themselves "to the Censure of all Mankind" and their province "to the Rage of the Heathen," they decided to leave the North Carolinians to their own devices.[8] An ashamed Spotswood considered bypassing the legislature and mobilizing the province's militia but instead spent the next two years apologizing for the behavior of his fellow Virginians and trying to arrange a treaty with the "neutral" Tuscarora towns.[9]

North Carolina's only hope for direct aid lay in the hands of the South Carolinians, a group that had previously done little to advance the cause of intercolonial unity. A month into the war, the North Carolina government sent Christopher Gale to Charles Town to give a detailed description of the Indian attack, an event he described as "the grossest piece of villainy that perhaps was ever heard of in English America." It took a great deal to move or disturb South Carolina's government officials, but Gale's account of the Tuscaroras' initial rampage—corpses left in grotesque poses and fetuses hanging from tree branches—did the trick nicely. Gale continued a masterful performance by claiming that the South Carolinians, more than any other group of colonists, knew that the only way to defeat a group of murderous savages "flushed with their first success" was to rely on the aid of "Indians who are acquainted with their manner of fighting." By the time of his return to North Carolina, Gale had secured a shipload of supplies and promises for a relief expedition to be made up of South Carolinians and their Indian allies.[10]

The task of assembling this force fell to John Barnwell, the scion of a prominent Dublin family who had immigrated to South Carolina in 1701 out of a restless search for adventure.[11] With the four thousand pounds Carolina money supplied by his government, Barnwell hired thirty-two whites from the colony's militia, many of whom, like himself, were veterans of the Florida campaigns.[12] It took him somewhat longer to round up the thousand or so Indians he intended to take into North Carolina; from an Indian's point of view, late fall and early winter were not ideal seasons for fighting. Barnwell was most familiar with the Yamasees and the Apalachees who lived near his Port Royal plantation, and he managed to persuade about 150 of these Indians to join one of his Native "companies." A few more Indians were hired from small "settlement" groups like the Cussaboes, but most joined the expedition as it made its way through the Carolina backcountry. Small Siouan groups like the Esaws, the Waterees, and the Catawbas probably needed little coaxing to fight against their traditional enemies to the east, and by January 1712 nearly eight hundred warriors from the Piedmont had volunteered to serve with the man who soon became known throughout South Carolina as "Tuscarora Jack."[13]

More than any campaign of Queen Anne's War, Barnwell's march through North Carolina in the winter and spring of 1712 displayed the arrogance of South Carolina imperialism. In his regular dispatches to Charles Town, Barnwell came across as one of his province's most tireless champions, noting how his campaign added to the "Glory of virtuous South Carolina[,] whose armies [were] the same winter gathering Laurells from the Cape Florida and from the Bay of Spiritta Sancta even to the Borders of Virginia."[14] He expressed nothing but disdain for the North Carolinians, whom he described as "the most impertinent, imperious, cowardly Blockheads that ever God created." Barnwell showed an equal contempt for the Virginians, who had possessed the nerve to "beg a most ignominious neutrality" of some of the Tuscarora towns.[15] Though Barnwell claimed that his army "struck the Dominion of Virginia into amazement and wonder," he was actually overstating the extent of its power and the unity of its cause.[16]

In fact, nearly half of the expedition's Indians had decided to head home rather than attempt a difficult crossing of the Cape Fear River into North Carolina.[17] When the remaining troops eventually got around to assaulting various

Tuscarora towns, they displayed little cooperation or solidarity. At a makeshift fort in the town of Norhunta, Barnwell and the white soldiers made a point of charging recklessly, showing off to the extent "that it was Terror for [their] own heathen friend to behold [them]."[18] After routing Norhunta's defenders—primarily women, children, and old men who had already begun negotiations with Virginia—Barnwell's troops revealed their primary motives for participating in the expedition.[19] In a mad scramble for scalps, captives, and assorted booty, the white troops came up short; Barnwell lamented that "our Indians got all the slaves and plunder" except for a single Tuscarora girl. After scouring a few outlying settlements for valuables, nearly all the Catawba warriors took their leave of Barnwell's expedition, their need for plunder and revenge evidently satisfied. Barnwell expressed surprise and dismay to see all these Indians "running away from [him, with] nothing left for the white men but their horses tired and their wounds to comfort them." His "Confusion was so great" that it took him a while to notice that the Catawbas had absconded with "10 bags of spare bullets."[20]

Barnwell felt fortunate that he could still rely on the "brave Yamasees," Indians who would "live and die with [him]" and "go wherever [he] led them."[21] Certainly there was no real danger of the Yamasees and the Apalachees following the Catawbas' lead. These Indians were much further from home, and some of them undoubtedly felt a personal affection for Barnwell. Nevertheless, their behavior during the remainder of the campaign showed that they had no intention of obeying Barnwell's every order. A few headmen from the "Yamasee company" actually told Barnwell that they were less than enthusiastic about proceeding into unfamiliar territory with a dramatically reduced army.[22] Barnwell assured them that it would be worth their while, and after a brief stop in Bath Town to pick up a contingent of sixty-seven North Carolina troops, the expedition continued on to Hancock's town, the nerve center for the Tuscarora resistance. Assisted by a fugitive black slave named Harry, Hancock and his followers had constructed an impressive log fortress, which held about three hundred Indian defenders and several dozen North Carolinian captives. Two separate assaults in March and April 1712 failed to take the fort, but the second engagement ended with the Tuscaroras and their allies agreeing to a conditional surrender.[23] For the next several weeks, they complied with Barnwell's terms by handing over thirty-two black and white captives along with several of their own leaders. Barnwell was prepared to head back to South Carolina, but many in his expedition—particularly the Yamasees—felt that they had been shortchanged. Under a flag of truce, they proceeded to ambush many of the recently surrendered Tuscaroras in Coree Town, thereby earning an additional prize of fifty scalps and two hundred slaves.[24]

With the betrayed Tuscaroras renewing their attacks on the North Carolina settlements, Barnwell's chaotic campaign came under harsh criticism from the North Carolina and Virginia governments. Some officials strongly implied that Barnwell's actions—by undermining ongoing peace deliberations—amounted to outright treason against fellow British subjects.[25] Barnwell, for his part, vehemently asserted his innocence in the disgraceful engagement at Coree Town. But even if the ambush had primarily been the work of the Yamasees and the Apalachees, the incident did not speak well for the South Carolinians' vaunted ability to control their Indian allies.[26]

Since discussions with the Virginia government had reached another impasse and North Carolina's own troops remained plagued by disorganization and desertion, North Carolina officials were soon forced to swallow their distaste for Barnwell's "sham" and send another plea to Charles Town.[27] In a message to the South Carolina Commons House, North Carolina's Governor Hyde admitted that South Carolina's Indian allies were—as potentially dangerous as they seemed—preferable to the even more fearsome Senecas offered by the New York government. Though Hyde appealed to the South Carolinians' sense of honor, he focused his sales pitch on "the great advantage [that] may be made of slaves," including "many hundreds of women and children."[28] Charles Craven, South Carolina's popular and charismatic new governor, enthusiastically consented to Hyde's request and initiated plans for a second relief expedition.[29] Barnwell agreed to remain behind in an advisory role, and command of the expedition was given to James Moore Jr., the leader in the 1708 campaign against the Savannahs. Moore rounded up his allotment of thirty-two white troops, and Craven instructed South Carolina's Indian traders to help fill the province's quota of a thousand Indian warriors.

After several months of recruiting, the number of Indian volunteers had reached only about 850. Craven viewed this shortcoming as an embarrassing affront to his government's authority. Taking the loyalty of his Indian allies for granted, the governor directed his anger at South Carolina's impertinent and unpatriotic traders, who allegedly "prevailed on several of them [the Indians] to stay at home, and others to go to war where they thought fitt." His singling out of eleven Cherokee and Ochese traders suggested that these groups had shown particularly disappointing turnouts.[30] Nevertheless, the conflicting accounts of Moore's expedition attest to the participation of Cherokee warriors, perhaps as many as three hundred of them. Mindful of their previous success, the Catawbas also joined in large numbers, with the remainder of the force being made up of about fifty Yamasees and an unspecified number of Ocheses and Apalachicolas.[31] Despite the diverse origins of Moore's army, nearly everyone involved was driven by a common pursuit of plunder. Some estimated that North Carolina held as many as four thousand potential Indian slaves.[32]

Upon arriving in North Carolina, the Indians in Moore's army were forced to spend a month foraging for corn and cattle in Albermarle County, an area that had been spared the ravages of war. According to the governor, the foraging of the South Carolina Indians was so unsettling that some colonists were "seemingly more ready to rise up against them than march out against the enemy."[33] To the great relief of the terrified North Carolinians, Moore and his troops saved their wrath for Fort Neoheroka, which had replaced nearby Fort Hancock as the Tuscaroras' main stronghold. On March 20, 1713, Moore's army and a supplement of eighty-five North Carolina troops launched a furious, three-day assault that left the fort in ruins. With a loss of twenty-two whites and thirty-five Indians, they managed to kill about half of the fort's 950 defenders and capture most of the survivors. By the time Moore could finish the reports of his triumph, all but 180 of his army's Indians had returned to their villages to sell their slaves and hold their own victory celebrations.[34]

Later that summer Moore also went home to a hero's welcome. The destruction of Fort Neoheroka had effectively ended the war, forcing most of the remaining Tuscaroras to flee North Carolina for a new home among the Iroquois Five Nations of New York. In earning the respect and gratitude of the North Carolinians, Moore's campaign smoothed over many of the hard feelings that had followed in the wake of Barnwell's army.[35] Taken as a whole, the Tuscarora War appeared to be the South Carolinians' greatest military success since their invasion of Apalachee. They had acquired some seven hundred Tuscarora slaves and proven their mettle to their Virginian and North Carolinian rivals. On the battlefield they had managed to take several enemy forts, a feat that they had not been able to accomplish during Queen Anne's War. Though the enemy had not been an imperial rival, the defeat of the Tuscaroras still marked a triumph for South Carolina imperialism. In a successful push along their northern frontiers, South Carolinians and their Indian allies had taken advantage of a golden opportunity for prestige and profits.

Amid the euphoria of victory, it was easy for South Carolinians to overlook some of the more disturbing implications of their latest offensives. By making separate treaties and exacerbating their rivalry among the Catawbas and the Cherokees, the Virginia and South Carolina governments had only darkened an already unfriendly relationship. More unsettling, however, were the obvious strains within South Carolina's own imperial sphere. Even a successful campaign against an external enemy could not conceal the many tensions between South Carolina imperialists and their Indian allies. In many ways the Barnwell and Moore expeditions had unfolded like free-for-alls, with whites and Indians often displaying more competition than cooperation. Even an apparently loyal group of warriors like the "brave Yamasees" could occasionally make a mockery of the South Carolinians' control.

The possibility of losing control over the Indian alliance network was all the more disturbing to officials who had begun to implement an ambitious and expensive system of frontier regulation during Queen Anne's War. This system had been built on the central premise that South Carolina's frontier influence flowed primarily from its Indian trade, and that the trade might devolve into irreparable chaos if allowed to continue without careful supervision. The race for spoils in the Tuscarora War suggested a need for South Carolina officials to build on their earlier efforts at trade reform. For most reformers the primary goal remained a system for curbing the abusive tendencies of a supposedly dissolute group of traders. All the while, some reformers hoped to improve South Carolina's frontier standing by introducing the southeastern Indians to men who, in theory, represented a more enlightened and compassionate side of the imperial power structure.

The Missionary Impulse

Unlike the French and the Spanish, the British were slow to use religion as a means to bolster their imperial authority. In 1701, however, the establishment of the Society for the Propagation of the Gospel in Foreign Parts (SPG) as the missionary branch of the revamped Anglican Church seemed to signal a bold new direction for the empire.[36] The ranks of the SPG included a number of important imperial officials, including most of the governors of Britain's North American colonies. The SPG quickly perceived North America as one of its greatest priorities but soon grew aware of the difficulties they faced there. Previous attempts at proselytizing had been limited to a few Puritan communities in Massachusetts, and no Englishman had ever been successful in converting Indians who lived beyond the colonial settlements. Though the SPG lacked a proper English model for frontier missionary work, it could look to the experiences of Britain's foremost imperial rival. For nearly seventy years Catholic missionaries from the Society of Jesus had been playing a remarkable role along the extensive frontiers of New France, claiming thousands of Indian converts and helping to establish a workable "middle ground" between Indians, fur traders, and French military officers. [37] The accomplishments of the Jesuits had already become the stuff of legend in colonial circles, even as far away as South Carolina. When SPG member Thomas Nairne sent his request for a few frontier missionaries "disinterested from all the wrangles of Trade," he probably hoped that the South Carolinians might acquire some reliable Protestants possessed of Jesuit-like dedication. [38]

Since the British generally believed that the Indians could only embrace Christianity after acquiring some familiarity with the "civilized" world, the Southeast initially seemed an ideal proving ground for the SPG. As Nairne explained, South Carolina's trade among the Indians was already so extensive that it would be "easier for [the South Carolinians] to undertake propagating the Christian faith among them, than it [was] for the Northern Colonies." [39] SPG officials in London were inclined to agree and sent dozens of missionaries to Charles Town over the course of Queen Anne's War. Like the traders and government officials, these missionaries varied considerably in strength, integrity, and dedication. [40] Regardless of their personal backgrounds and convictions, however, they could unanimously agree that South Carolina did not live up to their expectations.

Gideon Johnston, the SPG commissary in South Carolina, spoke for most of the missionaries when he lamented that he "never repented so much of anything, [his] Sins only excepted, as [his] coming to [that] Place." [41] For men schooled in the sleepy parishes of England, South Carolina seemed like some kind of cruel joke. In letters to the SPG's London headquarters, Johnston and several of his colleagues complained regularly about the heat, the food, their paltry salaries, and their failing health. For Johnston the worst thing about the place was its white inhabitants: "the Vilest race of Men upon the Earth . . . being a perfect Medley of Bankrupts, pirates, decayed Libertines, sectaries, and Enthusiasts of all sorts." [42] Even the more generous of the missionaries had to admit that the South Carolinians were overly preoccupied with "getting money and their worldly affairs" and that God was "very little adored and loved" among them. [43] Though many South Carolinians possessed religious convictions, it was hard to get them to attend church. Of the nearly five hundred communicants in Charles Town, only twenty-four bothered to show up for the Easter services performed in 1706 by one of the recently arrived missionaries. [44]

As rough and uncouth as they could be, however, the colonists seemed preferable to the Indians who lived on South Carolina's frontiers. As the first missionary to arrive in South Carolina, Samuel Thomas initially intended to work among the Yamasees, widely considered the most receptive of the province's Indian allies. After several colonists told him that the Yamasees "had neither leisure nor dispositions to attend Christian Instructions, and that a Missionary could not in [that] time of war reside among them without the utmost hazard to his life," Thomas gave up on his mission without ever setting foot in a Yamasee town.[45] Unlike the Jesuits, who relished physical deprivation of all kinds, he and the rest of the SPG missionaries were not anxious for martyrdom among the Indians. Thomas settled for a less adventurous life as Governor Johnson's distinguished houseguest and warned the SPG that "those Missionarys which they sen[t] among and confine[d] to the Indians [would] but lose time and receive their salaries for no service."[46] Another potential missionary to the Yamasees responded a bit more forthrightly than Thomas, claiming "that he might have 60[,] nay 100£ Sterling per Annum [and] he would not engage in it, being resolved to Stay where he then was, and to get his bread after a more Easy manner among the white folks."[47]

Throughout the colonial period, most of the SPG missionaries found enough to keep them busy among South Carolina's white population and generally refused to entertain thoughts of working among the Indians.[48] But South Carolina was not the only colony of the early eighteenth-century Southeast to experience such difficulties. Governor Spotswood limited his proselytizing efforts to the College of William and Mary, which provided religious instruction to only a handful of Virginia's "tributary" Indians. Even the experienced Bienville could not accomplish much and found himself pleading for some devoted Jesuits to replace the exceptionally corrupt and lazy priests who were stationed in Louisiana.[49] Despite the obvious dearth of frontier missionaries, however, Samuel Thomas and many of his colleagues were wrong to assume that the southeastern Indians would never embrace Christianity. The notable successes of the seventeenth-century Florida missions stood as evidence to the contrary. Though most of these missions had collapsed by the end of Queen Anne's War, an important part of South Carolina's frontier complex still carried the legacy of the Franciscans. A few of the SPG missionaries in South Carolina were astute enough to realize this legacy and committed enough to try to build on the religious influences that the Spaniards had instilled among some of the Southeast's Indians.

Foremost among these missionaries was Dr. Francis Le Jau, a French-born, university-trained Anglican minister who came to South Carolina in 1706. Conversant in six languages, Le Jau left behind a considerable paper trail that portrays him as a remarkably perceptive, articulate, and sensitive man.[50] Though Le Jau's tendency to view the Indians as innocent children of nature seems patronizing by today's standards, it set him apart from those missionaries who dismissed the Indians as hopeless barbarians. Along with a few fellow missionaries, Le Jau made an effort to learn about the Indians who inhabited some of the province's frontiers. Though they were rarely able to pay direct visits to these frontiers, they talked extensively to some of South Carolina's traders and officials, closely examined the "settlement" Indians, and did their best to communicate with some visiting Indian leaders. On one occasion a visiting headman from the Ochese town of Cussita showed interest in a Bible and agreed to consider sending two of his young children to be schooled by one of the missionaries.[51] It soon became apparent that the groups that seemed most willing "to have Clergymen living in their Settlements" were those—like the Yamasees, the Apalachees, and the Savannahs—that had formerly interacted with the Spanish.[52] Le Jau acknowledged the need to cleanse them of their Catholic predilections, but he and a few others remained optimistic enough to see the souls of these Indians as "fit Materials which [might] be easily polish't."[53]

Le Jau came up with a number of promising ideas for the conversion of South Carolina's Indian allies and even began to look into the possibility of translating the Bible into some of the Southeast's primary lingua francas.[54] At the same time, however, he and his most committed colleagues realized that they would have to depend on the aid of those South Carolinians who had the most experience living and working on the province's frontiers. Even the French Jesuits usually proved unsuccessful unless they had a trader or government official to help facilitate their introduction to Indian society. In South Carolina Le Jau and other SPG missionaries found most of the traders to be decidedly uncooperative.[55]

As their frustration increased, the missionaries grew more inclined to lend their voices to the chorus of attacks against the character of the traders. Only the "Scandalous Lives" of this "profligate, wicked sort of people" prevented the missionaries from gaining a foothold among the Indians.[56] The traders, they assumed, wanted no potential obstruction to their evil works, especially "those perpetual wars they promote[d] amongst the Indians for the only reason of making slaves to buy their trading goods."[57] Though greed probably contributed to the traders' reticence, other factors were at work as well. Very few of the South Carolina traders—even the most morally upright among them— were the kinds of men to relish the constant company of a sanctimonious minister. On an entirely different level, some of the uncooperative traders might have perceived something about the Indians that the missionaries, in their enthusiasm and inexperience, would have been likely to overlook. Even the Indian societies that appeared the most receptive to Christianity were actually home to some serious religious divisions. For every Yamasee or Apalachee who remembered his catechism and wanted his children baptized, there was another who had left Florida with some extremely hard feelings about the missions. Some of the traders probably feared that the arrival of an SPG missionary would upset many of the Indians and jeopardize their ties to them. According to one missionary, some of the traders opposed SPG activity because they believed that the Yamasees had left the protection of the Spanish "because they would not be Christians," and that the Yamasees might "return again to the Spaniards" if English missionaries pushed them too hard.[58]

Though the traders did little to help them, the missionaries ultimately suffered even more from a dearth of support from the South Carolina government. As the SPG's principal authority in the province, Gideon Johnston attempted to circumvent the traders by acquiring a position on the Board of Indian Trade Commissioners. Deeply averse to "a Clergyman's meddling in Secular Affairs," the board summarily denied Johnston's request, forcing him to consider more convoluted ways of bringing the gospel to the Indians.[59] In 1713 the SPG went so far as to sponsor the son of a Yamasee headman to travel to England, where he received baptism and two years of schooling.[60] By the time this "Yamasee prince" prepared to return to South Carolina, however, it was becoming clear that any constructive changes in trade reform or frontier affairs would have to come not from the missionaries but from the province's civil government.

The government's task was far from simple. South Carolina officials had begun to express frustration not only with the traders' behavior but also with their resistance to any kind of government supervision. On one level Governor Craven's spirited indictment of the traders during the planning of Moore's Tuscarora campaign was nothing new; his predecessors had been spouting similar charges for the previous twenty years. At the same time, however, Craven's portrayal of the traders' misconduct as a "growing evil" added more weight to his accusations. Indeed, many of South Carolina's most concerned imperialists shared Craven's deteriorating impression of the South Carolina traders and tended to hold the traders responsible for almost every perceived threat to the government's authority among the Indians. In yielding to this temptation, they ran the risk of overlooking some of the more fundamental problems that were coming to plague the Indian trade during South Carolina's most aggressive period of imperial expansion.

Scoundrels and Scapegoats

Though the Indian trade no longer dominated the colonial economy the way that it had during the 1670s and 1680s, it remained lucrative and dynamic well into the early eighteenth century. By the end of Queen Anne's War, exports of deerskins and Indian slaves outweighed the combined totals for the livestock, lumber, and naval-stores trades. [61] Even the rapid emergence of rice as South Carolina's dominant staple crop could not stall the Indian trade's growth. Because the wartime expansion of South Carolina's frontiers created a growing market, the trade's continued vitality simply depended on the accumulation of enough capital to finance longer and more frequent trips into the interior. With South Carolina's planters channeling more of their resources into rice production, Charles Town's growing merchant community stepped in to take up the slack. The years 1705–15 witnessed the arrival of men like Samuel Wragg, John Bee, and Samuel Eveleigh, merchants with valuable connections to England who were willing to invest their fortunes in cargoes of cloth, rum, utensils, and weapons. Joining forces with some of the most successful and experienced traders in South Carolina, they formed the firms and companies that helped make the Indian trade more profitable than it had ever been. [62]

Ultimately, however, the success of the trade lay in the hands of the people who negotiated and sealed the deals along the colony's frontiers. South Carolina's Indian traders of the second decade of the eighteenth century represented a wide range of ethnic and socioeconomic backgrounds. [63] Below the relatively wealthy and cultivated "master traders" like Thomas Nairne and Thomas Welch were the men who drove the trains of packhorses and canoes. Further down the ladder were skilled and unskilled laborers, whose ranks included a number of indentured servants and African slaves. As the Indian trade expanded, the number of white and black visitors to the Indian country increased apace. In the early eighteenth century, no position in the Indian trade ever remained open for long. Laborers and packhorse men earned good wages, anywhere from two to four times as much as those of the average laborer in Charles Town. Moreover, everyone but the slaves seemed to have a fair chance at advancement, possibly joining the circle of men who were fortunate enough to purchase plantations with their earnings. [64]

Of all the various kinds of traders, none stood out as conspicuously as the men who spent most of the year living and working among the Indians. By the end of Queen Anne's War, South Carolinians could boast nearly two hundred of these traders scattered throughout the Southeast at any given time. They were able to interact with far-flung groups of Indians in ways that were matched only by the legendary *coureurs de bois* of New France. Though the semiresident traders had proven invaluable to South Carolina's extensive sphere of influence, their extended stays among the Indians made them somewhat strange and suspect in the eyes of mainstream colonial society. Despite the recent growth of the large trading firms, many of these men remained self-employed, eking out profits that placed them in the poor to middling ranks of South Carolina's white society. Moreover, it was common knowledge that some of the frontier traders had chosen their profession as a way to pay off or avoid their creditors.[65] As a result it became relatively easy for merchants, master traders, and political officials to write them off as riffraff, and for future generations of historians to condescendingly describe them as "true types of the first American frontier" or as members of "a particularly disgusting group."[66] In reality these traders encompassed all kinds of "types": from wily veterans to inexperienced newcomers; from shady characters off the Charles Town docks to hardworking and ambitious young men just released from their indentures.

Those critics who perceived the traders as refugees and runaways had an outlook that was equally one-sided. In distancing themselves from one world, the traders became more immersed in another. Their initial entry into Indian communities was often facilitated by village headmen, who tended to view generosity and reciprocity as important expressions of power. Once introduced to an Indian town, however, a trader would have to do his best to pursue other important relationships.[67] South Carolinians generally found frontier life much more manageable and enjoyable when they shared it with Indian women. In addition to providing some welcome female companionship, Indian wives helped introduce the traders to Indian food, clothing, and languages. John Lawson claimed, "The English Traders are seldom without an Indian Female for his Bed-Fellow . . . [because] it makes them learn the Indian Tongue much the sooner, they being of the French-man's Opinion, how that an English Wife teaches her Husband more English in one Night, than a School-master can in a Week."[68] Since the influence of Indian women often extended beyond the domestic sphere, wives could also serve as indirect but valuable allies in a village's political arena. Perhaps most importantly women were also a gateway into the Indians' matrilineal and matrilocal kinship systems. As an honorary affiliate of his wife's clan, a trader acquired—in the words of Thomas Nairne—"relations in each Village from Charles Town to the Mississipi."[69] These "relations" could serve as valuable friends, protectors, and business partners, clearly demonstrating the advantages a trader could gain by "going native."

At the same time there were certain limits to any trader's immersion into Indian culture. Unlike the so-called white Indians who severed all ties to colonial society, South Carolina's traders belonged to two worlds at the same time. No matter how close they grew to their Indian hosts or how much scorn they drew from fellow colonists, they still maintained important connections to the colonial world, especially its mercantile economy. Many had numerous motives for living and working among the Indians, but all of them expected to make money for their efforts, whether they intended to pay off a debt, purchase a slave, or merely finance a drinking binge on their next trip to Charles Town. By no means was every trader a shrewd protocapitalist; their regular extension of credit to the Indians aggravated the Charles Town merchants no end. [70] Nevertheless, most traders were aware of the things that separated them from their customers. Whenever a trader's packhorses and storehouse were full, he usually found that his cooperation, his favors, and especially his trade goods were in great demand among the Indians. As one of the centers of a village's attention, he could bask in one of the Indian trade's most important fringe benefits: an exciting sense of power.

An overwhelming majority of South Carolina's traders had been born and raised in a society in which parents beat their children, teachers beat their pupils, officers beat their troops, and masters beat their slaves. When the traders obtained a sense of power—often for the first time in their lives—some of them found it natural to back it with force and violence. Though hardly uncommon by the standards of eighteenth-century Anglo-America, the abusive tendencies of these traders stood out more conspicuously among Indian societies that lived by markedly different standards.

When dealing with members of their own clans or villages, southeastern Indians generally avoided using coercion or corporal punishment. Traders might have seen clan membership as a route to economic and political connections, but when viewed from the perspective of the Indians, it appeared to be a good way to get traders to conform to Indian standards. Indian leaders who welcomed traders into their own towns and clans were not only getting satisfaction from a display of hospitality; they were also doing their best to make sure that the traders behaved themselves as kinsmen should. In this light acts of violence committed by traders against fellow clan members could prove especially problematic, particularly when committed against female clan members. Traders who married Indian wives in the Southeast often found that their own patriarchal authority conflicted with the Indian tendency to grant women a great deal of control in domestic affairs. One trader noted that among the Cherokees "the women Rule[d] the Rostt and [wore] the brichess," and Thomas Nairne commented that the Chickasaws frequently teased Ochese men for being overly deferential to their wives. [71] Among these Indian societies, violence against women was virtually unheard of, making it all the more glaring if an English trader used his fists to settle an argument with an "uppity" Indian wife. If the assaulted woman happened to share a clan connection with village leaders, the trader's misconduct could have serious consequences indeed—not only for his own status in the village but for the entire trade relationship between South Carolina and that particular group of Indians. [72]

Evidence suggests, however, that over time, some Indian leaders might have been finding it harder to clamp down on acts of violence—domestic or otherwise—committed by resident traders. Upon entering a village for the first time or dealing with an unfamiliar group of Indians, South Carolina traders usually behaved cautiously and deferentially, knowing that their success—or even their lives—could depend on making a good first impression. [73] A Henry Woodward among the Cowetas in 1685 or a John Stewart among the Chickasaws in 1693 would never have dreamed of doing what Alexander Nicholas, a trader among the Yamasees, did in 1712, when he beat his pregnant Yamasee wife to death and seriously injured the wife and sister of two important Yamasee leaders. Nicholas was either extremely foolhardy or confident enough to believe that Indians so beholden to the South Carolinians would never take it upon themselves to punish him. Indeed, when the "king" of the Yamasee town of Altamaha appeared before South Carolina authorities that fall, he claimed that "he would have bound him [Nicholas] and brought him to Town but that he feared the Displeasure of the Government." [74]

This story, and many others like it, has been preserved in the journal of South Carolina's Board of Indian Trade Commissioners. Extant from the years 1710–18, the journal shows a depressing litany of fraud, beatings, kidnappings, and rapes perpetrated by some of the colony's most ruthless traders. A careful examination of earlier records reveals that these abuses were hardly new to some of South Carolina's frontiers; the Altamaha king had filed a complaint over the kidnapping of one of his sons twenty years before the Nicholas incidents. On the whole, however, all of South Carolina's colonial records present problems for a thorough analysis of trade abuse. Even for those few years covered by a source as relatively rich as the commissioners' journals, it is safe to assume that many abuses went unreported or unrecorded. Despite these pitfalls it is reasonable to suggest some broad patterns in the behavior of South Carolina's early Indian traders. Though familiarity with Indian culture brought success to many traders, it could also breed overconfidence and contempt. A process that had begun as an exchange between relative equals was listing heavily to the side of the white men, more so in some parts of the Southeast than in others.

There was no question that trade abuse had become a more glaring problem over the previous several years. At the height of Queen Anne's War, the traders—despite their various misdeeds—had been treated as valuable agents of the government. But with South Carolina's enemies rapidly diminishing and its allies rapidly increasing, its Indian alliance network was becoming more vulnerable to disturbances like Indian slave raids. More than ever, it appeared that the traders' quest for private profits was falling out of step with what some government officials perceived as the public good.

This dilemma sparked Governor Craven's antitrader tirade in 1712 and reappeared even more prominently two years later in a dispute that involved Alexander Long and Eleazer Wiggan, traders among the Lower Cherokees who had, incidentally, been singled out in Craven's earlier indictments.[75] After meeting in Euchasee, one of the Lower Cherokees' principal war towns, Long and Wiggan hatched a plan to increase their fortunes and settle a personal score at the same time. Together the two men persuaded the warriors of Euchasee that a "brave Parcel of Slaves" awaited them in Chestowe, a nearby Yuchi town where Long had been partially scalped and totally humiliated a few years earlier. The Cherokees did not have to be asked twice to attack their traditional enemies; supplied with the necessary hardware by Long and Wiggan, they set out against Chestowe and came away with several Yuchi slaves, whom they handed over to the two traders as payment for their debts. The Cherokees explained that they would have returned with more had most of Chestowe's residents not chosen suicide over capture.[76]

Trader-sponsored raids between rival groups of Indians had long comprised an important, if unsavory, aspect of the South Carolina frontier complex. In 1691 the Commons House had essentially snickered at the news of a Savannah raid against the Cherokees. By 1714, however, the government was willing to take such a raid very seriously; Wiggan, Long, and several witnesses were quickly summoned before the Board of Commissioners for an official inquiry. After short deliberations the board decided to revoke the licenses of the two traders and recommend them for criminal prosecution. There were a number of reasons for this relatively swift and severe verdict. The Yuchis were long-standing allies who had expressed some dissatisfaction with the South Carolinians in recent years, and the government was justifiably alarmed at an incident that was bound to alienate them even more.[77] Probably more disturbing than the raid itself, however, was the way in which it had been carried out. According to another South Carolina trader, Long and Wiggan had shown the Cherokees a piece of paper disguised as an order from the governor. In fact, the governor's real order to the Cherokees—one that explicitly forbade them from disturbing the Yuchis—had been mysteriously delayed from crossing the mountains until after the raid on Chestowe. Wiggan adamantly insisted that the Cherokees would have attacked the Yuchis anyway, but his plaints fell on deaf ears. Rather than entertain thoughts of the Indians' insubordination, the board found it easier to charge the traders with that offense.[78]

In its response to the "Chestowe affair," the South Carolina government betrayed its growing reliance on a new cog in the provincial bureaucracy. While the governor and the two houses of assembly occasionally waded in with their opinions, the supervision of South Carolina's Indian affairs in the aftermath of Queen Anne's War fell mostly to the Board of Indian Trade Commissioners. The ideal commissioner was an influential member of the assembly who had gained at least some prior experience in dealing with South Carolina's Indian allies.[79] With the assistance of their agents in the field and a number of unofficial informants, the nine commissioners assumed responsibility for recognizing potential problems in the province's alliance network and taking the proper measures to remedy them. Though mandated by the Indian Act of 1707, the board did not hold its first meeting until 1710. Over the next five years, it compiled what could charitably be described as a mixed record. Several of the commissioners' most promising and judicious decisions were eventually compromised by shortcomings in the colonial legal system, as well as their own misunderstandings of frontier relations.

To their credit the commissioners were perceptive enough to realize that they would have to expand on the 1707 Indian act in order to address the most pressing problems on South Carolina's prominent frontiers. One significant step was to establish a separate agency for the most vulnerable and beleaguered allies of the province. John Wright, who had replaced Thomas Nairne as Indian agent in the aftermath of a 1708 political scandal, was informed by the board in 1712 that he no longer had the "Right to act as Agent amongst the Yamasee and those [Pallachacola] Indians."[80] Returning to a prominent position in South Carolina's regulatory system, Nairne took on the demanding task of visiting every town in the Combahee-Savannah basins every two months. Nairne was ordered not only to encourage the Indians to voice their grievances but also to hold the Yamasee and Pallachacola traders to some relatively rigid standards.[81]

These innovations reflected the board's growing concern for the area where South Carolina's Indian relations had been at their most intensive and volatile for the previous twenty-five years.

Indians in this region not only faced the intrusions that went along with heavy trade, but they also figured prominently in South Carolina's imperialistic strategies. Though South Carolina officials had been making an extra effort to appease these Indians since the beginning of Queen Anne's War, they remained troubled by the Indians' inability or unwillingness to settle their soaring debts to the South Carolina traders. The commissioners, however, were fully aware of the important role that groups like the Yamasees, the Pallachacolas, and the Ocheses had played against the Spanish and were therefore willing to meet them halfway in this area. In 1710 the board canceled a debt for two hundred pounds of powder and five hundred pounds of bullets that the Ocheses had incurred during their raids on the Choctaws, a decision that reportedly left the Indians "well satisfied." [82] The following year the commissioners announced the cancellation of all the Indians' "Rum Debts" (which stood at over one hundred thousand skins for the Yamasees alone), as well as any debts owed by their deceased relatives. These major concessions to the Indians seemed to bode well for the board's ability to mollify South Carolina's allies by making some significant economic and cultural adjustments. [83]

When examined closely, however, even some of the board's most outwardly impressive regulations seem encumbered by imprecision and internal contradictions. Admitting that they were powerless "wholy to restrane the Traders from [illegally] carrying up Rum," the commissioners implied that they could do nothing to prevent the accumulation of future rum debts among the Indians. [84] By 1712 the commissioners were also qualifying the decree that protected Indians from the debts of their deceased or insolvent relatives; if the Indians had previously known about or consented to these debts, they would now have to pay them. [85] When faced with pressure to settle their debts, Indians were more likely to resort to offering Indians from other areas as payment. Such practices prompted the board to decree in the summer of 1711 that "no Indian shall be deemed a Slave and bought as such unless taken in Warr" and also to impose a three-day waiting period on any trader purchasing slaves from the Indians. [86] These laws did nothing to allay the growing problems associated with the clandestine Indian slave trade and might even have served to encourage disturbing transgressions like the Coree Town massacre or the Cherokees' "war" on Chestowe. [87]

Despite their inherent flaws, these regulations might have acted as a useful salve to the Indian trade if the board had been able to enforce them to any significant extent. It was one thing for the commissioners to instruct the traders "to be loving and kind to the Indians and not to abuse them," but it was an entirely different matter to punish those traders who stepped out of line. [88] Though the board had the power to make regulations, it lacked the authority to prosecute South Carolinians for criminal offenses. If the commissioners suspected a trader of theft, rape, assault, treason, or murder, the most they could do was revoke his license to trade and refer his case to the colony's overworked and undependable attorney general. [89] It did not take long for the traders to view the board and its agents as paper tigers. On one occasion four traders who received arrest warrants from the board felt secure enough to rip them up before the eyes of the Indian agent. By 1714 the threats of the board carried so little legitimacy that few traders were even bothering to apply for licenses at all. [90]

Even in the relatively few cases where offenders were apprehended, tried, and punished, the penalties were almost never stringent enough to suit the crime. As much as they liked to point fingers at the wayward traders, South Carolina's government officials eventually had to admit that they could not get along without them. Eleazer Wiggan, the colony's most notorious black sheep following his role in the Chestowe incident, was out of action for no more than a few months before the government renewed his license and begged his assistance among the Cherokees. [91] John Musgrove, a trader indicted for several abuses among the Yamasees and the Ocheses, was deemed so inexpendable that he sat as an official interpreter during many of the board's sessions. [92] Even John Wright, one of the agents responsible for controlling the traders and appeasing the Indians, would eventually stand accused of numerous transgressions and abuses of his power. [93] It did not speak well for South Carolina's regulatory system that the officials who were supposedly making and enforcing regulations for the Indians' protection could not even understand the Indians without the help of men who were accused of hurting them.

Nor were the commissioners themselves beyond reproach. According to the 1707 Indian act, all members of the board were supposed to remain aloof from the financial concerns of the Indian trade. The regular presence of Samuel Eveleigh, one of the wealthiest and most influential merchants in South Carolina, suggests that the board could not always display the kind of impartiality that was expected of it. Indeed, most of South Carolina's political officials in the second decade of the eighteenth century maintained at least some financial stake in the Indian trade and were not likely to support any measures that impinged on its profitability.[94] The commissioners' concerns with cash flow might help explain their obsession with traders' licenses. In addition to symbolizing the board's authority over the traders, licenses were also expected to provide the revenue to support the entire regulatory system. The commissioners' journals often give the impression that they begrudged the traders more for shirking their license fees than for abusing their Indian customers. At one point Agent Nairne was ordered to crack down on "all such Persons *except such as have Lycenses* whom [he thought] burthensome to the Indians" (italics added).[95] A cynic might conclude that a license to trade on South Carolina's frontiers amounted to a license to ignore authority.

Other fragments of evidence also suggest that the commissioners were not showing a sufficient level of interest in South Carolina's Indian allies. Though the board had originally been designed to provide a forum for settling Indian-white and Indian-Indian disputes, it soon began to devote most of its attention to squabbles between South Carolinians. In November 1714, at a time of rising tension on South Carolina's frontiers, the board spent considerable time and energy resolving a conflict between two traders over the possession of an Indian boy.[96] As the board began to resemble a mouthpiece for South Carolina's wealthier merchants and traders, it became less and less convincing in its supervision of Indian relations. Even a case as dramatic and disturbing as the Chestowe affair revealed surprisingly little outrage or emotion on the part of the commissioners.[97] With a few notable exceptions—such as Governor Craven's angry tirade or Commissioner Charles Hart's forceful order to destroy all casks of rum among the Yamasees—it would appear that most of South Carolina's officials did not invest much of their energy in the task of trade regulation.[98] In December 1714 the transcript of the Indian act disappeared from the office of the provincial secretary, and the Commons House had to search long and hard before unearthing a person who could give them "some account" of what the document said.[99] The government's gradual detachment from Indian affairs extended to matters of diplomacy as well. In June 1714 the governor and council had to force some members of the Commons House to attend a ceremony confirming the colony's good relations with the Chickasaws and had to remind them that the Chickasaws were important allies who "ought to be shown some respect."[100]

Ultimately it would be futile to pin the blame for problems in South Carolina's Indian trade and diplomacy on any number of individuals, whether they be Indians, traders, trade commissioners, or politicians. By the second decade of the eighteenth century, tensions had far more to do with major "structural" flaws (e.g., deficits, market pressures, ecological quandaries) and deep cultural impasses than they did with the misdeeds of traders and the ineffectiveness of the men charged with managing them. [101] Realistically there was very little that anyone—colonial or Indian—could have done to "fix" things on South Carolina's troubled frontiers.

It should not be surprising that many officials were merely going through the motions of frontier regulation even as the South Carolina government continued to boast of its grand imperial ambitions. South Carolina's imperialists often expressed a desire for control, but imperialism has always involved a wide gap between rhetoric and reality. In the immediate aftermath of Queen Anne's War, South Carolinians were by no means blind to many of the problems on their frontiers; they were quick to point them out and in many cases knew what they had to do to address them. [102] But most of the people who railed against the evils of the Indian trade could suddenly find other things to do when the time came for putting their plans into action. With some exceptions they probably were less concerned with the state of the province's Indian buffer zone than they often let on. For many South Carolinians, it had become easier to take their Indian allies for granted, especially at a time when the colonists' anxieties had begun to shift away from their frontiers and toward their own settlements.

"The Moon Would Be Turned into Blood"

By the end of Queen Anne's War in 1713, South Carolina's frontiers had grown further removed from the everyday concerns of most colonists. In a little more than forty years, the province's colonial settlements had expanded from the immediate environs of Charles Town into a strip of territory that stretched nearly 150 miles along the coast and 40 miles into the interior. [103] Though some colonists on the far edges of this territory made their livings by raising cattle or cutting timber, a growing number—particularly in the most densely settled regions of Goose Creek and Colleton County—devoted their energies to farming. The most successful of their farms had burgeoned into plantations, extensive enterprises that brought together people of different backgrounds to labor for the good of the owner and his family. These plantations witnessed considerable interaction between people of different races and cultures, but the parameters of this cultural exchange were much more clearly defined than they were among the Southeast's largest and most powerful Indian societies. By law and their own reckoning, plantation owners were considered undisputed masters of their domains.

Though South Carolina's early eighteenth-century plantations did not constitute frontiers in the generally understood sense of the term, they still displayed a troubling sense of instability and uncertainty. Their expansion came at a great human cost, helping to complete South Carolina's transition to a slave society. Though South Carolina's slave population had begun to grow steadily in the 1690s, it exploded after 1700, when a dwindling supply of indentured servants encouraged planters to look to more convenient and cost-effective pools of labor. The Indian trade provided South Carolinians with one ready-made source. Most of the slaves purchased from the province's Indian trading partners had previously been exported to New England and the West Indies, but by the early eighteenth century, a growing number of Indian slaves were being put to work on South Carolina plantations.[104] Despite the increasing popularity of Indian slaves, South Carolinians tended to value them less than the black slaves imported from the Caribbean and Africa; in 1712 John Norris wrote, "An Indian Man or Woman may cost 18 or 20 Pound, but a good Negro is worth more than twice that Sum."[105] As a result of the cheaper prices brought on by the recent end of the Royal African Company's monopoly, planters throughout colonial North America gained easier access to shiploads of African slaves. The importation of blacks increased dramatically during Queen Anne's War, especially in South Carolina, where the number of slaves soon eclipsed the number of free white residents. According to historian Peter Wood's estimates, South Carolina's black population rose from twenty-eight hundred to eighty-six hundred between 1700 and 1715, during which time the white population rose from thirty-eight hundred to only fifty-five hundred.[106]

Though South Carolinians were coming to realize how much these slaves contributed to the strength and prosperity of their province, they found it hard to shake their nagging suspicions of them. Various bills and laws from the period clearly testify to the growing uneasiness of white South Carolinians in the early years of the eighteenth century. Along with their draconian slave codes of 1696 and 1712, a 1698 act for "the Encouragement of the Importation of White Servants" displayed their worries that a growing ratio of slaves to whites might "endanger the safety" of South Carolina.[107] Such concerns continued to prevail well into the second decade of the eighteenth century, when the South Carolina assembly passed two different import duties as a means to keep the slave population in check.[108] No legislative measure could impede a planter's quest for profits, and as slaves continued to flood into the province, officials were forced to tolerate them to a certain extent. During Queen Anne's War, the provincial government's fear of the French and the Spanish occasionally outweighed their mistrust of South Carolina's slaves. In 1703 and 1704, the government drew up provisions that allowed well-supervised slaves to bear arms and even passed a law to draft qualified black slaves into the militia. [109] Nevertheless, it is highly unlikely that South Carolina officials would have resorted to such measures if the province had contained enough eligible white men to meet its quotas. Their reservations about arming slaves were so great that they accompanied the 1704 militia act with an act that created South Carolina's first organized slave patrol. Except during the 1706 Franco-Spanish invasion, the South Carolina militia actually spent most of the war on the lookout for fugitive slaves. [110]

South Carolinians had shown great concern over the slaves who had escaped to Florida during the 1680s and 1690s, and the beginning of open warfare with the Spanish after 1702 probably did little to assuage their anxieties. Soon, however, it became apparent that any fears of a massive slave exodus to Florida were groundless. The dramatic weakening of the Spanish combined with the increasing aggressiveness of South Carolina's Yamasee and Ochese allies cut off many possible escape routes, but the ruthlessness of South Carolina's slave owners provided an equally effective deterrent. [111]

Though a few slaves were fortunate enough to serve as artisans, cowboys, or assistants in the Indian trade, it would be wrong to assume that frontier influence made early South Carolina slavery any less oppressive. [112] By the height of Queen Anne's War, a growing majority of South Carolina's slaves were stationed on low-country plantations, fully immersed in an exceptionally cruel and brutal institution. Reverend Francis Le Jau lamented that most masters of his acquaintance could not "be persuaded that Negroes and Indians [were] otherwise than Beasts, and use[d] them as such."[113] His observations in Goose Creek Parish left him horrified at the measures South Carolinians would take to exert their authority. One of his neighbors regularly stuck his slaves in a suffocating, coffinlike contraption for twenty-four hour periods, and another had one of his recalcitrant slaves burned alive not far from Le Jau's doorstep. [114] As the reins of slavery tightened in South Carolina, slaves began to lose their formerly significant place in the province's imperial struggles. At the same time, however, an increasing tension between masters and slaves appeared to foreshadow a new danger to the South Carolinians: that of slave insurrection.

South Carolinians clearly did not perceive all their slaves as equally menacing. Some Indian slaves had been punished for allegedly plotting an uprising in 1700, but on the whole they appeared much less suspicious than black slaves in the eyes of the colonial authorities. [115] A majority of Indian slaves were women and children from societies that had apparently been demoralized and subdued by South Carolina's Indian allies. Black slaves, on the other hand, generally appeared healthier and more robust and also possessed a racial phenotype that elicited profound, deeply ingrained feelings of revulsion and unease in most colonists. [116] As Le Jau suggested, few South Carolinians were willing to acknowledge the humanity of their black slaves. This tendency was revealed not only in the various pieces of oppressive legislation that singled out the "negroes" but also in the colonists' ongoing resistance to slave conversions. Though willing to support missionary activity along South Carolina's Indian frontiers, Thomas Nairne dismissed the SPG's "notion of converting the Goose Creek Negroes" as "perverted" and took no measures to introduce the gospel to his own black slaves. [117] Though a few South Carolinians took advantage of the 1712 law that allowed slave baptisms, the SPG missionaries admitted that "the Masters of Slaves [were] generally of the Opinion that a Slave [grew] worse by becoming a Christian." [118]

Le Jau baptized dozens of Goose Creek blacks over the next several years but admitted that he felt somewhat disturbed by his work. Even as he extolled the innocence of the Indians, he claimed that "the Negroes [were] generally very bad men, chiefly those that [were] Scholars." [119] Whether raised among West Africa's Islamic elite or instructed by Europeans in Africa and the West Indies, some slaves had learned enough theology to provide the SPG missionaries with an unwanted challenge. One such slave in Goose Creek Parish managed to come across a book "wherein he read some description of the several judgm[en]ts that Chastise Men because of their Sins in [those] latter Days." Deeply impressed by this book, the slave "told his Master abruptly [that] there would be a dimmed time and the Moon would be turned into Blood." By the time Le Jau could be summoned to set the slave straight, a rumor had begun to circulate among all the slaves of the parish "that an Angel [had come] and spoke[n] to the Man." [120] Needless to say, this sudden interest in apocalyptic themes did not sit well with the local white population.

Though this particular incident failed to blossom into the feared uprising, other episodes during this period seemed to confirm the worst fears of the South Carolina planters. In 1712 a brief but bloody slave rebellion claimed the lives of nine whites in the streets of New York. [121] South Carolinians were therefore all the more alarmed the following year when they learned of an abortive conspiracy in their own backyard. Led by an educated slave from Martinique, at least fifteen Goose Creek blacks had taken part in planning a violent uprising before being betrayed at the last minute by a recently baptized African slave named Job.[122] A short time earlier a band of fugitive slaves under the leadership of a "Spanish negroe" named Sebastian had set up a "maroon" settlement in the vicinity of Charles Town and had reportedly begun to plunder plantations and terrorize the local colonists. South Carolina officials easily crushed Sebastian's mini-rebellion with the help of an unspecified group of Indian warriors but were so disturbed by the incident that they began work on a new bill to "effectually prevent [those] fears and jealousies [they then lay] under from the insolence of the negroes."[123] Since many of them had spent time in the West Indies—a region where maroon communities and slave revolts were not to be scoffed at—they tended to remain hypersensitive to any kind of "insolence" on the part of South Carolina's growing black population.[124]

While the South Carolinians grew more nervous around blacks, residents of other British colonies had begun to express similar reservations about Indians.[125] Between 1712 and 1714, Massachusetts, Pennsylvania, Rhode Island, New Jersey, New Hampshire, and Connecticut all passed laws designed to curb or ban the importation of Indian slaves, with Connecticut citing the "divers conspiracies, outrages, barbarities, murders, burglaries, and notorious other crimes, [that] at sundry times, and especially of late, [had] been perpetrated by Indians and other slaves, within several of his Majesties plantations."[126] Obviously concerned that prisoners from the Tuscarora War might inspire recalcitrance in local Indian populations, several of these colonial legislatures went so far as to single out the "Carolina Indians" in their provisions.[127] By this time nearly every British colony from North Carolina to the Canadian borderlands had experienced some kind of disastrous run-in with the Indians. The Powhatan uprisings in Virginia, King Philip's War in New England, and the Iroquois "Beaver Wars" in New York had all contributed to an emerging image of Indians as deadly and devious predators.[128]

For the most part South Carolinians did not appear to share this perception of the Indians, an attitude that seems all the more surprising in light of their up-close look at the ravages of the Tuscarora War. In assisting their suffering neighbors, the South Carolinians never displayed the slightest concern that something similar might happen to them. To their way of thinking, the Indian allies and trading partners of South Carolina were somehow different from the other Indians on the continent. John Barnwell expressed a strong disdain for much of humanity but was willing to stake his life on the "brave Yamasees" who accompanied him into North Carolina. While other colonists fretted over the use of Indian slaves, South Carolinians continued to value them as a safe and convenient source of labor.[129] Once an Indian had become his ally or his prisoner, a South Carolinian no longer felt that he had any reason to be afraid of him.

Before dismissing the South Carolinians as smug and overconfident, we should keep in mind the various concerns they had to face from day to day. Despite a growing economy and a distinct advantage in the Southeast's imperial struggle, the South Carolina of the early eighteenth century was hardly an earthly paradise, even for its wealthiest and most influential inhabitants. In addition to logging long hours of arduous labor, South Carolinians also had to endure the occasional natural disaster, such as the 1711 yellow fever epidemic that killed roughly 5 percent of the total population, or the 1713 hurricane that killed seventy people, destroyed one hundred thousand pounds worth of crops, and left many of Charles Town's fortifications in ruins.[130] With so much uncertainty and instability in their lives, many South Carolinians proved perfectly willing to latch onto the few things that seemed dependable. No matter how difficult things became at home, South Carolina officials felt that they could always count on their Indian allies to bolster their frontiers and keep the province's growth on track.

A combination of distractions and prejudices made it relatively easy for South Carolinians to misunderstand and misrepresent the alliance network that had taken root over the previous thirty-five years. While the South Carolinians and the various Indian societies of the southeastern interior could still find occasions to further one another's interests, their cooperation almost always depended on the exploitation of a third party. In the absence of a convenient external enemy, tension between the allies was more likely to make its way to the surface. Though they became the major area of concern for Indian and colonial leaders, sporadic incidents of violence, dissent, and other forms of "unruliness" were merely symptoms of a deeper, underlying problem. Despite all the significant cultural adjustments they had been required to make, South Carolinians and their Indian allies were continuing to talk past each other, coming up with their own demands and expectations without really bothering to understand the other side. The South Carolinians, for their part, never had any doubts about which side was in the driver's seat. In 1712 the South Carolina government instructed its Indian agents to "strictly charge the Indians to be honest, loving and assistant, kind and obedient in all reasonable Demands to the white Men living and trading among them . . . giving the King and Head Men Advice in Relation to the managing of their People the better to keep them in Subjection, and with Example and Arguments drawn from a Parallel with our Government."[131] Staunch believers in their own superiority, South Carolinians sought, assumed, and even pretended to be in firm control of the exchange process. In so doing they underestimated or ignored the various shades of discontent proliferating on the other side of their frontiers.

4. Conspiracy Theories

INTER-INDIAN ALLIANCES AND THE
OUTBREAK OF THE YAMASEE WAR

The last official assessment of South Carolina's Indian buffer zone came in the early months of 1715, when provincial authorities commissioned a report on "the number and strength of all the Indian nations . . . subject to the government of South Carolina."[1] Culled from the notes and estimates of the province's most knowledgeable frontiersmen, this census listed a grand total of 28,041 friendly Indians scattered within a 640-mile radius of Charles Town. To the west and southwest of the capital—clumped within a hundred miles of each other—were the two towns of the Yuchis, the three towns of the Savannahs, the four towns of the Apalachees, the two towns of the Pallachacolas, and the ten towns of the Yamasees. To the north and northwest of Charles Town, the twelve towns of the Catawbas, the Cheraws, and the Congarees filled out the inner arc of South Carolina's defensive perimeter. A hundred miles further to the west, one would begin to encounter the largest and most powerful of South Carolina's Indian allies: the ten towns of "the Ocheses or Creeks," the thirty-two towns of the Tallapoosas, the Abeikas, and the Alabamas, and the sixty towns of the Lower, Middle, and Overhill Cherokees. Finally, the six remaining towns of the Chickasaws marked the outer fringes of the alliance network and South Carolina's thrust into the Mississippi Valley. Those South Carolina imperialists who had enough time to read this census undoubtedly saw it as a comforting confirmation of their power in the Southeast.

They would have taken much less comfort in another census that was conducted in the same general area at about the same time. Instead of determining the extent of South Carolina's Indian alliances, this second census claimed to count the number of Indian towns that were committed to destroying the province. Unaccustomed to paper and pen, these census takers used eight-yard-long strips of deerskin, tying a knot for every town that they deemed receptive to their plans. When Florida Governor Francisco Córcoles y Martínez received these strips from a delegation of Yamasee and Ochese leaders on May 28, 1715, he counted no fewer than 161 knots.[2] The South Carolinians did not need to see these knotted deerskins in order to make some significant revisions to their own census. By that time their desperate struggle to save themselves from their former Indian allies was already more than six weeks old.

The Yamasee War hit South Carolina as a horrifying shock that forced many colonists to reconsider everything that they had previously believed about the southeastern Indians. A certain degree of paranoia had always played a role in South Carolina imperialism, but no one had really expected such a disaster to occur during a period of relative peace and prosperity. While the suffering South Carolinians were quick to suspect their French and Spanish rivals, the most thoughtful commentators were not about to underestimate the strength and unity of South Carolina's new Indian enemies. For men like the Reverend Francis Le Jau, the first terrible weeks of the war suggested a "General Conspiricy of the Indians that Surround[ed them]—from the Borders of St. Augustin to Cape Fear."[3] From the murdered traders near the banks of the Mississippi to the charred ruins of Port Royal plantations, it appeared that South Carolina's Indian defense network had been turned completely on its head.

It is easy to imagine how the South Carolinians could have assumed that the entire Southeast had lined up against them, but it is more difficult to understand how future generations of scholars could perpetuate the colonists' first confused impressions of the Yamasee War. Over the years it has become fairly common to describe South Carolina's opposition as a wide-ranging "united front" of various Indian societies whose participation in the war resulted from some kind of shadowy, overarching "conspiracy."[4] While the Yamasee War certainly involved a number of important inter-Indian alliances, it did not stem from a conspiracy as formidable as the one that was initially assumed. Both the early reports of the panic-stricken colonists and the deerskin census of the defiant Yamasees greatly exaggerated the extent and unity of the Indian resistance. In the months that surrounded the outbreak of the Yamasee War, Indians and South Carolinians found their judgment clouded by a general state of confusion that forced them to simplify an extremely complicated picture.

During their worst crisis of the early colonial period, South Carolinians faced not a single, monolithic Indian enemy but a number of different Indian enemies who fought with different motives and different levels of intensity. Indians had developed many reasons to begrudge the traders and officials who intruded into their lives and homelands, but some southeastern groups had more cause for resentment than others. Moreover, the outbreak of the Yamasee

War was not simply an issue of cause and effect, with abuses and grudges automatically translating into a decision to destroy South Carolina. Commitment to the war was not easy for any group of Indians; it depended not only on anger, resentment, or panic but also on the prospects of support from other Indian and colonial societies. A more accurate picture of the Indians' opposition to the South Carolinians can only emerge when broken into distinct segments, allowing a close look at how the war erupted on its two major fronts.

The Southwestern Front

By the spring of 1715, South Carolina's traders and imperialists felt most at ease on the frontiers that extended to the southwest of the colonial settlements. Though the French and the Spanish still lingered on the other sides of these frontiers, Queen Anne's War had seemingly left them crippled and humiliated. Any white man who dared to stray too far from the forts of Mobile, Pensacola, or Saint Augustine risked falling into the hands of hostile Tallapoosas, Ocheses, or Yamasees, groups that the South Carolinians prized as devoted friends and servants. These were the Indian allies whom they knew best. Twenty to thirty years of intensive trade and cultural exchange had begun to convince most South Carolinians that the Indians on their southwestern frontiers were dependable, predictable, and even somewhat tractable.

Relationships that looked stable and comfortable from the South Carolinians' perspective seemed much different from the other side. The province's imperialists and government officials had never intended their relationships with the region's Indians to remain indefinitely on an equal footing. Since South Carolina imperialists considered it just and inevitable for their own authority to prevail in any frontier relationship, many of them found it easy to turn a blind eye to the increasing discomfort of their Indian allies. What seemed like a natural progression to colonial authorities seemed like an unsettling detour for most of the Indian societies that formed South Carolina's defensive perimeter. Contact with the South Carolinians had already taken a heavy toll, but it had also brought some compelling rewards. Having ridden the wave of prosperity that surged from South Carolina's most aggressive period of imperialistic expansion, many of these Indians suddenly found themselves in danger of losing the advantages to which they had grown accustomed.

Though certain problems had plagued the various South Carolina–Indian alliances from the very beginning, both sides had previously found these problems easier to cope with. The strain in these alliances—as in any fundamentally unstable relationship—was bound to be cumulative. As Indian societies throughout the Southeast began to suffer from the damaging effects of drink, debt, and disease, it became increasingly difficult for them to stand up to the demands of the South Carolinian visitors, who seemed to be growing stronger and more confident by the day. Though these inequities had begun to spread through much of the Southeast, they remained most glaring among those groups that continued to bear the brunt of South Carolina's colonial expansion. Other than the beleaguered remnants of the low-country "settlement" groups like the Seewees, the Cussaboes, and the Ittawans, no Indian society suffered more than the twelve hundred Yamasees who inhabited the "reservation" between the Combahee and Savannah rivers. Of all the groups in the Indian buffer zone, the Yamasees almost certainly had compiled the most grievances against the South Carolinians.

In the aftermath of Queen Anne's War, the friction between the Yamasees and the traditionally brusque Port Royal traders was palpable to anyone even remotely familiar with the Yamasee–South Carolina frontier. The Indians who had so impressed Lord Cardross in the 1680s were now finding themselves manhandled by the infamous Alexander Nicholas and a host of other drunks and reprobates. By this time many of the Yamasees had developed their own problems with alcohol, one of the commodities—along with clothing, firearms, and munitions—that had contributed to their astronomical trade deficit with the South Carolinians. Merchants, traders, and colonial officials had found it easier to defray or dissolve some of the Yamasees' debts during the recent imperial crisis, but with the Spanish holed up in their forts, the Yamasees' assistance no longer seemed worth the ten thousand pounds sterling that they owed to their creditors.[5] A new determination to collect the Yamasees' debts unquestionably contributed to the deteriorating manners of the traders and was the direct cause of at least some of the beatings, kidnappings, and robberies that made their way into the reports of the officials responsible for regulating the Indian trade.

Since these problems are relatively well documented, South Carolina's Indian traders and system of trade regulation have become primary scapegoats for the disaffection of the Yamasees. Traders had suffered from a bad reputation among many imperial officials even before 1715, and the Yamasee War did nothing to improve it. When the Board of Trade demanded an explanation for the Indians' attacks on South Carolina, Virginia's William Byrd II claimed that the war was "in great measure owing to the Carolinians themselves, for their traders ha[d] so abused and so imposed upon the Indians . . . that they ha[d] been thereby very much disgusted." Byrd was not the most impartial of observers; he cited the restrictions against Virginia traders as one of South Carolina's "abusive" practices. Several South Carolinians, however, also blamed the war on "the want of good government among the Indian traders . . . that trade at present being under no good regulation, and the laws which [were] made not being observed."[6]

The reports of prewar trade abuse combined with South Carolina's postwar efforts to overhaul the Indian trade have led many historians to believe that trade controversies and trader misconduct were the overriding cause of the Yamasee War.[7] But while the Indians had certainly developed numerous reasons to resent, fear, and even hate the traders, trade abuse was actually nothing more than the tip of the proverbial iceberg. By drawing what James Merrell has described as "a straight and bloody line from confidence to arrogance to abuses to uprising," the consensus formed by contemporaries and perpetuated by historians only sheds light on a limited aspect of the Yamasees' plight.[8] To the Yamasees trade was just one manifestation of an alien society that seemed to be closing in at an alarming rate.

Despite military triumphs from the Florida Keys to the North Carolina tidewater, the Yamasees had begun to suffer a marked decline in the previous decade. In 1713 Francis Le Jau observed that the Yamasees were "formerly very numerous but by degrees they [were] come to very little[;] they could muster eight hundred fighting men and now they [were] hardly four hundred." Population estimates from 1708 and 1715 appear to confirm this decline.[9] In addition to military casualties, these losses might also have reflected the Yamasees' shrinking resource base. By 1715 the "reservation" that had been granted to them eight years earlier had begun to seem less like a safe haven and more like a trap. No section of South Carolina was expanding more dramatically than the Port Royal region. In 1711 the construction of a road between Port Royal and Charles Town made the area even more accessible to prospective colonists, allowing a rush of newcomers to carve out farms and cattle ranches in the shadows of the huge plantations that belonged to men like Thomas Nairne, William Bray, and John Barnwell.[10] The Yamasees were soon experiencing more of the encroachments that had brought colonial authorities to mark off the reservation in the first place. Now, however, the Yamasees' complaints about "white Men settling among them" carried more urgency than ever.[11]

Though the clear-cut fields and wandering livestock of these white interlopers impinged on the Yamasees' territorial integrity, they posed an even greater threat to the Yamasees' livelihood. Those who downplayed the importance of the Yamasees' land failed to appreciate the nature of the Yamasees' dual economy, in which a crop-based agriculture managed by Yamasee women supplemented the hunting and trading activities of the Yamasee men. [12] When the white traders became more aggressive in their collection of debts, some of the Yamasees reportedly begged the South Carolina government for a chance to repay them in livestock, vegetables, and lard. [13] The illegal reduction of farmland not only took food from the Yamasees' mouths but also robbed them of a potential means to address their trade deficit. Perhaps even more devastating to the Yamasee economy was a dramatic decline in the region's deer population. While Indians like the Tallapoosas, the Catawbas, and even the Lower Cherokees continued to send prodigious quantities of deerskins to Charles Town, evidence suggests that the Yamasees had essentially given up on this aspect of the trade. Several decades of intensive hunting had probably contributed to the scarcity of deer, but it is possible that South Carolina's rice plantations and free-roaming cattle had also played an important part in the Yamasees' dilemma. As burdensome as the Yamasees' trade debts had become, they were clearly exacerbated by an ecological degradation. [14]

Government officials attempted to reassure the Yamasees that their fields and hunting grounds would not be taken away from them, but most South Carolina imperialists probably gave little thought to the Yamasees' ecological quandary. As far as the South Carolinians were concerned, the Yamasees were essentially useless in all but a military capacity. Given the decreasing likelihood of a Spanish invasion, slave hunting seemed to be the only remaining outlet for the Yamasees' martial skills and the only conceivable method for recouping the Yamasees' debts. South Carolina's increasing demand for Indian slaves meant that a human captive could fetch a sum worth as much as two hundred deerskins. [15] At the same time, however, the rising prices of Indian slaves also indicated that they were becoming harder to find. [16] By the end of Queen Anne's War, the supply of Timucuans and other Florida Indians had finally begun to dry up for the Yamasees. This shortage helps explain the behavior of the Yamasee warriors who participated in the Tuscarora expeditions; their apparently steadfast devotion to Barnwell and their treacherous conduct in the Coree Town massacre helped prevent a disastrous, empty-handed return to their villages. By then some of the South Carolina traders had allegedly begun to threaten that without a sufficient number of enemy captives, the Yamasees would soon find themselves on the auction block. [17]

Along with abusive traders, South Carolina's clandestine Indian slave trade has become another prevalent explanation for the disaffection of the Yamasees.

Fear of enslavement undoubtedly played a strong part in the Yamasees' decision to attack South Carolina; Yamasee warriors later asserted that they had acted primarily out of fear for their vulnerable women and children.[18] While scholars have been completely justified in drawing attention to this Indian slave trade, they have not sufficiently explained how the Yamasees suddenly could have become so averse to it. From the Yamasees' standpoint, the threats of the traders and the occasional kidnapping only constituted part of the problem. The specter of enslavement would not have seemed nearly as foreboding to the Yamasees had it not been accompanied by their diminishing confidence in the South Carolina government.

The enslavement of South Carolina's Indian allies was officially against South Carolina law, but so were assault, rape, the collection of rum debts, and trespassing on Indian land. While the Yamasees had once been eager to appeal for the government's assistance, they soon began to associate South Carolina's regulatory officials with the lawlessness that prevailed in their territory. At times the Indian agents seemed more abusive and threatening than the traders they were supposed to supervise. Before his removal by Governor Craven, Agent John Wright not only took the illegal step of building a house among the Yamasees but also forced the Indians to gather building materials and help raise it.[19] Thomas Nairne was initially regarded as a significant improvement over Wright, but several Yamasees expressed an unshakable fear that Nairne would personally "cause theire Lands to be taken from them."[20] To the Yamasees all the soothing replies sent down from Charles Town amounted to nothing but further evidence that the government's words no longer matched its actions. As South Carolina officials continued to heap praise and promises on the Yamasees, they constructed a fort near the newly zoned town of Beaufort, a structure that the Indians interpreted as a sign of the province's preparation for war.[21] With their suspicions aroused, the Yamasees could find ominous implications in all of the government's measures, no matter how innocuous they might have appeared to the South Carolinians.

According to some Indian residents of Saint Augustine in the early 1730s, the census conducted by the South Carolina government in early 1715 led the Yamasees to believe that "the object of the English was to make slaves of them."[22] While a number of merchants and Port Royal planters might have been receptive to this kind of outcome, it is highly unlikely that the government would have sanctioned a measure that would have required a costly and counterproductive war. Shortly after the outbreak of the Yamasee War, several prominent South Carolinians expressed surprise at the suggestion that the Yamasees might have feared enslavement and claimed that their govern-ment had never intended to pursue such a policy. [23] But even if South Carolina imperialists did not intend to turn against the Yamasees as they had turned against the Westoes thirty-five years earlier, there is every reason to believe that they would have allowed the Yamasees to suffer a more prolonged and less dramatic demise. For a likely example of their fate, the Yamasees would have had to look no further than the Cussaboes, a formerly powerful group of Indians on the South Carolina coast who were forced in 1712 to make a pathetic, heart-rending plea for the last small island that remained in their possession, claiming that they were "afraid of all other Indians and [knew] not how to dispose of themselves when dispossessed of [their] Land." [24] The Yamasees were already standing in the path of colonial "progress," and no one in South Carolina would have been surprised to find them appealing for the pity and charity of the government several years down the road.

Those who were willing to push the Yamasees aside had short memories indeed. Only a few years earlier, South Carolina authorities had often gone out of their way to accommodate the Yamasees, partly as a sign of respect for the fearsome reputations that many of these Indians had acquired while living under the influence of the Spanish. Astute students of the Southeast's recent history would have realized that the Indians who had once wrought havoc on the Guale and Timucuan missions were not the kind of people to tolerate an increasingly desperate situation. Indeed, it is possible to discern many similarities between the Yamasee uprising of 1715 and the various re-volts carried out against the Spanish by the Guales and the Timucuans in the sixteenth and seventeenth centuries, particularly in the ways in which all these groups prefaced their actions by warning other Indian societies about the evil intentions of the colonists.[25] Though fully capable of lashing out on their own, the Yamasees recognized the formidable power of the South Carolinians and therefore sought outside support for the counterstroke that some of them had been discussing for the last several years. By early 1715 the Yamasees had begun to spread the word about the treacherous plans for conquest and enslavement that lay hidden under South Carolina's cloak of friendship. [26]

Though the South Carolina government had made some attempts to set the Yamasees apart from the other Indian societies of the Southeast, the Port Royal reservation hardly restricted the Yamasees to a life of secret isolation. Yamasee hunters, warriors, and leaders regularly traveled beyond the bounds of their territory, and their Hitichi speech was mutually intelligible with other Musko-gean dialects and subgroups like Apalachee, Guale, and Muskogee proper. [27]

These linguistic ties made it relatively easy for them to communicate with most of the towns that stretched along the Savannah and Ocmulgee rivers. As important as these ties were, however, they did not automatically imply a greater cultural or political unity between different groups, just as major linguistic differences had not prevented alliances between the Indians and the English. In the connections between the various cultures of the Southeast, common experience was an even more important factor than common language. The Yamasees' experience with the Muskogean groups of the interior predated their connections to the English: in the previous fifty years they had traded together, fought together, and even lived together. Even into the second decade of the eighteenth century, there were still some strong cultural connections between the Port Royal Yamasees and the Muskogeans who had taken up residence on the Ocmulgee. In 1713 some Yamasees asked the government whether the Cheehaws, "who ware [sic] formerly belonging to the Yamasees and now settled at the Creek," might be persuaded to return to their people. [28] It is likely that many of the Yamasees had emerged from other southeastern Indian societies and would have been able to return to these societies when the need arose.

As the Yamasees relayed their grievances to the west, they encountered a number of small and troubled groups that had developed their own problems with their South Carolinian allies. Roughly a hundred miles up the Savannah River, the Pallachacolas (or Apalachicolas) inhabited a world much like that of the Yamasees; their languages and situations were so similar that South Carolina authorities sometimes conflated the two groups. [29] Though the circumstances of their removal from the Apalachicola to the Savannah River area remain unclear, it is possible that these Indians had not made the move to the Ocmulgee in 1690 and were later transported under duress to a location considered more strategic by the South Carolinians. [30] In this respect the Pallachacolas were much like the Apalachees, the Florida Indians who had been marched to the banks of the Savannah by James Moore's army in 1704. Though the Apalachees did not share the Yamasees' fear of encroaching colonial settlements, they had come to suffer much damage and abuse at the hands of the South Carolina traders. [31] As early as 1708, South Carolina's governor casually commented that the traders were using the Apalachees as beasts of burden, paying a few strips of cloth to any Indian who would agree to trot up to five hundred miles with sixty pounds of skins or trade goods strapped to his back. [32] While the Apalachees' population dropped from about 1,300 to 650 between 1705 and 1715, they did not fare much worse than the Savannahs and the Yuchis, two small groups that had endured an even longer partnership with the South Carolinians. Considered prime replacements for the Westoes in the 1670s and 1680s, both groups had suffered mightily in the early eighteenth century, becoming sitting ducks for aggressive English traders and Cherokee and Catawba slave hunters.

Like the Yamasees all these small and suffering Indian societies had the means to relay their grievances to the larger and more powerful groups that lived further into the southeastern interior, most notably the Ocheses. [33] Despite their occasional preference for the more remote and exotic Chickasaws, South Carolina imperialists generally recognized the "Creeks" as their colony's strongest and most productive allies. As early as the 1670s, the towns of these Indians had displayed an uncommon degree of unity, aided by what appeared to be the exceptional influence of a single charismatic leader. [34] Called "el gran cacique" by the Spanish and "emperor" by the English, the head war chief of the prestigious town of Coweta had seen his position bolstered even further by the economic and military influence that the South Carolinians had afforded him during Queen Anne's War. In truth the man the South Carolinians knew as "Emperor Brims" wielded no more than a small fraction of the authority that European observers attributed to him. Nevertheless, Brims could often rely on his personal prestige and reputation to make up for what he lacked in coercive power. [35] While very few Indians owed him any kind of political obligation, many Indians throughout the Southeast respected what he and his people had accomplished over the years. Since the 1680s the South Carolinians had relied on the Ocheses and their "emperor" to help solidify their connections to other groups, including those as powerful and distant as the Tallapoosas, the Abeikas, and the Chickasaws. Even though Brims and the Ocheses were less formidable than the South Carolinians had originally believed, their disaffection could have a disastrous effect on the province's frontier relations.

To most South Carolinians, however, it appeared that the Ocheses had relatively little cause for complaint. In comparison to the smaller groups further to the east, they did not seem to show much concern for the abuses and controversies that filled the slates of the colony's regulatory officials. More than two hundred miles from the nearest colonial settlement, the Ocheses shared none of the Yamasees' fear over cattle ranches and rice plantations. Unlike the more vulnerable Yuchis, Savannahs, and Apalachees, the Ocheses also remained largely (though not completely) immune from the incursions of enemy slave raiders. [36] Indeed, Queen Anne's War had established the Ocheses as some of the most fearsome and successful warriors in the Southeast. Raids on

Apalachee, Pensacola, and Choctaw country had lifted many of the Ocheses' leading men to an unprecedented level of prosperity.[37]

For many of the Ocheses, however, their diminishing military triumphs signaled a shift to a climate that was decidedly less comfortable than the one enjoyed by a few prominent war chiefs. From the time of their first transactions in the mid-1680s, the well-stocked South Carolina traders had been able to compromise the lives of these Indians in ways that their Spanish and Indian enemies had never done. Though the traders brought the weapons and finery that kept Ochese men and women secure and stylish, they also helped encourage a cycle of disease and debt that had become harder and harder to escape. During the halcyon days of Queen Anne's War, the Ocheses and the other Muskogean nations further to the west had earned glowing marks for their ability to repay their debts.[38] By 1712, however, they had begun to stumble into a slave-catching dilemma similar to that of the Yamasees: the dwindling supply of potential captives took away their primary means to satisfy their creditors. The Ocheses were well on their way to economic dependency on the South Carolinians.[39]

At the same time respectful traders in the model of Henry Woodward or Thomas Nairne were becoming relics from the past, replaced by men who did not hesitate to twist arms. Pressure from the traders became so great that it could even affect someone as prestigious as the headman of Cussita, who allegedly resorted to kidnapping other Ocheses "upon Pretence of paying some Town Debts."[40] Such complaints were probably becoming far more prevalent than the commissioners' journals would suggest. If anything the traders among the Ocheses and other groups further to the west were operating in an area that was even less conducive than the Savannah basin to government supervision. Several days before the outbreak of the Yamasee War, the Board of Commissioners for the Indian Trade received one of its only reports of trade abuse among the Ocheses, a warning that "the Creek Indians were dissatisfied with the Traders that were among them, and that they had made severall Complaints without Redress."[41] Though the Ocheses' situation remained much less desperate than that of the Yamasees, many of them had begun to show a new dissatisfaction, disquiet, and disgust, both with the traders who dared to disrespect them and with the government that refused to curb the traders' behavior.

By early 1715 the various shades of discontent that radiated from town to town had begun to blur around the edges. Different Indian societies had developed their own compelling reasons to resent, mistrust, or fear the South Carolinians, but the spread of information between these groups had also helped instill a more general uneasiness among them. Just as the Yamasees—and possibly the Apalachees and the Pallachacolas as well—had begun to speak out about their worst fears, they were also finding themselves on the receiving end of equally disturbing news. At some point in this chaotic period, all the Indians in the Savannah and Ocmulgee basins became privy to a rumor that the English traders had killed the usinjulo—the "beloved son" and successor of the great "emperor" of Coweta—for his inability to pay a debt.[42] The murder of such an important figure over such a trivial matter would have been a clear indication that the South Carolinians had finally lost their minds. That the rumor was possibly unfounded did not make its impact any less powerful. If nothing else it showed that the pall of suspicion had begun to spread across South Carolina's southwestern frontiers.

Evidence of widely circulating stories and rumors clearly hints at the existence of some kind of "conspiracy" between different Indian societies. In order to understand the conspiracy that caused the Yamasee War, however, it is necessary to modify the generally understood notions of the term. It is often assumed that every conspiracy has a definite center; that someone, or some group of people, is responsible for devising and orchestrating the plan. These commonly held assumptions help explain why scholars of the Yamasee War have usually sought to pin the conflict on a single Indian leader, a single Indian nation, or—at the very least—a "confederacy" of different Indian polities.[43] With varying degrees of skill and sensitivity, most of these accounts imply the kind of central decision-making body that did not yet exist on anything like a regional scale. This is not to say that the various Indian societies in the southern part of South Carolina's buffer zone did not establish certain connections to one another. Indeed, the various forms of cultural interaction that characterized this region in the late seventeenth and early eighteenth centuries often make it difficult to draw firm lines between different groups of Indians. Nevertheless, these different polities—and even the different towns that comprised them—always maintained a political autonomy that allowed them to filter their experiences through their own lenses. Cooperation could and did occur between these groups, but in a form that would be better to interpret as a temporary alliance rather than any kind of permanent political union.

The Yamasee War resulted not from the decision of any single group but from a number of different groups that came to their own conclusions, aided to some extent by their interaction with one another. Many of the Southeast's Indian societies had agreed that something needed to be done about the South Carolinians, but at the same time they were unable to agree on precisely when and how to do it. In the unlikely event that the Indian societies ranging from the Alabamas to the Yamasees had developed the seeds of a cohesive plan, they certainly had come up short in working out its details. From the perspective of the Board of Trade, the *Boston News-Letter*, or the colonists pinned down in Charles Town, the Yamasee War seemed like a conflict that had erupted with great decisiveness and precision. Hindsight and detachment allow for the reconstruction of a more balanced and accurate view of the war's outbreak. In their uneven transition from discontent to violence, the Indians on South Carolina's southwestern frontiers often gave the impression of being swept up in a situation that had spiraled out of control.

By the early spring of 1715, the groundswell in support of war had grown strong enough to make some Indians nervous. In fact, the best evidence of a "conspiracy" comes from the reports of those Indians who felt compelled to warn the South Carolinians of their impending danger. A Yamasee trader named John Fraser allegedly heard reports of the Indians' plans at least ten days before the outbreak of the war but returned to Charles Town without telling anyone what he had heard. [44] Other warnings did make their way to provincial officials, the clearest of which point to the Ocheses as the group that had made the most progress in developing some kind of plan for attacking the South Carolinians. In one case a Pallachacola Indian told trader Samuel Warner that the "Creek Indians" had been saying that "upon the first Afront from any of the Traders they would down with them and soe go on with itt." At about the same time, the wife of Port Royal planter and trader William Bray was approached by a friend of hers, a Yamasee Indian named Cuffy, who warned her that the Ocheses "had a Design to cut off the Traders first and then to fall on the Settlement, and that it was very neare" (Cuffy was later rewarded by the South Carolina assembly for his actions, and his wife and daughter were freed from slavery). When the Board of Commissioners received word of these designs on April 12, they were in no mood to find out exactly how "neare" they were to fruition. Instantly sobered, the Board sent Warner and Bray on a mission to the Yamasees and the Pallachacolas in order to obtain their assistance in arranging an emergency summit with Ochese leaders. [45] Their first stop on this mission was the Upper Yamasee town of Pocotaligo.

Despite the warnings relayed to Warner, Bray, and possibly Fraser, it is likely that the Indians' preparations for war had not yet reached their advanced stages. Whatever they had prepared for, they had not counted on having their hands forced so early in the game. As a result the Yamasee War—regardless of all the planning that might have gone into it—began as a sudden response to an unexpected confrontation. Yamasee warriors had certainly been aware of the Ocheses' battle plans, but we probably will never know the full extent of their involvement in them. One Spanish source, recorded after the outbreak of the Yamasee War, suggests that Brims paid a visit to Pocotaligo shortly before the arrival of the emergency English embassy, and that other Ochese leaders and warriors were present throughout the entire Pocotaligo conference.[46] But if the Ocheses had persuaded the Yamasees to attack the English, the South Carolinians had no knowledge of any such development. They fully expected that they could prevail on the Yamasees to distance themselves from the hotheaded Ocheses and come around to the position of the provincial government. When Warner and Bray reached Pocotaligo, they were quickly joined by several other South Carolinians who had learned of their mission, including Yamasee agent Thomas Nairne, former agent John Wright, and Seymour Burroughs, a resident of Port Royal and a captain in the Colleton County militia.[47]

Pocotaligo was generally recognized as the head town of the Yamasees, and leaders from various Yamasee towns had grown accustomed to convening there to pick up presents or hold their war councils. It was therefore a diverse collection of Yamasees who listened to the speeches of the South Carolina emissaries on the night of Thursday, April 14. Nairne, Wright, and the others urgently insisted that they would always remain kind to their Yamasee neighbors and that Governor Craven himself would soon be arriving to provide redress for all the Yamasees' complaints. After some ceremonial drinking, the South Carolinians went to bed firmly convinced that the Yamasees had taken their words to heart.[48]

But as the white men slept, the Indians' council fire continued to burn. Pocotaligo's council house soon became a cauldron of dissent and confusion; no one could seem to agree on the meaning of the South Carolinians' unexpected visit. It was clear that not all the Yamasees had fully pledged themselves to a war on the English.[49] For those with second thoughts, the recent promises of the South Carolinians must have come as something of a relief. For the malcontents and some of the fence-sitters, however, this latest embassy of South Carolina officials seemed less than reassuring. They had lost their faith in untrustworthy men like Wright and Nairne and had come to associate the South Carolina "officers" with the province's increasingly unreasonable demands.[50] The sudden appearance of these men, as well as the impending arrival of the governor, struck many Yamasees as proof that the South Carolina government was preparing to impose its final, dreaded punishment on them. Their suspicions were seemingly confirmed by an English-speaking Yamasee woman who arrived in Pocotaligo after midnight with the rumor that the South Carolinians had come not to mediate but to spy. For three Indian leaders in particular—the Yamasee headmen of Salkehatchie and Pocotaligo and an Ochese warrior named Yfallaquisca ("Brave Dog")—this intelligence was the final straw. [51] After applying red and black paint to their faces and bodies, these men and a number of their fellow warriors began their war songs and roused the white men from their sleep. Seymour Burroughs fled in a panic, suffering two bullet wounds before plunging into the Pocotaligo River and swimming his way to safety. Another unnamed South Carolinian successfully hid himself in some nearby woods. [52] Nairne, Wright, Warner, Bray, and the other ambassadors were never heard from again.

While a few wayward traders had been killed in the past, no South Carolina official had ever lost his life when dealing with a supposedly "friendly" group of Indians. The Yamasees clearly recognized the importance of the men who came to Pocotaligo; they reportedly respected Thomas Nairne so much that they devoted several hours to torturing him before ending his life. [53] They knew full well that their decision to kill the South Carolina ambassadors was a decision for war.

Since they had already passed the point of no return, the Yamasees decided to inflict as much damage as possible before their inevitable confrontation with Governor Craven and the South Carolina militia. [54] On the day of the Pocotaligo massacre, the Yamasees quickly organized several hundred of their men into two war parties, one of which fell on the colonial settlements of Port Royal. Earlier that morning the wounded Seymour Burroughs had managed to stumble to the nearby plantation of John Barnwell, who proceeded to raise a frantic alarm throughout the region. By the time the Yamasee warriors reached the Port Royal settlements, several hundred colonists had piled onto a small ship moored in the harbor, and dozens more had fled the area in canoes. The second Yamasee war party proved much more successful. Making its way through the farms and plantations of Saint Bartholomew's Parish, it managed to kill over a hundred colonists and slaves before returning to the Yamasee villages with a satisfying cargo of prisoners and assorted plunder. [55] Within a week a large contingent of Yamasee warriors was preparing to engage the South Carolinians near Salkehatchie, while the rest of the tribe headed south to find sanctuary in their makeshift forts.

The Yamasees bequeathed their name to South Carolina's most disastrous Indian war because it was their decision—and theirs alone—to take the drastic step of attacking the province's officials and civilians. Several months into the conflict, a South Carolina officer claimed that the war "was first fomented by some of the lower Creeke people but the first stroke was given by the Yamasees." Likewise, Francis Le Jau also expressed a belief that the Yamasees started the war "sooner than was designed among the Indians that surrounded [the South Carolinians]." These statements—as well as those of historians who have taken them at face value—miss the larger point of the Yamasee War's outbreak.[56] In throwing down the gauntlet, the Yamasees acted independently, following no order higher than their own consciences. The Yamasee War was not "fomented" by a single group of people or even by a single conspiracy. Regardless of all that had been said and done by the Indians in the weeks and months before April 15, the war was only made real by the disjointed actions of various leaders and warriors. Other Indian societies might have been prepared to make a similar plunge, but the fact remains that the Yamasees launched the conflict and dominated its most violent and memorable stages.

Nevertheless, they did not feel alone in their struggle. Knowing that they were not the only group with scores to settle, many of the Yamasees assumed that other Indians would follow their example and give the South Carolinians what they deserved. The Yamasees' deerskin census was just one reflection of their belief that the war against the English had spread throughout the region. After the South Carolinians' first successful engagement with the Yamasees, they reportedly discovered a semiliterate note on an enemy corpse, warning them that "all the Indians on the continent" were about to take up arms against the province.[57] Though the Yamasees did not directly lead or coordinate the war efforts of these other groups, they did become standard bearers in a conflict that eventually spread far beyond the South Carolina low country.

During the first weeks of the war, the Yamasees remained the most pressing concern for South Carolina's civilians and officials. Meanwhile many of South Carolina's Indian traders had their hands full with other, far-ranging Indian societies. For most of the traders, the end result proved just as harrowing as it had for the victims of the Yamasees. Authorities later estimated that the province lost ninety of the roughly one hundred traders who were in the field at the time of the war's outbreak, but little is known about when and where these men perished.[58] At the time of the Pocotaligo massacre, most of the traders at the Ocmulgee and points further west were probably still alive, though they might have already heard about the fate that was intended for them. Sixty years after the Yamasee War, a trader among the Lower Creek Indians told the naturalist William Bartram that "almost all the white traders then in the Nation were massacred" in a town "wither they had repaired from the different towns, in hopes of an asylum or refuge . . . having been timely apprised of the hostile intentions of the Indians by their temporary wives, they all met together in one house, under the avowed protection of the chiefs of the town, waiting the event; but whilst the chiefs were assembled in council . . . the Indians in multitudes surrounded the house and set fire to it; they all, to the number of 18 or 20, perished with the house in the flames."[59]

While the Ocheses undoubtedly carried through on their threats to "down" the traders among them, this story suggests that their implementation was probably not as swift, smooth, or sudden as accounts have often implied. Once these threats had been carried out, however, the Ocheses also found themselves committed to a war against the South Carolinians, a development that did not bode well for the traders working among the Southeast's other Muskogean provinces.

The Tallapoosas, the Abeikas, and the Alabamas had little in common with the Yamasees, the Apalachees, and the other small Indian societies that inhabited the Savannah River basin. They had, however, developed grievances that were similar to those of the Ocheses, a group that was far more familiar to them. Since the mid to late seventeenth century, Indians from the Coosa, Tallapoosa, and Alabama basins had been frequent visitors to towns like Coweta and Cussita, and some of them had likely joined the 1690 migration to the Ocmulgee. During their joint campaigns against the Indians of Louisiana and western Florida during Queen Anne's War, the western Muskogeans had developed an even greater respect for the fearless and well-provisioned leaders of the Ocheses. Given the long-standing interaction and alliances between the large Muskogean provinces, the Alabamas, the Abeikas, and the Tallapoosas had almost certainly been aware of the Ocheses' plans to make war on the South Carolinians. When the Ocheses committed themselves to action, these other Indians were soon ready to follow suit. [60] Though the western Muskogeans would never play anything more than a peripheral role in the rest of the war, they did kill most—if not all—of the English traders among them and were soon speaking of their powerful Ochese allies with more respect and deference than ever. [61] When South Carolinians learned that they had lost traders as far west as the Choctaws and the Chickasaws, some of them feared that their rupture with the Ocheses would have worse consequences than they had first imagined. [62]

Most South Carolinians, however, chose to interpret the wide extent of their early losses as proof of something far more sinister than a pan-Muskogean alliance. In London a group of visiting South Carolina merchants and planters commented that the southeastern Indian nations "never had policy enough to form themselves into alliances, and could not in all probability have proceeded so far at [that] time, had they not been incouraged by the Spaniards at St. Augustin, or the French at Moville."[63] In part this consensus among the South Carolinians stemmed from their refusal to believe that they could have done anything to make their Indian friends and servants hate them so much. Even more importantly, however, the province's imperialists found it difficult to question the deeply ingrained prejudice that viewed white men as worthy rivals and Indians as mere auxiliaries. Despite everything that they had learned about the military capabilities of their Native allies over the last fifteen years, many South Carolinians believed that the Indians lacked the bitterness, intelligence, and determination required to launch such a devastating blow against them. They were dead wrong.

At most Bienville and the French can be implicated in some of the damages that the South Carolinians sustained on their far-western frontiers. Following Bienville's successful overtures to the Alabamas at the end of Queen Anne's War, South Carolina imperialists had redoubled their efforts to establish economic and political influence among the Choctaws. Disturbed by the progress that English traders and strategists had begun to make among Louisiana's most important Indian allies, Bienville authorized the arrest of Pryce Hughes, a recent immigrant from Wales who was making some preliminary surveys for a large English colony on the Mississippi.[64] At the same time Bienville encouraged pro-French Choctaws to plunder or otherwise harass the South Carolina traders and the Indian leaders who had welcomed them. Nursing the grudges that they had acquired during Queen Anne's War, many of the Choctaws responded enthusiastically to Bienville's orders, sending him the heads of two pro-English leaders and killing several of the South Carolinians.[65] After his release from prison in Mobile, Hughes met an equally grisly fate at the hands of some Tohome Indians who had bitter recollections of English-sponsored slave raids.[66] In and of themselves, however, these violent actions do not prove French complicity in the outbreak of the Yamasee War. While the French wanted to remove the South Carolina traders from Choctaw country, they had no desire to provoke the English into another series of attacks on their weak and poorly provisioned colony. In 1714 Louisiana governor La Mothe de Cadillac, Bienville's new commanding officer, wryly commented that his only defense against an invasion would be to "throw sand in the eyes of the enemy."[67]

More than a month into the South Carolinians' war with their erstwhile

Indian allies, Bienville still gave the impression that neither he nor his Indian informants had any idea of what was happening. In a report to his superiors written in mid-June, Bienville merely summarized his recent actions against Hughes and the Choctaw traders while implying that the English might launch a counterattack against Louisiana at any time. [68] Only later would he discover that the "Alabamas, Abekas, Tallapoosas, and Cowetas" had forced the English back on their heels. Bienville was stunned by this sudden development and did not display any of the joy that the South Carolinians would have expected from him. After a largely unsuccessful attempt to ransom white captives from the Indians, Louisiana officials were forced to welcome a delegation of headmen from the four great Muskogean nations, who asked the French "to send traders into their country for them." Though Bienville "received them in the best way that it was possible for [him] to do," he nervously admitted to himself that "these Indians [would] not find the same advantage with [the French] that they had with the English." [69] This new alliance between Louisiana and the southeastern Muskogeans resulted not from any carefully fomented strategy on the part of the French but from Indian leaders whose recent actions had left them in need of new colonial partners.

A similar situation held true for the Spanish soldiers and officials who clung to Florida's coastline, who were in no condition to reach out to the Indian nations of the interior. For the last several years, Tallapoosa warriors had continued an incessant cycle of raids, subjecting the Spanish to conditions that were just as bad as anything they had experienced during their late struggle with the South Carolinians. In 1713 Pensacola's commandant, Salinas Varona, reported that his men were down to their last pound of flour and that the "infidel Indians" would not "give any person an opportunity to cease cannon firing for fear of being killed or made prisoner." Pensacola's prospects seemed so bleak that the viceroy of New Spain wondered if he should even bother to continue supplying it. [70] Having lost more than seventy men to Indian war parties, Varona finally mustered the courage to send several Spanish soldiers and twenty Christian Indians on an overland voyage to Charles Town to remind the South Carolinians that the war between Spain and England had ended. When the expedition was confronted by a large group of Tallapoosas on May 25, they learned for the first time that South Carolina was under attack. Several weeks later a party of forty Tallapoosa headmen and warriors approached Pensacola's fort with an "escort" of three Spanish soldiers, giving signs "of the good relations that they wished to observe with the Spaniards." Though Varona agreed to supply these Indians with as much powder, ball, and clothing as his garrison could spare, he found it hard to comprehend the dramatic turnabout he was witnessing.[71] For the Spanish in Pensacola, the Yamasee War was an amazing stroke of good fortune, not the culmination of any devious arrangement with the southeastern Indians.

Despite a lack of solid evidence, it is nevertheless tempting to speculate that the Spanish might have played some role in the outbreak of the Yamasee War. Unlike the French, the Spanish had once enjoyed a considerable degree of interaction with many of the Indian societies that played prominent roles in the war. Moreover, Florida officials made no apologies for the support they gave to many of these Indians once their war against the South Carolinians had begun in earnest. In response to a letter from Virginia governor Alexander Spotswood, Governor Córcoles y Martínez denied any involvement in the Yamasees' decision to go to war, claiming that "the destruction wrought by the Indians [was] due to their ill treatment by the Carolinians." He added that he could "by no means agree to [Spotswood's] proposal that [the Spanish] should not protect or trade with the Indians who fly for protection to Florida and return to their old allegiance to the Catholic King."[72] This riposte did little to clear Córcoles of suspicion in the eyes of the English. Generations of South Carolina historians would later seethe at how the Spanish received Yamasee war parties "with bells ringing and guns firing" through the streets of Saint Augustine, and how Córcoles allegedly entertained a delegation of South Carolina's Indian allies several months before the outbreak of the war.[73] While two such meetings did occur in February 1715, the records give no indication that the Indians revealed their battle plans or that the Spanish pledged their support to an Indian uprising. In his report to the king of Spain, Córcoles simply related that he had received "two very friendly visits" from "groups of pagan and Christian Indians," most likely the Yamasees.[74] Though the governor was encouraged enough by these visits to request an increase in his budget and hope for a "restoration of the lost provinces," he heard nothing else from the Yamasees or any of South Carolina's other Indian enemies until Yfallaquisca and several Yamasee leaders showed up on his doorstep with their knotted strips of deerskin.

The Indians who lashed out against South Carolina's traders, colonists, and officials certainly knew that they would have somewhere else to turn if the need arose. For this reason it would be safe to say that the French—and especially the Spanish—did have an indirect influence on the outbreak of the Yamasee War. At no time, however, did this influence amount to instigation. It is important to remember that the Indians took the initiative in all their meetings with Louisiana and Florida officials during the spring and summer of 1715. The Yamasee War would eventually take on important implications for the Southeast's three-way imperial struggle, but in its earliest and most critical stages, it remained nothing more or less than a conflict between a single colonial power and the various groups of Indians it had provoked and underestimated.

For more than forty years, South Carolinians had successfully faced down the intrigues of their French and Spanish rivals in the strategic expanse of territory between the Tennessee River and the Gulf of Mexico. The official maps and reports of their imperial triumphs gave them an inflated sense of control over the region and its indigenous peoples. While most of the Southeast's native societies had already begun to slide toward a crippling economic dependence on the South Carolinian newcomers, few of them had lost the will or the means to assert their fundamental political autonomy. Finding strength in their own desperation or anger, these Indian societies struck a series of disjointed but effective blows, tangling the South Carolinians in a web that they would only begin to unravel after a great deal of suffering. In the meantime the suddenly unsettled South Carolinians would find themselves mired in a similar crisis on a different range of frontiers.

The Northern Front

Though South Carolina's northern frontiers had recently ranked among the most violent places in North America, they appeared to be enjoying a rare period of peace and stability in the early months of 1715. For the past year the Cherokees and the Catawbas had been able to hunt deer and grow crops without disturbance from the war parties of the Iroquois Five Nations.[75] The Tuscaroras, another traditional foe, had all but vacated the region, and the few hostile Indians who remained in the Carolina borderlands had grown quiet at last. On April 13, Jonathan Urmstone, a curmudgeonly SPG missionary, wrote that he and his fellow North Carolinians were finally "at Peace, thanks be to God, with the Indians and among [themselves]."[76] Two days later the Pocotaligo massacre sparked several months of bloodshed and mayhem among his colonial neighbors to the south. While the South Carolinians fought for their lives around Port Royal and flooded into the streets of Charles Town, they briefly held out hope for some timely assistance from the northern part of their Indian alliance network.[77] After several weeks, however, the only people to emerge from the mountains and the Piedmont were a handful of ragged traders with some discouraging stories to tell. The news of dead Cherokee and Catawba traders came as a devastating blow and seemed to implicate all the northern Indians in the "conspiracy" against South Carolina.[78]

Given the severity of their crisis, the South Carolinians were not immediately inclined to question the nature of the Catawbas' and the Cherokees' connections to the Muskogean insurgents further to the south. While these different Indian societies were more familiar with one another than one might imagine, they never linked up in any single, undifferentiated plot against a common colonial enemy. A closer analysis of the violence on South Carolina's northern and northwestern frontiers reveals a markedly different conflict from the one that involved groups like the Yamasees, the Apalachees, and the Ocheses.

Compared to the various Muskogean societies of the Savannah, Ocmulgee, and Tallapoosa basins, the Indians who inhabited the northern backcountry were relatively recent acquaintances of the South Carolinians. Traders and government officials did not begin to show much interest in these Indians until well into Queen Anne's War, when the pressures of intercolonial rivalry sparked a concerted effort to bring them under firmer control. South Carolina imperialists had worked hard to make up for lost time, and by the time of the Tuscarora War, the Cherokees and the Catawbas had found themselves playing host to an unprecedented number of white visitors. Despite their increasingly intensive contact with the South Carolinians, these Indians still had a long way to go before they faced a situation as discouraging as that of the Yamasees. The Cherokees and the Catawbas soon developed a number of reasons to resent the aggressiveness of their South Carolinian allies, but their strength and geographic situation generally assured that their grievances would remain different from those of the province's other Indian allies.[79]

Though a scattering of colonial settlements had reached as far north as the Santee River by the time of the Yamasee War, few of the Catawbas and none of the Cherokees would have regarded these outposts as serious threats to their crops or hunting grounds.[80] Enemy slave raids had long provided a serious concern for these Indians, but since the turn of the eighteenth century, most of their worries had focused on the Tuscaroras, the Iroquois, and other Native peoples who had almost nothing to do with the South Carolinians. Some Cherokees and Catawbas continued to be held as slaves in South Carolina well into the second decade of the eighteenth century, but on the whole these Indians were finding that their more active participation in South Carolina's military ventures placed them on the profitable end of the province's Indian slave trade.[81] But while imperialism brought new rewards to the Cherokees and the Catawbas, it also introduced them to a new range of hassles. In exchange for newfound strength against their traditional Indian rivals, they had to put up with a disturbing lack of respect from many of South Carolina's traders and officials.

Unlike their counterparts among the Muskogeans, the traders who worked in Cherokee and Catawba country faced some significant competition from rivals who could undercut their prices. The unwelcome presence of the Virginians might have forced these traders to behave with more respect and caution than the traders who had strangleholds on the Yamasees and the Apalachees.[82] The journal of the Board of Commissioners makes few references to South Carolina's northern allies, but one somewhat cryptic entry from August 1711 suggests that the "Wacsaw and Esaw and Cuttabau Indians" might have developed more complaints than the board was inclined to acknowledge.[83] After the outbreak of the Yamasee War, Virginia traders like David Crawley and William Byrd II would eagerly testify about the rapes, thefts, and other transgressions committed by the "little tyrants" who worked among the Catawbas and other neighboring groups.[84] Even accounting for the obvious biases of these "witnesses," it is safe to assume that considerable friction had developed between the Catawbas and some of the South Carolina traders. The infamous "Chestowe incident" of 1714 suggests that indebtedness and abusive behavior were probably becoming even more serious among the Lower Cherokees, a group that the Virginians visited less frequently than the Catawbas.[85] As their contact with the South Carolinians grew more frequent and more intensive, the Indians of the northern buffer zone saw their initial eagerness and respect begin to give way to frustration and disillusionment.

It did not take long for these Indians to deduce that the South Carolinians were not as munificent as they had initially promised to be. Their alliance with the South Carolinians was motivated by something more than a thirst for European trade goods; they also hoped that their new friends would treat them with respect and help bolster them in their struggles against their traditional enemies. Though the Cherokees and the Catawbas had their own reasons for fighting the Savannahs and the Tuscaroras, they also saw their participation in these campaigns as acts of good faith and expected their colonial allies to reciprocate.[86] In the aftermath of the Tuscarora War, many of these Indians were bitterly disappointed to find that the South Carolinians "did not perform their promise" for cheaper trade goods and better protection.[87]

For the Catawbas the Tuscarora War also confirmed something about the fundamental weaknesses of the South Carolinians. For the previous ten years, the Catawbas had noticed that the different groups of white men who paid court to them seemed to do nothing but harass and slander one another even though they spoke the same language and carried the same kinds of goods. The bitter trade rivalry between the South Carolinians and the Virginians was convincing enough, but the Catawbas learned even more about the deep divisions between the different groups of colonists when they observed all the bickering and backstabbing that unfolded during North Carolina's darkest hours. According to Virginia governor Alexander Spotswood, these disputes helped convince the Indians that the various colonies were "under Distinct Sovereigns, as well as Governors, and that [Virginia] would no more assist Carolina than they [Virginia]." [88] Though some of the Catawbas might have hoped to parlay the Virginia–South Carolina rivalry into a favorable price war, the gulf between the colonies could also take on more ominous implications when the Indians finally decided that they had had enough of one province's representatives. [89]

During the Tuscarora War the Catawbas and the Cherokees had often behaved in ways that could be construed as disrespectful to their colonial "commanders." Though their frequent "desertions" indicated that they were less than awestruck by their English allies, many of these Indians probably felt a healthy respect for the people who had frequently proven themselves capable of ruthless acts of destruction. Like that of the Ocheses or the Tallapoosas, the Catawbas' and the Cherokees' growing resentment of the South Carolinians was more a function of dissatisfaction than abject desperation. Nevertheless, some of them were concerned enough by the South Carolinians' behavior to find credence in some of the disturbing rumors that began to come their way. [90] In the year before the Yamasee War, the Lower Cherokees received two separate warnings from two of South Carolina's "outlaw" traders, both of whom claimed that the South Carolina government "did design to kill all their head warriors." [91] Such a rumor might have had an even greater impact on the Cherokees if—as some people have speculated—they and the Catawbas had already begun to hear similar stories from the Yamasees and the Ocheses. One Lower Cherokee headman later claimed that the warnings from the renegade English traders were corroborated by some of South Carolina's "friendly Indians." [92]

It is likely that the Indians on South Carolina's northern and southern frontiers had at least some interaction in the months before the Yamasee War. Though they belonged to markedly different linguistic groups, they were hardly strangers to one another. Indeed, a few pieces of indirect evidence suggest that some of the Yamasees and the Lower Cherokees might have become intertwined in the old province of La Tama.[93] As was the case with the Yamasees and their Muskogean neighbors, however, the connections between different Indian societies could stem from common experience as well as common culture. Partly as a result of the South Carolinians' imperial ambitions, Indians from various parts of the province's buffer zone had recently begun to take part in joint military expeditions like the ones that entered North Carolina between 1711 and 1713. Some colonists later claimed that the South Carolina government's decisions to bring together these different groups of warriors led directly to the "general Conspiracy" that seemed to manifest itself in 1715.[94] Though it would—as one historian concedes—be a stretch to assume that the Yamasee War was "planned around the campfires of Tuscarora country," the Barnwell and Moore expeditions probably helped lay a foundation for the Muskogean messengers who made their way north some time later.[95]

As significant as they might have been, these visits did not necessarily implicate the Cherokees and the Catawbas in any kind of general plot. Far from cohesive among the closely related Muskogean groups, the "conspiracy" against South Carolina proved even flimsier when it extended to the northern Indians. No matter what they knew of the Ocheses' or the Yamasees' violent intentions, neither the Cherokees nor the Catawbas made the decision to strike out against the South Carolinians until most of the fighting on the southwestern front had already ended. Even then their uneven actions indicated that they were far from unified in their commitment to the war.

Among the Cherokees the anti-English faction was probably in the minority. Those Cherokees who favored a war against the South Carolinians hailed mostly from the lower towns, where the process of cultural exchange had taken its greatest toll. Soon after hearing of the Yamasees' rampage, some of the Lower Cherokees quickly showed their support by killing many of their traders in much the same way that the Ocheses probably did. One trader who escaped from Cherokee country claimed that he and six other traders had been assembled together by a group of Indians who initially promised to protect them but then proceeded to shoot them down at a feast held in the traders' honor.[96] The situation was probably less perilous, however, for the traders who were working among the Middle and Overhill Cherokees. Relatively isolated from the South Carolinians, these Indians had never reconciled themselves to the Ocheses, the Abeikas, and the Tallapoosas, and they would eventually play a major role in the important Cherokee–South Carolina alliance of 1716.[97]

For all the divisions among the Cherokees, there is reason to believe that the Indians of the Carolina Piedmont remained even less certain about their course of action. More than most of South Carolina's former Indian allies, the Catawbas had the luxury of weighing their options. According to two Virginia traders who were among the Catawbas at the time of the Yamasee uprising, "neither that Nation nor the others in their neighbourhood had any intention to quarrel with the English; but on the contrary were preparing to assist the people of South Carolina against the Yamasees."[98] This would explain why several South Carolina traders chose to stay among the Catawbas instead of fleeing to Charles Town. In time, however, a number of different factors caused many of the Catawbas to change their minds. Above all the Cheraws, the Waxhaws, and other southern Piedmont groups probably began to push for war on the basis of their vulnerability to South Carolinians, who had already "killed a great many of their Indians."[99] It was soon reported that a group of Catawbas carrying deerskins to Charles Town had fallen victim to the colonists' indiscriminate rage.[100]

If these rumors were not enough to stir the Catawbas into action, the Catawbas could also draw support from their connections to the Virginians. Some Virginia traders would later stand accused of goading the Catawbas into attacking the South Carolinians, but it is more likely that their mere presence as an alternative source of trade goods was enough to convince the Catawbas that they could live without the more demanding breed of Englishmen.[101] When they finally decided to kill the South Carolina traders, they decided to spare the Virginians. The Catawbas' entry into the Yamasee War was not an indiscriminate lunge against the forces of English imperialism, but neither was it the "mere accident" that they later described to colonial authorities.[102] Instead, it resulted from a calculated decision based on their early observations of South Carolina's vulnerability.

The South Carolinians did not become fully aware of the hostile intentions of their northern Indian allies until the end of May, when a large group of Catawba warriors killed a colonist named John Hearn on his Santee River plantation. Soon the four hundred or so Catawbas were joined by about seventy of the most militant Cherokees, forming a war party that was growing more confident by the day. By this time the Catawba and Cherokee warriors were drawing inspiration from a number of South Carolina's slaves, servants, and "settlement" Indians who carried valuable and encouraging news of the province's plight.[103] In the first week of June, a former Indian slave of James Moore Sr. approached a group of warriors with the news that Moore's son-in-law, Captain Thomas Barker, was leading a contingent of ninety mounted troops on a relief expedition to the Santee region. The next day this former slave, who had actually fought alongside the South Carolinians in their recent skirmishes with the Yamasees, reportedly fired the first shot in a devastating ambush that killed Barker and twenty-five of his "very pretty young men."[104] Shortly thereafter another Cherokee-Catawba war party surrounded a makeshift South Carolinian fort on Benjamin Schenkingh's plantation. Unable to breach the walls, they tricked the fort's commander into letting them in to discuss a truce and then proceeded to kill about twenty of the fort's thirty black and white defenders. With nothing standing between these Indians and the rich settlements of Goose Creek, South Carolina's formerly quiet northern frontiers soon became the primary focus of the province's war effort.[105]

Along with the reports of various "spies," the northern Indians' early experiences against South Carolina's confused colonists and relief expeditions might have convinced them that they were dealing with a beaten and demoralized enemy. If they expected to follow an easy route into the heart of South Carolina, they were in for a string of unpleasant surprises. The Indians' first setback occurred when the seventy Cherokees suddenly abandoned the expedition on the outskirts of Goose Creek Parish, having received word from their towns that the English were willing to make a favorable peace.[106] If the remaining Catawbas still had any intentions about proceeding further into the South Carolina settlements, they were soon dissuaded by about 120 black and white troops under the command of George Chicken, an accomplished Indian trader and a captain in the Goose Creek militia. On the evening of June 13, a few miles from a site known as the Ponds, Chicken's force ambushed the Catawbas' scout party and immediately launched a headlong charge into the main body of Indians. With only a handful of casualties, the South Carolinians managed to kill approximately forty to sixty Indians, including a number of women and children who had tagged along with the war party.[107]

Though superb guerrilla warriors, the Catawbas—like most of the southeastern Indians—were unaccustomed to fighting off an enemy that engaged them in such a bold and direct manner. The survivors of this rout quickly fled Goose Creek for the safety of their villages and interpreted their latest setback as a sign to reevaluate their role in the war.[108] Unlike the Yamasees, who would continue to fight the South Carolinians despite suffering even worse defeats, the Catawbas decided to cut their losses and acknowledge the enemy's superior firepower. Within a month Catawba leaders were in Williamsburg, informing the Virginia authorities of their willingness to "join with the Government of South Carolina in cutting off the Yamasees & others [of] their Enemies."[109]

By July 1715, just as the Yamasees and the Apalachees were beginning to join forces for another offensive into South Carolina's southwestern settlements, the war in the north had essentially come to an end. In the weeks after the sudden disappearance of the Cherokee and Catawba war parties, more and more South Carolinians began to grasp what a few of them had suspected all the long: that their Indian enemies were not as unified as they had briefly appeared to be. [110] While some South Carolinians continued to perceive all Indians as enemies or spies, others grew hopeful that the northern Indians would reestablish themselves as valuable "friends" of the province. [111] For the next several months, South Carolina's surviving traders and officials would vigorously pursue a new and better alliance with the Catawbas and Cherokees, making them vital components in the province's plans to subdue the more recalcitrant southern Indians.

The Yamasee War remained far from over, but the most optimistic colonists could finally see an end to their troubles somewhere on the horizon. In recognizing and exploiting the heterogeneous nature of the massive Indian "uprising," South Carolinians made a significant stride toward the resolution of their latest crisis. This breakthrough, however, only came after several damaging weeks of confusion and indecision. Unaccustomed to the pain, humiliation, and frustration of a major Indian war, South Carolinians were forced to realize that their sanity and survival would depend on their ability to adapt to the changing conditions on their frontiers.

5. Crisis and Change

WARTIME ADJUSTMENTS OF THE
SOUTH CAROLINIANS

Three weeks after losing his plantation to a pillaging band of Yamasee warriors, George Rodd was unable to take much solace in the fact that he was still alive. By May 1715 South Carolina's unexpected Indian war had burdened him with an array of troubles that seemed "a hundred times worse than death." The devastated plantation was the least of Rodd's worries. In a desperate letter to a friend in London, this future attorney general of South Carolina acknowledged that he was on the verge of losing his mind. Rodd had joined hundreds of other uprooted colonists in flocking to Charles Town, quickly transforming South Carolina's bustling capital into one of the most miserable places in North America. Widows and orphans wailed over their plight as they camped out in the town's stifling streets. Rodd could feel his nerves becoming more frayed by the day: he gripped a musket every waking moment and sought out hiding places for sleeping. Though Charles Town's walls and heavy guns made it the safest location in South Carolina, Rodd was consumed by the unspeakable fear of falling into the hands of the "damned Indians" who lurked somewhere in the surrounding countryside.[1]

The Yamasee War grew out of disagreements that had festered along South Carolina's various frontiers, but its impact quickly resounded into the very heart of the province. For a brief period every settlement in South Carolina was subjected to the uncertainty of a frontier power struggle. Faced with the omnipresent possibility of an Indian attack, South Carolinians were forced to take closer account of the presence and actions of cultural outsiders. Though most colonists did not remain in grave danger for more than a few months, fallout from the war continued to affect the South Carolinians even after they began to push back their enemies and repair their damaged settlements. Their lingering fear and humiliation cast a shadow not only over the traditional frontier issues of trade and military strategy but also over some problems that had long plagued the province as a whole. South Carolinians never stopped worrying about intercolonial rivalries, the Lords Proprietors, or the increasingly skewed ratio between blacks and whites, controversies that took on even greater urgency when combined with the crisis of an unexpected Indian war.

Perhaps the most difficult and frustrating aspect of this crisis was that the South Carolinians—despite their efforts to regain control of their frontiers as quickly as possible—could not bring a true sense of closure to the war. From some perspectives the Yamasee War seemed rather brief. The Lords Proprietors and some of their supporters considered the province to be out of mortal danger after the first few weeks. Many colonists felt that the war had come to a close in early 1716 with the establishment of a new South Carolina–Cherokee alliance, and others pointed to the government's treaty with the various Muskogean provinces in the fall of 1717. In reality the end of the war was far less certain than many South Carolinians would have liked to believe. Most of the province's major Indian enemies were neither cowed nor disarmed, and some of them—primarily the Yamasees and the Apalachicolas—would continue to raid the South Carolina settlements for another ten years. The task of rebuilding South Carolina's devastated economy, diplomacy, and defensive perimeter did not really fall under the rubric of postwar reconstruction, because the province in many ways still remained locked in a disturbing struggle against Indians and imperial rivals.

When examining the effects of the Yamasee War on South Carolina society, it is more appropriate to speak of a period roughly five years long (1715–20) during which the concerns of the war weighed most heavily on the province. During this period South Carolinians underwent important changes in their attitudes, tactics, and policies. Some of these changes were of a short-term nature, undertaken out of necessity and abandoned as soon as the worst crises had passed. At the same time the Yamasee War also inspired South Carolinians to make a number of long-term adjustments in their ways of dealing with Indians, slaves, and one another. By taking a closer look at how these different kinds of changes applied to the themes of colonial defense, imperial politics, and South Carolinian identity, one can begin to gauge the extent of the influence that flowed across South Carolina's frontiers during the course of the Yamasee War. Even though the war in some ways compelled South Carolinians to set themselves apart from potentially threatening "outsiders," the colonists remained inextricably linked to other groups and cultures throughout the region.

Defense and Trade

One of the Indians' most significant impacts was in forcing a sudden shift in South Carolina's military and mercantile trajectory. Driven by an expansionist mentality since their arrival in 1670, South Carolina imperialists had proven aggressive to the point of recklessness in the early years of the eighteenth century. While the South Carolinians had not ignored the need to establish an effective network for their own protection, they had focused most of their attention on stopping or dissuading their French and Spanish enemies. During their rapid expansion into the southeastern interior, South Carolinians had relied on Indian allies as a means to secure the province's inland frontiers against enemy invasion. In implementing this strategy, the South Carolinians had been well served by combining a military swagger with a lucrative Indian trade. The apparent collapse of the Indian alliance network in the spring of 1715 was a stunning blow to the advocates of these time-honored methods and briefly left South Carolinians at a loss for ways to restore control over their frontiers.

Ultimately the imperialistic successes of the several previous decades proved too compelling for the South Carolinians to ignore. Patterns of economic and military exchange were so deeply woven into the fabric of frontier interaction that no self-respecting imperialist could ever abandon them altogether. Between 1715 and 1720, efforts to rebuild South Carolina's frontier defense would remain closely linked to the restoration of the province's Indian trade. The basic framework for South Carolina's Indian relations would remain in place, but it was clearly unrealistic and unwise to attempt an exact replication of the prewar system. Most South Carolinians believed that they would have to implement a number of minor and major changes to prevent another shock from rocking the foundations of their province.

Early in the Yamasee War, however, no one in South Carolina was in a position to give serious consideration to these necessary reforms. Questions about future recovery temporarily took a backseat to concerns about South Carolina's very survival. Having suffered a series of demoralizing blows in the first few days of the war, South Carolinians were forced to do whatever they could to prevent their situation from worsening. Initial losses were so disturbing that many colonists wondered whether their efforts would be of any use. After reminding the Commons House of the government's need to keep its composure, Governor Craven proceeded to lament that he and his fellow South Carolinians were "almost naked and defenseless, and know not how soon some of us may be in the hands of those monsters of mankind, the Indians." [2] To Craven, George

Rodd, and a number of other South Carolinians, their new Indian enemies were mysterious and fearsome enough to inspire a barely controllable sense of dread. SPG Commissary Gideon Johnston claimed that the Indians had "nothing but the shape of Men to distinguish them from Wolves & Tygers," and another colonist agreed that the South Carolinians "may as well go to War with the Wolfs & Boars."[3] Even the normally levelheaded Reverend Francis Le Jau had to admit that "if this Torrent of Indians continue[d] to fall upon [them]," the disoriented colonists would soon be powerless to resist.[4]

Such helplessness was a new and previously unthinkable experience for a group of people who had projected strength, vitality, and an almost defiant sense of independence during the various conflicts of the previous fifteen years. In the South Carolinians' struggles against the French, the Spanish, and the Tuscaroras, their only assistance had come from the same Indian societies that now appeared to be lashing out against the province. The only Indians known with certainty to be friendly were "few in Number and bad Souldiers," making it necessary for the South Carolinians to swallow their pride and request supplies and manpower from other British dominions.[5] Confined to makeshift forts and despairing for their survival, the South Carolinians found themselves in a situation similar to the one that had plagued their North Carolinian neighbors a few years earlier.

The Tuscarora and Yamasee Wars began in much the same fashion, with the murder of experienced frontiersmen quickly followed by assaults on unsuspecting colonial settlements. Despite some striking parallels between them, however, the two conflicts ultimately followed distinct courses and ended with some noticeably different results. One major difference became apparent early in the Yamasee War, as the South Carolinians began to display a range of capabilities that the North Carolinians had largely lacked. Even as the South Carolinians continued to fear the worst and plead for outside assistance, they realized that their fate would have to rest primarily on their own shoulders.

In the intense and crucial engagements of the war's early weeks, the brunt of the action was borne by the South Carolina militia. Despite the government's efforts to improve the militia during Queen Anne's War, nothing in their monthly musters had prepared the men for the confusing, unregimented violence of an Indian war. In nearly every Indian war that had involved the North American colonies since the early seventeenth century, colonists were forced to endure painful periods of adjustment, suffering heavy losses to elusive enemies whom they could barely see, let alone fight.[6] During the early stages of the Yamasee War, South Carolina's militia sustained several of these humiliating setbacks, most notably the ambush of Thomas Barker's cavalry and the Catawbas' capture of Schenkingh's garrison. Though South Carolina's citizen-soldiers were thrown into occasional fits of confusion and panic by their Indian enemies, it should not be assumed that they spent the first part of the Yamasee War bumbling their way through the forests. Relative to other colonial fighting forces, the South Carolina militia compiled a rather impressive record in its first major test against Indian warriors.[7]

While the militia included an abundance of inexperienced farmers, laborers, and slaves, its ranks also contained several dozen soldiers and officers who knew what steps they would have to take to beat back the Indians' challenges.[8] This advantage became evident almost immediately, when Governor Craven led 240 members of the Colleton County militia on an expedition into the "Yamasee lands" less than a week after the Pocotaligo massacre. Craven's decisive action and confident command not only gave some badly needed encouragement to his troops but also left the Yamasees little chance to press the advantage that they had gained in the first few days of the war. As the South Carolinians approached the town of Salkehatchie—"Saltcatchers" to the English tongue—they forced the kind of engagement to which the Yamasees were poorly suited: a pitched battle on open terrain. Attacking the South Carolinians in a crescent formation of several hundred warriors, the Yamasees soon discovered that they would not be able to outflank the enemy columns without suffering heavy losses. The resolve of the South Carolinians and the deaths of several head warriors convinced the Yamasees to abandon the battle and disperse into the nearby swamps. Though casualties for the Salkehatchie fight were fairly even at about two dozen men per side, the Yamasees' hasty retreat provided the South Carolinians with their first taste of victory.[9]

Seizing momentum, the South Carolinians achieved a string of further victories on the strength of contingents that were smaller and less "traditional" than the force commanded by Craven. As the militia pressed into Yamasee country, several scout parties led by experienced frontier fighters sought to take on the Indians in their own towns. Having fought alongside the Yamasees during the Florida and Tuscarora campaigns, John Barnwell and Alexander MacKay knew that the element of surprise could sometimes prevail over superior numbers.[10] As Craven engaged the Yamasees at Salkehatchie, Barnwell led several men into the town of Pocotaligo, where they overwhelmed sentries and recovered some of the plunder that the Indians had acquired on their earlier raids. Further south MacKay directed an assault against some two hundred Yamasees who had taken refuge in a large, palisaded encampment. Though outnumbered the South Carolinians attacked ferociously; one "young stripling" named John Palmer led fifteen other men over the walls, fighting the Yamasees for several minutes before safely jumping back to the other side. When a second charge by Palmer convinced the Yamasees to flee out the back way, MacKay and a hundred of his men ambushed them with a deadly barrage of gunfire. Those Yamasees who escaped the attack were soon persuaded that they would be better off in moving south to the Altamaha River, further away from the maniacal South Carolinian "swamp hunters."[11]

Throughout the Yamasee War, South Carolinian forces proved most successful whenever they fought more like Indians than textbook militiamen. Always a staple tactic among the North American Indians, ambushes yielded particularly good results for the South Carolinians. MacKay's defeat of the Yamasees and Captain George Chicken's important victory over the Catawbas in the Battle of the Ponds both relied on the ambush. The tactic worked equally well for a scout boat crew in the "Daufuskie fight," a summer engagement in which the South Carolinians killed thirty-five Yamasees while suffering only a single casualty.[12] The South Carolinians' use of this successful tactic might have been facilitated to some extent by the assistance of a few loyal Indian allies, but it is more likely that they had become well acquainted with it even before the outbreak of the Yamasee War. Decades of frontier exchange had already left an indelible mark on an important segment of the South Carolina military. Without the experience that some of them had acquired in earlier conflicts, the South Carolinians might have been unable to win the timely victories that checked the early advances of the Yamasees and the Catawbas, giving the province some badly needed breathing room.

Despite its early successes, the militia could not completely assuage the anxieties that gripped South Carolina. Even after thwarting the Indians' initial offensives, the colonists remained maddeningly uncertain about when and where the next wave of attacks might strike. Several missionaries tried to give comfort to the tormented but had to admit that nearly six months after the war's outbreak, their "unsettled" parishioners "feared a second incursion upon every pretended uneasiness."[13] As the Yamasees and the Catawbas pulled away from the South Carolina settlements, it became more difficult for the militia to undertake the kind of preemptive offensive that had worked earlier in the war. Confined to an uneven ring of hastily fortified plantation houses, the militia proved that it was far less effective when placed on a strictly defensive footing.[14] Many of the men grew restless from whiling away long, tense hours in cramped quarters and began to worry that the Indians might bypass the widely scattered forts and attack their vulnerable women and children.[15] By the second month of the war, deserters were leaving the militia in alarming numbers, some of them attempting to protect their families, but others intending to abandon the province for parts unknown. South Carolina's Indian enemies— both real and imagined—appeared to be on the verge of dissolving the colony from within.[16]

The obvious need for greater order and discipline within the South Carolina militia allowed an energetic executive to tighten his hold on the colonial government. Twelve years earlier Governor Nathaniel Johnson had been able to use the emergency of Queen Anne's War as a means to implement his costly plans for South Carolina's coastal defenses. Far more popular and charismatic than Johnson, Governor Craven soon found that the South Carolina assembly was willing to issue him a blank check to guide the province through its darkest crisis yet.[17] Craven responded by initiating a string of forceful measures that he and his largely Whiggish legislature would have been extremely reluctant to support under less urgent circumstances. On May 13, the government authorized martial law, allowing the militia to impress supplies from the public and punish any able-bodied shirker with death.[18] In an attempt to swell the ranks of South Carolina's forces, the government also ordered the militia to admit and arm more black slaves than the previous militia acts had stipulated.[19] When the militia continued to experience problems in spite of these measures, Craven took an even more momentous step by temporarily replacing this cherished institution with the province's first professional army. By August the South Carolina government had hired roughly six hundred South Carolinians, four hundred black slaves, one hundred Indians "of the small Nations among us who never revolted," seventy "friendly" Tuscaroras from North Carolina, and three hundred troops from North Carolina and Virginia to serve in various sixty-man companies. The Commons House resolved to pay each white soldier a salary of eleven pounds Carolina money per month, while the master of each black soldier was to receive two pounds per month. Indians did not receive a salary; they were to be paid in clothing, with the possibility of a three-pound bonus for every enemy scalp taken.[20]

Any misgivings over the employment of "mercenaries" soon began to erode as it became apparent that a new kind of army was the best way for South Carolinians to cope with the changing nature of the war. By the end of 1715, most South Carolinians had grown thoroughly frustrated with their enemies' refusal to "come to a decisive battle." The Indians' "old method of Bush fighting"— an unpredictable combination of ambushes and raids—was best left to men who were more qualified to handle it.[21] Such was the primary rationale behind the South Carolina government's strategy to harness the military capabilities of Indian warriors; in addition to employing the Tuscaroras and "settlement Indians," they had also stepped up their efforts to capitalize on inter-Indian rivalries and bring important groups like the Cherokees and the Catawbas back into the fold. Throughout the Yamasee War, South Carolina officials would continue to use Indians as hired guns, but at the same time they also began to realize that certain colonial troops could handle the kinds of tasks that had once been the exclusive domain of the province's Indian allies.

In July Craven had taken a large contingent of South Carolinian troops on an expedition to quell the remaining hostile Indians in the Carolina Piedmont, only to leave the southern settlements open to a brief but terrifying incursion from five hundred Yamasee and Apalachee warriors.[22] Meanwhile the "marines" who patrolled the maze of waterways around Port Royal Sound were proving quite successful in defeating and deterring those Indians who attempted to raid the settlements by canoe. Though the South Carolina scout boat crews had served intermittently since the late seventeenth century, they saw extensive use in the Yamasee War, especially after a grateful government increased their number and stationed them in two new locations.[23] Soon the concept of the scout boats was being applied to South Carolina's land forces, as various ranger companies—groups of six to twelve mounted troops under a commanding officer—began to patrol the areas between frontier outposts.[24] Though the rangers left a good deal of ground uncovered, their occasional victories over small Indian raiding parties put Francis Le Jau's mind at ease, convincing him that they were "disposed in such a manner as to be able to hinder the Coming of the Enemy into [their] Inner settlements."[25] Inclined to agree with this assessment, the government would remember the effectiveness of the scouts and rangers even after South Carolina's situation began to take a pronounced turn for the better.

When the South Carolinians finally established a long-awaited alliance with the Cherokees in early 1716, the province's standing army was dismantled, and most of the South Carolinian troops returned home to regular militia duty. Though the worst appeared to be over, the colonial government was reluctant to conduct a total demobilization. In addition to sending a hundred troops to assist the Cherokees in their fight against the various Muskogean groups that were still at war with South Carolina, officials called upon 113 men to staff six strategically placed frontier garrisons.[26] The following year, convinced that the still "uncertain" state of the war made it as necessary as ever "to keep on foot certain companies of Soldiers, Rangers, and Garrisons," the government called up an additional 140 men for frontier service.[27] Many of these posts were filled by publicly owned servants, men who had been indentured to the South Carolina government as a result of their participation in Scotland's failed Jacobite uprising of 1715.[28] Given the average militiaman's reluctance to volunteer for dangerous work far away from his farm or family, the government had to fill the remaining slots with a special kind of South Carolinian. Their most likely candidates were unemployed Indian traders or other experienced frontiersmen, men who had fewer reservations about isolating themselves from colonial society. South Carolina officials did not necessarily intend for these frontier troops to replace departed Indian allies, but they did suggest that the idea of a professional soldiery—formerly regarded as a stop-gap measure and a necessary evil—was on its way to becoming a more permanent fixture in the province's defense network.

Coupled with this trend was the South Carolina government's new reliance on frontier fortifications. While forts had begun to emerge as an important part of Florida's and Louisiana's imperial strategies by the end of Queen Anne's War, South Carolinians had seen no need to finance such expensive projects as long as they could rely on the assistance of formidable Indian allies. The outbreak of the Yamasee War caused an immediate change of plans, forcing the South Carolinians to construct twenty-four different forts in less than two years, most of them little more than modified farmhouses or cattle pens designed to house troops on a temporary basis.[29] Throughout the first year of the war, the government frequently shifted the various garrisons in an effort to block the enemies' anticipated routes of attack. Though many of the provisional forts were abandoned by 1716, South Carolina officials elected to build or improve several larger structures as a means to lodge ranger companies and guard some of the principal passages into the colonial settlements.[30] Savannah Town, an old trade hub located about two hundred miles up the Savannah River, became the site of Fort Moore, built in November 1715 and expanded several times over the next two years. In 1717 the South Carolinians constructed Beaufort Fort on Port Royal Sound, intending it as a station for scout boats and a replacement for a smaller fort that had been built immediately before the Yamasee War. After covering the south and the west, the government sought to address some of the province's northern frontiers with the Congarees, a fort near present-day Columbia, which was designed in 1716 and completed two years later.[31]

Though more substantial than the makeshift structures built earlier in the

Yamasee War, the forts at Savannah Town, Beaufort, and the Congarees paled in comparison to European models or even the coastal forts at Charles Town, Mobile, Pensacola, and Saint Augustine. Fashioned of wooden walls around a few wooden barracks and storehouses, they were considered just sturdy enough to withstand the arrows and musket balls of an Indian attack. In promoting his scheme for a new southeastern colony in 1717, Sir Robert Montgomery claimed that "it [was] not necessary, that [forts] be of Bulk, like those of Europe; small Defence [was] strong against poor unskilled Natives of America: They . . . accomplish'd all their bloody Mischiefs by Surprizes, and Incursions, but durst never think of a Defyance to Artillery." [32] Forts were handy resources to have in a fight against Indians, but they were probably just as important for their symbolic value. As the South Carolinians fought and recovered from an agonizing Indian war, the new frontier forts were able to stand as solid bastions of the province's wounded imperial authority. Serving primarily as a warning to potential intruders, the forts also spoke to South Carolina's steady resurgence between 1716 and 1720. In time forts would play an even more prominent role on South Carolina's frontiers, continuing as symbols of a double-sided policy that attempted to balance an aggressive expansionism with a cautious defensiveness. [33]

By assuming a more direct and active role in the defense of South Carolina's frontiers, the government ameliorated one range of problems to the detriment of another. In the words of one frustrated South Carolinian, the Indian enemies were "freebooters" who could function perfectly well on "a little parched corn and puddle water," allowing them to prolong a war that had already put the colonists "to a vast Expence." [34] In 1710 Thomas Nairne had lauded the Indian buffer zone as a cost-effective means of defending the province. Seven years later the use of forts and rangers and the purchase of arms from abroad had helped double South Carolina's defense budget at a most inopportune time. [35] The government initially attempted to finance these new measures by collecting import duties on liquor, slaves, and luxury goods, levying an additional fifty thousand pounds in direct taxes, and printing a new supply of paper currency. Rampant inflation, staggering debts, and a heavily damaged infrastructure all combined to make these solutions impractical. [36] As of mid-1716 South Carolina's estimated prewar value of £709,763 sterling had "been diminished by desertion, destruction, etc. at least one third." [37] Rice production, concentrated in a region that sustained little damage during the war, returned to its former levels by 1718, but elsewhere the prospects remained gloomier. As much as half of the colony's arable land was rendered temporarily useless, and the cattle industry of the southwestern settlements would never recover.[38] Even after the worst fighting had passed, many South Carolinians worried that they might soon find themselves "reduced to the miserable condition of their Neighbours in the Bahama Islands."[39]

For all the damage inflicted on South Carolinian agriculture, another sector of the economy had suffered a setback that was even more potentially harmful to the province's recovery. Before the war the Indian trade had comprised a major cog in South Carolina's economy, accounting for a high percentage of exports while spurring the expansion of the province's frontiers. With the violence and distrust that escalated in the wake of the Pocotaligo massacre, this once-unstoppable trade was thrust into what one historian correctly refers to as a "period of utter confusion."[40] Nearly half of South Carolina's experienced traders lay dead; all of South Carolina's important trading partners had become either hostile or inaccessible; and the various hardships of the war allowed fewer opportunities for processing or marketing deerskins. The numbers of skins exported from Charles Town spoke for themselves: 60,451 in 1713, 50,781 in 1714, 55,806 in 1715, and 4,702 in 1716.[41] Faced with this drastic reduction, South Carolina's merchants, traders, and officials began a concerted effort to nurse the Indian trade back to its former profitability. The restoration of the Indian trade soon became a priority to the private and public sectors alike; in addition to helping some colonists recoup their personal fortunes, it could also help defray the government's rising frontier expenses.

Because the South Carolinians did not want to run the risk of supplying their enemies with tools, clothing, or weapons, the restoration of the Indian trade was contingent on making peace with those Indian societies that had apparently broken with the province. The opportunity for a new and improved trade emerged in mid-1716, as the wary South Carolinians finally became convinced that the Cherokees and most of the Piedmont Indians could be trusted.[42] In renewing their alliances with the South Carolinians, these powerful groups clamored for the trade goods that they had so dearly missed in the previous year. Reminded of the inseparable connections between economic and diplomatic exchange, the South Carolina government jumped back into the Indian trade with a vengeance. On June 30, the assembly ratified "An Act for the Better Regulation of the Indian Trade," a measure that dwarfed all of the government's previous attempts at trade legislation. This act was less a reform than a major overhaul. For the first time in South Carolina's history, the colonial government was to assume a monopoly over the Indian trade and manage it "for the sole Use, Benefit, and Behoof of the Publick."[43]

Though the government cast an eager glance on the potential revenue of the Indian trade, the most compelling justifications for the public monopoly had nothing to do with money. Since monopolies were no more attractive than standing armies in the eyes of many Englishmen, it stands to reason that many South Carolina officials only accepted the 1716 Indian Trade Act as an emergency measure. [44] The primary rationale behind the monopoly was to ensure the security of South Carolina's frontiers. Concluding that "the Indian Trade as formerly carried on by private Traders" had "tended [very] much to the great Damage and Detriment" of the province, the government decided that major changes were the only way to "prevent [such] Inconveniencies for the Future." The monopoly promised to "fortify" South Carolina's Indian trade by restricting it to three different "factories": one to be placed inside Fort Moore, the second in the Congarees garrison, and the third at the Santee River plantation-fort of Winyah. [45] The government "factors" in charge of these posts were expected to serve as both master traders and diplomatic officials, strictly monitoring the behavior of the Indians and lesser traders while keeping the province's supplies of trade goods under lock and key. [46] Like the Indian agents of the prewar system, the factors had the power to enforce the policies designed by a central board of commissioners, which in turn answered to the Commons House. The board mandated by the public trade act, however, appeared in many ways to be a new institution committed to a far more active role in the regulatory process. [47]

On paper the public monopoly appeared to be an ideal system for preventing former abuses and presiding over South Carolina's frontier recovery. Those in charge of the public trade certainly seemed to learn from past mistakes. Mindful of the massive debts that had been accumulated by some Indian societies in the years immediately before the Yamasee War, the commissioners issued strict orders that the government factors were "not on any Pretence whatsoever to give any Credit or Trust any Indians whatsoever, even for the value of one single skin." [48] The board proved equally reluctant to trust the traders, pegging them as convenient scapegoats for the province's recent miseries. [49] Not only did the board offer rewards of one hundred pounds Carolina money for information on abusive traders; it also adopted a tougher stance on punishment, requiring any lawbreaker to pay a fine of five hundred pounds Carolina money and forfeit all his trade goods to the public treasury. [50] It soon began to appear that the government's more active role in the Indian trade was paying valuable dividends. Reported cases of abuse and violence declined substantially, and the government turned profits as high as 400 percent on some of the items sold to the Indians. Deerskin exports climbed from an abysmal 4,702 in 1716 to a more respectable 21,713 the following year.[51] Eventually advocates of the public monopoly and several sympathetic historians would praise the new system for its effectiveness, crediting it with the newfound stability that seemed to prevail on South Carolina's frontiers.[52]

In all probability, however, these improvements stemmed more from the profound social and demographic dynamics of the war than the policies of a more sensitive and enlightened government. A clear case in point was the transformation of the Indian slave trade, formerly among the most problematic aspects of the South Carolina frontier complex. Like previous generations of South Carolina lawmakers, the commissioners in charge of the public trade expressly forbade colonists from enslaving or selling "Indians of any Nation . . . in Amity and under the Protection of [that] Government."[53] There is no evidence, however, that South Carolinians had come to object to the Indian slave trade on principle. Not only did they eagerly enslave those Yamasee, Santee, Waxhaw, and Winyah enemies whom they managed to capture during the war; they also made it legal to purchase prisoners taken by the Cherokees, the Catawbas, or other Indian allies.[54] At one point, when this traffic appeared too slow, the commissioners even raised the maximum age of Indians eligible for enslavement from fourteen to thirty.[55] Despite this measure the sale of Indian slaves in South Carolina underwent a veritable nosedive between 1715 and 1725, primarily as a function of the migrations and new alliances that many Indian societies were forced to make during the Yamasee War.[56] While this collapse undoubtedly had a soothing effect on the province's frontier relations, the South Carolinians themselves had little to do with it.

Few of the men who strove to rebuild South Carolina's frontier trade under the public monopoly were driven by humanitarian concerns for the Indians.[57] Most of the South Carolinian traders who gradually returned to action found it prudent to be on their best behavior. At the same time this healthy respect for the Indians could often blur into a pervasive fear that caused the South Carolinians to view all Indians—even their avowed allies and trading partners—as devious and deadly creatures.[58] According to the South Carolina government's agents in London, the Indians of the Southeast were universally "proud, revengefull, and bloody, Lovers of Warr and Mischiefe, and [were] no longer to be kept in Subjection [than] Necessity or Interest obliges them[,] which [might] be accomplished by prudent Methods and precautions, the Chiefe of which [was] making them Dependent for necessaries of all kinds, and in those keeping them bare and unstored."[59] To this way of thinking, a carefully managed trade amounted to a kind of weapon against the unpredictable people who were—for better or worse—an integral part of South Carolina's imperial destiny. The Yamasee War chastened the South Carolinians to a certain degree, but it did not startle them into abandoning their old beliefs in the fundamentally unequal nature of the exchange process. South Carolina officials never consulted with the Indians when they hammered out their public trade act; they simply presented it to them as a done deal and privately vowed to stick by their new system whether their Indian trading partners were "Satisfied or not."[60]

Unfortunately for its supporters, the monopoly could not always meet the rigid standards that were outlined in the halls of assembly. Though the commissioners seemed to be "honest [and] worthy Gentlemen," one trader felt that they were "not so well acquainted with the ways of Indians and their trade as might have been wished."[61] Imposing a new economic order on South Carolina's frontiers was a difficult enough task in and of itself, but it became even more challenging as the public trade began to reveal many of the problems that had hindered the old system. The commissioners did prove flexible enough to change some of their most unrealistic policies in response to various complaints; in addition to allowing the Indians to reestablish small lines of credit, they also required five assistant factors to leave Fort Moore and set up shop in various Cherokee towns.[62] Too often, however, the government's flexibility seemed suspect, as when Eleazar Wiggan—fined five hundred pounds for illegally trading with the Catawbas—successfully appealed his penalty based on his usefulness as an interpreter.[63] Government officials occasionally took a more direct role in the nefarious aspects of the trade, especially when it seemed to be in the government's best financial interest. After ordering the Fort Moore factor to water down the Indians' rum "according to the custom," the commissioners were forced to deal with delegations of angry Cherokees who voiced their own "customary" preference for undiluted liquor.[64]

Though the commissioners occasionally sought to use it to their own advantage, the power of custom proved to be the most formidable obstacle to the public monopoly. Many of the Indians and the South Carolinians began to look back fondly on the days when they could trade with one another without having to abide much interference from the government. Determined parties soon discovered that the public trade's array of restrictions was easy enough to bypass. Colonists who filtered back into the Santee River area in 1716 found the Catawbas eager to unload their deerskins on them, and the agent in charge of the nearby Winyah factory soon began complaining that several local planters were taking his business away by underselling the government.[65] Things were no better for the government agents around Fort Moore, where traders routinely dodged the factors by sending their slaves to deal with the Indians camped out in the surrounding countryside. Authorities tried to crack down on the transgressions of these "evil disposed" traders in December 1716 with "An Additional Act to an Act for the Better Regulation of the Indian Trade," but by then the public monopoly was already beyond saving.[66]

Around this time Alexander MacKay, one of South Carolina's greatest war heroes, did his best to sabotage the government's new system by informing the Cherokees that the commissioners were deliberately supplying them with goods of poor quality.[67] MacKay's controversial outburst showed that questions about the future direction of the Indian trade were beginning to spark passionate divisions among South Carolina's imperialists. Debate over the public monopoly grew even more intense and politicized following South Carolina's settlement with its Muskogean enemies in the fall of 1717, a development that placed the government's remaining "emergency" measures under heavy scrutiny.[68] Convinced that the province's frontiers were now as stable as they were going to get, many of South Carolina's wealthier traders and merchants immediately began to attack the monopoly as an unnecessary affront to their livelihoods.

South Carolina's planters, many of whom had been forced out of the Indian trade as a result of the Yamasee War, tended to support the public trade on the grounds that it gave them enough security to rebuild their agricultural enterprises. It is unlikely, however, that the debate was simply a question of greedy merchants on one side and far-sighted planters on the other.[69] One critic of the monopoly argued that the Indians themselves were "allready Averse to this manner of carrying on the Trade amongst them" and that South Carolina risked losing all its Indian trading partners because it had "engrossed the whole Trade thro a Mercenary and Ignorant Temper."[70] Because so many Indians had clearly become frustrated with the factor system, the continuation of the monopoly raised troubling concerns for many colonists who had no direct financial interest in the Indian trade.[71] By 1718 resistance from a diverse collection of Indians, merchants, planters, and frontiersmen had grown strong enough to help convince the Lords Proprietors to nullify the public monopoly. Though the government factories would remain in place until 1721, they were forced to tolerate legal competition from the private firms whose traders and packhorse men steadily crept back into the picture over the next several years.[72]

As South Carolinians gradually recovered from the Yamasee War, they found themselves wrestling with contradictory impulses on their province's frontiers. They sponsored an expensive new system of forts and semiprofessional troops even as they continued to court the skills and services of their once-and-future Indian allies. They clung to the concept of a tightly regulated, government-sponsored Indian trade even as they showed a renewed interest in the kind of largely unfettered traffic that had fueled the province's earlier expansion. Though puzzling at first glance, these paradoxes make more sense in light of the enormous tasks that faced South Carolina's imperialists during and immediately after the Yamasee War. Most of these men yearned for a return to their prewar glory days, but their dreams were clouded by abundant evidence that they no longer cut the same imposing figure among the Indians, their imperial rivals, or even their fellow British subjects.

Intercolonial Relations and "Royalization"

For all its dramatic effects on South Carolina's Indian alliance network, the Yamasee War did almost as much to transform the province's place within Britain's fledgling colonial empire. In the first fifteen years of the eighteenth century, South Carolina's burgeoning economy and rapid imperial expansion had helped establish it as the most dynamic colony in British North America, an accomplishment that did not go unnoticed by the South Carolinians themselves. Queen Anne's War and the Tuscarora campaigns had helped bring them somewhat closer to the concerns of other British colonies, but South Carolina authorities nevertheless found it hard to mask their growing arrogance. Thoroughly convinced of their superiority over the antiquated Virginians and the incompetent North Carolinians, they had even seen fit to test the limits of the mother country's imperial authority. Almost overnight the devastating Indian attacks of 1715 changed South Carolinians from cocky and self-reliant parvenus into desperate and humiliated supplicants. Dire circumstances forced them to accept whatever charity they could obtain during the early stages of the Yamasee War, opening the door to outside influences that would become more and more controversial over the course of South Carolina's gradual recovery.

Though the South Carolinians had managed to keep their heads above water during the first few weeks of the war, their efforts left them exhausted, confused, and frightened enough to feel a pressing need for outside assistance. When the assembly convened in early May, some of its first resolutions were to send agents as far north as New England in search of arms, provisions, and troops.[73] These measures did little to put anyone's mind at ease, for the South Carolinians could hardly have expected that their requests would be granted. Their recent assistance to the North Carolinians in the Tuscarora War had been something of an anomaly in colonial diplomacy. As of 1715 the weight of precedent was still *against* intercolonial cooperation. Among recent failures to cooperate were the New York–New England disputes during King Philip's and King William's Wars and the North Carolina–Virginia impasse during the Tuscarora War.[74] As the South Carolinians began to show signs of unraveling in the late spring, there remained a distinct possibility that their pleas for aid might fall victim to the British colonists' notorious reluctance "to undertake anything for the relief of their Neighbours."[75]

Upon receiving the news of the southeastern Indians' violent offensives, some colonists had precious little sympathy to spare for the South Carolinians. The materialistic appetites of the South Carolinians had become well known in colonial circles, as had their aggressive stance toward their Indian allies. Cotton Mather, the irrepressible spokesman of Puritan Massachusetts, pronounced that the South Carolinians had been punished "by the dreadful Judgments of God," and the Reverend William Andrews of New York concluded that the South Carolinians had "brought them [their troubles] upon themselves" through their "crying sins" and abuses.[76] In a more secular vein, William Byrd II almost seemed to revel in the misfortunes of his South Carolinian rivals, denouncing them for their crimes and adding the further insult that he and his fellow Virginians "were in no apprehension of the said Indians, [they] having always well treated them."[77]

Throughout Britain's North American colonies, a number of concerned officials expressed their dismay over the prevailing climates of self-interest. In North Carolina SPG missionary Jonathan Urmstone noted that many colonists were "unwilling to pay or return kindness" even though they were "still indebted to them [the South Carolinians] for their kind assistance in large sums."[78] In Virginia a sympathetic Alexander Spotswood found himself locked in a struggle with the most contentious and tightfisted assembly of his administration.[79] New York's governor Robert Hunter experienced similar problems with his own legislature, and his attempts to send Iroquois warriors to assist the South Carolinians were actively discouraged by New York's Indian traders, a group "more intent on their private profitt than the public good."[80] Hunter's situation bore striking similarities to Craven's dispute with the South Carolina traders in 1712, another indication that the cause of intercolonial unity had not made much progress in the years since the Tuscarora War.

This general reluctance to rush to South Carolina's aid did not necessarily mean that most British colonists were completely insensitive to the plight of the South Carolinians. Whether read in the *Boston News-Letter* or overheard at the local tavern, stories of the Pocotaligo massacre and the devastation of Saint Bartholomew's Parish were bound to stir unpleasant memories within colonies that were not too far removed from their own Indian wars. In such a context a colonist's sympathy for the South Carolinians could easily translate into a concern for his or her own safety. From North Carolina to New York, officials responded to news of the Yamasee War by examining the situations on their own frontiers and deciding that they had "too much reason to fear the worst."[81] Citing a number of mysterious movements among the Iroquois and the "Canada Indians," many colonists began to fear the existence of a "continental conspiracy" designed to drive all the British into the sea. As colonial authorities nervously took stock of their own military supplies, they acquired a convenient and plausible excuse to rebuff the South Carolinians' requests for material assistance.[82]

At the same time, however, some colonists were able to follow their fears to an altogether different conclusion: that aiding South Carolina in the short run would lead to greater security for all the British colonies in the long run. The most eloquent advocate of this new imperial logic was Alexander Spotswood, who saw the Yamasee War as an ideal opportunity to implement the kind of agenda that he had unsuccessfully pursued during the Tuscarora War. Unlike his cavalier councilman William Byrd—who was safely across the ocean on a business trip—Spotswood expressed great concern for Virginia's safety. Though his fears of a widespread "heathenish Combination" left him wary of sending too much materiel out of the province, Spotswood resisted the urge to retreat completely into a defensive shell.[83] He felt that a South Carolinian victory was the only way to preserve the aura of invincibility that was protecting all of Britain's North American colonies from the powerful Indian societies of the interior. To that end Spotswood sent messages to the governors of Maryland, Pennsylvania, and New York, urging them to send relief ships to South Carolina and join the Virginians in a united front against the Iroquois.[84] Correctly assuming that some governors might "think that the providing for the Security of their respective Provinces [was] all that [was] incumbent upon them," he also asked Whitehall to issue a royal order for better cooperation between colonial governments.[85] Unfortunately for Spotswood and South Carolina, no such orders were forthcoming. By the end of South Carolina's miserable summer, most of the British colonies had provided next to nothing in the way of meaningful assistance.[86]

Not surprisingly most of South Carolina's wartime aid came from its southeastern neighbors. With uncomfortably close views of some of the action, the

North Carolinians and the Virginians could find more reasons than others to lend a hand to the people who had previously acted as their most ardent colonial rivals. The North Carolinians, still licking their wounds from their last Indian war, grew fearful that South Carolina's enemies might spark another string of uprisings from the Corees, the Cape Fears, and other local Indians.[87] Despite some resistance from his legislature, North Carolina governor Charles Eden decided to act aggressively. In early July he ordered 150 militia troops and 70 "friendly" Tuscarora warriors to link up with Craven and 200 South Carolinian troops on a joint expedition through the Piedmont.[88]

The Virginia council also adopted a firm response to the crises on the Southeast's frontiers. In the second week of July, HMS *Valour* arrived in Charles Town Harbor from Virginia with 120 men, twenty-five casks of bullets, ten barrels of powder, 160 muskets, and promises for an additional 200 troops in the coming months.[89] This unprecedented display of generosity was a testament to Governor Spotswood's political skills. When the burgesses expressed their dismay over his rising expenditures, Spotswood responded by alternately flattering them, insulting them, and appealing to their notorious sense of self-interest. Assisting the South Carolinians was not only a question of preventing "Savage Pagans" from "inhumanely Butchering and Torturing [their] Brethren" but also an ideal opportunity "to acquire Glory, and appear to the Heathen the most formidable Dominion in America." In the long run this reputation would suffice to protect Virginia "better than some hundreds of Rangers kept in pay upon the frontiers."[90] For all his talk of a more unified British Empire, Spotswood continued to believe in his province's superiority and remained watchful for any chance to reassert Virginia's imperial leadership in the Southeast.

The South Carolinians had already begun to suspect that the Virginians' motives for helping them were not entirely altruistic. In early June 1715, South Carolina's Arthur Middleton traveled to Williamsburg to make arrangements for Virginia's entry into the war and emerged with a contract that seemed close to extortionate. The Virginia council began by informing Middleton that they could send as many as three hundred men to South Carolina, depending on how many Virginians they could recruit for such hazardous duty. In return Middleton's government would have to pay for the Virginians' salaries, transportation, food, and clothing: a coat, two shirts, stockings, and shoes. The council attempted to soften the terms by agreeing to feed the troops for as long as they remained in Virginia but quickly moved on to the most important part of the deal: the South Carolinians would also have to agree to send up a female black slave for every Virginian hired into their army. Any slave children born in Virginia would automatically become the property of their mothers' temporary masters. Middleton consented to this hard bargain and possibly proposed some of its clauses. Still, it is likely that he did so only out of desperation and with more than a little resentment toward his benefactors.[91]

As South Carolina's military outlook began to improve toward the end of 1715, the Virginians began to wonder if Middleton and his colleagues had ever intended to honor their part of the contract. The South Carolina government continued to ask for men, but a disappointed Spotswood vehemently denied these requests because of the "poor usage of those already sent."[92] Virginia's governor had begun to hear grievances from a number of his subjects who resented serving under South Carolinian officers or receiving payment in devalued South Carolina currency. The South Carolinians had also been lax in sending their slaves, prompting Virginia's planters and overworked farm wives to complain that Spotswood had "conspired to kidnap them [their servants and husbands] into the Service of another Province."[93] Faced with the impatient queries of the Virginia government, the South Carolinians initially attempted to seek refuge in excuses, claiming that they lacked the money to support the Virginian troops and could not afford to send the female slaves "by reason of the Discontent such Usage would have given their husbands."[94]

While the demands of the war made it difficult for the South Carolinians to uphold their arrangement with Virginia, other factors were probably at work as well. As the Virginians' assistance became less urgent, the South Carolinians decided that they could afford to renege on a contract that had never sat well with them. They certainly had few—if any—qualms about upsetting the Virginia government. South Carolinians had initially responded to Spotswood's "honourable" assistance with humble gratitude, but within a few months they grew more inclined to display some of their old contempt for their Virginian rivals.[95] In response to Spotswood's inaccurate claims that Virginia's troops had repeatedly "saved" South Carolina from its enemies, South Carolinians dismissed the Virginians as "poor Ragged fellows . . . unservicable and unexperienced in Armes."[96] According to one bemused South Carolinian, Virginia's soldiers were "the most ignorant creeping naked people that ever was seen for such a number together . . . many of them did not know how to load a gun and some of them did confess that they never did fire one." Virginia's gift of weapons had proven equally laughable, "so broke and out of order that above 3/4 of them were sent to the smiths to be mended."[97] Outraged, the Virginia council briefly considered confiscating the few South Carolinian slaves who had made their way into the province but eventually resorted to petitioning the home government, much as they had done during their prewar trade disputes with South Carolina.[98] Spotswood angrily vowed to make the South Carolinians look "as odious as he could both at home in England and in all the King's Governments in America" and warned that the South Carolinians' deplorable conduct would have an "ill Effect upon the dispositions of other Governments to assist one another on like occasions."[99]

The troop controversy dealt a crippling blow to Spotswood's vision of inter-colonial cooperation, but the South Carolinians' imperial fortunes remained closely tied to those of the Virginians as the Yamasee War dragged on. Though the South Carolinians would never acknowledge any kind of debt to Spots-wood, some of their most important efforts at frontier recovery bore a suspi-cious resemblance to models that had already been implemented by the Virginia governor. In 1714 Spotswood had unveiled a package of ambitious innovations for Virginia's frontier security, including a fort/trading post near the province's fall line, a "garrison town" of German immigrants who could double as frontier rangers, and a new joint-stock company that gave the gov-ernment an effective monopoly over Virginia's Indian trade.[100] Opposition to the public trade was even more vociferous in Virginia than in South Carolina; in addition to facing the predictable complaints from mercantile interests, Spotswood had to contend with unbloodied critics who had trouble under-standing the concepts and consequences of trade abuse and trade regulation. Most of Spotswood's frontier initiatives would eventually be struck down by the House of Burgesses and the Board of Trade at about the same time the Lords Proprietors were deciding to nullify South Carolina's government trade monopoly.[101]

Despite their basic similarities in direction, the South Carolina and Virginia governments found more room for argument than agreement in the realm of Indian affairs. Even as they looked on the Virginians as potential saviors in the summer of 1715, some South Carolinians had "too much Reason to fear that their private Indian Traders [would] have more regard to their own gain, than the Security of their distressed Neighbours."[102] While officials bickered over the use of the Virginia troops, they also argued over allegations that sev-eral Virginia traders had instigated and supplied some of South Carolina's Indian enemies.[103] It was not long before the South Carolinians' accusations of treachery began to extend to the Virginia government itself. Still resent-ful of the Virginians for their "neutral" role in the Tuscarora War, the South Carolinians' worried that Virginia would seize the war as an opportunity to "engross" its Indian trade and arrange separate treaties with hostile Indian groups, thereby supplying the Indians with the wherewithal to prolong their war against South Carolina. [104] These fears were never realized, mainly because the Virginia government was unwilling to go that far to achieve an advantage over its rivals. When some of the Piedmont Indians began to approach the Virginians in search of a favorable peace, South Carolina officials were present at the negotiations, forcing the Indians to realize that they would have to agree to South Carolina's terms in order to secure their desired supply of English trade goods. [105]

This truce between the two colonial rivals proved short-lived, however. As peace gradually returned to the Piedmont and mountains in 1716, the South Carolina–Virginia trade dispute began to resume its prewar intensity. With both governments running public trade monopolies, the imperial stakes of the contest seemed even higher this time around. The South Carolinians—fresh from their recent disasters—were especially eager to achieve a semblance of control over their newly reconciled allies. To the South Carolinians' consternation, the Virginia traders among the Catawbas managed to acquire twice as many deerskins in the period 1716–18 as they had in the entire decade before the Yamasee War. [106] This startling run of success convinced South Carolina officials that their authority among the Indians was in jeopardy and inspired them to employ certain South Carolina traders as spies against their Virginia counterparts. [107] The reports of Eleazar Wiggan and other semisecret agents proved instrumental in persuading the Board of Indian Trade Commissioners to alter some of its policies. The gradual phasing out of Indian burden bearers, the implementation of across-the-board price reductions, and the collapse of Spotswood's frontier policies all combined to help the South Carolinians regain and widen their advantage over the Virginians in the next several years. [108]

In general the Yamasee War and its immediate aftermath did little to improve diplomatic relations between the South Carolina and the Virginia government. [109] Troubling enough in times of peace, their rivalry became even more disruptive in times of military crisis, when mutual jealousies and suspicions could occasionally make the South Carolinians and Virginians seem like their own worst enemies. Indeed, the two groups of colonists continued to bristle at each other long after they had stopped fighting against most of the region's Indians. By 1720 their quarrels had become so exasperating that imperial authorities in London finally ordered the South Carolina and Virginia governors to patch up their differences and put their diplomatic affairs on a more common footing. [110] Ultimately the only things that prevented this fierce intercolonial rivalry from escalating even further in the years after the Yamasee War were the Virginians' gradual retreat from southeastern frontier affairs and the South Carolinians' growing respect for the directives of the royal government.

Prior to the outbreak of the Yamasee War, the relationship between South Carolinians and the imperial hierarchy in London had been tepid at best. By taking Virginia's side in its trade dispute with South Carolina, Whitehall had only confirmed the South Carolinians' wariness over the disruptive powers of the British Crown. The Indian assaults of 1715 quickly changed the South Carolinians' perceptions, forcing them to acknowledge the Board of Trade as a lifesaver instead of an obstacle. Realizing that other colonial governments might prove reluctant to help them, South Carolinians agreed with George Rodd's assertion that it was "up to Kings and great men to protect their states from falling into the hands of pagans and barbarians."[111] In early May the South Carolina assembly voted to "humbly supplicate" the newly crowned George I to order his royal colonies "to give [them] such a timely Assistance of Men and Arms as they [were] capable of Affording."[112] The assembly also dispatched former council member Richard Berresford as an official agent to London, where he joined several South Carolina merchants in begging direct assistance from the British government. As the South Carolinians submitted their requests for five hundred men, three hundred barrels of powder, fifteen hundred muskets, forty mortars, six field pieces, and twelve months' provisions, they took care to present themselves as loyal "subjects of Great Britain," abandoning all signs of their former truculence.[113]

Mingled with the South Carolinians' pleas for royal assistance were indictments against the Lords Proprietors, the small clique of noblemen who officially owned and ruled the colony. Many of Britain's imperial officials had long been in the habit of castigating proprietary governments for their refusal to "take any due care for their own defense and security against an enemy."[114] These accusations were apparently confirmed by the Carolina proprietors' negligible responses to Queen Anne's War and the Tuscarora insurgency. South Carolinians were well acquainted with the proprietors' inability or refusal to send adequate military assistance in times of need, and on at least one occasion they had appealed over the proprietors' heads for royal protection.[115] Reluctant to compromise their considerable leeway in imperial affairs, the South Carolinians refused to follow up on this petition once they realized that they had gained the upper hand in Queen Anne's War. Six years later, however, the southeastern Indians were able to do what the French and the Spanish could not. By August 1715 South Carolina officials felt desperate enough to take another crucial step toward the royal government. Convinced that the proprietors were "not capable of supporting [them] in a Warr of this nature," the South Carolina Commons House announced its intention to "unanimously throw [themselves] under [his] Majesties imediate protection."[116]

Back in London discussions about "royalizing" the South Carolina government were already under way. As reports of South Carolina's crisis began to reach the metropolis in the first week of July, the Board of Trade was disturbed enough to organize an official inquiry into the province's military, economic, and political situation. [117] The testimony of Lords Ashley and Carteret—the most organized and informed of the Carolina proprietors—did little to inspire the board's confidence. In addition to displaying a shocking ignorance of British military policy, the proprietors admitted that they lacked the funds to purchase or transport the necessary supplies for their suffering province. When the board asked them if they would offer their charter as collateral for government credit, the proprietors claimed that they would only do it "for an equitable consideration and not otherwise."[118] This blatant act of moneygrubbing helped convince the board that South Carolina's proprietors were "not able, or at least not inclined" to assist their subjects and that "so valuable a Province" deserved the kind of care that only the king's government could provide.[119] Before they could pursue this recommendation, however, members of the Board of Trade and the Privy Council ran into an immovable obstacle in Parliament, where Whiggish delegates rallied around the proprietors' "vested rights" to their charters. This impasse would drag on for several years, leaving South Carolina's political future up in the air and effectively preventing any relief ships from leaving the British Isles. [120]

South Carolina's constitutional crisis continued to escalate even as its military prospects gradually improved. Throughout the years 1716–18, the South Carolina Commons House continued to send its uncharacteristically groveling petitions to the king, providing further evidence that many South Carolinians had come to perceive royal protection as a long-term solution for the province's security. [121] At the same time the Lords Proprietors—stirred by the military threat to their colony and the political threat to their titles—were attempting to reassert the authority and responsibility that they had previously neglected. [122] By now they certainly knew that a growing number of South Carolinians were lining up against them, ready to protest any measures that the proprietors might propose. Instead of heeding the "insolent" warnings of Joseph Boone and Richard Berresford, the South Carolina assembly's agents in London, the proprietors chose to believe what their secretary and a few sympathetic merchants told them: that they were powerful enough to impose their will on any recalcitrant subjects.[123]

In their political struggle against the South Carolina Commons House, the proprietors' greatest weapon was their power to veto or nullify any measures passed by the colonial government. Having failed to exercise this power in the previous twenty years, the proprietors decided to reestablish it at the worst possible time, challenging acts that were designed to expedite South Carolina's recovery from the Yamasee War. The proprietors' veto of the public Indian trade in 1718 is often cited as their most egregious intrusion into the colony's imperial affairs, but in reality they took this step with the tacit approval of the British government and a considerable segment of South Carolina's population.[124] Far less forgivable was the proprietors' opposition to the "Act to Appropriate the Yamasee Lands," the Commons House's plans to transform the Yamasees' abandoned reservation into a defensive zone peopled by Protestant immigrants from Great Britain and the West Indies. The assembly ratified the act in June 1716 based on the principle that immigration "enriches in times of peace" and "strengthens in time of war," and that South Carolina's security would be improved if colonists settled closer to one another.[125] Despite South Carolina's crying need to recruit new settlers, the act was nullified as an unlawful "Encroachment upon the property of . . . the Lords proprietors," who later announced their intention to turn the Yamasee lands into personal "baronies."[126] The proprietors insisted that they would be better equipped to sponsor any projects of colonization, but their excuses rang hollow, and their plans struck almost everyone as an impractical and insensitive solution to South Carolina's reconstruction needs.[127]

By 1719 the proprietors were on decidedly shaky ground within South Carolina, not so much for any particular policy as for their general callousness toward the colonists' predicaments. While the proprietors tended to dismiss the complaints against them as "the business of a faction and party," their opposition had actually spread well beyond the parameters of a typical political struggle.[128] South Carolina's rival political factions had been approaching a "unified anti-Proprietary 'harmony'" since the latter stages of Queen Anne's War, and the Yamasee War only served to reduce the proprietors' support even further.[129] According to the proprietors, the South Carolina Commons House was exaggerating the province's plight in order to advance its own antiproprietary agenda. Though the proprietors probably had just cause to suspect the colonists of harboring ulterior motives in their petitions to King George, they made a grave mistake in underestimating the level of fear and paranoia that had gripped the South Carolinians during the Yamasee War. As far as the proprietors were concerned, the war had ended with the South Carolina–Cherokee alliance of early 1716, and at no point in the struggle had the province been "in so apparent a danger of being lost, as was suggested."[130] Though some colonists were admitting by 1717 that things had finally become "pretty Easy in relation to the Indian war," a number of private and official observations suggested that the insecurity and economic instability brought on by the war were continuing to weigh heavily on the minds of many South Carolinians.[131]

According to the South Carolina merchant Francis Yonge, the colonists' most serious gripe against the proprietors was "the same thing that made them not fear them, i.e. their Inability to succour and protect them, either from their own Intestine Enemies, the *Indians*, or from the *Spaniards*, with whom at that time there was a War."[132] The outbreak of another war in Europe caused grave concern among South Carolinians, who worried about the apparent resurgence of their enemies in Louisiana and Florida. Concern turned to panic in the early summer of 1719, when a South Carolinian spy in Cuba learned that the Spanish were planning to invade the province with an army of six hundred Indians and a fleet from Havana.[133] The Franco-Spanish battle over Pensacola diverted this invasion force at the last minute, but the South Carolinians' hysteria was bolstered by another disturbing rumor: that the Lords Proprietors were unconcerned about the Spanish invasion, feeling that "if the Inhabitants were destroyed the Country might be settled by a better People."[134] Whether unfounded or not, rumors could fuel heated emotions and reactions among the South Carolinians, just as they had among the southeastern Indians prior to the Yamasee War. This climate of rumor and resentment—combined with a rash order to dissolve the South Carolina assembly—caused the proprietors to lose their last vestiges of support from the planters, merchants, militia, and practically everyone else who wielded any power within the province.[135]

In December 1719, following a brief struggle that was more comic than violent, a session of the assembly was transformed into a convention to appoint a new governor in the name of King George.[136] Alexander Spotswood was just one of the observers who appeared satisfied with this development, claiming that "if they [the South Carolinians'] Proprietors [were] unable or unwilling to protect them, it [would] deserve the attention of his Majesty's Ministers to preserve so considerable a Province from falling into the hands of a foreign Power."[137] Imperial officials in Whitehall found themselves in complete agreement with Spotswood, and their growing appreciation of South Carolina's economic and strategic value led them to support the kind of political coup against the proprietors that they might not have been willing to condone even ten years earlier.[138] After the Board of Trade gathered memorials from the South Carolina government for evidence in their case against the proprietors, the Privy Council placed South Carolina under the control of the Crown in August 1720. Carolina's proprietors would retain their title to the soil for another nine years, but their role in the colony's government affairs had come to an inglorious end.[139]

South Carolina's "Revolution of 1719" was actually far less sudden or dramatic than its name might suggest. The political struggle against the Lords Proprietors had been building since the days of the first "Goose Creek men" in the early 1680s, and the South Carolinians had begun to make some tentative strides toward the royal government as early as Queen Anne's War.[140] As South Carolina began its new existence as a royal colony, it remained uncertain whether the South Carolinians' supplication before the Crown was genuine or merely a strategy for acquiring enough protection to allow themselves to pursue their old brand of semiautonomous imperialism. Despite these qualifications, however, it is undeniable that South Carolina moved closer to the mainstream of the British Empire between 1715 and 1720, and that the main catalyst for this shift was the economic, political, and psychological fallout from the Yamasee War.[141] In launching their attacks against the province, Indians helped widen the path to a new political identity for the South Carolinians.

The Entrenchment of a White Minority

Political leanings are among the most explicit aspects of a group's identity and are fairly easy to trace through petitions, legislative proceedings, and other written records. The ways in which people perceive themselves in other matters are usually much more difficult to discern. This difficulty holds especially true for the South Carolinians of the early colonial period, a group of people who were not generally inclined to mull over their feelings in writing. More often than not, South Carolinians revealed most about themselves when they confronted groups that they considered threatening to their personal safety or prosperity. South Carolinians had long been accustomed to upholding themselves against outsiders, but at the same time they had been unable to offer any consensus on the proper criteria for "otherness." By presenting the South Carolinians with an array of unprecedented challenges, the Yamasee War managed to recast the issue in terms that seemed a good deal clearer. In so doing the war helped the South Carolinians develop a better sense of how they fit into the Southeast's changing cultural mosaic.

On at least one level, the war's impact on South Carolina society was crystal clear. South Carolinians suffered greatly and often in more ways than one. Several hundred colonists lost their lives as a result of the Yamasees' initial rampages, the early engagements of 1715, and the various raids and skirmishes that continued for years afterward. In killing 7 percent of South Carolina's white population, the Yamasee War compiled a mortality rate nearly twice as high as that of King Philip's War, a conflict that is frequently mentioned as the bloodiest in American history. [142] In many ways the Yamasee War seemed even harder on those colonists who survived, as George Rodd indicated in his vivid letter to London. By the summer of 1715, British authorities could draw a bleak but accurate picture of South Carolinians "driven from their Plantations, imprisoned between mud Walls[,] stifled with excesive heats, oppressed with Famine, sickness, the Desolation of their country [and] Death of their friends, [apprehensive] of their own fate, despairing of Relief, and destitute of any hopes to escape." [143]

Even after the twin risks of Indian warriors and "flux & feaver" began to diminish, South Carolina's weakened condition made recovery an arduous task. With many of the inland settlements damaged by the war and many of the coastal settlements vulnerable to a new epidemic of piracy from the likes of Stede Bonnet and Blackbeard, food was often hard to come by, leaving some colonists "ready to Eat up one another for Want of provisions." [144] Those who could not subsist on their own suffered greatly from inflation. Living on a fixed income from the SPG, Reverend Francis Le Jau lamented in the summer of 1716 that he was being forced to pay "5 or 600 percent" on goods brought from England and the South Carolina countryside. [145] Some of the more indigent colonists—such as Mary Atkins, a lame and sick mother of three young children who had lost her husband and three eldest daughters to the Indians—were forced to seek the charity of their neighbors. [146] Others attempted to establish lines of credit, only to find that "not everybody . . . was willing to trust in such times of distress and danger, not knowing how soon [they would] be forced away." [147] The financial and psychological burdens of the war did indeed prove too great for some colonists. Despite strict laws against emigration, a number of South Carolinians decided that they would "rather choose to leave their Homes and Land . . . than endure a lingering War and an Insupportable Tax." [148] Of the roughly 1,400 white families in South Carolina on the eve of the Yamasee War, 150 disappeared from the province over the next three years, some of them relocating with their slaves to Virginia or the Bahamas. [149]

Those South Carolinians who did not flee the province tended to close ranks and become even more rigid than they had been before the war. One group that had long been disturbed by the hard-driven, materialistic personalities of the South Carolinians was the SPG missionaries. To their way of thinking, the plague of miseries that descended on South Carolina was nothing less than divine punishment for the colonists' "evil Spirit of Covetousness and self Interest," as well as their reluctance to introduce their "heathen" slaves to the gospel. [150] Initially the missionaries hoped that the war would make the South Carolinians' see the error of their ways. In May 1715 Reverend Thomas Hassell found himself riding out the storm with a militia company in one of the plantation garrisons of Saint Thomas's Parish. Attempting to "preach upon such subjects as [were] proper under the . . . dismal circumstances," Hassell found a particular relevance in Leviticus 26:25: "And I will bring a sword upon you, that shall avenge the quarrel of my covenant: and when ye are gathered together within your cities, I will send the pestilence among you, and ye shall be delivered into the hand of the enemy." [151] But unlike many of the New England Puritans who endured the horrors of King Philip's and Queen Anne's Wars, the South Carolinians generally showed little patience for jeremiads. Ministers complained that even in the midst of the most pressing crises, few colonists appeared to be "separating themselves from the Crowd of willful Transgressors." [152] According to Commissary Gideon Johnston, most South Carolinians were "so bent upon Revenge" that they chose to ignore the clergy's exhortations for humility and forgiveness. [153] While numerous South Carolinians did beg God for mercy throughout the Yamasee War, they often found it more practical to beg the rest of the British Empire for the food, money, and ammunition that would allow them to punish their enemies and carry on with the task of rebuilding their lives.

For many South Carolinians begging assistance from anyone was a profoundly unsettling experience. Even before 1715 South Carolinians had grown to distrust various kinds of outsiders. This wariness had often resulted in a confrontational and counterproductive style of diplomacy, but it had also helped South Carolinians smooth over some of the long-standing political and cultural rifts within the province. The various controversies that had threatened to divide the South Carolinians from the 1680s through the early 1700s—Anglicans versus Dissenters, Goose Creek Tories versus Colleton County Whigs, transplanted Barbadians versus Huguenot refugees—became less pressing as the colonists began to shift their concern to their imperial rivals and the new "black majority." [154] The outbreak of the Yamasee War only served to accelerate this trend. As South Carolinians struggled to cope with this unexpected threat to their survival, they became even more particular about distinguishing those people they could trust from those they could not. While South Carolinians continued to argue with one another over certain political issues, they no longer attempted to expel their political opponents from the province. Instead, they reserved exclusion and persecution for those whom they viewed as potential traitors or saboteurs.

The criteria for these categories were not necessarily based on race. As South Carolina officials attempted to entice white immigrants to settle the abandoned Yamasee lands in 1716, they made a point of specifying that only certain kinds of white immigrants would be welcome. They firmly refused to accept "persons of lewd or profligate lives," an obvious attempt to discourage the British government from unloading more of its convicted felons on the province. [155] Unfortunately the South Carolinians were in no position to be so selective. The miseries of the Yamasee War instantly discredited the promotional tracts of Thomas Nairne, John Norris, and other boosters and effectively prevented any prosperous British yeomen from coming to South Carolina of their own volition. Most of the five hundred or so white immigrants who arrived in South Carolina between 1716 and 1720 did so as indentured servants, a group of people who often struck the South Carolina authorities as more trouble than they were worth. [156] Though the Jacobite prisoners stationed at Fort Moore served the province well, other servants tended to shirk their duties or "run away to remote plantations." [157] Irish Catholics seemed especially problematic; one young man named Kelley was even accused of freeing several Indian slaves and fleeing to the Catawbas in early 1717, where he allegedly spread some disturbing rumors about the intentions of the South Carolina government. [158] Later that year the South Carolina assembly was finally persuaded to pass an "Act for Better Governing and Regulating White Servants," a measure that imposed extra service time for any absences and corporal punishment for the smallest of offenses. [159]

The act reserved its harshest penalties for those servants convicted of consorting or absconding with blacks, indicating that South Carolinians were still anxious over the rising number and increasing "insolence" of their slaves. [160] They continued to harbor these anxieties even as they watched the black majority play a major role in defending South Carolina from its enemies. Not only were unprecedented numbers of blacks drafted into the South Carolina militia during the first few months of the Yamasee War; slaves also came to comprise nearly a third of the colony's "professional" army. Some of these slaves were able to parlay their backwoods experience as cattle ranchers and Indian traders into important positions within the military, acting as scouts or translators for some of the most crucial expeditions of the war. [161] Nor did the slaves' skills as frontier soldiers go unnoticed. In confirming his people's alliance with the South Carolinians, one Cherokee leader specifically requested the assistance of thirty black troops, claiming that they would be "very servicable to them in running after the enemy." [162] Reverend Francis Le Jau, a man who harbored many nagging suspicions about the Goose Creek blacks, had to admit that some of the "poor Negroe men" from his parish conducted themselves "bravely and to Admiration upon all Occasions." [163] Other South Carolinians quietly implied that they could never have held out against the Indians without help from their black slaves. [164]

Nevertheless, some colonists expressed strong reservations over the government's decision to furnish black men with weapons. One group of petitioners warned that "there must be great Caution used, lest [their] Slaves when armed might become [their] Masters." [165] For men such as these, the hundreds of slaves who fought with bravery and distinction would always be overshadowed by the relatively few slaves who fled their owners or offered their services to the hostile Indians. As the Yamasee War dragged on, many of the Indian insurgents withdrew further into the southeastern interior and became less threatening to the South Carolinians' security. Meanwhile South Carolina's black population remained firmly rooted in the colonial settlements, their numbers increasing by the day. The vast majority of these slaves served neither with nor against the South Carolinians during the war. Most of them simply carried on with their lives in ways that proved inscrutable to their frustrated and anxious owners.

The government's solution to this mystery was to assume the worst: that all blacks had the potential to "endanger the safety" of South Carolina. [166] Though the Commons House freed at least one slave during the Yamasee War, most of the several hundred blacks who served on behalf of South Carolina were unceremoniously returned to their plantations by the war's end. [167] Authorities passed an act in 1719 that allowed them to recall "Trusty Slaves" into the militia in the event of an emergency, but conventional wisdom still held that blacks were less reliable soldiers than whites. [168] The South Carolina government not only endeavored to keep a grip on the thousands of slaves who were already residing in the province but also continued its earlier efforts at curbing the importation of blacks. Though the Lords Proprietors did not take long to stop viewing the southeastern Indians as a menace, they steadfastly refused to repeal the government's prohibitive duties on slaves, claiming that a new flood of Africans would put all South Carolinians at risk.[169] But just as government legislation had been unable to prevent South Carolinians from illegally trading with the Indians, the stiff import duties could not discourage many South Carolina merchants and planters from placing their own prosperity above the government's concerns. The collapse of the Indian slave trade and a boom in rice production caused the importation of black slaves to skyrocket. By 1717 this traffic had eclipsed its prewar levels, throwing the province's black-white ratio even further out of balance. The ratio stood at about twelve thousand blacks to fifty-six hundred whites in 1720, as opposed to eighty-six hundred blacks to fifty-five hundred whites five years earlier.[170] Unlike South Carolina's native- or West Indian–born slaves, most of these new arrivals came directly from Africa, bringing customs and dialects that made them even more disturbing in the eyes of many South Carolinians.[171]

Nevertheless, most South Carolinians failed to show any new interest in acculturating their slaves. Francis Le Jau happily mentioned that a few Goose Creek planters were allowing their slaves to be baptized and instructed by missionaries, but in general the SPG faced even more obstacles in South Carolina than it had before the war.[172] Half of South Carolina's parishes were torn apart by the early campaigns of the war, and many of the missionaries were left without the kind of financial and moral support that they needed to carry on with their efforts at proselytizing. Most of the missionaries who did attempt to convert South Carolina's blacks found themselves actively discouraged by the slave owners, who were more reluctant than ever to waste their slaves' energy on a project that they had long mistrusted.[173] Colonists were not alone in their suspicion of the missionaries' work. Reverend John Lapiere complained that the greatest impediment to his conversion of the young "Heathen" was "the strong prejudices of them who [were] grown in years," and another missionary admitted that the few slaves who "prayed and read some part of their Bibles in the field and in their Quarters" were facing persecution from "profanne men who laught at their Devotions."[174] By 1720 the rate of slave conversions in South Carolina had slowed from a trickle to a drip.[175]

The travails of the SPG and its scattered slave converts indicated that South Carolinians were continuing to hold blacks at a distance while regarding them as an alien and potentially dangerous group. Given the obvious instability on their Indian frontiers, South Carolinians had even more reason to worry about the omnipresent threat of slave rebellion. Nearly 150 years after the Yamasee War, the distinguished South Carolina historian William Rivers would insist "that a natural antipathy was felt by the Indians against the negroes, and that to their unconquerable aversion the colonists for a long period owed much of their safety." [176] For the colonists themselves, however, a large-scale alliance between blacks and Indians remained a very real and very terrifying possibility. Though South Carolinians were powerless to remove the Indians from their frontiers or the black slaves from their settlements, many of them believed that they could successfully "make Indians and Negro's a cheque upon each other."[177] South Carolina authorities never adopted an official "divide and rule" policy, but they did occasionally suggest certain strategies to that effect: using blacks as Indian fighters, hiring Indians as slave hunters, and restricting slaves' access to the province's frontiers.[178] As long as they could promote tension and discourage cooperation between blacks and Indians, South Carolinians felt that they could survive as a white minority stuck between two hostile majorities.

Blacks and Indians never did combine forces to the extent that many South Carolinians feared, but it would be a mistake to ascribe too much influence to the Machiavellian strategies of the South Carolinians. The notion of "divide and rule" inherently assumes that blacks and Indians could not make important judgments about each other without the help of white intermediaries. There was, in fact, a great deal of direct contact between blacks and Indians both during and after the Yamasee War. Contrary to any assertions of a "natural antipathy" or "natural sympathy" between the two groups, black-Indian interaction in this period never adhered to any hard and fast pattern.[179]

On many occasions blacks and Indians acted with hostility toward one another. Numerous blacks died during the course of the war, whether in the Yamasees' early assaults on Port Royal and Saint Bartholomew's Parish, the Catawba-Cherokee raids on the Santee region, or the violent collapse of Schenkingh's garrison. Indians, for their part, also died at the hands of slaves, such as the forty black troops who took part in South Carolina's lopsided victory in the Battle of the Ponds.[180] Even a number of black noncombatants found themselves drawn into South Carolina's struggle against the Indians. In 1716 a black slave named Buff Moore petitioned the South Carolina Commons House for his freedom on the grounds that he had "made his escape from the Indian enemy." [181] The stories of Moore and several other slaves suggest that at least some Indians had begun to adopt the whites' derogatory opinions of blacks, seizing them as contraband and later attempting to resell them for profit.[182] Indians could also keep black slaves as valuable bargaining chips. As the Lower Creeks attempted to make peace with the South Carolinians in 1717, they offered to return five hundred stolen horses and forty stolen slaves as an act of good faith.[183] Such actions were hardly apt to sow the seeds of harmony between Indians and blacks.

Still, the climate of violence and confusion did not automatically preclude blacks and Indians from establishing close connections during and after the Yamasee War. Soon after the Yamasees launched their initial attacks against the South Carolinians, a small group of black and Indian slaves reportedly attempted to seize the Charles Town powder magazine. Though this failed uprising has led one historian to speculate about a major alliance between the Yamasees and South Carolina's slaves, his theory seems undermined by the fact that the Yamasees killed large numbers of slaves in the early days of the war.[184] At the same time evidence does indicate that small numbers of black and Indian slaves—often singly or in pairs—escaped to the frontiers in order to combine with South Carolina's Indian enemies.[185] Escape was never easy under any circumstances, but in certain parts of South Carolina, a slave's chances improved to some extent after the outbreak of the Yamasee War. When coming to terms with the Virginia and South Carolina governments, the Catawbas were asked to hand over several black and Indian slaves who had settled among them and encouraged their attacks against the South Carolinians.[186] Of the ninety-eight South Carolinian slaves who found freedom in Saint Augustine during the second half of 1715, most came from the estates of John Barnwell, John Cochran, Robert Graham, William Bray, and other Port Royal planters.[187] In all likelihood none of these slaves could have completed his overland journey to Florida without the active—or even forceful—assistance of the Yamasees, the same Indians who had formerly served as South Carolina's most valued slave hunters.[188] By 1720 the specter of the Yamasee "kidnappers" was still strong enough to discourage many South Carolinians from bringing slaves into the Port Royal region, fanning a sense of insecurity that would persist well into the next decade.[189]

The unpredictability of black-Indian relations was reflected in an incident that rocked South Carolina in the spring of 1720. On May 6, a group of black slaves escaped from a plantation on the Upper Ashley River and killed three members of a nearby white family. Terrified South Carolinians soon began to believe that this minor insurrection was part of a much larger plot designed to extend throughout the countryside and into Charles Town. As the South Carolinians rounded up an unspecified number of slave "conspirators" on dubious evidence, a small group of Waccamaw Indians on the Santee River made matters worse by taking up arms against the local colonists. Though the Waccamaws were quickly subdued and enslaved by a combined force of South

Carolinians and Winyah Indians, the timing of the Waccamaw insurrection raised some disturbing speculations about black-Indian solidarity. [190] Shortly thereafter, however, some of these fears were allayed by the news that fourteen fugitives from the black "uprising" had shown up "half starved" at Fort Moore following their unsuccessful attempt to persuade some Lower Creek Indians to "pylott" them to Saint Augustine. [191]

Though the South Carolinians expressed relief at this outcome, their behavior in the wake of the 1720 insurrections showed that there were no easy solutions to their lingering paranoia. Brutal punishments of the slave "conspirators" and additional restrictions on slave behavior could not help the South Carolinians nor could their appeals to their royal protector. While South Carolinians continued to worry about some of their recent Indian enemies, many of them also remained convinced that the "whole Province was . . . in danger of being Massacred by their Own Slaves." [192] South Carolinians had sought to take precautions against the supposedly "barbarous natures" of their slaves as early as the 1690s, but their fears had never been quite as vivid or explicit as they were in the aftermath of the Yamasee War. By the early 1720s fears of "Secret Poisonings and bloody Insurrections" had become so rampant that South Carolinians were more reluctant than ever to trust their slaves. One SPG missionary caustically noted that it would be "almost impracticable to convert any but here and there a favourite house Slave." [193] If the South Carolinians' supposedly trustworthy Indian allies could turn against them in the blink of an eye, who could pretend to know what further atrocities lay in store?

Five years after the outbreak of the Yamasee War, the South Carolinians' traditional mistrust of outsiders had begun to soften in some ways and harden in others. The backbreaking challenges of the war quickly forced South Carolinians to realize that they could no longer afford to keep everyone but their closest cronies at bay. Their concept of the people they could rely on became somewhat more inclusive; by 1720 many South Carolinians were more willing to cooperate with other British subjects. At the same time, however, the Yamasee War also caused South Carolinians to grow even more suspicious of those groups that did not fit this bill: not only blacks and Indians but also Britain's traditional "Papist" enemies. South Carolinians became less inclined to perceive white Anglo-Saxon Protestants as potentially hostile "foreigners," but all the while they continued to display a sense of wariness that even "royalization" was powerless to expunge. Though they would never again assert their autonomy as starkly or forcefully as they had in the years immediately before the Yamasee War, South Carolinians still believed that they would have to count primarily on themselves.

Despite the early concerns of George Rodd and other colonists, South Carolina's world was not turned upside down by its Indian attackers. South Carolinians managed to keep upright and afloat through the worst parts of the storm, but only because they were able to make some important changes in their course. In cases where these changes clearly contributed to the strength and security of the province—such as the adoption of a more professional military system or the overthrow of the proprietors—South Carolinians had little trouble deciding to make them. Some changes—such as martial law and the public monopoly on the Indian trade—were far less palatable to many South Carolinians but proved easy enough to reverse when people became too uncomfortable with them. Other changes, however, were far more difficult to control. Many South Carolinians were dragged kicking and screaming into their "acceptance" of higher taxes, intrusions from other governments, and the renewed influx of African slaves. As far as most South Carolinians were concerned, these negative influences far outweighed any constructive changes that might have been inspired by the Yamasee War. During their first forty-five years in South Carolina, colonists had grown accustomed to doing things on their own terms. With their sudden and frightening assaults, the Yamasees, the Catawbas, and other Indians instantly dispelled the colonists' illusions of control by pushing the South Carolinians into the kind of unpredictable free fall that they had always dreaded but never really expected.

The Yamasee War's greatest impact on South Carolinians was in demonstrating that they did not fit the high standards that they had built for themselves. The war left deep emotional scars that were probably made even worse by the South Carolinians' general unwillingness to acknowledge their pain. Despite everything they had endured in the space of five years, most South Carolinians were not about to make apologies for being an extremely ambitious group of people willing to advance their fortunes at the expense of others. The painful setbacks of the war only made some of them more determined than ever to slam the lid on their boiling frontiers and renew their quest for control. Their various adjustments to the damages wrought by the war were an important step toward realizing this aim, but they were only half the battle. As South Carolina imperialists attempted to reassert their authority during their first decade as champions of a new royal colony, they would be forced to learn that the different groups they hoped to court or intimidate had undergone important changes of their own.

6. Distances Bridged and Widened

WARTIME ADJUSTMENTS OF THE SOUTHEASTERN INDIANS

Shortly after the outbreak of the Yamasee War, many observers considered the South Carolinians to be at a distinct disadvantage. While the South Carolina government could place no more than fifteen hundred men in the field, it was widely assumed that the "enemy" included anywhere from three thousand to seventeen thousand elusive, highly trained killers. [1] These odds seemed even more lopsided in light of the South Carolinians' tendency to exaggerate the power and cohesiveness of the Indians who attacked them. Their mistaken assumptions eventually helped give rise to another commonly held misconception about the Yamasee War: that the Indians began the fight with the upper hand, only to be foiled by their own organizational and tactical shortcomings. In truth not all the southeastern Indians were interested in destroying South Carolina, and those who did take on the task faced an extremely daunting challenge.

The South Carolinians bore little resemblance to the Mobilians, the Tohomes, the Timucuans, or any other groups that had provided easy targets for Ochese, Tallapoosa, and Yamasee warriors in the previous twenty years. Though the Carolinians had regularly delegated many of their military tasks to their Indian allies, they remained better armed than their Indian adversaries and ruthlessly committed to holding their ground. Once the Indian insurgents lost the advantage of surprise, their chances for success became even more remote. It did not take long for them to discover that the South Carolinians could inflict punishment even better than they could absorb it.

South Carolinians were not the only people who had something to lose from participating in the Yamasee War. The various attacks and reprisals of 1715 triggered a cycle of disruption and devastation that spread throughout the entire southeastern frontier complex. In the years prior to the Yamasee War, most of the Southeast's Indian societies had grown all too familiar with intertribal violence, and many of them had faced disturbing threats from colonial imperialists. When Indians joined the war against the South Carolinians, however, they often traded one kind of vulnerability for another. If they managed to rid their villages of abusive intruders and avoid punishment from vengeful colonists, they often had to fend off attacks from Indian enemies without the benefit of valuable material assistance from the South Carolinians. Even those Indians who stayed out of the fray or withdrew during its early stages found themselves sucked into the widening whirlpool of the Yamasee War, struggling under the weight of old and new pressures.

The disruptive effects of warfare and colonial expansion had never extended equally throughout the Southeast, and the Yamasee War proved no exception. Just as the war seemed to have no hard and fast conclusion for the South Carolinians, many of the Southeast's Indian societies also found their status up in the air. The Yamasee War proved far longer and more destructive for some groups of Indians than for others, but nearly all of the region's Indian societies had to make adjustments, many of them even more drastic than those made by the South Carolinians. Between 1715 and 1720 Indians had to look for new homes, new allies, and new ways of procuring the goods that were growing more and more essential to their security. As the southeastern Indians sought these things, they not only altered the shapes of their own societies but also helped redraw the parameters of the region's ongoing imperial struggle. Groups like the Yamasees, the Cherokees, the Catawbas, and the so-called Creeks emerged from the Yamasee War with markedly different outlooks, causing more frustration for those colonists who continued to search for a single, overarching solution to the various problems associated with frontier exchange.

The Yamasees

The Yamasee Indians fully deserved to have the war named after them. After setting the entire conflict in motion, they proceeded to fight longer and harder than any other group. It had taken years of broken promises and painful second-guessing for the Yamasees to grow disillusioned with their English partners, but once they had been pushed past the breaking point, many of them regarded the South Carolinians with naked and unwavering hatred. Though the Yamasees probably had no immediate plans for a full-scale assault on Charles Town in April 1715, they did prepare for an extended push against the South Carolina settlements. The Yamasees' initial attacks on Port Royal and

Saint Bartholomew's Parish unfolded more like raids than typical marches of conquest, but they also formed the closest thing to an "invasion" that the South Carolinians had to endure during the entire war.

As the Yamasees regrouped for another offensive, they also began to prepare for the inevitable South Carolinian counterattack. These defensive preparations marked the Yamasees' first major adjustment of the war. The Yamasees had not been forced to fend off an invasion since the collapse of Guale in the 1680s, and most of their younger warriors had no firsthand experience in defensive tactics. Despite this disadvantage the Yamasees managed to get off to an impressive start. In a little over a week, Yamasee war chiefs assembled a force of several hundred fighting men near their northernmost town of Salkehatchie and set their remaining warriors to fortifying some of their encampments. South Carolinian accounts suggest that several hundred Yamasees sought refuge in camps surrounded by wooden palisades, and at least one report claims that the Yamasees began to build a large, two-acre fort but did not have enough time to complete it before the arrival of the South Carolinian forces. [2] Though the Yamasees had never used fortifications on their South Carolina "reservation," some of them had lived near small Spanish forts in Guale and Apalachee, and others had seen the Tuscaroras make effective use of forts in their war against North Carolina. Had the Yamasees been able to spend more time working on their own fortifications, their resistance to the South Carolinians might have proven more successful.

Though the Yamasees later attempted to claim victory in the engagement outside Salkehatchie, they found it impossible to put a positive spin on the capture and destruction of their unfinished forts.[3] By the end of April the South Carolinians had killed or enslaved as many as three hundred Yamasees, nearly one-fourth of the tribe's total population.[4] Heavy by any standards, these losses proved especially difficult for a group of people who had always taken great care to minimize their military casualties. This serious setback did not force the Yamasees to concede defeat, but it did convince them to evacuate the area that had been their home for the previous eight years. By early May all the remaining Yamasees had disappeared from the Combahee-Savannah basin and moved south toward the Altamaha River, one of their several ancestral homelands. [5] But just as enemy raids had forced the dispersal of La Tama in the 1660s and 1670s, the Yamasees of 1715 found it equally difficult to put down permanent roots on the Altamaha. Once again the Yamasees had become refugees, a harried and hunted group of people on the verge of splintering in several different directions.

The Yamasees had frequently interacted with the Apalachees, the Apalachicolas, and the Ocheses even before the outbreak of the war, and the Yamasees' brief respite on the Altamaha allowed them to get closer—both geographically and emotionally—to these other groups. But even though the Yamasees shared a common enmity for the South Carolinians, they were not of a single mind when it came to dealing with their Indian allies. Some Yamasees proved more willing than others to establish closer ties to the Muskogean and Hitichi groups along the Savannah and Ocmulgee rivers. Indeed, a significant percentage of the Yamasees—perhaps as many as one-third of them—chose to settle among the other groups and lend their assistance to an Ochese-directed war effort.[6] Most of the Yamasees, however, hesitated to make concessions to other groups of Indians. Though Yamasee headmen willingly communicated with Ochese and Apalachicola leaders, several of them felt that they might find better land and more supplies by moving closer to the Spanish. Bearing messages of goodwill from the "great cacique of Coweta," the headmen of the Yamasee towns of Yoa, Pocotaligo, Ocute, Pocosabo, and Altamaha ushered several hundred of their people to Saint Augustine during the late spring and early summer of 1715.[7] Wary of all outsiders, the leader of the Huspah Yamasees temporarily remained in limbo on the Altamaha but finally headed down to Florida in the fall, barely avoiding a South Carolinian expedition that had set out to seize him.[8]

After the small force commanded by Lieutenant Governor Robert Daniel failed to find anyone on the Altamaha, the South Carolinians felt that they had been duped by their informants and temporarily found themselves at a loss to explain just what had happened to the Yamasees.[9] Many of them suspected some kind of collusion with the Spanish, a suspicion that was confirmed several months later when a second South Carolinian expedition succeeded in capturing the "Yoa King" and thirty other Yamasees on the outskirts of Saint Augustine.[10] Though the Yamasees no longer posed the same kind of threat that they had a year earlier, the South Carolinians expressed dismay at the reports that began to reach them in the spring of 1716. Hugh Bryan, a Port Royal planter who had been held captive by the Yamasees in Saint Augustine for nearly a year, testified that he had "been an Eye-witness to the Spaniards furnishing the Yamasees with whatever they wanted to carry on the War against [the South Carolinians]."[11] For once the South Carolinians had good reason to suspect the Spanish. Emboldened by a royal donation of six thousand pesos and one thousand firearms, Florida authorities had begun to provide the Yamasees with weapons and purchase captives from them.[12] When South Carolina's James

Cochran paid an official visit to Saint Augustine in the summer of 1716, he was outraged to find several of his "kidnapped" slaves there. Florida officials attempted to tiptoe around the issue, but the Yamasees themselves readily admitted to their new arrangement with the Spanish.[13] They seemed to know that nothing short of a costly and unlikely war between Great Britain and Spain could remove them from their new home.

From the Yamasees' standpoint, their alliance with the Spanish almost marked a return to business as usual. Even if the Yamasees could no longer hope to force the English out of South Carolina, they could make a respectable living at the expense of their former employers. Every plantation the Yamasees raided and every slave they "liberated" reminded them of the respect and importance that they had commanded during their early years in South Carolina.[14] Those Yamasees who came to Saint Augustine in search of Spanish protection achieved a special status and initially remained somewhat aloof from the other Indians in the area. According to a census conducted by the Spanish in 1717, the Yamasees worked hard to preserve elements of their old political structure, entrusting each of their settlements to the care of a principal headman and several distinguished advisors. They settled almost exclusively with other Yamasees, usually alongside men, women, and children from their old towns in South Carolina. Perhaps most importantly, most of the Yamasees also proved extremely slow or reluctant to adopt Christianity. While 86 percent of the Guales, Timucuans, and Apalachees living around Saint Augustine were listed as Christians, fewer than 20 percent of the Yamasees fell into this category. In a space of more than two years, only thirteen of the nearly four hundred Yamasees in Florida had offered their souls to the Catholic Church. Having spent several decades fighting the Spanish and their Christianized Indian allies, many Yamasees evidently harbored reservations about blending in with the rest of Saint Augustine's population.

The Spanish appeared content just to have the Yamasees on their side and did not want to risk the possibility of alienating their new allies by forcing Catholicism down their throats. In general the presence of the Yamasees allowed the Spanish to become more relaxed and confident in their relationships with all their Indian allies. In 1711 the Spanish had claimed authority over a mere 401 Indians in seven small settlements, all of them grouped "within a pistol shot" of the Castillo de San Marcos. Six years later their 946 Indian allies lived in ten different villages, some of them located as far as fifteen miles outside Saint Augustine.[15]

As much as the Spanish appreciated the Yamasees, however, they still mistrusted them and aimed to manipulate them into better behavior. Like the South Carolinians, Florida authorities attempted to arrange Indian settlements in a pattern that suited their own defensive needs. The Yamasees were allowed to live further away from Saint Augustine, but in exchange for this freedom, they had to abide the presence of small Spanish garrisons in two of their villages.[16] Though the garrisons were ostensibly intended to assist the Yamasees in fending off outside attacks, the Indians easily could have construed them as part of a Spanish strategy to keep them in line. Having spent nearly three decades as part of the South Carolina buffer zone, the Yamasees had become all too familiar with interference from imperial strategists. Even the relatively subtle machinations of the Spanish upset at least some of the Yamasees.

After several months in Florida, one Yamasee leader grew frustrated enough to consider the possibility of returning to South Carolina. In the spring of 1716 the headman of Huspah sent word to Charles Town that he and the rest of his town had done no wrong to the South Carolinians and hoped to return to their old lands.[17] The South Carolina government jumped at the request. In the words of House Speaker Thomas Broughton, the reintegration of the Huspah Yamasees would "in some measure lessen the charge of the war, and likewise be a present security to [their] southern settlements."[18] At first the South Carolinians wanted to make sure that these particular Indians had "not been instrumental in dipping their hands in the blood of [their] people," but after several more months of enduring the hardships of war, they became less inclined to split hairs.[19] By the end of 1716 the assembly was convinced that the time had come to end the war "as well by fair means, as by open force." Remarkably, it proceeded to offer a reward of five hundred pounds to anyone who could persuade the "Huspah King" or "any other Yamosee Indians" to come back to South Carolina.[20]

Unfortunately for the South Carolinians, the few colonists who visited Saint Augustine in the fall and winter of 1716 could not find any trace of the Huspah king. Some South Carolinians speculated that the Spanish had killed him for wanting to defect to the English, but the truth of the matter was that he had simply changed his mind.[21] A few years later the South Carolinians would learn from a Spanish prisoner that the Huspah king was living near Saint Augustine to get food and ammunition from the Spanish, but that he remained hard to pin down because "when he talk[ed] of going to one place he Comonly [went] to Another."[22]

Though the South Carolinians had difficulty keeping tabs on the Yamasees, they could ill afford to ignore them altogether. From their new base in Florida, the Yamasees continued to lash out at the people whom they no longer deemed worthy of their trust. In the summer of 1716, they managed to turn the tables on the vaunted South Carolinian scout boat system, ambushing a crew commanded by Major Henry Quintyne. The sole survivor—a physician named Rose—lost his scalp and part of his nose to the Indian attackers. The following year the Yamasees jumped a supply boat on its way up the Savannah River, killing all seven crewmembers and strewing their corpses along the shoreline. All the while the Yamasees continued to steal horses and "kidnap" slaves from South Carolina's vulnerable "out settlements," killing the occasional colonist who strayed too far from his neighbors. The Yamasees' attacks proved so profitable and satisfying that they continued to send raiding parties into South Carolina well after the rest of the southeastern Indians had sued for peace.[23]

In early 1719 John Barnwell—by now the leading spokesman for South Carolina's frontier affairs—decided to make one last pitch to the elusive Huspah king, entrusting the mission to several Lower Creek Indians who claimed to know the Yamasee leader.[24] Barnwell's contacts managed to approach the Huspah king in Saint Augustine but reportedly "found him in such a temper, that they durst not deliver their Errand; the Spaniards haveing made him Chief Generall of 500 and odd Indians to come immediately against [them], he was carried about the town in triumph with drums and Trumpets before him."[25] Since Great Britain and Spain had recently declared war on each other, Barnwell was inclined to believe the news that the Spanish had offered to "buy [their] heads and horses at the same price." Barnwell was so convinced that a force was on the way from Florida that he claimed to see the campfires of the enemy as he wrote his letter to the governor.[26] Though the expected Spanish-Indian invasion never materialized, the Yamasees did launch several small-scale assaults on Port Royal over the course of the summer. In one raid they struck the residence of South Carolina war hero Seymour Burroughs, kidnapping his wife and killing his small child. Having spent several months on pins and needles, Barnwell and many other South Carolina authorities finally lost patience with the Yamasees.[27]

In September 1719 Barnwell helped organize a punitive expedition composed of a white trader, two "half-breed or Mustees," and a diverse collection of fifty Indian warriors, primarily Cussabos and Tuscaroras from among the South Carolina settlements.[28] After leaving their canoes at the Saint Johns River, they proceeded overland to the edge of the Yamasee settlements and arrived undetected a few hours before dawn on the morning of October 12. The expedition seemed poised for a complete rout, but several of the party's scouts claimed to have friends and family members in the town of Pocotaligo and felt the need to give them some kind of warning. News of the attack quickly spread between the various villages, allowing them to mount a reasonably effective resistance. The attackers did manage to kill about five Indians, take twenty-four Yamasee prisoners, and seize some silver from a village church before they noticed "50 or 60 Spaniards in full march after them." After the Spanish ignored their flag of truce, the South Carolinian expedition made a nimble attack on the Spanish flanks, killing fourteen and capturing ten. Three of the Spanish captives were transported to South Carolina; the others were stripped naked and forced to make the humiliating walk back to their fort. When Barnwell learned of the expedition's success, he gleefully relayed the news of it to Governor Robert Johnson. [29]

The South Carolina–sponsored raid revealed that the Yamasees living near Saint Augustine were more vulnerable than previously believed. As pressure from the South Carolinians and their Indian allies began to build, the Yamasees also had to cope with a different set of pressures from another direction. After several years of living in the shadow of another European settlement, the Yamasees began to succumb to new diseases, making it easier for the Spanish to chip away at their proud sense of independence. Census information from the early 1720s reveals that many of the remaining Yamasees in Saint Augustine saw fit to make another major cultural adjustment. Spanish Franciscans managed to baptize 105 Yamasee men, women, and children in the mission of Candelaria between 1717 and 1723, a period that witnessed the loss of an additional ninety Yamasee warriors. [30] Within five years of beginning their war against the South Carolinians, the Florida Yamasees were finding it harder and harder to keep themselves from slipping down the steep slope to extinction.

Though the South Carolinians took notice of their enemies' plight, they also learned that their troubles with the Yamasees remained far from over. In the grand scheme of things, the 1719 raid on the Yamasees was nothing more than a qualified success. Even if the South Carolinians could continue to strike an occasional blow against their tormentors, they realized that it would be extremely difficult to extinguish them altogether, especially if the Yamasees could continue to take advantage of their close ties to some of South Carolina's Lower Creek allies. And while the Spanish had proved less than awe inspiring as "protectors" of the Yamasees, the South Carolinians felt that they would have to remain somewhat wary of them as long as Florida authorities could continue to entice fugitive slaves or provide weapons to vindictive Indians. [31] Indeed, the South Carolinians still had ample reason to fear for their safety. A few months after Barnwell's punitive expedition, the Yamasees sought revenge through another series of violent raids, not only against the South Carolinians but also against some of South Carolina's Indian allies.[32] This quick and forceful rebound was indicative of the Yamasees' great tenacity in the face of rising adversity. Though the Yamasees had long since begun to lose their struggle against the damaging effects of colonial imperialism, they refused to behave like a group whose days were numbered.

The Cherokees

While the Yamasees became notorious for their determination to resist the South Carolinians to the bitter end, other groups proved more willing to assist the South Carolinians in their hours of greatest need. Just as the Yamasees and their Muskogean allies would later take most of the blame for starting and prolonging the war, the Cherokees would receive much of the credit for bringing South Carolina's crisis to a close. The Cherokees' entry into a stronger military and economic alliance with South Carolina quickly transformed them into a powerful new force in the region, putting them in a position to exert more influence on the complex struggle between different groups of colonists and Indians. By choosing to cooperate with the South Carolina imperialists, the Cherokees embarked down a path that initially promised to be safer and more lucrative than the one selected by the Yamasees. Over the next five years, however, the Cherokees gradually realized that the costs of a closer relationship with the South Carolinians could often outweigh its rewards.

At the outbreak of the Yamasee War, the Cherokees and the South Carolinians were still relatively unfamiliar with each other. The South Carolinians knew enough to recognize the vast potential of what was—with the possible exception of the French-allied Choctaws—the largest Indian society in the Southeast, but they found it next to impossible to form an accurate impression of the Cherokees' allegiances.[33] The Cherokees themselves had difficulty deciding where they would stand in the Yamasee War; for the first several months of the conflict, they remained strongly divided in their views of the South Carolinians. Some Cherokees, primarily those from the lower towns, felt angry or frightened enough to kill several South Carolina traders and take part in the Catawbas' attacks on the Santee River settlements. At the same time, however, a few Cherokees made a conscious effort to reach out to the South Carolinians by assisting them in their fight against the Yamasees and attempting to convince concerned South Carolina officials that the rest of the Cherokees would soon come to terms.[34]

It initially appeared that these Cherokee emissaries might prove good to their word. Within a month of their appearance before the Commons House, they managed to persuade seventy Cherokee warriors to withdraw from the Catawba war party that had begun to advance on Goose Creek Parish. The South Carolinians heard nothing more of the Cherokees in the next several months, but this silence did not necessarily put their minds at ease. Even if the South Carolinians did not interpret the Cherokees' silence as a sign of their involvement in the Indian "conspiracy," they yearned for the Cherokees to offer them something more substantial than cautious neutrality. The South Carolina government put such a high premium on Cherokee aid that it offered a reward of five hundred pounds Carolina money to two adventurous traders who claimed that they could bring the Cherokees into a firm alliance with the province.[35]

Eleazar Wiggan and Robert Gilcrest were among the handful of Indian traders who had managed to return alive from South Carolina's frontiers, and their decision to lead a train of packhorses back into the towns of the Middle and Overhill Cherokees must have struck many South Carolinians as a courageous but foolhardy move.[36] However, Wiggan and Gilcrest were not as reckless as they might have appeared. These Indians had not only protected the two of them from danger a few months earlier but were also providing shelter for Wiggan's friend Alexander Long, a trader who had gone into exile from South Carolina in 1714.[37] Though some of the Middle and Overhill Cherokees had already grown familiar with the South Carolinians' potential for abusive and intrusive behavior, any resentment that they might have felt toward the South Carolinians was outweighed by the enmity that they felt toward other groups.[38]

For years the Middle and Overhill Cherokees had struggled to hold their own in wars against the Catawbas to the east, the Abeikas and the Tallapoosas to the southwest, and Iroquois raiders from the north. After the Cherokees killed twelve Frenchmen and fifty Kaskaskia Indians during a raid into the Illinois country in late 1714, the threat of French retaliation made their situation even more precarious.[39] While the Indians contacted by Wiggan and Gilcrest had little cause to join some of their traditional enemies in a war against South Carolina, they had compelling reasons to seek out the kind of military assistance that they could gain through a more active relationship with the South Carolinians.

In October 1715 eight Cherokee headmen, twelve head warriors, and over a hundred warriors of lesser rank accompanied Wiggan and Gilcrest on their triumphant return to Charles Town. Brought before an elated Governor Craven and his council, the Cherokee visitors offered peace pipes and animal skins as signs of their undying friendship for the English. When Craven asked the Cherokees if they would contribute warriors to a large, two-pronged expedition against the various groups of hostile Muskogeans, they readily pledged their assistance, promising to link up with the South Carolinian army near the new fort at Savannah Town. Starved for good news of any kind, the South Carolinians greeted this arrangement with an outpouring of relief and jubilation.[40] The following month, however, their optimism quickly gave way to a familiar sense of frustration. After waiting in vain for several weeks at the designated meeting point, the South Carolinians concluded that their Cherokee allies had reneged on their agreement.[41]

This was not the first diplomatic misunderstanding between the South Carolinians and the southeastern Indians, nor would it be the last. While the South Carolinians' expectations appeared clear enough, it is more difficult to know how the Cherokees reacted to the "treaty" made in Charles Town. Though it is possible that the Cherokees—like the Huspah king in Florida—simply experienced second thoughts about joining the South Carolinians, it is more likely that the Indians who had agreed to Governor Craven's terms had been forced to confront a good deal of opposition when they returned to their villages. [42] The South Carolinians would soon learn that the Cherokees remained far from unanimous in their support for a war against the Muskogeans. Factionalism was becoming an increasingly important part of Cherokee political culture, but the increasingly desperate South Carolinians had little patience for it. Shortly after the South Carolina troops stopped waiting for the Cherokees at Savannah Town, the colonial government decided to send three hundred heavily armed men into the mountains in an effort to help the Cherokees make up their minds once and for all.[43]

When the South Carolinian expedition reached Cherokee country at the end of December 1715, it split into small segments and took up positions in various Lower, Middle, and Overhill towns. The leaders of the expedition—a group that included George Chicken, John Herbert, Theophilus Hastings, and several other experienced frontiersmen—kept a running correspondence with one another and gradually developed a better picture of the major political camps among the Cherokees. The most outspoken advocate of the South Carolinians appeared to be Caesar, a headman from the Middle town of Echota who had taken part in the treaty ceremony at Charles Town a few months earlier. Even though Caesar had spent several years as a slave in South Carolina, he took it on himself to circulate between different Cherokee towns in an attempt to drum up support for an active military alliance with the English.[44] On January 2 in the Lower town of Nagouchee, Caesar reminded a large audience of "his promeases to ye Govner and ye nessesseateas of going to war against the Creek Indians." Three weeks later in the Overhill town of Quanassee, he delivered an impassioned speech that dripped with animosity for the Ocheses.[45]

Wherever Caesar spoke, the "warriors and the young men" seemed to react with unbridled enthusiasm, dancing throughout the night and preparing themselves for war. For young men seeking to advance within the Cherokee military hierarchy, success in battle was the quickest way to garner prestige and self-esteem. By the time of the Yamasee War, the pursuit of material profit had become an equally important concern. Several young Cherokee warriors admitted to George Chicken that without a new opportunity for going to war, "they should have no way in getting of Slaves to buy amunition and cloathing." The hated "Creeks"—the wealthiest and most aggressive Indians in the Southeast—seemed as good a target as any.[46]

For a while, however, these enthusiasts were kept in check by another group of Cherokees who urged caution and patience. When young warriors began their dances, some older men of great respect could come up with "severall reasons for them to desist att present." One of the most persuasive of the moderates was Charitey Hagey, a prestigious military and spiritual leader whom the South Carolinians frequently referred to as "the Conjurer." Charitey Hagey hailed from Tugaloo, the Cherokee town closest to the South Carolina settlements. While Charitey Hagey probably had shown some sympathy for the Yamasees and the Ocheses in the early months of the war, he managed to convince the South Carolinians who visited his town on December 30 "that he and the English was all one [and] that he nore none of his men should ever fitte against [the English] any more." But even if Charitey Hagey and his supporters had decided to dismiss the war against South Carolina as a lost cause, they expressed a strong reluctance to fight against anyone but their most bitter enemies, the Yuchis and the Savannahs. They claimed to have sent a "flag of truce" to the "headmen of the Crick," who in turn had promised to come to the Cherokee towns as soon as possible. Cherokee leaders like Charitey Hagey were seemingly offering to broker a settlement between the South Carolinians and their Muskogean enemies. These Indians proved so persuasive that the South Carolinians altered their policy on the spot and spent the next several weeks trying to prevent Caesar and his young followers from taking to the warpath.[47]

The impending arrival of the Muskogean leaders made one South Carolinian confident enough to claim, "[I]n all Probability we shall have a Peace with all our Indians again . . . and our Trade with them may Flourish again as it has done in times past." The South Carolinians saw themselves taking control of a precarious situation, but throughout their stay in the mountains, they remained largely out of the loop, seeing only what the Indians were willing to show them. While traveling between two Cherokee towns on January 13, Maurice Moore and John Herbert came across two Ochese warriors who informed them that the scouts of Brims, the "great cacique of Coweta," were watching the South Carolinians "every day and night." Though the South Carolinians seemed unfazed by this news, an even greater surprise lay in store for them. On January 27 the South Carolinians were hastily summoned back to the town of Tugaloo, where they found the Cherokees standing over the corpses of eleven Muskogean leaders and keeping a twelfth "to be shott at night." Only then did the South Carolinians learn that the "Creek" delegation had already made its arrival, bringing nearly five hundred Yamasee and Ochese warriors within striking distance of the scattered South Carolinian expedition. By the time Chicken and the rest of the unsettled officers could organize an attack, however, the enemy force had already fled back toward the Ocmulgee, dispelling any hopes for a quick and easy resolution to the war.[48]

Though the aborted parlay between Ochese and Cherokee leaders clearly stood as one of the most pivotal episodes of the Yamasee War, its details remain shrouded in mystery. According to colonial authorities, the Cherokees had reached an agreement to join the Ocheses in destroying the South Carolinian expedition, but "as providence order'd it[,] they chang'd their minds" at the last minute.[49] Though the Cherokees probably had a hand in arranging the clandestine meeting at Tugaloo, they did not necessarily have any prior knowledge of what their visitors would say to them. Much like the Yamasees' attacks on the English delegation at Pocotaligo, the Tugaloo murders probably resulted from a heated, pressure-packed situation that allowed a strong-willed and aggressively pro-English or anti-Ochese minority to make up the minds of an uncertain majority.[50] If the Cherokees present at Tugaloo were going to have to choose between the Ocheses and the English, some of them were perfectly willing to walk out of the council house, grab their weapons, and give their answer right then and there.

While most of the Cherokees had no direct role in the Tugaloo massacre, all of them eventually had to deal with its repercussions. As word of the murders quickly spread through the Muskogean heartland, the Cherokees lost any remaining hopes for a neutral role in the Yamasee War. The Ocheses now re-garded them as treacherous enemies and were likely to attack at any time.[51] Short of civil war only one option appeared to remain open to the Cherokees: an active cooperation with the South Carolinians.

At first glance the stage seemed set for a firm and lasting alliance grounded on mutual interest. The ecstatic South Carolinians believed that the Cherokees would assume much of the province's military burden while providing a ma-jor boost to a moribund Indian trade. Many of the Cherokees, for their part, believed that they had secured powerful partners who could supply them with the coveted trade goods that would make them more powerful than their var-ious enemies. On a deeper level, however, the reaffirmed connection between the Cherokees and the South Carolinians was unlike any alliance that either group had heretofore experienced. Though both the Cherokees and the South Carolinians generally realized that they would have to rely on each other to an unprecedented degree, neither group was comfortable enough with the other to allow the alliance to maintain a level of predictability. Not all the Cherokees felt exactly the same way about the South Carolinians, and not all the South Carolinians felt exactly the same way about the Cherokees. Since the alliance had to include a number of conflicting expectations and interpretations, it was bound to experience some difficult moments.

For the Cherokees the alliance with the South Carolinians was sealed in blood. Though most Cherokees had become well acquainted with intertribal warfare by the early eighteenth century, their intervention in the Yamasee War forced them to fight as they had never fought before.[52] Some of the Cherokees' new engagements were not all that far out of character; in 1716 they launched a devastating attack on the Abeikas, a western Muskogean group that they had long regarded as enemies.[53] In general, however, the Cherokees' war against the Muskogeans rarely went so smoothly. Many Cherokees—particularly those from the Lower and Middle towns—found it harder and harder to deal with the Lower Creeks, the assemblage of Ocheses and allied groups that had relocated to the Chattahoochee River in the wake of the Tugaloo massacre. Following a few mildly successful raids in 1716 and early 1717, the Cherokees began to feel the sting of Lower Creek reprisals, one of which practically annihilated the Lower Cherokee town of Nagouchee.[54] The increasing frequency and intensity of Lower Creek raids made it more and more difficult for Cherokee men to ven-ture from their villages and often discouraged them from hunting or trading.[55]

In exchange for their sacrifices, the Cherokees clearly expected to reap cer-tain rewards from their colonial partners. After a year of arduous fighting, the

Cherokees grew more inclined to remind the South Carolinians that "it was upon their account that they made War on the Creek Indians, depending upon the Promise of the White People to supply them plentifully with what they wanted."[56] Occasionally the South Carolinians lived up to these expectations by granting the kind of material assistance and respectful treatment that the Cherokees desired. Since the South Carolinians tended to gravitate toward any prominent Indian leaders who expressed the slightest pro-English leanings, certain Cherokee headmen and head warriors managed to do fairly well under the revamped alliance. After renouncing the South Carolinians' Muskogean enemies, Charitey Hagey became a particular favorite of the colonial government and found that the various gifts provided by the English could help him accrue more respect and influence among his people.[57] Despite such "success" stories, however, some Cherokees reaped a less than fair return on their deal with the South Carolinians. Even Caesar of Echota—a man who probably received more favors than anyone from the South Carolina government—could find several bones to pick with the colonial officials who had pledged to help him.[58] While some of the controversies between the Cherokees and the South Carolinians emerged as early as the week after the Tugaloo massacre, most of them resulted from the dramatic overhaul of South Carolina's Indian trade system in the summer of 1716. As the first major Indian society to come to terms with the South Carolinians, the Cherokees effectively became guinea pigs for the public trade, forced to adjust to the new economic and diplomatic policies that were foisted on them.

Despite the best intentions of its architects, the public trade usually catered more to the anxieties of the South Carolina government than to the needs of its Indian allies. While the South Carolinians balked at sending packhorses to the Cherokee towns for fear of enemy raiding parties, they had no problem asking the Cherokees to send their own men to serve as burden carriers on the long and dangerous journey to and from the Fort Moore trading factory.[59] The Cherokees consented to this arrangement when the South Carolinians promised to build another fort and factory closer to their settlements, but the Congarees fort—completed after more than two years of frustrating delays—did not seem to make their voyages much safer or easier.[60] While the Cherokees feared for their safety, they also expressed dismay over other aspects of the factor system. As neglected piles of dressed deerskins began to decompose in the villages and factories, the Cherokees questioned the efficiency of the public trade and wondered aloud whether they would "be supplyed with as much Goods as formerly."[61] It also appeared to many Cherokees that the prices of

"Duffels, Hatchets, Caddice [lace], Belts, and several other small things" had gone through the roof, and that the liquor sold to them was far less potent than the kind they had purchased before the war.[62] The Cherokees frequently found it cheaper and more convenient to deal with the South Carolinians on the sly, but clandestine trading often left them even more vulnerable to swindlers. Several Cherokees, including the venerable Charitey Hagey, attempted to appeal to the government after someone cheated them out of skins, blankets, and a horse, only to meet with a stern rebuke for "not hearkening to the Great Men's talk to them" and "choosing rather to deal with private Persons."[63]

Understandably the Cherokees tended to bristle whenever the South Carolinians treated them like misguided children. While the Cherokees were clearly growing more attached to some European goods, such as textiles, and more dependent on others, such as liquor and munitions, they were not necessarily willing to suffer a full range of indignities in order to acquire these things. Like most relatively large Indian societies of the early colonial period, the Cherokees did not become passive cogs in an inexorable "world system." For them economic exchange remained replete with a variety of cultural meanings that most colonists could not begin to understand.[64] Sometimes the Cherokees viewed trade as a community rite rooted in reciprocity and mutual respect, and sometimes they regarded it as the "moral equivalent of war," a kind of contest meant to boost one's ego or social standing.[65] Either way the Cherokees were bound to take offense at a relationship in which condescension was often the best thing they could expect. In many cases the South Carolinians could appear downright rude or hostile, showering the Cherokees with insults, denying them access to forts and plantations, and deliberately and defiantly shortchanging them for various services.[66]

Though stung by such affronts, the Cherokees remained proud and powerful enough to respond to them. Many Cherokees could come up with some cutting insults of their own, berating the South Carolina traders "like so many Oyster Women." Some went a step further by threatening the most offensive South Carolinians with bodily harm, threats that they might have carried out on occasion, if the mysterious disappearance of several "rogue" traders is any indication. Cherokee factor William Hatton related that on one occasion Caesar of Echota stopped by his house and casually mentioned that he "did not expect to find [him] alive," since he had heard "severall consultations in the path about killing [him] and the rest of [them] that was in the Nation."[67] When attempting to vent their various grievances, however, the Cherokees generally had more success with a more subtle form of intimidation. Caesar made the situation perfectly clear during a meeting with Governor Robert Daniel in early 1717: if the South Carolinians continued to cheat and disrespect the Cherokees, the Cherokees would be "forced to go to those that [would] seek their friendship." [68] When nothing else worked, the threat of Indian defection invariably caused South Carolina officials to sit bolt upright in their chairs.

The South Carolinians reserved their deepest concern for the French, but the most serious challenge to their alliance with the Cherokees actually came from a different group of imperial rivals. One day in 1717 several Cherokees returned from a visit to the Catawbas with the news that "the Virginians was arrived there with 2 or 300 horses loaded with goods and was designed to the Charikees to Trade and would Sell to them much Cheaper than those from South Carolina, adding that [the South Carolinians] made Horses [of] 'em to carrie Skins, but . . . they had brought Horses [in] abundance to ease them of that trouble. This News so Elevated them . . . that they looked as Cheerfull, and apeared like Men eased of a Burthen not to be born." [69] Though the Virginians never arrived in the mountains in significant numbers, they made an effort to spread rumors of their own largesse, "fine stories such as they knew would please Indians, especially those who had an Inclination to be pleased by them." Before long Cherokees were going out of their way to announce that "the Virginians were very good, but [that] they valued [the people] of Carolina no more than dirt." [70] Many of them began to make preparations for the impending arrival of the Virginians, stockpiling food and setting aside their best deerskins. Close to panic, Cherokee factor William Hatton helped convince the Board of Commissioners to authorize some significant price discounts and then "ventured to stretch [his] orders" by making even greater discounts on his own. [71] Though Hatton's Indian customers soon "began to be better humored" with him, he had the uneasy feeling that the Cherokees were playing him and his fellow South Carolinians like a bunch of cheap fiddles. [72]

Whenever the Cherokees attempted to assert themselves, the South Carolinians voiced new reservations about their partnership. Like the South Carolinians, the Cherokees could often come across as troublesome, duplicitous, and a bit unstable. When Cherokee burden bearers left Fort Moore or the Congarees with a hundred pounds of South Carolina trade goods strapped to their backs, they frequently made detours off the beaten path, sometimes absconding with as much as a third of their cargo. [73] Cherokees also made a habit of paying unscheduled visits to Charles Town, where diplomatic custom dictated that they receive some kind of "present" from the government. [74] As the Cherokees grew more expensive to their financially strapped allies, they also began to test the South Carolinians' patience in the political arena. Since their earliest days of imperial expansion, the South Carolinians had preferred to have the southeastern Indians tied up in neat, orderly packages. Despite their overarching linguistic and cultural commonalties, the Lower, Middle, and Overhill Cherokees frequently rebuffed the South Carolinians' efforts to have them "joyn and come together for their better security," often preferring to regard each other with jealousy and animosity.[75] South Carolina officials were greatly disturbed to see Charitey Hagey and Caesar engaged in heated arguments during an official visit to Charles Town and later expressed dismay at the news that some of Charitey Hagey's supporters "had beaten Cesar very much, and threatened to kill him" upon their return to the mountains.[76]

The South Carolinians did not like to see the Cherokees fighting among themselves when they were supposed to be fighting against other groups of Indians. From the standpoint of the colonial government, the most problematic aspect of the alliance was the Cherokees' performance in the war against South Carolina's remaining Indian enemies. Though the Cherokees proved instrumental in persuading the Catawbas and other Piedmont groups to come to terms with the South Carolinians, one colonist lamented that the Cherokees' campaigns against the Lower Creeks "so often Disappointed [them] that [they] could but little Depend on them in that affair."[77] To the South Carolinians, the Cherokees' military shortcomings reflected a lack of will rather than a lack of ability. As early as February 1716, Charitey Hagey had warned that many of the Cherokees would be "slack in going to war" unless the South Carolinians provided them with enough material aid to justify their efforts.[78] In early 1717 Caesar agreed to head an expedition against the Yamasees in Florida, only to return empty-handed a mere two weeks later, demanding his payment in rum.[79] Colonial officials found it harder and harder to reconcile the Cherokees' apparent foot-dragging with their increasingly "unreasonable" demands. Concerned that they were in danger of becoming "Tributaries" of the Cherokees, South Carolinians began to wonder if they should continue to invest so heavily in their most important Indian allies.[80]

For the Cherokees the South Carolinians' change of heart came at a most inopportune time. The province's settlement with the Lower Creeks in late 1717 was soothing to the South Carolinians but disastrous for the Cherokees. The Lower Creeks vowed to step up their raids against the Cherokees and even approached the dreaded Iroquois for assistance.[81] Pressured from the north and the south, the Cherokees unsuccessfully petitioned South Carolina authorities for three hundred colonial troops.[82] Failing to secure this assistance was bad enough, but the Cherokees grew even more disheartened by what some of them claimed to notice during one of their run-ins with the Lower Creeks.[83] It appeared that the South Carolinians—the self-proclaimed "best friends" and protectors of the Cherokees—had begun to supply the Cherokees' enemies with new weapons. Though the South Carolinians tried to hide the conditions of their peace with the Creeks, the Cherokees had every reason to fear the worst.[84] Even before the settlement, the South Carolina government had begun to look on the Creeks as the only possible defense against the increasingly volatile and aggressive Cherokees. Once peace was made, the South Carolinians could proceed with their plan "to hold both [groups] as [their] friends, for some time, and assist them in Cutting one another's throats without offending either."[85]

The Cherokees easily saw through this strategy and were, in fact, greatly offended by it. They had no real objections to fighting the Creeks, but they did resent the fact that their supposed allies were putting them at such a great disadvantage in this ongoing struggle.[86] The South Carolinians, however, had no intentions of cutting off the Cherokees altogether. Their even greater fear of the newly reconciled Lower Creeks often compelled them to go out of their way to try to allay the Cherokees' suspicions by giving them better bargains on firearms and other essential trade goods.[87] Whenever the Cherokees began to appear especially "jealous" of South Carolina's other Indian allies, they could frequently expect a new shipment of gunpowder or bullets to keep them from falling even further out of line.[88]

While the Cherokees remained free to push the envelope of their alliance with South Carolina, they also began to see that their challenges to colonial authority could only go so far. By 1720 their options were clearly limited. The Virginians, initially hailed by the Cherokees as a trump card, had already begun to pull out of the mountains. Soon the Cherokees' concern would lead several headmen to far-off Williamsburg in a futile quest to attract more Virginia traders.[89] Meanwhile the Cherokees were forced to deal with the increasingly confident South Carolinians, a group that now possessed more trump cards of their own. William Hatton briefly showed his hand during a discussion with Charitey Hagey in the summer of 1718, informing the Cherokee leader that "the Government [would] not make use of the Interest they [had] with the Creeks, to his Detriment, unless his people gave Occasion for it."[90] In other instances the South Carolinians could be even more blunt. After receiving complaints that the Indians of Quanasseee and Terrequa towns had become dangerously "inofficious to the White Men who dwell[ed] among them," the Board of Commissioners warned the Cherokees that if their poor behavior continued, they would lose all their trade with South Carolina and "be made a Prey of by their Enemies." [91] Such warnings were actually nothing more than well-rehearsed bluffs, but the Cherokees were no longer in a position to call them.

Though the Cherokees probably were nursing more grievances than ever against the South Carolinians, their chance for serious resistance appeared to have already come and gone. When the Cherokees had come upon an opportunity to challenge the South Carolinians in 1715, most of them had spurned it, preferring instead to take a different path to security and prosperity. Five years later it would have been difficult to convince the Cherokees that they had fought on the "winning" side of the Yamasee War. [92] On the surface the Cherokees managed to get through the war in fairly good shape, preserving their territorial integrity while losing a relatively small percentage of their population. [93] But while groups like the Yamasees had already come to grips with the worst that war and imperial expansion had to offer, the Cherokees' problems in these areas had only begun.

The Catawbas

The Cherokees' increasing vulnerability between 1715 and 1720 stood in stark contrast to the relative isolation that many of them had enjoyed prior to the Yamasee War. This isolation had made the Cherokees something of an anomaly within the Southeast: they alone had been able to take full advantage of the natural protection provided by the rugged Appalachian Mountains. Within the foothills and upcountry that stretched to the east of this range, an ethnically diverse collection of small to mid-sized Indian societies had been forced to withstand an unsettling onrush of outside pressures since the turn of the eighteenth century. While these pressures helped draw the Piedmont Indians into a closer relationship with colonial imperialists, they had also helped make them tougher, warier, and more combative than many of South Carolina's Indian allies. The Cherokees found themselves roughly jostled by their involvement in the Yamasee War, but the Piedmont Indians appeared to be in a position for an even bumpier ride.

By 1715 South Carolinians had already begun to refer to the various groups of the northern backcountry and Piedmont under a single name: the Catawbas. At the same time, however, the South Carolinians continued to employ a number of other names as well, indicating that they could not help but notice some of the cultural distinctions between these groups. [94] The Catawbas were just the largest and most powerful group in an assemblage that also included Cheraws, Congarees, Santees, Pee Dees, Waxhaws, Waterees, Wacca-maws, and Winyahs. At the outbreak of the Yamasee War, these groups—like the Cherokees—remained undecided about the course they should pursue. After more than a month of arguing, waiting, and vacillating, they finally committed themselves to a war against their erstwhile allies in South Carolina. Having worked together in a number of joint military campaigns against the Tuscaroras and other traditional enemies, the Piedmont Indians probably had little trouble combining forces for an extended raid into the settlements of their new enemies.[95] Some of these Indians had further to travel than others in order to reach the South Carolinians, but once they crossed the Santee River, they began to enjoy the kind of success that made even the longest excursions worthwhile.

While the initial advance into South Carolina probably presented little challenge to the various Piedmont groups, everything began to change as soon as they ran up against stronger colonial defenses. In June 1715 the Piedmont Indians' crushing defeat in the Battle of the Ponds forced them to reconsider their options, thereby leading to a gradual unraveling of their war effort.[96] Like the Yamasees the Piedmont Indians realized that they could no longer send large war parties into the South Carolina settlements. Unlike the Yamasees, however, they had a hard time reshaping their strategies for carrying on with the war. If they had any hope of keeping up the fight, they would have to find a new source for guns and ammunition, not to mention a secure base for protecting themselves from South Carolinian reprisals. While evidence suggests that a handful of the Catawbas may have accompanied the Yamasees on their exodus to Saint Augustine, most of the Piedmont Indians were in no position to appeal to a group as remote and alien as the Spanish.[97] Their only viable alternative to the South Carolinians lay several hundred miles to the north. Not surprisingly the Piedmont Indians decided to approach the Virginia government for solutions to the various problems that had begun to plague them by the summer of 1715.

From the outset Virginia officials made it perfectly clear that they would never supply the Indians with the means to kill fellow British subjects. Once the Piedmont Indians realized that a settlement with South Carolina was the only way for them to acquire the English goods that they so desperately needed, they treated the Virginians as peace brokers, sending three large delegations to Williamsburg over the course of the next year.[98] But just as the Piedmont Indians had entered the Yamasee War with varying degrees of enthusiasm and conviction, their exit from the war proved even more uncertain and uneven. Eager for English trade and pressured by South Carolina's Cherokee and Iroquois allies, the Catawbas played the most active role in the peace negotiations and soon rendered their "submission" to authorities in Williamsburg and Charles Town in July 1715.[99] This development spelled disaster for several smaller groups that wished to continue the struggle against the South Carolinians. After the Santees and the Waxhaws killed several colonists and slaves in early 1716, the South Carolina government asked the Catawbas to "fall upon them and cut them off as enemies to them and [South Carolina]."[100] The Catawbas complied by launching a series of ruthless attacks that played out much like the famous "mourning wars" of their Iroquoian enemies: warriors gave vent to pent-up feelings of anguish and grief while simultaneously acquiring Santee and Waxhaw captives that could be adopted into Catawba society and offset recent losses in Catawba population. The Catawbas' attacks on their Piedmont neighbors not only enhanced the Catawbas' status in the eyes of the South Carolinians but also fulfilled some of their own cultural and diplomatic needs.[101]

Unfortunately for the South Carolinians, however, not every group in the Piedmont and northern backcountry seemed as compliant as the Catawbas or as expendable as the Santees. Leaders of the Pee Dees, the Waccamaws, and the Winyahs eventually came down to Charles Town to renew their "Articles of Alliance" with the South Carolina government in the fall of 1717, but the Cheraws still refused to submit. Rumors of the Cheraws' continuing hostility caused North and South Carolina leaders to ask the Virginia government for assistance in a joint campaign against these Indians, but Spotswood adamantly refused, and the plan was summarily dropped. The South Carolina government elected to do nothing but issue a half-hearted ban on trading with the Cheraws and continued to hold out hope that the Cheraws would come to town to make their apologies.[102] South Carolina's northern frontiers appeared much more secure than they had a year earlier, but they remained clouded by a lingering sense of mistrust and uncertainty.

Despite their misgivings the South Carolinians felt compelled to reestablish their presence among these Indians. As the South Carolinians showed in their attempts to recall the Yamasees from Florida, they were much more inclined to forgive their Indian enemies if they feared losing them to an imperial rival. The South Carolinians and the Virginians were fresh from an unprecedented display of diplomatic cooperation, but at its heart their relationship remained as tense and adversarial as ever. According to a report issued by the Board of Trade in 1720, the intense competition between Virginia and South Carolina in the aftermath of the Yamasee War caused many Indians to "look upon them as not under the same Government."[103] As the Yamasee War began to wind down by the spring of 1717, both groups set their sights on the Piedmont, an area of tremendous strategic importance. The renewal of the long-standing trade war between Virginia and South Carolina promised innumerable headaches for colonial traders and authorities, but it meant something far more palatable to their Indian customers and "tributaries." While the Piedmont Indians seemed to have lost their last chance to throw off all traces of South Carolinian authority, many of them continued to benefit from a "buyer's market," a circumstance that would allow them to maintain considerable leeway in their ties to colonial imperialists.[104]

Shortly after returning to the Piedmont, South Carolina traders began to realize that they would have to bend over backward to keep their Indian customers content. Though little more than an enticing rumor to the Cherokees, the Virginia traders were a pleasant reality for the Catawbas, the Cheraws, and other nearby groups. The South Carolinians could not impose the rigors of their public trade system on groups of Indians who simply had too many options at their disposal. The Piedmont Indians not only had "no Trouble at all" working with the Virginians who visited them but also took advantage of a vigorous private trade with South Carolinian planters in the Santee region.[105] To bring any of the Piedmont trade through the government factors, South Carolina officials had to sell goods at a loss and invest in an expensive stable of packhorses. The South Carolina government abandoned the controversial "burdener" system among the Catawbas in 1717, a full year before making a similar concession to the Cherokees.[106]

Though the Piedmont Indians reaped great benefits from the presence of an alternative market, they drew concessions from the South Carolina government in other ways as well. Many of these Indians had an aggressive, slightly dangerous air about them, qualities that tended to elicit respect from the wary South Carolinians. While the Cherokees were frequently prevented from entering the Congarees garrison and trading post, the Catawbas had "Regress and Freegress as they pleased" and often took full advantage of the South Carolinians' hospitality.[107] The Piedmont Indians also appeared to have free run of the Winyah garrison, where they bullied factor Meredith Hughes to the point where he frantically appealed for his government's assistance. The Board of Commissioners responded by advising Hughes to mask his "Resentment" of the Indians, lest he provoke them into further transgressions.[108] The commissioners proved equally cautious when they received a rare convoy of Catawba burden bearers in the fall of 1717. After the Catawbas brazenly cheated the government out of 150 skins, the commissioners decided that it would be best to say nothing. [109]

Despite the flexibility of their relationship with South Carolina, the Piedmont Indians—like the Cherokees—soon realized that there were definite limits to the generosity of colonial officials. If the Catawbas or other Piedmont groups started to play out too much line, the South Carolinians were not averse to giving the occasional tug. [110] Whether snubbing a headman's request for presents or hastily shooing away a delegation of Catawba leaders to make room for a visiting party of Lower Creeks, the South Carolinians showed that they could assert themselves in ways that were far more subtle than their "extirpation" of the troublesome Santees. [111] In general, however, the South Carolinians' most effective leverage against the Piedmont Indians was the indirect and often unconscious pressure that they exerted on a regular basis. After 1715 most of the Indians on South Carolina's northern frontiers had to worry about losing a good deal more than their pride and dignity.

The pressure weighed heaviest on those groups that lived closest to South Carolina's northernmost settlements. Unlike the devastated war zone around Port Royal, the northern settlements attracted an influx of uprooted colonists once South Carolina's military prospects began to improve. Colonists not only returned to the Santee River but also began to cross it for the first time, carving new plantations and cattle ranches out of the countryside. With this expansion previously independent groups like the Waccamaws, the Pee Dees, and the Winyahs faced a dark new future as "settlement Indians," groups dependent on the patronage and charity of whites. The Winyahs along the Santee were forced to pay new duties on the land that they cultivated, and the Waccamaws found themselves preying on the cattle of nearby colonists. [112] The South Carolina government—mindful of similar actions undertaken by the Yamasees a few years earlier—expressed great concern over the latter development, fearing that it might be a prelude to another massive insurrection. While some of the Waccamaws and their neighbors would indeed launch small and utterly futile uprisings in the next several years, most of the Indians who felt threatened by colonial expansion took the less drastic step of moving to a more secure location. [113] In the winter of 1717–18, many of the Winyahs and the Waccamaws pulled up stakes and moved closer to the Cheraws, citing "the Hardship they [had] met with, in living among the white people." [114]

But even if the Indians could manage to get out of range of the expanding colonial settlements, they could never outrun colonial microbes. In 1718 an unspecified disease (likely smallpox) cut a swath through the northern backcountry, reaching as far as the Virginia Piedmont.[115] During a visit to Fort Christanna, Virginia Governor Alexander Spotswood observed the effects of the disease on a nearby encampment of Catawbas. Unlike the Cherokees, who seemed to be an "increasing people," the Catawbas had apparently "become much lessened, by a remarkable dispensation of Providence . . . as if Heaven designed by the diminution of these Indian neighbors, to make room for [the colonists'] growing settlements."[116] Between 1718 and 1720, the various Piedmont groups probably lost more people on sickbeds than they had in all the engagements of the Yamasee War.[117]

This is not to say that the Piedmont Indians remained free from military strife once they made their uneasy peace with South Carolina. Like the Yamasees they had to deal with external enemies as they tried to cope with pressures from colonial society. Though the Piedmont Indians did not object to warfare on principle, they did have trouble withstanding the conflicts that engulfed them in the aftermath of the Yamasee War. The Catawbas' alliance with the South Carolinians and Cherokees brought a respite from some of their problems, but it also led to a range of new troubles by pitting the Catawbas against the dangerous Lower Creeks. On at least one occasion, Lower Creek raiding parties were so thick around the Catawbas that the South Carolinians felt compelled to put a hold on their packhorse trains.[118] All the while the Catawbas had to keep up a running battle with an even more formidable enemy. The Iroquois had already been raiding the "Flathead" groups of the Carolina Piedmont for several decades when New York's Governor Robert Hunter asked them to go to South Carolina's aid in the summer of 1715. That fall a party of Senecas destroyed one of the Cheraws' towns, and by the following year the various groups of the Piedmont were forced to admit that the "Mohacks [had] been very hard upon them of late."[119] The Iroquois—aided by the advice and assistance of their newest addition, the Tuscaroras—had no intention of letting up simply because the Catawbas had reached some kind of settlement with some strange groups of Englishmen.[120] The Catawbas were skilled and accomplished warriors who often more than held their own against the Iroquois, but in time the relentless raids from the north began to wear them down. When a group of Catawbas was struck just outside the walls of Virginia's Fort Christanna in the spring of 1717, they realized that they were far more vulnerable than they had been a few years earlier.[121]

With their numbers rapidly diminishing and their positions more exposed than ever, the Piedmont Indians were forced to adopt new strategies for survival. They began by taking steps to make their villages more secure. When a runaway Irish servant approached the Catawbas in the spring of 1717 with the rumor that the South Carolina government had plans to destroy them, the Indians reportedly leapt to the task of "building and erecting Forts to defend themselves." In responding to this false alarm, they also revealed a strategy that was soon to become an even more important security measure within the Piedmont. The Catawbas' estimated prewar population of five hundred fighting men had suddenly risen to more than seven hundred, suggesting that different groups from the region had "gathered together" to find safety in numbers. [122]

By the end of the Yamasee War, the various peoples of the Piedmont had already gone to great lengths to protect themselves. Some Indians in the region allowed themselves to fall in with the South Carolinians and assume an unflattering new identity as "settlement Indians." [123] Other Indians disappeared entirely from the colonists' view. According to a report issued by South Carolina governor Robert Johnson in 1720, several of the small groups along the fringes of the Piedmont had been "utterly extirpated" as a result of their role in the Yamasee War. [124] Johnson and many other South Carolinians did not realize that many of these Indians had simply elected to seek shelter among stronger and more remote Indian societies. Some Indians initially flocked to the Cheraws, but most tended to seek out the Catawbas. Within a few years even the Cheraws would begin to move closer to the Catawba-Wateree basin. [125]

Though the Catawbas allowed the other Indians to settle around them, they did not rush to absorb them into their own society. Linguistic differences and past disputes initially compelled the Catawbas to keep some distance from their new neighbors, but the gravity of their situation quickly inspired them to bridge some of the gap. Nearby groups soon began to convene with the Catawbas to make decisions about joint military expeditions, colonial trade, or other matters that concerned the Piedmont Indians as a whole. In the words of a Shawnee Indian who regularly raided the Piedmont groups from his home in Pennsylvania, it now appeared that the Catawbas consisted of "many nations under that name." [126] Though the emerging "polyglot society" in the Catawba-Wateree basin was based first and foremost on an alliance of expediency, it paved the way for the political and cultural consolidation that would occur on an even greater scale over the next several decades. By 1720 the stage was already set for what historian James Merrell has described as "a more populous, more diverse Catawba nation." [127]

In 1721 a "King" appointed to speak on behalf of the Catawbas and their neighbors traveled to Charles Town to present a deerskin map of his homeland to newly arrived Governor Francis Nicholson. Like all cartographers of the day, the Catawba mapmaker imbued his work with his own cultural prejudices and understandings, positioning his own society in the center of things and relegating less familiar groups to the sketchy margins.[128] In this particular case he depicted a vision that seemed surprisingly confident in light of the severe hardships that many of the Piedmont groups had recently experienced. An official copy of the Catawbas' deerskin map shows a number of different groups represented as circles. Some of these circles are clearly larger and more prominent than others, but all of them are connected into a single entity that occupies a position of power and importance between Virginia and South Carolina, the two colonies drawn unobtrusively into the corners of the map. Though Governor Nicholson graciously accepted the Catawbas' gift, neither he nor his fellow officials seemed to understand it entirely. In future years the South Carolinians would remain content to gloss over the different circles on the map in the belief that one of them—that of the Catawbas—spoke for all.[129] But even as the South Carolinians continued to harbor their own misconceptions about Catawba identity, they were forced to admit that the Indians of the Piedmont, in spite of their various problems, were somehow managing to make a new name for themselves.[130]

In their relations with South Carolina, the Catawbas had always maintained a kind of distance that belied their geographic proximity to the province. Though the Yamasee War forced these Indians to realize that they could not make a complete escape from the colonial shadows, it did not destroy their determination to preserve some measure of autonomy and self-respect. For many Indians in the Piedmont, this defiance involved overwhelming struggles and sacrifices, subjecting them to a level of suffering that was unsurpassed anywhere in the Southeast. Even more than the Yamasees, however, the Catawbas and their neighbors were able to salvage a renewed sense of strength and vitality from the darkest of circumstances. For all their travails, they became living proof that defeat in the Yamasee War did not have to mean disaster.

The Creeks

The Catawbas and the Yamasees proved their resourcefulness beyond any measure of doubt, but as they entered the 1720s, their persistence was more an issue of tenacity than of prosperity. While no southeastern Indian society could rightfully claim victory over the South Carolinians, some hostile groups did manage to emerge from the war in better shape than the Catawbas and the Yamasees. Like the Indians of the Carolina Piedmont, the "Creeks" were a group that consisted of diverse cultures and polities. By 1715 they comprised several distinct, largely Muskogean provinces between the Alabama and Ocmulgee rivers. Though the Indians from the different Muskogean provinces generally rebuffed the Europeans' attempts to shape them into a more cohesive entity, they did enjoy some strong connections with one another, especially as military allies. Cooperation in battle fostered a mutual respect between all Muskogeans, but the various campaigns associated with Queen Anne's War had helped bring one particular group to the forefront.

By virtue of their proximity to South Carolina, the Ocmulgee Muskogeans—or "Ocheses"—often acted as conduits between the English and the Tallapoosas, the Abeikas, and the Alabamas, who lived further to the west. This circumstance helped transform the Ocheses into South Carolina's most valuable Indian allies, but it also put them in an altogether different position once the Indians of the southeastern interior began to grow disillusioned with the South Carolinians. While all the Muskogean provinces participated in the Yamasee War to some extent, the Muskogean war effort in many ways belonged to the Ocheses. No other Muskogean group invested more in the war or reaped more changes from its investment.

At first blush it might appear that most of the Ocheses' problems on the eve of the Yamasee War stemmed from their single-minded attachment to the South Carolinians. After abandoning the Spanish and moving to their new home along the Ocmulgee, the Ocheses made themselves more available to South Carolina traders and more vulnerable to the traps and intrusions of the South Carolina government. Despite the Ocheses' growing reliance on English trade goods, however, it would be misleading to assume that the South Carolinians were their only significant allies between 1690 and 1715. The Ocheses also worked hard to build a kind of "buffer zone" of their own, forging and maintaining an alliance network with various Indian societies throughout the Southeast. This network did not necessarily help the Ocheses acquire guns, duffels, or Jamaican rum, but it did give them leverage against outside threats or incursions. While these Indian alliances probably played a major role in the formation of the anti–South Carolina "conspiracy," the Ocheses would only begin to take full advantage of their Indian connections after the first blow against South Carolina had already been struck.

From the outset of the Yamasee War, the Ocheses discovered that they benefited from the assistance of the smaller and more vulnerable Indian groups that lived between the Ocmulgee and the South Carolina settlements. The Yuchis, the Savannahs, the Apalachees, the Apalachicolas, and the Yamasees had been fairly close neighbors of the Ocheses for several decades and had developed a healthy respect for them. While some of the Indians from these groups probably took part in the Ocheses' hazy plans to make war on the South Carolinians, all of them had the autonomy and incentives to strike out on their own. The early clashes of the war were dominated by the smaller tribes of the Savannah basin, not only the Yamasees but also the Apalachees, the Savannahs, and the Apalachicolas. In July 1715 the Apalachees led a joint assault on South Carolina's southwestern parishes, killing sixteen colonists, taking several prisoners, and burning the bridge over the Pon Pon River.[131] While a handful of Ochese warriors might have participated in the early raids on the South Carolina settlements, it appears that the vast majority of them were absent from the engagements of the spring and summer of 1715.[132] After killing nearly all the English traders among them, the Ocheses adopted a more cautious approach to the war once the South Carolinians proved determined to defend themselves. Fearing reprisals from the South Carolinians, the survivors from small tribes of the Savannah basin began to flee further into the interior. Most of them headed toward the Ocmulgee, where they joined the Ocheses in regrouping for the next stage of the war.[133]

While the Ocheses were bolstered by the arrival of several hundred refugees from the Savannah River tribes, they drew just as much confidence from their alliance with the other Muskogean provinces. The Ocheses had strong and long-standing connections to the Tallapoosas and a solid working relationship with the Abeikas and the Alabamas. The western Muskogeans displayed great respect for the strength and accomplishments of the prestigious Ochese leaders, a respect that probably convinced them to go along with the Ocheses' attacks on the South Carolina traders. Unlike the Apalachees, the Savannahs, and the Apalachicolas, however, the Alabamas, the Abeikas, and the Tallapoosas remained strong and secure enough to keep the Ocheses at a distance. Several hundred miles from the nearest South Carolina settlement, they had no immediate fears of English retaliation. Instead, their greatest concern during the early stages of the Yamasee War was the sudden shortage of European trade goods. The western Muskogeans continued to look to the Ocheses for diplomatic and military advice, but at the same time they also expressed their willingness to establish stronger relations with the French and Spanish settlements along the Gulf Coast.

The Ocheses actually encouraged their allies to search for new colonial markets. Upon hearing that the Tallapoosas were thinking about sending emissaries to Pensacola, Brims, the principal headman of Coweta, urged them "to make friendship with the Spaniards with whom they desired good relations."[134] Though reluctant to make their own commitments to Louisiana and Florida authorities, the Ocheses were perfectly willing to have other Indians test the waters for them. The Tallapoosas quickly established themselves as an important link to the Spanish in western Florida, sending ninety headmen and a hundred warriors to visit the Pensacola garrison during the summer of 1715.[135] They also joined the Alabamas in making a number of trips to and from Mobile, where French authorities readily handed out guns, ammunition, and other "considerable presents."[136] Like the Yamasees who sought refuge in Saint Augustine, the western Muskogeans were able to secure a new lease on life by making some perfunctory "submissions" to the French and Spanish governments.

As these Indians cemented their ties to their new colonial allies, all of them claimed that a larger and more powerful group lay waiting in the wings. French and Spanish officials eagerly anticipated further word from the "great cacique of Coweta" and the rest of the Ocheses, but after a few months their hopes began to fade.[137] Despite the generous receptions accorded to the Alabamas, the Tallapoosas, and the Yamasees, the Ocheses were apparently reluctant to compromise their autonomy by paying tribute to the "empires" that they had raided and harassed for the previous twenty years. Though now at war with the enemies of France and Spain, the Ocheses were determined to fight the South Carolinians on their own terms for as long as it remained in their power to do so.

By the end of 1715 the Ocheses realized that it would take more than a few scattered raids to mount an effective challenge to South Carolina. With the Catawbas and other Piedmont groups gradually withdrawing from the war, the South Carolinians were taking new steps to shore up the defenses along their southwestern frontiers, thereby putting more pressure on the Ocheses and their Yamasee, Apalachee, and Apalachicola allies. While the western Muskogeans had several thousand warriors at their disposal, they balked at the prospect of traveling long distances to join a fight for which they had never had much interest.[138] The Ocheses also had some valuable connections to the fearsome Chickasaws of the Mississippi Valley, but the Chickasaws had quickly taken pains to distance themselves from the anti-English insurgency and were actively attempting to regain the trust and trade of the South Carolinians.[139] Faced with a pressing need for additional Indian manpower, the Ocheses and their depleted allies had to set their sights on the Cherokees, the numerous and apparently "neutral" mountain dwellers who held as much promise for the South Carolinians' enemies as they did for the South Carolinians themselves.

The massacre at Tugaloo in January 1716 not only dashed the Ocheses' hopes for an alliance with the Cherokees but also signaled a major change in the Muskogean war effort. Though hardly the most formidable warriors in the Southeast, the Cherokees became a much more imposing foe when bolstered by South Carolina troops and English weapons. For the first time during the Yamasee War, the Ocheses were forced to confront the likely possibility of an enemy invasion.[140] Though colonial officials correctly assumed that the "Crick Indians" would be "very much disheartened" by the South Carolina–Cherokee alliance, they were premature in assuming that the Ocheses and their allies would soon crawl back to Charles Town on their knees.[141] Like several of South Carolina's Indian enemies, the Ocheses discovered that they could continue to mount an effective resistance by making certain strategic adjustments. The traditionally aggressive Ocheses quickly got to work on a series of defensive preparations, rising to the kind of logistical challenge that had defied several other insurgent groups.

Above all the Ocheses' strategies hinged on their ability to put protective distance between themselves and the South Carolinians, an adjustment that had benefited the Yamasees and eluded—at least initially—the various groups of the Piedmont. In the spring of 1716 the Ocheses conducted their second major migration in twenty-five years, returning to their old homeland along the banks of the Chattahoochee. In moving away from the Ocmulgee basin, they appeared to assume a new identity, thereby inspiring European observers to come up with new names for them. To Florida authorities it appeared that a restoration of the old province of "Apalachicola" was in the works.[142] While many of the Muskogean and Hitichi towns did return to the vicinity of the sites that they had occupied prior to their rupture with the Spanish in 1690, the composition and arrangement of these towns had changed markedly in the intervening years. When the Ocheses moved back to the Chattahoochee, they brought along some of the Yamasees, as well as the tattered remnants of the Yuchis, the Savannahs, the Apalachees, and the Apalachicolas.[143] The Muskogeans and the Hitichis of the Lower Chattahoochee basin had welcomed diverse groups of refugees among them as far back as the mid-seventeenth century, but the fallout from the Yamasee War eclipsed all precedents.[144] With more refugees moving into Muskogean towns or settling nearby for protection, the stage seemed set for a new province peopled by a larger and more diverse group of Indians, a group that the South Carolinians would thereafter know as the "Lower Creeks."

While the Yamasee War inspired many important changes in Indian identity, the Lower Creeks did not fashion themselves into a new, improved, and more cohesive polity overnight. Despite the gradual emergence of "provincial" identities in the years before the Yamasee War, the Muskogeans—like most southeastern Indians—continued to reserve their strongest political loyalties for their individual "towns."[145] The idea of a self-conscious "confederacy" still lay several decades in the future, and for many years different "Lower Creeks" would continue to refer to themselves as Cowetas, Cussitas, Apalachicolas, Tuskeegees, and so on. Throughout the Yamasee War and its aftermath, the towns along the Chattahoochee often displayed considerable autonomy in their political and military affairs. The threat of Cherokee, Catawba, and South Carolinian raids persuaded many towns to surround themselves with palisades or other fortifications.[146] On at least one occasion, the pro-Spanish leaders of one Lower Creek town were inspired to expand their fortifications to protect themselves against pro-English Indians from other Lower Creek towns.[147] During especially stressful periods, the Lower Creek towns could often take on the appearance of isolated islands in a turbulent sea.

Despite recurrent tensions, however, the different towns were not completely cut off from one another. In military affairs, at least, cooperation between the towns was far more common than disagreement. Many of the Lower Creeks had long been accustomed to combining forces in large-scale military operations, a practice that in recent years had been reinforced even further by the South Carolina trader-imperialists. Continuing the prominent role it had displayed during Queen Anne's War, the prestigious "founding town" of Coweta played host to many of the Lower Creeks' military councils during the Yamasee War. As the "great cacique" Brims organized war parties to send against the Cherokees or South Carolinians, he was aided by a cadre of military advisors from various Lower Creek towns. According to Spanish sources, one of Brims's most esteemed "war captains" was Cherokeeleechee, a Hitichi-speaking Apalachicola leader whose ethnic stock differed from that of the Lower Creek "emperor."[148] While some of the connections between the Lower Creeks' various towns and ethnic groups certainly predated the Yamasee War, it is reasonable to venture that the presence of a major outside threat encouraged further cooperation between Lower Creek leaders, much as it did between politically active South Carolinians.[149]

By relocating to the Chattahoochee, fortifying their villages, and displaying a more cohesive military front, the Lower Creeks managed to defend themselves with great success in the two years after the Tugaloo disaster. At least part of their success was due to the unexpectedly light pressure exerted by their enemies; the massive campaigns that the South Carolinians and the Cherokees had planned during the winter of 1715–16 never materialized, and the few raiding parties that did set out against the Lower Creeks soon got more than they had bargained for.[150] To the Cherokees, the Catawbas, and the South Carolinians, the Lower Creeks appeared to grow stronger as the war dragged on. Given new breathing room by their defensive adjustments, the Lower Creeks quickly returned to the aggressive raids and guerilla tactics that had always served them most effectively. In addition to harassing the villages and supply lines of South Carolina's Indian allies, they continued to target the settlements of the South Carolinians themselves.[151] During a short stay among the Lower Creeks in 1716, a Spanish officer named Diego Peña ransomed two English captives and saw a war party make a triumphant return to Coweta with the horses of four South Carolina rangers.[152] In time the Lower Creeks' negotiations with the competing imperial powers would reveal that they had accumulated an impressive quantity of plunder, most of it in the form of slaves, horses, and captured colonists.[153]

For all their apparent vitality, however, many of the Lower Creeks and their western Muskogean allies were beginning to struggle under the burdens of the Yamasee War. Their continued military success masked a major problem that had already begun to hinder their fighting ability. For several decades the various Muskogeans had grown more and more dependent on guns for waging war. Bows remained reasonably effective weapons: Indians had adopted metal-tipped arrows and other technological advancements since the seventeenth century, and a skilled archer could still get off several well-placed shots in the time it took to reload a musket. Nevertheless, the European firearms that began to enter the market after 1700 or so were demonstrably superior to Indian weapons in terms of range, power, and accuracy.[154] Of the nearly thirty-five hundred Muskogean warriors who took part in the campaigns against the Choctaws in 1711 and 1712, over twenty-seven hundred were described as "gun men" by the South Carolina government.[155]

While the Muskogeans had acquired an abundance of flintlock muskets by 1715, they did not have free rein to use these guns for as long as they wished. The typical "trade guns" purchased by the Indians were shorter and shoddier than the weapons allotted for European use, "consumable" tools that required considerable maintenance to remain in working order. Even weapons patched together by ad hoc Indian gunsmiths were useless without a steady supply of powder and bullets.[156] Though the Lower Creeks, the Tallapoosas, the Abeikas, and the Alabamas managed to fulfill some of their needs through their direct and indirect connections to the French and the Spanish, the supply from these sources could never keep pace with the Indians' demands.[157] This shortage did not bode well for the Muskogeans, especially when compared to the seemingly unlimited supply of military hardware that the Cherokees and the Catawbas had at their disposal.

For all their problems, the South Carolinians enjoyed a mercantile advantage that was recognized by nearly everyone in the Southeast. From the earliest stages of the Yamasee War, some of the South Carolinians clung to the hope that their Indian enemies would eventually wear down from lack of essential English trade goods. After a large Apalachee-Yamasee war party struck the southwestern settlements in July 1715, Francis Le Jau took solace in the observation that many of the warriors "had only bows and Arrows," a possible sign that the Indians "want[ed] ammunition and [were] not able to mend their Arms."[158] The lure of English trade goods soon proved instrumental in bringing the Catawbas and several other enemies to terms with South Carolina, and there was reason to believe that it might have a similar effect on the more stubborn Muskogeans. Pro-English elements probably began to emerge within the various Muskogean provinces as early as the spring of 1715, and by the following year they had grown visible enough to worry French and Spanish authorities.[159] By early 1717 the trend had come to include Muskogean leaders as influential as Brims. That spring the ascendant "anglophile factions" among the Lower Creeks and the Tallapoosas sent two headmen and two South Carolinian prisoners on a mission to Charles Town, where they delivered the Muskogeans' first tentative feelers for peace.[160]

The South Carolinians suddenly found themselves in a situation strikingly similar to the one they faced with the Huspah king and the rest of the Yamasees around Saint Augustine. Though many colonists continued to yearn for vengeance, most of them had grown sick and tired of the war and were willing to take the first available exit.[161] They eagerly awaited the reports of John Jones, the South Carolina trader who had bravely traveled to the Chattahoochee after receiving word of the possible breakthrough. After speaking with Brims and several other Lower Creek leaders, Jones came away convinced that the Muskogeans were willing to make amends to South Carolina and renounce their ties to the Yamasees, whom they had apparently "resolved to destroy though under the walls of Saint Augustine for having drawn them into a war with [the colonists]."[162] This news was more than good enough for South Carolina authorities, who quickly set a time and place for a peace conference. Upon reaching the designated meeting point, however, the South Carolina delegation realized that their negotiations with the Muskogeans would not go as smoothly as they initially had hoped. Instead of the venerable Brims with all his attendants, they were met by a single Lower Creek messenger who claimed that his people could not make peace "until their corn was ripe."[163] This was in all probability a reference to the Green Corn Ceremony, an important annual ritual of spiritual, economic, and political renewal practiced by the Muskogeans and many other Indian cultures throughout the Southeast. To the impatient South Carolinians, however, the whole thing smacked of foot-dragging and bore an uncanny resemblance to the impasse with the Cherokees in the fall of 1715. Once again the South Carolinians found themselves on the short end of a diplomatic misunderstanding that turned their buoyant optimism into grave concern.

Like the Cherokees a year and a half earlier, the Muskogeans were far from unanimous in their support of a settlement with South Carolina. Even as some of them initiated contact with the South Carolinians, others were engaged in a last-ditch effort to win the war on their own terms. In the fall of 1716 the various Muskogean provinces had sent emissaries on a long trip to New York to engage the assistance of the Iroquois Six Nations. With studied arrogance these emissaries portrayed themselves as representatives of "50 Nations of Indians" who had "done great Damage" to the "English of Carolina" and warned their hosts "not to assist them [the South Carolinians] lest they might kill some of their People which they would not willingly do." Duly impressed by this backhanded invitation, the Iroquois sent twenty of their own "ambassadors" to accompany the Muskogeans on their return home. [164] Though the Muskogeans and the Iroquois were primarily intent on planning attacks against their mutual Indian enemies, the Cherokees and the Catawbas, the South Carolina government was thrown into an instant panic.[165] According to Commons House speaker George Logan, the "union of two such powerful nations" under any circumstances posed an intolerable threat "to all the English colonies on the main." Should the "Creeks" successfully use the Iroquois to help them defeat the Cherokees and the Catawbas, "they might fly off and renew their hostilities against [the South Carolina] government."[166]

This disturbing possibility prompted the South Carolinians to jump-start their stalled negotiations with the Muskogeans. But while the government had employed three hundred troops in a similar situation with the Cherokees, it entrusted its Muskogean mission to a smaller and more subtle group of agents. In the summer of 1717 the experienced frontiersman Theophilus Hastings led a caravan of eleven traders, one black slave, and twelve heavily laden packhorses toward the Chattahoochee. [167] The arrival of these emissaries proved deeply upsetting to many of the Lower Creeks. The town of Cussita kept the South Carolinians at bay by displaying a red warning flag, and a number of pro-Spanish Indians—primarily Apalachees and Apalachicolas who still harbored an intense hatred of the English—talked about capturing the visitors and delivering them to Saint Augustine. [168] Ultimately, however, these malcontents chose not to challenge those Lower Creeks who seemed to welcome the South Carolina traders as long-lost friends. One of the traders, the well-traveled John Musgrove, brought along his half-Muskogean son Johnny, who—as legend has it—was promptly paired off with one of Brims's young nieces. [169]

Despite the importance of these human ties, the success of the South Carolinians' mission rested primarily on the backs of their packhorses. According to a disgruntled Spanish correspondent, many of the Lower Creeks, including Brims and his wives, reacted with unrestrained delight at the sight of the fine cloth and beads that the English had brought with them. [170] Shortly thereafter the stock of the South Carolinians rose even further when two Lower Creek headmen returned to their villages with stories of the lavish treatment they had received during a late-summer visit to Charles Town. During their stay the two leaders received two pounds of powder, six pounds of bullets, coats, hats, and striped blanket. When one of the Indians expressed interest in seeing an English ship, they were escorted to the harbor and given a three-gun salute. [171] By the fall of 1717 many of the Tallapoosas and the Lower Creeks trusted the South Carolinians enough to send a delegation of eleven headmen to treat with Governor Robert Johnson and his council.

That November the governor and the Muskogean emissaries reached an agreement to end all hostility between their respective peoples. The South Carolina government would agree to send trade goods to the Muskogeans as long as the Muskogeans could guarantee their safety. Though the Indians responded favorably to these terms, they took care not to promise too much. They not only claimed that they would have to confirm the treaty with the other headmen back home but also warned that they had "no power to conclude anything" for the Alabamas, who evidently remained aloof from the proceedings. [172] Despite these reservations Governor Johnson treated these negotiations as an unqualified success. Within a matter of weeks, the government factor at Fort Moore received permission to trade with the "Creeks" and was even encouraged to outdo the French and the Spanish in providing them with guns. [173]

South Carolina officials expressed further satisfaction at the Lower Creeks' request "that fifty white men [might] be sent up with them . . . to show the French and Spaniards that they [did] not want for friends to assist them."[174] By early 1718 the fifty South Carolina traders were not only hard at work among the towns of the Lower Creeks but were also traveling as far west as the Alabamas, who reportedly greeted their arrival with enthusiasm.[175] Optimists within the South Carolina government assumed that they were well on their way to reabsorbing the various Muskogeans and even began efforts to systematize them into a single "Creek" nation with lower, middle, and upper sections.[176] But given the South Carolinians' difficulties in implementing a similar strategy among the Cherokees, they were bound to have an even harder time with the Muskogeans. Not only were the far-flung "Creeks" less politically cohesive than the Cherokees; they also stood in a much better position to assert themselves against outside interference.

The Lower Creeks proved especially eager to show the South Carolinians the kind of alliance they had in mind. Though they did not actually dictate the conditions of their settlement with South Carolina, they managed to secure some extremely favorable terms. More than anything else, their renewed attachment to the South Carolinians meant access to more and better firearms—a new pipeline to the military hardware that would allow them to continue fighting the wars that meant the most to them. One of the provisions in their treaty with South Carolina required the South Carolinians' to assist the Indians in repairing their broken firearms.[177] Some South Carolinians probably fooled themselves into believing that their prodigal sons would not use their new guns against South Carolina's other Indian allies, but the Cherokees knew all too well that the Lower Creeks were applying for peace "not out of Love but [a] Want to be supplyed."[178] In the final analysis most South Carolinians simply did not care if their Cherokee or Catawba allies suffered, as long as the Lower Creeks would reopen themselves to trade and keep their raiding parties away from the colonial settlements. During every stage of negotiation, the Muskogeans were forthright about their intentions to continue fighting the Cherokees and the Catawbas under any circumstances.[179] During a ceremony held at Coweta in January 1718, the Lower Creeks presented the South Carolinians with a broken bow that symbolized their peace with the English and a bloodstained knife that symbolized their ongoing war with the Cherokees. The Lower Creeks then announced that if the South Carolinians broke the peace by assisting the Cherokees in any way, they would "without hesitation wage war against them as well."[180]

Though this warning did not stop the South Carolinians from providing arms to the Cherokees, it spoke volumes about the strength and self-confidence of the Lower Creeks. Several months after restoring South Carolina's alliance with the Lower Creeks, Governor Johnson finally had to admit that "treatys with them [were] very precarious."[181] Though their forebears had been considered the most valuable and trustworthy parts of the South Carolina buffer zone, the Lower Creeks had become the most unpredictable and intimidating of the province's Indian allies. Even if the South Carolinians chose to believe that the Yamasees had "drawn" the Lower Creeks into the war, they could not forget that the Lower Creeks had fought South Carolina to a standstill for more than two years. The Lower Creeks knew that they frightened the South Carolinians, and—like Indians throughout the Southeast—they occasionally used the South Carolinians' fear to their own diplomatic or economic advantage. The Cherokees and the Catawbas, however, demonstrated that intimidation could only go so far. Ultimately what distinguished the Lower Creeks from these other Indians was their ability to put more geographic and emotional distance between themselves and the South Carolina imperialists.[182]

The Cherokees gradually discovered that a protective mountain barrier and a proud tradition of independence could not forestall their troubling reliance on the South Carolinians. The Catawbas, despite their relative proximity to the South Carolina settlements, could often find relief from the South Carolinians by turning to the Virginians, but even this option had its limits. While the Piedmont groups could benefit from a "buyer's market," the various Muskogean groups found themselves in a veritable "bargain basement." In the South Carolinians' efforts to shore up their alliances with the "Creeks," nothing caused them more concern than the looming presence of the French and the Spanish.

An Imperial Rivalry Renewed

South Carolina officials had regarded the French as their most dangerous rivals since the days when Louisiana had consisted of little more than a few wooden shacks and a handful of Canadian fur traders. When Louisiana began to experience its first significant growth in the immediate aftermath of the Yamasee War, the French suddenly became even more imposing in the eyes of the South Carolinians. After losing Newfoundland and Acadia in Queen Anne's War, French imperial authorities grew determined to make Louisiana a bulwark against further British incursions.[183] In 1717 they conceded the direction of Louisiana to the Company of the Indies, a joint-stock venture that promised immediate improvement in the colony's strength and profitability. In Louisiana's first year under company management, its white population increased from 300 to 550, and over the next four years, forty-three ships brought an additional 6,000 settlers, 1,000 soldiers, and 2,000 black slaves to the colony.[184] Even after sustaining significant losses from death and desertion, Louisiana's population stood at roughly 5,400 whites and 600 blacks by 1721, figures that rekindled the South Carolinians' old fears of French "encirclement."[185]

Above all the South Carolinians worried that Louisiana's resurgence would put an end to their hard-earned dominance in southeastern Indian affairs. Though the South Carolinians had no proof that the French had incited the Yamasee War, they readily believed that Bienville and his cohorts would try to take full advantage of it. South Carolina officials not only suspected the French of luring the Lower Creeks toward the Chattahoochee but also assumed that the French would try to recoup the Chickasaws and win over the Cherokees.[186] Virginia's governor Alexander Spotswood initially dismissed these fears as "ill grounded," claiming that the French were still too "small" to penetrate "the fastness of the great mountains."[187] In truth the South Carolinians had far more confidence in the French than the French had in themselves. At the beginning of the Yamasee War, Bienville expressed doubts in his ability to maintain a strong alliance with the Muskogeans who approached his government and accurately predicted that "these Indians [would] not find the same advantage with [the French] that they had with the English, who sold them merchandise very cheap."[188] Though the influx of more money and manpower after 1717 made it easier for Louisianans to engage in the Indian trade, they soon discovered that an expanded trade carried more potential for the kinds of fraud, abuse, and misunderstanding that haunted South Carolina's system.[189] Louisiana's sudden expansion also brought a burgeoning rivalry with the new Spanish colony of Texas, tension between French settlers and the Natchez Indians, and the arrival of a new governor who had little interest or ability in Indian affairs.[190] The highly competent Bienville, now relegated to a subordinate position within the government, must have longed for the simpler days when he could rule Louisiana's frontiers from his dinner table. He and his experienced colleagues knew that the South Carolinians would not stay down for long and that the French would have to be content with modest imperial victories.[191]

Throughout the Yamasee War, the French often had a hard time making headway among the Indians in their own backyard. While the Choctaws remained close allies of the French, the Chickasaws—mortal enemies of the Choctaws—expressed no interest in abandoning their close and profitable relationship with the South Carolinians.[192] However, the French did manage to build a stronger relationship with the Alabamas and the Tallapoosas, the Indians who most actively courted French assistance after breaking with the South Carolinians. By the end of 1715 the French had begun to send boats along the network of rivers that reached up from Mobile, a means of access more efficient and less intrusive than South Carolina's overland system.[193] The western Muskogeans provided a definite boost to Louisiana's Indian trade, but in order to take better advantage of this new market, the French felt that they would have to establish a more permanent presence along their eastern frontiers.[194] Queen Anne's War had convinced the French of the value of forts as frontier institutions, and French officials had drawn up plans for a fort at the confluence of the Coosa and Tallapoosa rivers (present-day Montgomery, Alabama) as early as 1714. The outbreak of the Yamasee War cleared the way for this project, but the Louisiana government hesitated for another two years, primarily because it did not want to be accused by the British government of instigating the southeastern Indians into their war against South Carolina. They finally completed Fort Toulouse in the summer of 1717, only months before the first South Carolina traders began returning to the area.[195]

A three-hundred-square-foot log stockade with four towers and six field pieces, Fort Toulouse was neither imposing enough to quell the local Indians nor efficient enough to saturate the local trade market. The Alabamas and the Tallapoosas who flocked to the area often conducted business with the South Carolina traders within sight of the fort's walls.[196] At the same time, however, the Indians seemed determined to keep Fort Toulouse in operation. Since the French made a conscious effort to keep prices lower at the fort than at any of their other trading posts, the Indians could often find satisfying bargains. River travel made it easier for the French to transport heavier items such as gunpowder and bullets, and the Indians tended to buy those goods at the fort whenever possible.[197] The French outpost not only gave the western Muskogeans a badly needed alternative to the resurgent English but also ensured that the South Carolina traders would remain on their best behavior.[198] Though French officials expressed disappointment in the leaky fort and its garrison of sixty ragged, scurvy-ridden troops, the South Carolinians were not privy to this inside information. From their distant perspective, Fort Toulouse seemed like an infectious sore on South Carolina's western frontiers, a base from which the French could "dayly encroach upon [them] and draw away [their] Indians."[199] Despite the ire of the South Carolinians and the fort's myriad weaknesses, the French—with the valuable assistance of the western Muskogeans—would continue to hold their position on the Coosa-Tallapoosa for another forty-five years.[200]

Warts and all, Fort Toulouse represented a step in the right direction for French imperialists. As Louisiana continued to expand over the next several years, Bienville and other officials gradually became more confident of their ability to challenge their imperial rivals. While South Carolina authorities correctly assumed that the French would try to build another post even further to the east, they did not foresee the direction of the next French offensive. In 1718 Bienville's attempt to erect a fort at the mouth of the Apalachicola River indicated that his government had new designs on Spanish Florida.[201] The following year the outbreak of the War of the Quadruple Alliance in Europe thrust the French and the Spanish into a heated contest for Pensacola.[202] As part of their eastward advance, the French began to establish their first meaningful contact with the Lower Creeks. French agents even managed to persuade Brims's son and several other Lower Creek leaders to visit Mobile, where Bienville reportedly entertained them in grand style.[203] According to one French observer, the Lower Creeks "had begun to say that [they] had lost spirit, which [was] their favorite term." By 1720, however, these Indians had apparently developed "a very high opinion of the French."[204] The French could not yet compete with the South Carolinians as purveyors of cheap and high-quality trade goods, but some of the Lower Creeks had begun to see them as an intriguing new option.

Though the French looked like the real upstarts in the Tallapoosa and Chattahoochee basins, the Spanish benefited even more from the wartime adjustments of the Tallapoosas and the Lower Creeks. By early 1715 the Spanish—pinned within their forts by recurrent Indian raids—had all but withdrawn from the Southeast's imperial struggle. When the Tallapoosas broke with the South Carolinians, they breathed new life into the pathetic Spanish settlement at Pensacola. The commandant of Fort San Carlos was compelled to give most of his meager supplies to an endless stream of Tallapoosa visitors, but his men could finally venture beyond the walls in relative safety. With overland communications at a standstill, however, the residents of Florida's other Spanish enclave remained largely unaware of the encouraging developments along the Gulf Coast.[205] Spanish officials in Saint Augustine still seethed over the loss of their extensive "provinces" during Queen Anne's War and hungered for a chance to regain them from the South Carolinians. The arrival of the Yamasees in the late spring and early summer of 1715 certainly gave the Spanish some encouragement, but at the same time it merely whetted their desire to win over Brims and the rest of the Lower Creeks.

While the Yamasees claimed to have connections to the venerable "great cacique of Coweta," the Apalachees and the Apalachicolas eventually proved even more helpful in bridging the gap between the Spanish and the Lower Creeks. Though the Apalachees and the Apalachicolas had turned their backs on the Florida missions during the 1690s and early 1700s, many of them had developed an even stronger dislike of the South Carolinians in recent years. As late as 1735, the Apalachicola headman Cherokeeleechee continued to show his contempt for the South Carolinians, proudly admitting that he had "done the English all the harm [he] could" during the Yamasee War.[206] When the Yamasee refugees first came to Saint Augustine in May 1715, they hinted that Cherokeeleechee, a confidant of the "great cacique of Coweta," wanted to establish a closer relationship with the Spanish.[207] Cherokeeleechee confirmed these hints in the fall of that year by traveling to Saint Augustine and smoking a peace pipe with Governor Córcoles. The two men reportedly struck up a quick and strong friendship, hoping that each could bolster the other's position among the Ocheses.[208] After the Ocheses and their allies moved away from the Ocmulgee in the spring of 1716, Cherokeeleechee and some of his Apalachee neighbors made an effort to stay in touch with the Spanish officials in Saint Augustine.

By this time the Spanish had already begun to consider moving Florida's capital from Saint Augustine to the abandoned province of Apalachee, another indication of how badly they coveted the Lower Creeks' assistance.[209] In July 1716 they sent Lieutenant Diego Peña and four other Spanish soldiers to accompany Cherokeeleechee on a mission to the Chattahoochee. Peña's orders were simple: to get the "great cacique" to renew his obedience to the Spanish Crown and persuade him to move his people to Apalachee. Brims and the other Lower Creek leaders received Peña with the utmost courtesy, realizing that they could not afford to keep the Spanish at bay forever. But whereas the Spanish of the 1680s had attempted to extract Brims's obedience at gunpoint, the Spanish of 1716 seemed far less threatening and overbearing. During the Yamasee War the Spanish obedience drill became little more than a harmless exercise, a chance to acquire Spanish goods and favors in exchange for a few token pledges. Conversing with Peña, Brims duly pledged his loyalty to Spain and politely agreed to consider a move to Apalachee.[210] Several curious Lower Creeks accompanied Peña back to Saint Augustine to deliver Brims's replies. When they returned to the Chattahoochee several months later, their glowing reviews of the governor's hospitality convinced many of the Indians that they should render their obedience more often.[211]

Throughout 1717 and 1718 the Lower Creeks and the Tallapoosas did much to strengthen their ceremonial ties to the Spanish officials in Saint Augustine and Pensacola. In April 1717 newly appointed Governor Juan de Ayala y Escobar played host to a large delegation of 157 Lower Creek, Apalachee, and Tallapoosa headmen led by Sepeycoffee, the "beloved son" and designated successor of the "great cacique of Coweta." Sepeycoffee claimed to be acting on Brims's authority and explained his father's absence on the basis of "his great age and [his] being preoccupied with taking care of his places." Governor Ayala enthusiastically accepted the "goodwill, submission, and obedience" of his guests and agreed to their request for a new Spanish fort along the Gulf Coast. [212] Meanwhile the viceroy of New Spain, who had begun to reevaluate his earlier dismissals of Pensacola, entertained seven Tallapoosa and Apalachee headmen at his palace in Mexico City. [213] Tixjana, the war chief of the Tallapoosa town of Tallassee, returned from Mexico with a new Christian name and a new commission to serve as the "Lord" and "Campmaster General" of the Tallapoosas. In January 1718 Spanish officials organized a ceremony at the Tallapoosa town of Teguale in which they vested Sepeycoffee and Tixjana with "rods of office." They also asked the other Lower Creek and Tallapoosa headmen to move closer to Pensacola, where the Spanish would instruct them "in the things of which they were ignorant" and allow them to "wield greater authority and become richer than the common people." [214] From the Spanish perspective, these various ceremonies marked the restoration of the "republic of Indians," a quasi-feudal system of patronage and vassalage that would allow the Spanish to rule through Indian leaders. [215]

But the Muskogeans clearly had their own interpretations of the Spanish obedience rituals. At the large 1717 ceremony in Saint Augustine, the Indians even brought their own crown to place on the head of the bemused Spanish governor. In the subsequent negotiations, Sepeycoffee and the other Lower Creek and Tallapoosa leaders showed that the real purpose of their visit was not to render submission but to smoke the governor's cigars, drink Spanish liquor, and ask for more military supplies. [216] Once the Indians returned to their own villages, the Spanish often hesitated to pursue them, fearing that if they did not bring good presents with them, the Indians would "accuse them of being basehearted." [217] In the words of Pensacola commandant Salinas Varona, the Indians of the region would "become final allies of him who gives them most." [218] Though Spanish officials could keep a good table, they never had enough financial support to provide the Indians with quality goods on a regular basis. When the Spanish finally constructed the rather small and unimposing Fort San Marcos at the mouth of the Apalachee River in 1718, only six Lower Creek towns—primarily those of Apalachee and Apalachicola stock—showed any interest in moving nearby.[219] The Spanish emissaries who visited the towns along the Chattahoochee expressed dismay at what they perceived as a lack of respect on the part of the Lower Creeks. Brims and other leaders frequently snubbed the Spanish in favor of French or English invitations, leading Diego Peña to conclude that "little confidence [could] be placed in their friendship."[220]

Officials in Louisiana and South Carolina grew equally frustrated in their attempts to win the loyalty of the various "Creeks." After watching the Alabamas and the Tallapoosas use the South Carolina traders as leverage against Fort Toulouse, the French saw proof that the Indians were "savages only in name" and had "as much discernment and shrewdness as [could] be expected from people without education."[221] After several years of trying to restore South Carolina's influence among the Muskogeans, Governor Johnson was forced to admit that the South Carolinians had "not above half of the trade and number of Indians subject to this government as [they] had in 1715." Like their French and Spanish rivals, South Carolina imperialists expected nothing less than total obedience from their Indian allies and trading partners. Johnson could come up with only one explanation for the Creeks' impertinent behavior: they were "affecting a newtrallity, yet makeing their advantages of the differences happening between the European nations."[222]

Whenever Indians hesitated to comply with suggestions or dabbled with more than one imperial power at the same time, they appeared "neutral" in the eyes of frustrated colonial officials. Many of the Southeast's Indian societies fit this definition of neutrality to some extent, but the Muskogean provinces— situated directly in the middle of the English-Spanish-French triangle—fit it better than any others. In the aftermath of the Yamasee War, the Muskogeans were unquestionably "neutral" in the sense that they recognized the dangers of attaching themselves too firmly to a single nation of white men. All the Muskogeans—but especially the Lower Creeks—knew that an overreliance on the South Carolinians or anyone else would make their lives "as unhappy as that of a poor fellow, who had only one perverse wife, and yet must bear with her forward temper."[223] Like the Cherokees and the Catawbas, many of the Creeks took advantage of every opportunity to trade or negotiate with competing groups of Europeans.

In part this dabbling resulted from conscious decisions made by Indian leaders, especially Brims and some of his fellow Lower Creeks. The town of Coweta even hosted a diplomatic conference on the merits of tripart neutrality in the spring of 1718.[224] More often, however, the Alabamas, the Tallapoosas, and the Lower Creeks gave the impression of neutrality simply because they had a hard time reaching the kind of consensus that they needed in order to carry out major political decisions or commitments. Like the Cherokees' "neutrality" in the early months of the Yamasee War, the Creeks' version resulted primarily from the "political paralysis" caused by competition between internal factions.[225] After reaching agreements with small parties of sympathetic Indians, colonial officials often assumed that they had gained valuable footholds within entire Indian nations. The Indians themselves often encouraged them to think this way, knowing that optimistic officials would be more inclined to provide them with material assistance. When a governor thought that he was buying the Lower Creeks' loyalty, he actually was doing nothing more than upping his stock among a limited segment of the Lower Creek population. Just as a pro-English Lower Creek faction could ask South Carolina's governor "to show the French and Spaniards that they [did] not want for friends to assist them," a pro-Spanish faction could tell Florida's governor that "it was important that the English should see their [the Lower Creeks'] friends and protectors."[226] In this way imperial competition and Indian factionalism could reinforce each other almost indefinitely: new options led to new divisions, which in turn inspired the rival colonial powers to make themselves even more available to the Indians.

Though the various Muskogean provinces had long histories of internal debate and dissent, they had never experienced anything quite like the kind of factionalism that began to emerge during and immediately after the Yamasee War.[227] The inner workings of these factions remained largely invisible to colonial observers, but they often proved confusing to the Indians themselves. The lines between factions were difficult to define, cutting across provinces, towns, clans, families, and even individuals.[228] Since Indians rarely shared the black-and-white worldviews of European imperialism, they frequently left room in their lives for different kinds of friends and enemies. More frequently the diplomatic views of the southeastern Indians followed a "red and white" dichotomy: "red" towns and leaders were associated with military activity, and "white" towns and leaders were associated with peacetime functions. The lines between red and white were often just as hazy and fluid as lines between political factions; leaders and towns could frequently change their "color" at a moment's notice.[229] Many of the Muskogeans felt no compunctions about belonging to more than one faction at the same time, as long as it served their own sense of stability. By 1717, however, every Muskogean required some kind of European connection in order to feel secure. At no time after the Yamasee War did the Muskogeans give rise to a truly neutralist, anti-European faction comparable to the one that emerged among the Iroquois Five Nations in the mid-seventeenth century.[230] Individual "Creeks" were clearly capable of playing the French, the Spanish, and the English against each other on occasion, but it was impossible for them to remain completely neutral in their hearts and minds.

No episode demonstrated this tenet more clearly than Diego Peña's visit to the Lower Creeks in the summer of 1717. When Peña demanded to know why the Lower Creeks were entertaining English traders after pledging their obedience to Spain, Brims initially tried to explain that the South Carolinians had come "on invitation of some men who had been circulating evil talk without his knowledge." Dissatisfied, Peña continued to press his complaint until "the great cacique"—to Peña's utter astonishment—hung his head and wept, tearfully claiming that the Spanish were "as white as they [the English] were and that he [Peña] should reach an agreement with the said English." Brims would have been completely content to live out his life sampling the wares of different colonial markets, but Peña's complaints served to remind Brims that the rival groups of white men would never stop hounding him or his people. Despite their best efforts to maintain contact with the Spanish, Brims and most of the other leaders from Coweta began to list heavily toward the better-provisioned South Carolinians.[231]

Brims's pro-English tendencies proved exasperating to other Lower Creeks who continued to harbor strong reservations about the South Carolinians, including Brims's "beloved son," Sepeycoffee, who once walked into the Pensacola garrison and asked a Spanish official "why the Spaniards, who were such good Christians, remained at peace with the English, who were such bad men."[232] During Peña's 1717 visit, Sepeycoffee frequently expressed his disgust at the vacillations of his father and other Lower Creek leaders. When Sepeycoffee learned that Hastings, Musgrove, and the other South Carolina traders were trying to persuade Brims to kill Peña and his Spanish cohorts, he reportedly grew so incensed "that he was on the point of taking up arms against his father." Though Sepeycoffee held his temper in check, he did escort the Spanish expedition to safety, warning Peña "that the words of his father should not be trusted, that he was a traitor and that he received the English because of the gifts which they gave him."[233]

Though factionalism eventually worked to the Lower Creeks' diplomatic advantage, it often left them as angry, tense, and confused as the Europeans who courted them.[234] The Yamasee War allowed the Muskogeans to distance themselves from the South Carolina imperialists, but it did not unlock the door to a neutral paradise. After more than two years of fighting the South Carolinians, the Alabamas, the Tallapoosas, and the Lower Creeks still maintained enough strength and vitality to intimidate nearly every Indian and European in the Southeast. But even though the Muskogeans no longer had to deal with aggressive traders calling in their debts, they continued to withstand a great deal of unwelcome pressure, not only from resurgent colonial imperialists but also from the Cherokees and the Catawbas, traditional enemies who looked on the Muskogeans with more hatred and suspicion than ever. As the Creeks attempted to rebuild in the aftermath of the Yamasee War, they still had a number of inner and outer demons to exorcise.

The South Carolinians generally spent little time contemplating the hidden problems and motives of the Indians who opposed or assisted them during the Yamasee War. Throughout the war and its immediate aftermath, the overwhelming concern of the South Carolinians was to distinguish the Indians they could trust from those they could not. Only the doggedly hostile Yamasees and the steadfastly loyal Chickasaws seemed cut and dried; the Cherokees, the Catawbas, and especially the Creeks continued to display signs of aloofness, mistrust, and outright hostility even after reaching their settlements with the South Carolina government. When South Carolinians surveyed the southeastern interior in 1720, they got the unsettling impression that the war had not yet run its full course: that "many of [their] Indians [were] still uneasy and dissatisfied."[235] The war lived on not only in the South Carolinians' own vivid fears but also in the divisions, grudges, and misgivings that cast new shadows over the groups of Indians that they had once claimed to know so well. There was no hope of fitting these beleaguered, disgruntled, distant, and "precarious" allies into anything like a single, airtight buffer zone. On the factious and volatile frontiers of the 1720s, South Carolina imperialists would learn only one thing with absolute certainty: that they would never be able to pick up where they thought they had left off on the morning of April 15, 1715.

7. Inchoate Resistance

INDIANS AND IMPERIALISTS IN
THE CREEK-CHEROKEE WAR

William Hatton, South Carolina's agent among the Cherokees, was making his rounds one November day in 1724 when he heard that a major crisis had erupted in the nearby town of Tugaloo. Hatton gathered up all the men and guns he could find on such short notice but arrived far too late to stop an act of destruction as disturbing as anything he had witnessed during the Yamasee War. Under ordinary circumstances, Hatton would not have been too surprised to behold such a scene in the town where the Creek-Cherokee War had effectively begun nearly nine years earlier. But this time, instead of finding dead and grieving Cherokees, Hatton's gaze fell on John Sharp, an experienced South Carolina trader who had operated a successful private store in Tugaloo for several years.

Hatton found Sharp nursing a bullet wound and shivering amid the ransacked rubble of his trading post. The details of Sharp's predicament slowly came to light. The culprits were members of a Creek war party that had slipped into Tugaloo in the early morning hours, rousing Sharp from his sleep by breaking into his home and shooting him in the leg. As the warriors loaded up with merchandise, Sharp desperately attempted to remind his attackers "that the White people and they were friends." Only after the robbers had finished cleaning him out did they pause to voice their own interpretation of South Carolina–Creek relations. One of them reportedly approached Sharp "and [shook] him by the hand and [told] him he was a Tallapoosa, and [took] off his coat; another [cried] out Euchee and [took] off his shirt, and others too Egellahs, Coweatahs, and Yomahitas, till they had stript him out of all his Cloathes." Though Hatton disliked Sharp as a person, he shared his humiliation as a South Carolinian. Hatton's shame quickly gave way to anger when he learned that the Cherokees of Tugaloo had spent the entire morning barricaded in their houses, refusing to lift a finger to defend or assist their resident trader.

After patiently withstanding Hatton's rebukes, the headmen of Tugaloo boldly asked why Hatton and his armed entourage had not set off in pursuit of the Creeks, adding "that they [did] believe that [the South Carolinians] are as much afraid of the Creeks as they [were], and that if they had been guilty of doing half so much to the white people as the Creeks had done they was sure [the white people] should soon Come to Warr upon them." Though stung by this insult, Hatton appeared even more troubled by the fact that the Creeks and the Cherokees—on this occasion, at least—had left each other in peace. Under the smug scrutiny of his Cherokee hosts, Hatton added up all the evidence and delivered his unsettling conclusion in a report to his superiors. Unless things improved in a hurry, the Cherokees and the Creeks would soon "joyn together and send their forces Against the White People."[1]

The fear, uncertainty, and outrage that surrounded the assault on John Sharp were par for the course in the Creek-Cherokee War, a struggle that was in many ways inseparable from the larger conflict that had spawned it. The Yamasee War ended for most South Carolinians in the fall of 1717, but its legacy continued to weigh heavily on most of South Carolina's frontiers for at least another decade. Throughout the 1720s the Creek-Cherokee War set the parameters of frontier exchange between South Carolina imperialists and the various Indian societies of the southeastern interior and gave new life to the region's long tradition of frontier violence.

Though the South Carolinians and their Indian allies continued to share a number of important bonds, they often revealed dramatically different interpretations of the Creek-Cherokee War. The South Carolina imperialists had grown decidedly more circumspect as a result of the Yamasee War, but their caution was often offset by a new sense of confidence that stemmed from their stronger connections to the British Crown. The series of policies and reforms launched during the early 1720s showed that South Carolina officials still had faith in their ability to shape and dictate conditions on their province's far-flung frontiers. At the height of their diplomatic initiatives, however, these officials found themselves struggling to deal with evidence of their own shortcomings. Though South Carolinian and British imperialists attempted to reassert their authority over the southeastern interior through major peace accords in 1727 and 1730, their efforts could not mask an underlying and all too familiar sense of frustration and instability. Once again South Carolinians found themselves up against walls of Indian resistance, walls far less visible but ultimately no less effective than those erected during the Yamasee War.

Reescalation

Though no longer as desperate as they had portrayed themselves in their first petitions to King George I, South Carolinians remained anxious over the "precarious" state of the southeastern interior. Since the outbreak of the Yamasee War, most of South Carolina's political, economic, and frontier policies had been fashioned on an emergency or provisional basis, but the prospect of royal protection in 1720 finally appeared to clear the way for the completion of the province's postwar recovery. Above all South Carolina imperialists hoped that a stronger relationship with the British Crown would help break their stand off with the French, the Spanish, and the Southeast's most powerful Indian societies. Significantly one of their first actions after the antiproprietary "revolution" was to send John Barnwell to London in an effort to help Crown officials sketch out a blueprint for the future of South Carolina imperialism.[2]

Barnwell's twenty years of service as a trader, soldier, and diplomat made him the logical heir to the late Thomas Nairne as South Carolina's foremost authority on the southeastern frontier complex. In meetings with the Board of Trade that stretched through the summer and early fall of 1720, Barnwell revealed that many South Carolinians still lived in mortal terror of the southeastern Indians, believing that the only thing that kept them at peace with the Creeks was "the Warr that [was] between them [the Creeks] and the Cherokees."[3] In many ways Barnwell simply restated what British merchants and imperial officials had learned from five years of letters, reports, and unpaid debts: that the South Carolinians were having a hard time rebounding from the Yamasee War. At the same time, however, Barnwell also brought along a refreshing sense of confidence, indicating that he and his fellow South Carolinians finally stood in a position to put their frontier troubles behind them once and for all. The crux of his mission was to find a similar vein of optimism in his English hosts, thereby laying the groundwork for a new and expensive campaign to "retrieve the desolation of Carolina."[4]

Barnwell had the good fortune to share many of the Board of Trade's predilections and prejudices. His recommendation to pattern South Carolina's frontier policies on French models struck England's leading imperialists as fundamentally sound. Whitehall had just recently begun to buy into the myth of France's *génie coloniale* and felt that it would make sense for the English dominions to borrow a few French ideas. Barnwell's primary reason for evoking the French was to win the board's support for a new ring of frontier forts, but he also proposed French strategies as a means to exert more influence over important Indian leaders.[5] Though every colonial power had its own favorite methods of bribing the Indians, the French had become the first to develop a system that allowed prominent headmen to wear their loyalties around their necks. Barnwell obviously had the French "medal system" in mind when he recommended that His Majesty's government send a shipment of English coins "to be strung on red ribbons and wore by the chiefs" of the major southeastern tribes. For good measure he also insisted that the South Carolinians start distributing small portraits of the royal family to their Indian allies.[6] Barnwell was not naive enough to think that he could buy the loyalty of Indian leaders with a few trinkets, nor did he believe that the English could, or should, exactly replicate a French approach to Indian diplomacy whose success depended on the relatively few demands and pressures that it exerted on the Indians. For the men determined to rebuild South Carolina's imperial power, the real appeal of the "medal system" lay in its symbolic power. Medals, ribbons, and cheap engravings not only served as important icons for the "royalization" of South Carolina but also spoke to the South Carolinian and English imperialists' belief that the time had arrived for the South Carolinians to make a new push into the southeastern interior.

Though Barnwell did not leave England with as much material assistance from Whitehall as he would have liked, he and other South Carolinians nevertheless had reason to believe that the Crown would stand more firmly behind them in their quest to gain control of the Southeast. The clearest proof of this support was the Board of Trade's decision to appoint Francis Nicholson, a grizzled old soldier with more than thirty years of experience in colonial administration, as South Carolina's first provisional royal governor. During terms of service in New York, Maryland, and Virginia, Nicholson had demonstrated both a firm loyalty to the Crown and an unwavering confidence in the might of the British Empire.[7] When the royal warship carrying Barnwell and Nicholson pulled into Charles Town Harbor in May 1721, it was challenged by a party of 120 proprietary sympathizers who had taken positions on one of the city bastions. Nicholson quickly dispatched this "counterrevolution" by waving his royal credentials and ordering his crew to fire a few warning shots over the heads of the malcontents.[8] From his first day in South Carolina, Nicholson established himself as the type of governor who would sit rigidly in his chair and look for some heads to knock together.

Nicholson did not have to wait long to show his mettle again. In July 1721 he got his first look at the Lower Creeks and the Cherokees, the strongest and most problematic of South Carolina's Indian allies. As soon as the Lower

Creek delegation was ushered into the council chamber, Nicholson lit into the leader of the group, Ouletta of Coweta, a son of the "emperor" Brims and a staunch supporter of the South Carolinians. From now on Ouletta and his "whole Nation" were to know that none of the Creeks were to give the South Carolinians any "further occasions of Complaints" now that their "late differences" were behind them. Nicholson closed by warning Ouletta that he would become even more upset unless every Creek town sent a headman to Charles Town to hear his "Talk."[9] Later that month Nicholson greeted a party of nine Cherokee headmen with a similar message, albeit a slightly less forceful one. Nicholson was under orders to treat the Cherokees with extra respect in order to keep them in the English interest.[10] To that end he smoked the calumet with them and politely sat through one of their war dances before sending them on their way. The Cherokee leaders returned to their towns carrying portraits of King George and the royal coat of arms and, no doubt, spreading the word about South Carolina's curious new governor.[11]

Nicholson's aggressive approach to the Creeks and the Cherokees stood in stark contrast to the conduct of his predecessor, Robert Johnson, a man whose confidence and enthusiasm had been drained by the various crises of the second decade of the eighteenth century. While Nicholson's energetic personality was an important new factor in frontier affairs, it did not inspire a complete overhaul of South Carolina imperialism. Many South Carolinians shared Nicholson's desire to wield greater economic and political influence on the Southeast's frontiers, but few shared his unwavering devotion to the Union Jack. Despite their increasing receptiveness to the trappings of the British Empire, South Carolinians continued to cling to many of their own peculiar notions of imperial expansion.

Few people learned more about the gap between British and South Carolinian imperialism than Francis Varnod, a young, energetic, and idealistic SPG missionary who settled in Goose Creek Parish in the early 1720s. Varnod was determined to introduce the "poor pagans" along South Carolina's frontiers to the wonders of Anglicanism and immediately set out to learn all he could about the religious customs and predilections of the Indians.[12] Not content with the beleaguered Indians of the South Carolina low country, Varnod set his sights further afield, first on the Cherokees and then on the Creeks, a "great Nation" whose language was reportedly "understood further upon the main land than any other."[13] Varnod's enthusiasm evoked some of the better missionaries who came to South Carolina during Queen Anne's War, but by the time of Varnod's arrival, Francis Le Jau, Gideon Johnston, and almost every other missionary with the slightest interest in Christianizing the Indians had either died or moved on to another British dominion. [14] Had these men been present to see Varnod ask the South Carolina assembly to sponsor a "discreet young man" to preach on the frontiers, they probably would have told him to save his breath. [15] Within a year of his petition, the young zealot stopped mentioning the Indians in his reports to SPG headquarters.

Varnod could have avoided his disappointment had he taken the time to converse with colonial authorities in Virginia. These men would have told him that the South Carolinians, despite their new ties to the British Crown, remained as arrogant, contentious, avaricious, and shortsighted as ever. Though the South Carolina and Virginia governments had reached a brief truce around the time of the antiproprietary "revolution," any feelings of good will were shattered in November 1721, when the South Carolina assembly passed a law to impose taxes and license fees on any Virginians who traded among the "western Indians." [16] When the South Carolina government had attempted a similar maneuver in 1711, the Virginians had managed to prevail against it by drawing on the support of the imperial hierarchy in London. Given South Carolina's new status as a royal colony, however, the protests of the Virginia government were now far less likely to make an impression on the Board of Trade. The South Carolina imperialists, working under the cover of the British flag, finally had their Virginian rivals right where they wanted them. Unable to respond in any practical way, the Virginia authorities could do nothing but vent their frustration by proclaiming that the "unjust and impudent proceedings" of the South Carolina government were "founded upon the private Interest of their Traders, and not with any view to the General Tranquility of his Majesty's other plantations." [17]

The Virginians had every reason to resent the policies of their rivals, but they went a little too far in accusing the South Carolina government of reckless behavior. Still recovering from an exhausting Indian war, South Carolina officials did not wish to do anything to threaten the safety of their own or any other British province. Though they jealously guarded South Carolina's markets, they continued to harbor strong reservations about the character of South Carolina's Indian traders. When Nicholson assumed office, he was unprepared for the strength or extent of the South Carolina government's bitterness toward the traders. During one session of the assembly in early 1722, Nicholson suggested that the best traders among the Creeks and the Cherokees should receive powers to act as official government representatives. The members of the assembly coolly informed him that they had "found it by experience to be very inconvenient to entrust the Traders with any particular powers[,] for they [had] always made use of such powers to their particular advantage and not to the benefit of the public."[18] Nicholson now knew that he had another major challenge on his hands. He waded into the task with his trademark zeal, shifting the prerogative of trade regulation from the Commons House to the council.[19]

Nicholson soon discovered just how difficult it would be to keep all the traders and their Indian customers in line. By the early 1720s South Carolina's Indian trade had risen from a temporary lull to become more extensive and complicated than ever. The revocation of the public monopoly and the reopening of western markets inspired Charles Town's merchant community to jump back into the trade with both feet.[20] With other sectors of the South Carolina economy continuing to slump, the Indian trade remained one of the few viable options for landless men.[21] The number of new traders more than made up for the number of traders lost during the Yamasee War, giving the southeastern Indians some welcome new options. In the summer of 1723 a large group of Lower Creeks approached trader John Worth with fifteen hundred deerskins at his store near the Ocmulgee River. After briefly perusing Worth's wares, the Indians decided to move on to another nearby trader recently arrived from Charles Town, a man who was likely to have better merchandise on his hands.[22]

Unfortunately for everyone involved, however, the privatization and subsequent expansion of the Indian trade caused a range of familiar and unfamiliar problems. The end of the ill-fated public monopoly made the trade somewhat more convenient for the Indians, but it also left them open to some of the most frustrating aspects of free enterprise. Things were especially hard for the Cherokees, a group with no real alternatives to the South Carolina market. On numerous occasions Cherokee leaders petitioned the South Carolina government for a return to the fixed-price schedule that had existed under the public monopoly. Invariably they found their requests denied on the grounds that "the goods were not the Governments" or that "the goods sent amongst them belong[ed] to each Particular trader."[23] Indians often grumbled about prices, but the South Carolina traders knew that they would usually choose to pay rather than go without an essential item. Despite the South Carolinians' increasing investments in the trade, the supply of trade goods never came close to matching the Indians' growing demand.[24]

The Indians usually managed to procure the goods they wanted, but with greater and greater difficulty. While records of deerskin exports indicate that there were still plenty of deer to be found in the southeastern interior, they do not begin to show how hard and disruptive it had become for the Indians to hunt these animals successfully.[25] Indians had to travel further and further from home to reach decent hunting grounds and often found themselves locked in intense competition with men from other towns or tribes. Indian hunters also had to cope with the Creek-Cherokee War, a conflict that not only placed their own lives in jeopardy but also made them reluctant to leave their families and villages unguarded for any considerable length of time.[26] To stop hunting altogether was simply out of the question, for an Indian's ability to hunt was as much a sign of his manhood as his ability to fight his enemies. All the while, however, his sense of honor and masculinity was dampened by the economic leverage that the white traders continued to hold over him. In the likely event that an Indian hunter did not have enough skins to meet a trader's price, his only option was to run up an account. Against all orders from the colonial government and their merchant employers, the South Carolina traders of the early 1720s usually complied with their customers' requests for credit, allowing individual Indians to compile enormous debts.[27]

News of these debts led government authorities to believe that the traders were selfishly encouraging the kind of licentious behavior that had supposedly given rise to the Yamasee War. The extension of credit was only one of the strikes against the traders. Though no longer as rigid as they had been under the government monopoly, South Carolina officials still expected the traders to pay their license fees and treat the Indians and government agents with respect. By 1723 the council's newly established Committee on Indian Affairs heard so many complaints of unlicensed traders among the Cherokees that it considered sending a detachment of troops from Fort Moore to round up the culprits.[28] The traders seemed to be getting equally out of hand among the Lower Creeks, where Agent Theophilus Hastings accused John Coleman and several other traders of opening his mail and "mak[ing] it their business to ridicule [him] to the Indians."[29] Following a welcome display of manners during and immediately after the Yamasee War, the traders had begun to show their traditional disdain for most of the government's rules.

For all their anger over the lack of respect shown by the traders, South Carolina authorities grew even more upset at evidence that some of the traders were once again wearing out their welcome among the Indians. In the words of one highly respected Cherokee elder, it was a "shame [for] the white men [to be] more debauched and more wicked than the beatest [sic] of [their] young fellows."[30] In many cases it was actually a tossup as to which group was the more "debauched." More often than not, the confrontations and disputes between the traders and the Indians had something to do with mutual intoxication. The Indians of the Southeast had consumed alcohol for decades, but by the 1720s they appeared to be drinking a good deal more of it. The traders among the Cherokees met some of this demand by building the first in a long line of Smokey Mountain moonshine stills, and the Alabamas and the Tallapoosas reportedly developed such a fondness for brandy that they were willing to trade back their English cloth for it.[31] With the wholesale murders of 1715 still fresh in their minds, South Carolina officials understandably feared that all this liquor—combined with the general "lawlessness" of the traders—might bring out the worst instincts in everyone and prove extremely detrimental to the province's imperial interests.[32]

According to the Board of Trade, the most effective solution to frontier instability would be "to recommend in the strongest terms to the Indian traders to be just and reasonable in their dealings with the Native Indians."[33] Though most South Carolinians knew from experience that it was much easier to talk about trade regulation than to implement it, they continued to believe that they could solve their problems through new legislation. Between 1721 and 1725, the South Carolina assembly passed three new "Acts for the Better Regulation of the Indian Trade," a series of measures that sought to control the traders by adding new punishments and licensing restrictions. Traders not only faced heavy fines for operating without a license, issuing credit, or threatening the Indians with the use of force, but also found themselves restricted to trading with a single "nation" of Indians. The 1725 act also raised license fees to thirty pounds, a step intended to restrict the Indian trade to the "better sort" of South Carolinians. Traders were allowed to share the cost of a license, but in so doing they would have to share the license as well and spend only half or a third as much time engaged in trading. In essence the South Carolina government decided that the easiest way to reduce frontier tensions was to minimize contact between the Indians and a certain "class" of trader.[34]

The trade regulations of the early 1720s shared much in common with the regulations proposed twenty or even thirty years earlier, but they also bore the influence of the Yamasee War. The government now had more disdain than ever for the poorer and less cultivated traders, a group pegged as convenient scapegoats for many of the problems that had plagued South Carolina since 1715. But while the South Carolina authorities undoubtedly harbored strong prejudices against many of the traders, they remained even more concerned about the attitudes and behavior of the Indians. On the one hand, the commissioners of the Indian trade encouraged the Indians to voice their grievances and ostensibly pledged themselves to protect the Indians' interests. On the other hand, they also authorized the use of corporal punishment against any Indian found guilty of disturbing the peace, a sentence they dared not mete out to the most wayward of the white traders.[35] Though there is no evidence that government officials actually carried out such a sentence against an Indian in the 1720s, the very fact that they authorized it suggests that they perceived the Indians as unequal partners at best and potential enemies at worst. While restrictions against the traders might bring a temporary reprieve to frontier problems, South Carolina's imperialists felt that a more durable solution would depend on their ability to achieve greater control over the Indians.[36]

Like James Moore, Maurice Matthews, and other "Goose Creek men" of the late seventeenth century, the imperialists of the early 1720s sought to shore up their power by establishing greater economic and political influence over the southeastern Indians. Whereas most of the early South Carolina imperialists had focused primarily on expanding the Indian trade, some of those influenced by the Yamasee War tended to emphasize the political dimensions of imperialism. To men like Governor Nicholson and his close advisors, South Carolina's recent frontier troubles appeared to be a product of the Indians' increasing willingness to challenge English political authority. Unwilling to admit that this authority had never been strong, South Carolina imperialists convinced themselves that they could push their unstable Indian allies back in line by reminding them who their true "fathers" were.[37]

In Nicholson's mind the deerskin trade was of little use to the well-being of South Carolina and the British Empire unless it helped strengthen South Carolina's political hold on the Indians. On this rationale he finally persuaded the South Carolina assembly to accept his strategy for using two trustworthy traders as government "agents" among the Creeks and the Cherokees.[38] In addition to monitoring the Indian traders, the agents would also watch over the Indians, traveling from town to town and relaying the governor's messages. After a year in South Carolina, Nicholson concluded that the Creek and Cherokee leaders who came to Charles Town could not always be counted on to relay messages accurately to their people.[39] Nicholson correctly perceived a wide communication gap between the South Carolina government and the Indians of the southeastern interior, but he never bothered to understand it in any detail and therefore proved unable to bridge it.

Though Nicholson realized that his "Talk" carried much less weight on the frontiers than in the council chamber, he continued to give it with greater force and frequency to the Indian leaders who visited him. With customary bluntness Nicholson carried on with his campaign to formalize South Carolina's Indian relations by drawing a straighter line between King George and certain Indian leaders. In addition to distributing British flags and portraits of the royal family, Nicholson also took it upon himself to "commission" Ouletta as the successor to "Emperor Brims" and to name several sympathetic headmen as "kings" of the Lower, Middle, and Upper Cherokees. [40] Once Nicholson and his council finished handing out their gifts and commissions, they expected to see quick results and inevitably became upset as soon as they learned that the Indians were continuing to visit the French and the Spanish, insult the South Carolina traders, or engage in any other kind of unacceptable behavior.

On some level the South Carolina imperialists probably realized that many of their frustrations sprung from Indian factionalism. After receiving numerous rebukes from Nicholson, an exasperated Ouletta finally tried to explain that there were "many Divisions among those of [his] own Collour" and that neither he nor his father had the power to coerce those Lower Creeks who disagreed with them. [41] On another occasion Nicholson and the council learned that two headmen were locked in a heated and counterproductive struggle to determine the true "king" of the Lower Cherokees. [42] Although the policies of the South Carolina government in many ways helped promote factionalism among the Indians, Nicholson, like his predecessors, had little patience for it. To him Indian factionalism was a Gordian knot that the South Carolina government could cut by offering the Creeks and the Cherokees two stark alternatives: they could either toe the line and continue to receive all the wonderful material benefits of English "friendship," or they could persist in their double-dealing and lose access to the trade goods that had made them "a warlike and great people." [43] Nicholson was clearly a man who knew no middle ground. To show the Lower Creeks that he meant business, in 1723 he temporarily restricted the South Carolina traders to the "dependable" town of Cussita, an action that stunned and outraged many of the Indians. [44]

Even Nicholson himself undoubtedly realized that there were some heavy risks involved with these aggressive strategies. Given the prevailing cultural prejudices of the day, however, Nicholson probably felt that he had no choice but to plow ahead and hope for the best. In the eyes of most early eighteenth-century imperialists, Indians were—and always would remain—inferior to white men. For men committed to restoring South Carolina's frontier influence, it was unthinkable to let the Indian trade and Indian politics continue along their chaotic courses. Every day the South Carolinians spent without a firm grip on their Indian allies gave their imperial rivals another chance to wrest the Indians from their grasp. In the decade after the Yamasee War, most South Carolinians continued to see imperialism as the kind of zero-sum contest that they had waged during Queen Anne's War. Now, however, they had a much more vivid idea of the horrors that awaited them if they lost.

In the contest over the Creeks and the Cherokees, the South Carolinians feared one rival above all others: the French. The Virginians, once considered a troublesome presence among the Cherokees, no longer appeared to be much of a threat. [45] Economic woes and an apathetic assembly took a heavy toll on Virginia's western Indian trade, prompting South Carolina's agent among the Cherokees to write in 1725 that the Virginia traders could "not do any prejudice to [theirs] in the way of Trade, there not being above two or three of them and their goods no ways Sortable or Comparable" to the South Carolinians'. [46] The French, however, had already begun to make new inroads among the Alabamas, the Tallapoosas, and the Lower Creeks. In a 1721 report to King George I, the Board of Trade lamented that thirty-four hundred "Creek" warriors "whom [the English] formerly traded with are entirely debauched to the French Interest by their new settlement and Fort at the Alabamas." Another two thousand or so warriors reportedly traded "indifferently" with both the French and the English, but the board feared "that these likewise [would] be debauched" unless proper countermeasures were taken. [47]

As usual the English imperialists were exaggerating the strength and offensive capabilities of their French rivals. They did not seem to realize that the French envied and feared the military might and commercial clout of the English, or that many of the French troops in Louisiana were desperate to escape to South Carolina. [48] In the summer of 1721, about forty troops attempted to flee overland from Fort Toulouse but were hunted down by a party of 250 Alabama warriors hired by the fort's officers. The Alabamas killed eighteen of the troops outright and dragged the remainder back to the fort to face punishment. [49] Despite the perils involved, a number of French deserters did make it to South Carolina over the next several years. These deserters all gave similar descriptions of Louisiana's poverty, referring to it as a country with "neither Money nor Provisions" and describing how the troops at Fort Toulouse were forced to trade most of their ammunition to the Indians for food. [50]

Louisiana officials could entertain no immediate hopes of winning over the Lower Creeks or the Cherokees, but they did embark on a policy that promised to bring greater disruption and disorder to South Carolina's far-western frontiers. [51] The French had originally come to the Southeast with a plan to frustrate the South Carolinians by making peace between the Choctaws and the Chickasaws. Twenty years later, however, Bienville and his cohorts found themselves losing ground among Louisiana's two largest Indian societies and became convinced that "the sole and only way to establish any security in the colony" was "to put these barbarians into play against each other."[52] When a party of Chickasaws killed a French officer on the Mississippi River in 1720, Louisiana officials had a perfect excuse to encourage the Choctaws to attack their bitter enemies to the north. By 1723 the Choctaw-Chickasaw War had taken on a life of its own, becoming far easier for the French to prolong than to stop.[53]

The Choctaws and the Chickasaws had fought each other longer than anyone could remember, but in the engagements of the early 1720s, the Chickasaws—a group whose warriors had long been regarded as the most fearsome, respected, and successful in the Southeast—finally discovered how it felt to be on the short end of the red stick. After making it through the Yamasee War relatively unscathed, the Chickasaws sustained heavy losses at the hands of the better-provisioned and better-supported Choctaws: Bienville boasted that one massive raid in 1722 took four hundred Chickasaw scalps and a hundred Chickasaw prisoners.[54] When the Chickasaws appealed for help from the English, they saw just how quickly their star had fallen among the South Carolina imperialists, men who now had their hands full with less remote groups of Indians. The South Carolinians essentially shrugged their shoulders to their loyal allies, claiming that the most they could do was to offer the Chickasaws sanctuary in the shadows of Fort Moore and Port Royal.[55] While a handful of Chickasaws did agree to serve as human shields for the South Carolina settlements, hundreds more sought refuge among the Cherokees and the Abeikas, determined to carry on their struggle against the French and the Choctaws.

The French made peace with the remaining Chickasaws in the Mississippi Valley in 1724, but by then the Choctaw-Chickasaw War had become intertwined with the ongoing conflict between the Creeks and the Cherokees.[56] At a time when the colonial powers of the Southeast officially considered themselves at peace, the Indian societies of the region found themselves becoming even more militaristic. With the escalation in intertribal warfare, South Carolinians began to notice some significant changes in Indian culture, particularly among the "closest" of their allies, the Cherokees. Traditionally spiritual leaders had occupied a preeminent place in the Cherokee world and played a crucial role in preserving Cherokee notions of social hierarchy and harmony. By the early 1720s, however, Cherokee shamans had begun to lose their grip on their increasingly truculent "young people" and no longer exerted the same influence in the council house.[57] The great Charitey Hagey of Tugaloo, who died in 1719, was the last "conjurer" to play a prominent role in the Cherokees' political and military affairs. Cherokee war chiefs, following in the footsteps of Caesar of Echota, began to command more and more influence among their people, often taking full advantage of the colonial "commissions" that increased their ability to acquire and redistribute coveted English trade goods.[58]

To South Carolinian observers, it appeared that the Cherokees and the other Indians of the southeastern interior spent most of their time planning military expeditions of one kind or another.[59] When not on the attack, the Indians often busied themselves in making defensive preparations. One visitor among the Overhill Cherokees remarked that the Indians living in the "very compact and thick Settled" town of Great Tellico had to protect themselves with spike-filled ditches and "Muskett proof" houses, "otherwise they would be Cut off by the Enemy who [were] Continually within a Mile of the Town lurking about the Skirts thereof."[60] In and of itself, the rise in intertribal violence did not necessarily strike South Carolina imperialists as problematic. The South Carolina government not only did its best to keep the Creeks and the Cherokees occupied with each other but also gave active encouragement to the Upper Cherokees' war against the "French Indians" of Illinois and to the Tallapoosas' and Lower Creeks' raids against the remaining Yamasees in Florida.[61] As long as the South Carolinians could keep Indian warriors pointed in the right direction, they had no trouble accepting—or even exacerbating—the increasing militarization of Indian culture. The real difficulty, of course, was in making sure that their well-armed and highly proficient allies continued to fight against the right people. When examined alongside the issues of trader unruliness and Indian "disobedience"—problems that continued to plague the southeastern interior despite the stern warnings and aggressive policies of Governor Nicholson— the wars between the Indians began to seem much less manageable and much more dangerous. By 1724 many officials had become far more sensitive to any signs of impending disaster.

That fall a rumor that the Cherokees and the Catawbas were on the verge of war was relayed to Charles Town by William Hatton, who lamented that without the combined strength of the Cherokees and the Catawbas, "there [was] no doubt by the help of God But Carolina [would] be able to deale with the Creeks."[62] Talk of a Cherokee-Catawba split seemed bad enough, but it hardly compared to the troubling news that the South Carolinians themselves were falling victim to Indian warriors. As South Carolina officials attempted to deal with the assault and robbery of John Sharp in late 1724, they received word of a similar attack carried out against trader John Worth at his store on the Altamaha River. [63] Though these incidents were probably the work of nothing more than a limited number of overzealous Muskogean warriors, the South Carolina government chose to regard them as calculated "insults" on the part of the entire Creek "Nation." With the Cherokees openly questioning the manhood of the English, the time had come for the South Carolina government to "right [them]selves and Comply with [their] talk with the Cherokees in Treating the Creeks as Enemies." [64] Somehow, the Creeks had to learn that the South Carolinians were willing to back up their warnings and threats, even if it meant "enter[ing] into a Warr with that Nation, unless future satisfaction [were] made." [65] This challenge seemed tailor-made for Governor Nicholson, but unfortunately for the South Carolinians, the old "war captain" had left on official business to England a few months earlier. President of the council Arthur Middleton did his best to fill the void by placing Fort Moore on full alert and proposing the construction of a new fort on the Ocmulgee, a hundred miles closer to the troublesome Lower Creeks. [66] By the spring of 1725, the South Carolinians teetered on the brink of a military showdown with the group of Indians whom they had tried so hard to court, control, and arm for the last eight years.

In the end, however, cooler heads and empty coffers prevailed. The assembly rejected the idea of the Ocmulgee fort out of hand, and no one stepped up to fund the project out of his own pocket. Middleton requested help from the Board of Trade, but any response was bound to be slow and insufficient. [67] For all their talk of the need for another Indian war, South Carolina officials were highly unlikely to follow up on it as long as there remained any possibility of saving face in a less direct and expensive manner. As far as the provincial government was concerned, the cause of South Carolina's problems with the Creeks—and to a lesser extent with the Cherokees—seemed obvious: the Indians had become spoiled through their acquisition of English trade goods and refused to show a sufficient respect for English authority. [68] South Carolina officials assumed that if the "agents" appointed by Nicholson could not redress this imbalance, the job would only have to be entrusted to more capable men with sterner messages. By replacing Creek agent Theophilus Hastings and Cherokee agent William Hatton with Tobias Fitch and George Chicken—two proven frontiersmen who had "no stake in trade"—the South Carolina imperialists showed faith in their ability to manage their western frontiers through diplomatic channels. [69] Though born of high anxiety, the great Creek and Cherokee missions of 1725–26 also reflected South Carolina's vigorous frontier ambitions.

The Missions of George Chicken and Tobias Fitch

On the surface the missions to Cherokee and Creek country signaled a new departure in South Carolina's frontier diplomacy. For the first time since the Yamasee War, the South Carolina government was sending agents to talk with the Indians, not trade with them. The Cherokees and the Creeks both referred to these agents as "beloved men," their general term for the handpicked messengers of any great and respected leader. When Chicken and Fitch reached their destinations, many of the Indians remarked that they had gone a long time without seeing a beloved man of the "Great King of the English" among them.[70] For some of the Tallapoosas, Abeikas, and Alabamas, Fitch was probably the first English official to come calling since Thomas Nairne in 1708. Before the Yamasee War, Nairne, Thomas Welch, Pryce Hughes, and other English beloved men had acted more as private adventurers than official representatives, often traveling with only the vaguest sanction of the South Carolina government. Chicken and Fitch, however, had orders to maintain as much contact as possible with Charles Town and each other.[71] These two new beloved men embodied the South Carolina government's quest to wield a more direct, active, and coordinated presence in the southeastern interior.[72]

Fitting with this new sense of purpose, the government sponsored the Chicken and Fitch missions with some specific goals in mind. Colonel Chicken—a hero of the Yamasee War and the province's newly appointed Indian trade commissioner—had the responsibility of keeping the Cherokees in the South Carolina camp by preventing them from making any separate treaties with the French or the Creeks.[73] The younger and less experienced Captain Fitch, another respected planter and Yamasee War veteran, had the more hazardous and difficult of the two missions. The job fell into his lap only after it was turned down by Captain John Herbert, a more cautious and less ambitious member of the assembly.[74] Fitch was required to travel into what many South Carolinians considered hostile territory and knew that he could not return home without getting the Creeks to make amends for their recent attack on trader John Sharp. For good measure Fitch also had orders to straighten out the twisted lines of communication between South Carolina and the Lower Creeks, a crucial step toward bringing those powerful Indians away from the French and Spanish interests.[75]

Chicken and Fitch also differed from other frontier emissaries of the early colonial period in that they did not set out to gain a better understanding of the Indians' cultural or political predilections. Indeed, these two new beloved men—thanks to an abundance of correspondence from South Carolina traders and some of their own past observations—probably assumed that they knew everything they needed to know about the Cherokees and the Creeks, right down to the number of men, women, and children who resided in each and every town. As they saw it, the purpose of their missions was not to introduce the Indians to a curious English audience but to reintroduce English authority to a wayward Indian audience.

Such a task required Chicken and Fitch to take a page from Francis Nicholson's book and adopt the role of the stern father figure to the Cherokees and the Creeks. Chicken's reports frequently mention that he felt compelled to speak "after a Sharp Manner" to the Cherokees, but even so he rarely proved as blunt as Fitch did in his conversations with the Creeks.[76] When an Abeika headman attempted to welcome Fitch to his village with a gift of deerskins, Fitch tersely informed him, "[M]y Great King did not Send me here to get presents, [and] neither do I want them."[77] Fitch made it abundantly clear that he intended to deliver a tongue-lashing to his hosts, and that he expected them to be men enough to accept it, since his Great King "did not send Talks to please Women and Children."[78] Before a large audience of Tallapoosa headmen, Fitch showed signs of a lighter but no less manipulative touch, plaintively asking them how they could "set no greater Value" on their good friends the English than they did on their "greatest Enemies."[79] Like an exasperated parent, Fitch alternated seamlessly between shaming and threats in his quest to get the Indians to listen to him.

Like Nicholson and other South Carolina imperialists, Chicken and Fitch persuaded themselves that a direct and aggressive approach was the only way to get through to the Indians. Throughout their missions it often appeared that this approach was yielding positive results. From what Chicken could see, the Cherokees were practically falling over themselves to please him, fanning him with eagle wings and giving him the seat of honor in all their councils. Whenever Chicken gave them a warning, he rarely had to repeat it and frequently received the very response that he expected. In one meeting a council of headmen in the Overhill Cherokee town of Tennessee promised that they would "never Suffer any French Man Whatsoever to come amongst them, because they never had any love [for] them."[80] The Long Warrior of Tennessee town even went a step further by standing up and announcing that the Cherokees "must now mind and Consider that all their Old men were gone, and that they ha[d] been brought up after another Manner than their forefathers and that they must Consider that they could not live without the English." [81] Chicken could not have said it any better himself.

Among the Tallapoosas and the rest of the so-called Upper Creeks, Fitch encountered a number of Indians who seemed equally eager to please the English. When Fitch began to inquire after the whereabouts of the warriors who had assaulted John Sharp in Tugaloo, some of these Indians gladly pointed him in the direction of Steyamasiechie, a Tallapoosa headman known to the English as "Goggle Eyes." [82] Fitch told Steyamasiechie that he had little interest in tracking down those warriors who had actually robbed Sharp, "they Being a parcell of Inferiour Fellowes." Fitch claimed that his real goal was to extract restitution from the headmen of these warriors, and that "Nothing Else [could] prevent [his] Kings makeing a Warr with [the Indians]." Steyamasiechie apologized profusely for the behavior of his young "rogues" and pledged to return as many of Sharp's goods as he could find. [83] Upon returning to the same town several months later, however, Fitch learned that several of the Alabamas and Tallapoosas had taken exception to the brusque tone of his previous "talk" and had begun to discuss the possibility of killing him. Fitch wasted no time in confronting the malcontents, warning them, "[I] would not have you think that I am affeared to Dye . . . for if you was to do me any hurt I do assure you that my King would never forgive you while one of you was Liveing." [84] The Indians backed down. Whenever Fitch encountered any signs of truculence during his travels through the various Muskogean provinces, he usually left the Indians staring at the ground, shuffling their feet, or promising to do better in the future.

While there can be little doubt that some of the Cherokees and Creeks were intimidated or shamed by the imperious conduct of Chicken and Fitch, the Indians' outward compliance did not necessarily indicate their submission before the forces of South Carolina imperialism. Cherokee and Creek leaders frequently stood up to the demands and impositions of Chicken and Fitch, but often in ways that were hard for South Carolina's beloved men to understand. Indians were rarely able—or willing—to speak much English. John Fontaine, an Irish soldier who traveled among some of Virginia's "tributary Indians" in the aftermath of the Yamasee War, observed that even those Indian leaders who were capable of speaking good English "would not treat but in their own language, and that by an interpreter, nor [would they] answer to any question made to them without it be in their own tongue." [85] Chicken and Fitch, who probably knew no more than a few Cherokee or Muskogean phrases, essentially had to depend on what their "linguisters"—usually South Carolina traders—were willing to tell them.[86] But even though these interpreters had a vested interest in keeping the beloved men happy—and even though Chicken and Fitch had a vested interest in filing reports that kept their own superiors happy—they could not mask the sense of frustration they experienced in dealing with the Indians.

Problems associated with the rapidly expanding Indian trade proved especially exasperating to Captain Chicken. When Chicken reached Cherokee country, he had his government's permission not only to inform against wayward traders but also to indict, prosecute, and punish them.[87] Chicken nursed the typical wealthy planter's disdain for the "loose and Vagabond sort of people" that traded among the Cherokees and seemed to take pleasure in setting them straight. When several Cherokee headmen complained that some of the traders' horses were destroying the local corn crop, Chicken gave them leave to shoot the horses if the problem persisted and then tersely informed the traders of his decision.[88] Though Chicken was an imposing presence who often seemed capable of controlling the traders by sheer force of will, he expressed doubts in his ability to effect a permanent solution to trader unruliness.[89] As the Long Warrior reminded him, most of South Carolina's rules "would be minded as long as [Chicken] stayed among them, but when [he] was gone, it would be as the Traders pleased."[90] Fitch possessed few of Chicken's regulatory powers, but even if he had, he might not have bothered to implement them. During his 1726 mission, Fitch essentially threw up his hands, claiming that the traders had "got to such a hight, that they mind[ed] neither Law, nor nothing else." In his opinion the only real way for the government to manage the traders would be to send them all home.[91]

Both Chicken and Fitch observed that it had become "customary" for the South Carolina traders to flout many of the rules and regulations hammered out in Charles Town. While they placed much of the blame for this problem on the poor character of the traders, they also noticed that the Indians themselves played a strong role in forging the "customs" of disobedience. When Fitch expressed horror at a trader who had trusted one Lower Creek warrior for more than three hundred deerskins, he was informed that most Indians would not even agree to trade with the South Carolinians unless they were offered strong lines of credit.[92] When Chicken and Fitch tried to find out why too many untreated deerskins were making their way to Charles Town, they learned that many of the Cherokees and Creeks had begun to demand stiff fees for dressing their skins, a service that they previously had performed free of charge. [93] Since these unexpected twists on the Indian trade did not sit well with South Carolina's merchants and government officials, Chicken and Fitch attempted to push the Cherokees and the Creeks back in line, threatening to remove the traders if the Indians persisted in the "ill Custome" of amassing debts and turning in "raw" skins. [94] These threats, however, were hollow. With the province's sluggish economy leaning heavily on the trans-Atlantic leather trade, it seemed obvious that the South Carolinians would have to comply with the Indians' demands for credit and "service charges" if they had any hope of maintaining a marketable supply of deerskins. [95]

For frustrated South Carolina imperialists, the challenge of holding the Cherokees and the Creeks to the principles of English mercantilism was compounded by the utter impossibility of confining them within English political models. Throughout the early 1720s, Nicholson and other South Carolina officials had worked toward the further "nationalization" of the Cherokees, hoping that the appointment of new Cherokee "kings" would make the different Cherokee towns and sections into a more manageable and dependable polity. During his 1725 mission, Chicken attempted to go a step further by appointing an intelligent and sympathetic headman named Crow to serve as king of all the Cherokees and summoning all Cherokee leaders to the Middle Cherokee town of Ellijay to take part in the first nationwide Cherokee council on record. [96] Chicken's ability to organize this council was a strong testament to the growing influence of the South Carolinians, not to mention his own considerable charisma. At the same time, however, the Ellijay council also revealed some stubborn foot-dragging on the part of Cherokee leaders, as well as some glaring flaws in South Carolina's imperial strategy.

Many of the Lower Cherokee leaders arrived in Ellijay exceptionally late and unusually sullen, prompting Chicken to deduce that they "had not any regard for their King, he being a man (As [he] have been informed) that they never could rely on for the truth[,] which [made] them so dubious of their being sent for at any time to hear the English talk." [97] King Crow, for his part, proved equally skeptical of many of his Cherokee "subjects," particularly those whom the South Carolinians had outfitted with "commissions" in recent years. Many of the Cherokees who traveled to Charles Town and conversed with the governor only did so "in hopes of having some cloath given them" and frequently forgot or ignored the governor's instructions once they returned to their towns. [98] Crow apologetically informed Chicken that the Cherokees "would work as they pleased and go to Warr as they pleased, notwithstanding his saying all he could to them, and that they were not like white men." [99] Chicken merely interpreted this well-founded warning as a confirmation that the "King" was "more under the Commands of his Subjects than they [were] under him," and that the South Carolinians would simply have to find a more suitable replacement. [100] Like Francis Nicholson, Chicken persisted in believing that the Cherokees would eventually hear and understand the "English talk" as long as it was delivered to them at the right pitch and volume.

Further south Fitch had his own problems attempting to secure some dependable political footholds among certain groups of Muskogeans, particularly the Lower Creeks. In the town of Coweta, South Carolina's new methods of granting commissions were called into question by the great Brims, who scolded Fitch with uncharacteristic directness: "I am Old yet I am the head of this Nation and my mouth is good. I do not know the meaning that your King has left of his former Customs for theire was never a head man made here but such as I would Recommend to your King. But now any young Fellow that goes Down and Tells a fine Story they [get] a Commission and then they Come here and are head Men and at the same Time are No more [fit] for it than Dogs." Fitch reportedly replied that Brims had no grounds to criticize the English King for "appointing unproper men to be headmen . . . for by what [he could] see the most of [them were] in one mind this day and another the next." [101] Despite the many risks inherent in granting commissions to apparently unstable characters, Fitch felt that he had no choice but to continue the practice, especially since Brims's son Ouletta—a man considered one of South Carolina's most valuable supporters—had recently lost his life in a skirmish with the Yamasees. Fitch sought to fill this void by looking to Ouletta's half-brother Sepeycoffee, granting him a commission to serve as the "Commander in Chief of [the Lower Creeks] under his Father Emperor Brims' Derections . . . to Take all orders that [should] come from [the English] King, to hear no Talk but what [came] from him, and to be sure to put all his Orders in Execution." [102] Though Fitch had many reservations about entrusting such responsibility to an Indian leader with notoriously strong connections to the French and the Spanish, he hid them well. In the end he was more concerned with fulfilling his orders in the immediate present than with contemplating any potential problems in the near or distant future.

During his travels through the various Muskogean "provinces," Fitch actually encountered less interference from the French and the Spanish than he originally had feared. When Fitch expressed some concern about Fort Toulouse, a Tallapoosa headman wryly informed him that the fort's troops would have deserted to the English long ago "if they had not been such Crippells that they could not walk." [103] But even though Fitch rarely met with any French or Spanish agents in person, he constantly observed the traces of intercolonial intrigue, primarily in the form of Indian factionalism. Wherever Fitch went, he encountered pro-English Indians who were anxious to make his stay as pleasant as possible, even to the point of challenging or threatening those less hospitable Indians who glowered at the South Carolina beloved man and whispered behind his back. [104] Several Abeika and Tallapoosa headmen went so far as to tell Fitch that they would no longer stay among their people "unless they [would] be more Governable," for wherever their people decided to "go when they please[d] and commit Trespasses on the English," the headmen were held accountable. [105]

Despite the disturbing presence of anti-English sentiment among the Abeikas and the Tallapoosas, Fitch remained convinced that the "upper people" were far more reliable than the Lower Creeks, most of whom "seem[ed] to be very Indifferent and [did] not care whether they came to hear the talk or not." [106] Of all the Lower Creek towns, only Cussita consistently supported the South Carolinians. Fitch tried to capitalize on the Cussitas' "loyalty" by using them as leverage against the other Lower Creeks. At one point Fitch even led a small army of ten traders and a hundred Cussita warriors across the Chattahoochee to frighten Coweta leaders into handing over a fugitive slave whom some of their townspeople were accused of hiding. [107] Like Nicholson, Fitch assumed that the proper combination of bribery and intimidation would bring troublesome Indians to heel, inspiring them to be "as good Friends to [his] King as the Cusseatawes [were]." [108] He never seemed to consider that the practice of playing favorites might only serve to deepen the divisions between pro-English and anti-English Indians.

Chicken and Fitch obviously came up short in their attempts to iron out the Indian trade and refashion Cherokee and Creek politics. In many ways, however, it was surprisingly easy for South Carolina imperialists to gloss over these shortcomings as long as the Indians remained dependable on the battlefield. For the South Carolina authorities and their superiors in London, the bottom line was their ability to control the military activities of their most powerful Indian allies. By the mid-1720s every self-respecting imperialist could see that the Creek-Cherokee War had begun to get out of hand, making South Carolina's western frontiers less safe and stable than at any time since the Yamasee War. When Chicken and Fitch left on their missions, they had orders to see what they could do to bring the war to a halt while discouraging the Creeks and the Cherokees from entering into an "abrupt peace" with each other. [109] To prevent resentful Cherokees and Creeks from getting together to "send their forces against the white people," any Creek-Cherokee peace would have to come at South Carolina's initiative and on South Carolina's terms.

The South Carolinians' belief that they could dictate the terms of a Creek-Cherokee peace rested on their mistaken assumption that they had dictated the terms of the Creek-Cherokee War. When Chicken and Fitch proposed the idea of a peace to their Indian hosts, they received a number of conflicting responses, a strong indication that different groups of Creeks and Cherokees had developed their own unique views of the war. Some of the Upper Cherokees expressed interest in the possibility of a peace with the Creeks, claiming that "if they were in Unity with the Southward Indians they should have no Enemy to look after but the French Indians who they could send out against and then Venture to leave their Women and Children at home and also that they could have room to Hunt." [110] Though the Middle and Lower Cherokees were even more vulnerable to Creek raiding parties, they had no interest in ending the war and even seemed somewhat offended that an English beloved man could suggest such a fainthearted option. At the great Ellijay council, Lower Cherokee headmen reminded Chicken that "the Creeks [did] not only Abuse them, but also the English (their brothers)." In a clear reference to the Yamasee War, they also warned that "the Creeks [might] knock them [the South Carolinians] on the head notwithstanding they [were] at peace with the English." According to most of the Cherokees, the Creeks were a bloodthirsty and perfidious people, and the English were only asking for trouble by deluding themselves that they could "Continue in Friendship" with them. [111]

Fitch also had strong doubts about the trustworthiness of many of the Creeks, but these doubts did not prevent him from trying to impose a peace on them. During his brief stay among the towns of the Coosa basin, Fitch observed that the Abeikas and the rest of the so-called Upper Creeks were "Dayly Terrified by the Cherokeys and Chick'saws who [were] in Conjunction with them." [112] Though the Abeikas and the Tallapoosas had suffered extensive losses in the last few years—including a number of "leading men" and "principal warriors"—they informed Fitch that they would only accept the mediation of the South Carolina government once they had finished reaping their vengeance against their tormentors from the northeast. [113] Fitch's proposal met with a more vehement rejection among the Lower Creeks, where he attempted to sell the idea of a Creek-Cherokee peace by lying that the Upper Creeks had already consented to it. Unfazed, Brims replied, "[T]he Tallapoosas and Abecas may do as they please[,] But we have Nothing of Makeing a peace with the

Cherokeys[;] for them men that was killed by the Cherokeys of Mine When the White people were there is not over with Me as yet, nor never shall be while there is a Cowwataid [Coweta] Liveing." [114]

For Lower Creeks like Brims, the war against the Cherokees was an important way of gaining satisfaction for the treachery that had occurred at Tugaloo in early 1716. The "emperor's" remark revealed not only an undying hatred for the Indians who had betrayed him but also an undying resentment for the "white people" who had been there to revel in this betrayal. A cloud of tension and unrest continued to hang over Coweta two weeks later, when a small party of Seneca beloved men arrived to renew the Creek-Iroquois alliance. The Senecas told Brims and the rest of their hosts to drop their resentment of Fitch: "[K]eep a peace with the English[;] you once had a warr with them and you gott little by it and had you [continued] it Longer it would have Been the worse for you." In the same breath, however, the Senecas also reminded the Lower Creeks that they were not "upon any pretence Whatever [to] Conclude a peace with the Cherokeys," lest they themselves become enemies of the Senecas. [115] For Fitch this warning must have confirmed the impression that the South Carolinians were not the only group trying to call the shots in the Creek-Cherokee War.

The war seemed a good deal more complex and convoluted to Fitch and Chicken than it did to most of the frontier policymakers in Charles Town. While Fitch listened to the Iroquois messengers, Chicken found himself dealing with another group of outsiders who wanted to throw their weight into the conflict. For years the Chickasaws of the Mississippi Valley had enjoyed a fairly close relationship with many of the Muskogeans in the Coosa, Tallapoosa, and Chattahoochee basins, groups that they had often thought of as their "Youngest Brothers." [116] Following the renewal of the Choctaw-Chickasaw War in the early 1720s, however, many of the Chickasaws had sought refuge among the Cherokees and along the Upper Savannah River, where they frequently got in the way of Creek raiding parties. By the time of Chicken's mission, some of the Creeks had also begun to ally with the Choctaws, giving the fiercely proud Chickasaws an even stronger case for retaliation. [117] During a brief stop at Fort Moore in October 1725, Chicken came across a sizeable Chickasaw war party on its way to attack the Lower Creeks and did his best to convince it to turn back. The Chickasaws patiently held their tongues when Chicken likened them to a pack of "Wild Wolves in the Woods" and then continued on their mission, claiming that they "intend[ed] to take their revenge and hope[d] the white people [would] not take it at heart." [118] In essence the

Chickasaws were politely telling Chicken the same thing King Crow of the Cherokees had told him a month earlier: that the Indians would "have their own way of Warring and that it would be good if the English would let them alone and see what they [would] do of themselves."[119]

For once Chicken and Fitch seemed almost willing to heed the Indians' advice. In light of their recent observations, it appeared that they would never be able to get all the Creek and Cherokee towns to agree on a mediated settlement. As soon as South Carolina authorities realized that there was no danger of the Creeks and the Cherokees making an alliance against the English, they allowed their agents to abandon the peace project for the time being.[120] But while Chicken and Fitch found it easy to relinquish their roles as peacemakers, they could not bring themselves to stay out of the Creek-Cherokee War altogether. If the Indians were so intent on killing each other, then Chicken and Fitch felt that they might as well help the friendlier Indians hold their own against the more truculent ones.[121] Fitch advised Chicken to warn the Cherokees about the impending arrival of a large Creek war party, and Chicken returned the favor by notifying Fitch and the Lower Creeks about the Chickasaw war party he had encountered at Fort Moore.

While these duplicitous warnings earned the gratitude of the Cherokees, they did little to improve the South Carolinians' stock among the Creeks.[122] Several months after issuing his warning to Chicken, Fitch was confronted by a party of forty frustrated Abeika warriors who had spent fifteen days outside a fortified Cherokee village without managing to take a single scalp. The Abeikas wondered what kind of "strange friendship" could have prompted Fitch to "apraize the Cherokeys of [their] Designes against them." After a few tense moments, Fitch assured them that he would never dream of favoring the Cherokees over the Creeks and explained that the news of the attack must have been leaked by one of the unscrupulous traders.[123] Fitch was confident that his lies had worked and soon shifted his attention to matters he considered more important.

By the time Chicken and Fitch returned to Charles Town in the winter of 1725–26, the war between the Creeks and the Cherokees no longer seemed as dangerous as it had a year earlier. After reading the journals and reports associated with the missions, the South Carolina assembly concluded that Chicken and Fitch had acquitted themselves "Honourably" and in a manner "highly to the advantage of the Province."[124] A major crisis had been averted, and the government seemed well on its way to recouping some of the prestige and authority that it had lost in the years since the Yamasee War. Though many of Chicken's and Fitch's reports raised some important doubts and begged significant questions, this unsettling subtext easily escaped the notice of South Carolina's government officials, many of whom were more concerned with their own plantations and counting houses than with the conditions on far-off frontiers. [125] For men such as these, the hefty rewards handed out to Chicken and Fitch brought a sense of closure to the problems associated with the Creek-Cherokee War. As always, however, South Carolina's imperialists found it impossible to let down their guard for long. Sooner or later a disaster of one kind or another was bound to erupt within the southeastern interior, reawakening every South Carolinian to the dangers of imperial complacency.

In March 1726 a large war party of Cherokees and Chickasaws set out against the Lower Creeks. Confident in the support of their South Carolinian "brothers," they carried with them a large British flag, which they proudly brandished during the course of a devastating attack on the town of Cussita. The South Carolina council feared that the French and the Spanish now had a golden opportunity to win over the bewildered and offended Creeks. [126] No longer could anyone in South Carolina afford to pretend that the Chicken and Fitch missions had solved the province's most important frontier problems. Indeed, the greatest testament to the shortcomings of the 1725 missions was the government's need to send Chicken and Fitch back to the western frontiers just a few months later. This time, however, the missions had one overwhelming objective: to put a stop to the Creek-Cherokee War before it escalated into something far worse. [127]

The Cherokee-Chickasaw attack on Cussita reminded South Carolinians that war with the Creeks was a very real possibility and instantly dredged up unpleasant memories of the Yamasee War. Francis Nicholson was still officially recognized as governor of South Carolina, but he had not yet returned from London and would soon die there. As acting governor Arthur Middleton sought the assembly's authorization for a new round of missions to the Creeks and the Cherokees. He mentioned that he did not need to remind anyone of "the deplorable consequence of an Indian Warr, the effects of that [they had] allredy felt not being yet wore out of [their] minds." [128] After unsuccessfully trying to hide from his impatient superiors, Tobias Fitch finally consented to return to Creek country, but only with an escort of ten armed men. [129] When Fitch and his escort reached their destination, they discovered that they were not the only ones reliving the horrors of the Yamasee War. Many of the South Carolina traders who had rebuffed Fitch a year earlier now begged him for the government's protection. Rumor had it that the Creeks—at the suggestion of the Spanish—had begun to make plans to kill all the English traders among them.[130] Several traders had already been robbed by the Indians, and one trader named Edmund Maxey had been "Terrified with fear" to hear a group of Creeks planning to kill him and "lay it on the Chigasaws."[131] Though the Creeks had not yet risen up en masse against the English, few of the traders were willing to express much confidence in their own personal safety.

Despite this growing sense of panic, Fitch managed to see that there was no real danger of a massive Creek uprising against the English. Though the atmosphere seemed more tense than it had during his last visit, the Creeks' situation seemed remarkably similar at heart, with some of the Indians actively supporting the South Carolinians and others coming across as torn and uncertain. According to Fitch, many of the Abeikas and Tallapoosas were "not a Little rejoyced that the Cussetaws [had] taken Share in their Suffering" and seemed confident that the Lower Creeks' recent misfortune would make them see the wisdom of a peace with the Cherokees. Pro-English Abeikas and Tallapoosas even went so far as to inform Fitch that they would be willing to make their own settlement with the Cherokees if the Lower Creeks remained intransigent.[132] For Fitch and the rest of the South Carolina imperialists, however, the loyalty of the Upper Creeks was less important than the need to win over the Lower Creeks.[133] The urgency of South Carolina's situation demanded that Fitch take one last run at overriding the evils of Indian factionalism by getting the different groups of Creeks to answer his demands in a single voice. Through a combination of inducements (for the Abeikas and the Tallapoosas) and trade boycotts (for the Lower Creeks), Fitch got headmen from the various Creek "provinces" to assemble in the Tallapoosa town of Tuckabatchee for a "national council" along the lines of the one Chicken had called for the Cherokees in 1725.

In compliance with his government's policies, Fitch recognized three major divisions among the Creeks and ordered each of these divisions to appoint its own spokesman. Though Fitch had confidence in the choices of the Abeikas and the Tallapoosas, he was unfamiliar with the leader whom the Lower Creeks selected to speak on their behalf. Since Brims's advanced age kept him confined to Coweta, Fitch expected to deal with Sepeycoffee, the "beloved son" whom he had named as Brims's second-in-command during the previous year's mission. At some point during Fitch's absence, however, Sepeycoffee had "taken by force a Cagg of Rum from a trader and drank himself dead," leaving a void that had been filled by his uncle Chigelly, head warrior of Coweta and guardian of Brims's two young sons.

Throughout the Tuckabatchee council, Fitch found himself astonished by Chigelly's bold opposition to a peace with the Cherokees and immediately perceived that he, like Brims, was having a hard time getting over the 1716 Tugaloo massacre. Fitch initially tried to defuse the tension head on, telling Chigelly that it was "high time to have done with that which was done when [they] was in Warr." When this frontal assault failed, Fitch attempted to pick at Chigelly's credentials, claiming that as a representative of the "red" or "bloody" town of Coweta, he had no authority to discuss matters of peace. Fitch invited another Lower Creek headman to step up and take Chigelly's place, but no one was willing to challenge the enormous prestige of someone so intimately connected to the great headman of Coweta. Fitch had hoped that the arguments of the Abeikas and the Tallapoosas would "overpower" the recalcitrant Lower Creeks, but he finally had to admit that "what ever he [Chigelly] said was as Law at [their] Great meeting . . . that very man [could] sway this Nation as he [thought] fit." Though Fitch exaggerated the coercive power of his newest adversary, he correctly perceived that Chigelly and his inner circle were major obstacles to South Carolina's authority among the Lower Creeks. In Fitch's opinion the only way to get Chigelly to agree to a Creek-Cherokee peace would be to purchase his loyalty by granting him a commission.[134]

Meanwhile Fitch's counterpart among the Cherokees was attempting to play a remarkably similar game. Though the Cherokees seemed a good deal more compliant than the Lower Creeks, Colonel Chicken knew that most of them had proven adamantly opposed to a peace with the Creeks during the 1725 mission. When Chicken returned to Cherokee country in July 1726, he immediately called another general council, this one in the Lower Cherokee town of Tuckseegee. Standing before the headmen of thirty-eight Cherokee towns, Chicken attempted to sell the idea of a Cherokee-Creek peace by wrapping it in a paternalistic, sugarcoated package. Chicken announced that his great king had decided to put a stop to the incessant skirmishes with the Creeks, a war that threatened to make the Cherokees "a small people, which would make [them] Sorry to see or hear." If the Cherokees accepted this offer, they would "have free hunts and get great Quantitys of Skinns to Cloath [their] Women and Children." Chicken gave them time to prepare a response "in one voice," but made it clear that he was not about to accept no for an answer. When the Cherokees' negotiations appeared to stall, Chicken decided to speed up the process by handing out a number of "small presents." One Cherokee leader who continued to hold out against peace was won over in an even less subtle manner; Chicken took him aside, flattered his abilities, and offered him a new commission, along with all the future favors that it implied. When the Indian nodded his assent, Chicken could finally rest easy, figuring that he had him and the rest of the Cherokees "pretty much at [his] Command."[135]

Chicken and Fitch expressed outward confidence in their repair jobs even as they worried that their work might not stand up to the next stiff breeze. After sustained pressure from Fitch, Chigelly finally consented to send a string of white beads to the Cherokees but vowed to smear some of the beads with blood to signify his undying hatred for the Chickasaws living in the Cherokee towns.[136] The Cherokees responded to this halfhearted offer by sending their own string of white beads but warned that they would not agree to expel the Chickasaws from their towns unless the Creeks persuaded the Iroquois to stop their raids into the Appalachians.[137] Chicken and Fitch took this exchange of beads as a sign of the Cherokees' and Creeks' willingness to accept their "English father's" peace. At the same time, however, Chicken felt that "it [could] not be Expected that [the Cherokees] could live without warring, at one place or Another," and Fitch continued to believe that it was imperative for the untrustworthy Creeks to be "deverted in warr some way or other."[138]

Chicken and Fitch managed to cast aside their doubts long enough to inform their superiors that the Cherokees and the Creeks had agreed to come to Fort Moore for an official settlement. In this respect the 1726 missions seemed to mark another victory for South Carolina's frontier diplomacy. Once again few South Carolinians were willing or able to realize that their heroic agents had, in fact, made remarkably little progress in imposing their authority on the Indians. If the South Carolinians had taken the time to analyze the shortcomings of the 1725 and 1726 missions, they probably would have placed the blame on the Indians and the traders. Chicken and Fitch—the best and brightest men the government had to offer—seemed beyond reproach. But in spite of all their undeniable energy and courage, Chicken and Fitch, like all South Carolina imperialists, were hampered by one overwhelming flaw: an immutable belief in their own intellectual and cultural superiority.

To be sure, the two beloved men proved capable of making certain compromises and even managed to pick up on some of the nuances of Indian political and military culture. All the while, however, they never stopped believing that they could mold the Cherokees and the Creeks into dependable servants of the South Carolina government and the British Empire. Ideally the South Carolinians would never have to suffer the indignities of meeting any group of Indians halfway. The South Carolina government doggedly stuck by this principle when it came time to make the arrangements for the upcoming

Cherokee-Creek peace conference. Though the governor and the council knew from experience that it was "much better treating with them [the Indians] amongst themselves in their own Towns than in [the colonists'] settlements," they nevertheless decided to change the site of the conference from Fort Moore to Charles Town to spare themselves the inconveniences of travel.[139] By the end of 1726, the South Carolina imperialists found themselves in an all too familiar position, attempting to rule their distant frontiers by imposing a *pax Caroliniana* on groups of people who—in the simple but profound words of King Crow—were "not like white men."

Peace Accords in Charles Town and London

Arthur Middleton, Francis Nicholson's de facto replacement as governor, had some high expectations for the Charles Town peace conference. During his preliminary discussions with Indian leaders, Middleton showed that stopping the Creek-Cherokee War was only one of his many concerns. More importantly the conference would also allow the South Carolinians to prove themselves benevolent but mighty fathers by handing out lace-trimmed coats, firing the heavy guns of their fort, and showing off the bustle of a busy seaport.[140] In turn the Indian visitors would have a chance to prove themselves dutiful and responsible children. The Cherokees would have to make the noble sacrifice of forgiving their enemies for the sake of their English friends and providers. The Lower Creeks, as South Carolina's wayward sons, would have the more substantial obligations of removing the Yamasees from Florida and resisting the advances of the French and the Spanish. If the Lower Creeks wanted to give even further proof of their friendship, they could move back to their old homes along the Ocmulgee, closer to the South Carolina settlements. As Middleton explained it, the supreme wish of the South Carolinians was that "all those who were [their] friends before the Warr, should be united in Peace, to be on guard against" the French. In sum, the South Carolinians hoped for nothing less than the restoration of the old Indian buffer zone, a hugely ambitious goal that hinged on their ability to expunge the troubling legacy of the Yamasee War.[141]

Middleton and his cohorts clung to these ambitions even as they watched most of their carefully constructed plans for the conference begin to unravel. The Cherokee contingent arrived in late December 1726 under the leadership of the Long Warrior of Tennessee, the new favorite of Colonel Chicken. The pro-English Abeikas appeared in town shortly thereafter, and the two groups—

anxious to please their hosts—agreed to a peace with little fanfare or cere-mony. [142] The Tallapoosas declined to make the trip to Charles Town but en-trusted their mission to the Lower Creek contingent, around which the most important part of the conference was to revolve. After several weeks the Abei-kas, the Cherokees, and the South Carolinians began to give up on the Lower Creeks, but the Lower Creeks had no problem keeping everyone waiting. [143] The homesick Cherokees expressed their desire to return to the mountains, and the South Carolina Commons House was perfectly willing to let them go, "they being at a very great Expence to the Publick, and daily falling sick from their irregular living in Charles Town." [144] The designs of the South Carolina council were on the verge of collapse when Chigelly and a surprisingly small party of Lower Creek headmen came sauntering into Charles Town on January 24, almost a full month late.

By the time everyone convened in the council chamber two days later, the Cherokees and the South Carolinians had exhausted their reserves of good will. A ceremony originally intended to serve as a confirmation of harmony quickly turned into an inquisition of the Lower Creeks. After the members of the coun-cil and the Commons House took their seats, the Long Warrior walked into the room and took the place of honor at the main table, directly to the right of Pres-ident Middleton. When Chigelly took his own seat a few minutes later, Middle-ton began by scolding him for bringing so few of his people along and then or-dered him to stand up and make his speech to the Cherokees. Chigelly started his speech but directed it to the white audience, forcing Middleton to interrupt him. Chigelly paused, turned to the Long Warrior, held up a white eagle's wing, and uttered a few perfunctory words. The Long Warrior turned to Middleton in astonishment, asking, "Is this all they have to say?" Chigelly replied with a simple "yes" and placed the wing on the table. The Long Warrior delivered his withering response without even bothering to leave his chair: "You appear here and Talke before the Governour, but you do not mind what you Promise when you come home. I see your white Wing there, but shall not receive it till I find you'll be good to the White People. . . . It is now come to this. We are the red People now mett together. Our flesh is both alike, but we must have noe further Talke with you[;] wee shall see when we goe home whether any of Our People have been killed, and whether you are Rogues. If soe, wee shall Know what to do." Accounts of the conference suggest that these two Indian spokesmen had precious little enthusiasm for a Creek-Cherokee peace. [145] Even the stubbornly optimistic Middleton had to recognize that the Cherokees and the Lower Creeks might return to war in the not too distant future.

For the time being, however, he and the rest of the South Carolina officials simply hoped that Chigelly and the Long Warrior would have the good graces to complete the ceremony. With hundreds of impatient eyes on him, Chigelly solemnly promised to abandon the French and the Spanish and to honor the English as the only true friends of his people. He completed his smooth recovery by picking up a glass of wine and proposing a toast to Middleton's health. Temporarily disarmed, the South Carolinians murmured their approval, and the Long Warrior and the rest of the Cherokees consented to shake hands with Chigelly and his small entourage. After another round of toasts to King George and the royal family, the conference adjourned to the sound of a cannon salute. Middleton distributed presents to the Indian leaders and allowed them to repair to the outskirts of town to smoke the calumet and cement the peace in their own way.[146]

The conference did not end with an actual treaty, at least in the generally understood sense of the term. Neither Chigelly nor the Long Warrior left his signature, or even his mark, on any kind of official document. Throughout the conference everyone understood that one's "word," or spoken promise, was one's bond. The South Carolinians and the Cherokees agreed to accept Chigelly's word, even though many of them doubted his willingness to keep it. At the same time, however, the South Carolinians made much of their ability to bring some extra leverage to the table, a special power that allowed them to act as guarantors of all the Indians' promises. At the beginning of the treaty ceremony, Middleton pointed to his copy of the "journal" of George Chicken's recent missions, reminding the Cherokee contingent that he would "allwayes [be] assured of [their] Friendship"[:] "I have it in these Papers in Writeing, wee can never forget it." Middleton also made a similar, if more ominous, observation to the Lower Creeks, informing Chigelly that his pledges were being preserved by a government scribe and would "always be remembered by [them]."[147] On the surface the minutes of the 1727 Charles Town peace conference reveal a healthy mixture of diplomatic traditions: white wings and wooden tables, wine goblets and peace pipes. But even as the South Carolina officials gave the Cherokees and the Creeks enough leeway to indulge in some of their own customs, they also meant to leave no doubt as to which side had real control over the proceedings.

Though a clear expression of English power, the written word could also serve as a kind of refuge for colonial diplomats. Ultimately the transcripts of the treaty were just another way for the South Carolinians to "paper over" their frontier problems. Just as all the commissions offered by Nicholson, Chicken, and Fitch had failed to overhaul Indian political culture or untie the knots of Indian factionalism, a treaty arranged and imposed by the South Carolina government did not have the power—in and of itself—to put a stop to the Creek-Cherokee War. Despite their adoption of firearms and other implements of European military culture, the Indians of the southeastern interior continued to fight in ways that baffled European observers and defied European control.

Wars between Indians were not contests for territory and resources as much as they were self-sustaining cycles of raids and counterraids fueled by the desire for revenge and other forms of emotional catharsis. Most South Carolina imperialists of the late 1720s knew enough to recognize some of the fundamental differences between Indian and European warfare, but by the end of the great Charles Town conference, they nevertheless had convinced themselves that the Creeks and the Cherokees would channel their "Sudden Passions" for vengeance into government-sanctioned attacks on the "French Indians" or the rootless, wandering, and increasingly troublesome Chickasaw refugees living in the Savannah River basin.[148] Within months of the conference, South Carolina officials found themselves surprised and offended by rumors coming out of the Chattahoochee basin, where Chigelly and some of the other Lower Creeks apparently had begun to boast that no treaty arranged by the English could prevent them from fighting whenever, wherever, and whomever they pleased.[149]

The South Carolina government should have realized more clearly than ever that it could not dictate the terms of cultural exchange in the southeastern interior. By the summer of 1727, many of the Lower Creeks had not only determined to keep fighting the Cherokees but had also failed to follow through on Chigelly's promises to bring the Yamasees back to South Carolina.[150] Always the greatest concern of the South Carolina imperialists, the Lower Creeks quickly became the center of a new crisis, one that shall be examined at greater length in the next chapter. Even as the South Carolinians worried about the Lower Creeks, however, they could not help but notice an onslaught of unwelcome challenges from the supposedly loyal and subservient Cherokees. More than anything else, these challenges revealed the shortcomings of South Carolina's diplomatic initiatives.

From the outset the South Carolina–Cherokee alliance was never as smooth or seamless as the South Carolinians wished to believe. By 1720 or so the escalation of the Creek-Cherokee War and the retreat of the Virginia traders—along with the relentless influx of English trade goods—had combined to make the Cherokees less openly defiant of the South Carolinians. All the while, however, the Cherokees continued to assert their fundamental political autonomy. While the spirit of resistance ran deep among the Cherokees throughout the entire 1720s, it did not become apparent to most South Carolina imperialists until the great peace "treaty" of 1727 began to come apart at the seams.

This ironic twist had at least some connection to the Cherokees' growing sense of disillusionment. In September 1727 the South Carolina government, once again on the verge of war with the Lower Creeks, sent Colonel John Herbert to convince the Cherokees to break the treaty that they had so recently made. The Cherokees, Herbert averred, had been right all along: the Lower Creeks were "Shee Rogues," unworthy of anyone's patience or friendship. [151] When asked to renew their attacks against their old enemies, some of the Cherokee headmen responded with poorly concealed disgust, not only for the Lower Creeks but also for Herbert and the South Carolinians. One of the headmen who had participated in the Charles Town ceremony reminded Herbert that the Cherokees "wanted to return home without making peace with them," but the South Carolina government had pressured the Cherokees to wait in Charles Town for the Lower Creek delegation. [152] Choatehee, a head warrior from the Upper Cherokee town of Great Tellico, agreed to set out against the Lower Creeks but insisted that Herbert accompany him. When Herbert predictably stalled, Choatehee scoffed that "he believed the English were afraid of the Creeks." [153] South Carolina's newest beloved man found his very honor in question, a situation uncomfortably similar to the one that had plagued agent William Hatton a few years earlier. Though the Cherokees complied with the request to mobilize against the Lower Creeks, their insolent tone must have struck Herbert and some of his superiors as ominous.

In the eyes of the Long Warrior, Choatehee, and several other Cherokees who had supported the English in recent years, Herbert could not begin to fill the shoes of George Chicken, who died of unspecified causes in the summer of 1727. Colonel Chicken, for all his shortcomings, had earned a great deal of respect and formed some genuine friendships among the Cherokees. Before the Long Warrior took his seat in the great Charles Town ceremony, he scanned the council chamber for Chicken and was visibly piqued to find his "country man" relegated to an unobtrusive spot in the background. [154] Chicken's untimely death not only upset many of the Cherokees but also spelled trouble for South Carolina's agenda of frontier regulation. [155] Colonel Herbert—a man who had turned down an earlier mission to Indian country—found himself walking into a tough situation and clearly lacked the skills, reputation, and charisma of his predecessor. The abrupt change in personnel not only helped raise tensions between the Cherokees and the South Carolinians but also made it all the more difficult for the South Carolina government to remedy its preexisting problems with the Cherokees.

As usual these problems were hardest to overlook in the Indian trade, where none of the government's recent regulations seemed to have had the slightest impact on either the traders or their Indian customers. Though Herbert assumed all the regulatory powers that had belonged to the late Commissioner Chicken, he proved far less effective at enforcing them.[156] When the headmen of Tugaloo complained about a trader named John Facey for "turning [them] out of his house at times and looking on them as boys," Herbert attempted to take action, only to drop the matter when Facey replied that "he was Obliged to use some harsh means with some of them in defence of himselfe."[157] It often fell on the traders themselves to keep government officials in Charles Town abreast of troubling developments. In the fall of 1727, the experienced Eleazar Wiggan informed President Middleton that some of the traders were "trusting the Indians . . . to the value of 16 or 18 hundred skins," and that those who "refused to do the like" were forced to "bear the insults of some impudent fellows."[158] With another potentially disastrous credit crisis in the works, Middleton attempted to wipe the slate clean by canceling many of the Cherokees' debts.[159] Shortly thereafter the assembly's Committee on Indian Affairs made a thinly veiled suggestion to return to the old government monopoly, claiming that it would be "impracticable" to impose any further regulations as long as the Indian trade was "caryed on in Divers Interests."[160] These acts of semidesperation indicated that the South Carolina government had finally begun to doubt its ability to keep the Cherokees under control.

Tension increased even further when government officials realized that some of the Cherokees were not satisfied with pulling South Carolina's purse strings. While South Carolina imperialists almost expected the Cherokees to tinker with the trade, they never dreamed that the Cherokees would defy the British alliance system. For years the South Carolinians had pounded home the message that they would "not Suffer them [the Cherokees] to make peace with foreign Nations without [their] Consent and upon [their] Termes, for [they knew] what [was] best for them."[161] Above all they insisted that the Cherokees avoid making peace with the "French Indians" of the Mississippi Valley, an order that the Long Warrior and other Cherokee leaders had readily accepted during their 1727 visit to Charles Town.[162] Within a year, however, Middleton and the council began to hear disturbing rumors that the Long Warrior had joined several other Cherokee headmen in advocating peace and free trade with their former enemies in Illinois.[163] Though upset that important leaders like the Long Warrior were no longer paying as much attention to them, South Carolina officials were even more disturbed by the prospect of French influence over the Cherokees, a scenario that was one of their worst imperial nightmares.[164]

Such a scenario no longer seemed as far-fetched as it had even a few years earlier. In 1725 Louis XV poured an additional three hundred thousand livres into the Company of the Indies, which finally agreed to entrust Louisiana's Indian affairs to experienced and capable agents. Disturbed by the threat of English influence among the Choctaws, these agents decided to strike back by launching the first French initiatives among the Cherokees.[165] Compared to the South Carolinians, the French could offer little in the way of useful material goods. Nevertheless, their first tentative approaches—whether made directly through a few adventurous French agents or indirectly through the Illinois Indians—managed to generate considerable interest in Cherokee country.

The situation that began to emerge in the Appalachians after 1727 bore remarkable similarities to the South Carolina–Virginia rivalry of the second decade of the eighteenth century, a time when the mere rumor of the Virginia traders had sufficed to whet the appetite of any Cherokee who held the slightest grudge against the South Carolinians. The French became an important new trump card, not only for Cherokees alienated from the South Carolinians but also for pro-English Cherokees who hoped to curry favor by depicting themselves as heroic bulwarks against French expansion.[166] The late 1720s witnessed a new explosion of Indian factionalism, a phenomenon that had lain fairly dormant among the Cherokees for nearly a decade. With a trace of panic, South Carolina officials noted that the Cherokees were "very divided amongst themselves" and beset by "great distractions" that might persuade them to "destroy the Traders" among them.[167] By the end of 1728, the Cherokees suddenly seemed a good deal more like the Lower Creeks than the steady and dependable allies whom the South Carolinians had once claimed to know.

Though the South Carolina imperialists perceived a pressing need to reassert their authority, they hesitated to do anything drastic for fear of driving the Cherokees into the French camp. In a major departure from the optimistic diplomatic initiatives of the early and mid-1720s, no one in South Carolina even pretended to come up with a simple solution to the province's frontier problems. This time it fell on an irrepressible and uninitiated "outsider" to step in and save the day.[168]

Sir Alexander Cuming, the man who single-handedly took up the challenge of cowing the Cherokees, shared all the ethnocentric assumptions of Middleton, Fitch, Chicken, and other South Carolina diplomats but carried them to an even further extreme. Like Francis Nicholson, Cuming came to South Carolina directly from Britain, bringing along a strong attachment to the Crown and the wider British Empire. Unlike Nicholson, however, Cuming had absolutely no direct experience with the North American colonies, not to mention the tricky business of Indian affairs. Cuming was a dyed-in-the-wool eccentric, a minor Scottish nobleman who sailed to Charles Town at his own expense and initiative after his wife had a dream that foretold great things for him in South Carolina. After several months of idleness among the low-country gentry, Cuming learned of the government's growing crisis with the Cherokees and suddenly knew where his destiny would lie.[169]

Even though "it was given out in the English settlements . . . that the Traders would not venture to return among them [the Cherokees] for fear of being murdered," Cuming managed to find several men who agreed to guide him into the mountains.[170] They left Charles Town in early March 1730, embarking on a month-long circuit that took them through nearly every Cherokee village. According to Cuming's version of the trip, the Cherokees were unruly but impressionable children who only needed a firm hand to guide them along the proper path. At his first stop, the Lower Cherokee town of Keowee, Cuming reportedly marched into a packed council house "armed with three Cases of Pistols, a Gun, and his Sword" and got three hundred or more Cherokees to "Owe Obedience to him on their Knees."[171] This bold action established Cuming as a force to be reckoned with, not only in the eyes of the awe-struck traders but also among the rest of the Cherokees. Cuming's reputation apparently preceded him to the town of Tassatche, where a headman told him several days later that "he knew he was come amongst them to rule, and that their whole Nation must do whatever he bid them."[172]

Cuming's journey culminated on April 3 with a great Cherokee council in the Upper Cherokee town of Neguassie, where Moytoy, head warrior of Great Tellico and the primary rival of the pro-French Long Warrior, received a commission to serve as emperor of the Cherokees "by the unanimous consent of the whole People; and to whom at Sir Alexander's Desire, they all gave an unlimited Power over them, and he to answer to Sir Alexander." At the conclusion of the conference, Cuming, seated in a ceremonial chair and fanned with thirteen eagle wings, ordered everyone "to acknowledge themselves dutiful Subjects and sons to King George . . . calling upon everything that was terrible to destroy them, and that they might be no People, if they violated their Promise and Obedience." Satisfied with his handiwork, Cuming turned his gaze to a nearby coterie of traders, who "declared they would not have believed such a thing possible, if they had not seen it."[173]

But at least one South Carolinian remained highly skeptical even after witnessing all of Cuming's adventures. Ludovick Grant, a trader who served as a guide and translator throughout the entire expedition, eventually became familiar with Cuming's version of the story and proved eager to shoot several gaping holes in it. According to Grant, Cuming was always very explicit about his credentials, repeatedly informing the Cherokees that he was "not sent either by the Great King or any of his Governors . . . and only came for his own private Satisfaction to see the Country." Cuming rarely stayed "above two or three hours" in any village and usually appeared satisfied with the most superficial understandings of his hosts. Whenever Cuming met a Cherokee and shook his hand, he would "take his name down in his pocket book saying that he had made a Friend of him." At Neguassie, Cuming simply sat in on a run-of-the-mill ceremony for naming a new Cherokee headman, and at Keowee he simply proposed a toast to King George on bended knee, an action that the Indians mimicked out of politeness. Grant admitted that Cuming had carried his sword and pistols into the Keowee council house but chalked the deed up to foolishness rather than bravery. When one of the traders upbraided him for this breach of etiquette, Cuming "answered with a Wild look, that his intention was if any of the Indians had refused the King's health to have taken a brand out of the fire that Burn[ed] in the middle of the room and have set fire to the house." In Grant's account "Sir Alexander" comes across not only as a self-aggrandizing neophyte but also as a bit mentally unsound.[174]

The Cherokees, though beset with internal factions and outside pressures, remained confident enough in their own rituals and institutions to accommodate the missteps of an enthusiastic and somewhat intriguing visitor. Given the fundamental stability of Cherokee political culture—not to mention Cuming's colorful personality—it is easy to decide which of the two conflicting accounts of Cuming's mission is more believable. Despite all the controversy, however, no one could dispute that the core of Cuming's agenda was to forge a stronger connection between London and the Cherokees and advance his own political career. Eventually, Cuming would attempt to pursue these goals with a scheme to settle three hundred thousand Jewish families in the Cherokee mountains.[175] For the time being, however, he was content to take some of his new Cherokee "friends" back to England with him. Several Cherokees politely turned him down, but several others jumped at the offer. As early as 1722, pro-English Cherokees had asked the South Carolina government for a chance to go across the Great Water, claiming that it would allow them "to see all things and how they [were] made."[176] Though the idea of a Cherokee embassy to London was not original to Cuming, he deserves credit for getting the idea off the ground. South Carolina officials, reluctant to spend their province's money on such an undertaking, were perfectly content to let Cuming fund the trip out of his own pocket. On May 4, 1730, Cuming booked passage on the man-of-war *Fox*, accompanied by six Cherokees and a curious Catawba whom the party had met on its way back to Charles Town. They arrived in England a month later, kicking off a visit that has appropriately been described as a "diplomatic *tour de force*."[177]

The Indians made the most of their summer in England, visiting George II at Windsor Palace, having their portrait painted in Covent Garden, and becoming a hot topic among London socialites. [178] Along the way they also found time for an audience with the Board of Trade, which seized on the visit as an ideal opportunity to cement the British Empire's authority over the entire Cherokee nation. On September 7 the board drew up a series of "Articles of Friendship and Commerce" intended to weld the Cherokees to the British mercantile, military, and legal systems. In exchange for twenty guns, forty-eight kettles, seventy-two hatchets, 120 belts, 144 knives, four hundred pounds of powder, a thousand pounds of bullets, and ten thousand flints, the six overwhelmed Cherokees duly agreed to protect the English from their enemies, to trade with no one but the English, to return any fugitive English slaves, and to abide by the English penalty for murder. The Cherokees' designated spokesman summed up the occasion with predictable modesty: "The Great King George's Enemies shall be our Enemies, his people and ours shall always be one, and shall die together. We came hither naked and poor as the Worm of the Earth; but you have every thing, and we that have Nothing must love you, and can never break the chain of Friendship which is between us." On that note the Cherokees affixed their marks to the articles, completing the first written treaty between the southeastern Indians and the British imperial hierarchy.[179]

Over the years it has been tempting for historians to share the Board of Trade's perspective on the 1730 Cherokee treaty, viewing it as a reflection of South Carolina's "royalization," a capstone of the South Carolina–Cherokee alliance, and a welcome antidote to the frontier instability that had grown out of the Yamasee War. [180] In some ways the treaty—along with the two dramatic missions that led to it—did mark a turning point in Anglo-Cherokee relations. It would be fair to conclude, in the words of Verner Crane, that the visit of the Cherokees and the signing of the treaty "dramatised for many Englishmen the existence of a frontier of empire of which few had yet been aware."[181] Moreover, the various ceremonies of 1730 also made a considerable impression on the Cherokees. The six Cherokee travelers not only returned to the mountains with a large load of presents and an inexhaustible supply of stories but also held on to their copy of the treaty, a parchment that they would continue to display as a sign of the Great King's friendship for many years to come.[182]

Though the treaty and the events that surrounded it probably increased English prestige among the Cherokees, they did little if anything to increase British authority. To be sure, Sir Alexander Cuming's ability to visit the Cherokees, intrude in their political affairs, and escort some of them to England was a function of the considerable influence achieved by the South Carolinians over the previous fifteen years. Someone like Cuming would not have lasted ten minutes among the Cherokees in the spring of 1715. Nevertheless, one should not rush to interpret the events of 1730 as a triumph of British imperial might. In essence the Cuming mission and the treaty hammered out by the Board of Trade carried on South Carolina's fifty-year-old pattern of arrogance and misunderstanding, albeit on a much grander scale.

The popular image of American frontier diplomacy is based largely on the treaties of the late eighteenth and nineteenth centuries, documents in which white men compelled Indians to concede land, sovereignty, or other important privileges. In the early eighteenth century, however, European diplomats usually approached Indians from a position of anxious uncertainty rather than confident strength.[183] In 1730 South Carolina and British imperialists lacked the firepower—or even the believable threat thereof—to persuade the Cherokees to surrender their most basic freedoms. In all probability the Cherokees who went to England fully intended to uphold the promises that they made to the Board of Trade. At the same time these men in no way spoke for all ten thousand of the Cherokees; only two of the six "ambassadors" were headmen, and not even the most prestigious Cherokee leaders possessed the power to force their people to live by foreign codes.[184] The Articles of Commerce and Friendship, a binding treaty in the eyes of the Board of Trade, became little more than an interesting conversation piece once they were carried into the Cherokee mountains. For those Cherokees who adamantly supported the English, the articles might have served as a reminder to stand by their friends and providers. For those who adamantly resented the English and the pro-English Cherokees, they might have served as another unwelcome example of English nagging. For most of the Cherokees, however, the articles were probably nothing more than a parchment decorated with undecipherable symbols.

Officials in London remained content to emphasize their own imperial rhetoric over the realities of the southeastern frontier complex, but officials in Charles Town could no longer afford the luxury of this simple but fruitless approach. The South Carolina imperialists had remarkably little to do with the great Anglo-Cherokee peace treaty of 1730. Far better than the Board of Trade, they understood that the Cherokees—no matter how much some of them might seem to comply with English demands—would continue to go their own way once everything was said and done. [185] By itself a treaty could do nothing to prevent traders and Indians from coming to blows or the French from making overtures to South Carolina's Indian allies. After stumbling their way through the bold diplomatic initiatives of the 1720s, South Carolina imperialists finally began to abandon their search for a perfect solution to their frontier anxieties.

Instead of looking for signs that point to the end of the era of the Yamasee War in the southeastern interior, it would be better to emphasize the continuation of Indian resistance. Despite the enormous physical and cultural pressures associated with trade, warfare, and other products of imperial expansion, the Cherokees, the Creeks, and other relatively large Indian societies continued to assert their own fundamental autonomy, even to the point of reworking some of the arrangements they had made with the South Carolinians before, during, and after the Yamasee War. The South Carolinians, blinded by their own prejudices and assumptions, often had a hard time detecting this resistance or understanding what made it work. Unable or unwilling to understand the Indians, they could only plead with them or pressure them. Ultimately the sustained pressure of disease, trade goods, and intertribal warfare would make significant inroads against Creek and Cherokee independence. In the meantime, however, the South Carolina imperialists were forced to wield far less control than they would have liked along certain far-off frontiers. On frontiers closer to home, they convinced themselves that their future would have to rest on something far more solid than an uncomfortable stalemate and a patchwork paper trail.

8. Designs on a Debatable Land

THE WATERSHED OF SOUTH
CAROLINIAN EXPANSION

Istawekee never forgot his homeland. Long after the South Carolinians had driven him and his people away from the inlets of Port Royal Sound, he continued to make frequent and unscheduled visits to the area. Some of the local colonists were more hospitable than others; one man named Blakeway often took the illegal risk of sheltering Istawekee and his compatriots and buying their deerskins. During one such transaction in the fall of 1723, Blakeway and his guests suddenly discovered that Colonel John Barnwell was on his way to take them into custody. Istawekee managed to flee in the nick of time, but after a few weeks on the lam, he ran out of luck when a terrified family on Parris Island informed against him. Cornered by Barnwell and a ten-man posse, the "runagado Yamasee" finally turned and stood his ground.

Istawekee attempted to explain that he had only come to Port Royal to hunt and trade, but his story made little impression on his captors. As far as most South Carolinians were concerned, Istawekee was a menace, an "intolerable Insolent" warrior rumored to have fought alongside the infamous Cherokeeleechee during the Yamasee War. Barnwell was fairly well acquainted with Istawekee, having reminded him on numerous occasions that the Yamasees were legally forbidden to visit the South Carolina settlements. This time, however, Istawekee startled Barnwell and everyone else by responding that "he had as much right to the Land as [they,] for Land was free as Air and Water to everybody." Barnwell's only response to this heresy was to seize Istawekee's gun and break it before his eyes. Humiliated and enraged, Istawekee reportedly let out a "Warr hoope" and lunged for Barnwell's throat, only to be restrained at the last instant. Istawekee had come to Port Royal as a free, proud, and daring young man. He left in leg irons and shackles, a common prisoner relegated to the dark recesses of South Carolina history. [1]

While many South Carolina imperialists set their sights hundreds of miles into the southeastern interior during the 1720s, most of them realized that they had more pressing concerns closer to home. For all the damage done to English interests along the Alabama and Tennessee rivers, the crippling legacy of the war weighed heaviest on the province's southernmost settlements, where colonists found it impossible to forget the harrowing and humiliating incursions of the Yamasees and the Lower Creeks. To these South Carolinians, Indians like Istawekee not only posed intolerable challenges to English notions of law and property but also served as unwelcome reminders of the province's vulnerability. As long as the Yamasees and the Lower Creeks could continue to pass through the southern settlements and flaunt their autonomy, the South Carolinians would never be able to complete the unbearably slow process of recovery.

Throughout the 1720s South Carolina imperialists equated recovery with control and strove to assert their authority in every tenuous or ambiguous situation. Along many of South Carolina's far-western frontiers, imperialists had to operate through the channels of trade and diplomacy and often found themselves frustrated by immovable cultural obstacles. Though the South Carolinians drew on similar strategies in their quest to stabilize their war-torn southern frontiers, they quickly realized that they could establish control over this region in other ways as well. When the Yamasees and the Lower Creeks migrated to Florida and the Chattahoochee basin in 1715–16, they unwittingly cleared the way for a new chapter in South Carolina's imperial expansion. The vulnerable settlements of Saint Bartholomew's and Saint Helena Parishes now bordered on a vast expanse of uninhabited forests, plains, and swamps. Claimed by both the English and the Spanish for more than fifty years, the "debatable land" of present-day Georgia soon became the primary focus of the South Carolina imperialists and their superiors in London.[2] Like the ongoing conflict between the Creeks and the Cherokees in the southeastern interior, the contest for the debatable land fanned the embers of the Yamasee War. Nevertheless, the South Carolinians asserted themselves far more forcefully and effectively in this contest than they did in the Creek-Cherokee War. As they waged and eventually won the struggle for the debatable land, they revealed the ruthless determination that had fueled a half-century of frontier expansion, as well as the deeply rooted fears that would shape their future frontier policies.

A Fort up in Flames

Following the overthrow of the proprietors in 1720, most South Carolina officials felt confident in their ability to regain the level of prosperity that had existed before the Yamasee War. As they looked at certain sections of the province, however, they realized that they still had a good deal of work ahead of them. In 1722 Francis Yonge, a successful South Carolina merchant and the province's newly appointed agent in London, published an influential pamphlet on the state of the South Carolina economy, reserving his harshest criticism for Port Royal and the other "southward" settlements. Yonge firmly placed the blame for the region's sluggishness on "the late Indian War, which not only destroyed the stocks of cattle, but drove most of the inhabitants . . . from their plantations, who dare[d] not yet return for fear of the Yamazee Indians, who frequently disturb[ed] the settlements near Port Royal, murder[ed] the planters, [and] carr[ied] the slaves to St. Augustin." Port Royal's Saint Helena Parish, home to several hundred white residents before the war, now contained no more than thirty. According to Yonge such paltry numbers left the southernmost colonists unable to "defend themselves against their own slaves, much less a Spanish or French enemy."[3]

No one recognized Port Royal's vulnerability more than its most famous and influential resident, John "Tuscarora Jack" Barnwell. By the time Yonge wrote his pamphlet, Barnwell was already immersed in a plan to expedite Port Royal's recovery by rebuilding South Carolina's defensive perimeter. Along with several members of the South Carolina assembly, Barnwell believed that the South Carolinians needed to establish a more direct presence along their frontiers by constructing a ring of new frontier outposts, forts that would eventually serve as centerpieces for clusters of new homesteads.[4] While the scheme for new "garrison towns" drew on similar models implemented by the Massachusetts and Virginia governments, it also grew out of South Carolina's own wartime experience, during which the success of Fort Moore and other structures had helped win converts to the concept of frontier fortification.[5] Overall, however, Barnwell's greatest inspiration came from the French, whose new forts in Louisiana and Canada had become the envy of English imperialists everywhere. In 1717–18 the construction of Louisiana's Fort Toulouse and Florida's Fort San Marcos posed an even more immediate challenge to South Carolina's frontier strategists. Barnwell contended that by replicating their enemies' policies of fortification, the South Carolinians would acquire the means "not only to preserve [their] Trade with the Indians and their Dependance on [the colonists], but also to preserve [their] Boundaries." [6] Here, in Barnwell's mind, was the ultimate solution to all of South Carolina's frontier concerns.

During his important conferences with the Board of Trade in the summer and fall of 1720, Barnwell asked the British Crown to sponsor new or improved forts in five highly strategic southeastern locations: Savannah Town, Port Royal, the Chattahoochee and Tennessee rivers, and the mouth of the Altamaha. The board, deeply concerned by the threat of French expansion in the Southeast, eagerly embraced Barnwell's proposal on the grounds that "a penny [then] laid out [might] save pounds [t]hereafter." [7] Upon further consideration, however, the board decided that it did not have enough pennies on hand to finance all five forts at once. For the time being, the South Carolinians would have to make do with one fort, constructed at the site of greatest priority. If given the choice, Barnwell and the rest of the South Carolinians probably would have preferred to build at Port Royal or even at the old Apalachicola towns along the Savannah River. [8] The board was concerned that the French, after losing their brief hold on Pensacola, were looking for a new port of entry into the Southeast. To preempt the most dangerous site that the French might select, the board fixed its sights on the Altamaha. Though somewhat disappointed, Barnwell knew better than to complain. A fort on the Altamaha could serve as a bulwark against Yamasee incursions while acting as an advance guard for South Carolina's beleaguered southern settlements. More importantly His Majesty's government would be footing the bill, having agreed to provide tools, military hardware, and a battalion of independent troops to build and staff the fort.

By the time Barnwell set sail for South Carolina, however, he had even greater cause for disappointment. His ship carried tools to build the fort, but no engineer to plan and direct construction. Instead of a crack battalion, he had only a hundred ragged troops taken from the dregs of the British army, most of whom contracted scurvy during the rough trip across the Atlantic. [9] Barnwell realized that he would have to take charge of the project and began to patch together his own outfit as soon as he returned to Port Royal in June 1721. After finding six Lower Creek Indians to scout and hunt for the party, he recruited the Port Royal scout boat crews to ferry supplies and help with the construction. [10] Barnwell proudly remarked that these hardened frontiersmen could work faster and shoot straighter than anyone but also lamented that they were often "drunk as beasts" and "ready for the Run on the least disgust." [11]

The detail proved to be a thoroughly disgusting one. The site chosen for the fort—a marshy riverbank roughly one mile east of present-day Darien,

Georgia—was almost unlivable during the steamy months of summer. Men worked chest-deep in malarial water, swatting mosquitoes and living off rancid meat. The six Lower Creeks took one look at the situation and headed for home; most of the other men somehow stuck it out. By the end of the summer, they finished work on a twenty-six-foot compound made of cypress planks and palmetto leaves and adorned with several cannon and a Union Jack. Barnwell christened it Fort King George and proudly reported its completion to the authorities in Charles Town.[12]

Francis Nicholson, South Carolina's new royal governor, shared Barnwell's pride but also knew that the fort could not solve all of the province's frontier problems by itself. Since Nicholson believed that the stabilization of South Carolina's southern frontiers would have to depend on a reconciliation with the Yamasees, he quickly made these Indians the focus of his aggressive Indian policy. In June 1721, even before his first dramatic meetings with the Lower Creeks and the Cherokees, Nicholson issued an order "to get some of the Creek Indians to carry the Broad Seal of the province as an Assurance in Writing to the Yamasee Indians" that if they would consent to make peace with South Carolina, they would be "kindly received" and permitted to "settle on such Lands as [might] be Ordered them by the Government."[13] This was Nicholson at the height of his arrogance, fresh off the boat and largely insensitive to the intense feelings of hatred that the Yamasees had developed for the South Carolinians in recent years. He not only expected the Yamasees to forget all about the punitive expedition sent down by the South Carolinians in 1719 but also assumed that a written document with a "broad seal" would convince them to return to the subservient status they had rebelled against six years earlier.

Nicholson got a rude awakening when he heard from Matthew Smallwood, a trader sent down to Apalachicola Town to receive the Yamasees' answer. The Lower Creek messengers bluntly informed Smallwood that the Yamasees had refused even to consider Nicholson's proposal. They warned Smallwood not to try to bring South Carolina's great seal to Saint Augustine on his own, for the Yamasees "would kill him if he should offer it." The Huspah king, now in charge of the Yamasees living around Saint Augustine, apparently had built three new forts to protect himself against the English and had pledged "to kill any of his people that threatened to desert." Smallwood, at a loss for how to proceed, sent a messenger up to Coweta to get the opinion of the "Emperor" Brims. Shortly thereafter the messenger returned with the advice that "it would be best for him to return and not proceed any farther for it would be all to no purpose."[14]

According to Nicholson and other South Carolina officials, the Creeks had no right to tell the South Carolinians what they should or should not do in respect to the Yamasees. Nicholson made this point abundantly clear to Brims's son Ouletta during a conference in the spring of 1722. Nicholson ordered Ouletta to make one last attempt at bringing the Yamasees to South Carolina and tried to assure him that "on their coming . . . [the South Carolinians would] be friends with them . . . forgetting all that [was] past." If the Yamasees happened to refuse again, however, Ouletta and the Creeks were to "use them as [their] own enemy."[15] When Ouletta agreed to his demands, Nicholson automatically expected the rest of the Creeks to fall in line. In one stroke the Creeks' relations with the Yamasees became a benchmark of their loyalty to the South Carolinians. By putting so much stock in the Creeks, however, the South Carolinians only wound up complicating and exacerbating the problems along their southern frontiers. Since the various divisions and factions among the Creeks could never begin to live up to Nicholson's unrealistic expectations, it was only a matter of time before they grew even more frustrating and threatening in the eyes of the South Carolina authorities.

Once it became clear that no one could persuade the Yamasees to surrender by peaceable means, the South Carolina government began to offer new inducements for Yamasee scalps. By the early 1720s most of the Yamasees who had accompanied the Lower Creeks on their 1716 migration to the Chattahoochee resided in the vicinity of San Marcos de Apalachee, the new Spanish outpost along the Gulf Coast. The Yamasees of Apalachee soon became a relatively easy and convenient target for the Tallapoosas, who, unlike many of the Lower Creeks, did not have close familial or political ties to the Yamasees. Even some of the pro-English Lower Creeks, particularly the Yuchis and the Cussitas, found it hard to resist the temptation.[16] By the summer of 1723, these "infidel" raiders had grown bold and successful enough to worry the handful of Spanish troops at San Marcos and to force most of the surviving Yamasees to flee to Saint Augustine.[17] That fall a party of ten Tallapoosa headmen visited Charles Town, where the members of the Commons House provided them with coats, hats, guns, powder, and bullets as a reward "for the late Services done against the Yamasees." The Tallapoosas thanked the South Carolinians for the gifts and assured them that all the Alabama, Abeika, and Lower Creek towns had "agreed to Prosecute the War."[18]

As much as the South Carolinians would have liked to believe them, they had a good deal of evidence to the contrary. Theophilus Hastings, South Carolina's agent among the Creeks, joined a number of concerned traders in reporting that some of the Lower Creeks were attempting to protect the Yamasees.[19] When a party of Tallapoosas from the town of Tuckabatchee passed along the Chattahoochee on their way to attack the Yamasees, several Lower Creeks tried to divert them with "the false report that the Cherekees were discovered in the Woods." Undaunted, the Tallapoosas continued on their course and even issued an angry challenge when another group of Lower Creeks from Coweta tried to dissuade them. Some of the Lower Creeks were so impressed by the Tallapoosas' resolve that they decided to join the war party, but others rushed ahead to spread an alarm among the Yamasees. The expedition ended in failure, sparking considerable resentment between the different groups of Creeks.[20]

By 1724 such episodes had helped convince the South Carolina government "that the lower Creeks design[ed] to support the Yamasees." Some officials even went so far as to speculate that certain Lower Creek leaders, instead of hunting down the Yamasees, had "rather encouraged them to continue [as their] enemies."[21] Cherokeeleechee, the Lower Creek headman who had played a significant role in the formation of the Creek-Spanish alliance during the Yamasee War, remained the primary target of the South Carolinians' suspicions. One of the Yamasees arrested at Port Royal in the fall of 1723 defiantly boasted "that Cherokeeleechee had three hats full of money from the Spaniards" for scalps and slaves that he had collected during recent raids into South Carolina.[22] Enraged by the Lower Creeks' "treacherous" collusion with the Yamasees, Nicholson decided to adopt a hard-line approach and issued his controversial order to restrict all of South Carolina's Lower Creek traders to the town of Cussita.[23] This bold action, however, did nothing to solve the problem of Indian factionalism nor to dispel South Carolina's fears that the Creeks were falling into the Spanish interest and preparing for war. The disturbing connections between the Yamasees and the Lower Creeks continued to gnaw at South Carolina imperialists and emerged as one of the major concerns of Captain Tobias Fitch during his crucial mission to Creek country in the summer of 1725.

At first Fitch used relatively subtle means to persuade the Lower Creeks to attack the Yamasees at Saint Augustine, but he grew frustrated when his speeches continued to meet with resistance.[24] Fitch finally lost patience when some of the Lower Creeks allegedly threatened to kill Tickhoneby, a pro-English Tallapoosa headman, to avenge the death of one of their Yamasee friends. In a meeting with forty-five Lower Creek headmen in the town of Coweta, Fitch angrily ordered anyone who wished "Satisfaction for the Death of a Yamasee" to step forward. It was obvious, claimed Fitch, that the Yamasees only continued to attack South Carolina because they "knew they had [the Lower Creeks] to uphold them." When no one stood to admit his guilt, Fitch continued his tirade, announcing that the Great King of the English was growing "weary of this uncerton peace" between South Carolina and the Creeks and needed to know once and for all "who amongst [them was their] Friends and who [was] not." Following this terse ultimatum, Fitch had the satisfaction of seeing several large expeditions—including one from Coweta and another from "Cherokeeleechee's town"—set out for Saint Augustine by the end of the summer.[25]

Though Fitch briefly believed that he had forced the Creeks to turn over a new leaf, it soon became clear that these new expeditions made little departure from the routine established over the last several years. Many warriors were perfectly willing to attack the Yamasees without the benefit of a lecture from South Carolina's "beloved man." These included not only Tallapoosas like Tickhoneby who looked to collect bounties and vent their martial energies but also quite a few Lower Creeks who wanted revenge for damage suffered in recent run-ins with the Yamasees. According to Theophilus Hastings, many of the Creeks fought the Yamasees with considerable success and enthusiasm throughout the summer of 1725, returning from Saint Augustine with fifty scalps and thirty prisoners.[26] The largest and most ambitious raid, led by the Tallapoosa headman Steyamasiechie, struck Saint Augustine in early November. Though most of the Yamasees were able to take refuge in the Castillo de San Marcos, Steyamasiechie's party managed to inflict about twenty casualties while taking some silver from a mission church and putting a real scare into the Huspah king and his Spanish protectors.[27]

But even as some Creeks proved themselves "true friends" to the English, others remained friendly with the Spanish and the Yamasees in spite of Fitch's various pleas, threats, and inducements. It did not take Fitch long to notice that for every expedition that ended in reasonable success, another turned out suspiciously disappointing. One expedition reportedly broke apart when a black slave in the employ of the French convinced seventy Lower Creek warriors to turn back.[28] The Coweta war party, led by Brims's son Sepeycoffee, returned home empty-handed, as did the expedition from Cherokeeleechee's town. Both parties apologized for their lack of success and claimed that they had given up only after finding all the Yamasees "in forted" in Saint Augustine. Though their stories were plausible, Fitch remained uneasy and attempted to allay his suspicions by arranging a parlay with Cherokeeleechee. But a thorough search failed to turn up the elusive headman; evidently he had taken refuge among the Spanish, who had convinced him that Fitch had come to send him and his family "over the great water." To Fitch all evidence suggested that too many of the Lower Creeks were allowing their minds to be poisoned by the French and the Spanish. As Fitch took his leave from the Lower Creeks in December 1725, he warned Brims and Sepeycoffee to do a better job of rooting out the "spies" among them and added that "amonge [the English] Such a man would be Tied to four mad horses and Drawn to pieces."[29]

While Fitch and other South Carolina imperialists continued to complain about foreign influence over the Creeks, they never stopped to consider that the Spanish might have become even more flustered with the behavior of these Indians. The Spanish had initially made promising strides among the Creeks as a result of the Yamasee War, but by the early 1720s, they—like the English— had great difficulty distinguishing the Indians they could trust from those they could not. Some of the Tallapoosas and Lower Creeks who had rendered obedience in 1717 were now proving themselves inveterate enemies of the Spanish Empire.[30] Not even the pro-Spanish sympathies of Cherokeeleechee, Sepeycoffee, Chigelly, and other important Lower Creek leaders could prevent certain Indians from continually harassing the Yamasees and endangering the Spanish settlements. Though the kingdoms of Spain and Great Britain officially remained at peace, Florida authorities grew convinced that they were actually locked in a state of undeclared warfare with the aggressive and dangerous South Carolinians.

Just as they had during the troubles of the 1690s, the Spanish Floridians initially tried to protest through official channels. In 1721 they got the Council of the Indies in Madrid to inform Whitehall that the "Inhabitants of Florida could not stir out of their houses to Cultivate their lands, nor turn out their Cattle without apparent danger from [the South Carolina] Indians."[31] King George I, desirous of Spain's assistance against the French, had Secretary of State Lord Carteret order the South Carolina government to put a stop to the raids. A year later Carteret sent the same order, diplomatically assuming that the first had been lost in transit because the raids had not stopped.[32] By this time the impatient and pressured officials in Saint Augustine had decided to take matters into their own hands, sending the governor's secretary, Francisco Menéndez, on an official mission to Charles Town. While there Menéndez happened to overhear a reference to the new fort at the mouth of the Altamaha, a discovery that whipped his superiors into a state of even greater agitation.[33]

The South Carolinians had built Fort King George primarily to discourage the French, giving little thought to the uproar that it might cause among the

Spanish. The incessant raids from English-sponsored Indians were troubling enough, but the Spanish could never abide English encroachments into territory that they considered their own.[34] In late 1722 Florida officials sent thirty emissaries on a mission to Charles Town to solidify their claims to the Georgia coast. There they advanced a number of sound arguments, pointing to the 1670 Treaty of Madrid as well as the precedents established by the Guale missions, Spanish settlements that had stood near the Altamaha as recently as the 1680s.[35] The Spanish soon discovered, however, that South Carolina officials were prepared to do anything to prevent supposed rules of "international law" from getting in their way. The South Carolinians pretended not to remember the Guale missions, an absurd claim given that some of their fathers and grandfathers had played an active role in destroying them. Some South Carolinians took the farce even further, asserting that the English had right of first discovery to the Georgia coast by virtue of John Cabot's 1497 voyage, an expedition that never went further south than Newfoundland.[36]

When pressed too far by the Spanish diplomats, Nicholson and the assembly simply decided to expel them from the province. A follow-up expedition in 1724 met with an even ruder reception; the Spanish emissaries spent several weeks confined to Charles Town jail cells before returning to Saint Augustine in frustration.[37] In Madrid the Council of the Indies shared Governor Benavides's anger but essentially told him to swallow his pride and keep trying.[38] Benavides's last-ditch attempt came in 1725, when he sent two more agents to Charles Town with an offer to pay for all the fugitive slaves harbored in Florida if the South Carolinians would agree to destroy their fort on the Altamaha. Nicholson scoffed at the proposal, and the final attempt for a diplomatic solution to the Fort King George controversy ended with hard feelings on both sides.[39]

The South Carolinians stonewalled the Spanish because they knew that they could afford to do so. They also, in their own way, felt entirely justified in their aggressive and uncompromising stance. Throughout the colonial period, the English and the Spanish tended to hold conflicting views on the proper protocol for establishing territorial claims. While the Spanish generally put more stock in staking claims by way of treaties, exploration, or wooden crosses erected along abandoned shores, the English often emphasized the importance of actual, sustainable settlement.[40] Since the Spanish had turned their backs on the old province of Guale, they had, in the English estimation, left it up for grabs. The South Carolina imperialists did not see Fort King George as an illegal intrusion but as a case of "finders keepers." At the same time there also came a point where the South Carolinians felt that they no longer had to justify their claims to the debatable land by responding to questions about treaties and other legal precedents. Even if they had "taken" the Altamaha from the Florida government, they knew that there was precious little that the Spanish could do about it, short of going to war against Great Britain. Though the king and the Board of Trade might continue to voice their displeasure over the recurrent Indian raids into Florida, the South Carolinians correctly assumed that the Crown, having helped them build Fort King George in the first place, would support their claims to the debatable land. [41]

In the late seventeenth century, the South Carolinians' incursions into Spanish territory had stemmed from an arrogant program of expansionism. Though they often affected the same arrogant demeanor throughout the 1720s, they did so mainly to mask an increasingly powerful sense of insecurity. The Spanish and the French, after a brief falling out during the War of the Quadruple Alliance (1719–20), seemed well on their way to a rapprochement, causing the South Carolinians to speculate that their two Catholic rivals would soon return to "playing their old game" of combining their forces against the English. [42] Though the South Carolinians traditionally disdained the Spanish, the prospect of French support threw a different light on the situation. The Spanish might suddenly gain the confidence to launch new offensives against South Carolina, not only in the form of Yamasee and Lower Creek raiding parties but also by instigating the province's exploding population of black slaves into flight or insurrection. The early 1720s saw dozens of slaves make their way to Saint Augustine, and one group of ten runaways even managed to join forces with Yamasee warriors on occasional raids of the South Carolina settlements. [43] When the South Carolinians observed members of the 1722 and 1725 Spanish delegations trying to strike up conversations with black slaves in the streets of Charles Town, it seemed clear that they could "have no other motive than to entice them from their masters." [44] Amid a climate of such suspicion and hostility, orderly and respectful negotiations were all but impossible.

The Crowns of Spain and Great Britain remained at peace, but the South Carolina imperialists, like their adversaries in Florida, felt as if they were engaged in a kind of covert and unofficial war over the debatable land. As a result they were prepared to do whatever it took to hold on to their newly constructed outpost at the mouth of the Altamaha. Surrendering Fort King George would not only compromise South Carolina's honor and territorial integrity, but would also be tantamount to "owning that all the Creek Indians [were] depending on the Spaniards." [45] If the South Carolina or the British government stooped to make these concessions, it would only be a matter of time before the southern settlements—and perhaps the rest of the province as well—collapsed under relentless pressure.

According to many South Carolina imperialists, there were only two ways to hold back the impending Franco-Spanish onslaught: greater economic and diplomatic leverage over the southeastern Indians, and a determined campaign to guard and occupy the debatable land. Though the former strategy remained more reliable and cost-effective in the eyes of most officials, the latter strategy was unquestionably gaining ground. The death of John Barnwell in late 1724 was mourned as a "great loss" to the province's defensive network, but other officials quickly stepped in to champion the program of frontier fortification.[46] When Arthur Middleton assumed command of the South Carolina government in place of the departed Francis Nicholson, he not only proved himself committed to preserving Fort King George but also proposed a scheme to build another fort further up the Altamaha, at its confluence with the Ocmulgee. By the end of 1725, Middleton had become convinced that holding the line in the debatable land was the best way to "overawe" the Spanish, the Yamasees, and the Lower Creeks.[47]

But despite Middleton's best efforts, the line would not hold. A number of demoralizing crises soon exposed the fragility of the South Carolina government's bold new frontier initiatives. In the summer of 1725, cost-conscious members of the assembly balked at Middleton's proposal for another Altamaha fort, preferring instead to send Tobias Fitch on his mission into Creek country. Fitch returned home to accolades, but the South Carolina authorities had hardly finished congratulating him when they received the disturbing report that Fort King George—a supposed bulwark against Creek insolence—had gone up in flames. The fort's commander, Captain Edward Massey, deemed the fire accidental but admitted that "the Men were not so active as they might have been in extinguishing [it]."[48] Though the fire was welcomed by the bored, sick, and hungry troops stationed at the fort, it struck Middleton and many other officials as nothing short of disastrous. As they scrambled to rebuild the fort, their anxiety rose even further at the news of the infamous flag-waving raid on Cussita made by the Cherokees and the Chickasaws in March 1726. With the fort destroyed and the Creek-Cherokee War spinning dangerously out of control, the government felt that it had no choice but to send Captain Fitch back into the inferno.

Upon returning to the Chattahoochee, Fitch discovered that the Spanish— after repeated humiliations from the South Carolina government—had redoubled their efforts to expel the English from the old province of Guale. In January 1726 Spanish officials welcomed several prestigious Lower Creek leaders into San Marcos de Apalachee and Saint Augustine, where they received further displays of "obedience" on behalf of the "great cacique" and cemented a "peace" between the Creeks and the Yamasees. [49] While Fitch managed to get several of the Lower Creek leaders to renounce their agreement with the Yamasees and the Spanish, he was unable to wipe the slate entirely clean. During an audience with Chigelly in the town of Coweta, Fitch was surprised by the arrival of Cherokeeleechee and three Yamasees from Saint Augustine. To a "great deal of pomp and ceremony," Cherokeeleechee and the Yamasees strolled into the town square and whisked Chigelly into a remote corner of the village. Their message was "kept so private" that Fitch, despite his best efforts, could not uncover it. Fitch left Coweta in a huff and proceeded to circulate among his "best friends in the lower Towns," offering a handsome reward to anyone who would kill Cherokeeleechee and his three Yamasee companions. No one dared to accept. Even as Fitch eventually got Chigelly to agree to attend the great Creek-Cherokee peace conference, he worried that Cherokeeleechee and his followers would continue to exert a dangerously corrupting influence over many of the Lower Creeks. [50]

Despite Fitch's grave concerns, most South Carolina imperialists felt that the winter of 1726–27 would give them the opportunity to regroup. Though primarily arranged as a means to stop the Creek-Cherokee War, the Charles Town peace conference also had major implications for the future of the debatable land. As the South Carolina officials spent several long weeks waiting for the arrival of the Lower Creeks, they used the time to address the concerns of panic-stricken colonists from Port Royal and the other southern settlements. In addition to their usual cry for more forts, the southernmost colonists had also lodged requests for "friendly" Indians to act as rangers and protective buffers against any potential attacks from Florida. [51] To that end the Commons House stepped up its efforts to bring groups like the Cape Fears and the Chickasaws closer to the most vulnerable settlements and even suggested that the Abeikas who had come to town for the conference could prove themselves better friends to the English by relocating from the Coosa River to the "Pallachacola Old Towns" along the Savannah. [52]

When Chigelly and the small Lower Creek contingent finally arrived in Charles Town, Middleton wasted no time in asking them about their relationship to the Yamasees. Chigelly responded that while the Lower Creeks had some "kindred" among the Yamasees, the two groups were indeed "Different Nations." Middleton then reminded Chigelly that he expected the Creeks to follow through on their oft-repeated promises to "remove" the Yamasees. Chigelly assured him that the Yamasees would soon come begging the English for mercy and even added that Cherokeeleechee had recently agreed to move himself and his followers closer to Coweta, where their pro-Spanish tendencies would be easier to counteract. [53] With the Lower Creeks agreeing to Middleton's preliminary demands, the rest of the conference could proceed as planned. Most of the agreements reached during the conference, however, were no sturdier than the paper they were recorded on. Just as the conference failed to erase the enmity between the Creeks and the Cherokees, it also failed to stop the bleeding on South Carolina's southernmost frontiers.

While the South Carolina imperialists attempted to lay down the law in Charles Town, Florida officials threw down the gauntlet. The outbreak of another war between the Crowns of Spain and Great Britain in 1727 allowed the Spanish to offer new bounties for English scalps and black slaves. [54] As a result the residents of Port Royal and the other southern settlements found themselves subjected to an even deadlier wave of attacks throughout the summer and fall of 1727. Though these raiding parties consisted primarily of Yamasees and Lower Creeks, they also included an occasional fugitive black slave or Spanish militia officer. All told, the raiders killed or captured at least twenty white South Carolinians and captured or liberated at least two dozen black slaves. [55] They inflicted even greater damage on the South Carolinians' peace of mind, forcing some colonists to send their slaves to the north and others to abandon their homes and live in the "utmost extremity." [56] In the words of a deeply concerned Governor Middleton, the southern settlements had virtually no hope for economic and demographic recovery as long as the local residents remained "obliged to hold the Plough in one hand and the sword in the other." [57]

Though disturbed by the plight of the southern settlements, a number of South Carolina officials seemed even more upset by their growing vulnerability in the debatable land. In July 1727 a raiding party composed of twenty-six Yamasees and eight Lower Creeks overwhelmed a profitable and well-armed South Carolinian trading post on the Altamaha. The Indians killed Matthew Smallwood and six other traders and took one prisoner and over three thousand deerskins back to Saint Augustine. For outraged South Carolina imperialists, the loss of the men and the deerskins was made worse by the fact that the attack occurred so close to the rebuilt Fort King George. [58] Suddenly nearly everyone could see that the fort, while important to English territorial claims, was practically worthless in a military sense. According to its frustrated commander, Fort King George was "incapable of defense," a pathetic and pestilential structure that "might as usefully have been placed in Japan" for all the good it did for the South Carolina settlements.[59] The inhabitants of Port Royal agreed, warning South Carolina officials "that unless His Majesty's Independent Company [were] speedily removed thither for their protection . . . all the Settlements in those parts must be abandoned to their utter ruin and destruction, they being in hourly danger of their lives and in no condition of defending themselves."[60] Under additional pressure from the Board of Trade, Middleton and the council reluctantly gave orders to burn the fort and relocate the troops to Port Royal.[61]

This inglorious retreat from the debatable land threatened all the ambitious projects advanced earlier in the decade by Barnwell, Nicholson, and the Board of Trade. With no immediate plans to replace the smoldering outpost on the Altamaha, nervous South Carolinians suddenly found themselves back at square one. By late 1727 South Carolina imperialists were suffering some of the same diplomatic and strategic setbacks in the debatable land as they were further into the southeastern interior. Along South Carolina's southern frontiers, however, the frightening memories of the Yamasee War had bubbled even closer to the surface. South Carolina imperialists knew that in order to gain control of a frustrating situation, they would have to come up with more effective ways of getting their message across to the groups of people who dared to defy them.

The Defeat of the Yamasees

As the South Carolinians suffered from a new wave of Indian incursions in the summer of 1727, many of them recalled the standards that had guided earlier generations of colonists in times of crisis. During the darkest days of the Yamasee War, the South Carolinians had managed to stave off further disaster by launching a series of quick and decisive counterstrokes against their attackers. Now, with a number of unrepentant Florida Indians seemingly intent on rekindling old flames, the South Carolina government decided that the province's best defense would lie in a good offense. Though tactically sound, the decision to take the fight to the Indians was more a product of raw emotion than cool, levelheaded strategy. Upon learning of the bold Yamasee–Lower Creek attack on the Altamaha, South Carolina officials yearned for vengeance.[62] In the halls of the assembly, support for a new military offensive ran so high that no one even paused to worry about how much it might cost. The same officials who earlier in the year had rejected a proposal for a punitive expedition now began the task of assembling two new armies: one to strike against the Yamasees living near Saint Augustine, and the other to "reduce Cherokee Lechey and bring the Creeks to reason."[63]

By late August 1727 the South Carolina assembly had agreed to fund a two-hundred-man man expedition for service against the Yamasees.[64] The second expedition proved more difficult to organize, primarily because the South Carolinians approached it with a far greater sense of caution. According to Governor Middleton, the offensive against the Lower Creeks could only go forward after a great deal of careful planning, "for should [the South Carolinians] there miscarry lett the success of that [expedition] against the Yamasees prove ever so great It would not be putting an End to [their] Troubles."[65] Middleton and his council initially suggested that as many as 500 South Carolinian troops would have to make the trip to the Chattahoochee. Though they reduced their estimate to 280 after a few weeks of further consideration, they also decided that they would need to bolster the expedition by recruiting more than seven hundred Cherokee and Catawba warriors.[66] If everything went according to plan, Cherokeeleechee, Chigelly, and the rest of the recalcitrant Lower Creeks would find themselves confronted by the largest and most intimidating army to march through the Southeast since the days of Hernando de Soto.

Fortunately for the Lower Creeks, the South Carolinians could not organize and deploy such a large force on short notice. The intervening weeks and months provided South Carolina officials with ample time to cool their tempers and reconsider their options. Even as they sent Colonel John Herbert on a mission to secure the military assistance of the Cherokees, they also decided to give the Lower Creeks one last chance to follow through on their oft-repeated promises to renounce the Yamasees and the Spanish. Though increasingly pessimistic about their chances, Middleton and several other officials continued to hope that a single, well-respected agent might be able to do the work of an entire army, thereby sparing the province a considerable expense. The government decided to overlook Tobias Fitch in favor of Charlesworth Glover, an experienced trader and Yamasee War veteran who had spent several years in command of the garrison at Fort Moore.[67] In his new capacity as a "beloved man," Glover found himself in the most dangerous and challenging situation of his life, ordered to succeed at a task that had defeated several of South Carolina's best frontier diplomats.

Upon arriving among the Creeks in January 1728, Glover immediately took up position in the Upper Creek town of Oakfuskee, where local headman had promised that the English could "depend upon the Abeccas and Tallapoosas to stand to their words in being true to [their] Government in Peace and War." [68] Tired of incurring South Carolina's displeasure because of the "roguish doings" of certain Lower Creek warriors, Abeika and Tallapoosa leaders "sent very severe Messages down by them to the Cowetaws and Pallachacolas threatening them that if they did not comply with their Promises to the English that they would oblige them to it." [69] The protection and support offered by the Upper Creeks gave Glover the confidence to get tough with the recalcitrant towns along the Lower Chattahoochee. He began in dramatic fashion, ordering all South Carolinians to withdraw from the Lower Creek towns. Though normally reluctant to bend to government authority, most of the traders evidently complied on this occasion. The resulting embargo made an immediate impression among the Lower Creeks, whose rapidly dwindling supplies of powder and ammunition made them "prodigious[ly] afraid" of the prospect of an attack from the South Carolinians and Cherokees. [70] Over the next several months, Chigelly and a number of other important Lower Creek leaders were persuaded to visit Glover in Oakfuskee, hoping "to see how to make it straight" between themselves and the English. [71]

In the course of their meetings, Glover and the various Lower Creek leaders proved much more forthright with each other than was typical of most frontier missions and conferences. While Fitch, Nicholson, Middleton, and others could speak just as bluntly or menacingly as Glover, none of them could match his eloquence in explaining just what the Great King of the English expected of his Indian children. During one of his "talks" to Lower Creek leaders, Glover warned, "[A]lthough you and several others among you never hurt an Englishman, yet there is some among you that have, and it is your business to find them out, or the blood they have spilt [will] fall on all your Heads as the Rain falls on the good and bad." [72] In addition to renouncing the Spanish, hunting down the Yamasees, and turning in the "rogues" among them, the Lower Creeks would also have to stop the incessant bickering and infighting that plagued their councils. Unless they acted as "one mind one Tongue and one people," they would wind up "just like the Chickesaws" and "fall to the ground like a House that is supported by some pieces of Rotten wood." [73]

Though Glover pushed the Lower Creeks toward a stable relationship with the South Carolinians, he realized that they faced many temptations to stray from the English path. Like most South Carolina imperialists, however, Glover had trouble understanding the factors that prevented the Lower Creeks from making a total commitment to the English. Glover adhered to Thomas Nairne's old adage that the Indians would belong to "him who sells best cheap" and doggedly believed that the Lower Creeks would comply with South Carolina's demands once they realized that it was in their own best economic interest to do so. He not only continued South Carolina's long-standing practice of plying Indian leaders with rum, clothing, and other gifts but also gave impassioned speeches to extol the superiority of the English trade.[74] "Show me one of your Women or Children cloathed by the French or Spaniards," he challenged, "and I'll show you 500 cloathed by the English." While the Spanish officials in Saint Augustine often spent several months anxiously awaiting their next shipment of trade goods, the South Carolinians would never deign to "get out of [their] Chairs to go and look at so foolish a thing as one ship."[75] Though Glover's speeches seem somewhat wry in retrospect, at the time they had a rather sharp edge. By reminding the Lower Creeks how much they stood to gain from the English trade, he also meant to show them how much they would suffer without it.

The weight of Glover's embargo was undeniable. After rushing north to meet the new English beloved man, the Long Warrior of Coweta admitted that his people were "poor and low and [didn't] know what to think of it," noting, "I am like a Man in love with a young wife, and can't forbear coming to see you."[76] Despite the enormous economic pressure exerted by Glover, however, several Lower Creek leaders continued to question and challenge the unrealistic expectations of the English. After his initial supplication, the Long Warrior asked Glover "what harm it did to receive Spaniards, French or any white people." When Glover responded with a standard diatribe against Spanish treachery, the Long Warrior claimed that he could "not help what the Spaniards" did to the South Carolinians.[77] Though visibly annoyed with this reply, Glover found Chigelly to be even bolder in his responses. Upbraided for the "wild" and unpredictable behavior of his people, Chigelly deflected the blame to the South Carolina traders, claiming that their heavy-handed tactics forced some of the Lower Creeks "away to [Saint] Augustine and so to killing the English to pay [their] Debts that way."[78] Chigelly could not understand why the South Carolinians urged him to control his people when they obviously had a hard enough time trying to keep reins on their own men.

While the Long Warrior, Chigelly, and other Lower Creek leaders clearly had a great deal of fear and respect for the English, they freely admitted that "they did not know what to make of [them]." During one meeting between Glover and Chigelly, a raiding party returned to Oakfuskee from an attack on some Spanish and Indian cattle drovers in Apalachee. Of the eight guns included among their plunder, seven were of English manufacture. According to Chigelly, these guns—having recently come to the Spanish by way of an English trading sloop—stood as clear proof of the South Carolinians' hypocrisy. How could the Lower Creeks ever bring themselves to cast their lot with a group of people who would bargain with the Spanish from one side of their mouths while conspiring to destroy them from the other?[79]

In many ways the openness of the discussions between Glover and Chigelly only served to highlight the vast, seemingly unbridgeable distances that separated the South Carolina imperialists from the Lower Creeks. Even after Glover warned that he was the last Englishman who would come out to discuss things peacefully with the Lower Creeks, some of the Indians refused to yield, claiming that they were "loath to make any promise for fear of disappointing [him]."[80] Glover could take little solace in the frankness of the Lower Creeks as long as they continued to resist complying with his government's demands. Not only did the Long Warrior and Chigelly fail to bring in Cherokeeleechee or any of the Yamasees, but they also ignored Glover's request that they "punish one or two of [their] Rogues" as an act of good faith.[81] Given the sense of urgency that had prompted his mission in the first place, Glover had precious little patience for another stalemate. After more than a month of frustration, Glover confided to several Upper Creek headmen that he had decided to give up on the lower people and would advise his superiors to exact vengeance on them as they saw fit.[82]

Back in Charles Town, however, the prospect of a military offensive against the Lower Creeks no longer seemed as certain as it had six months earlier. Despite Middleton's insistence that the Lower Creeks take first priority, most South Carolinians continued to view the Yamasees as a more immediate threat. By the end of 1727, a number of disturbing developments suggested that the southernmost settlements would not last much longer if left to their own devices. The South Carolina government's campaign to rebuild and restock Fort King George was making little headway among imperial officials in London.[83] The Chickasaws living around Port Royal and Fort Moore appeared far more interested in hunting deer than in chasing bounties for Yamasee scalps.[84] The government could not even count on the local colonists to protect South Carolina's soft underbelly. Indeed, the inhabitants of Port Royal proved so lax in volunteering for guard duty that the Commons House was forced to institute a draft from the region's militia companies.[85]

With the South Carolina militia on call for the first time since 1717, it was only a short jump for provincial officials to dust off the punitive expedition that they had authorized the previous summer.[86] Any reservations about sending this force into action abruptly disappeared in February 1728, when the South Carolinians suffered a pair of fresh outrages, including the deadly ambush of a scout boat crew by a Yamasee war party at the southern tip of Daufuskie Island.[87] Shortly thereafter Middleton and the council received "a very impudent sawcy letter" from Governor Benavides in Saint Augustine. In the past Benavides had always feigned ignorance of the Yamasees' raids, shrugging his shoulders and blaming the attacks on pirates.[88] On this occasion, however, he could not resist the temptation to taunt the South Carolinians, asking Middleton why he "suffered his Frontier plantations to be cut off, and his people carryed away prisoners by the Indians." According to one eyewitness, Middleton managed to smile at Benavides's boldness, undoubtedly thinking of the even stronger message that he had in store for the Spanish.[89]

Aside from a few scattered raids—most recently by the small expedition organized by Barnwell in 1719—the South Carolinians had not invaded Florida since the early stages of Queen Anne's War. With the exception of Moore's unsuccessful siege of Saint Augustine in 1702, the South Carolinians had never descended on Florida in large numbers, preferring instead to delegate most of the dirty work to their Indian allies. In light of these earlier precedents, the most striking aspect of the 1728 expedition was the relatively small number of Indians who took part in it. Whereas the South Carolinians had managed to employ upward of a thousand Muskogean warriors during the 1704 sack of Apalachee, this time they had great difficulty rounding up a mere one hundred Indians, most of them Chickasaws, Tuscaroras, Cape Fears, and Ittawans from the fringes of the South Carolina settlements.[90] These warriors were joined by an equal number of South Carolinians pulled from the province's militia rolls and commanded by John Palmer, an experienced scout boat captain and Indian fighter.

Just as he had as one of Alexander MacKay's "swamp hunters" in the early days of the Yamasee War, Palmer demonstrated considerable expertise in hit-and-run tactics. Though composed of a large number of whites, the Palmer expedition unfolded much like a typical southeastern Indian raid and bore a striking resemblance to the attack that Steyamasiechie and the Tallapoosas had launched against Saint Augustine in the fall of 1725. But whereas the Yamasees had received a timely warning that protected most of them from Steyamasiechie's attack, the Palmer expedition took them almost completely by surprise. Arriving at the outskirts of Saint Augustine in the early morning of March 9, 1728, Palmer's force silently surrounded the principal Yamasee town of Nombre de Dios Chiquito, a newly built mission settlement about a half-mile from the Castillo de San Marcos. They struck at daybreak. In a matter of a few violent minutes, they killed thirty Yamasees, took fourteen captives, and set fire to the Indians' homes and chapel. The survivors, many of them grievously wounded, ran to the Spaniards' great stone fortress. Palmer's expedition lingered for several days, hoping for the Yamasees to show themselves. Though the town's free-black militia bravely skirmished with some of the attackers, the Indians remained hidden, and the Spanish responded with nothing more than a few token cannon blasts from their fort. Palmer, under strict orders to avoid direct engagements with the Spanish, decided to head for home. The hero's welcome that he encountered in South Carolina was even more heartfelt than those that George Chicken and Tobias Fitch had received upon returning from their great frontier missions several years earlier. The scalps and prisoners that Palmer brought with him were tangible proof that the South Carolinians, after years of frustration, had finally asserted themselves. [91]

Over the course of their thirteen years in Saint Augustine, the Yamasees had suffered a fairly steady demographic decline, their numbers occasionally replenished by the arrival of Yamasee refugees from San Marcos de Apalachee and the Chattahoochee basin. By the mid-1720s, however, sporadic raids by the Tallapoosas, the Chickasaws, and the Lower Creeks had begun to take an irreversible toll, and the outbreak of a deadly epidemic in 1727 had left Saint Augustine's Indian settlements in an even weaker state. [92] The furious assault of the South Carolinians reduced the number of Yamasee towns from four to one and wiped out as much as one-third of their remaining Yamasee population. [93] Regardless of its exact demographic impact, the Palmer expedition broke the back of the Yamasee resistance. Within a year or two, the Yamasees had all but disintegrated as a distinct nation. Many of the survivors found it hard to stay in Saint Augustine; according to one Franciscan missionary, "So great was the fear they had of the infidels, that for the slightest cause they would move from place to place without ever having a permanent residence." [94] Some of them moved west to seek refuge with Cherokeeleechee and their Lower Creek allies. Others stayed rooted to the Spanish settlement, farming small and sandy plots, performing odd jobs, and sliding into alcoholic obscurity. [95]

For all the harm it did to the Yamasees, the Palmer expedition proved nearly as demoralizing for the Spanish. In explaining the raid to his superiors, Benavides exaggerated the size of the attacking force, estimating it at three hundred whites and one hundred Indians. [96] No matter how much he doctored his report, however, he could not conceal a tone of shame and disgust. On the one hand, Benavides was deeply troubled that "el gran cacique de Caveta" and his other supposedly loyal friends among the Lower Creeks could allow the English to invade Spanish territory. On the other hand, he was probably even more dismayed that the Spanish themselves had proven so helpless and ineffective at the hour of reckoning, hiding in their fort and locking many of their Yamasee allies outside. To Benavides the entire incident was nothing short of a *desgrazia*, a humiliating punctuation to a string of recent setbacks. He had good reason to worry that this latest outrage would do great damage to Spanish prestige in the Southeast.[97]

It did not take long for news of the Palmer expedition to reach the Chattahoochee and Flint rivers; a few Coweta Indians had been in Saint Augustine at the time of the attack, and Glover eagerly filled in other details as soon as he learned them from his superiors.[98] As far as Glover could tell, most of the pro-Spanish Lower Creeks reacted with trepidation. Once again the Spanish had failed to deliver on their oft-repeated claims that they were powerful enough to protect their Indian allies from their enemies. More importantly everyone now recognized that the South Carolinians, contrary to the image that they had projected in the previous ten years, were perfectly capable of backing up their threats with violent and ruthless actions.[99] Those Lower Creeks who counted on stonewalling or intimidating the English suddenly became less sure of themselves. During a visit to Coweta in mid-April, Glover penned a triumphant report to Middleton, claiming, "Colonel Palmers success has intirely convinced these People that yr. honr. is now in earnest, and [they] believe Cherokee Letchee thought it would be his turn next."[100]

As Palmer's victory sank in, Glover discerned a marked improvement in the attitudes of Chigelly and other previously recalcitrant Lower Creeks. In the town of Cussita, warriors presented the English beloved man with a highly symbolic gift of two scalps: one Yamasee and one Spanish. The principal headman of Cussita buried his long-standing resentment of Chigelly, and the two leaders promptly sent a joint message down to Cherokeeleechee, warning him that unless he turned himself in to Glover, they would "come and spoil him."[101] Glover remembered the hundreds of colonial troops and Cherokee warriors that his government supposedly had waiting in the wings and opined to his superiors "that there [would] be no need for them." An armed invasion was bound to be costly, dangerous, and excessive. If the South Carolinians had any hope of "governing" the Lower Creeks, they would have to do it through the Indian trade.[102] To that end Glover made the unilateral decision—"for the good of the publick by [his] Commission as Agent"—to lift the trade embargo. He personally delivered the good news to Brims and Chigelly, hoping that this gesture would convince them that the South Carolinians "[didn't] want to throw [them] quite away."[103]

With these cavalier words, Glover depicted the South Carolinians as magnanimous caretakers and the Lower Creeks as groveling supplicants. Despite his bluster, however, Glover knew that lifting the embargo was a concession to the considerable power and leverage that the Lower Creeks continued to possess. As long as the Lower Creeks were willing to trade with the English and make a few token acknowledgments of South Carolina's power, Glover found it wise to take the path of least resistance, clinging to the hope that Chigelly and the other leaders would "comply with what they promise[d]."[104] Glover worried that if the South Carolinians overplayed their hand by continuing the embargo or sending in an army, the Lower Creeks would only "fly to the French."[105] In some ways Glover had much in common with South Carolina's previous frontier diplomats, men who strove to exert their control by bribing Indian leaders and glossing over wide cultural gaps. At the same time, however, Glover was also one of the first government officials to explicitly acknowledge South Carolina's imperial limitations. More than any of his predecessors, he recognized that along certain frontiers, the pursuit of complete control was not only impractical but also dangerously counterproductive.

To be sure, not every English imperialist was ready to make this significant mental leap. Impatient and exasperated after more than a dozen years of frontier stalemates and setbacks, many South Carolina authorities continued to slip toward a policy of clumsy and provocative extremism. After reading Glover's reports, the South Carolina assembly's Committee on Indian Affairs concluded that the Lower Creeks had not been sufficiently punished for their role in the Altamaha raid. In July 1728 they ordered Glover to arrest a Lower Creek leader and hold him as a hostage until the rest of the Lower Creeks honored their promises to make satisfaction for the murders of Matthew Smallwood and the other South Carolina traders. Governor Middleton, however, viewed their order as too extreme and gave Glover permission to back out of it.[106] Middleton was one important official who saw the logic of Glover's position, agreeing that further pressure against the Lower Creeks might only serve to weaken South Carolina's influence in the long run.

Though South Carolina officials submitted to Middleton's stance on the Lower Creeks, they showed a good deal of resistance to his position on the Yamasees. In the immediate aftermath of the Palmer expedition, Middleton prepared to disband South Carolina's scout boat system but was dissuaded by the

Commons House, which wanted to keep at least fifty of Palmer's men on perpetual guard against the "Bloody and Vengeful" Yamasees.[107] Though Palmer had reportedly destroyed three Yamasee towns, he had left one "consisting of several Enemy Indians that escaped him which [might] probably come upon [South Carolina's] Southern Frontiers to Commit Murders and Robberies."[108] The more the Commons House thought about it, the more they wanted to send a few hundred men down to Saint Augustine to finish the job that Palmer had started. After several days of heated argument, Middleton finally got the assembly to strike a compromise: the scout boats could stay in operation, but another assault on Saint Augustine was out of the question. Since the British imperial hierarchy would not look kindly on a full-scale war between South Carolina and Florida, the South Carolinians would simply have to accept the fact that their punitive campaign against the Yamasees was "at an end."[109]

Many South Carolinians undoubtedly found it hard to live with the lack of a tidy resolution to all the frontier challenges that they had faced in the previous thirteen years. Some of them might have felt a little better if they had managed to capture and execute Cherokeeleechee or the Huspah king, but in all likelihood not even these actions would have erased all their disturbing memories. A half-century earlier, New England colonists had not cured their frontier anxieties by killing the defiant sachem Metacom and displaying his head on a cemetery gate.[110] For the South Carolinians of the late 1720s, the situation remained even more open-ended than it had been for the New England Puritans. The Cherokees, the Chickasaws, and the Lower Creeks differed greatly from what little remained of the Narragansetts, the Nipmucks, and the Wampanoags after King Philip's War. More than a decade after the "end" of the Yamasee War in 1717, these groups continued to prove that the South Carolina imperialists could not impose their will over all the Indians who dared to resist them.

Nevertheless, it gradually became clear in the several years after the Palmer expedition that the English would not have to brook the same kinds of frustrations and stalemates in the debatable land that they were forced to tolerate in more remote areas. Though scout boat crews continued their patrols and many residents of the southern settlements remained nervously on guard, no one could deny that the frightening raids from Florida had stopped.[111] The Yamasees, it appeared, had at last been beaten. Along their southern frontiers, the South Carolinians had finally managed to prevail through the application of flintlock diplomacy.

Settled and Unsettled

In the colonial Southeast, as in the rest of colonial America, a number of factors contributed to the resolution of frontier power struggles. But while the cumulative, destructive effects of trade, disease, and military pressure always proved crucial to the defeat of Indian societies, the factor that ultimately cemented the process was the expansion of colonial settlement. With the decimation of the Yamasees and the humbling of the Spanish, the English found themselves in an ideal position to stake a new claim on the debatable land and soon began to build new forts and communities in the area from which they recently had been forced to withdraw.[112] The founding of Georgia in the early 1730s, which established an effective British buffer south of the Savannah River, brought the South Carolinians as close as they would get to experiencing a real end to the Yamasee War. Still, the lingering effects of the recent struggle would never completely leave the South Carolinians. Even as the growth of new colonial settlements helped put some anxieties to rest, other issues and controversies remained as vivid and disturbing as ever.

By the late 1720s the shortcomings of forts, ranger patrols, and Indian alliance networks had convinced many officials that the most effective way to secure South Carolina's frontiers was through the expansion of white settlement. The idea of settlements as a defensive perimeter had a long tradition in English imperialism, stretching as far back as the "garrison towns" of seventeenth-century Ireland and New England. Efforts to apply the concept to the Southeast began to intensify shortly after the outbreak of the Yamasee War. In 1717 Sir Robert Montgomery, a restless and somewhat eccentric English courtier, petitioned the Lords Proprietors with a fantastic scheme to establish the "Margravate of Azilia," a grid of uniform lots and fences surrounding a fortified castle on South Carolina's vulnerable southwestern frontiers.[113] Seven years later Swiss entrepreneur Jean Pierre Purry made a more practical appeal to the British Crown for permission to settle the Protestant refugees of Europe in a string of fortified towns between South Carolina and the Mississippi River.[114] Meanwhile, South Carolina officials were trying to implement John Barnwell's 1722 act, which granted gifts of land, tools, and tax exemptions to any whites who would agree to settle around the new frontier forts that the Board of Trade had recently pledged to sponsor.[115]

Despite the widespread support that greeted Purry's and Barnwell's schemes, the expansion of white settlement toward the south and southwest faced a number of formidable obstacles throughout the 1720s. Though the recurrent raids of the Yamasees and the Lower Creeks provided the most obvious deterrent, South Carolina's broader demographic, economic, and political situations also inhibited such expansion. With the exception of the Indian trade, South Carolina's economy struggled mightily; by the end of the decade, small farmers and the naval-stores industry faced imminent financial ruin. [116] Floundering South Carolinians pressed for more paper currency to help them pay off their debts, a measure that most of the South Carolina merchants adamantly opposed. The resulting controversy caused riots in the countryside and threatened to bring the provincial government to its knees, adding to South Carolina's already unsavory reputation among prospective white immigrants. [117] Even those few immigrants and South Carolina residents who intended to settle on the province's frontiers were forced to wait in limbo while the government attempted to sort out its various problems. To make matters worse, South Carolina's Lords Proprietors, though no longer a direct factor in provincial policymaking, continued to hold titles to the soil, effectively preventing government authorities from parceling out plots of land on South Carolina's frontiers. [118]

Most of these stubborn obstacles to the expansion of British settlement in the Southeast gradually fell aside during the watershed period of 1728–32. To the south the threat of enemy invasion diminished with the defeat of the Yamasees and Glover's uneasy settlement with the Lower Creeks. In Charles Town and London, Samuel Wragg and a number of other highly influential merchants helped resolve the paper-currency crisis by ushering in an effective compromise. Whitehall followed by restoring a government bounty on naval-stores production and removing export restrictions on rice, measures that provided a huge boost to the South Carolina economy. Perhaps the most significant breakthrough of all occurred in 1729, when Crown officials succeeded in convincing the Lords Proprietors to sell their land rights, the step that finalized South Carolina's transformation into a royal colony. [119]

Whitehall immediately celebrated this windfall by appointing a new royal governor to take the place of the late Francis Nicholson and his temporary stand-in, Arthur Middleton. Their choice, Robert Johnson, was no longer the young, inexperienced, and overwhelmed official who had been removed by the antiproprietary "revolution" of 1719. In the intervening decade he had established important contacts on both sides of the Atlantic and given serious thought on how to pull South Carolina out of its protracted slump. [120] Convinced that South Carolina's future development would hinge on frontier security, Johnson made the establishment of new frontier settlements his top priority. Within weeks of assuming office, he went before the Board of Trade with a detailed and considerate proposal that later came to be known as "Johnson's township scheme," his single greatest administrative achievement.

Johnson borrowed liberally from the plans advanced by Barnwell eight years earlier but made them even more ambitious, calling for ten frontier settlements instead of five. Like Barnwell, Johnson proposed that the South Carolina government offer various incentives to help fill the new towns with sober, industrious, Protestant farmers. Each of the ten towns would consist of 250 centrally located house lots surrounded by several hundred plots of seventy-five to a hundred acres each. All the townships would occupy strategic locations, overlooking the major river routes into South Carolina: three on the Savannah, two on the Santee, and one each on the Pon Pon, the Wateree, the Black, the Peedee, and the Waccamaw. While these towns would strengthen the South Carolina militia and discourage outside incursions, they would also help address what had recently become South Carolina's most pressing internal security issue: the increasingly lopsided ratio of black slaves to whites. Taken as a whole, the townships would provide, in Johnson's words, the protection that had been "almost fatally wanting during the Yamasee revolt." [121]

Johnson's proposal made a good impression on his superiors. By 1730 their enthusiasm for expansion in the Southeast was once again on the rise after a brief lull surrounding the Fort King George debacle of 1727. With Alexander Cuming and his Cherokee companions making themselves the toast of English society, Crown officials found it easy to focus more attention on South Carolina's frontier concerns. They not only gave Johnson permission and support to implement all his proposed townships but also insisted that he establish two more settlements south of the Savannah River. Despite sustained pressure from angry Spanish diplomats, the British imperial hierarchy clearly had no intention of abandoning its claims to the debatable land south of the Carolinas. [122]

Johnson arrived in Charles Town to great fanfare in December 1730 and quickly set about confirming the South Carolina assembly's approval of the township scheme. By the spring of 1732 the first group of prospective settlers were provisioned and transported to the east bank of the Savannah River, where they established the town of Purrysburg. [123] But before Johnson could get around to expanding South Carolinian settlement below the Savannah, his mantle was seized by a group of British imperialists and social reformers under the leadership of James Oglethorpe, a young and energetic member of Parliament. Oglethorpe and his colleagues presented themselves to George II as trustees for a projected colony in the debatable land, named—appropriately enough—for the king who held the key to the entire project. George II consented by granting them a charter in the summer of 1732, a document that gave the Georgia trustees the right to all the land below the Savannah, above the Altamaha, and as far west as the Pacific Ocean.[124]

Oglethorpe wasted no time in getting the new province off the ground. He personally led the first group of several hundred prospective colonists across the ocean, arriving at the mouth of the Savannah by way of Charles Town and Port Royal in February 1733. Though he and the other trustees intended for Georgia to serve as a refuge for English debtors and the persecuted Protestants of Europe, Oglethorpe also adhered to doctrines espoused by Nairne, Barnwell, Nicholson, and other notable South Carolina imperialists.[125] He firmly believed that America was there for the taking, and "that Occupancy is the most unquestionable Title by the Law of Nature."[126] Oglethorpe quickly supervised the layout and construction of several settlements as a means to cement his claim. By the mid-1730s Georgians had settled the port of Savannah several miles up the river of the same name, the military post of Frederica on Saint Simons Island, and the town of Darien near the mouth of the Altamaha and the ruins of Fort King George.

Though Oglethorpe worried surprisingly little about the complaints and opposition expressed in Spanish Florida, he felt the need to make a sound impression on the people whom he believed to hold the most valid claims to the territory he intended to settle.[127] Right from the beginning, Georgia officials realized that the success of their venture would depend on their ability to get along with the Lower Creek Indians. For one thing they knew from the example of South Carolina that the Indian trade would probably serve as a major sector of the Georgia economy until they could establish a viable agricultural enterprise. At the same time they also knew that the cooperation and goodwill of the Indians would be essential to assuring that their advance proceeded without the exhausting struggles that had hindered the southward expansion of South Carolina in recent decades.[128]

The first Indians encountered by the Georgia colonists were Yamacraws, a group of about one hundred Lower Creek refugees who had moved from the Flint River to the mouth of the Savannah some time around 1730.[129] Oglethorpe went out of his way to treat the Yamacraws with respect and managed to form close personal bonds with many of them, especially Tomochichi, an important Yamacraw headman with roots in the Lower Creek town of Apalachicola. Tomochichi and his advisors readily gave the Georgians access to coastal lands and even accompanied Oglethorpe to London in 1734, where they pledged their friendship before Britain's imperial hierarchy.[130] Tomochichi and the Ya-macraws proved even more useful to the Georgians as a connection to the Indi-ans of the Chattahoochee basin; Oglethorpe knew that the assistance of the Ya-macraws would mean little unless backed up by the rest of the Lower Creeks.[131] In May 1733 the newly arrived Georgians were elated to receive a delegation of headmen from Coweta and other Lower Creek towns. The resulting treaty was vague and ambiguous; though it granted important trading privileges to the Lower Creeks, it made no specific reference to the land cession that Oglethorpe desired.[132] Still, the amicable conference that produced the treaty was a sign that the Georgians had managed to make more progress among the Lower Creeks within the space of a few months than the South Carolinians had been able to make in the previous fifteen years.

A number of different factors help explain why the Creeks and the Georgians were able to warm to each other so quickly. The Lower Creeks now had access to a new source of relatively inexpensive and high-quality British trade goods without having to deal with overbearing traders and officials from South Carolina. Fifty years earlier the Creeks' ancestors had done much the same thing for the early Carolinians, viewing them as a welcome alternative to the Spanish. By the 1730s the Lower Creeks had grown quite skilled at perceiving and exploiting distinctions between different groups of colonial imperialists. Even though Oglethorpe and his followers spoke the same language as the South Carolinians—and even though they were often accompanied by several South Carolinian advisors—the Lower Creeks hoped to find important differ-ences between them. Yahoulakee, the new guardian of Brims's children and the head spokesman for the Lower Creek diplomats who visited Oglethorpe in the spring of 1733, claimed that he had "often desired to go down to Charlestown, but would not go down, because [he] thought that [he] might die in the Way." Despite his wariness of the English, however, he could not resist making the twenty-five-day journey to Savannah when he "heard that [the Georgians] were come, and that [they] were good men."[133]

For the Georgians the establishment of a sound working relationship with the Lower Creeks was made easier by their ability to fit themselves into preex-isting patterns of frontier exchange. The two people who probably did more than anyone to smooth over Georgia's early Indian relations were Johnny and Mary Musgrove, the couple that had been formed as part of South Carolina's reconciliation with the Lower Creeks back in 1717. Johnny, the half-Muskogean son of longtime South Carolina trader John Musgrove, and Mary, the niece of the venerable Brims of Coweta, had opened a trading store in South Carolina shortly after their marriage but relocated to the Savannah River at the invitation of the Yamacraws in 1732, where they managed to do a booming business in deerskins for the next several years. In the Musgroves, Oglethorpe had a pair of veteran, bilingual merchants and cultural mediators who not only offered valuable assistance in the Indian trade but also served as translators and advisors in Georgia's early treaties with the Lower Creeks.[134]

As careful students of South Carolina's experienced Indian traders, Oglethorpe and other Georgia officials knew what kinds of things they could reasonably expect from the Indians and what kinds of things the Indians would want from them in return. To facilitate their nascent Indian trade, the Georgians had the good sense and good fortune to build settlements on ports with convenient river access to the southeastern interior.[135] Georgians also showed experience beyond their years in Indian diplomacy. Oglethorpe not only proved quick to learn the protocol of conferences with Indian leaders in Savannah and London but also appointed an officer to supervise the traders and serve as a liaison to the Indian settlements of the interior.[136] On the whole such strategies allowed Georgians to avoid the awkward introductory period that had plagued the Indian relations of most other British colonies.

For all of Oglethorpe's careful planning and good fortune, however, the establishment of Georgia and the early development of Georgia-Creek relations would not have gone as smoothly as they did if not for the South Carolinians' initial enthusiasm for their new neighbors. Though South Carolina officials had directives from the Board of Trade to assist Oglethorpe in setting up the new colony, they did not need any urging to agree with Governor Johnson's assertion that the founding of Georgia would work out to "the greatest advantage to the welfare and safety of [that] Province."[137] South Carolina officials played generous hosts to Oglethorpe for over a month, and when the first group of settlers headed south to the site of Savannah, they were accompanied by South Carolina council member William Bull Sr., who actively assisted Oglethorpe in surveying the town and setting up the Indian trade.[138] In their earliest months of settlement, Georgians subsisted on cattle, hogs, and rice donated by sympathetic South Carolina planters who knew that it was in their own best interest to keep new buffer settlements on their southern flank. Many of the planters and officials who contributed aid and advice to the Georgians were undoubtedly relieved at the opportunity to devote more of their attention to domestic concerns after suffering through a generation's worth of frontier headaches.[139]

The establishment and early development of Georgia coincided with a period of unprecedented growth and prosperity for South Carolina. In his first treatise on Georgia, Oglethorpe lauded the good fortunes that the South Carolinians had experienced in recent years, claiming that "the wide extent of their Rice Trade; the amazing Encrease of their Stock of Negroes and Cattle; and the encouraging Essays they have made in Wine and Silk, render[ed] South-Carolina a new Country to Geographers."[140] With the province's return to political and economic stability, immigrants from Europe and other American colonies finally began to arrive in substantial numbers, helping to bring South Carolina's white population from approximately ninety-eight hundred to fifteen thousand between 1730 and 1740.[141] The decade of the 1730s also witnessed the construction and settlement of nine new garrison towns in the "middle country" between the tidewater and the fall line. This perimeter not only marked a significant improvement in South Carolina's defensive network but also acted as a precedent for other settlements that would proliferate in the South Carolina Piedmont in ensuing decades.[142]

Though South Carolinians no longer had to worry much about the prospects of an enemy invasion, these defensive improvements did not satisfy every need, urge, and phobia of the South Carolina imperialists. For more than fifty years, South Carolina's economic, political, and territorial expansion had been driven by a diverse collection of impulses, many of which continued to burn just as hot in the 1730s as they had in the 1680s. It was impossible for most South Carolinians to dismiss all their old ambitions, jealousies, and anxieties as relics of a more turbulent past. South Carolina underwent important transformations after the founding of Georgia, but its leading inhabitants did not grow markedly more serene or enlightened in their outlooks.

By the early 1730s plantation owners had already begun to dominate South Carolina society and had largely extricated themselves from the business of Indian affairs. Nevertheless, not even this increasingly powerful and secure class of people could afford the luxury of letting down its guard. Even as the economic boom of the early 1730s turned rice into gold, it also made at least one of South Carolina's traditional security problems seem all the more glaring. Black slaves, a group that had comprised the majority of South Carolina's population since the early 1700s, became even more prevalent throughout the province as planters purchased rising numbers of human chattels to keep pace with rapid agricultural expansion. Charles Town merchants had imported an average of 275 slaves per year during the second decade of the eighteenth century and 900 per year during the 1720s; in the 1730s the annual average climbed to well over 2,000.[143] Though South Carolina officials continued to express concern over the province's exploding slave population, their measures to impose what they considered a satisfactory ratio of blacks to whites proved wholly inadequate. Even after the substantial influx of white immigrants in the 1730s, this ratio was far more unbalanced in 1740 (36,000 to 15,000) than it had been ten years earlier (20,000 to 10,000).[144]

South Carolina planters and officials would have shown less concern for the rising slave population had they not continued to harbor the same visceral fear and loathing of blacks that they had displayed since the earliest years of the province. Indeed, the trend toward importing slaves directly from Africa during the 1720s and 1730s served to make South Carolina's black population all the more alien and threatening in the eyes of most whites.[145] The days of black cowboys and Indian traders were becoming a distant memory as whites made a conscious and rigorous effort to keep their slaves under strict control.[146] SPG missionaries intent on converting the slaves complained that masters had become more adamantly opposed than ever to their efforts, fearing that the regular religious assembly of blacks would lead directly to insurrection.[147] By the early 1730s South Carolinians had begun to perceive—with some justification—a "thickening" of insurrectionary plots.[148] In the next several years South Carolinians revamped their slave patrol system and nervously read newspaper accounts of massive slave uprisings in the Caribbean, convinced that only constant vigilance would protect them from the naturally "hot and violent spirit of the negroes."[149]

The situation appeared especially dangerous in the southern parts of the province, which saw a rapid influx of planters and their slaves following the final defeat of the Yamasees and the founding of Georgia.[150] Though the Georgians outlawed slavery in their own province, they pledged to return any fugitive slaves to South Carolina and even got the Lower Creeks to promise to do the same.[151] These reassurances notwithstanding, many South Carolina planters from Port Royal and surrounding settlements continued to worry about the threat posed by Spanish Florida. In Saint Augustine, Governor Benavides, disgusted by the decline of the Yamasees and the vacillations of the Lower Creeks, began to believe that fugitive slaves from South Carolina were better auxiliaries than the Indians.[152] Blacks had become the most stalwart component of the Florida militia, and Florida officials even went as far as to consider paying them bounties for South Carolinian scalps. Though South Carolina did not sustain any attacks from black raiding parties, Saint Augustine continued to act as a magnet for South Carolina's runaways, occasionally with violent consequences.[153] In September 1739 a group of twenty black slaves from a parish southwest of Charles Town killed twenty-five white South Carolinians during an attempt to reach freedom in Saint Augustine. Though crushed by South Carolina troops, the Stono Rebellion, the bloodiest slave uprising in the history of colonial North America, caused enormous unrest at a time of unprecedented economic prosperity and clearly fit a pattern that extended back to the unstable era of the Yamasee War.[154]

Even as old problems and controversies continued to weigh heavily on South Carolina's planters, they proved even more immediate to those South Carolinians who maintained a vested interest in frontier trade and diplomacy. Though more and more South Carolinians had begun to spend less and less time thinking about the Indians of the Southeast, a significant number of merchants, traders, and officials still remained intent on exploiting the Indians in the manner of the previous half-century. When Governor Johnson died in 1735 after several highly successful years in office, he was succeeded by council member Thomas Broughton, a wealthy merchant with considerable financial stake in the South Carolina Indian trade. As a young trader thirty years earlier, Broughton had incurred the wrath of Thomas Nairne and other reformers for his illegal enslavement of South Carolina's Indian allies. Despite Broughton's new trappings of respectability, his appointment to South Carolina's highest office promised to evoke memories of a more aggressive and contentious period in South Carolina imperialism.[155]

South Carolinians not only grew jealous of the quick success enjoyed by the Georgia traders but also expressed outrage at some new restrictions imposed by the Georgia government. Georgia's 1735 act to regulate its Indian trade essentially replicated the standing Indian act of South Carolina, including the clause that imposed license fees on traders from other colonies.[156] Experienced South Carolina traders found it easy enough to avoid paying these fees, but they nevertheless resented the intrusions of Georgia's zealous authorities, especially its Indian agent, Patrick MacKay. By 1738 South Carolina and Georgia officials were "all to pieces 'bout the Indian trade," exchanging such venomous charges and countercharges that the Board of Trade finally felt compelled to step in and abolish all intercolonial license fees.[157] Even though this particular conflict reached an uneasy resolution, it showed that South Carolina imperialism had changed little since the bitter South Carolina–Virginia disputes of the previous generation.[158] True intercolonial cooperation in the Indian trade and other frontier affairs would have to wait another twenty years, until the exigencies of the Seven Years War finally prompted a wealthier and more experienced British Crown to seize direct control of the regulatory process.

Though the establishment of Georgia brought a new group of players to the table, the imperial contest in the Southeast in many ways remained a destructive, maddeningly uncertain stalemate between the French, the Spanish, and the British. The capture of the debatable land and the expansion of British settlement in the Southeast did not pay immediate dividends for those British imperialists who sought to subjugate the region's Indians and overwhelm their French and Spanish rivals. While officials in London, Charles Town, and Savannah hoped for the tide to turn, some of the people caught in the middle of this ongoing imperial struggle remained equally confident that the situation would not change. During a visit to Coweta in March 1735, Georgia's Indian agent, Patrick MacKay, came face to face with the elusive Cherokeeleechee, "the Craftiest, most cunning, and the boldest spoken Indian" he had the honor to meet. "Your King allways threatens to demolish [Saint] Augustine and Conquer the French att Movile," he reminded MacKay, "and the Cutt cheek King (meaning the Governor of Augustine) threatens to destroy Charlestown, and the King of Movile says he'll destroy both, but I shall never see the day that the one shall Conquer the other."[159]

Cherokeeleechee was a bold and occasionally rash man, but he was not a stupid one. He knew full well that he, his people, and his various Indian neighbors had undergone major changes in the course of his lifetime, and he undoubtedly realized that they would undergo a good many more before he died. In his three decades as a warrior and headman, he had seen the English of South Carolina increase dramatically in number, wealth, power, and influence. Nevertheless, Cherokeeleechee did not see them as an immovable or inexorable force destined to overwhelm everything in their path. He not only had faith in his own resourcefulness but also had enough experience to know that the "advance" of various colonial frontiers had been an uncertain struggle every step of the way. Like many Indians of the southeastern interior, Cherokeeleechee had no reason to believe that this struggle would soon end.

Though Cherokeeleechee never witnessed the British conquest of the Southeast, he only made it with a few years to spare. In 1763, shortly after the great headman's death, Great Britain's victory in the Seven Years War drove the Spanish out of Florida and the French out of Louisiana. By then even a group of Indians with the power and leverage of the Lower Creeks had to realize that the British imperialists of South Carolina, Georgia, and East and West Florida possessed cultural advantages that eventually would allow them to prevail in all their frontier power struggles. Still, traces of Indian resistance continued to smolder, even on those frontiers long since overrun by encroaching Europeans.

By the time the celebrated English naturalist William Bartram made an excursion to the eastern edge of Okefenokee Swamp in the summer of 1776, Georgia had been in British hands for more than forty years. The Spanish had left Florida for Cuba and Vera Cruz, taking with them the handful of Yamasee Indians who still remained under their protection. Few people, white or Indian, had firsthand memories of the old conflicts that formerly had raged over the debatable land. Nevertheless, those who traversed this particular part of Georgia continued to tell some fascinating stories, especially about a spectral band of "fierce men" whose "incomparably beautiful" wives were rumored to give aid to any wayward travelers stuck in Okefenokee's "inextricable swamps and bogs." According to Bartram's Lower Creek confidants, these swamp dwellers were "the posterity of a fugitive remnant of the ancient Yamasees, who escaped massacre after a bloody and decisive conflict between them and the Creek nation (who, it is certain, conquered, and nearly exterminated, that once powerful people) and [had] found an asylum, remote and secure from the fury of their proud conquerors." [160]

One can only imagine that this tale might have brought some vindication to Istawekee, the homesick Yamasee arrested for trespassing by John Barnwell some fifty years earlier. In the harsh light of reality, debates were won by those with the most handcuffs and guns, and land belonged to those who took it. In the powerful realm of imagination, however, claims belonged to anyone willing to take a stand and able to say something memorable.

Conclusion

THE SIGNIFICANCE OF
THE YAMASEE WAR

The Lower Creeks who described the mysteries of Okefenokee Swamp to William Bartram in 1776 were storytellers, no less so than William Gilmore Simms, the South Carolinian who crafted his own "romance" of the Yamasees nearly fifty years later. Like Simms, Bartram's Lower Creek guides drew from a deep well of local legends to explain an important and tumultuous episode from the past. Unlike Simms, however, they did not choose to tell their story of the Yamasee War as a lengthy, meandering, and florid celebration of South Carolina's triumphs. Bartram's vignette about the Lower Creeks and the Yamasees provides little room for literary analysis, but it speaks volumes from a historical standpoint. On the one hand, it provides an all too rare glimpse of the ways in which eighteenth-century Indians viewed their history. On the other hand, this brief story proves more tantalizing than instructive, leading readers to reflect on a massive documentary void. For every surviving relation, memory, and interpretation of the Yamasee War, there were many others that never found their way onto paper.

The Yamasee War gave rise to an abundance of fundamentally different written and unwritten stories, none of which succeed in conveying the entire story. The more one learns about the complexity of ethnicity, trade, diplomacy, and warfare along South Carolina's early frontiers, the easier it becomes to spot the shortcomings in those works, like Simms's *Yemasee*, that attempt to depict the Yamasee War as a single, momentous episode in southeastern history.[1] A more satisfying synthesis must move beyond Simms's ethnocentrism by evaluating more carefully what the war meant to the various Indians of the Southeast. Those Native societies were not mere stooges or appendages of the Europeans, but autonomous communities that made their own decisions. Given the fundamental autonomy of all parties involved in the Yamasee War, the crucial task is to show that everyone—European and Indian alike—made their decisions and acted in a larger context: a network of multilateral frontier relationships that evolved in the region over an extended period.

Wars have the ability to transform landscapes and cultures through their sheer destructive power. Though subject to numerous perspectives and interpretations, the Yamasee War also had a very real and tangible impact on those who took up arms to punish, destroy, or defend South Carolina. The numerous attacks and counterattacks associated with the war killed thousands of people, inflicting losses that were demoralizing to groups as large as the South Carolinians and the Cherokees and nothing short of disastrous to smaller and more vulnerable societies like the Yamasees, the Santees, and the Apalachees. For every person killed in the Yamasee War, many others were left maimed, widowed, orphaned, or otherwise traumatized. Even the physically unwounded often found themselves dealing with other disturbing losses, such as slaughtered livestock, uprooted crops, pillaged homesteads, and burned-out villages. In many cases the infrastructural damage sustained during the Yamasee War proved beyond repair, compelling survivors of all races and cultures to rebuild their lives from scratch.

By forcing so many people to begin anew, the Yamasee War brought significant changes to the physical and human geography of the Southeast. The war had an especially strong influence on the region's settlement patterns. The Ocheses, the Yamasees, the Apalachees, the Apalachicolas, and several other groups took pains to find new homes further from their enemies and closer to potential allies. In so doing they drastically reduced their presence in some parts of the Southeast while intensifying it in others. The "debatable land" between the Savannah and Altamaha rivers became devoid of human settlement for more than fifteen years after the Yamasee War, but the Lower Chattahoochee basin witnessed the proliferation of towns established and strengthened by refugees. A similar process occurred around the Catawba River in the Carolina Piedmont, where small and beleaguered tribes like the Ittawans and the Cheraws began to congregate to bolster themselves against outside incursions. The myriad pressures of the Yamasee War caused Indians not only to relocate but also to alter the shape and structure of their settlements. Throughout the entire Southeast—from the Appalachian Mountains to the plains of the Gulf Coast—the surge in intertribal warfare brought Indians to surround their towns with ditches, palisades, and other protective features.

At the same time the Yamasee War also led to similar defensive adjustments among the South Carolinians. While the South Carolina government adopted its first program of frontier fortification, hundreds of colonists elected to flee from vulnerable outlying settlements. The Indian raids that began during the Yamasee War delayed South Carolina's expansion into the "debatable land" of the Savannah River basin by nearly twenty years. When South Carolinians finally began to resume the settlement of their highly strategic southwestern frontiers, they proceeded with far more caution than they had displayed in the several years before the Yamasee War.

The efforts of Europeans and Indians to cope with the destructiveness of the Yamasee War also had a significant impact on the mercantile and military competition between the Southeast's three colonial powers. The new attitudes, settlements, and obstacles that were introduced by the war presented the English, the Spanish, the French, and several southeastern Indian societies with new challenges and opportunities. For the South Carolinians the Yamasee War came as a terrifying shock that temporarily forced them to abandon their imperial offensive and focus on protecting the very heart of their province. This sudden reversal not only allowed their imperial rivals some badly needed breathing room but also gave these rivals opportunities to conduct offensives of their own. At most the French and the Spanish played only a small and indirect role in inciting the Yamasee War. Once the conflict had begun, however, they did their utmost to capitalize on South Carolina's misfortune. From a European perspective, the most visible signs of French and Spanish retaliation were the strategic outposts that they built, staffed, and supplied at key locations in the southeastern interior. Though not the most imposing of structures, Fort Toulouse at the confluence of the Coosa and Tallapoosa rivers and Fort San Marcos in the old province of Apalachee were deemed threatening enough to compel British imperialists to respond with Fort King George on the Altamaha and eventually with the new colony of Georgia. This new triangle of frontier outposts spoke to the general shift that had occurred in the region's balance of power. The imperial contest that the South Carolinians had nearly won during Queen Anne's War became a stalemate that lasted another fifty years, largely as a result of the setbacks that South Carolina suffered during the Yamasee War.

All the while Indians continued to show that they remained far more than mere auxiliaries in this three-way imperial struggle. Indeed, early European advancements into the southeastern interior depended on Indian support: frontier outposts like Fort Toulouse and Fort San Marcos were in many ways akin to naked pawns on a chessboard, untenable without economic and military assistance from local or visiting Indians. Europeans often discovered to their chagrin that Indians could not always be counted on to cooperate with imperial strategies. This frustration proved especially acute in situations where Indians were confronted or courted by emissaries from more than one colonial power. While many of the Southeast's most powerful Indian societies had begun to gravitate almost exclusively toward the English by 1715, the Yamasee War offered some of them the incentive to reach out to the French and the Spanish. Few of the Alabamas, Abeikas, Tallapoosas, or Lower Creeks remained completely "neutral" in their hearts and minds, but their willingness to take advantage of rival traders and diplomats often served to frustrate South Carolina's attempts to gain an imperial monopoly over the Southeast.

While imperial rivalry remained a constant presence in the Southeast in the years before, during, and after the Yamasee War, the participants in this struggle underwent important changes in their outlooks and attitudes. These changes were especially evident in the character of South Carolina imperialism. For the first several decades of South Carolina's frontier expansion, traders, opportunists, and private adventurers imposed themselves on different Indian groups while suffering very little supervision from the provincial government. South Carolina began attempting to control its frontier expansion as early as the 1680s, but the Yamasee War forced the government to make dramatic overhauls in its regulation of the Indian trade and Indian diplomacy. Within two years the government's insistence on a tightly managed "public" trade collapsed in a storm of controversy, a development that betrayed a strong streak of stubbornness in many of South Carolina's frontiersmen. Though the quest for riches and personal glory always motivated South Carolina's traders and officials to a certain extent, many of them gradually learned to fall more in step with the concerns of their province and the wider British Empire. South Carolina's constitutional rebellion against the Lords Proprietors in 1719–20, an episode sparked primarily by economic and psychological fallout from the Yamasee War, helped clear the way for the greater influence of Crown officials in the province's frontier affairs.

Though the southeastern Indians did not have written laws or constitutions to redraft, they also experienced important changes in the ways in which they viewed their relationships to other groups. For nearly all the region's Native societies, the Yamasee War entailed more fighting against other Indians than against the South Carolinians. In certain cases the Yamasee War triggered intertribal conflicts that eventually took on destructive lives of their own. Following the Tugaloo massacre of January 1716, the Lower Creeks and the Cherokees—two of the region's most powerful Indian societies—embarked on nearly a century of intermittent warfare, prolonging a struggle that drew in other Native powers like the Chickasaws and the Choctaws and inflicted untold suffering in the southeastern interior. At the same time the pressures of the Yamasee War also inspired many southeastern Indian groups to form more amicable associations with one another. As different groups fragmented, relocated, and consolidated, they furthered a blurring of ethnic lines. Even before the Yamasee War, interaction with Europeans had begun to drive a "tribalization" process by grouping towns and clans into quasi-"national" entities. During and after the Yamasee War, some of these polities began to combine and congregate into multitribal, multiethnic "confederacies" like those of the Lower Creeks and the Catawbas. Though it remains impossible to determine precisely how the different peoples of the early eighteenth-century Southeast defined themselves, it seems safe to conclude that the Yamasee War helped push Indians toward the acceptance of new political and cultural identities.

For the white colonists of South Carolina, the Yamasee War proved less significant in transforming cultural identities than in reinforcing them. Since the earliest days of the colony, South Carolinians had largely defined themselves in opposition to those whom they considered culturally inferior. Slavery, an institution that drew sharp divisions between colonists and racial and cultural "others," had always been an important mechanism of white dominance in South Carolina. Even before the Yamasee War, South Carolinians had grown acutely conscious of being outnumbered by an alien and disturbing population of black slaves. Though the South Carolinians also exported and held significant numbers of Indian slaves, they were mysteriously quiet about their views of these slaves, even after the outbreak of the Yamasee War generated a new fear and loathing of Indians. When the most potentially dangerous Indian enemies began to distance themselves from South Carolina's colonial settlements, the colonists seemed to channel much of this fear onto the large numbers of black slaves who remained among them. The substantial increase in African slave imports between 1717 and 1740 was not solely a result of the Yamasee War, but it did raise issues that exacerbated the war's aftershocks. In the more vulnerable settlements of Port Royal and the Santee region, a lingering frontier instability caused colonists to worry more than ever about the threat of slave insurrection. South Carolina's frenzied responses to the Stono Rebellion—as well as other, far less serious acts of slave resistance—were due in large part to an underlying climate of terror left over from the Yamasee War.

For numerous cultures throughout the early colonial Southeast, the Yamasee War cast a long and cold shadow. It cut a wide swath of destruction and reconstruction, not only within the colonial settlements of South Carolina but also within the wide expanse of frontiers that enfolded the province. The changes wrought by the Yamasee War had a profound effect on the entire southeastern frontier complex and fully deserve to hold a prominent place in the region's history. Nevertheless, students of early colonial South Carolina should resist the temptation to see the conflict as a major "turning point" in southeastern history. It would be dramatic but ultimately far too simplistic to conclude that when Thomas Nairne met his grisly fate in the Pocotaligo town square on that April morning in 1715, an entire imperialistic way of life went up in flames with him. Such logic comes perilously close to viewing the Yamasee War as a transition between a reckless and problematic "before" and a more measured and orderly "after."

For generations historians of the Whiggish persuasion tended to assume that wars had clear beginnings, courses, and endings, thereby constituting acts of conflict and resolution. Today most scholars know the risks inherent in ascribing too much rationality to human conflict, the kind of approach that led nineteenth-century Prussian theorist Carl von Clausewitz to describe warfare as "the continuation of policy . . . by other means."[2] This maxim fails to do justice even to the most highly regimented conflicts that scoured Europe in the nineteenth and twentieth centuries, not to mention the multinational campaigns of the early twenty-first century. Few would dare to argue, for example, that the First World War really ended with the Treaty of Versailles or that the current war on terrorism will come to a clear and irrevocable conclusion. While numerous historians and pundits continue working to revise understandings of westernized warfare, they have been slower to apply these revisions to wars that did not involve well-drilled columns or modern military technology.

As some scholars have noted, Europeans in the colonial period were often struck by the strangeness and unpredictability of warfare in North America. Indians throughout the continent tended to fight in ways that frustrated, insulted, and frequently terrified white soldiers, who had their own deeply ingrained notions about what constituted fair play on the battlefield.[3] Because the Yamasee War conformed to this pattern in many ways, it is plausible to draw some parallels between it and some of the other European-Indian conflicts of the colonial period. At the same time, however, such comparisons have serious limitations. King Philip's War in New England, the Popé uprising in New Mexico, the Powhatan Wars in Virginia, and even the Tuscarora War in North Carolina all pitted unique groups of colonists and Indians against each other.[4] Moreover, close examination of many of these conflicts only makes it harder to generalize about them. Frontier warfare in colonial North America could display great variety, not only from conflict to conflict but also within the *same* conflict.

This tenet holds especially true for the Yamasee War, a conflict with a wider geographic scope than any other Indian war of the colonial period. It engulfed not just a colony but an entire region, thousands of square miles occupied by three imperial powers and dozens of different Indian societies. When regarded on such a massive scale, the Yamasee War initially seems to leave little choice but to clump its combatants into solid, easily distinguishable blocks. Only after zooming in for a closer look does one begin to appreciate the kaleidoscopic complexity of the early eighteenth-century "Southern frontier," a place of fluid identities and ambiguous alliances. A more thorough examination of South Carolina's diverse and sundry frontiers makes it harder to accept the sweeping generalizations that have emerged from most studies of the early colonial Southeast.

According to one of the most enduring and influential of these misconceptions, the Yamasee War amounted to a confrontation between champions of a dynamic and expansive "English" way of life, on one side, and defenders of a timeless, traditional, and utterly doomed "Indian" way of life, on the other. This stark juxtaposition not only trivializes the differences between colonial and Indian cultures but also glosses over variations within both. To one degree or another, the outbreak of the Yamasee War had ramifications for every British colonist and every Native American who lived in the Southeast. As different groups prepared to join or avoid the struggle, however, they confirmed that the region was far too diverse and unstable to divide itself into two seamless camps.

On the side of the colonists, it would be imprudent to assume that all English-speaking residents of the late seventeenth-century and early eighteenth-century Southeast belonged to a cohesive British Empire. Tensions between South Carolina, North Carolina, and Virginia hindered intercolonial unity and cooperation not only in times of relative peace and prosperity but even in times of serious crisis. Throughout the era of the Yamasee War, colonial governments were nowhere near powerful, wealthy, or efficient enough to carry out the designs of a few ambitious imperial architects. Authorities such as Charles Craven, Thomas Nairne, Alexander Spotswood, and John Barnwell could pay homage to the British Crown even as they continued to scheme against rival British provinces. Moreover, these officials usually had more than they could handle in trying to keep track of the traders, planters, and roustabouts who circulated along the frontiers of their own provinces. The first frenzied months of the Yamasee War in some ways forced South Carolina's frontiersmen and officials closer together, but in the long run many of the old divisions remained in place. As in the rest of British North America, the British imperialism of the early colonial Southeast was of a peculiar, polycentric sort, one that often allowed provincial politics and personal ambition to stand in the way of imperial purpose.

While the southeastern Indians often perceived and exploited the tensions within and between the British provinces, they remained subject to internal divisions of their own. Ideally the Yamasees, the Lower Creeks, the Cherokees, and other Indian societies sought to govern their affairs through consensus, but in reality such consensus was often extremely difficult or impossible to reach. Nevertheless, a lack of consensus seldom stopped different Indians from embarking on different courses of action. By the early eighteenth century, most of the Southeast's Indian societies were changing at an unprecedented rate as a result of their various frontier relationships, developing a range of new needs, ambitions, and behaviors that made it next to impossible for any town or tribe to speak with a single voice. Factionalism played an increasingly prominent role among all the southeastern "nations," from the ten closely grouped towns of the Yamasees to the sixty widely dispersed towns of the Cherokees. Indian factionalism came into play throughout the era of the Yamasee War, even during the most intense stages of the war itself. In the wake of the Pocotaligo massacre, for example, one group of Yamasees decided to execute another group of Yamasees who refused to take part in the war against South Carolina.

If controversy and dissension could plague a tribe as seemingly dedicated and determined as the Yamasees, it would follow that there would be even greater obstacles to a tenable, regionwide alliance between different Indian cultures. Of all the prevailing misconceptions about the Yamasee War, the one in greatest need of revision is that which posits a pan-Indian "conspiracy" against South Carolina. Indians from different parts of the Southeast did establish alliances with one another, but they never managed to develop a coordinated plan of attack. While the Yamasees, the Apalachees, and the Apalachicolas threw themselves at the South Carolina settlements, other groups like the Catawbas waited nearly six weeks to join the fray and were among the first to come to terms as soon as the tide of battle shifted in South Carolina's favor. Some of the Cherokees wavered for a few anxious months but ultimately decided to marshal their forces against South Carolina's most determined enemies. This dearth of cooperation between different Indian societies clearly proved crucial to South Carolina's survival. Still, the inability of these different societies to form a "united front" against South Carolina should not be viewed as a failure or shortcoming on the part of the southeastern Indians. Instead, one should simply see it as a reflection of the Southeast's highly fractured political and cultural landscape, recognizing that the region's different Indian groups had undergone different experiences and transformations in the decades before the outbreak of the Yamasee War. They all pursued their interests, but these interests were not identical and were often incompatible.

In addition to these factions and divisions, a number of other factors point to the pitfalls of treating the Yamasee War as a single, cataclysmic "showdown" between whites and Indians. To be sure, there was much about the Yamasee War that allowed South Carolinians and Indians to distinguish it from previous conflicts like Queen Anne's War and the Tuscarora War. For the first time the South Carolinians had become the targets rather than the instigators or beneficiaries of frontier warfare. The Yamasee War made such a strong impression on the South Carolinians that they became too distracted to fully appreciate its complexity. Many of them *were* inclined to clump all their Indian enemies into a single camp and to understand the war as a simple struggle against savagery. In retrospect it is easy to forgive the South Carolinians for oversimplifying the Yamasee War; even from a safe distance, it remains all but impossible to determine exactly where one fight ended and another began. When, for example, did the Cherokees start fighting the Creeks more for their own reasons than those of their South Carolinian allies? For the most part, however, South Carolinians did not bother themselves with such questions, choosing instead to believe that their treaties with the Creeks in the fall of 1717 were authoritative enough to bring a close to the Yamasee War. But a war that the South Carolinians tried desperately to put behind them was a war that several other groups refused to stop fighting. In the end the Yamasee War could not fit neatly between temporal bookends. Though known to the South Carolinians and their descendants as a single conflict, the spate of frontier violence that wracked the Southeast between 1715–17 actually marked the temporary confluence of a number of different conflicts with roots and branches that extended far beyond the two years in question.

Indeed, the Yamasee War loses many of its sharp edges when viewed as part of the larger context of frontier relations in the early colonial Southeast. The South Carolinians proved more ruthless and destructive than most conquerors, but even before they first chose to venture into the southeastern interior, warfare had been an inseparable part of frontier exchange within the region. While the South Carolinians unquestionably altered the scope and shape of the Southeast's alliance networks, they did little to alter the fundamental nature of the alliances themselves. The arrival and expansion of the South Carolina imperialists caused intercultural conflict to unfold with greater intensity and more destructive results, but at its heart the story remained remarkably consistent during the several decades before and after the Yamasee War. The various cultures of the Southeast never lost the urge to increase their strength and hold off their enemies, and no amount of loss or suffering could bring them to imagine a world without warfare.

Frontier exchange and conflict obviously meant different things to different people, a realization that makes it impractical for scholars to apply general models to their study of early colonial frontiers.[5] To a certain extent, however, the history of the South Carolina frontier complex in the era of the Yamasee War *can* be summarized in a single, universal statement. In essence all residents of the late seventeenth- and early eighteenth-century Southeast—whether black or white, Spanish or English, Chickasaw or Cherokee—were intent on the same thing: making the best of an alien and rapidly changing world. Some encountered this alien world as they expanded their horizons, meeting and courting new groups of people as a means of self-empowerment. Others had an alien world thrust on them, sometimes in the form of enticing goods and promises, but often in the form of unwanted diseases, debts, and obligations. Wherever these alien worlds came together, they formed a shifting and unstable crosshatch that required all concerned to watch their step or fall flat on their faces.[6]

But in spite of all the significant frontier transformations brought on by new trade networks, new weapons, new alliances, and new colonial settlements, most groups of people in the Southeast managed to maintain at least some hold over the traits and beliefs that distinguished them from other groups. No matter how much these groups "borrowed" from a different culture, their economic, military, and diplomatic relations with that culture always had to pass through the filter of their own assumptions and prejudices. Throughout the era of the Yamasee War, frontier exchange in the Southeast remained a fundamentally adversarial process. Though different groups could and did make concessions to each other in their quests for greater security and prosperity, the "middle ground" reached through these concessions never achieved any kind of long-term stability. On frontiers where South Carolinians and Indians did reach mutually agreeable arrangements, they really fashioned nothing more than a precarious equilibrium, in much the same way that two children playing on a see-saw can momentarily stay level with each other.

While trade, warfare, and diplomacy were rarely the stuff of fun and games, this metaphor bears some pursuing. Frontiers, like seesaws, can give the illusion of balance between players of unequal weight and leverage. When a seesaw moves back and forth, its predictable, oscillating rhythm makes it easy to forget that one child almost always weighs more than the other. If the heavier child grows tired of the game and decides to bring his weight to bear, it is only a matter of time before the balance begins to tip toward his side. At such a time the other child has only a few basic options at hand. He might try to jump off the seesaw and find someone else to play with. He might give in to the pressure and allow himself to be lifted further off the ground. Before going either way, however, he is likely to try leaning back in his seat in an effort to keep his own end down.

As South Carolinians expanded into the Southeast, they came as strangers to a number of alien and dangerous worlds. Most of them quickly realized that their determination to penetrate these worlds would require them to execute some intricate balancing acts. At the same time, however, the South Carolina imperialists never had any doubt as to which end of the seesaw they wanted and expected to occupy. Even in the stage of tentative first contact—a time when they found it prudent to obey the standards and demands of their Indian hosts—they entertained dreams of conquest. Even as South Carolina officials made occasional gifts or concessions to their Indian allies and trading partners, they did so as a means to impose or restore their own sense of order. However important a particular group of Indians could appear to South Carolina's short-term economic or military goals, it could never aspire to true equality in the minds of most South Carolinians. To most of South Carolina's imperial strategists, Indians amounted to little more than objects that could be moved or manipulated to meet the province's needs. Throughout most of the late seventeenth and early eighteenth centuries, South Carolinians applied conscious and unconscious pressure to every frontier situation they happened to enter and assumed that even the most stubbornly independent of groups would eventually have to yield to the demands of colonial expansion.

Though these assumptions never disappeared altogether, they did occasionally give way to periods of painful uncertainty. For the South Carolinians, of course, the most distressing of these periods centered around their desperate struggle to save themselves and their property from the unexpected attacks of their Indian allies. Even after withstanding these challenges, however, South Carolina's imperialists could not manage to cauterize their deepest wound, a psychological gash that seemed to break open every time the Indians, the

French, or the Spanish issued a firm challenge to British authority. With every reminder of their apocalyptic wartime experience, South Carolina officials were forced to lower the blinders that they usually wore in the formulation of frontier policy. Only in these instances of extreme discomfort did the South Carolinians even begin to admit that their triumph over the various peoples of the Southeast was not as inevitable as they wanted to believe.

In the complicated, unbalanced, and often torturous process of frontier exchange, violence—or the believable threat thereof—often proved to be the only message that all groups could understand. When different Indian societies found their own reasons to make war on South Carolina, they stated in no uncertain terms that the dynamics of the exchange process had become unacceptable to them. Likewise, the South Carolinians showed that they could also resort to violent threats and reprisals when the communication gap that separated them from their frontier adversaries grew too wide to bridge. To be sure, messages from the competing cultures of the Southeast were inspired by different motives, a spectrum that ranged from desperation to outrage to maddening impatience. Ultimately, however, all these cultures chose to fight in order to make themselves understood. In the final analysis, then, the Yamasee War's greatest significance—one that can be applied to the entire southeastern frontier complex—was as a collection of tragic but temporarily effective forms of expression.

While a multitude of expressions once resounded throughout the Southeast, most of them have faded away. As scholars explore this region across a chasm of nearly three centuries, the first and loudest voices they encounter come to them through the written records of the South Carolinians and their European rivals. Though not always the most eloquent or loquacious of men, the Southeast's colonial imperialists did possess an effective means of revealing their worldviews and preserving them for posterity. What they have bequeathed is their ceaseless quest for familiarity and order: their determination to construct a solid scaffold for assuaging their anxieties and fulfilling their dreams. Like their acknowledged rivals, the South Carolinians gradually strove to build this scaffold of straight lines and right angles, drawing maps, naming tribes, taking censuses, scheduling conferences, fixing prices, and granting commissions. In the midst of these tasks, they also fought a war, a multifaceted conflict that helps define an extensive period in the Southeast's early frontier history. More than anything else, the era of the Yamasee War should be remembered as the last time when some of the region's most forgotten groups had the capacity to draw lines of their own.

Notes

Abbreviations

Col. Office Records   British Public Record Office, Colonial Office.

Commons House Transcript   Journals of the Commons House of Assembly of South Carolina.

Council Transcript   Journals of the Governor's Council of South Carolina, 1671–1721.

CRNC   *The Colonial Records of North Carolina*, ed. William L. Saunders.

CSP   *Calendar of State Papers, Colonial Section, America and West Indies*, ed. W. Noel Sainsbury, J. W. Fortescue, and Cecil Headlam.

EJCCV   *Executive Journals of the Council of Colonial Virginia*, ed. J. P. Kennedy and H. R. McIlwaine.

Indies Archives   Archives of the Indies, Audiencia of Santo Domingo.

JCHASC   *Journals of the Commons House of Assembly of South Carolina*, ed. Alexander Salley.

JCIT   *Journals of the Commissioners of the Indian Trade, September 20, 1710–August 29, 1718*, ed. W. L. McDowell.

JCTP   *Journal of the Commissioners of Trade and Plantations*, Great Britain, Public Record Office.

JHBV   *Journals of the House of Burgesses of Virginia, 1619–1776*, ed. J. P. Kennedy and H. R. McIlwaine.

MPAFD   *Mississippi Provincial Archives, French Dominion*, ed. Dunbar Rowland and A. G. Sanders.

SC Records   Records in the British Public Record Office Relating to South Carolina.

SPG Letter Books   Society for the Propagation of the Gospel in Foreign Parts, Letter Books.

Upper House Journals   Journals of the Upper House of Assembly of South Carolina.

Introduction

1. John Caldwell Guilds and Carolina Caldwell, eds., *William Gilmore Simms and the American Frontier* (Athens: University of Georgia Press, 1994).

2. Wood, *Black Majority*, 127.

3. Turner, *History, Frontier, and Section*.

4. Crane, *Southern Frontier*, xix.

5. For examples of some of the most significant work in New Western history, see Worster, "New West, True West," 141–56; Cronon, "Revisiting the Vanishing Frontier," 157–76; Limerick, *Legacy of Conquest*; and White, *"It's Your Misfortune and None of My Own."*

6. Gallay, *Indian Slave Trade*, especially pp. 1–19, 315–57.

7. See Axtell, *European and the Indian*; Merrell, *Indians' New World*; Richter, *Ordeal of the Longhouse*; Usner, *Indians, Settlers, and Slaves*. For a good overview of the New Indian history's definition of frontiers, see Cayton and Teute, "On the Connection of Frontiers," 5–9.

8. For more on the etymology and usage of the word "frontier," see Juricek, "American Usage of the Word 'Frontier'"; Nobles, *American Frontiers*, 3–16, 252–55.

9. Axtell, *European and the Indian*, 245–305.

10. Forbes, "Frontiers in American History," 213.

11. Cayton and Teute, "On the Connection of Frontiers," 9–15; Nobles, *American Frontiers*, 251–74.

1. Builders and Borrowers

1. Weir, *Colonial South Carolina*, 47–52.

2. Hudson, *Southeastern Indians*, 77–97; Worth, *Timucuan Chiefdoms*, 5; Anderson, *Savannah River Chiefdoms*, 1–107; Widmer, "Structure of Southeastern Chiefdoms," 125–55.

3. Hudson, *Knights of Spain*, 238–48; Hudson, *Southeastern Indians*, 102–19; Corkran, *Creek Frontier*, 41–47. For an interpretation of the de Soto *entrada* that differs from that of Hudson, see Galloway, *Hernando De Soto Expedition*. For detailed analysis of another Spanish expedition into the southeastern interior, see Hudson, *Juan Pardo Expeditions*.

4. Milner, "Epidemic Disease," 41–42; Dobyns, *Their Number Become Thinned*, 270.

5. One scholar has recently argued that some of the virgin-soil epidemics, most notably smallpox, did not have their greatest impact on the Southeast until the late seventeenth century, and that the "period between 1526 and 1696 is best described as the false dawn of epidemiological disaster." See Kelton, "Great Southeastern Smallpox Epidemic," 28–30.

6. M. Smith, "Aboriginal Depopulation," 270.

7. Rayson, " 'Great Matter to Tell,'" 87.

8. M. Smith, *Coosa*, 96–117.

9. Swanton, *Early History*, 11.

10. Boyd, "Expedition of Marcus Delgado," 26–27.

11. Cline, *Florida Indians*, 1:39; Bushnell, *King's Coffer*, 1–14; Worth, *Timucuan Chiefdoms*, xvii.

12. Weber, *Spanish Frontier*, 95.

13. Bushnell, *Situado and Sabana*, 23–26.

14. Wenhold, "17th Century Letter," 8–9; Boyd, "Enumeration," 181–88.

15. Wenhold, "17th Century Letter," 14.

16. Bushnell, *Situado and Sabana*, 95–103.

17. Merrill, "Conversion and Colonialism," 154.

18. Hann, *Apalachee*, 214–16; Wenhold, "17th Century Letter," 7.

19. Hann, "Apalachee of the Historic Era," 340.

20. Bushnell, "Ruling the 'Republic of Indians,'" 134–50; Hann, "Political Leadership," 188–208; Axtell, *Indians' New South*, 28–30; Worth, *Timucuan Chiefdoms*, 37, 77.

21. Milanich, *Florida Indians*, 178–203; Bushnell, *Situado and Sabana*, 28.

22. McEwan, "San Luis de Talimali," 56.

23. Hann, *History of the Timucua Indians*, 200–220; Hann, *Apalachee*, 16–20; Bushnell, *Situado and Sabana*, 128–33.

24. Worth, *Timucuan Chiefdoms*, 111; Weber, *Spanish Frontier*, 118.

25. McEwan, "San Luis de Talimali," 55.

26. Waselkov, "Seventeenth-Century Trade," 117–33.

27. Dickinson, *God's Protecting Providence*, 52–53.

28. Waselkov, "Seventeenth-Century Trade," 118–19; Boyd, "Expedition of Marcus Delgado," 15.

29. Bolton, "Spanish Resistance," 119; Corkran, *Creek Frontier*, 49–50; Durschlag, "First Creek Resistance," 99.

30. Crane, *Southern Frontier*, 11.

31. Crane, *Southern Frontier*, 16–17.

32. Reding, "Plans for the Colonization and Defense," 173–74.

33. Matter, "Missions in the Defense," 31; Worth, *Struggle for the Georgia Coast*, 26; Milanich, *Florida Indians*, 272.

34. Lanning, *Spanish Missions of Georgia*, 141; Worth, *Struggle for the Georgia Coast*, 37–42; Bushnell, *Situado and Sabana*, 161–65.

35. Crane, *Southern Frontier*, 24.

36. Martin, "Southeastern Indians," 306; Barker, " 'Much Blood and Treasure,' " 40.

37. Bolton, "Spanish Resistance," 120.

38. Juricek, "Indian Policy," 128–32; Juricek, "Westo Indians," 138; Crane, *Southern Frontier*, 20–21; Gallay, *Indian Slave Trade*, 40–69.

39. Braund, *Deerskins and Duffels*, 26–30.

40. Boyd, "Expedition of Marcus Delgado," 27; Waselkov, "Seventeenth-Century Trade," 121.

41. See Hahn, "Miniature Arms Race," 65.

42. Bushnell, *Situado and Sabana*, 60–66; Rayson, " 'Great Matter to Tell,' " 55.

43. Bushnell, *Situado and Sabana*, 69.

44. Crane, *Southern Frontier*, 15.

45. Worth, *Struggle for the Georgia Coast*, 17–19; Bushnell, *Situado and Sabana*, 134.

46. Report of Antonio Matheos, quoted in Hann, "Late Seventeenth-Century Forebears," 76; Francis Le Jau to the SPG secretary, in Klingberg, *Carolina Chronicle of Francis Le Jau*, 87; Hann, "St. Augustine's Fallout," 188–89.

47. Antonio Matheos, quoted in Boyd, "Enumeration," 185; Green, "Search for Altamaha," 2–3; McKivergan, "Migration and Settlement," 29; Worth, *Struggle for the Georgia Coast*, 22.

48. Worth, *Struggle for the Georgia Coast*, 22.

49. Governor Quiroga y Losada to the king, April 1, 1688, Indies Archives, 227B (microfilm); Barcía, *Chronological History*, 312; Rayson, " 'Great Matter to Tell,' " 283; Worth, *Timucuan Chiefdoms*, 197.

50. Quoted in Worth, *Struggle for the Georgia Coast*, 112.

51. Green, "Search for Altamaha," 5; Crane, *Southern Frontier*, 25; Bushnell, *Situado and Sabana*, 165–66.

52. "Examanacon of Severall Yamasse Indians," May 6, 1685, in SC Records, 2:66.

53. Caleb Westbrooke to Deputy Governor Godfrey, February 21, 1684/1685, in CSP, 12, 28.

54. Cardross to the Lords Proprietors, undated, in Jones, *Port Royal under Six Flags*, 90–91.

55. Worth, *Struggle for the Georgia Coast*, 43.

56. Rowland, Moore, and Rogers, *History of Beaufort County*, 72.

57. Deposition of John Edenburgh, May 6, 1685, in SC Records, 2:63.

58. Crane, *Southern Frontier*, 30–31; Gallay, *Indian Slave Trade*, 80–84.

59. William Dunlop to the Lords Proprietors, September 1686, in Jones, *Port Royal under Six Flags*, 95.

60. Worth, *Struggle for the Georgia Coast*, 146.

61. Dickinson, *God's Protecting Providence*, 86–87. For more on the success of the Spanish retaliation, see Worth, *Struggle for the Georgia Coast*, 146–53, 162–63.

62. Lords Proprietors to James Colleton, March 3, 1686/1687, in SC Records, 2:184; Lords Proprietors to James Colleton, October 10, 1687, in SC Records, 2:222.

63. Carolina Commons House to Seth Sothell, undated, in CRNC, 2:846–47; Rowland, Moore, and Rogers, *History of Beaufort County*, 73.

64. Reding, "Plans for Colonization and Defense," 169–71; Lanning, *Spanish Missions of Georgia*, 175.

65. Hann, *Apalachee*, 200.

66. Hann, "Late Seventeenth-Century Forebears," 72–74.

67. Boyd, "Expedition of Marcus Delgado," 27.

68. Governor Juan Cabrera to King Carlos II, March 20, 1686, Indies Archives, 852 (microfilm).

69. Quoted in Bolton, "Spanish Resistance," 122; Crane, *Southern Frontier*, 35.

70. Cabrera to King Carlos II, November 8, 1686, Indies Archives, 227B (microfilm).

71. Antonio Matheos, quoted in Hann, "Late Seventeenth-Century Forebears," 76; also see Swanton, *Early History*, 221; Durschlag, "First Creek Resistance," 116.

72. Serraño y Sanz, *Documentos historicos*, 220; Quiroga y Losada, quoted in Pearson, "Anglo-Spanish Rivalry," 51.

73. Governor Losada to King Carlos II, April 1, 1688, Indies Archives, 227B (microfilm).

74. Bolton, "Spanish Resistance," 124; Crane, *Southern Frontier*, 36.

75. John Stewart to William Dunlop, April 27, 1690, in Dunlop, "Letters from John Stewart," 30; Gallay, *Indian Slave Trade*, 89.

76. John Stewart to William Dunlop, April 27, 1690, in Dunlop, "Letters from John Stewart," 30; Corkran, *Creek Frontier*, 51.

77. Boyd, "Documents Describing the Second and Third Expeditions," 139.

78. Wood, *Black Majority*, 96–130.

79. Duncan, "Servitude and Slavery," 636–45; Landers, "Black-Indian Interaction," 149–50; Te Paske, "Fugitive Slave," 3.

80. See Dunlop, "William Dunlop's Mission," 1–30; Crane, *Southern Frontier*, 33.

81. Wood, "Changing Population," 38.

82. Worth, *Struggle for the Georgia Coast*, 170.

83. The 1696 slave code is no longer extant, but a reenactment passed in 1712 can be found in Cooper and McCord, *Statutes*, 7:352; also see Duncan, "Servitude and Slavery," 756.

84. Sirmans, *Colonial South Carolina*, 50.

85. Wright, *Only Land They Knew*, 108.

86. Clowse, *Economic Beginnings*, 83.

87. Lords Proprietors to Joseph West, March 13, 1684/1685, in SC Records, 2:33.

88. Lords Proprietors to Seth Sothel, May 13, 1691, in CSP, 13:1,497; Sirmans, *Colonial South Carolina*, 50.

89. Barker, " 'Much Blood and Treasure,'" 89–126; Le Fave, "Time of the Whitetail," 6; P. Brown, "Early Indian Trade," 118–28.

90. Salley, *Journal of the Grand Council*, 31.

91. Beverly, *History and Present State of Virginia*, 182.

92. J. Lawson, *New Voyage*, 18, 210–12.

93. J. Lawson, *New Voyage*, 56.

94. Archdale, "New Description," 290.

95. John Stewart to William Dunlop, June 23, 1690, in Dunlop, "Letters from John Stewart," 94.

96. Lords Proprietors to James Colleton, October 18, 1690, in SC Records, 2:292–93.

97. Salley, *Journal of the Grand Council*, 55.

98. Salley, *Journal of the Grand Council*, 31.

99. Quoted in Crane, *Southern Frontier*, 33.

100. JCHASC, January 13, 1692/1693, 11–12; JCHASC, January 14, 1692/1693, 12–13.

101. Swanton, *Early History*, pl. 3; Juricek, "Westo Indians," 138; Dickinson, *Journal*, 84.

102. Lords Proprietors to Joseph West, March 13, 1684/1685, in SC Records, 2:28–33; Lords Proprietors to Joseph West, May 5, 1685, in SC Records, 2:59; Cooper and McCord, *Statutes*, 2:64–68; Vaughan and Rosen, *Carolina and Georgia Laws*, 111–14; Crane, *Southern Frontier*, 141.

103. Salley, *Journal of the Grand Council*, 45–46.

104. Friedlander, "Indian Slavery," 17; Snell, "Indian Slavery," 27; Willis, "Colonial Conflict," 19.

105. Perdue, *Slavery and the Evolution of Cherokee Society*, 19–35; Rayson, " 'Great Matter to Tell,' " 259; Merrell, *Indians' New World*, 37.

106. JCHASC, January 13, 1692/1693, 12–13.

107. Archdale, "New Description," 300–301.

108. Lords Proprietors to John Archdale, June 28, 1695, in SC Records, 3:159.

109. Dickinson, *Journal*, 16, 48.

110. Quoted in Worth, *Struggle for the Georgia Coast*, 174.

111. Letters of Governor Ayala to the king, June 27, 1697, and March 11, 1695, Indies Archives, 839 (microfilm).

112. Axtell, *Indians' New South*, 26.

2. Contested Empires

1. Hann, "Leturiondo's Memorial," 174.

2. Crane, *Southern Frontier*, 64–65; Governor Torres y Ayala to the Viceroy, May 15, 1699, Indies Archives, 839 (microfilm); Joseph Blake to Proprietors, June 28, 1699, in SC Records, 4:91.

3. Hann, "Leturiondo's Memorial," 174.

4. Iberville in Margry, *Découvertes et Etablissements*, 4:322–23.

5. Iberville in Margry, *Découvertes et Etablissements*, 4:310, 546, 550–51.

6. Arnade, "English Invasion," 29.

7. Francis Nicholson to the Board of Trade, June 10, 1700, in CSP, 18:523.

8. JCHASC, August 14, 1701, 4.

9. Commons House Transcript, March 31, 1702, 1:338.

10. Margry, *Découvertes et Etablissements*, 4:594–95.

11. Commons House Transcript, January 15, 1701/1702, 1:284.

12. Kelton, "Great Southeastern Smallpox Epidemic," 21–37; Wood, "Impact of Smallpox," 34; Commons House Transcript, March 31, 1702, 1:338.

13. Commons House Transcript, January 29, 1701/1702, 1:310.

14. Gallay, *Formation of a Planter Elite*, 11.

15. Commons House Transcript, March 31, 1702, 1:308.

16. JCHASC, November 16, 1700, 22–23; JCHASC, January 24–25, 1701/1702, 121; see also Crane, *Southern Frontier*, 144.

17. JCHASC, August 14–15, 1701, 5–7.

18. Sirmans, *Colonial South Carolina*, 83.

19. Crane, *Southern Frontier*, 74.

20. JCHASC, February 22, 1700/1701, 15; JCHASC, August 27, 1701, 24.

21. Haefeli and Sweeney, "Revisiting *The Redeemed Captive*"; Richter, *Ordeal of the Longhouse*; Demos, *Unredeemed Captive*; and Melvoin, *New England Outpost*.

22. JCHASC, August 20, 1702, 64.

23. Arnade, *Siege of St. Augustine*, 32; Crane, *Southern Frontier*, 76. Others among these Indians fled south to Saint Augustine; see Worth, *Struggle for the Georgia Coast*, 181.

24. Covington, "Migration of Seminoles," 341; Gallay, *Indian Slave Trade*, 127.

25. Arnade, "English Invasion," 33; Crane, *Southern Frontier*, 76.

26. Boyd, "Siege of St. Augustine," 345–52.

27. Arnade, *Siege of St. Augustine*, 59.

28. Bolton, "Mission as a Frontier Institution," 42–61; Matter, "Missions in the Defense," 18–38; Matter, *Pre-Seminole Florida*; Weber, *Spanish Frontier*, 145–46; and Chatelain, *Defenses of Spanish Florida*, 38.

29. Hann, "Leturiondo's Memorial," 178.

30. Covington, "Apalachee Indians," 369–70.

31. Matter, *Pre-Seminole Florida*, 119–50.

32. Hann, "Leturiondo's Memorial," 178; also see letter of Apalachee caciques to the king, February 12, 1699, in Boyd, Smith, and Griffin, *Here They Once Stood*, 24.

33. Corkran, *Creek Frontier*, 52.

34. Hann, "Leturiondo's Memorial," 177.

35. Apalachee caciques to King Carlos II, February 12, 1699, in Boyd, Smith, and Griffin, *Here They Once Stood*, 26.

36. Hann, "Leturiondo's Memorial," 176; JCHASC, September 15, 1703, 121.

37. Letter of Jacinto Roque Perez to Governor Zúñiga, May 25, 1703, in Boyd, Smith, and Griffin, *Here They Once Stood*, 9–10; Covington, "Apalachee Indians," 371; Pearson, "Anglo-Spanish Rivalry," 57; Bolton, "Spanish Resistance," 126; Crane, *Southern Frontier*, 74.

38. Hann, *Apalachee*, 190. For accounts of the battle, see Carroll, *Historical Collections of South Carolina*, 2:351; also Pearson, "Anglo-Spanish Rivalry," 57–58; Crane, *Southern Frontier*, 74n.

39. Sirmans, *Colonial South Carolina*, 84–85.

40. Arnade, "English Invasion," 34–35.

41. JCHASC, September 15, 1703, 121.

42. Durschlag, "First Creek Resistance," 227.

43. Hann, *Apalachee*, 271.

44. See Franciscan testimony before Saint Augustine Council of War, June 1705, in Boyd, Smith, and Griffin, *Here They Once Stood*, 76; letter from Juan Solana to Governor Zúñiga, July 8, 1704, in ibid., 53.

45. Hann, *Apalachee*, 264–83, 294; Moore's letters to Governor Johnson and Lords Proprietors, April 16, 1704, Col. Office Records, no. 5/283, 82–86.

46. Commons House Transcript, April 27–28, 1704, 1:401.

47. Solana to Zúñiga, July 8, 1704, in Boyd, Smith, and Griffin, *Here They Once Stood*, 54.

48. See Arnade, "English Invasion," 35–36, for evidence of a disastrous Spanish defeat in early 1705.

49. Bienville to Pontchartrain, July 28, 1706, in MPAFD, 2:25; Bienville to Pontchartrain, September 6, 1704, in MPAFD, 3:27.

50. "An Account of the Invasion of South Carolina by the French and Spaniards in the Month of August 1706," in SC Records, 5:164.

51. See Cole, "Organization and Administration," 41–42; Jabbs, "South Carolina Colonial Militia," 250–54; Quarles, "Colonial Militia and Negro Manpower," 643–52.

52. Nairne, "Letter from South Carolina," 52.

53. Zúñiga to King Philip V, September 15, 1704, in Boyd, Smith, and Griffin, *Here They Once Stood*, 69; Royal *cedula* of May 2, 1705, Indies Archives, 836 (microfilm).

54. SC Records, 2:161–70; also Crane, *Southern Frontier*, 87; Jabbs, "South Carolina Colonial Militia," 262.

55. The Yamasees, for example, were given a present of gunpowder and shot to help persuade them to drop some charges they had raised about the conduct of an abusive trader; see JCHASC, February 17, 1702/1703, 47.

56. For deerskin exports, see table 1 in Crane, *Southern Frontier*, and table 3 in Clowse, *Economic Beginnings*.

57. Thomas Nairne to the Earl of Sunderland, July 28, 1708, in CSP, 24:662.

58. JCHASC, December 11, 1706, 21–23; JCHASC, April 29, 1703, 75–78; Col. Office Records, no. 5/306, 4.

59. Moore, "Carolina Whigs," 1–9.

60. Sirmans, *Colonial South Carolina*, 78.

61. Defoe, "Party Tyranny," 241.

62. Moore, "Carolina Whigs," 90–94; Crane, *Southern Frontier*, 122; Stumpf, "Merchants of Colonial Charles Town," 51.

63. JCHASC, July 5, 1707, 81.

64. JCHASC, December 20, 1706, 35; JCHASC, January 31, 1706/1707, 42; JCHASC, July 4, 1707, 78; JCHASC, July 5, 1707, 81; Sirmans, *Colonial South Carolina*, 90–91.

65. Cooper and McCord, *Statutes*, 2:309–16; Vaughan and Rosen, *Carolina and Georgia Laws*, 136–43; JCHASC, July 18, 1707, 98; Crane, *Southern Frontier*, 148–50; L. R. Smith, "South Carolina's Indian Trade Regulations," 25–30.

66. For biographical information on Nairne, see Alexander Moore's introduction to *Nairne's Muskhogean Journals*; also see Gallay, *Indian Slave Trade*, 168–70.

67. Moore, *Nairne's Muskhogean Journals*, 33, 69.

68. Crane, *Southern Frontier*, 133.

69. Waselkov and Cottier, "European Perceptions," 23–45. For a firsthand account of the Spanish classification of the Muskogean nations, see the deposition of a Spanish officer in Governor Martínez's letter to the king, January 22, 1710, Indies Archives, 841 (microfilm).

70. Swanton, *Social Organization*, 276; Hudson, *Southeastern Indians*; Lankford, "Red and White," 57.

71. Knight, "Formation of the Creeks," 374–86; Swanton, "Social Significance," 333.

72. Ferguson and Whitehead, "Violent Edge of Empire," 4–23.

73. "Kings, Princes, Generals, Etc. to the Crown of England," in Hayes, *Indian Treaties and Cessions*, 1–2; Gallay, *Indian Slave Trade*, 138–39.

74. Crane, *Southern Frontier*, 82–83.

75. Moore, *Nairne's Muskhogean Journals*, 35. Since Oakfuskee was actually the principal town of the Abeikas, Nairne was probably using "Tallapoosa" as a catchall term on this occasion.

76. Governor Johnson to the Board of Trade, September 17, 1708, in Merrens, *Colonial South Carolina Scene*, 34.

77. JCHASC, March 28, 1706, 43.

78. JCHASC, November 28, 1707, 46.

79. Cooper and McCord, *Statutes*, 2:317–18; Vaughan and Rosen, *Carolina and Georgia Laws*, 144–45.

80. McKivergan, "Migration and Settlement," 35, 218.

81. Green, "Search for Altamaha," 24; Crane, *Southern Frontier*, 164; Swanton, *Early History*, 97.

82. McKivergan, "Migration and Settlement," 230.

83. McKivergan, "Migration and Settlement," 220.

84. Cooper and McCord, *Statutes*, 2:318.

85. Johnson to the Board of Trade, September 17, 1708, in Merrens, *Colonial South Carolina Scene*, 35; also Commons House Transcript, November 28, 1707, 3:342.

86. Commons House Transcript, April 9, 1707, 3:144–45.

87. JCHASC, June 12, 1707, 27; JCHASC, February 7, 1707/1708, 62; Crane, *Southern Frontier*, 148n.

88. Crane, *Southern Frontier*, 81.

89. Thomas Nairne to the Earl of Sunderland, July 11, 1708, in Moore, *Nairne's Muskhogean Journals*, 75; Nairne, "Letter from South Carolina," 53.

90. Governor Córcoles y Martínez to King Philip V, January 6, 1708, March 20, 1708, April 18, 1708, Indies Archives, 841 (microfilm); also letter of viceroy to king, August 25, 1709, Indies Archives, 841.

91. Hann, "St. Augustine's Fallout," 182; Hann, *History of the Timucua Indians*, appendix.

92. Pénicaut, *Fleur de Lis and Calumet*, 11.

93. Moore, *Nairne's Muskhogean Journals*, 90.

94. John Stewart to William Dunlop, October 20, 1693, in Dunlop, "Letters from John Stewart," 170.

95. Galloway, "Henri de Tonti," 160.

96. Woods, *French-Indian Relations*, 4.

97. Galloway, "Henri de Tonti," 158.

98. Crane, "Projects for Colonization," 23–27; Crane, *Southern Frontier*, 50.

99. Goss, "French and the Choctaw Indians," 33.

100. Woods, *French-Indian Relations*, 6; reports of Spanish officials in Madrid, September 3, 1701, Indies Archives, 840 (microfilm).

101. Letter of Lavasseur, 1700, quoted in Higginbotham, *Old Mobile*, 41–42.

102. Iberville, quoted in Higginbotham, *Old Mobile*, 77.

103. Crane, *Southern Frontier*, 70.

104. Pénicaut, *Fleur de Lis and Calumet*, 65.

105. Higginbotham, *Old Mobile*, 124.

106. Pénicaut, *Fleur de Lis and Calumet*, 72; Bienville to Pontchartrain, September 6, 1704, in MPAFD, 3:22; Bienville to Pontchartrain, April 10, 1706, in MPAFD, 3:33–34.

107. Crane, *Southern Frontier*, 69; Higginbotham, *Old Mobile*, 77.

108. MPAFD, 3:34; Moore, *Nairne's Muskhogean Journals*, 63.

109. Moore, *Nairne's Muskhogean Journals*, 38–48.

110. White, *Roots of Dependency*, 36.

111. Moore, *Nairne's Muskhogean Journals*, 63.

112. Morris, "Bringing of Wonder," 332.

113. Barker, " 'Much Blood and Treasure,'" 212.

114. Moore, *Nairne's Muskhogean Journals*, 56.

115. Moore, *Nairne's Muskhogean Journals*, 57.

116. Thomas Nairne to the Earl of Sunderland, July 10, 1708, in Moore, *Nairne's Muskhogean Journals*, 75.

117. Moore, *Nairne's Muskhogean Journals*, 56.

118. Wood, "Changing Population," 38.

119. Foret, "French Colonial Indian Policy," 87–88; Gallay, *Indian Slave Trade*, 128–29.

120. Bienville to Pontchartrain, February 20, 1707, in MPAFD, 3:37.

121. Foret, "French Colonial Indian Policy," 83–84; Crane, *Southern Frontier*, 84.

122. Pénicaut, *Fleur de Lis and Calumet*, 25; Woods, *French-Indian Relations*, 10; Bienville's 1726 memoir of his service in Louisiana, in MPAFD, 3:539.

123. Higginbotham, *Old Mobile*, 126.

124. JCHASC, November 22, 1707, 49.

125. Duclos to Pontchartrain, October 25, 1713, in MPAFD, 2:126–27.

126. Higginbotham, *Old Mobile*, 355.

127. Foret, "French Colonial Indian Policy," 88.

128. Duclos to Pontchartrain, October 25, 1713, in MPAFD, 2:127; also Bienville's 1726 memoir, in MPAFD, 3:539.

129. Bienville to Pontchartrain, October 12, 1708, in MPAFD, 2:41.

130. Bienville to Pontchartrain, February 20, 1707, in MPAFD, 3:37; Bienville to Pontchartrain, October 12, 1708, in MPAFD, 2:68.

131. Bienville to Pontchartrain, February 25, 1708, in MPAFD, 3:113.

132. See Moore, *Nairne's Muskhogean Journals*, 56; Bienville to Pontchartrain, October 12, 1708, in MPAFD, 2:39; Bienville to Pontchartrain, November 12, 1708, in MPAFD, 2:40.

133. Quoted in Galloway, "Henri de Tonti," 169.

134. Moore, *Nairne's Muskhogean Journals*, 57; Governor Johnson to the Board of Trade, September 17, 1708, in Merrens, *Colonial South Carolina Scene*, 35.

135. Moore, *Nairne's Muskhogean Journals*, 38–45.

136. Bienville to Pontchartrain, September 6, 1704, in MPAFD, 3:22.

137. Bienville to Pontchartrain, April 10, 1706, in MPAFD, 3:34.

138. Quoted in Crane, *Southern Frontier*, 96.

139. JCHASC, November 22, 1707, 50.

140. Thomas Nairne to Secretary of State Sunderland, July 11, 1708, in Moore, *Nairne's Muskhogean Journals*, 74.

141. Ford, *Triangular Struggle*, 78–87; Crane, *Southern Frontier*, 88–91.

142. Governor Córcoles y Martínez to King Philip V, January 22, 1710, Indies Archives, 841 (microfilm).

143. Bienville to Pontchartrain, September 1, 1709, in MPAFD, 3:133; Tivas de

Gourville to Pontchartrain, June 1712, in MPAFD, 2:68; Bienville to Pontchartrain, August 20, 1709, in MPAFD, 3:136.

144. Reynolds, "Alabama-Tombigbee Basin," 73.

145. Higginbotham, *Old Mobile*, 460.

146. Bienville to Pontchartrain, October 27, 1711, in MPAFD, 3:161; Reynolds, "Alabama-Tombigbee Basin," 86.

147. Bienville to Pontchartrain, October 27, 1711, in MPAFD, 3:161.

148. Merrell, *Indians' New World*, 51.

149. D. Brown, *Catawba Indians*, 1.

150. Merrell, *Indians' New World*, 18–25.

151. J. Lawson, *New Voyage*, 27, 38.

152. Merrell, *Indians' New World*, 31, 86.

153. J. Lawson, *New Voyage*, 46–47.

154. J. Lawson, *New Voyage*, 48–49; Merrell, *Indians' New World*, 6. For accounts of disease in the Piedmont, see J. Lawson, *New Voyage*, 34.

155. JCHASC, November 12, 1697, 21; JCHASC, October 7, 1698, 25.

156. JCHASC, February 13, 1700/1701, 8.

157. Merrell, *Indians' New World*, 63.

158. Dodson, *Alexander Spotswood*, 16; Crane, *Southern Frontier*, 154; Rothrock, "Carolina Traders," 4; D. Brown, *Catawba Indians*, 102; and Chapman, "Indian Relations," 46.

159. Greene, *Selling a New World*, 8; JCHASC, February 6, 1700/1701, 3; JCHASC, September 16, 1703, 123.

160. EJCCV, October 19, 1708, 194.

161. Franklin, "Virginia and the Cherokee Indian Trade," 4–6; D. Brown, *Catawba Indians*, 53.

162. Merrell, *Indians' New World*, 36; Martin, "Southeastern Indians," 307–8.

163. Journal of the House of Burgesses, May 19, 1699, in CSP, 17:399.

164. EJCCV, March 3, 1703/1704, 351.

165. Merrell, *Indians' New World*, 53.

166. JCHASC, February 20, 1700/1701, 15.

167. Crane, *Southern Frontier*, 154; Ward, *Unite or Die*, 154.

168. EJCCV, April 28, 1708, 177–78.

169. EJCCV, April 28, 1708, 178.

170. D. Brown, *Catawba Indians*, 113.

171. E. Randolph to the Board of Trade, March 5, 1700/1701, in CSP, 19:208.

172. EJCCV, October 28, 1708, 201; JCTP, 1:546–50; JCTP, 2:397.

173. Crane, *Southern Frontier*, 156.

174. D. Brown, *Catawba Indians*, 109; Johnson to the Board of Trade, September 17, 1708, in Merrens, *Colonial South Carolina Scene*, 35–36.

175. D. Brown, *Catawba Indians*, 24.

176. J. Lawson, *New Voyage*, 10.

177. Commons House Transcript, April 21, 1709, 3:415.

178. Merrell, " 'Their Very Bones Shall Fight,' " 122.

179. Richter, *Ordeal of the Longhouse*, 32–38, 237–39.

180. Crane, *Southern Frontier*, 156; Franklin, "Virginia and the Cherokee Indian Trade," 10.

181. Merrell, *Indians' New World*, 54–55.

182. EJCCV, October 28, 1708, 201; Crane, *Southern Frontier*, 156.

183. Merrell, *Indians' New World*, 55–59; Chapman, "Indian Relations," 63.

184. Hatley, *Dividing Paths*, 6–7.

185. Bloom, "Acculturation of the Eastern Cherokee," 324; Goodwin, *Cherokees in Transition*, 94.

186. Rothrock, "Carolina Traders," 5.

187. Hatley, *Dividing Paths*, 8; Wood, "Changing Population," 38.

188. Willis, "Colonial Conflict," 25, 35; Commons House Transcript, November 11, 1698, 1:208.

189. Nairne to Sunderland, July 10, 1708, in Moore, *Nairne's Muskhogean Journals*, 76.

190. Johnson to the Board of Trade, September 17, 1708, in Merrens, *Colonial South Carolina Scene*, 35.

191. Goodwin, *Cherokees in Transition*, 115; Commons House Transcript, April 21, 1709, 3:415.

192. Pryce Hughes to the Duchess of Ormond, October 15, 1713, in Pryce Hughes Letters.

193. Johnson to the Board of Trade, September 17, 1708, in Merrens, *Colonial South Carolina Scene*, 35.

194. Robinson, "Virginia and the Cherokees," 26–27.

195. Crane, *Southern Frontier*, 157; Robinson, "Virginia and the Cherokees," 27; L. R. Smith, "South Carolina's Indian Trade Regulations," 42. The act was ratified on June 28, 1711; see Cooper and McCord, *Statutes*, 2:357–59; Vaughan and Rosen, ed., *Carolina and Georgia Laws*, 153–54.

196. Cooper and McCord, *Statutes*, 2:357.

197. Cooper and McCord, *Statutes*, 2:358.

198. Ward, *Unite or Die*, 256.

199. Peckham, *Colonial Wars*, 73–74.

3. Beneath the Buffer Zone

1. Nairne, "Letter from South Carolina," 52–54.

2. Dill, "Eighteenth-Century New Bern," 295–98.

3. Dill, "Eighteenth-Century New Bern," 299–311; Nash, *Red, White, and Black*, 147; and Lee, *Indian Wars in North Carolina*, 19–20.

4. See Cristophe De Graffenreid's account in CRNC, 1:933–35; also see Dill, "Eighteenth-Century New Bern," 309–10; Lee, *Indian Wars in North Carolina*, 25–26; and Chapman Milling, *Red Carolinians*, 114–16.

5. Ward, *Unite or Die*, 256; Crane, *Southern Frontier*, 158.

6. Spotswood to the Board of Trade, October 15, 1711, in *Official Letters*, 1:117.

7. Byrd, *Secret Diary*, 417–18.

8. Spotswood to the Board of Trade, November 1711, in Brock, *Official Letters*, 1:135; JHBV, December 19, 1711, 355.

9. Byrd, *Secret Diary*, 518; Dodson, *Alexander Spotswood*, 32; Crane, *Southern Frontier*, 158; Spotswood to the Earl of Dartmouth, February 11, 1712/1713, in *Official Letters*, 2:7; Spotswood to Secretary of State Nottingham, February 8, 1711/1712, in *Official Letters*, 1:146.

10. For Gale's account of his mission to Charles Town, see CRNC, 1:827–28. Also see Lee, *Indian Wars in North Carolina*, 27; and Parramore, "With Tuscarora Jack," 115–17.

11. John Page to John Harleston, December 1, 1708, in letter book compiled by Catharine O. Barnwell, South Carolina Historical Society, Charleston.

12. Cole, "Organization and Administration," 46.

13. John Barnwell, "Journal," 394.

14. John Barnwell, "Journal," 398.

15. John Barnwell, quoted in Parramore, "With Tuscarora Jack," 131.

16. John Barnwell, "Journal," 400.

17. Parramore, "With Tuscarora Jack," 118.

18. John Barnwell, "Journal," 395.

19. Parramore, "With Tuscarora Jack," 124; Byrd, *Secret Diary*, 499.

20. John Barnwell, "Journal," 395–99.

21. John Barnwell, "Journal," 397.

22. John Barnwell, "Journal," 399.

23. Parramore, "With Tuscarora Jack," 129–32. For Barnwell's account of these engagements, see the second part of his Tuscarora journal, 44–50.

24. Parramore, "With Tuscarora Jack," 134; Lee, *Indian Wars in North Carolina*, 31; Gallay, *Indian Slave Trade*, 274–75.

25. Governor Pollock to the Lords Proprietors, September 20, 1712, in CRNC, 1:874–75; also Baron de Graffenreid's account of the Tuscarora War in CRNC, 1:956.

26. Parramore, "With Tuscarora Jack," 135; Spotswood to the Board of Trade, September 26, 1712, in *Official Letters*, 1:171.

27. Spotswood to the Board of Trade, July 26, 1712, in *Official Letters*, 1:169; also Dodson, *Alexander Spotswood*, 28–29; Governor Pollock to the Lords Proprietors, September 20, 1712, in CRNC, 1:874–75.

28. Commons House Transcript, August 6, 1712, 4:93–96; also quoted in Milling, *Red Carolinians*, 128; and Grinde, "Native American Slavery," 40.

29. Joseph Barnwell, "Second Tuscarora Expedition," 46.

30. Commons House Transcript, November 20, 1712, 4:109–10; Commons House Transcript, December 1, 1712, 4:133.

31. Lee, *Indian Wars in North Carolina*, 34; Crane, *Southern Frontier*, 160; JCIT, May 20, 1714, 57.

32. Commons House Transcript, August 6, 1712, 4:96; Nash, *Red, White, and Black*, 147; Snell, "Indian Slavery," 81.

33. Joseph Barnwell, "Second Tuscarora Expedition," 36; CRNC, 1:879; CRNC, 2:16.

34. CRNC, 1:892–93; CRNC, 2:30; Joseph Barnwell, "Second Tuscarora Expedition," 39–40; Lee, *Indian Wars in North Carolina*, 35–36; and Crane, *Southern Frontier*, 161.

35. Commons House Transcript, November 19, 1713, 4:181.

36. Wright, *Only Land They Knew*, 182; also Eliades, "Indian Policy," 111.

37. White, *Middle Ground*, 23, 26–28; Axtell, *Invasion Within*, 93.

38. Thomas Nairne to the SPG secretary, August 20, 1705, in SPG Letter Books, series A, 2:156.

39. Thomas Nairne to the SPG secretary, August 20, 1705, in SPG Letter Books, series A, 2:156; also see John Blair to the SPG secretary, 1704, in Salley, *Narratives of Early Carolina*, 218. For more on the British approach to Indian conversions, see Axtell, *Invasion Within*, 133–36.

40. Wright, *Only Land They Knew*, 190.

41. Gideon Johnston to the SPG secretary, September 20, 1708, in Klingberg, *Papers of Commissary Gideon Johnston*, 19.

42. Gideon Johnston to the SPG secretary, September 20, 1708, in Klingberg, *Papers of Commissary Gideon Johnston*, 22; also quoted in Klingberg, "Indian Frontier in South Carolina," 483–84.

43. Edward Marston to the SPG secretary, February 2, 1702/1703, in SPG Letter Books, series A, 1:60; Francis Le Jau to the SPG secretary, April 12, 1711, in Klingberg, *Carolina Chronicle of Francis Le Jau*, 89.

44. Carroll, *Historical Collections of South Carolina*, 2:539–40.

45. Samuel Thomas, "Account of the Church in South Carolina," in "Documents Concerning Rev. Samuel Thomas," 41; Wright, *Only Land They Knew*, 191.

46. S. Thomas, "Account of the Church," 44; also see Samuel Thomas to Dr. Woodward, January 29, 1702/1703, in "Letters of Rev. Samuel Thomas," 225–26.

47. Gideon Johnston to Jonathan Chamberlaine, May 28, 1712, in Klingberg, ed., *Papers of Commissary Gideon Johnston*, 109.

48. Sirmans, *Colonial South Carolina*, 100.

49. Spotswood to the bishop of London, November 11, 1711, in *Official Letters*,

1:126–27; Bienville to Pontchartrain, February 25, 1708, in MPAFD, 3:120; also Bienville to Pontchartrain, February 20, 1707, in MPAFD, 3:40.

50. Pennington, "Reverend Francis Le Jau's Work," 1–17; Wright, *Only Land They Knew*, 190; Klingberg, *Carolina Chronicle of Francis Le Jau*, 1–12.

51. Reverend Haig to the SPG secretary, read July 15, 1715, in SPG Letter Books, series A, 10:82.

52. Le Jau to the SPG secretary, April 22, 1708, in Klingberg, *Carolina Chronicle of Francis Le Jau*, 39; Le Jau to the SPG secretary, March 13, 1707/1708, in ibid., 37; Le Jau to the SPG secretary, March 22, 1708/1709, in ibid., 54.

53. Le Jau to the SPG secretary, October 20, 1709, in Klingberg, *Carolina Chronicle of Francis Le Jau*, 61.

54. See S. Thomas, "Account of the Church," 43–44; Wright, *Only Land They Knew*, 191; Le Jau to the SPG secretary, August 30, 1712, in Klingberg, *Carolina Chronicle of Francis Le Jau*, 121; also Le Jau to the SPG secretary, February 9, 1710/1711, in ibid., 87.

55. Crane, *Southern Frontier*, 152; Friedlander, "Indian Slavery," 47.

56. Johnston to the SPG secretary, July 5, 1710, in Klingberg, ed., *Papers of Commissary Gideon Johnston*, 53; Reverend Haig to the SPG secretary, undated, in SPG Letter Books, series B, 10:83; also see Klingberg, "Indian Frontier in South Carolina," 484–85.

57. Le Jau to the bishop of London, May 27, 1712, in Klingberg, *Carolina Chronicle of Francis Le Jau*, 116; also Le Jau to the SPG secretary, September 15, 1708, in ibid., 41; Le Jau to the SPG secretary, October 20, 1709, in ibid., 61.

58. Edward Marston to the SPG secretary, February 2, 1702/1703, in SPG Letter Books, series A, 1:60; Oldmixon, "History of the British Empire," 372.

59. Johnston to the SPG secretary, January 27, 1710/1711, in Klingberg, *Papers of Commissary Gideon Johnston*, 129.

60. Klingberg, "Mystery of the Lost Yamasee Prince," 18–32.

61. Crane, *Southern Frontier*, 110.

62. Clowse, *Economic Beginnings*, 163–65; Stumpf, "Merchants of Colonial Charles Town," 42–43; Le Fave, "Time of the Whitetail," 11; Crane, *Southern Frontier*, 120–21.

63. Barker, " 'Much Blood and Treasure,' " 92; Braund, *Deerskins and Duffels*, 81–82.

64. P. Brown, "Early Indian Trade," 127; Clowse, *Economic Beginnings*, 165.

65. Crane, *Southern Frontier*, 125.

66. Crane, *Southern Frontier*, 124; L. R. Smith, "South Carolina's Indian Trade Regulations," 29.

67. Merrell, " 'Customes of Our Countrey,' " 125; Rayson, " 'Great Matter to Tell,' " 156.

68. J. Lawson, *New Voyage*, 35–36; Barker, " 'Much Blood and Treasure,'" 150.

69. Moore, *Nairne's Muskhogean Journals*, 60–61.

70. Stumpf, "Merchants of Colonial Charles Town," 101; Corkran, *Carolina Indian Frontier*, 22–23.

71. Corkran, "Alexander Long's 'A Small Postscript,' " 30; Moore, *Nairne's Muskhogean Journals*, 48.

72. For more on the repercussions of traders' actions with Indian women, see Ramsey, " 'Something Cloudy in Their Looks,' " 50–51; Perdue, *Cherokee Women*, 63–80; Braund, "Guardians of Tradition," 239–53; and Martin, *Sacred Revolt*, 76–79.

73. Merrell, " 'Our Bond of Peace,' " 198–202; Merrell, *Indians' New World*, 86–87.

74. JCIT, October 25, 1712, 37–38.

75. Commons House Transcript, December 1, 1712, 4:133.

76. JCIT, May 4–7, 1714, 53–57; Rayson, " 'Great Matter to Tell,' " 248–49; Reid, *Better Kind of Hatchet*, 44.

77. Commons House Transcript, May 15, 1712, 4:29; also JCIT, May 14, 1712, 24.

78. JCIT, May 5–7, 1714, 55–57.

79. Crane, *Southern Frontier*, 150.

80. JCIT, June 28, 1712, 29.

81. JCIT, December 8, 1712, 40.

82. JCIT, October 28, 1710, 5.

83. JCIT, July 27, 1711, 11; P. Brown, "Early Indian Trade," 121.

84. JCIT, July 27, 1711, 11.

85. JCIT, July 9, 1712, 33–34.

86. JCIT, August 3, 1711, 15–16.

87. Friedlander, "Indian Slavery," 42.

88. JCIT, July 9, 1712, 31.

89. JCIT, September 13, 1711, 18; JCIT, July 17, 1713, 47.

90. JCIT, March 9, 1710/1711, 6; Reid, *Better Kind of Hatchet*, 49; L. R. Smith, "South Carolina's Indian Trade Regulations," 30–31.

91. Reid, *Better Kind of Hatchet*, 44.

92. JCIT, September 10, 1710, 4; JCIT, March 24, 1712/1713, 41; JCHASC, December 11, 1706, 23.

93. JCIT, March 24, 1712/1713, 42; JCIT, August 31, 1714, 59.

94. Crane, *Southern Frontier*, 50; Sirmans, *Colonial South Carolina*, 104.

95. JCIT, July 10, 1712, 36; JCIT, April 10, 1712, 22.

96. JCIT, November 19, 1714, 62.

97. P. Brown, "Early Indian Trade," 126; Barker, " 'Much Blood and Treasure,' " 110; Rayson, " 'Great Matter to Tell,' " 276.

98. JCIT, August 19, 1713, 50.

99. Commons House Transcript, December 17, 1714, 4:334.

100. Commons House Transcript, December 17, 1714, 4:272.

101. Ramsey, " 'Something Cloudy in Their Looks,' " 57–65.

102. Eliades, "Indian Policy," 103–4.

103. Greene, *Selling a New World*, 8.

104. William Ramsey, " 'All & Singular the Slaves,' " 168–69; also Menard, "Africanization of the Low Country Labor Force," 90; Gallay, *Indian Slave Trade*, 288–314.

105. Norris, "Profitable Advice for Rich and Poor," 106.

106. Wood, "Changing Population," 38.

107. Cooper and McCord, *Statutes*, 2:153; Donnan, "Slave Trade in South Carolina," 804.

108. Duncan, "Servitude and Slavery," 164–65.

109. Cooper and McCord, *Statutes*, 7:33, 347–49; Quarles, "Colonial Militia and Negro Manpower," 648–49.

110. Jabbs, "South Carolina Colonial Militia," 218, 256.

111. Wood, *Black Majority*, 263.

112. Wood, *Black Majority*, 59–62, 95, 205.

113. Le Jau to the SPG secretary, March 22, 1708/1709, in Klingberg, *Carolina Chronicle of Francis Le Jau*, 55.

114. Le Jau to the SPG secretary, February 20, 1711/1712, in Klingberg, *Carolina Chronicle of Francis Le Jau*, 108.

115. Duncan, "Servitude and Slavery," 759.

116. For an informed discussion of racism in early Anglo-America, see Winthrop Jordan, *White over Black*, 1–63. In the early colonial period, colonists tended to have better opinions of the Indians and generally regarded them as racially superior to people of African ancestry; Byrd, *Histories of the Dividing Line*, 3; Vaughan, "From White Man to Redskin," 917–53.

117. Nairne, quoted in Klingberg, *Appraisal of the Negro*, 9; also see Samuel Thomas's accusation of Nairne in Thomas's "Remonstrance," in "Documents Concerning Rev. Samuel Thomas," 47.

118. Johnston to the SPG secretary, undated, in SPG Letter Books, series A, 11:477; also in Klingberg, *Appraisal of the Negro*, 6–7; and Duncan, "Servitude and Slavery," 303. Also see William Treadwell Bull to the SPG secretary, January 20, 1714/1715, in SPG Letter Books, series A, 10:90–91; Wood, *Black Majority*, 133–42.

119. Le Jau to the SPG secretary, April 15, 1707, in Klingberg, *Carolina Chronicle of Francis Le Jau*, 24.

120. Le Jau to the SPG secretary, February 1, 1709/1710, in Klingberg, *Carolina Chronicle of Francis Le Jau*, 70.

121. Aptheker, *American Negro Slave Revolts*, 168.

122. Le Jau to the SPG secretary, January 22, 1713/1714, in Klingberg, *Carolina Chronicle of Francis Le Jau*, 137; Aptheker, *American Negro Slave Revolts*, 174.

123. Commons House Transcript, June 20, 1711, 3:565; Commons House Transcript, October 10, 1711, 3:579; also see Duncan, "Servitude and Slavery," 589.

124. Aptheker, "Maroons Within the Present Limits," 168–69; Duncan, "Servitude and Slavery," 762.

125. Eliades, "Indian Policy," 40–41.

126. Hoadly, *Public Records*, 5:516.

127. Ramsey, " 'All & Singular the Slaves,' " 178; Friedlander, "Indian Slavery," 61–62.

128. Nash, "Image of the Indian," 219–22; Ferling, *Wilderness of Miseries*, 32–34; Lepore, *Name of War*, 48–68.

129. Menard, "Africanization of the Low Country Labor Force," 100.

130. Le Jau to the SPG secretary, January 4, 1711/1712, in Klingberg, *Carolina Chronicle of Francis Le Jau*, 104; Le Jau to the SPG secretary, January 22, 1713/1714, in Klingberg, *Carolina Chronicle of Francis Le Jau*, 137; Johnston to the SPG secretary, November 6, 1711, in Klingberg, *Papers of Commissary Gideon Johnston*, 99; Johnston to the SPG secretary, 1714, in Klingberg, *Papers of Commissary Gideon Johnston*, 144.

131. JCIT, July 9, 1712, 32.

4. Conspiracy Theories

1. For a transcript of the census, see Governor Robert Johnson to the Board of Trade, January 12, 1719/1720, in SC Records, 7:233–50; also in Merrens, *Colonial South Carolina Scene*, 60–61.

2. Governor Córcoles y Martínez to King Philip V, July 5, 1715, Indies Archives, 843 (microfilm).

3. Le Jau to the SPG secretary, May 10, 1715, in Klingberg, *Carolina Chronicle of Francis Le Jau*, 152. Also see Governor Charles Craven to Secretary of State Lord Townshend, May 23, 1715, in CRNC, 2:177; William T. Bull to the SPG secretary, August 10, 1715, in SPG Letter Books, series B, 1:49.

4. Swanton, *Early History*, 101; Crane, *Southern Frontier*, 162; Durschlag, "First Creek Resistance," 419; also Rayson, " 'Great Matter to Tell,'" 319.

5. Green, "Search for Altamaha," 73.

6. JCTP, July 15–16, 1715, 3:54–57; Byrd, *Histories of the Dividing Line*, 303–4; South Carolina merchants to the Board of Trade, July 18, 1715, in CRNC, 2:197.

7. Crane, *Southern Frontier*, 162; Swanton, *Early History*, 97; Milling, *Red Carolinians*, 135–45; Sirmans, *Colonial South Carolina*, 100; Haan, " 'Trade Do's Not Flourish as Formerly,' " 342–43, 351.

8. Merrell, " 'Our Bond of Peace,' " 207–8.

9. See Le Jau to the SPG secretary, August 10, 1713, in Klingberg, *Carolina Chronicle of Francis Le Jau*, 134; also Governor Nathaniel Johnson to the Board of Trade, September

17, 1708, in Merrens, *Colonial South Carolina Scene*, 34; Governor Robert Johnson to the Board of Trade, January 12, 1719/1720, in Merrens, *Colonial South Carolina Scene*, 60–61.

10. Rowland, Moore, and Rogers, *History of Beaufort County*, 81–84; McKivergan, "Migration and Settlement," 117; Crane, *Southern Frontier*, 164–65.

11. JCIT, May 14, 1711, 9; JCIT, June 28, 1711, 11; JCIT, August 3, 1711, 14–15; JCIT, June 12, 1712, 27–28.

12. McKivergan, "Migration and Settlement," 6; Eliades, "Indian Policy," 113.

13. Córcoles y Martínez to King Philip V, July 5, 1715, Indies Archives, 843 (microfilm).

14. Haan, " 'Trade Do's Not Flourish as Formerly,' " 347–49; Silver, *New Face on the Countryside*, 88–93; Otto, "Origins of Cattle-Ranching," 123; Otto, *Southern Frontiers*, 37–38.

15. JCIT, April 17, 1712, 23; Haan, " 'Trade Do's Not Flourish as Formerly,' " 344.

16. Menard, "Africanization of the Low Country Labor Force," 100.

17. Córcoles y Martínez to the king, July 5, 1715, Indies Archives, 843 (microfilm); Landers, "Black-Indian Interaction," 150; Haan, " 'Trade Do's Not Flourish as Formerly,' " 343.

18. Córcoles y Martínez to the king, July 5, 1715, Indies Archives, 843 (microfilm).

19. JCIT, March 24, 1712/1713, 42; Milling, *Red Carolinians*, 139n. For more on Wright's deficiencies, see Gallay, *Indian Slave Trade*, 245.

20. JCIT, June 20, 1712, 27.

21. Córcoles y Martínez to the king, July 5, 1715, Indies Archives, 843 (microfilm); Ivers, "Scouting the Inland Passage," 125.

22. Quoted in Swanton, *Early History*, 100.

23. London merchants and Carolina planters to the Board of Trade, July 18, 1715, in CSP, 28:524.

24. Commons House Transcript, November 27, 1712, 4:130–31.

25. See Rayson, " 'Great Matter to Tell,' " 55; Worth, *Timucuan Chiefdoms*, 90–110.

26. Córcoles y Martínez to the king, July 5, 1715, Indies Archives, 843 (microfilm).

27. See Swanton, *Early History*, 11; Barker, " 'Much Blood and Treasure,' " 26; Weir, *Colonial South Carolina*, 12–13, 28–29; Hann, "Late Seventeenth-Century Forebears," 67, 76; Hann, "St. Augustine's Fallout," 188–89.

28. JCIT, March 25, 1712/1713, 42; Swanton, *Early History*, 167–69.

29. JCIT, July 10, 1712, 35; also Milling, *Red Carolinians*, 177.

30. Swanton, *Indians of the Southeastern United States*, 92; Hann, *Apalachee*, 399–400.

31. JCHASC, December 11, 1706, 21–23; JCIT, September 21, 1710, 3–4; Hann, *Apalachee*, 297–300; Covington, "Apalachee Indians," 378.

32. Nathaniel Johnson to the Board of Trade, September 17, 1708, in Merrens, *Colonial South Carolina Scene*, 35; D. L. Johnson, "Yamasee War," 58.

33. Governor Johnson to the Board of Trade, September 17, 1708, in Merrens,

Colonial South Carolina Scene, 35; Hann, *Apalachee*, 397–400; Covington, "Apalachee Indians," 376; Swanton, *Early History*, 177.

34. Hann, "Late Seventeenth-Century Forebears," 72–73.

35. Hahn, "Invention of the Creek Nation," 211–13; Durschlag, "First Creek Resistance," 88.

36. Durschlag, "First Creek Resistance," 277–82.

37. Patrick MacKay to Governor Oglethorpe, March 29, 1735, in Juricek, *Georgia Treaties*, 50.

38. Moore, *Nairne's Muskhogean Journals*, 34–35.

39. Hahn, "Mother of Necessity," 82.

40. JCIT, June 12, 1712, 26.

41. JCIT, April 12, 1715, 65.

42. Córcoles y Martínez to the king, July 5, 1715, Indies Archives, 843 (microfilm); Hahn, "Invention of the Creek Nation," 240–41.

43. Rowland, Moore, and Sanders, *History of Beaufort County*, 95; Weir, *Colonial South Carolina*, 28–29; Rayson, " 'Great Matter to Tell,' " 55; Leach, *Arms for Empire*, 169; D. L. Johnson, "Yamasee War," 86; Swanton, *Early History*, 226; Crane, *Southern Frontier*, 169; Corkran, *Creek Frontier*, 58; Durschlag, "First Creek Resistance," 7–8.

44. Kirk, *Yamasee War of 1715*, 7; Hewatt, *Historical Account*, 1:214.

45. JCIT, April 12, 1715, 65; Commons House Transcript, August 13, 1715, 4:434.

46. Córcoles y Martínez to King Philip V, July 5, 1715, Indies Archives, 843 (microfilm); Hahn, "Invention of the Creek Nation," 239–43.

47. Rodd to "a Gentleman in London" (hereafter cited as Rodd's "Relation"), May 8, 1715, in SC Records, 6:75. The original version of Rodd's "Relation" is written in French; an English translation can be found in CSP, 28:166–69. For the Yamasees' account, see Córcoles y Martínez to the king, July 5, 1715, Indies Archives, 843 (microfilm).

48. Rodd, "Relation," 75.

49. Francis Le Jau to the SPG secretary, May 14, 1715, in Klingberg, *Carolina Chronicle of Francis Le Jau*, 156.

50. Green, "Search for Altamaha," 33.

51. Córcoles y Martínez to the king, July 5, 1715, Indies Archives, 843 (microfilm); Hahn, "Invention of the Creek Nation," 239–43.

52. Rodd, "Relation," 75–77.

53. Rodd, "Relation," 78.

54. Córcoles y Martínez to the king, July 5, 1715, Indies Archives, 843 (microfilm).

55. Rodd, "Relation," 75–78; Milling, *Red Carolinians*, 141–42.

56. Cheeves, "Journal of the March," 337; Le Jau to the SPG secretary, May 14, 1715, in Klingberg, *Carolina Chronicle of Francis Le Jau*, 155; Crane, *Southern Frontier*, 169; D. L. Johnson, "Yamasee War," 86; Nash, *Red, White, and Black*, 150.

57. Córcoles y Martínez to the king, July 5, 1715, Indies Archives, 843 (microfilm); Rodd, "Relation," 80.

58. *Boston News-Letter*, June 13, 1715; reprinted in Carroll, *Historical Collections of South Carolina*, 2:572.

59. Bartram, "Travels Through North and South Carolina," 91n.

60. Fitch, "Journals," 189–90.

61. Salinas Varona to Governor Ayala, July 24, 1717, in Boyd, "Documents Describing the Second and Third Expeditions," 127.

62. Alexander Spotswood to Secretary of State Stanhope, July 15, 1715, in Brock, *Official Letters*, 2:122.

63. London merchants and Carolina planters to the Board of Trade, July 18, 1715, in CSP, 28:523. For similar comments, see Governor Craven to Secretary of State Townshend, May 23, 1715, in CRNC, 2:178; Rodd, "Relation," 81; Le Jau to the SPG secretary, August 23, 1715, in Klingberg, *Carolina Chronicle of Francis Le Jau*, 165–66.

64. Crane, *Southern Frontier*, 99–103.

65. Bienville's 1725 "Memoir," in MPAFD, 3:490–92; Pénicaut, *Fleur de Lis and Calumet*, 162–63; Corkran, *Creek Frontier*, 56–57; Giraud, *History of Louisiana*, 327–29.

66. Pénicaut, *Fleur de Lis and Calumet*, 163.

67. Crane, *Southern Frontier*, 106–7; Moore, *Nairne's Muskhogean Journals*, 20; Durschlag, "First Creek Resistance," 340–41; Reynolds, "Alabama-Tombigbee Basin," 91.

68. Bienville to Pontchartrain, June 15, 1715, in MPAFD, 3:166–69.

69. Bienville to Pontchartrain, September 1, 1715, in MPAFD, 3:188.

70. Varona to the viceroy, July 16, 1713, in Mary Letitia Ross Papers (microfilm), section 4–3B, folder 110, no. 1, Georgia Department of Archives and History, Atlanta; also La Mothe de Cadillac to Pontchartrain, October 26, 1713, in MPAFD, 2:173.

71. Varona to Governor Ayala, July 24, 1717, in Boyd, "Documents Describing the Second and Third Expeditions," 127.

72. Córcoles y Martínez to Spotswood, May 30, 1715, in CSP, 29:545.

73. Hewatt, *Historical Account*, 214; Rivers, *Sketch of the History*, 260–61; Carroll, *Historical Collections of South Carolina*, 1:198–99; Simms, *Yemassee*.

74. Córcoles y Martínez to the king, February 22, 1715, Indies Archives, 843 (microfilm).

75. Wraxall, *Abridgement of Indian Affairs*, 107–8; Willis, "Colonial Conflict," 42.

76. Jonathan Urmstone to the SPG secretary, April 13, 1715, in CRNC, 2:176.

77. Commons House Transcript, May 7, 1715, 4:393.

78. Crane, *Southern Frontier*, 170.

79. Reid, *Better Kind of Hatchet*, 55.

80. Crane, *Southern Frontier*, 162.

81. Perdue, *Slavery and the Evolution of Cherokee Society*, 38–39.

82. Merrell, " 'Our Bond of Peace,' " 208; also see his *Indians' New World*, 68.

83. JCIT, August 3, 1711, 14; also D. Brown, *Catawba Indians*, 136.

84. Byrd, *Histories of the Dividing Line*, 303–4; David Crawley to William Byrd II, July 30, 1715, in SC Records, 6:110–11; also in Milling, *Red Carolinians*, 138–39.

85. Willis, "Colonial Conflict," 42; Cheeves, "Journal of the March," 335.

86. Merrell, *Indians' New World*, 54.

87. Wraxall, *Abridgement of Indian Affairs*, 107–9.

88. Spotswood to the Board of Trade, October 15, 1711, in *Official Letters*, 1:118; also see Dodson, *Alexander Spotswood*, 82.

89. Merrell, " 'Our Bond of Peace,' " 208; Merrell, *Indians' New World*, 69–71.

90. Merrell, " 'Our Bond of Peace,' " 209.

91. Cheeves, "Journal of the March," 334–35.

92. Cheeves, "Journal of the March," 331–37; Merrell, *Indians' New World*, 72; Milling, *Red Carolinians*, 235.

93. Cheeves, "Journal of the March," 330; Swanton, *Early History*, 184–91; Crane, *Southern Frontier*, 15; and Milling, *Red Carolinians*, 104.

94. Spotswood to the Board of Trade, June 4, 1715, in *Official Letters*, 2:114; William Treadwell Bull to the SPG secretary, August 16, 1715, in SPG Letter Books, series A, 11:61.

95. Merrell, *Indians' New World*, 74–75.

96. Rodd, "Relation," 81.

97. Hatley, *Dividing Paths*, 24.

98. Alexander Spotswood to Robert Hunter, March 2, 1715/1716, in Robinson, *Virginia Treaties*, 229.

99. EJCCV, October 18, 1715, 412; Cheeves, "Journal of the March," 330.

100. Spotswood to Hunter, March 2, 1715/1716, in Robinson, *Virginia Treaties*, 230.

101. Spotswood to the Board of Trade, February 16, 1715/1716, in *Official Letters*, 2:141; D. Brown, *Catawbas*, 107; Merrell, *Indians' New World*, 50, 69–71, 74–75.

102. Spotswood to the Board of Trade, August 9, 1715, in *Official Letters*, 2:127.

103. EJCCV, February 22, 1715/1716, 421–22; also Robinson, *Virginia Treaties*, 237.

104. William Treadwell Bull to the SPG secretary, August 16, 1715, in SPG Letter Books, series A, 11:58; Le Jau to the SPG secretary, August 22, 1715, in Klingberg, *Carolina Chronicle of Francis Le Jau*, 159; D. L. Johnson, "Yamasee War," 96.

105. Le Jau to the SPG secretary, August 16, 1715, in Klingberg, *Carolina Chronicle of Francis Le Jau*, 158–63; Crane, *Southern Frontier*, 172; Milling, *Red Carolinians*, 144; D. L. Johnson, "Yamasee War," 96–97; and Carroll, *Historical Collections of South Carolina*, 1:196–97.

106. Samuel Eveleigh to John Boone and Richard Berresford, July 19, 1715, in SC Records, 6:103–4.

107. Le Jau to the SPG secretary, August 22, 1715, in Klingberg, *Carolina Chronicle of*

Francis Le Jau, 162–63; also Crane, *Southern Frontier*, 172; D. L. Johnson, "Yamasee War," 97.

108. Merrell, *Indians' New World*, 75–77.

109. EJCCV, July 18, 1715, 406.

110. Le Jau to the SPG secretary, May 14, 1715, in Klingberg, *Carolina Chronicle of Francis Le Jau*, 156; William Guy to the SPG secretary, September 20, 1715, in SPG Letter Books, series A, 11:68.

111. Bull to the SPG secretary, August 16, 1715, in SPG Letter Books, series A, 11:58; Le Jau to the SPG secretary, October 3, 1715, in Klingberg, *Carolina Chronicle of Francis Le Jau*, 167; Eveleigh to Boone and Berresford, July 19, 1715, in SC Records, 6:107; Bull to the SPG secretary, October 31, 1715, in SPG Letter Books, series A, 11:95.

5. Crisis and Change

1. Rodd, "Relation," May 8,1715; CSP, 28:166–69.

2. Commons House Transcript, May 6, 1715, 4:389.

3. Gideon Johnston to the SPG secretary, October 13, 1715, in Klingberg, *Papers of Commissary Gideon Johnston*, 147; Nicholas Trott to the bishop of London, June 17, 1715, Fulham Papers in the Lambeth Palace Library, Colonial Section, section A, 9:48 (microfilm).

4. Francis Le Jau to the SPG secretary, May 21, 1715, in Klingberg, *Carolina Chronicle of Francis Le Jau*, 158; also see William Hassell to the SPG secretary, May 1715, in SPG Letter Books, series B, 10:97; Le Jau to the SPG secretary, May 10, 1715, in Klingberg, *Carolina Chronicle of Francis Le Jau*, 151; Rodd, "Relation," 84.

5. Le Jau to the SPG secretary, May 10, 1715, in Klingberg, *Carolina Chronicle of Francis Le Jau*, 153; Commons House Transcript, May 7–8, 1715, 4:392–402.

6. Malone, *Skulking Way of War*, 107–17; Leach, *Flintlock and Tomahawk*, 50–72; Mahon, "Anglo-American Methods," 259–64; Ferling, *Wilderness of Miseries*, 40–43.

7. Cole, "Brief Outline," 19.

8. Crane, *Southern Frontier*, 170.

9. D. L. Johnson, "Yamasee War," 90–94; Crane, *Southern Frontier*, 171; Rodd, "Relation," 79–80; Le Jau to the SPG secretary, May 14, 1715, in Klingberg, *Carolina Chronicle of Francis Le Jau*, 155; *Boston News-Letter*, June 13, 1715, reprinted in Carroll, *Historical Collections of South Carolina*, 2:571–73; Charles Craven to Secretary of State Townshend, May 23, 1715, in CRNC, 2:178.

10. The governor of North Carolina even singled out MacKay for his skillful command of a Yamasee contingent in Bath County; see William Pollock to Charles Craven, May 25, 1713, in CRNC, 2:45.

11. D. L. Johnson, "Yamasee War," 95–97; Crane, *Southern Frontier*, 171; Milling, *Red Carolinians*, 143–44; *Boston News-Letter*, June 13, 1715, in Carroll, *Historical Collections of South Carolina*, 2:572–73.

12. Rowland, Moore, and Rogers, *History of Beaufort County*, 98; Ivers, "Scouting the Inland Passage," 117; Milling, *Red Carolinians*, 147–48; Samuel Eveleigh to the Lords Proprietors, October 7, 1715, in sc Records, 6:118–19.

13. William Guy to the SPG secretary, September 20, 1715, in SPG Letter Books, series B, 11:69; William Bull to the SPG secretary, October 7, 1715, in Pennington, "South Carolina Indian War," 260.

14. Cole, "Organization and Administration," 48. For the names and locations of these early frontier garrisons, see Ivers, *Colonial Forts of South Carolina*, 6–9.

15. Commons House Transcript, May 8, 1715, 4:399.

16. Commons House Transcript, May 7–10, 1715, 4:397–406; JCTP, July 28, 1715, 64–65.

17. Moore, "Carolina Whigs," 168; Commons House Transcript, May 8, 1715, 4:400.

18. See Cooper and McCord, *Statutes*, 2:624–26; also Commons House Transcript, May 13, 1715, 4:413.

19. Commons House Transcript, May 7, 1715, 4:392; Quarles, "Colonial Militia and Negro Manpower," 652.

20. William Hassell to the SPG secretary, December 1, 1715, in Waddell, *Indians of the South Carolina Lowcountry*, 209; Cole, "Organization and Administration," 48–49; Crane, *Southern Frontier*, 178; Milling, *Red Carolinians*, 145–46; D. L. Johnson, "Yamasee War," 100. See Commons House Transcript, August 9, 1715, 4:424–25.

21. Jonathan Dale to the Prince of Wales, September 10, 1715, in sc Records, 6:126; Nicholas Trott to the bishop of London, June 17, 1715, Fulham Papers of the Lambeth Palace Library, Colonial Section, section A, 9:47–48 (microfilm); Crane, *Southern Frontier*, 178.

22. William Bull to the SPG secretary, August 1715, in SPG Letter Books, series B, 10:112; D. L. Johnson, "Yamasee War," 102; Crane, *Southern Frontier*, 173.

23. Ivers, "Scouting the Inland Passage," 124–25; Rowland, Moore, and Rogers, *History of Beaufort County*, 97–98.

24. Ivers, *Colonial Forts of South Carolina*, 33–36.

25. See Le Jau to the SPG secretary, October 3, 1715, in Klingberg, *Carolina Chronicle of Francis Le Jau*, 167; also Samuel Eveleigh to the Lords Proprietors, October 7, 1715, in sc Records, 6:119.

26. Cooper and McCord, *Statutes*, 2:634–41; Ivers, *Colonial Forts of South Carolina*, 11.

27. Cooper and McCord, *Statutes*, 3:23–24.

28. Jabbs, "South Carolina Colonial Militia," 309–10; Duncan, "Servitude and Slavery," 161–62; Weir, *Colonial South Carolina*, 207; Barker, " 'Much Blood and Treasure,' " 261. For lists of the transported Scottish prisoners, whose ranks included a number of future Indian traders and frontier policymakers, see CSP, 29:166–67.

29. See Ivers, *Colonial Forts of South Carolina*, 6–9, especially his map on p. 8.

30. Cooper and McCord, *Statutes*, 2:636–37, 3:24; Vaughan and Rosen, *Carolina and Georgia Laws*, 193–96, 205–6.

31. Ivers, "Scouting the Inland Passage," 125; D. L. Johnson, "Yamasee War," 104; Crane, *Southern Frontier*, 187–90; Milling, *Red Carolinians*, 152; Sirmans, *Colonial South Carolina*, 114.

32. Montgomery, *Azilia*, 19; Ivers, *Colonial Forts of South Carolina*, 27–29.

33. Crane, *Southern Frontier*, 191, 229–34; Crane, "Projects for Colonization," 30–31.

34. Jonathan Dale to the Prince of Wales, September 10, 1715, in SC Records, 6:127.

35. Jabbs, "South Carolina Colonial Militia," 320; Sirmans, *Colonial South Carolina*, 115. For a table of the annual expenses incurred by the South Carolina government between 1701 and 1716, see SC Records, 6:270–71.

36. Cooper and McCord, *Statutes*, 3:30; Stumpf, "Merchants of Colonial Charles Town," 114–18; Francis Le Jau to Jonathan Chamberlain, September 22, 1715, in Klingberg, *Carolina Chronicle of Francis Le Jau*, 162; William Bull to the SPG secretary, May 16, 1716, in SPG Letter Books, series A, 11:150.

37. Richard Berresford to the Board of Trade, June 23, 1716, in CSP 29:230; D. L. Johnson, "Yamasee War," 120.

38. Clowse, *Economic Beginnings*, 186, 207; Crane, *Southern Frontier*, 184; Merrens, *Colonial South Carolina Scene*, 69; Weir, *Colonial South Carolina*, 85, 150.

39. Richard Berresford to the Board of Trade, June 26, 1716, in CRNC, 2:233.

40. Barker, " 'Much Blood and Treasure,' " 228.

41. Clowse, *Economic Beginnings*, 257–58.

42. JCIT, August 7, 1716, 96; JCIT, November 23, 1716, 129.

43. For a complete transcript of the act, see Vaughan and Rosen, *Carolina and Georgia Laws*, 193–96.

44. Crane, *Southern Frontier*, 193.

45. Vaughan and Rosen, *Carolina and Georgia Laws*, 195–96.

46. Crane, *Southern Frontier*, 187, 194; Reid, *Better Kind of Hatchet*, 92.

47. JCIT, ix, 325; Crane, *Southern Frontier*, 193.

48. JCIT, July 24, 1716, 86.

49. Vassar, "Some Short Remarkes," 405.

50. JCIT, 327.

51. P. Brown, "Early Indian Trade," 123; Clowse, *Economic Beginnings*, 257–58.

52. Resolution of the South Carolina Commons House, May 6, 1720, in SC Records, 7:309; L. R. Smith, "South Carolina's Indian Trade Regulations," 41; Corkran, *Carolina Indian Frontier*, 23; Crane, *Southern Frontier*, 196–97.

53. JCIT, July 23, 1716, 86.

54. Commons House Transcript, November 27, 1716, 5:183; January 25, 1716/1717, 5:230. Also see Claudius Phillipe de Richebourg to the SPG secretary, February 12,

1715/1716, in SPG Letter Books, series A, 11:141; Snell, "Indian Slavery," 92; Crane, *Southern Frontier*, 172.

55. JCIT, November 23, 1716, 129–30; Ramsey, " 'All & Singular the Slaves,' " 178.

56. Ramsey, " 'All & Singular the Slaves,' " 179–80; Rayson, " 'Great Matter to Tell,' " 317; P. Brown, "Early Indian Trade," 124; Braund, "Creek Indians, Blacks, and Slavery," 606; Grinde, "Native American Slavery," 41.

57. Barker, " 'Much Blood and Treasure,' " 206.

58. JCIT, August 9, 1716, 101.

59. John Boone and Richard Berresford to the Board of Trade, December 5, 1716, in SC Records, 6:265.

60. Commons House Transcript, January 23, 1716/1717, 5:227; Reid, *Better Kind of Hatchet*, 89.

61. Vassar, "Some Short Remarkes," 405.

62. JCIT, November 7, 1716, 123; JCIT, November 16, 1716, 125.

63. JCIT, January 28, 1717/1718, 252; JCIT, March 21, 1717/1718, 262; JCIT, October 1, 1716, 114; JCIT, November 16, 1716, 128; JCIT, December 15, 1716, 140.

64. JCIT, August 9, 1716, 102; JCIT, September 10, 1717, 205.

65. JCIT, October 18, 1716, 119; JCIT, November 26, 1716, 132.

66. Cooper and McCord, *Statutes*, 2:691–94; Vaughan and Rosen, *Carolina and Georgia Laws*, 197–99.

67. JCIT, January 16, 1716/1717, 147–48.

68. JCIT, ix; L. R. Smith, "South Carolina's Indian Trade Regulations," 41.

69. Crane, *Southern Frontier*, 198; Stumpf, "Merchants of Colonial Charles Town," 102–5; Sirmans, *Colonial South Carolina*, 116; Eliades, "Indian Policy," 120.

70. See Samuel Godin to the Board of Trade, December 17, 1717, in SC Records, 7:71–72.

71. Vassar, "Some Short Remarkes," 421; Reid, *Better Kind of Hatchet*, 122–24.

72. Crane, *Southern Frontier*, 198–99.

73. Commons House Transcript, May 7, 1715, 4:392–93, 402.

74. Caleb Heathcoate to Lord Townshend, July 12, 1715, in CRNC, 2:190–91; Leach, *Arms for Empire*, 173; Ward, *Unite or Die*, 168.

75. Alexander Spotswood to the Earl of Dartmouth, February 11, 1712/1713, in *Official Letters*, 2:7.

76. Mather quoted in Crane, *Southern Frontier*, 206; William Andrews to the SPG secretary, July 12, 1715, in SPG Letter Books, series A, 10:187.

77. JCTP, July 15, 1715, 54.

78. Urmstone to the SPG secretary, June 12, 1715, in CRNC, 2:186.

79. Dodson, *Alexander Spotswood*, 36; also see JHBV, September 7, 1715, 170; Spotswood to the Board of Trade, August 9, 1715, in *Official Letters*, 2:128.

80. Hunter to the Board of Trade, September 29, 1715, in CSP, 28:629.

81. Urmstone to the SPG secretary, June 21, 1715, in CRNC, 2:187.

82. Dodson, *Alexander Spotswood*, 33; Crane, *Southern Frontier*, 167, 206; Caleb Heathcoate to Lord Townshend, July 12, 1715, in CRNC, 2:191; Samuel Eveleigh to John Boone and Richard Berresford, October 7, 1715, in CSP, 28:642; Spotswood to Secretary of State Stanhope, July 15, 1715, in *Official Letters*, 2:124.

83. Spotswood to Secretary of State Stanhope, May 27, 1715, in SC Records, 6:89–90.

84. Spotswood to Stanhope, July 15, 1715, in *Official Letters*, 2:122–23; EJCCV, May 26, 1715, 399; Ward, *Unite or Die*, 171.

85. Spotswood to Stanhope, July 15, 1715, in *Official Letters*, 2:124–25.

86. Spotswood to Stanhope, July 15, 1715, in *Official Letters*, 2:124; Robert Daniel and Arthur Middleton to John Boone and Richard Berresford, August 20, 1715, in SC Records, 7:134; Crane, *Southern Frontier*, 173; Pennington, "South Carolina Indian War," 268–69.

87. Jonathan Urmstone to the SPG secretary, June 21, 1715, in CRNC, 2:187; Report of North Carolina Council, September 13, 1715, in CRNC, 2:200.

88. Alexander Spotswood to Secretary of State Stanhope, July 15, 1715, in *Official Letters*, 2:125; Samuel Eveleigh to the Lords Proprietors, July 19, 1715, in SC Records, 6:105; Crane, *Southern Frontier*, 173; Lee, *Indian Wars in North Carolina*, 40–41.

89. EJCCV, July 8, 1715, 405; Spotswood to the Board of Trade, July 15, 1715, in *Official Letters*, 2:119–20; Samuel Eveleigh to the Lords Proprietors, July 19, 1715, in SC Records, 6:104; Crane, *Southern Frontier*, 173.

90. JHBV, August 4, 1715, 122–23.

91. EJCCV, June 20, 1715, 402–4; Dodson, *Alexander Spotswood*, 35; D. L. Johnson, "Yamasee War," 102–3; Crane, *Southern Frontier*, 174–75.

92. Spotswood to Stanhope, October 24, 1715, in *Official Letters*, 2:131.

93. EJCCV, May 16, 1718, 472; EJCCV, May 2, 1719, 505; also Spotswood to the Board of Trade, October 24, 1715, in *Official Letters*, 2:136; Spotswood to the Board of Trade, April 16, 1717, in *Official Letters*, 241–42; Spotswood to the Board of Trade, May 24, 1716, in *Official Letters*, 165.

94. Joseph Boone and Richard Berresford to the Board of Trade, March 15, 1715/1716, in SC Records, 6:160; Boone and Berresford to the Board of Trade, December 5, 1716, in SC Records, 6:263; Nash, *Red, White, and Black*, 210.

95. South Carolinian merchants to the Board of Trade, September 16, 1715, in CSP 28:622; Samuel Eveleigh to the Lords Proprietors, July 19, 1715, in SC Records, 6:104; Joseph Boone and John Barnwell to the Board of Trade, November 23, 1720, in CRNC, 2:396.

96. Spotswood to the Board of Trade, October 24, 1715, in *Official Letters*, 2:136; Boone and Berresford to the Board of Trade, March 15, 1715/1716, in SC Records, 6:162; Kirk, *Yamasee War of 1715*, 10.

97. Extract from a letter from South Carolina dated April 21, 1716, and included in Boone and Berresford to the Board of Trade, December 5, 1716, in CRNC, 2:253–54.

98. EJCCV, November 1, 1715, 416; EJCCV, November 7, 1715, 418.

99. Boone and Berresford to the Board of Trade, March 15, 1715/1716, in SC Records, 6:161; Spotswood to Stanhope, October 24, 1715, in *Official Letters*, 2:131–32.

100. Spotswood to the Board of Trade, July 21, 1714, in *Official Letters*, 2:70; Robinson, "Virginia and the Cherokees," 25.

101. Dodson, *Alexander Spotswood*, 84–86, 89–93.

102. South Carolina merchants to the Board of Trade, September 16, 1715, in CSP 28:622.

103. CRNC, 2:251–53; EJCCV, July 8, 1715, 405–6.

104. South Carolina Council to the Board of Trade, August 30, 1715, in CSP 29:413; Robert Daniel and Arthur Middleton to Joseph Boone and Richard Berresford, August 20, 1715, in SC Records, 6:131–32; Boone and Berresford to the Board of Trade, August 6, 1716, in SC Records, 6:241; Boone and Berresford to the Board of Trade, December 5, 1716, in SC Records, 6:255–56.

105. EJCCV, October 18, 1715, 412; Merrell, *Indians' New World*, 77–79; Merrell, " 'Our Bond of Peace,' " 210; Crane, *Southern Frontier*, 176–78.

106. See "a Comparison of the quantity of skins and furs imported from Carolina and Virginia for the three years before and after the late war," in Col. Office Records, no. 5/1,317, 36; also Robinson, "Virginia and the Cherokees," 29.

107. JCIT, September 20, 1717, 211–12; JCIT, May 22, 1718, 275–76.

108. JCIT, May 8, 1717, 272; JCIT, July 19, 1718, 306.

109. Crane, *Southern Frontier*, 158.

110. See memorandum from Board of Trade, September 15, 1720, in SC Records, 8:183; Crane, *Southern Frontier*, 203–4.

111. Rodd, "Relation," 84.

112. South Carolina Commons House to King George I, May 1715, in SC Records, 6:86–87.

113. Lonn, *Colonial Agents*, 67–70; Moore, "Royalizing South Carolina," 202; JCTP, July 28, 1715, 64–65; JCTP, July 16, 1715, 57; Board of Trade to Secretary of State Stanhope, July 19, 1715, in SC Records, 6:100.

114. Board of Trade to King William III, March 26, 1701, in CRNC, 1:537; Colonel Quarry to the Board of Trade, March 26, 1702, in CSP, 20:260.

115. Petition of the South Carolina Commons House to Queen Anne, 1709, in CSP, 24:870; South Carolina Commons House to the Lords Proprietors, February 25, 1701/1702, in SC Records, 5:35–36.

116. South Carolina Commons House to King George I, August 1715, in SC Records, 6:117.

117. SC Records, 6:137–43.

118. JCTP, July 13, 1715, 53; JCTP, July 15, 1715, 55–56.

119. Board of Trade to Stanhope, July 19, 1715, in SC Records, 6:98–99.

120. Crane, *Southern Frontier*, 207–8.

121. South Carolina Commons House's petitions to King George I, April 28, 1716, in SC Records, 6:186; June 12, 1716, in ibid., 6:167–68; November 30, 1716, in ibid., 6:256–59; spring 1717, in ibid., 7:24; March 7, 1717/1718, in ibid., 7:98–100; also Crane, "Projects for Colonization," 28.

122. Moore, "Royalizing South Carolina," 314; Sirmans, *Colonial South Carolina*, 118.

123. Lords Proprietors to South Carolina Commons House, March 3, 1715/1716, in SC Records, 6:150; Sirmans, *Colonial South Carolina*, 118, 124.

124. Yonge, "Narrative," 154; P. Brown, "Early Indian Trade," 124; Sirmans, *Colonial South Carolina*, 124–25; Crane, *Southern Frontier*, 214; Lords Proprietors to the South Carolina Commons House, July 22, 1718, in SC Records, 7:145.

125. See Commons House Transcript, April 25, 1716, 5:97; Commons House Transcript, April 18, 1717, 5:264; Cooper and McCord, *Statutes*, 2:641–46.

126. See Lords Proprietors to the South Carolina Commons House, July 22, 1718, in SC Records, 7:144; April 17, 1719, in SC Records, 7:183.

127. Sirmans, *Colonial South Carolina*, 124–25; Crane, *Southern Frontier*, 214–15; Carroll, *Historical Collections of South Carolina*, 1:205.

128. South Carolina Commons House to King George I, November 30, 1716, in SC Records, 6:259.

129. Moore, "Carolina Whigs," 58; Moore, "Royalizing South Carolina," 199.

130. JCTP, May 31, 1717, 236; Lords Proprietors to the Board of Trade, June 4, 1717, in SC Records, 7:55; Sirmans, *Colonial South Carolina*, 115.

131. See William Bull to the SPG secretary, June 20, 1717, in SPG Letter Books, series A, 12:97; Francis Le Jau to the SPG secretary, July 1, 1716, in Klingberg, *Carolina Chronicle of Francis Le Jau*, 180; South Carolina Commons House to Charles Craven, July 13, 1716, in SC Records, 6:211–12; South Carolina Commons House to the king, March 7, 1717/1718, in SC Records, 7:98–100; church wardens of Goose Creek Parish to the SPG secretary, November 26, 1716, in SPG Letter Books, series A, 12:55; Joseph Boone to the Board of Trade, May 13, 1718, in SC Records, 7:126; Clowse, *Economic Beginnings*, 226; Cole, "Organization and Administration," 50.

132. Yonge, "Narrative," 161.

133. Governor Robert Johnson to the Board of Trade, November 6, 1719, in SC Records, 7:209–15; Thomas Hassell to the SPG secretary, May 13, 1719, in SPG Letter Books, series A, 13:227; Crane, *Southern Frontier*, 217–18.

134. "A True State of the Case between the Inhabitants of South Carolina, and the Lords Proprietors," February 3, 1719/1720, in SC Records, 7:287–88.

135. Cole, "Organization and Administration," 50; Sirmans, *Colonial South Carolina*,

126–28; Stumpf, "Merchants of Colonial Charles Town," 132; Jabbs, "South Carolina Colonial Militia," 345.

136. Yonge, "Narrative," 167; Moore, "Royalizing South Carolina," 327–55; Sirmans, *Colonial South Carolina*, 126–28.

137. Spotswood to the Board of Trade, May 20, 1720, in *Official Letters*, 2:337.

138. Crane, *Southern Frontier*, 185–86; Leach, *Arms for Empire*, 74.

139. Crane, *Southern Frontier*, 218–20.

140. Crane, *Southern Frontier*, 217; Moore, "Royalizing South Carolina," 197–98.

141. Sirmans, *Colonial South Carolina*, 116.

142. Robert Johnson to the Board of Trade, January 12, 1719/1720, in SC Records, 7:234; Weir, *Colonial South Carolina*, 85; Nash, *Red, White, and Black*, 153.

143. South Carolina merchants to the Board of Trade, July 18, 1715, in CRNC, 2:197.

144. Richard Berresford to the Board of Trade, April 1717, in SC Records, 7:19; Sirmans, *Colonial South Carolina*, 124.

145. Le Jau to the SPG secretary, July 1, 1716, in Klingberg, *Carolina Chronicle of Francis Le Jau*, 180; Le Jau to Jonathan Chamberlain, August 22, 1715, in ibid., 162.

146. Commons House Transcript, August 4, 1716, 5:161–62.

147. Gideon Johnston to the SPG secretary, January 27, 1715/1716, in Klingberg, *Papers of Commissary Gideon Johnston*, 155.

148. South Carolina Council to the Board of Trade, January 26, 1716/1717, in SC Records, 7:4.

149. JHBV, August 8, 1715, 129; Proclamation of the Virginia Council, June 15, 1715, in CSP, 28:652; South Carolina Commons House to King George I, March 7, 1717/1718, in SC Records, 7:100; Jabbs, "South Carolina Colonial Militia," 319.

150. Le Jau to the SPG secretary, August 22, 1715, in Klingberg, *Carolina Chronicle of Francis Le Jau*, 166; William Bull to the SPG secretary, August 16, 1715, in SPG Letter Books, series A, 11:60; Pennington, "South Carolina Indian War," 254.

151. Thomas Hassell to the SPG secretary, May 1715, in SPG Letter Books, series B, 10:97.

152. Le Jau to the SPG secretary, March 19, 1715/1716, in Klingberg, *Carolina Chronicle of Francis Le Jau*, 173–74.

153. Johnston quoted in Pennington, "South Carolina Indian War," 262; see also Le Jau to the SPG secretary, May 10, 1715, in Klingberg, *Carolina Chronicle of Francis Le Jau*, 153.

154. Rayson, " 'Great Matter to Tell,' " 232–41.

155. Cooper and McCord, *Statutes*, 2:641–49; Duncan, "Servitude and Slavery," 68–70, 80.

156. Robert Johnson to the Board of Trade, January 12, 1719/1720, in SC Records, 7:234; Crane, *Southern Frontier*, 184.

157. Cooper and McCord, *Statutes*, 3:16; Duncan, "Servitude and Slavery," 61–62.

158. JCIT, May 9, 1717, 177.

159. Cooper and McCord, *Statutes*, 3:15–19.

160. Cooper and McCord, *Statutes*, 3:17, 20; Duncan, "Servitude and Slavery," 277; Wood, *Black Majority*, 99.

161. Porter, "Negroes on the Southern Frontier," 57; Landers, "Black-Indian Interaction," 149–50; Wood, *Black Majority*, 124–28.

162. Cheeves, "Journal of the March," 348; Willis, "Divide and Rule," 167.

163. Le Jau to the SPG secretary, August 23, 1715, in Klingberg, *Carolina Chronicle of Francis Le Jau*, 165.

164. Richard Berresford to the Board of Trade, June 23, 1716, in CSP, 29:230.

165. South Carolina merchants to the Board of Trade, July 18, 1715, in CRNC, 2:197.

166. Cooper and McCord, *Statutes*, 2:646; Wood, *Black Majority*, 130.

167. Commons House Transcript, December 4, 1716, 5:204; Duncan, "Servitude and Slavery," 378, 393.

168. Cooper and McCord, *Statutes*, 3:108–11; Montgomery, *Azilia*, 22.

169. Duncan, "Servitude and Slavery," 164–66.

170. Wood, "Changing Population," 38–39; Wood, *Black Majority*, 146–49. Ramsey, " 'All & Singular the Slaves,' " 167, 179; Grinde, "Native American Slavery," 41; Donnan, "Slave Trade in South Carolina," 805; Menard, "Africanization of the Low Country Labor Force," 84–85.

171. Menard, "Africanization of the Low Country Labor Force," 86; Littlefield, *Rice and Slaves*, 152–55.

172. Le Jau to the SPG secretary, March 19, 1715/1716, in Klingberg, *Carolina Chronicle of Francis Le Jau*, 173; Klingberg, *Appraisal of the Negro*, 41n; Klingberg, "Indian Frontier in South Carolina," 498; Wood, *Black Majority*, 141.

173. Gilbert Jones to the SPG secretary, April 6, 1716, in SPG Letter Books, series A, 12:143.

174. Lapiere to the SPG secretary, May 15, 1716, in SPG Letter Books, series B, 4:69; Le Jau to the SPG secretary, March 19, 1715/1716, in Klingberg, *Carolina Chronicle of Francis Le Jau*, 174.

175. Thomas Hassell to the SPG secretary, October 11, 1718, in SPG Letter Books, series A, 13:192; Hassell to the SPG secretary, October 1721, in ibid., series A, 16:62.

176. Rivers, *Sketch of the History*, 48n.

177. Richard Ludlum to the SPG secretary, March 1725, in SPG Letter Books, series A, 19:85; also quoted in Willis, "Divide and Rule," 165.

178. Cooper and McCord, *Statutes*, 2:691–94; JCIT, July 16, 1716, 80; Willis, "Divide and Rule," 158–61; Willis, "Anthropology and Negroes,", 42–43; Perdue, *Slavery and the Evolution of Cherokee Society*, 59; Eliades, "Indian Policy," 105; Weir, *Colonial South Carolina*, 31.

179. Wood, *Black Majority*, 114–16; Eliades, "Indian Policy," 105; Rayson, " 'Great Matter to Tell,' " 187–99; Nash, *Red, White, and Black*, 294.

180. Claudius Phillipe de Richebourg to the SPG secretary, February 12, 1715/1716, in SPG Letter Books, series A, 11:141; Francis Le Jau to the SPG secretary, May 21, 1715, in Klingberg, *Carolina Chronicle of Francis Le Jau*, 158–60; Le Jau to the SPG secretary, August 22, 1715, in Klingberg, *Carolina Chronicle of Francis Le Jau*, 161–63; Porter, "Negroes on the Southern Frontier," 56–57.

181. Commons House Transcript, August 2, 1716, 5:155.

182. JCIT, November 30, 1717, 235; Braund, "Creek Indians, Blacks, and Slavery," 608; Littlefield, *Africans and Creeks*, 10.

183. Lords Proprietors to the Board of Trade, June 4, 1717, in SC Records, 7:54; Duncan, "Servitude and Slavery," 605–6.

184. Wright, *Only Land They Knew*, 278.

185. See Landers, "Black-Indian Interaction," 151–52; also EJCCV, July 18, 1715, 405–6; EJCCV, February 22, 1715/1716, 421–22.

186. EJCCV, July 18, 1715, 405–6; EJCCV, February 22, 1715/1716, 421–22; Robinson, *Virginia Treaties*, 237.

187. See the list enclosed in the South Carolina council's letter to the Board of Trade, March 19, 1720/1721, in SC Records, 10:39; also see Rowland, Moore, and Rogers, *History of Beaufort County*, 99.

188. Landers, "Black-Indian Interaction," 151; Porter, "Negroes on the Southern Frontier," 59–60.

189. South Carolina Commons House to Joseph Boone, June 24, 1720, in CSP, 32:125; Gallay, *Formation of a Planter Elite*, 16.

190. Wright, *Only Land They Knew*, 275.

191. South Carolina Council to Joseph Boone, June 24, 1720, in SC Records, 8:24–27, quoted at length in Aptheker, *American Negro Slave Revolts*, 175.

192. South Carolina Commons House to the Board of Trade, August 20, 1720, in SC Records, 8:99.

193. See Richard Ludlum to the SPG secretary, July 2, 1724, in SPG Letter Books, series B, 4:181; also Klingberg, *Appraisal of the Negro*, 43–47.

6. Distances Bridged and Widened

1. Charles Craven to Lord Townshend, May 23, 1715, in CRNC, 2:178; Alexander Spotswood to Secretary of State Stanhope, July 15, 1715, in *Official Letters*, 2:122; JCTP, July 15, 1715, 54.

2. *Boston News-Letter*, June 13, 1715, in Carroll, *Historical Collections of South Carolina*, 2:571–73; Francis Le Jau to the SPG secretary, May 14, 1715, in Klingberg, *Carolina Chronicle of Francis Le Jau*, 155–56; Ivers, "Scouting the Inland Passage," 124.

3. Francisco Córcoles y Martínez to King Philip V, July 5, 1715, Indies Archives, 843 (microfilm).

4. For the 1715 census information, see Governor Robert Johnson to the Board of Trade, January 12, 1719/1720, in Merrens, *Colonial South Carolina Scene*, 60–61. For the 1717 Spanish census, see Governor Juan de Ayala y Escobar to King Philip V, April 18, 1717, Indies Archives, 843 (microfilm); also summarized in Hann, "St. Augustine's Fallout," 184–86.

5. Córcoles y Martínez to King Philip V, July 5, 1715, Indies Archives, 843 (microfilm).

6. Covington, "Yamasee Indians in Florida," 121–22; Cheeves, "Journal of the March," 336; also Boyd, "Diego Peña's Expedition," 1, 24–25; also Diego Peña to Governor Juan de Ayala y Escobar, October 8, 1717, in Boyd, "Documents Describing the Second and Third Expeditions," 134.

7. Córcoles y Martínez to the king, July 5, 1715, Indies Archives, 843 (microfilm); Hann, "St. Augustine's Fallout," 184–86.

8. Samuel Eveleigh to the Lords Proprietors, October 7, 1715, in SC Records, 6:119; Ivers, "Scouting the Inland Passage," 125; Milling, *Red Carolinians*, 148.

9. William Bull to the SPG secretary, May 16, 1716, in SPG Letter Books, series A, 11:149.

10. Gideon Johnston to the SPG secretary, January 27, 1715/1716, in Klingberg, *Papers of Commissary Gideon Johnston*, 154–60; Rowland, Moore, and Rogers, *History of Beaufort County*, 98; Crane, *Southern Frontier*, 184n; Milling, *Red Carolinians*, 148.

11. Testimony of Hugh Bryan before the South Carolina Assembly, August 6/1716, in SC Records, 6:237. For more on Bryan's experience as a Yamasee "slave" in Saint Augustine, see Gallay, *Formation of a Planter Elite*, 17.

12. See King Philip V to Governor Córcoles y Martínez, February 17, 1716, Indies Archives, 843 (microfilm); Te Paske, *Governorship of Spanish Florida*, 198; Covington, "Yamasee Indians in Florida," 121.

13. Testimony of James Cochrane, Robert Daniel, and George Duckett before the South Carolina assembly, August 13, 1716, in SC Records, 6:245–46.

14. Landers, "Black-Indian Interaction," 150.

15. Hann, "St. Augustine's Fallout," 182–86.

16. Hann, "St. Augustine's Fallout," 182–83; Landers, "Black-Indian Interaction," 151.

17. Milling, *Red Carolinians*, 153.

18. Commons House Transcript, May 2, 1716, 5:93.

19. Commons House Transcript, May 3, 1716, 5:94.

20. Cooper and McCord, *Statutes*, 2:695–96; Vaughan and Rosen, *Carolina and Georgia Laws*, 200–201; Commons House Transcript, November 22,1716, 5:174.

21. Hugh Bryan's testimony before the South Carolina Assembly, August 6, 1716, in SC Records, 6:237; Hann, "St. Augustine's Fallout," 185.

22. Governor Johnson's interrogation of Spanish prisoner Antonio Eleanore, November 10, 1719, in SC Records, 8:7.

23. Francis Le Jau to the SPG secretary, July 1, 1716, in Klingberg, Carolina Chronicle of Francis Le Jau, 180; JCIT, April 11, 1717, 173; Ivers, "Scouting the Inland Passage," 126; Rowland, Moore, and Rogers, History of Beaufort County, 99; Milling, Red Carolinians, 151.

24. William Rhett to William Rhett Jr., April 28, 1719, in SC Records, 7:188–89.

25. John Barnwell to Governor Robert Johnson, April 20, 1719, in SC Records, 7:186.

26. John Barnwell to Governor Robert Johnson, April 20, 1719, in SC Records, 7:187.

27. Thomas Hassell to the SPG secretary, August 1, 1719, in SPG Letter Books, series A, 13:239; Milling, Red Carolinians, 154.

28. Barnwell's relation of the attack in his letter to Governor Johnson, April 1720, in SC Records, 8:1.

29. Barnwell to Johnson, April 1720, in SC Records, 8:1–5; Milling, Red Carolinians, 154–57.

30. See Hann, "St. Augustine's Fallout," 192; also Governor Johnson's interrogation of a Spanish prisoner, November 10, 1719, in SC Records, 8:7–8; Milling, Red Carolinians, 152–53.

31. Governor Johnson to the Board of Trade, January 12, 1719/1720, in Merrens, Colonial South Carolina Scene, 62–63.

32. South Carolina Commons House to Joseph Boone, June 24, 1720, in SC Records, 8:25; Milling, Red Carolinians, 158.

33. The 1715 South Carolina census estimated the Cherokees' population at 11,530, a figure that has been modified to 11,200 by Peter Wood's demographic study of the colonial Southeast. See Johnson to the Board of Trade, January 12, 1719/1720, in Merrens, Colonial South Carolina Scene, 60–61; also Wood, "Changing Population," 38–39.

34. Commons House Transcript, May 8, 1715, 4:404–7.

35. Commons House Transcript, August 6, 1715, 4:429.

36. Commons House Transcript, May 24, 1715, 4:409–10; Crane, Southern Frontier, 179.

37. Corkran, "Alexander Long's 'A Small Postscript,' " 1–2; Reid, Better Kind of Hatchet, 57.

38. Willis, "Colonial Conflict," 45–46; Hatley, Dividing Paths, 24.

39. Cheeves, ed., "Journal of the March," 331; Bienville to Raudot, January 20, 1715, in MPAFD, 3:200.

40. For accounts of the treaty ceremony and the South Carolinians' reactions to it, see Samuel Eveleigh to Joseph Boone and Richard Berresford, October 24, 1715, in SC Records, 6:118–20; South Carolina Commons House to Boone and Berresford, March 16, 1715/1716, in SC Records, 6:156–57; Gideon Johnston to the SPG secretary, December 19, 1715, in Klingberg, *Papers of Commissary Gideon Johnston*, 150–51; Crane, *Southern Frontier*, 179–80.

41. Crane, *Southern Frontier*, 180.

42. Reid, *Better Kind of Hatchet*, 57.

43. Eliades, "Indian Policy," 116; Durschlag, "First Creek Resistance," 366–67; D. L. Johnson, "Yamasee War," 102; Crane, *Southern Frontier*, 180; Milling, *Red Carolinians*, 149–50.

44. Perdue, *Slavery and the Evolution of Cherokee Society*, 38–39.

45. Cheeves, "Journal of the March," 332, 342; Crane, *Southern Frontier*, 180–81.

46. Cheeves, "Journal of the March," 342–43.

47. Cheeves, "Journal of the March," 330–32, 342; Crane, *Southern Frontier*, 181–82.

48. Cheeves, ed., "Journal of the March," 337–39, 345–46; Crane, *Southern Frontier*, 182.

49. South Carolina Commons House to Joseph Boone and Richard Berresford, March 15, 1715/1716, in SC Records, 6:157.

50. Durschlag, "First Creek Resistance," 369; Reid, *Better Kind of Hatchet*, 66–70.

51. Durschlag, "First Creek Resistance," 370.

52. Bloom, "Acculturation of the Eastern Cherokee," 333; Hatley, *Dividing Paths*, 27.

53. JCIT, December 21, 1716, 141; Swanton, *Early History*, 253.

54. Vassar, "Some Short Remarkes," 413.

55. JCIT, November 23, 1717, 231; Vassar, "Some Short Remarkes," 409; Goodwin, *Cherokees in Transition*, 142–48.

56. Vassar, "Some Short Remarkes," 420.

57. JCIT, August 1, 1716, 157; JCIT, November 30, 1716, 135.

58. Cheeves, "Journal of the March," 349.

59. JCIT, July 10, 1716, 75; JCIT, July 24, 1716, 84.

60. JCIT, July 10, 1716, 73; Crane, *Southern Frontier*, 188.

61. Vassar, "Some Short Remarkes," 410, 413; JCIT, January 16, 1716/1717, 152; JCIT, November 1, 1716, 120; Reid, *Better Kind of Hatchet*, 105–9.

62. JCIT, September 10, 1717, 205; Reid, *Better Kind of Hatchet*, 115.

63. JCIT, January 23, 1716/1717, 149–52.

64. Miller and Hammell, "New Perspective on Indian-White Contact," 318–22; White, *Roots of Dependency*, xv, 36.

65. Rayson, " 'Great Matter to Tell,' " 154–84; Hatley, *Dividing Paths*, 10.

66. Vassar, "Some Short Remarkes," 407, 415–17.

67. Vassar, "Some Short Remarkes," 409–10, 419.

68. Commons House Transcript, January 17, 1716/1717, 5:222.

69. Vassar, "Some Short Remarkes," 406.

70. Vassar, "Some Short Remarkes," 407–8; Franklin, "Virginia and the Cherokee Indian Trade," 113–17.

71. JCIT, July 19, 1718, 306; Crane, Southern Frontier, 196–97; Barker, " 'Much Blood and Treasure,' " 113; Morris, "Bringing of Wonder," 185.

72. Vassar, "Some Short Remarkes," 411.

73. Vassar, "Some Short Remarkes," 406; JCIT, December 2, 1717, 236.

74. JCIT, July 24, 1716, 84.

75. JCIT, July 24, 1716, 84; JCIT, November 2, 1716, 122–23; Reid, Better Kind of Hatchet, 94–95.

76. JCIT, February 27, 1716/1717, 168; JCIT, May 9, 1717, 178.

77. Richard Berresford to the Board of Trade, February 6, 1716/1717, in SC Records, 7:21; Benjamin Godin, Ralph Izard, and Edward Hyrne to the Board of Trade, August 6, 1716, in SC Records, 6:241; D. Brown, Catawba Indians, 146.

78. Commons House Transcript, February 29, 1715/1716, 5:8.

79. JCIT, February 5, 1716/1717, 158.

80. South Carolina Council to the Lords Proprietors, January 26, 1716/1717, in SC Records, 7:3.

81. Commons House Transcript, June 25, 1717, 5:325.

82. Commons House Transcript, January 17, 1716/1717, 5:222–24; Commons House Transcript, January 22, 1716/1717, 5:225–27.

83. JCIT, June 11, 1718, 290.

84. JCIT, June 11, 1718, 290–91.

85. Joseph Boone to the Board of Trade, April 25, 1717, in SC Records, 7:15–16; Crane, Southern Frontier, 263; Eliades, "Indian Policy," 125.

86. Vassar, "Some Short Remarkes," 419–21; Hatley, Dividing Paths, 27; Willis, "Colonial Conflict," 50.

87. Price schedules for the Cherokees and the Lower Creeks compared in Crane, Southern Frontier, appendix.

88. Berresford to the Board of Trade, April 27, 1717, in SC Records, 7:18; JCIT, July 5, 1718, 300.

89. Robinson, "Virginia and the Cherokees," 30–31; EJCCV, October 1721, 554–55; Willis, "Colonial Conflict," 49; Franklin, "Virginia and the Cherokee Indian Trade," 15–16.

90. JCIT, June 11, 1718, 290–91.

91. JCIT, December 2, 1717, 236–37.

92. Reid, Better Kind of Hatchet, 73.

93. Goodwin, Cherokees in Transition, 110.

94. See the 1715 South Carolina census in Johnson to the Board of Trade, January

12, 1719/1720, in Merrens, *Colonial South Carolina Scene*, 60–61; also Merrell, *Indians' New World*, 95–96.

95. Merrell, *Indians' New World*, 102.

96. Merrell, " 'Our Bond of Peace,' " 210; Merrell, *Indians' New World*, 68.

97. "Milling, *Red Carolinians*, 235; Governor Johnson's interrogation of a Spanish prisoner, November 10, 1719, in SC Records, 8:7–8; Hann, "St. Augustine's Fallout," 185.

98. Alexander Spotswood to the Board of Trade, February 16, 1715/1716, in *Official Letters*, 2:141; Merrell, *Indians' New World*, 79; Crane, *Southern Frontier*, 176–77.

99. JCIT, February 20, 1716/1717, 163; Spotswood to the Board of Trade, April 16, 1717, in *Official Letters*, 2:237–38; Crane, *Southern Frontier*, 184; D. Brown, *Catawba Indians*, 146.

100. Commons House Transcript, November 27, 1716, 5:183; Claudius Phillipe de Richebourg to the SPG secretary, February 12, 1715/1716, in SPG Letter Books, series A, 11:141.

101. Commons House Transcript, November 27, 1716, 5:180–82, 208; Merrell, *Indians' New World*, 103.

102. Council Transcript, September 12, 1717, 122; JCIT, February 20, 1716/1717, 163; JCIT, January 31, 1717/1718, 24; JCIT, February 26, 1717/1718, 257.

103. Board of Trade to King George I, September 10, 1720, in SC Records, 8:183.

104. Merrell, " 'Our Bond of Peace,' " 211.

105. JCIT, May 8, 1718, 272; JCIT, October 18, 1716, 119; JCIT, November 26, 1716, 132; JCIT, July 5, 1718, 298; Merrell, " 'Our Bond of Peace,' " 211.

106. JCIT, September 20, 1717, 210–12; Crane, *Southern Frontier*, 194.

107. Vassar, "Some Short Remarkes," 416.

108. JCIT, August 10, 1717, 202; JCIT, August 11, 1717, 206; JCIT, January 31, 1717/1718, 254.

109. JCIT, September 20, 1717, 211; Merrell, *Indians' New World*, 82–83.

110. Merrell, " 'Our Bond of Peace,' " 213.

111. JCIT, November 2, 1717, 223; Merrell, *Indians' New World*, 88–89.

112. JCIT, December 10, 1716, 137–38; JCIT, September 12, 1717, 208.

113. Merrell, *Indians' New World*, 80.

114. JCIT, September 12, 1717, 208; JCIT, April 11, 1718, 264–65.

115. JCIT, April 12, 1718, 266.

116. Spotswood to the Board of Trade, December 22, 1718, in CSP, 30:800.

117. Merrell, *Indians' New World*, 97.

118. JCIT, January 26, 1716/1717, 153; JCIT, October 9, 1717, 217; Milling, *Red Carolinians*, 235–36.

119. William Guy to the SPG secretary, September 20, 1715, in SPG Letter Books,

series A, 11:68; Francis Le Jau to the SPG secretary, July 1, 1716, in Klingberg, *Carolina Chronicle of Francis Le Jau*, 180; Merrell, *Indians' New World*, 78–79.

120. EJCCV, August 13, 1717, 451; Merrell, " 'Their Very Bones Shall Fight,' " 118; Boyce, "As the Wind Scatters the Smoke,' " 162.

121. Spotswood to Mr. Popple, April 16, 1717, in *Official Letters*, 2:237; Merrell, *Indians' New World*, 89.

122. JCIT, May 9, 1717, 177; Milling, *Red Carolinians*, 235; Merrell, *Indians' New World*, 80.

123. Merrell, *Indians' New World*, 106.

124. Johnson to the Board of Trade, January 12, 1719/1720, in Merrens, *Colonial South Carolina Scene*, 58–59.

125. D. Brown, *Catawba Indians*, 147; Merrell, *Indians' New World*, 113.

126. Merrell, *Indians' New World*, 110, 113–17.

127. Merrell, " 'Their Very Bones Shall Fight,' " 120; Merrell, *Indians' New World*, 133.

128. Waselkov, "Indian Maps of the Colonial Southeast," 303; also see Nobles, "Straight Lines and Stability," 9–35.

129. Merrell, *Indians' New World*, 93–94.

130. Joseph Boone to the Board of Trade, August 23, 1720, in SC Records, 8:70–71; Adair, *History of the American Indians*, 421–23.

131. South Carolina Commons House to Boone and Berresford, August 20, 1715, in SC Records, 6:129–30; William Bull to the SPG secretary, August 1715, in SPG Letter Books, series B, 10:112; Covington, "Apalachee Indians," 376; Crane, *Southern Frontier*, 164; D. L. Johnson, "Yamasee War," 99; Hann, *Apalachee*, 397–400.

132. Corkran, *Creek Frontier*, 52.

133. Martin, *Sacred Revolt*, 49; Cheeves, "Journal of the March," 336; Swanton, *Early History*, 101, 125; Francis Le Jau to the SPG secretary, March 19, 1715/1716, in Klingberg, *Carolina Chronicle of Francis Le Jau*, 174–75.

134. Salinas Varona to Juan de Ayala y Escobar, July 24, 1717, in Boyd, "Documents Describing the Second and Third Expeditions," 127.

135. Ford, *Triangular Struggle*, 94.

136. South Carolina Commons House to the Board of Trade, March 15, 1715/1716, in SC Records, 6:159; Pénicaut, *Fleur de Lis and Calumet*, 164.

137. See Francisco Córcoles y Martínez to King Philip V, July 5, 1715, in Indies Archives, 843 (microfilm); Te Paske, *Governorship of Spanish Florida*, 199; Bienville to Ministre de la Marine Pontchartrain, September 1, 1715, in MPAFD, 3:188.

138. Duclos to Pontchartrain, June 7, 1716, in MPAFD, 3:205.

139. Cheeves, "Journal of the March," 335–38; Crane, *Southern Frontier*, 182.

140. Crane, *Southern Frontier*, 183.

141. Francis Le Jau to the SPG secretary, March 19, 1715/1716, in Klingberg, *Carolina Chronicle of Francis Le Jau,* 174–75.

142. See Boyd, "Diego Peña's Expedition," 5; Te Paske, *Governorship of Spanish Florida,* 200.

143. Covington, "Migration of Seminoles," 344–45; Corkran, *Creek Frontier,* 60; Crane, *Southern Frontier,* 254.

144. Crane, *Southern Frontier,* 254; Swanton, *Early History,* 101, 177.

145. Debo, *Road to Disappearance,* 9; Lankford, "Red and White," 57; Martin, *Sacred Revolt,* 11.

146. Governor Juan de Ayala y Escobar to King Philip V, April 1, 1717, Indies Archives, 843 (microfilm). John Barnwell's 1722 map of the Southeast bears the legend of a fort built in 1716 in the town of Apalachicola near the confluence of the Flint and Chattahoochee Rivers; see Cumming, *Southeast in Early Maps,* pl. 48; also see Crane, *Southern Frontier,* 255.

147. Diego Peña to Governor Juan de Ayala y Escobar, October 8, 1717, in Boyd, "Documents Describing the Second and Third Expeditions," 133.

148. Governor Córcoles y Martínez to King Philip V, July 5, 1715, Indies Archives, 843 (microfilm); Governor Ayala y Escobar to the king, April 1, 1717, Indies Archives, 843 (microfilm).

149. Durschlag, "First Creek Resistance," 84.

150. Crane, *Southern Frontier,* 184.

151. South Carolina Commons House to Joseph Boone, June 8, 1717, in SC Records, 7:51.

152. Boyd, "Diego Peña's Expedition," 9–10.

153. Pénicaut, *Fleur de Lis and Calumet,* 165, 205; Lords Proprietors to the Board of Trade, June 4, 1717, in SC Records, 7:53–54.

154. Given, *Most Pernicious Thing,* 107; Durschlag, "First Creek Resistance," 147.

155. Commons House Transcript, June 22, 1711, 3:570; Commons House Transcript, May 24, 1712, 4:43.

156. Burke, "Eighteenth-Century Trade Guns," 6–7; Hahn, "Miniature Arms Race," 17.

157. Barker, " 'Much Blood and Treasure,' " 230; Ayala y Escobar to the king, April 1, 1717, Indies Archives, 843 (microfilm); Duclos to Pontchartrain, June 7, 1716, in MPAFD, 3:205.

158. Le Jau to the SPG secretary, August 22, 1715, in Klingberg, *Carolina Chronicle of Francis Le Jau,* 162.

159. Le Jau to the SPG secretary, May 14, 1715, in Klingberg, *Carolina Chronicle of Francis Le Jau,* 156; William Guy to the SPG secretary, September 20, 1715, in SPG Letter Books, series A, 11:68; Cheeves, "Journal of the March," 336; Duclos to Pontchartrain,

June 7, 1716, in MPAFD, 3:205; Boyd, "Diego Peña's Expedition," 26; Le Maire, *Mémoire Inédit*, 28; Crane, *Southern Frontier*, 184; Swanton, *Early History*, 101.

160. Richard Berresford to the Board of Trade, April 27, 1717, in SC Records, 7:18; Crane, *Southern Frontier*, 257.

161. Corkran, *Creek Frontier*, 64–65.

162. Commons House Transcript, May 24, 1717, 5:275; Commons House Transcript, May 25, 1717, 5:280; Crane, *Southern Frontier*, 257.

163. South Carolina Commons House to Joseph Boone, June 8, 1717, in SC Records, 7:50–51; Crane, *Southern Frontier*, 257.

164. Wraxall, *Abridgement of Indian Affairs*, 117–18.

165. South Carolina Commons House to Joseph Boone, June 8, 1717, in SC Records, 7:50; Durschlag, "First Creek Resistance," 345–46.

166. Commons House Transcript, June 14, 1717, 5:325.

167. Crane, *Southern Frontier*, 257.

168. Diego Peña to Governor Ayala y Escobar, September 20, 1717, in Boyd, "Documents Describing the Second and Third Expeditions," 117.

169. Braund, *Deerskins and Duffels*, 35; Barker, " 'Much Blood and Treasure,' " 239; Fisher, "Mary Musgrove," 50–52; Baine, "Myths of Mary Musgrove," 428–35.

170. Peña to Ayala y Escobar, September 20, 1717, in Boyd, "Documents Describing the Second and Third Expeditions," 118; Barcía, *Chronological History*, 358.

171. Council Transcript, September 11, 1717, 121–22.

172. Minutes of the treaty are no longer extant, and the only accounts of the meetings come from Governor Johnson's reports to the Commons House, in Commons House Transcript, November 15, 1717, 5:368; Braund, *Deerskins and Duffels*, 35; and Crane, *Southern Frontier*, 259.

173. JCIT, December 4, 1717, 241; JCIT, December 21, 1717, 246; JCIT, January 16, 1717/1718, 248.

174. Commons House Transcript, November 22, 1717, 5:376.

175. Bienville to Minister of Commerce Hubert, September 19, 1717, in MPAFD, 3:222–23; Crane, *Southern Frontier*, 257.

176. JCIT, July 19, 1718, 308.

177. Commons House Transcript, November 14, 1715, 5:366.

178. Richard Berresford to the Board of Trade, April 27, 1717, in SC Records, 7:18.

179. Commons House Transcript, May 24, 1717, 5:275.

180. Barcía, *Chronological History*, 364.

181. Robert Johnson to the Board of Trade, June 18, 1718, in SC Records, 7:135.

182. Waselkov, "Historic Creek Indian Responses," 125.

183. Reynolds, "Alabama-Tombigbee Basin," 102; Crane, *Southern Frontier*, 256.

184. Le Gac, *Immigration and War*, 51–52; Usner, *Indians, Settlers, and Slaves*, 32–33; Giraud, *History of French Louisiana*, 123.

185. JCTP, August 16, 1720, 198; Robert Johnson to the Board of Trade, January 12, 1719/1720, in Merrens, *Colonial South Carolina Scene*, 63; Alexander Spotswood to the Board of Trade, February 1, 1720/1721, in *Official Letters*, 2:229–31.

186. William Bull to the SPG secretary, May 16, 1716, in SPG Letter Books, series A, 11:149–50; Cheeves, "Journal of the March," 336; Cooper and McCord, *Statutes*, 3:39–41.

187. Spotswood to the Board of Trade, December 22, 1718, in CSP, 30:800.

188. Bienville to Pontchartrain, September 1, 1715, in MPAFD, 3:188.

189. Le Maire, *Mémoire Inédit*, 22–27.

190. Woods, *French-Indian Relations*, 141; Giraud, *History of Louisiana*, 170; Reynolds, "Alabama-Tombigbee Basin," 107.

191. Bienville to Hubert, September 19, 1717, in MPAFD, 3:222–23; Giraud, *History of Louisiana*, 330; Barker, " 'Much Blood and Treasure,' " 230.

192. Woods, *French-Indian Relations*, 50; Braund, *Deerskins and Duffels*, 34.

193. Richard Berresford to the Board of Trade, February 6, 1716/1717, in SC Records, 7:21.

194. South Carolina Commons House to the Board of Trade, March 15, 1715/1716, in SC Records, 6:159; D. Thomas, "Fort Toulouse," 147.

195. Reynolds, "Alabama-Tombigbee Basin," 81; D. Thomas, "Fort Toulouse," 151; Usner, *Indians, Settlers, and Slaves*, 28; and Crane, *Southern Frontier*, 256.

196. Heldman, "Fort Toulouse," 165–67; D. Thomas, "Fort Toulouse," 150; Waselkov, "Historic Creek Indian Responses," 127.

197. D. Thomas, "Fort Toulouse," 174–75; Waselkov, "Historic Creek Indian Responses," 127.

198. Durschlag, "First Creek Resistance," 399.

199. Robert Johnson to the Board of Trade, January 12, 1719/1720, in Merrens, *Colonial South Carolina Scene*, 63. For more on the South Carolinians' distorted impressions of Fort Toulouse, see D. Thomas, "Fort Toulouse," 163; Woods, *French-Indian Relations*, 52; Adair, *History of the American Indians*, 277–78.

200. Griffith, "South Carolina and Fort Alabama," 261–62.

201. Johnson to the Board of Trade, January 12, 1719/1720, in Merrens, *Colonial South Carolina Scene*, 64; Crane, *Southern Frontier*, 261.

202. Faye, "Contest for Pensacola Bay," 188–95; Folmer, *Franco-Spanish Rivalry*, 81–83; Ford, *Triangular Struggle*, 107–24; Crane, *Southern Frontier*, 262.

203. Barcía, *Chronological History*, 365, 375; Crane, *Southern Frontier*, 256.

204. Delaney, "Newly Found French Journal," 152.

205. Peña to Ayala y Escobar, September 20, 1717, in Boyd, "Documents Relating to the Second and Third Expeditions," 124.

206. Patrick MacKay to James Oglethorpe, March 29, 1735, in Juricek, *Georgia Treaties*, 50.

207. Córcoles y Martínez to the king, July 5, 1715, Indies Archives, 843 (microfilm).

208. Te Paske, *Governorship of Spanish Florida*, 199.

209. Te Paske, *Governorship of Spanish Florida*, 123–24.

210. Boyd, "Diego Peña's Expedition," 24–25.

211. Boyd, "Diego Peña's Expedition," 12; Te Paske, *Governorship of Spanish Florida*, 201.

212. Ayala y Escobar to the king, April 1, 1717, Indies Archives, 843 (microfilm); Te Paske, *Governorship of Spanish Florida*, 201.

213. Salinas Varona to Ayala y Escobar, July 24, 1717, in Boyd, "Documents Relating to the Second and Third Expeditions," 128; Crane, *Southern Frontier*, 255.

214. Barcía, *Chronological History*, 359–61.

215. Bushnell, "Ruling the 'Republic of Indians,' " 134–50.

216. Ayala y Escobar to King Philip V, April 1, 1717, Indies Archives, 843 (microfilm).

217. Barcía, *Chronological History*, 375.

218. Salinas Varona to Ayala y Escobar, September 7, 1717, in Boyd, "Documents Describing the Second and Third Expeditions," 130; also see Salinas Varona to Ayala y Escobar, July 24, 1717, in ibid., 128.

219. Peña to Ayala y Escobar, October 8, 1717, in Boyd, "Documents Describing the Second and Third Expeditions," 134; Crane, *Southern Frontier*, 255; Te Paske, *Governorship of Spanish Florida*, 205; Covington, "Migration of Seminoles," 345.

220. Governor Antonio Benavides to King Philip V, September 28, 1718, in Boyd, "Documents Describing the Second and Third Expeditions," 139; Barcía, *Chronological History*, 365; Te Paske, *Governorship of Spanish Florida*, 203.

221. Hubert to Royal Council, October 26, 1717, in MPAFD, 2:249; Le Maire, *Mémoire Inédit*, 28.

222. Johnson to the Board of Trade, January 12, 1719/1720, in Merrens, *Colonial South Carolina Scene*, 59.

223. Adair, *History of the American Indians*, 277.

224. Hahn, "The Invention of the Creek Nation," 286–91.

225. See Waselkov, "Historic Creek Indian Responses," 126; Braund, *Deerskins and Duffels*, 22. An exemplary study of the role of factionalism in Indian diplomacy is Richter's *Ordeal of the Longhouse*; see especially pp. 6–7, 46.

226. Commons House Transcript, November 14, 1717, 5:368; Barcía, *Chronological History*, 363–64.

227. Waselkov, "Historic Creek Indian Responses," 125–26.

228. Richter, *Ordeal of the Longhouse*, 117.

229. Lankford, "Red and White," 63; Hudson, *Southeastern Indians*, 185.

230. Corkran, *Creek Frontier*, 53; Richter, *Ordeal of the Longhouse*, 153.

231. Peña to Ayala y Escobar, September 20, 1717, in Boyd, "Documents Relating to the Second and Third Expeditions," 120–22; also Braund, *Deerskins and Duffels*, 35.

232. Barcía, *Chronological History*, 362.

233. Barcía, *Chronological History*, 358; Peña to Ayala y Escobar, October 8, 1717, in Boyd, "Documents Relating to the Second and Third Expeditions," 133; Peña to Ayala y Escobar, September 20, 1717, in ibid., 121.

234. Martin, *Sacred Revolt*, 81; Braund, *Deerskins and Duffels*, 22.

235. Thomas Hassell to the SPG secretary, August 1, 1719, in SPG Letter Books, series A, 13:239.

7. Inchoate Resistance

1. William Hatton to the South Carolina Council, November 14, 1724, in SC Records, 11:272–76.

2. Sirmans, *Colonial South Carolina*, 135.

3. Response to the Board of Trade queries, March 1719/1720, in SC Records, 7:259; also see Crane, *Southern Frontier*, 263; Eliades, "Indian Policy," 125; Cooper and McCord, *Statutes*, 3:91–94; Vaughan and Rosen, *Carolina and Georgia Laws*, 214–24.

4. English merchants to the Board of Trade, October 27, 1720, in SC Records, 8:226–27.

5. Crane, *Southern Frontier*, 229–31.

6. Barnwell and Joseph Boone to the Board of Trade, August 16, 1720, in SC Records, 8:176–78.

7. Webb, "Strange Career of Francis Nicholson," 547–48; Sirmans, *Colonial South Carolina*, 137; Crane, *Southern Frontier*, 264.

8. Moore, "Royalizing South Carolina," 390–92.

9. Council Transcript, July 1721, 1:132; Crane, *Southern Frontier*, 265.

10. Board of Trade to Francis Nicholson, August 30, 1720, in SC Records, 8:130.

11. Council Transcript, July 11, 1721, 1:134–36.

12. Francis Varnod to the SPG secretary, January 16, 1723/1724, in SPG Letter Books, series A, 17:121; Klingberg, "Indian Frontier in South Carolina," 494–95.

13. Varnod to the SPG secretary, January 13, 1723/1724, in SPG Letter Books, series A, 18:74.

14. Klingberg, *Appraisal of the Negro*, 140–42.

15. Varnod to the SPG secretary, January 15, 1723/1724, in SPG Letter Books, series A, 17:121–22.

16. L. R. Smith, "South Carolina's Indian Trade Regulations," 43.

17. EJCCV, June 13, 1722, 18.

18. Upper House Journals, January 20, 1721/1722, 158; Upper House Journals, August 26, 1721, 72–73.

19. Board of Trade to Nicholson, August 30, 1720, in SC Records, 8:130; L. R. Smith, "South Carolina's Indian Trade Regulations," 43.

20. Stumpf, "Merchants of Colonial Charles Town," 105; Braund, *Deerskins and Duffels*, 35–36.

21. Clowse, *Economic Beginnings*, 238.

22. John Worth to John Bee, July 30, 1723, in SC Records, 10:128.

23. Commons House Transcript, November 8, 1723, 6:304; Minutes of the Committee on Indian Affairs, November 3, 1723, in SC Records, 10:193.

24. Willis, "Colonial Conflict," 56; Corkran, "Alexander Long's 'A Small Postscript,' " 26.

25. The number of deerskins that passed through customs in Charles Town numbered 24,355 in 1720, 35,171 in 1721, 33,939 in 1722, 59,827 in 1723, 64,315 in 1724, 61,124 in 1725, and 79,753 in 1726; see Clowse, *Economic Beginnings*, 256–57.

26. Goodwin, *Cherokees in Transition*, 148; Willis, "Colonial Conflict," 148.

27. Cooper and McCord, *Statutes*, 3:143.

28. Commons House Transcript, November 8, 1723, 6:302.

29. Theophilus Hastings to the South Carolina Council, October 9, 1723, in SC Records, 10:187.

30. Corkran, "Alexander Long's 'A Small Postscript,' " 20.

31. Commons House Transcript, February 2, 1723/1724, 6:411; Perier and La Chaise to the directors of the Company of the Indies, January 30, 1729, in MPAFD, 2:613.

32. South Carolina Council Journal, September 27, 1722, in Col. Office Records, no. 5/425, 361.

33. Board of Trade to Nicholson, August 30, 1720, in SC Records, 8:130.

34. Cooper and McCord, *Statutes*, 3:141–46, 229–32; Vaughan and Rosen, *Carolina and Georgia Laws*, 256–59; also Hatley, *Dividing Paths*, 36; Barker, " 'Much Blood and Treasure,' " 246; L. R. Smith, "South Carolina's Indian Trade Regulations," 43; Crane, *Southern Frontier*, 201–3.

35. Cooper and McCord, *Statutes*, 3:144.

36. Reid, *Better Kind of Hatchet*, 187–88.

37. Nicholson's speech to Ouletta and the Lower Creeks, Upper House Journals, May 25, 1722, 8.

38. Upper House Journals, June 14, 1722, 11–16.

39. Commons House Transcript, May 26, 1722, 6:3.

40. Upper House Journals, February 3, 1721/1722, 166; Upper House Journals, May 25, 1722, 7–10; Crane, *Southern Frontier*, 265, 275.

41. Ouletta's speech to the South Carolina council, November 19, 1723, in SC Records, 10:183–84; Crane, *Southern Frontier*, 265; minutes of the Committee on Indian Affairs, November 16, 1723, in SC Records, 10:180; Theophilus Hastings to the council, October 9, 1723, in SC Records, 10:188.

42. Committee on Indian Affairs, November 6, 1723, in SC Records, 10:190–91.

43. Commons House Transcript, November 8, 1723, 6:301; Upper House Journals, May 25, 1722, 9–10.

44. Ouletta's speech to the council, October 25, 1723, in SC Records, 10:177; Nicholson's speech to Ouletta, November 16, 1723, in SC Records, 10:182; Upper House Journals, June 10, 1724, 275–76.

45. EJCCV, October 23, 1721, 554–55; EJCCV, October 25, 1721, 1–2.

46. Chicken, "Journals," 137.

47. Board of Trade to the king, September 8, 1721, in CRNC, 2:422; John Barnwell to the Board of Trade, August 18, 1720, in SC Records, 8:60; JCHASC, June 5, 1724, 13.

48. Minutes of the Superior Council of Louisiana, May 28, 1723, in MPAFD, 3:399; de la Chaise to the directors of the Company of the Indies, October 28, 1723, in MPAFD, 3:383–84; Charlevoix, "Pierre de Charlevoix's Journal,", 87–88.

49. Bienville to Conseille de la Marine, April 26, 1722, in MPAFD, 3:316; Reynolds, "Alabama-Tombigbee Basin," 128.

50. Upper House Journal, February 11, 1722/1723, 302.

51. See Bienville's memoir of his service in Louisiana, 1726, in MPAFD, 3:536–39.

52. Bienville to the Conseille de la Marine, February 1, 1723, in MPAFD, 3:343; Phelps, "Chickasaw, the English, and the French," 122–23.

53. Minutes of the Superior Council of Louisiana, July 20, 1723, in MPAFD, 3:355–58, 381; Reynolds, "Alabama-Tombigbee Basin," 124; Crane, Southern Frontier, 273.

54. Phelps, "Chickasaw, the English, and the French," 122–23.

55. Upper House Journal, June 21, 1722, 41; Commons House Transcript, June 21, 1722, 6:37; Milling, Red Carolinians, 188.

56. Minutes of the Superior Council of Louisiana, December 1, 1724, in MPAFD, 3:457–58.

57. Corkran, "Alexander Long's 'A Small Postscript,' " 18.

58. De Brahm, "Philosphico-Historico-Hydrogeography," 222; Nash, Red, White, and Black, 257; Willis, "Colonial Conflict," 214–21.

59. See Theophilus Hastings to the council, October 9, 1723, in SC Records, 10:186–87; Hastings to Governor Nicholson, September 7, 1723, in SC Records, 10:146–47; Gerald Monger to Nicholson, September 24, 1723, in SC Records, 10:156–57.

60. Chicken, "Journals," 111–12, 150.

61. Upper House Journals, June 13; 1724, 287; JCHASC, June 12, 1724, 36.

62. Hatton to the council, November 14, 1724, in SC Records, 11:278.

63. Upper House Journals, March 6, 1724/1725, 249.

64. Upper House Journals, May 29, 1725, 23–24.

65. Upper House Journals, April 9, 1725, 333.

66. Upper House Journals, April 9, 1725, 334.

67. Upper House Journals, April 9, 1725, 333; ibid., June 3, 1725, 29.

68. JCHASC, May 13, 1725, 113.

69. Upper House Journals, March 19, 1724/1725, 270; JCHASC, March 18, 1724/1725, 52–53; JCHASC, March 15, 1724/1725, 117; Reid, *Better Kind of Hatchet*, 133; Barker, " 'Much Blood and Treasure,' " 249; Crane, *Southern Frontier*, 201, 267.

70. Chicken, "Journals," 101; Fitch, "Journals," 178.

71. Upper House Journals, June 1, 1725, 46–48; ibid., undated (probably summer 1725), 49–50.

72. Rayson, " 'Great Matter to Tell,' " 339.

73. Upper House Journals, June 1, 1725, 46–48; Chicken, "Journals," 95–96.

74. JCHASC, May 29, 1725, 133.

75. Upper House Journals, undated (probably summer 1725), 49–50.

76. Chicken, "Journals," 110–11; Debo, *Road to Disappearance*, 28.

77. Fitch, "Journals," 177–78.

78. Fitch, "Journals," 196.

79. Fitch, "Journals," 181–88.

80. Chicken, "Journals," 118.

81. Chicken, "Journals," 113.

82. Barker, " 'Much Blood and Treasure,' " 256.

83. Fitch, "Journals," 178–80, 192–93.

84. Fitch, "Journals," 196–97.

85. Fontaine, *Journal*, 93.

86. Upper House Journals, August 1725, 68; Rothrock, "Carolina Traders," 12.

87. Chicken, "Journals," 102; Reid, *Better Kind of Hatchet*, 134, 155; Crane, *Southern Frontier*, 201–3.

88. Chicken, "Journals," 154–58.

89. Chicken, "Journals," 107.

90. Chicken's report to the council, October 26, 1726, in Col. Office Records, no. 5/429, 75.

91. Fitch's report to the council, September 1, 1726, in Col. Office Records, no. 5/429, 14–15.

92. Fitch's report to the council, in Upper House Journals, August 4, 1725, 59.

93. Chicken's report to the council, October 26, 1726, in Col. Office Records, no. 5/429, 75.

94. Chicken, "Journals," 129; Fitch's report to the council, September 23, 1726, in Col. Office Records, no. 5/429, 38.

95. Reid, *Better Kind of Hatchet*, 174; Clowse, *Economic Beginnings*, 207.

96. Chicken, "Journals," 109–11; Reid, *Better Kind of Hatchet*, 174.

97. Chicken, "Journals," 125.

98. Chicken, "Journals," 153.

99. Chicken, "Journals," 155.

100. Chicken, "Journals," 136, 165.

101. Fitch, "Journals," 195.

102. Fitch, "Journals," 209.

103. Fitch's report to the council, in Upper House Journals, August 1725, 67.

104. Fitch, "Journals," 177; Fitch's report to the council, in Upper House Journals, July 20, 1725, 51.

105. Fitch's report to the council, in Upper House Journals, August 1, 1725, 65.

106. Fitch's report to the council, in Upper House Journals, August 1, 1725, 66.

107. Fitch, "Journals," 185–86.

108. Fitch, "Journals," 186.

109. Upper House Journals, June 1, 1725, 117; JCHASC, May 15, 1725, 117.

110. Chicken, "Journals," 114.

111. Chicken, "Journals," 127.

112. Fitch, "Journals," 190.

113. Fitch, "Journals," 181; Fitch's report to the council, in Upper House Journals, July 20, 1725, 54.

114. Fitch, "Journals," 182.

115. Fitch, "Journals," 188–89.

116. Chicken, "Journals," 169.

117. Fitch's report to the council, in Upper House Journals, August 4, 1725, 57.

118. Chicken, "Journals," 170–72.

119. Chicken, "Journals," 154.

120. Upper House Journals, August 1725, 60.

121. Chicken, "Journals," 144, 157.

122. Chicken, "Journals," 168; Fitch, "Journals," 199.

123. Fitch, "Journals," 198–99.

124. JCHASC, November 2, 1725, 4; JCHASC, November 17, 1725, 21; JCHASC, February 4, 1725/1726, 85.

125. Barker, " 'Much Blood and Treasure,' " 249.

126. Crane, *Southern Frontier*, 268–69; Sirmans, *Colonial South Carolina*, 157.

127. Upper House Journals, April 28, 1726, 297; JCHASC, April 29, 1726, 102.

128. JCHASC, April 26, 1726, 88.

129. Upper House Journals, April 20, 1726, 281; JCHASC, April 27, 1726, 93–94.

130. Arthur Middleton to Francis Nicholson, June 7, 1726, in SC Records, 12:63–64.

131. Fitch's report to the council, September 1, 1726, in Col. Office Records, no. 5/429, 12; South Carolina Council Journal, October 30, 1726, in Col. Office Records, no. 5/429, 75.

132. Fitch's report to the council, September 1, 1726, in Col. Office Records, no. 5/429, 12–13.

133. Upper House Journals, April 28, 1726, 297.

134. Fitch's report to the council, September 23, 1726, in Col. Office Records, no. 5/429, 35–45.

135. Chicken's report to the council, September 1, 1726, in Col. Office Records, no. 5/429, 2–6.

136. Fitch's report to the council, September 23, 1726, in Col. Office Records, no. 5/429, 43–46; Fitch's report to the council, September 1, 1726, in Col. Office Records, no. 5/429, 13.

137. Chicken to Fitch, October 26, 1726, in Col. Office Records, no. 5/429, 73–75.

138. Chicken's report to the council, September 1, 1726, in Col. Office Records, no. 5/429, 3; Fitch's report to the council, September 13, 1726, in Col. Office Records, no. 5/429, 34–35.

139. JCHASC, April 28, 1726, 95–96; South Carolina Council Journal, September 1, 1726, in Col. Office Records, no. 5/429, 11–12.

140. JCHASC, December 13, 1726, 34–35; JCHASC, December 21, 1726, 45–46.

141. South Carolina Council Journal, January 24–25, 1726/1727, in Col. Office Records, no. 5/387, 131–37.

142. JCHASC, January 11, 1726/1727, 62.

143. JCHASC, January 21, 1726/1727, 82.

144. Upper House Journal, January 13, 1726/1727, in Col. Office Records, no. 5/429, 123; Crane, *Southern Frontier*, 269–70.

145. South Carolina Council Journal, January 26, 1726/1727, in Col. Office Records, no. 5/387, 138–39.

146. South Carolina Council Journal, January 26, 1726/1727, in Col. Office Records, no. 5/387, 139–42; also Crane, *Southern Frontier*, 269–70.

147. South Carolina Council Journal, January 25–26, 1726/1727, in Col. Office Records, no. 5/387, 136–37.

148. South Carolina Council Journal, January 24–25, 1726/1727, in Col. Office Records, no. 5/387, 133–35.

149. Salley, *Journal of Colonel John Herbert*, 11; Charlesworth Glover to the South Carolina council, January 24, 1727/1728, in SC Records, 13:106.

150. Salley, *Journal of Colonel John Herbert*, 13; Crane, *Southern Frontier*, 270–71.

151. Salley, *Journal of Colonel John Herbert*, 9; Milling, *Red Carolinians*, 274.

152. Salley, *Journal of Colonel John Herbert*, 10.

153. Salley, *Journal of Colonel John Herbert*, 25–26.

154. South Carolina Council Journal, January 26, 1726/1727, in Col. Office Records, no. 5/387, 133.

155. Reid, *Better Kind of Hatchet*, 188–89; Cooper and McCord, *Statutes*, 3:273.

156. Salley, *Journal of Colonel John Herbert*, 28; L. R. Smith, "South Carolina's Indian Trade Regulations," 47.

157. Salley, *Journal of Colonel John Herbert*, 28.

158. Wiggan to Middleton, October 7, 1727, in sc Records, 13:73.

159. Willis, "Colonial Conflict," 59.

160. Commons House Journal, July 13, 1728, in Col. Office Records, no. 5/430, 109.

161. South Carolina Council Journal, September 1, 1726, in Col. Office Records, no. 5/429, 19; also see Chicken's report to the council, October 30, 1726, in Col. Office Records, no. 5/429, 72–73.

162. South Carolina Council Journal, January 24, 1726/1727, in Col. Office Records, no. 5/387, 133.

163. Upper House Journal, August 29, 1727, in Col. Office Records, no. 5/429, 167–68; Upper House Journal, July 13, 1728, in Col. Office Records, no. 5/430, 109; Salley, *Journal of Colonel John Herbert*, 24.

164. Corkran, *Carolina Indian Frontier*, 26–27; Crane, *Southern Frontier*, 272.

165. Bienville's 1726 memoir, in MPAFD, 3:495–98; Reynolds, "Alabama-Tombigbee Basin," 136–37; Crane, *Southern Frontier*, 272; Milling, *Red Carolinians*, 275.

166. John Savoy to the Board of Trade, September 18, 1728, in CSP, 36:396.

167. Commons House Journal, April 12, 1728, in Col. Office Records, no. 5/430, 83; Commons House Journal, January 31, 1728/1729, in Col. Office Records, no. 5/430, 121.

168. Crane, *Southern Frontier*, 276.

169. Crane, *Southern Frontier*, 276–77; Cuming, "Account," 115–21.

170. Cuming, "Account," 124.

171. Cuming, "Account," 125.

172. Cuming, "Account," 125, 132–33.

173. Cuming, "Account," 126–27.

174. Grant, "Historical Relation," 54–57.

175. Crane, *Southern Frontier*, 277; Grant, "Historical Relation," 55n.

176. Upper House Journals, February 1, 1721/1722, 160; Upper House Journals, February 8, 1721/1722, 275; John Savoy to the Board of Trade, September 18, 1728, in CSP 36:396.

177. Crane, *Southern Frontier*, 280.

178. Foreman, *Indians Abroad*, 44–56; Cuming, "Account," 128–29; Crane, *Southern Frontier*, 295–98.

179. JCTP, September 7, 1730, 140–46; portions reprinted in Crane, *Southern Frontier*, 300–301.

180. See Eliades, "Indian Policy," 140–41; Hatley, *Dividing Paths*, 68; Crane, *Southern Frontier*, 280, 299–302; Milling, *Red Carolinians*, 275–77.

181. Crane, *Southern Frontier*, 280.

182. Grant, "Historical Relation," 57.

183. Willis, "Colonial Conflict," 59.

184. Grant, "Historical Relation," 57; Crane, *Southern Frontier*, 279.

185. Grant, "Historical Relation," 58.

8. Designs on a Debatable Land

1. John Barnwell to Francis Nicholson, October 2, 1723, in sc Records, 10:149–51; Milling, *Red Carolinians*, 157–58.

2. Bolton and Ross, *Debatable Land*, especially pp. 1–5.

3. Yonge, "View of the Trade," 69–73. For more on the plight of the southern settlements, see Upper House Journals, January 5, 1721/1722, 151; also Rowland, Moore, and Rogers, *History of Beaufort County*, 107.

4. Meriwether, *Expansion of South Carolina*, 11; Chestnutt, "South Carolina's Expansion," 9; Lanning, *Diplomatic History of Georgia*, 10.

5. Crane, *Southern Frontier*, 282–83.

6. jctp, August 16, 1720, 198; Crane, *Southern Frontier*, 229.

7. Quoted in Crane, *Southern Frontier*, 231.

8. 1722's "Act for the Better Strengthening and Securing the Frontiers of This Province;" see Cooper and McCord, *Statutes*, 3:178–83; Vaughan and Rosen, *Carolina and Georgia Laws*, 252–55.

9. Crane, *Southern Frontier*, 235.

10. Ivers, "Scouting the Inland Passage," 127.

11. Barnwell to the South Carolina Council, July 3, 1721, in sc Records, 9:59; also see Joseph Barnwell, "Fort King George," 193–94.

12. Joseph Barnwell, "Fort King George," 189–203; Crane, *Southern Frontier*, 235–36; Ivers, *Colonial Forts of South Carolina*, 52–55, especially map on p. 53.

13. Sainsbury, *Journal of His Majesty's Council*, 18.

14. Upper House Journals, September 14, 1721, 107–8.

15. See Nicholson's speech to Ouletta and the Lower Creeks in Upper House Journals, May 25, 1722, 7–9.

16. Gerald Monger to Francis Nicholson, September 24, 1723, in sc Records, 10:156–57; Theophilus Hastings to the South Carolina Council, October 9, 1723, in sc Records, 10:186; John Worth to John Bee, July 30, 1723, in sc Records, 10:131–32.

17. Governor Antonio Benavides to King Philip V, August 18, 1723, in Brooks, *Unwritten History*, 171; Covington, "Yamasee Indians in Florida," 122; Hann, "St. Augustine's Fallout," 186.

18. Commons House Transcript, October 3, 1723, 6:281.

19. Minutes of the Committee on Indian Affairs, November 16, 1723, in sc Records, 10:182.

20. Monger to Nicholson, September 24, 1723, in sc Records, 10:156–57.

21. Upper House Journals, June 10, 1724, 275–76.

22. Barnwell to Nicholson, October 2, 1723, in sc Records, 10:151; Upper House Journals, February 11, 1722/1723, 185; Hastings to the South Carolina Council, October 9, 1723, in sc Records, 10:187; Patrick MacKay to James Oglethorpe, March 29, 1734/1735, in Juricek, Georgia Treaties, 50.

23. Upper House Journals, June 10, 1724, 275–76.

24. Fitch's report to the council, in Upper House Journals, July 20, 1725, 56.

25. Fitch, "Journals," 182–83.

26. Hastings to the South Carolina council, July 17, 1725, in Upper House Journals, August 1725, 68–70.

27. Fitch, "Journals," 204–5; Covington, "Yamasee Indians in Florida," 123; Hann, "St. Augustine's Fallout," 192.

28. Fitch, "Journals," 193–94; Porter, "Negroes on the Southern Frontier," 53–78.

29. Fitch, "Journals," 193, 202–9.

30. Benavides to King Philip V, August 18, 1723, in Brooks, Unwritten History, 171–72.

31. Lord Carteret to Francis Nicholson, September 6, 1721, in sc Records, 11:39–42; also see Lanning, Diplomatic History of Georgia, 12.

32. Commons House Transcript, February 22, 1722/1723, 6:213.

33. Benavides to King Philip V, April 21, 1722, in Brooks, Unwritten History, 168–70; Lanning, Diplomatic History of Georgia, 14–15.

34. Crane, Southern Frontier, 238–39.

35. Te Paske, The Governorship of Spanish Florida, 126–27; Crane, Southern Frontier, 241.

36. South Carolina agents Francis Yonge and John Lloyd to the Board of Trade, May 28, 1728, in sc Records, 13:54; also see Lanning, Diplomatic History of Georgia, 3.

37. Te Paske, Governorship of Spanish Florida, 129–30.

38. Council of the Indies' responses to the testimonials of Florida officials, June 10–August 18, 1724, in Serraño y Sanz, Documentos historicos, 243–60.

39. Crane, Southern Frontier, 243–44; Te Paske, Governorship of Spanish Florida, 130; Lanning, Diplomatic History of Georgia, 20–26; Bolton and Ross, Debatable Land, 69–71.

40. Patricia Seed, "Taking Possession and Reading Texts," 183–209; Juricek, "English Territorial Claims," 7–22.

41. Te Paske, Governorship of Spanish Florida, 127–28.

42. South Carolina Assembly to Yonge and Lloyd, May 9, 1722, in sc Records, 9:126; also see Francis Nicholson to the Board of Trade, August 25, 1724, in csp, 34:215.

43. Landers, "Black-Indian Interaction in Spanish Florida," 150–51; Duncan, "Servitude and Slavery," 653.

44. Upper House Journals, February 28, 1722/1723, 200; Crane, Southern Frontier, 243.

45. Upper House Journals, September 10, 1725, 106–7; Arthur Middleton to Francis Nicholson, September 10, 1725, in SC Records, 11:345–46.

46. Joseph Barnwell, "Fort King George," 190.

47. Middleton to Nicholson, September 10, 1725, in SC Records, 11:345; Upper House Journals, June 12, 1724, 278; Upper House Journals, April 15, 1725, 307.

48. Massey to the Board of Trade, April 26, 1727, in SC Records, 12:249; Crane, Southern Frontier, 245.

49. Benavides to King Philip V, February 26, 1726, Indies Archives, 844 (microfilm); Benavides to the king, March 30, 1727, Indics Archives, 844 (microfilm); Report of the Council of the Indies, July 1727, Indies Archives, 844 (microfilm); Te Paske, Governorship of Spanish Florida, 206–7.

50. Fitch's report to the council, October 26, 1726, in Col. Office Records, no. 5/429, 76.

51. JCHASC, April 9, 1725, 81; JCHASC, December 7, 1726, 26; Upper House Journal, October 7, 1726, in Col. Office Records, no. 5/429, 29–30.

52. JCHASC, April 29, 1726, 103; JCHASC, January 11, 1726/1727, 61.

53. South Carolina Council Journal, January 25, 1726/1727, in Col. Office Records, no. 5/387, 134–35.

54. Te Paske, Governorship of Spanish Florida, 130.

55. Middleton to Secretary of State Newcastle, June 13, 1728, in SC Records, 13:62–67; South Carolina Council Journal, February 10, 1727/1728, in Col. Office Records, no. 5/430, 8; Lewis Jones to the SPG Secretary, January 27, 1727/1728, in SPG Letter Books, series A, 20:117–18; Duncan, "Servitude and Slavery," 653.

56. Lewis Jones to the SPG Secretary, December 10, 1729, in SPG Letter Books, series B, 4:239; Francis Varnod to the SPG Secretary, March 22, 1727/1728, in SPG Letter Books, series A, 21:85; Commons House Journal, September 15, 1727, in Col. Office Records, no. 5/429, 231; Crane, Southern Frontier, 247.

57. Middleton to Newcastle, June 13, 1728, in SC Records, 13:62.

58. Middleton to Newcastle, June 13, 1728, in SC Records, 13:64; Barker, " 'Much Blood and Treasure,' " 265; Crane, Southern Frontier, 248; Milling, Red Carolinians, 159.

59. Captain Edward Massey to the Board of Trade, April 26, 1727, in SC Records, 12:247–49; Crane, Southern Frontier, 246–47.

60. Massey to Secretary of War Henry Pelham, August 3, 1727, in SC Records, 12:239–40.

61. South Carolina Assembly to Massey, September 6, 1727, in CSP, 35:691; Crane, Southern Frontier, 248.

62. Upper House Journal, August 3, 1727, in Col. Office Records, no. 5/429, 159–60.

63. JCHASC, January 20, 1726/1727, 74, 81; Commons House Journal, August 30, 1727, in Col. Office Records, no. 5/429, 221.

64. Middleton to Newcastle, June 13, 1728, in sc Records, 13:67; Milling, *Red Carolinians*, 160.

65. Commons House Journal, September 23, 1727, in Col. Office Records, no. 5/429, 240.

66. Upper House Journal, August 3, 1727, in Col. Office Records, no. 5/429, 160; Commons House Journal, August 30, 1727, in ibid., 221; Upper House Journal, September 13, 1727, ibid., 173; Upper House Journal, September 23, 1727, in ibid., 185.

67. Salley, *Journal of Colonel John Herbert*, 4n.

68. Herbert to Middleton, September 13, 1727, in sc Records, 13:71.

69. Glover to the council, February 12, 1717/1728, in sc Records, 13:113.

70. Glover to the council, January 13, 1727/1728, in sc Records, 13:98; Barker, " 'Much Blood and Treasure,' " 268.

71. Glover to the council, January 16, 1727/1728, in sc Records, 13:86.

72. Glover to the council, January 16, 1727/1728, in sc Records, 13:92.

73. Glover to the council, March 5, 1727/1728, in sc Records, 13:126–27.

74. Glover to the council, January 16, 1727/1728, in sc Records, 13:93; Glover to the council, February 1727/1728, in sc Records, 13:119.

75. Glover to the council, March 14, 1727/1728, in sc Records, 13:130–31.

76. Glover to the council, January 16, 1727/1728, in sc Records, 13:87.

77. Glover to the council, January 16, 1727/1728, in sc Records, 13:93–94.

78. Glover to the council, March 15, 1727/1728, in sc Records, 13:145.

79. Glover to the council, March 15, 1727/1728, in sc Records, 13:145.

80. Glover to the council, January 16, 1727/1728, in sc Records, 13:96.

81. Glover to the council, January 13, 1727/1728, in sc Records, 13:89.

82. Glover to the council, February 8, 1727/1728, in sc Records, 13:108.

83. Board of Trade to King George II, December 1, 1727, in sc Records, 12:269–71.

84. Herbert to Middleton, October 26, 1727, in sc Records, 13:77–79.

85. Commons House Journal, February 9, 1727/1728, in Col. Office Records, no. 5/430, 7.

86. Jabbs, "The South Carolina Colonial Militia," 409–10.

87. Rowland, Moore, and Rogers, *History of Beaufort County*, 107; Ivers, "Scouting the Inland Passage," 128.

88. Duncan, "Servitude and Slavery," 656.

89. Crane, *Southern Frontier*, 249–50.

90. Milling, *Red Carolinians*, 160.

91. Middleton to Newcastle, June 13, 1728, in sc Records, 13:70; also Swanton, *Early History*, 341; Crane, *Southern Frontier*, 250; Landers, "Black-Indian Interaction," 152; Milling, *Red Carolinians*, 160–61; Te Paske, *Governorship of Spanish Florida*, 131.

92. Report of the Council of the Indies, February 1727, Indies Archives, 844 (microfilm); Hann, "St. Augustine's Fallout," 192.

93. Covington, "Yamasee Indians in Florida," 124; also Swanton, *Early History*, 104.

94. Quoted in Swanton, *Early History*, 340.

95. Covington, "Yamasee Indians in Florida," 124–25; Hann, "St. Augustine's Fallout," 194–200.

96. Benavides to Conde de Salazar, October 15, 1728, Indies Archives, 844 (microfilm); Middleton to Newcastle, June 13, 1728, in sc Records, 13:70; also Hann, "St. Augustine's Fallout," 197.

97. Benavides to Conde de Salazar, October 15, 1728, Indies Archives, 844 (microfilm); Te Paske, *Governorship of Spanish Florida*, 131–32; Crane, *Southern Frontier*, 250–51; Milling, *Red Carolinians*, 161.

98. Glover to the council, April 15, 1728, in sc Records, 13:164.

99. Corkran, *Creek Frontier*, 77–78.

100. Glover to the council, April 15, 1728, in sc Records, 13:168.

101. Glover to the council, March 17, 1727/1728, sc, 13:118.

102. Glover to the council, March 17, 1727/1728, sc, 13:120.

103. Glover to the council, April 15, 1728, in sc Records, 13:164–67.

104. Glover to the council, March 17, 1727/1728, in sc Records, 13:118.

105. Glover to the council, March 17, 1727/1728, in sc, 13:144; Glover to the council, April 15, 1728, in sc Records, 13:168.

106. Commons House Journal, July 13, 1728, in Col. Office Records, no. 5/430, 110.

107. Commons House Journal, April 5, 1728, in Col. Office Records, no. 5/430, 17.

108. Commons House Journal, April 4, 1728, in Col. Office Records, no. 5/430, 16.

109. Commons House Journal, April 6, 1728, in Col. Office Records, no. 5/430, 18.

110. Lepore, *Name of War*, 173–75.

111. Francis Varnod to the SPG secretary, March 22, 1727/1728, in SPG Letter Books, series A, 21:85; Lewis Jones to the SPG secretary, December 10, 1729, in SPG Letter Books, series B, 4:239; Rowland, Moore, and Rogers, *History of Beaufort County*, 108.

112. Crane, *Southern Frontier*, 251.

113. Montgomery, *Azilia*; Coleman, "Southern Frontier," 166; Crane, *Southern Frontier*, 210–14.

114. Coleman, "Southern Frontier," 166–67; Crane, *Southern Frontier*, 283–85; Crane, "Projects for Colonization," 31.

115. Cooper and McCord, *Statutes*, 3:176–83; Meriwether, *Expansion of South Carolina*, 11; Crane, *Southern Frontier*, 282–83; Crane, "Projects for Colonization," 32.

116. Sirmans, *Colonial South Carolina*, 155; Clowse, *Economic Beginnings*, 226–29.

117. Stumpf, "Merchants of Colonial Charles Town," 138; Weir, *Colonial South*

Carolina, 109–10; Sirmans, *Colonial South Carolina*, 158–59; Meriwether, *Expansion of South Carolina*, 8–9.

118. Hughes, "Populating the Back Country," viii; Crane, *Southern Frontier*, 288–89; Coleman, "Southern Frontier," 168; Meriwether, *Expansion of South Carolina*, 11.

119. Weir, *Colonial South Carolina*, 111; Stumpf, "Merchants of Colonial Charles Town," 140; Sirmans, *Colonial South Carolina*, 163; Crane, *Southern Frontier*, 290.

120. Sherman, *Robert Johnson*, 97–105; Crane, *Southern Frontier*, 292.

121. Johnson quoted in Crane, *Southern Frontier*, 293; Hughes, "Populating the Back Country," 4–6; Meriwether, *Expansion of South Carolina*, 13; Sherman, *Robert Johnson*, 108–9; Crane, "Projects for Colonization," 32; Weir, *Colonial South Carolina*, 111–12; Duncan, "Servitude and Slavery," 89.

122. Crane, *Southern Frontier*, 294–95; Lanning, *Diplomatic History of Georgia*, 32.

123. Hughes, "Populating the Backcountry," 8.

124. Crane, *Southern Frontier*, 303–25. For a transcript of the charter itself, see Vaughan and Rosen, *Carolina and Georgia Laws*, 359–63.

125. Crane, *Southern Frontier*, 251; Lanning, *Diplomatic History of Georgia*, 4.

126. Oglethorpe, "New and Accurate Account," 210.

127. For discussions of Oglethorpe's extensive arguments with the Spanish over his settlement of the Georgia coast, see Bolton and Ross, *Debatable Land*, 72–76; Lanning, *Diplomatic History of Georgia*, 35–54.

128. Juricek, *Georgia Treaties*, xxi; Spalding, "Georgia and South Carolina during the Oglethorpe Period," 54; Corry, *Indian Affairs in Georgia*, 70–71; Foret, "On the Marchlands of Empire," 94; Sonderegger, "Southern Frontier," 121; Gallay, *Indian Slave Trade*, 350–51.

129. Swanton, *Early History*, 109; Juricek, *Georgia Treaties*, 2.

130. Foreman, *Indians Abroad*, 60–67; Foret, "On the Marchlands of Empire," 97–100.

131. Juricek, *Georgia Treaties*, 3.

132. For a transcript of the treaty, see Juricek, *Georgia Treaties*, 15–17. For more on the Lower Creeks' first visit to Savannah, see Gordon, *Journal*, 48–49; Spalding, "Georgia and South Carolina during the Oglethorpe Period," 56–57; and Corry, *Indian Affairs in Georgia*, 70.

133. Juricek, *Georgia Treaties*, 12–14.

134. Braund, *Deerskins and Duffels*, 35, 41. For more on the life of Mary Musgrove, see Fisher, "Mary Musgrove."

135. Foret, "On the Marchlands of Empire," 94; Sonderegger, " Southern Frontier," 121.

136. Corry, *Indian Affairs in Georgia*, 49.

137. Johnson quoted in Spalding, "Georgia and South Carolina during the Oglethorpe Period," 14.

138. Gordon, *Journal*, 37–42; Weir, *Colonial South Carolina*, 116.

139. Chestnutt, "South Carolina's Expansion," 13; Spalding, "South Carolina and Georgia," 83, 93; Crane, *Southern Frontier*, 302.

140. Oglethorpe, "New and Accurate Account," 206.

141. Wood, "Changing Population," 38; Wood, *Black Majority*, 146–52; Menard, "Africanization of the Low Country Labor Force," 104.

142. Hughes, "Populating the Back Country," 10; Weir, *Colonial South Carolina*, 208. For more on South Carolina's territorial expansion in the mid-eighteenth century, see G. L. Johnson, *Frontier in the Colonial South*.

143. Menard, "Africanization of the Low Country Labor Force," 93, 107; Wood, *Black Majority*, 151.

144. Wood, "Changing Population of the Colonial South," 38; also Wood, *Black Majority*, 152.

145. Menard, "Africanization of the Low Country Labor Force," 86–87.

146. Wood, *Black Majority*, 165–66, 232–33.

147. Francis Varnod to the SPG secretary, January 13, 1723/1724, in SPG Letter Books, series A, 18:71; South Carolina missionaries' responses to SPG questionnaire, 1724, in Manross, *Fulham Papers*, 138–39; William Guy's report to the SPG, 1727, in Merrens, *Colonial South Carolina Scene*, 84; Klingberg, *Appraisal of the Negro*, 52, 124.

148. Aptheker, *American Negro Slave Revolts*, 181; Porter, "Negroes on the Southern Frontier," 63–64; Wood, *Black Majority*, 301–7.

149. Francis Varnod, quoted in Klingberg, *Appraisal of the Negro*, 56; also see Wood, *Black Majority*, 218–24. For a transcript of the 1734 slave patrol act, see Cooper and McCord, *Statutes*, 3:395–99.

150. Weir, *Colonial South Carolina*, 115–16; Chestnutt, "South Carolina's Expansion," 10; Rowland, Moore, and Rogers, *History of Beaufort County*, 111.

151. Spalding, "Georgia and South Carolina during the Oglethorpe Period," 57; Juricek, *Georgia Treaties*, 5.

152. Te Paske, "Fugitive Slave," 7.

153. Wood, *Black Majority*, 259–60; Landers, "Black-Indian Interaction," 152–58.

154. Wood, *Black Majority*, 308–26; Porter, "Negroes on the Southern Frontier," 77; Aptheker, *American Negro Slave Revolts*, 187–89.

155. Spalding, "South Carolina and Georgia," 95; Barker, " 'Much Blood and Treasure,' " 280; Eliades, "Indian Policy," 159–60.

156. Compare the transcript of the 1731 South Carolina act, in Cooper and McCord, *Statutes*, 3:327–34, to the 1735 Georgia act, in Vaughan and Rosen, *Carolina and Georgia Laws*, 363–69. Also see Juricek, *Georgia Treaties*, 29.

157. Mr. Garden to Mr. Quincy, July 20, 1736, in SPG Letter Books, series B, 4:284; Corry, *Indian Affairs in Georgia*, 52–60; Foret, "On the Marchlands of Empire," 102–12; Sonderegger, "Southern Frontier," 130–32.

158. Byrd, *Histories of the Dividing Line*, 246; also Corry, *Indian Affairs in Georgia*, 57–58.

159. Patrick MacKay to James Oglethorpe, March 29, 1735, in Juricek, *Georgia Treaties*, 50.

160. Bartram, "Travels Through North and South Carolina," 36–37.

Conclusion

1. West, "American Frontier," 39.

2. Keegan, *History of Warfare*, 3–12.

3. See especially Lepore, *Name of War*, 112–13; Malone, *Skulking Way of War*, 25–27.

4. Verner Crane was justified in offering a criticism of previous scholars who tended to gloss over the differences between the various Indian wars; see Crane, *Southern Frontier*, 162. More recently general overviews of the colonial Indian wars have tended to display greater sensitivity to these differences; see, for example, Steele, *Warpaths*; Utley and Washburn, *Indian Wars*.

5. Martin, "Southeastern Indians," 305; Wood, "Circles in the Sand," 3, 14.

6. Merrell, " 'Our Bond of Peace,' " 201–3; Merrell, " 'Customes of Our Countrey,' " 120.

Bibliography

Manuscripts and Archival Selections

Archives of the Indies, Audiencia of Santo Domingo. Stetson Collection, P. K. Yonge
Library of Florida History, University of Florida, Gainesville. (Cited as Indies
Archives.)

Barnwell Letter Book. Compiled by Catharine O. Barnwell. South Carolina Historical
Society, Charleston.

British Public Record Office, Colonial Office. CO 5: Original Correspondence,
America and West Indies. South Carolina Department of Archives and
History, Columbia. (Cited as Col. Office Records.)

Fulham Papers in the Lambeth Palace Library, Colonial Section. Woodruff Library,
Emory University, Atlanta.

Journals of the Commons House of Assembly of South Carolina. Vols. 1–6.
Transcribed by John Green. South Carolina Department of Archives and
History, Columbia. (Cited as Commons House Transcript.)

Journals of the Governor's Council of South Carolina, 1671–1721. Transcribed by John
Green. South Carolina Department of Archives and History, Columbia.
(Cited as Council Transcript.)

Journals of the Upper House of Assembly of South Carolina. Compiled by William S.
Jenkins. South Carolina Department of Archives and History, Columbia.
(Cited as Upper House Journals.)

Mary Letitia Ross Papers. Georgia Department of Archives and History, Atlanta.

Pryce Hughes Letters. South Caroliniana Library, University of South Carolina,
Columbia.

Records in the British Public Record Office Relating to South Carolina. Vols. 1–13.
Transcribed by W. Noel Sainsbury. South Carolina Department of Archives
and History, Columbia. (Cited as SC Records.)

Society for the Propagation of the Gospel in Foreign Parts. Letter Books: Series A and
B. Pitts Theology Library, Emory University, Atlanta. (Cited as SPG Letter
Books.)

Articles, Books, and Dissertations

Adair, James. *The History of the American Indians: Particularly Those Nations Adjoining to the Mississippi, East and West Florida, Georgia, South and North Carolina, and Virginia; Containing an Account of their Origin, Language, Manners, Religious and Civil Customs.* New York: Johnson Reprint, 1968.

Anderson, David. *The Savannah River Chiefdoms: Political Change in the Late Prehistoric Southeast.* Tuscaloosa: University of Alabama Press, 1994.

Aptheker, Herbert. *American Negro Slave Revolts.* New York: International Publishers, 1963.

——. "Maroons Within the Present Limits of the United States." *Journal of Negro History* 24 (April 1939): 167–84.

Archdale, John. "A New Description of That Fertile and Pleasant Province of Carolina." In *Narratives of Early Carolina, 1650–1708,* edited by Alexander Salley Jr., 277–312. New York: Charles Scribner's Sons, 1911.

Arnade, Charles. "The English Invasion of Spanish Florida, 1700–1706." *Florida Historical Quarterly* 41 (July 1962): 29–37.

——. *The Siege of St. Augustine in 1702.* Gainesville: University Press of Florida, 1958.

Axtell, James. *The European and the Indian: Essays in the Ethnohistory of Colonial North America.* New York: Oxford University Press, 1981.

——. *The Indians' New South: Cultural Change in the Colonial Southeast.* Baton Rouge: Louisiana State University Press, 1997.

——. *The Invasion Within: The Contest of Cultures in Colonial North America.* New York: Oxford University Press, 1985.

Baine, Rodney. "Myths of Mary Musgrove." *Georgia Historical Quarterly* 76 (Summer 1992): 428–35.

Barcía, Andres de. *Chronological History of the Continent of Florida.* Translated by Anthony Kerrigan. Gainesville: University Press of Florida, 1951.

Barker, Eirlys. " 'Much Blood and Treasure': South Carolina's Indian Traders, 1670–1755." PhD diss., College of William and Mary, 1993.

Barnwell, John. "Journal of John Barnwell." *Virginia Magazine of History and Biography* 5 (April 1898): 391–402.

——. "Journal of John Barnwell, Part II." *Virginia Magazine of History and Biography* 6 (July 1898): 42–55.

Barnwell, Joseph, ed. "Fort King George: Journal of Colonel John Barnwell in the Construction of the Fort on the Altamaha in 1721." *South Carolina Historical and Genealogical Magazine* 27 (October 1926): 189–203.

——. "The Second Tuscarora Expedition." *South Carolina Historical and Genealogical Magazine* 10 (January 1909): 33–48.

Bartram, William. "Travels Through North and South Carolina, East and West Florida, the Cherokee Country, the Extensive Territories of the

Muscogulges, or Creek Confederacy, and the Country of the Chactaws; Containing an Account of the Soil and Natural Productions of Those Regions, Together with Observations on the Manners of the Indians." In *William Bartram on the Southeastern Indians*, edited by Gregory Waselkov and Kathryn Holland Braund, 33–132. Lincoln: University of Nebraska Press, 1995.

Beverly, Robert. *The History and Present State of Virginia*. Chapel Hill: University of North Carolina Press, 1947.

Bloom, Leonard. "The Acculturation of the Eastern Cherokee: Historical Aspects." *North Carolina Historical Review* 19 (October 1942): 323–58.

Bolton, Herbert. "The Mission as a Frontier Institution in the Spanish-American Colonies." *American Historical Review* 23 (October 1917): 42–61.

———. "Spanish Resistance to Carolina Traders in Western Georgia." *Georgia Historical Quarterly* 9 (June 1925): 115–36.

Bolton, Herbert, and Mary Ross. *The Debatable Land: A Sketch of the Anglo-Spanish Contest for the Georgia Country*. Berkeley: University of California Press, 1925.

Boyce, Douglas. " 'As the Wind Scatters the Smoke': The Tuscaroras in the Eighteenth Century." In *Beyond the Covenant Chain: Iroquois and Their Neighbors in Indian North America, 1600–1800*, edited by Daniel K. Richter and James H. Merrell, 151–63. Syracuse NY: Syracuse University Press, 1987.

Boyd, Mark F., ed. and trans. "Diego Peña's Expedition to Apalachee and Apalachicola in 1716." *Florida Historical Quarterly* 28 (July 1949): 1–27.

———, ed. and trans. "Documents Describing the Second and Third Expeditions of Lieutenant Diego Peña to Apalachee and Apalachicola in 1717 and 1718." *Florida Historical Quarterly* 31 (October 1952): 109–39.

———, ed. "Enumeration of Florida's Spanish Missions in 1675." *Florida Historical Quarterly* 27 (October 1948): 181–88.

———, ed. and trans. "The Expedition of Marcus Delgado from Apalachee to the Upper Creek Country in 1686." *Florida Historical Quarterly* 16 (January 1937): 3–48.

———, ed. *Here They Once Stood: The Tragic End of the Apalachee Missions*. Gainesville: University Press of Florida, 1951.

———, ed. and trans. "The Siege of St. Augustine by Governor Moore of South Carolina in 1702 as Reported to the King of Spain by Don Joseph Zúñiga y Zerda, Governor of Florida." *Florida Historical Quarterly* 26 (April 1948): 345–52.

Braund, Kathryn Holland. "The Creek Indians, Blacks, and Slavery." *Journal of Southern History* 57 (November 1991): 601–36.

———. *Deerskins and Duffels: The Creek Indian Trade with Anglo-America, 1685–1815*. Lincoln: University of Nebraska Press, 1993.

————. "Guardians of Tradition and Handmaidens to Change: Women's Roles in Creek Economic Social Life in the Eighteenth Century." *American Indian Quarterly* 14 (Summer 1990): 239–58.

Brooks, A. M., ed. *The Unwritten History of Old St. Augustine, Copied from Spanish Archives in Seville by Miss A. M. Brooks*. Translated by Annie Avarette. Saint Augustine FL: Saint Augustine Historical Society, 1909.

Brown, Douglas. *The Catawba Indians: The People of the River*. Columbia: University of South Carolina Press, 1966.

Brown, Philip. "Early Indian Trade in the Development of South Carolina: Politics, Economics, and Social Mobility during the Proprietary Period, 1670–1719." *South Carolina Historical Magazine* 76 (April 1975): 118–28.

Burke, Lee. "Eighteenth-Century Trade Guns in the South: Or, The Carolina Gun, Its Time and Place in History." *The American Society of Arms Collectors Bulletin* 65 (September 1991): 3–16.

Bushnell, Amy Turner. *The King's Coffer: Proprietors of the Spanish Florida Treasury, 1565–1702*. Gainesville: University Press of Florida, 1981.

————. "Ruling the 'Republic of Indians' in Seventeenth-Century Florida." In *Powhatan's Mantle: Indians in the Colonial Southeast*, edited by Peter Wood, Gregory Waselkov, and M. Thomas Hatley, 134–50. Lincoln: University of Nebraska Press, 1989.

————. *Situado and Sabana: Spain's Support System for the Presidio and Mission Provinces of Florida*. Anthropological Papers of the American Museum of Natural History, vol. 74. New York: American Museum of Natural History, 1994.

Byrd, William, II. *Histories of the Dividing Line betwixt Virginia and North Carolina*. New York: Dover, 1967.

————. *The Secret Diary of William Byrd of Westover, 1709–1712*. Edited by Louis B. Wright and Marion Tinling. Richmond: Virginia Historical Society, 1941.

Carroll, Bartholomew, ed. *Historical Collections of South Carolina: Embracing Many Rare and Valuable Pamphlets, and Other Documents, Relating to the History of That State, From Its First Discovery to Its Independence, in the Year 1776*. New York: Harper & Brothers, 1836.

Cayton, Andrew R. L., and Fredrika J. Teute. "On the Connection of Frontiers." In *Contact Points: American Frontiers from the Mohawk Valley to the Mississippi, 1750–1830*, edited by Andrew R. L. Cayton and Fredrika J. Teute, 1–15. Chapel Hill: University of North Carolina Press for the Omohundro Institute of Early American History and Culture, 1998.

Chapman, Martha. "Indian Relations in Colonial North Carolina, 1584–1754." MA thesis, University of North Carolina, 1937.

Charlevoix, Pierre de. "Pierre de Charlevoix's Journal." In *Early Travels in the Tennessee*

Country, 1540–1800, edited by Samuel Cole Williams, 85–92. Johnson City TN: Watauga Press, 1928.

Chatelain, Verne. *The Defenses of Spanish Florida, 1565–1763*. Washington DC: Carnegie Institution of Washington, 1941.

Cheeves, Langdon, ed. "Journal of the March of the Carolinians into the Cherokee Mountains, 1715–1716." In *Yearbook of the City of Charleston*, 324–54. Charleston SC: Walker, Erono, & Cogswell, 1894.

Chestnutt, David R. "South Carolina's Expansion into Colonial Georgia." PhD diss., University of Georgia, 1973.

Chicken, George. "Journals of Captain George Chicken's Mission from Charleston to the Cherokees, 1725." In *Travels in the American Colonies*, edited by Newton Mereness, 93–172. New York: Macmillan, 1916.

Cline, Howard. *The Florida Indians*. New York: Garland, 1974.

Clowse, Converse. *Economic Beginnings in Colonial South Carolina, 1670–1730*. Columbia: University of South Carolina Press, 1971.

Cole, David. "A Brief Outline of the South Carolina Colonial Militia System." *Proceedings of the South Carolina Historical Association* 24 (1954): 14–23.

———. "The Organization and Administration of the South Carolina Militia System." PhD diss., University of South Carolina, 1953.

Coleman, Kenneth. "The Southern Frontier: Georgia's Founding and the Expansion of South Carolina." *Georgia Historical Quarterly* 56 (Summer 1972): 163–74.

Cooper, Thomas, and David J. McCord, eds. *The Statutes at Large of South Carolina*. Vols. 1–10. Columbia: State of South Carolina, 1836–41.

Corkran, David, ed. "Alexander Long's 'A Small Postscript on the Ways and Manners of the Indians Called Cherokees.'" *Southern Indian Studies* 21 (October 1969): 1–49.

———. *The Carolina Indian Frontier*. Columbia: University of South Carolina Press, 1970.

———. *The Creek Frontier, 1540–1783*. Norman: University of Oklahoma Press, 1967.

Corry, John P. *Indian Affairs in Georgia, 1732–1756*. Philadelphia: George Ferguson, 1936.

Covington, James. "The Apalachee Indians, 1704–1763." *Florida Historical Quarterly* 50 (April 1972): 366–84.

———. "Migration of Seminoles into Florida, 1700–1820." *Florida Historical Quarterly* 46 (April 1968): 340–57.

———. "The Yamasee Indians in Florida, 1715–1763." *The Florida Anthropologist* 23 (September 1970): 119–28.

Crane, Verner. "Projects for Colonization in the South, 1684–1732." *Mississippi Valley Historical Review* 12 (June 1925): 23–35.

————. *The Southern Frontier, 1670–1732*. Durham NC: Duke University Press, 1928. Reprint, New York: Norton, 1981.

Cronon, William. "Revisiting the Vanishing Frontier: The Legacy of Frederick Jackson Turner." *Western Historical Quarterly* 18 (Spring 1987): 157–76.

Cuming, Sir Alexander. "Account of the Cherokee Indians, and of Sir Alexander Cuming's Journey Amongst Them." In *Early Travels in the Tennessee Country, 1540–1800*, edited by Samuel Cole Williams, 115–46. Johnson City TN: Watauga Press, 1928.

Cumming, William P. *The Southeast in Early Maps, with an Annotated Check List of Printed and Manuscript and Regional and Local Maps of Southeastern North America during the Colonial Period.* Chapel Hill: University of North Carolina Press, 1958.

Debo, Angie. *The Road to Disappearance.* Norman: University of Oklahoma Press, 1941.

De Brahm, William. "Philosophico-Historico-Hydrogeography of South Carolina, Georgia, and East Florida." In *Documents Connected with the History of South Carolina*, edited by Plowden Weston Jr., 208–41. London: by the author, 1856.

Defoe, Daniel. "Party Tyranny." In *Narratives of Early Carolina, 1650–1708*, edited by Alexander Salley Jr., 219–64. New York: Charles Scribner's Sons, 1911.

Delaney, Caldwell, ed. "A Newly Found French Journal, 1720." *Alabama Review* 19 (April 1966): 146–53.

Demos, John. *The Unredeemed Captive: A Family Story from Early America.* New York: Alfred A. Knopf, 1994.

Dickinson, Jonathan. *Jonathan Dickinson's Journal: Or, God's Protecting Providence.* New York: Garland, 1977.

Dill, Alonzo Thomas, Jr. "Eighteenth-Century New Bern: Rebellion and Indian Warfare." *North Carolina Historical Review* 22 (July 1945): 293–319.

Dobyns, Henry. *Their Number Become Thinned: Population Dynamics in Eastern North America.* Knoxville: University of Tennessee Press, 1983.

Dodson, Leonidas. *Alexander Spotswood, Governor of Colonial Virginia, 1710–1722.* Philadelphia: University of Pennsylvania Press, 1932.

Donnan, Elizabeth. "The Slave Trade in South Carolina Before the Revolution." *American Historical Review* 33 (July 1928): 804–28.

Dowd, Gregory E. "The Panic of 1751: The Significance of Rumors on the South Carolina-Cherokee Frontier." *William and Mary Quarterly*, 3rd ser., 53 (July 1996): 527–60.

Duncan, John Donald. "Servitude and Slavery in Colonial South Carolina, 1670–1776." PhD diss., Emory University, 1970.

Dunlop, J. G., ed. "Letters from John Stewart to William Dunlop." *South Carolina Historical and Genealogical Magazine* 32 (January 1931): 1–33.

————. "William Dunlop's Mission to St. Augustine in 1688." *South Carolina Historical and Genealogical Magazine* 34 (January 1933): 1–30.

Durschlag, Richard. "The First Creek Resistance: Transformations in Creek Indian Existence and the Yamasee War, 1670–1730." PhD diss., Duke University, 1995.

Ehrenreich, Barbara. *Blood Rites: Origins and History of the Passions of War*. New York: Metropolitan Books, 1997.

Eliades, Davis K. "The Indian Policy of Colonial South Carolina, 1670–1767." PhD diss., University of South Carolina, 1981.

Fausz, J. Frederick. "An 'Abundance of Blood on Both Sides': England's First Indian War, 1609–1614." *Virginia Magazine of History and Biography* 98 (January 1990): 3–56.

Faye, Stanley. "The Contest for Pensacola Bay and Other Gulf Ports, 1698–1722." *Florida Historical Quarterly* 24 (January 1946): 167–95.

Ferguson, Brian R., and Neil Whitehead. "The Violent Edge of Empire." In *War in the Tribal Zone: Expanding States and Indigenous Warfare*, edited by Brian R. Ferguson and Neil Whitehead, 4–23. Santa Fe NM: School of American Research Press, 1992.

Ferling, John E. *A Wilderness of Miseries: War and Warriors in Early America*. Westport CT: Greenwood Press, 1980.

Fisher, Doris Behrman. "Mary Musgrove: Creek Englishwoman." PhD diss., Emory University, 1990.

Fitch, Tobias. "Journals of Captain Tobias Fitch's Missions from Charleston to the Creeks, 1726." In *Travels in the American Colonies*, edited by Newton Mereness, 177–212. New York: Macmillan, 1916.

Folmer, Henry. *Franco-Spanish Rivalry in North America, 1529–1763*. Glendale CA: A. H. Clark, 1953.

Fontaine, John. *The Journal of John Fontaine: An Irish Huguenot Son in Spain and Virginia, 1710–1719*. Edited by Edward P. Alexander. Williamsburg VA: Institute of Early American History and Culture, 1972.

Forbes, Jack. "Frontiers in American History and the Role of the Frontier Historian." *Ethnohistory* 15 (Spring 1968): 203–35.

Ford, Lawrence Carroll. *The Triangular Struggle for Spanish Pensacola, 1689–1739*. Washington DC: Catholic University of America Press, 1939.

Foreman, Carol. *Indians Abroad, 1493–1938*. Norman: University of Oklahoma Press, 1943.

Foret, James Michael. "French Colonial Indian Policy in Louisiana, 1699–1763." In *Proceedings of the Eighth Meeting of the French Colonial Historical Society*, 82–90. Washington DC: University Presses of America, 1985.

————. "On the Marchlands of Empire: Trade, Diplomacy, and War on the

Southeastern Frontier, 1733–1763." PhD diss., College of William and Mary, 1990.

Franklin, W. Neil. "Virginia and the Cherokee Indian Trade, 1673–1752." *East Tennessee Historical Society Publications* 4 (January 1932): 3–21.

Friedlander, Amy. "Indian Slavery in Proprietary South Carolina, 1671–1795." MA thesis, Emory University, 1974.

Gallay, Alan. *The Formation of a Planter Elite: Jonathan Bryan and the Southern Colonial Frontier*. Athens: University of Georgia Press, 1989.

———. *The Indian Slave Trade: The Rise of the English Empire in the American South, 1670–1717*. New Haven CT: Yale University Press, 2002.

Galloway, Patricia. "Confederacy as a Solution to Chiefdom Dissolution: Historical Evidence in the Choctaw Case." In *The Forgotten Centuries: Indians and Europeans in the American South, 1521–1704*, edited by Charles Hudson and Carmen Chaves Tesser, 393–420. Athens: University of Georgia Press, 1994.

———. "Henri de Tonti du village des Chacta, 1702: The Beginning of the French Alliance." In *La Salle and His Legacy: Frenchmen and Indians in the Lower Mississippi Valley*, edited by Patricia Galloway, 146–75. Jackson: University Press of Mississippi, 1982.

———, ed. *The Hernando De Soto Expedition: History, Historiography, and "Discovery" in the Southeast*. Lincoln: University of Nebraska Press, 1997.

Gannon, Michael. *The Cross in the Sand: The Early Catholic Church in Florida, 1513–1870*. Gainesville: University Press of Florida, 1965.

Gatschet, Albert. *A Migration Legend of the Creek Indians*. Vol. 1. New York: Kraus Reprint, 1969.

Giraud, Marcel. *A History of French Louisiana, 1715–1717*. Baton Rouge: Louisiana State University Press, 1974.

———. *A History of Louisiana: Reign of Louis XIV, 1699–1715*. Baton Rouge: Louisiana State University Press, 1974.

Given, Brian J. *A Most Pernicious Thing: Gun Trading and Native Warfare in the Early Colonial Period*. Ottawa: Carleton University Press, 1994.

Goodwin, Gary. *Cherokees in Transition: A Study of Changing Culture and Environment Prior to 1775*. Chicago: University of Chicago Press, 1977.

Gordon, Peter. *The Journal of Peter Gordon, 1732–1735*. Edited by E. Merton Coulter. Athens: University of Georgia Press, 1963.

Goss, Charles Wayne. "The French and the Choctaw Indians, 1700–1763." PhD diss., Texas Tech University, 1977.

Grant, Ludovick. "Historical Relation of Facts Delivered by Ludovick Grant, Indian Trader, to His Excellency the Governor of South Carolina." *South Carolina Historical and Genealogical Magazine* 10 (January 1909): 54–68.

Great Britain. Public Record Office. *Journal of the Commissioners of Trade and Plantations.* Vols. 1–6. London: His Majesty's Stationery Office, 1920. (Cited as JCTP.)

Green, William. "The Search for Altamaha: The Archaeology of an Early Eighteenth-Century Yamasee Indian Town." MA thesis, University of South Carolina, 1991.

Greene, Jack P., ed. *Selling a New World: Two Colonial South Carolina Promotional Pamphlets.* Columbia: University of South Carolina Press, 1988.

Griffith, Lucille. "South Carolina and Fort Alabama, 1714–1763." *Alabama Review* 12 (October 1959): 258–71.

Grinde, Donald, Jr. "Native American Slavery in the Southern Colonies." *Indian Historian* 10 (Spring 1977): 38–42.

Haan, Richard L. "The 'Trade Does Not Flourish as Formerly': The Ecological Origins of the Yamasee War of 1715." *Ethnohistory* 28 (Fall 1982): 341–58.

Haefeli, Evan, and Kevin Sweeney. "Revisiting *The Redeemed Captive*: New Perspectives on the 1704 Attack on Deerfield." *William and Mary Quarterly*, 3rd ser., 52 (January 1995): 3–46.

Hahn, Steven C. "The Invention of the Creek Nation: A Political History of the Creek Indians in the South's Imperial Era, 1540–1763." PhD diss., Emory University, 2000.

———. "A Miniature Arms Race: The Role of the Flintlock in Initiating Indian Dependency in the Southeastern United States, 1656–1730." MA thesis, University of Georgia, 1995.

———. "The Mother of Necessity: Carolina, the Creek Indians, and the Making of a New Order in the American Southeast, 1670–1763." In *The Transformation of the Southeastern Indians, 1540–1760*, edited by Robbie Ethridge and Charles Hudson, 79–114. Jackson: University Press of Mississippi, 2002.

Hann, John H. *Apalachee: The Land Between the Rivers.* Gainesville: University Press of Florida, 1988.

———. "The Apalachee of the Historic Era." In *The Forgotten Centuries: Indians and Europeans in the American South, 1521–1704*, edited by Charles Hudson and Carmen Tesser, 327–49. Athens: University of Georgia Press, 1994.

———. *A History of the Timucua Indians and Missions.* Gainesville: University Press of Florida, 1996.

———. "Late Seventeenth-Century Forebears of the Lower Creeks and Seminoles." *Southeastern Archaeology* 15 (1996): 68–89.

———. "Political Leadership among the Natives of Spanish Florida." *Florida Historical Quarterly* 71 (October 1992): 188–208.

———. "St. Augustine's Fallout from the Yamasee War." *Florida Historical Quarterly* 68 (Winter 1989–90): 180–200.

———. "Translation of Alonso Leturiondo's Memorial to the King of Spain." *Florida Archaeology* 2 (1986): 165–225.

Hatley, M. Thomas. *The Dividing Paths: Cherokees and South Carolinians through the Era of Revolution*. New York: Oxford University Press, 1993.

Hayes, J. E., ed. *Indian Treaties and Cessions of Land in Georgia, 1705–1837*. Atlanta: WPA Project No. 7158, 1941.

Heldman, Donald. "Fort Toulouse of the Alabamas and the Eighteenth-Century Indian Trade." *World Archaeology* 5 (October 1973): 163–69.

Hewatt, Alexander. *An Historical Account of the Rise and Progress of the Colonies of South Carolina and Georgia*. London: A. Donaldson, 1779.

Higginbotham, Jay. *Old Mobile: Fort Louis de la Louisiane, 1702–1711*. Tuscaloosa: University of Alabama Press, 1991.

Hinderaker, Eric. "The 'Four Indian Kings' and the Imaginative Construction of the First British Empire." *William and Mary Quarterly*, 3rd ser., 53 (July 1996): 487–526.

Hoadly, Charles, ed. *The Public Records of the Colony of Connecticut*. Hartford: Case, Lockwood, & Brainard, 1870.

Hudson, Charles. *The Juan Pardo Expeditions: Explorations of the Carolinas and Tennessee, 1566–1568*. Washington DC: Smithsonian Institution Press, 1990.

———. *Knights of Spain, Warriors of the Sun: Hernando de Soto and the South's Ancient Chiefdoms*. Athens: University of Georgia Press, 1997.

———. *The Southeastern Indians*. Knoxville: University of Tennessee Press, 1976.

Hughes, Kaylene. "Populating the Back Country: The Demographic and Social Characteristics of the Colonial South Carolina Frontier, 1730–1760." PhD diss., Florida State University, 1985.

Ivers, Larry E. *Colonial Forts of South Carolina, 1670–1775*. Columbia: University of South Carolina Press, 1970.

———. "Scouting the Inland Passage, 1685–1787." *South Carolina Historical Magazine* 73 (April 1972): 117–29.

Jabbs, Theodore. "The South Carolina Colonial Militia, 1663–1733." PhD diss., University of North Carolina, 1973.

Johnson, David L. "The Yamasee War." MA thesis, University of South Carolina, 1980.

Johnson, George Lloyd, Jr. *The Frontier in the Colonial South: South Carolina Backcountry, 1736–1800*. Westport CT: Greenwood Press, 1997.

Jones, Katherine, ed. *Port Royal under Six Flags*. New York: Bobbs-Merrill, 1963.

Jordan, Winthrop. *White over Black: American Attitudes toward the Negro*. Chapel Hill: University of North Carolina Press, 1968.

Juricek, John T. "American Usage of the Word 'Frontier' from Colonial Times to Frederick Jackson Turner." *Proceedings of the American Philosophical Society* 110 (1966): 10–34.

—————. "English Territorial Claims in North America under Elizabeth and the Early Stuarts." *Terrae Incognitae* 7 (1975): 7–22.

—————, ed. *Georgia Treaties, 1733–1763.* Vol. 11 of *Early American Indian Documents: Treaties and Laws, 1607- 1789,* edited by Alden T. Vaughan. Frederick MD: University Publications of America, 1989.

—————. "Indian Policy in Proprietary South Carolina, 1670–1693." MA thesis: University of Chicago, 1962.

—————. "The Westo Indians." *Ethnohistory* 11 (Winter 1964): 134–73.

Keegan, John. *A History of Warfare.* London: Hutchinson, 1993. Reprint, New York: Vintage Books, 1994.

Kelton, Paul. "The Great Southeastern Smallpox Epidemic, 1696–1700: The Region's First Major Epidemic?" In *The Transformation of the Southeastern Indians, 1540–1760,* edited by Robbie Ethridge and Charles Hudson, 21–38. Jackson: University Press of Mississippi, 2002.

Kennedy, J. P., and H. R. McIlwaine, eds. *Executive Journals of the Council of Colonial Virginia.* Vols. 1–6. Richmond: Virginia State Library, 1925–66. (Cited as EJCCV.)

—————, eds. *Journals of the House of Burgesses of Virginia, 1619–1776.* Vols. 1–13. Richmond: Virginia State Library, 1905–1915. (Cited as JHBV.)

Kirk, Francis Marion. *The Yamasee War of 1715: A Page from South Carolina's Colonial History.* Mount Pleasant SC: Society of Colonial Wars in the State of South Carolina, 1970.

Klingberg, Frank. *An Appraisal of the Negro in Colonial South Carolina.* New York: Associated Publishers, 1941.

—————, ed. *The Carolina Chronicle of Francis Le Jau.* University of California Publications in History, vol. 53. Berkeley: University of California Press, 1956.

—————, ed. *Carolina Chronicle: The Papers of Commissary Gideon Johnston, 1707–1716.* University of California Publications in History, vol. 35. Berkeley: University of California Press, 1946.

—————. "The Indian Frontier in South Carolina as Seen by the S.P.G. Missionary." *Journal of Southern History* 5 (November 1939): 128–65.

—————. "The Mystery of the Lost Yamasee Prince." *South Carolina Historical Magazine* 63 (January 1962): 18–32.

Knight, James Vernon. "The Formation of the Creeks." In *The Forgotten Centuries: Indians and Europeans in the American South, 1521–1704,* edited by Charles Hudson and Carmen Tesser, 373–92. Athens: University of Georgia Press, 1994.

La Harpe, Bernard de. "Historical Journal of the Establishment of the French in Louisiana." Translated by Benjamin F. French. In *Historical Collections of*

Louisiana, vol. 3, edited by Benjamin F. French, 9–118. New York: D. Appleton & Co., 1851.

Landers, Jane. "Black-Indian Interaction in Spanish Florida." *Colonial Latin American Historical Review* 2 (Spring 1993): 141–62.

Lankford, George E. "Red and White: Some Reflections on Southeastern Symbolism." *Southern Folklore* 50 (Spring 1993): 53–80.

Lanning, John Tate. *The Diplomatic History of Georgia: A Study of the Epoch of Jenkins' Ear.* Chapel Hill: University of North Carolina Press, 1936.

————. *The Spanish Missions of Georgia.* Chapel Hill: University of North Carolina Press, 1935.

Lawson, John. *A New Voyage to Carolina.* Edited by Hugh Talmage Lefler. Chapel Hill: University of North Carolina Press, 1967.

Lawson, Murray G. "An Act for the Better Regulation of the Indian Trade, 1714." *Virginia Magazine of History and Biography* 55 (October 1947): 329–32.

Leach, Douglas. *Arms for Empire: A Military History of the British Empire, 1607–1763.* New York: Macmillan, 1973.

————. *Flintlock and Tomahawk: New England in King Philip's War.* New York: Macmillan, 1958.

Lee, Lawrence E. *Indian Wars in North Carolina, 1663–1763.* Raleigh: Carolina Charter Tercentenary Commission, 1963.

Le Fave, Donald. "The Time of the Whitetail: The Charles Town Indian Trade, 1690–1715." *Studies in History and Society* 5 (Fall 1973): 5–15.

Le Gac, Charles. *Immigration and War, Louisiana, 1718–1721.* Edited and translated by Glen R. Conrad. Lafayette: University of Southwestern Louisiana Press, 1970.

Le Maire, Francois. *Mémoire Inédit sur la Louisiane, avec une Introduction de M. le Dr. G. Devron.* New Orleans: L'Athenée Louisianais, 1899.

Le Page du Pratz. *The History of Louisiana; Translated from the French of M. Le Page du Pratz.* Edited by Joseph G. Treagle Jr. Baton Rouge: Louisiana State University Press, 1975.

Lepore, Jill. *The Name of War: King Philip's War and the Origins of American Identity.* New York: Alfred A. Knopf, 1998.

Limerick, Patricia Nelson. *The Legacy of Conquest: The Unbroken Past of the American West.* New York: Norton, 1987.

Littlefield, Daniel. *Africans and Creeks.* Westport CT: Greenwood Press, 1979.

————. *Rice and Slaves: Ethnicity and the Slave Trade in Colonial South Carolina.* Baton Rouge: Louisiana State University Press, 1981.

Lonn, Ella. *The Colonial Agents of the Southern Colonies.* Chapel Hill: University of North Carolina Press, 1945.

Mahon, John K. "Anglo-American Methods of Indian Warfare, 1676–1794." *Mississippi Valley Historical Review* 45 (September 1958): 254–75.

Malone, Patrick. *The Skulking Way of War: Technology and Tactics of the New England Indians*. Baltimore: Johns Hopkins University Press, 1991.

Manross, William. *The Fulham Papers in the Lambeth Palace Library: American Colonial Section, Calendar and Indexes*. Oxford: Clarendon Press, 1965.

Margry, Pierre, ed. *Découvertes et Etablissements des Francais dans l'Ouest et dans le Sud de l'Amerique Septentrionale (1614–1754), Mémoires et Documents Originaux Recuellis et Publiés*. Paris: D. Jaoust, 1886.

Martin, Joel W. *Sacred Revolt: The Muskogees' Struggle for a New World*. Boston: Beacon Press, 1991.

——. "Southeastern Indians and the English Trade in Skins and Slaves." In *The Forgotten Centuries: Indians and Europeans in the American South, 1521–1704*, edited by Charles Hudson and Carmen Chaves Tesser, 304–24. Athens: University of Georgia Press, 1994.

Matter, Robert Alan. "Missions in the Defense of Spanish Florida." *Florida Historical Quarterly* 53 (July 1975): 18–38.

——. *Pre-Seminole Florida: Soldiers, Friars, and Indian Missions, 1513–1763*. New York: Garland, 1990.

McDowell, W. L., ed. *Journals of the Commissioners of the Indian Trade, September 20, 1710–August 29, 1718*. Columbia: South Carolina Archives Department, 1955. (Cited as JCIT.)

McEwan, Bonnie. "San Luis de Talimali: The Archaeology of Spanish-Indian Relations at a Florida Mission." *Historical Archaeology* 25 (Fall 1991): 36–60.

McKivergan, David. "Migration and Settlement among the Yamasee in South Carolina." MA thesis, University of South Carolina, 1991.

Melvoin, Richard I. *New England Outpost: War and Society in Colonial Deerfield*. New York: Norton, 1989.

Menard, Russell. "The Africanization of the Low Country Labor Force, 1670–1738." In *Race and Family in the Colonial South*, edited by Winthrop Jordan and Sheila Skemp, 81–108. Jackson: University Press of Mississippi, 1987.

Meriwether, Robert. *The Expansion of South Carolina, 1729–1765*. Kingsport TN: Southern Publishing, 1941.

Merrell, James H. " 'The Customes of Our Countrey': Indians and Colonists in Early America." In *Strangers within the Realm: Cultural Margins of the First British Empire*, edited by Bernard Bailyn and Philip Morgan, 117–56. Chapel Hill: University of North Carolina Press for the Institute of Early American History and Culture, 1994.

——. *The Indians' New World: Catawbas and Their Neighbors from European Contact through the Era of Removal.* Chapel Hill: University of North Carolina Press for the Institute of Early American History and Culture, 1989.

———. " 'Our Bond of Peace': Patterns of Intercultural Exchange in the Carolina Piedmont, 1650–1750." In *Powhatan's Mantle: Indians in the Colonial Southeast,* edited by Peter Wood, Gregory Waselkov, and M. Thomas Hatley, 196–222. Lincoln: University of Nebraska Press, 1989.

———. " 'Their Very Bones Shall Fight': The Catawba-Iroquois Wars." In *Beyond the Covenant Chain: The Iroquois and Their Neighbors in Indian North America, 1600–1800,* edited by Daniel K. Richter and James H. Merrell, 115–34. Syracuse NY: Syracuse University Press, 1987.

Merrens, Roy, ed. *The Colonial South Carolina Scene: Contemporary Views, 1697–1774.* Columbia: University of South Carolina Press, 1977.

Merrill, William L. "Conversion and Colonialism in Northern Mexico: The Tarahumara Response to the Jesuit Mission Program, 1601–1767." In *Conversion to Christianity: Historical and Anthropological Perspectives on a Great Transformation,* edited by Robert W. Hefner, 129–63. Berkeley: University of California Press, 1993.

Milanich, Jerald T. *Florida Indians and the Invasion from Europe.* Gainesville: University Press of Florida, 1995.

Miller, Christopher L., and George R. Hammell. "A New Perspective on Indian-White Contact: Cultural Symbols and Colonial Trade." *Journal of American History* 73 (Winter 1986–87): 318–22.

Milling, Chapman. *Red Carolinians.* Columbia: University of South Carolina Press, 1969.

Milner, George R. "Epidemic Disease in the Postcontact Southeast: A Reappraisal." *Mid-Continental Journal of Archaeology* 5 (Spring 1980): 39–56.

Montgomery, Sir Robert. *Azilia: A Discourse by Sir Robert Montgomery, 1717, Projecting a Settlement in the Colony Later Known as Georgia.* Edited by Max J. Patrick. Atlanta: Emory University Library, 1948.

Moore, Alexander. "Carolina Whigs: Colleton County Members of the South Carolina Commons House of Assembly, 1692–1720." MA thesis, University of South Carolina, 1981.

———, ed. *Nairne's Muskhogean Journals: The 1708 Expedition to the Mississippi River.* Jackson: University Press of Mississippi, 1988.

———. "Royalizing South Carolina: The Revolution of 1719 and the Transformation of Early South Carolina Government." PhD diss., University of South Carolina, 1991.

Morris, Michael Pate. "The Bringing of Wonder: The Effect of European Trade on the Indians of the Southern Backcountry, 1700–1783." PhD diss., Auburn University, 1993.

Nairne, Thomas. "A Letter from South Carolina." In *Selling a New World: Two Colonial South Carolina Promotional Pamphlets*, edited by Jack P. Greene, 33–76. Columbia: University of South Carolina Press, 1989.

Nash, Gary. "The Image of the Indian in the Southern Colonial Mind." *William and Mary Quarterly*, 3rd ser., 29 (April 1972): 197–230.

———. *Red, White, and Black: The Peoples of Early America*. Englewood Cliffs NJ: Prentice Hall, 1974.

Nobles, Gregory H. *American Frontiers: Cultural Encounters and Continental Conquest*. New York: Hill & Wang, 1997.

———. "Straight Lines and Stability: Mapping the Political Order of the Anglo-American Frontier." *Journal of American History* 80 (June 1993): 9–35.

Norris, John. "Profitable Advice for Rich and Poor." In *Selling a New World: Two Colonial South Carolina Promotional Pamphlets*, edited by Jack P. Greene, 77–147. Columbia: University of South Carolina Press, 1989.

Oglethorpe, James Edward. "A New and Accurate Account of the Provinces of South Carolina and Georgia." In *The Publications of James Edward Oglethorpe*, edited by Rodney M. Baine, 200–240. Athens: University of Georgia Press, 1994.

Oldmixon, Edward. "History of the British Empire in North America." In *Narratives of Early Carolina, 1650–1708*, edited by Alexander Salley, 313–74. New York: Charles Scribner's Sons, 1911.

Otto, John S. "The Origins of Cattle-Ranching in Colonial South Carolina." *South Carolina Historical Magazine* 87 (April 1986): 117–24.

———. *The Southern Frontiers: The Agricultural Evolution of the Colonial and Antebellum South*. New York: Greenwood Press, 1989.

Parramore, Thomas. "With Tuscarora Jack on the Back Path to Bath." *North Carolina Historical Review* 64 (April 1987): 115–38.

Pearson, Fred Lamar, Jr. "Anglo-Spanish Rivalry in the Chattahoochee Basin and West Florida, 1685–1704." *South Carolina Historical Magazine* 79 (January 1978): 50–59.

Peckham, Howard. *The Colonial Wars, 1689–1762*. Chicago: University of Chicago Press, 1964.

Pénicaut, André. *Fleur de Lis and Calumet: Annals of Louisiana from 1698–1732*. Translated by Richebourg McWilliams. Baton Rouge: Louisiana State University Press, 1953.

Pennington, Edgar Legare. "Reverend Francis Le Jau's Work among Indians and Negro Slaves." *Journal of Southern History* 1 (November 1935): 442–58.

———. "The South Carolina Indian War of 1715 as Seen by the Colonial Missionaries." *South Carolina Historical and Genealogical Magazine* 32 (October 1931): 251–69.

Perdue, Theda. "Cherokee Relations with the Iroquois in the Eighteenth Century." In

Beyond the Covenant Chain: The Iroquois and Their Neighbors in Indian North America, 1600–1800, edited by Daniel K. Richter and James H. Merrell, 135–49. Syracuse NY: Syracuse University Press, 1987.

———. Cherokee Women: Gender and Culture Change, 1700–1835. Lincoln: University of Nebraska Press, 1998.

———. Slavery and the Evolution of Cherokee Society, 1540–1866. Knoxville: University of Tennessee Press, 1979.

Phelps, Dawson. "The Chickasaw, the English, and the French, 1699–1744." *Tennessee Historical Quarterly* 16 (June 1957): 117–33.

Porter, Kenneth. "Negroes on the Southern Frontier, 1670–1713." *Journal of Negro History* 33 (October 1948): 53–78.

Quarles, Benjamin. "The Colonial Militia and Negro Manpower." *Mississippi Valley Historical Review* 45 (March 1959): 643–52.

Ramsey, William, " 'All & Singular the Slaves': A Demographic Profile of Indian Slavery in Colonial South Carolina." In *Money, Trade, and Power: The Evolution of Colonial South Carolina's Plantation Society*, edited by Jack P. Greene, Rosemary Brana-Shute, and Randy J. Sparks, 166–86. Columbia: University of South Carolina Press, 2001.

———. " 'Something Cloudy in Their Looks': The Origins of the Yamasee War Reconsidered." *Journal of American History* 90 (June 2003): 44–75.

Rayson, David T. " 'A Great Matter to Tell': Indians, Europeans, and Africans from the Mississippian Era Through the Yamasee War in North American Southeast, 1500–1720." PhD diss., University of Minnesota, 1996.

Reding, Katherine, ed. and trans. "Plans for the Colonization and Defense of Apalachee, 1675." *Georgia Historical Quarterly* 9 (June 1925): 169–75.

Reid, John Philip. *A Better Kind of Hatchet: Law, Trade, and Diplomacy in the Cherokee Nation during the Early Years of European Contact.* University Park: Pennsylvania State University Press, 1976.

Reynolds, Alfred Wade. "The Alabama-Tombigbee Basin in International Relations, 1701–1763." PhD diss., University of California, 1928.

Richter, Daniel K. *The Ordeal of the Longhouse: The Peoples of the Iroquois League in the Era of European Colonization.* Chapel Hill: University of North Carolina Press for the Institute of Early American History and Culture, 1992.

Richter, Daniel K., and James H. Merrell, eds. *Beyond the Covenant Chain: The Iroquois and Their Neighbors in Indian North America, 1600–1800.* Syracuse NY: Syracuse University Press, 1987.

Rivers, William. *A Sketch of the History of South Carolina to the Close of the Proprietary Government by the Revolution of 1719.* Charleston SC: McCarter, 1856.

Robinson, W. Stitt, Jr. "Virginia and the Cherokees: Indian Policy from Spotswood to

Dinwiddie." In *The Old Dominion: Essays for Thomas Perkins Abernathy*, edited by
Darrett Rutman, 21–40. Charlottesville: University Press of Virginia, 1964.

———. *Virginia Treaties, 1607–1722*. Vol. 4 of *Early American Indian Documents: Treaties
and Laws, 1607–1789*, edited by Alden T. Vaughn. Frederick MD: University
Publications of America, 1983.

Rothrock, Mary. "Carolina Traders among the Overhill Cherokees, 1670–1770." *East
Tennessee Historical Society Publications* 1 (January 1929): 3–18.

Rowland, Dunbar, and A. G. Sanders, eds. *Mississippi Provincial Archives, French
Dominion, 1704–1743*. Vols. 1–3. Jackson: Press of the Mississippi
Department of Archives and History, 1927–32. (Cited as MPAFD.)

Rowland, Lawrence Sanders, Alexander Moore, and George C. Rogers. *The History of
Beaufort County, South Carolina*. Vol. 1, 1514–1861. Columbia: University of
South Carolina Press, 1996.

Salley, Alexander. "The Creek Indian Tribes in 1725." *South Carolina Historical and
Genealogical Magazine* 32 (July 1931): 241–42.

———, ed. *Journal of Colonel John Herbert, Commissioner of Indian Affairs for the Province of
South Carolina, October 17, 1727, to March 19, 1727–28*. Columbia: State, 1936.

———, ed. *Journals of the Commons House of Assembly of South Carolina*. 21 vols.
Columbia: Historical Commission of South Carolina, 1907–49. (Cited as
JCHASC.)

———, ed. *Journal of the Grand Council of South Carolina*. Columbia: Historical
Commission of South Carolina, 1907.

———, ed. *Narratives of Early Carolina, 1650–1708*. New York: Charles Scribner's &
Sons, 1911.

———, ed. *Records in the British Public Record Office Relating to South Carolina, 1663–1776*.
Vols. 1–5. Transcribed by W. Noel Sainsbury. Columbia: Historical
Commission of South Carolina, 1947.

Sainsbury, W. Noel, ed. *Journal of His Majesty's Council for South Carolina, May 29,
1721–June 10, 1721*. Atlanta: Foote & Davies Co., 1930.

Sainsbury, W. Noel, J. W. Fortescue, and Cecil Headlam, eds. *Calendar of State Papers,
Colonial Section, America and West Indies*. Vols. 12–37. London: Her Majesty's
Stationery Office, 1860–1919. (Cited as CSP.)

Saunders, William L., ed. *The Colonial Records of North Carolina*. Vols. 1–4. Raleigh: P. M.
Hale, 1886–90. (Cited as CRNC.)

Seed, Patricia. "Taking Possession and Reading Texts: Establishing the Authority of
Overseas Empires." *William and Mary Quarterly*, 3rd ser., 49 (April 1992):
183–209.

Serraño y Sanz, Manuel, ed. *Documentos historicos de la Florida y la Luisiana, siglos XVI al
XVIII*. Madrid, 1912.

Service, Elman R. *Primitive Social Organization: An Evolutionary Perspective*. New York: Random House, 1962.

Sherman, Richard. *Robert Johnson: Proprietary and Royal Governor of South Carolina*. Columbia: University of South Carolina Press, 1966.

Silver, Timothy. *A New Face on the Countryside: Indians, Colonists, and Slaves in South Atlantic Forests, 1500–1800*. New York: Cambridge University Press, 1990.

Simms, William Gilmore. *The Yemassee: A Romance of Carolina*. New York: Harper & Brothers, 1835.

Sirmans, M. Eugene. *Colonial South Carolina: A Political History, 1663–1763*. Chapel Hill: University of North Carolina Press, 1966.

Smith, Louis R. "South Carolina's Indian Trade Regulations, 1670–1756." MA thesis, University of North Carolina, 1968.

Smith, Marvin. "Aboriginal Depopulation in the Postcontact Southeast." In *The Forgotten Centuries: Indians and Europeans in the American South, 1521–1704*, edited by Charles Hudson and Carmen Tesser, 257–75. Athens: University of Georgia Press, 1994.

———. *Coosa: The Rise and Fall of a Southeastern Mississippian Chiefdom*. Gainesville: University Press of Florida, 2000.

Snell, William. "Indian Slavery in Colonial South Carolina, 1671–1795." PhD diss., University of Alabama, 1972.

Sonderegger, Richard. "The Southern Frontier from the Founding of Georgia to King George's War." PhD diss., University of Michigan, 1964.

Spalding, Billups Phinizy. "Georgia and South Carolina during the Oglethorpe Period, 1732–1743." PhD diss., University of North Carolina, 1963.

———. "South Carolina and Georgia: The Early Days." *South Carolina Historical Magazine* 69 (April 1968): 83–96.

Spotswood, Alexander. *The Official Letters of Alexander Spotswood*. 2 vols. Edited by Robert A. Brock. Richmond: Virginia Historical Society, 1882–85.

Steele, Ian K. *Warpaths: Invasions of North America*. New York: Oxford University Press, 1994.

Stumpf, Stuart Owen. "The Merchants of Colonial Charles Town, 1680–1756." PhD diss., Michigan State University, 1971.

Swanton, John R. *Early History of the Creek Indians and Their Neighbors*. Washington DC: U.S. Government Printing Office, 1922.

———. *Indians of the Southeastern United States*. Washington DC: U.S. Government Printing Office, 1946.

———. *Social Organization and Social Uses of the Indians of the Creek Confederacy*. The 42nd Annual Report of the Bureau of American Ethnology. Washington DC: U.S. Government Printing Office, 1924–25.

―――. "Social Significance of the Creek Confederacy." *Proceedings of the International Congress of Americanists* 19 (1917): 327–34.

Te Paske, John Jay. "The Fugitive Slave: Intercolonial Rivalry and Spanish Slave Policy, 1697–1764." In *Eighteenth-Century Florida and Its Borderlands*, edited by Samuel Proctor, 1–2. Gainesville: University Press of Florida, 1975.

―――. *The Governorship of Spanish Florida, 1700–1763*. Durham NC: Duke University Press, 1964.

Thomas, Daniel. "Fort Toulouse: The French Outpost at the Alibamas on the Coosa." *Alabama Historical Quarterly* 22 (Fall 1960): 141–230.

Thomas, Samuel. "Documents Concerning Rev. Samuel Thomas, 1702–1707." *South Carolina Historical and Genealogical Magazine* 5 (January 1904): 21–55.

―――. "Letters of Rev. Samuel Thomas, 1707–1710." *South Carolina Historical and Genealogical Magazine* 4 (July 1903): 278–85.

Turner, Frederick Jackson. *History, Frontier and Section: Three Essays by Frederick Jackson Turner*. Introduction by Martin Ridge. Albuquerque: University of New Mexico Press, 1993.

Usner, Daniel. *Indians, Settlers, and Slaves in a Frontier Exchange Economy: The Lower Mississippi Valley before 1783*. Chapel Hill: University of North Carolina Press for the Institute of Early American History and Culture, 1992.

Utley, Robert M., and Wilcomb E. Washburn. *Indian Wars*. New York: American Heritage Press, 1985.

Vassar, Rena, ed. "Some Short Remarkes on the Indian Trade in the Charikees and the Management thereof since the Year 1717." *Ethnohistory* 8 (Fall 1961): 401–23.

Vaughan, Alden T. "From White Man to Redskin: Changing Anglo-American Perceptions of the American Indian." *American Historical Review* 87 (Fall 1982): 917–53.

Vaughan, Alden T., and Deborah A. Rosen, eds. *Carolina and Georgia Laws*. Vol. 16 of *Early American Indian Documents: Treaties and Laws, 1607–1789*, edited by Alden T. Vaughan. Frederick MD: University Publications of America, 1998.

Waddell, Gene. *Indians of the South Carolina Lowcountry, 1582–1751*. Spartanburg SC: Reprint Co.: 1980.

Ward, Harry. *Unite or Die: Inter-Colony Relations, 1690–1793*. New York: Kennikat Press, 1971.

Waselkov, Gregory. "Historic Creek Indian Responses to European Trade and the Rise of Political Factions." In *Ethnohistory and Archaeology: Approaches to Postcontact Change in the Americas*, edited by J. Daniel Rogers and Samuel M. Wilson, 123–31. New York: Plenum Press, 1993.

―――. "Indian Maps of the Colonial Southeast." In *Powhatan's Mantle: Indians in the Colonial Southeast*, edited by Peter Wood, Gregory Waselkov, and M. Thomas Hatley, 292–343. Lincoln: University of Nebraska Press, 1989.

————. "Seventeenth-Century Trade in the Colonial Southeast." *Southeastern Archaeology* 8 (Winter 1989): 117–33.

Waselkov, Gregory, and John Cottier. "European Perceptions of Eastern Muskogean Ethnicity." *Proceedings of the Annual Meeting of the French Colonial Historical Society* 10 (1984): 23–45.

Washburn, Wilcomb E. *The Indian in America.* New York: Harper & Row, 1975.

Webb, Stephen Saunders. "The Strange Career of Francis Nicholson." *William and Mary Quarterly,* 3rd ser., 23 (October 1966): 513–48.

Weber, David J. *The Spanish Frontier in North America.* New Haven CT: Yale University Press, 1992.

Weir, Robert. *Colonial South Carolina: A History.* Millwood NY: KTO Press, 1983.

Wells, Robin. "Frontier Systems as a Socio-Cultural Type." *Papers in Anthropology* 14 (Spring 1973): 6–15.

Wenhold, Lucy, ed. "A 17th Century Letter of Gabriel Diaz Vara Calderón, Bishop of Cuba, Describing the Indians and Indian Missions of Florida." In *The Missions of Spanish Florida,* edited by David Hurst Thomas, 105–18. New York: Garland, 1991.

West, Elliott. "The American Frontier: Romance and Reality." In *William Gilmore Simms and the American Frontier,* edited by John Caldwell Guilds and Carolina Caldwell, 27–43. Athens: University of Georgia Press, 1994.

White, Richard. *"It's Your Misfortune and None of My Own": A New History of the American West.* Norman: University of Oklahoma Press, 1991.

————. *The Middle Ground: Indians, Empires, and Republics in the Great Lakes Region, 1650–1815.* New York: Cambridge University Press, 1991.

————. *The Roots of Dependency: Subsistence, Environment, and Social Change among the Choctaws, Pawnees, and Navajos.* Lincoln: University of Nebraska Press, 1983.

Widmer, J. Randolph. "The Structure of Southeastern Chiefdoms." In *The Forgotten Centuries: Indians and Europeans in the American South, 1521–1704,* edited by Charles Hudson and Carmen Tesser, 125–55. Athens: University of Georgia Press, 1994.

Willis, William S., Jr. "Anthropology and Negroes on the Southern Colonial Frontier." In *The Black Experience in America,* edited by James C. Curtis and Lewis L. Gould, 33–50. Austin: University of Texas Press, 1970.

————. "Colonial Conflict and the Cherokee Indians, 1710–1760." PhD diss., Columbia University, 1955.

————. "Divide and Rule: Red, White, and Black in the Southeast." *Journal of Negro History* 48 (July 1963): 157–76.

Wood, Peter H. *Black Majority: Negroes in South Carolina from 1670 through the Stono Rebellion.* New York: Norton, 1974.

————. "The Changing Population of the Colonial South: An Overview by Race and

Region." In *Powhatan's Mantle: Indians in the Colonial Southeast*, edited by Peter Wood, Gregory Waselkov, and M. Thomas Hatley, 35–103. Lincoln: University of Nebraska Press, 1989.

———. "Circles in the Sand: Perspectives on the Southern Frontier at the Arrival of James Oglethorpe." In *Oglethorpe in Perspective: Georgia's Frontier After 200 Years*, edited by Phinizy Spalding and Harvey Jackson, 5–21. Tuscaloosa: University of Alabama Press, 1989.

———. "The Impact of Smallpox on the Native Population of the Eighteenth-Century Colonial South." *New York State Journal of Medicine* 87 (January 1987): 30–36.

Woods, Patricia. *French-Indian Relations on the Southern Frontier, 1699–1762*. Ann Arbor: University of Michigan Press, 1980.

Worster, Donald. "New West, True West: Interpreting the Region's History." *Western Historical Quarterly* 18 (Spring 1987): 141–56.

Worth, John E. *The Struggle for the Georgia Coast: An 18th-Century Spanish Retrospective of Guale and Mocama*. Anthropological Papers of the American Museum of Natural History, vol. 75. New York: American Museum of Natural History, 1995.

———. *Timucuan Chiefdoms of Spanish Florida*. Vol. 1, *Assimilation*. Gainesville: University Press of Florida, 1998.

Wraxall, Peter. *An Abridgement of Indian Affairs, Contained in Four Folio Volumes, transacted in the Colony of New York, from the Year 1678 to the Year 1751*. Edited with an introduction by Charles H. McIlwain. Cambridge MA: Harvard University Press, 1915.

Wright, J. Leitch, Jr. *The Only Land They Knew: The Tragic Story of Indians in the Old South*. New York: Free Press, 1981.

Yonge, Francis. "Narrative of the Proceeding of the People of South Carolina in the Year 1719." In *Historical Collections of South Carolina: Embracing Many Rare and Valuable Pamphlets, and Other Documents, Relating to the History of That State, From Its First Discovery to Its Independence, in the Year 1776*, edited by Bartholomew Carroll, vol. 2. New York: Harper & Brothers, 1836.

———. "A View of the Trade of South Carolina, With Proposals Humbly Offered for Improving the Same." In *The Colonial South Carolina Scene: Contemporary Views, 1697–1774*, edited by Roy Merrens, 68–74. Columbia: University of South Carolina Press, 1977.

Index

Boone, Joseph, 163
Boston News-Letter, 156
Bray, William, 124, 125
Broughton, Thomas, 181, 296
Bryan, Hugh, 179
buffer zone: South Carolina's perceptions of, 83, 110–11, 112, 142; weaknesses in, 114–15
Bull, William, Sr., 293
Burroughs, Seymour, 125, 126, 182
Byrd, William, I, 75
Byrd, William, II, 86, 115–16, 134, 156

Cabrera, Juan, 28
Caesar of Echota, 186–87, 190, 191, 193, 236
Cardross, Henry, 26, 28
Carlos II, 40
Carolina. *See* South Carolina
Cary's Rebellion, 85
Catawba Indians: acceptance of refugee groups of, 201–2, 303; alliance with South Carolina of, 197–202; attack on Savannah refugees by, 59, 77; and early relations with South Carolina, 77–78; and Indian slavery, 133; raided by Iroquois Indians, 77, 132, 200; relations with Virginia of, 77–78, 134, 161, 196, 198; relations with Yamasee and Ochese Indians of, 135, 196; trade abuse among, 134; in Tuscarora War, 87–88; in Yamasee War, 137–38, 196–97. *See also* Piedmont Indians
censuses: of Florida Indians, 60, 180; of South Carolina's Indian allies, 112; of South Carolina's Indian enemies, 112–13
Charitey Hagey, 187, 190, 191, 193, 194, 235
Charles Town peace conference, 252–54, 276–77
Chatot Indians, 40
Cheraw Indians, 137, 197–98. *See also* Piedmont Indians
Cherokee Indians: alliance with South Carolina of, 186, 189–95, 255–58; attacked by Creek Indians, 223–24; at Charles Town peace conference, 252–54; divisions among, 79; early relations with

South Carolina of, 78–79; and embassy to Britain, 260–61; and first encounters with Europeans, 78; and Indian slavery, 133; and Indian trade, 190–91, 229, 257; and missions of George Chicken, 237–47, 250–51; raids on Creek Indians by, 189–90, 193, 245, 248; and relations with Illinois Indians, 185, 236, 257–58; and relations with Louisiana, 258; and relations with Virginia, 80, 134, 192, 194; and relations with Yamasee Indians, 135–36; and slave raid on Yuchis, 100–101; trade abuse among, 134, 190; and Tugaloo massacre, 188–89; in Yamasee War, 136–37, 184–95
Cherokeeleechee, 207, 217, 264, 270, 271, 272, 276, 277, 284, 285, 297
Chestowe affair, 100–101, 134
Chickasaw Indians: and Indian slave trade, 62, 64–65; as refugees among Cherokees, 235; as refugees in South Carolina, 235, 255, 282; and relations with Choctaw Indians, 62–63, 234–35; and relations with Creek Indians, 246, 248; and relations with Louisiana, 68–69, 71; and relations with South Carolina, 62, 68–69, 104, 235; in Yamasee War, 205
Chicken, George: death of, 256; first mission to Cherokees, 237–47; second mission to Cherokees, 250–51; in Yamasee War, 138, 145, 186
chiefdoms, 15
Chigelly, 249–50, 251, 253–54, 255, 276–77, 281, 282, 285, 286
Child, James, 15
Choatehee, 256
Choctaw-Chickasaw War, 234–35, 246, 302–3
Choctaw Indians: and relations with Chickasaw Indians, 62–63, 234–35; and relations with Louisiana, 63, 68–69, 129, 235
clans, 15, 97
Cofitachique, 73
Coleman, John, 230
Committee on Indian Affairs, 230, 257, 286

fortifications: of Catawba Indians, 201; of Cherokee Indians, 236; of Lower Creek Indians, 207; of South Carolinians, 52, 145, 147–49, 225–26, 266–68; of Tuscarora Indians, 90; of Yamasee Indians, 178, 268

Fort Christanna, 160, 200

Fort King George: construction of, 267–68, 301; controversy between South Carolina and Florida, 272–75; destruction of, 275, 277–78

Fort Moore, 148, 151, 246, 252

Fort Neoheroka, 90

Fort San Carlos, 216

Fort San Marcos, 28, 47–48, 284, 301

Fort San Marcos de Apalachee, 218, 266, 269

Fort Toulouse, 215, 234, 243, 266, 301

Franciscans, 16–17, 93

Fraser, John, 124

French. See Louisiana

frontiers: definition of, 4–7; in North American Southeast, 308–10

frontier complex, 7–8

Gale, Christopher, 86

Gallay, Alan, 5

George I, 162, 271

George II, 261, 290

Georgia: founding of, 288, 291; and Indian trade, 293, 296; relations with Florida, 291; relations with Lower Creek Indians, 291; relations with South Carolina, 293–94, 296

Gilcrest, Robert, 185

Glover, Charlesworth, 279–82, 285–86

Goggle Eyes. See Steyamasiechie

Goose Creek men, 35, 53, 232

Grant, Ludovick, 260

Green Corn Ceremony, 210

Guale Indians: dispersal from missions of, 22; revolts against Spanish of, 24

Hart, Charles, 104

Hassell, Thomas, 168

Hastings, Theophilus, 70, 186, 210, 230, 237, 269, 271

Hatton, William, 191–92, 194, 223–24, 236–37, 256

Hearn, John, 137

Herbert, John, 186, 238, 256

Hughes, Meredith, 198

Hughes, Pryce, 129, 238

Hunter, Robert, 156, 200

Huspah King, 179, 181, 268

Illinois Indians, 185, 236

imperialism: in British empire, 162–63, 165, 225–26, 261–63, 302, 305–6; in South Carolina, 42, 76, 80–82, 87, 142, 155, 165, 225–26, 227, 232, 233–34, 263, 273–75, 286, 294, 302, 305, 309

indentured servants: association with slaves, 169; importation of, 106, 148, 169; opposition to, 169

Indian alliances: of Ocheses, 120–22, 203–6; role in Yamasee War, 123; of Yamasees, 113

Indian factionalism: among Abeikas, 244; among Catawbas, 137; among Cherokees, 136, 186, 193, 233, 242–43, 258; among Lower Creeks, 209, 220–21, 233, 243–44; among Tallapoosas, 244; among Yamasees, 126, 306

Indian politics, 55–56, 97, 240, 242–43

Indian slavery, 21–22, 53, 64–65, 84, 88–90, 100, 102, 107–8, 109, 110, 117, 122, 152, 303

Indian trade: and alcohol, 36–37, 102, 153; and cultural conflict, 73–74, 98–99; embargo of, 281–82, 285–86; and firearms, 23, 25, 208–9; impact on Native cultures of, 19–20, 36–37, 64–65, 229–30; and imperial defense, 53–55, 142; and indebtedness, 102, 115, 151, 230; public monopoly of, 150–55; regulation of, 38, 46, 53–55, 228, 229–32, 296; role in South Carolina economy, 96, 149–50; role of Indian women in, 97; and Yamasee War, 150–55, 190–91, 198

repartmiento, 25, 48
Rodd, George, 140, 167, 175
Royal African Company, 106

Saint Augustine: Indian raids on, 182–83, 271; South Carolinian raids on, 182–83, 283–85; siege of, 47–48
Salkehatchie fight, 126, 144, 178
San Luis de Talimali, 30
Santee Indians, 52, 197
Savannah Indians: flight from South Carolina by, 59–60; and war with Westo Indians, 23; in Yamasee War, 204
Savannah Town, 148
Schenkingh's garrison, 138
scout boats, 145, 147, 267–68, 283, 286–87
Seneca Indians, 89
Sepeycoffee, 218, 221, 243, 249, 271
Seven Years War, 296, 297
Sharp, John, 223–24, 236, 238
Simms, William Gilmore, 2, 299
slavery: economic value of, 106; government concern over, 290, 294–95, 303; legal codes, 34–35, 106; oppressiveness of, 107. See also Indian slavery
slaves: as fugitives from South Carolina, 33–35, 174, 244, 274, 277, 295; importation of, 106, 171, 294–95, 303; manumission of, 172; rebellions of, 108–9, 173–74, 295–96; relations with Indians of, 172–74, 244, 274, 277; religious conversions of, 107–8, 171, 295; sent to Virginia, 158–59; in South Carolina army, 146; in South Carolina militia, 107, 146, 170
Smallwood, Matthew, 268, 277
Smith, George, 32
Smith, Marvin T., 15
Society for the Propagation of the Gospel in Foreign Parts (SPG): arrival in South Carolina of, 91–92; and efforts at slave conversion, 107–8, 295; and efforts at trade reform, 94–95; interaction with Indians of, 93–94, 95, 227–28; and reactions to Yamasee War, 168
Sothel, Seth, 35
South Carolina: assistance from other colonies for, 157–62; conflicts with Spanish Florida, 21, 28, 39–41, 165, 272–75, 277; diplomacy with Indians, 37–38, 46–47, 53–60, 65–66, 104, 186–189, 193, 209–13, 232–34, 237–58, 263, 268–72, 279–82; economy of, 96, 105, 149–50, 266, 289, 293–94; emigration from, 167; founding of, 12; government changes in, 146; immigration to, 169, 289, 294; and Indian trade, 23, 30, 35–38, 46, 53–55, 96, 100–105, 150–55, 208–9, 228, 257, 281–82; petitions to royal government, 162–63; relations with Georgia, 293–94; relations with Virginia, 74–78, 80, 135, 158–62, 198, 228, 234; slavery in, 105–9, 169–171; and Township Scheme, 288, 290, 294; in Tuscarora War, 87–91; in Yamasee War, 127–28, 137–39, 140–41, 167–69, 299–310
South Carolina army, 146–47, 279
South Carolina militia: in Queen Anne's War, 52, 107; slaves in, 107, 146; in Yamasee War, 128, 138, 143–45, 146, 282–83
Spanish. See Florida
Spotswood, Alexander, 80, 86, 93, 131, 135, 156, 157, 158–60, 165, 198, 200, 214
Stanyarne, James, 46
Steyamasiechie, 240, 271, 283
Stono Rebellion, 295–96, 303
Stuart's Town: competition with South Carolina, 27–28; destruction of, 28; establishment of, 26

Tallapoosa Indians: and mission of Charlesworth Glover, 280; and missions of Tobias Fitch, 239–40, 243–45; politics among, 55–56; raids on Pensacola by, 70–71; raids on Yamasee Indians by, 269–70, 271; and relations with Florida, 216, 217–18; in Yamasee War, 128, 130–31, 205. See also Upper Creek Indians
talwa, 57
Teguale, 218
territorial claims, 273–74
Texas, 214

Thomas, Samuel, 93
Tickhoneby, 270
Timucuan Indians: attacked by Yamasees, 44, 60; and Florida missions, 18–19, 44
Tixjana, 218
Tohome Indians, 129
Tomochichi, 291–92
de Tonti, Henri, 62
trade. *See* Indian trade
treaties: between British empire and Cherokee Indians, 261–62; between Georgia and Lower Creek Indians, 292; between South Carolina and Cherokee Indians, 186; between South Carolina and Creek Indians, 57–58, 211–13
Treaty of Madrid (1670), 21, 273
Treaty of Utrecht, 81
Tuckabatchee, 57
Tuckabatchee council, 249–50
Tuckseegee council, 250–51
Tugaloo: attacked by Creeks, 223–24; massacre in, 188–89, 246
Turner, Frederick Jackson, 4
Tuscarora Indians: enslavement of, 88, 90; merger with Iroquois Indians, 90; relations with North Carolina, 84–85; in Tuscarora War, 86–89; in Yamasee War, 146, 158
Tuscarora War: first South Carolina expedition in, 87–89; outbreak of, 85–86; outcome of, 90–91; second South Carolina expedition in, 89–90; and Yamasee War, 135, 136

Upper Creek Indians: and relations with Lower Creek Indians, 249, 250, 280; and relations with South Carolina, 244; and war with Cherokees, 245
Urmstone, Jonathan, 132, 156
usinjulo, 123

Varnod, Francis, 227–28
Varona, Salinas, 130, 218
Virginia: and frontier defense, 160; and Indian trade, 74–76, 78, 161, 234; in Queen Anne's War, 76; and relations

with South Carolina, 74–78, 80, 135, 137, 158–62, 198, 228, 234; in Tuscarora War, 86
von Clausewitz, Carl, 304

Waccamaw Indians, 174, 199. *See also* Piedmont Indians
warfare: European views of, 9, 244, 255; Indian views of, 9, 70, 235–236, 255
War of the Quadruple Alliance, 216
Warner, Samuel, 124
Waxhaw Indians, 137, 197. *See also* Piedmont Indians
Welch, Thomas, 62, 65–66, 238
Westo Indians: and alliance with South Carolina, 21–22; as refugees, 38; and war with South Carolina, 23
Wiggan, Eleazar, 100–101, 153, 161, 185, 257
Winyah garrison, 151, 153, 198
Wood, Peter, 106
Woodward, Henry, 23, 31, 62
Worth, John, 229, 236
Wragg, Samuel, 289
Wright, John, 101, 103, 125, 126

Yahoulakee, 292
Yamacraw Indians, 291–92
Yamasee Indians: and alliance with Spanish Florida, 179–80; demographic decline of, 284; ecological crises among, 116–17; and Indian slave trade, 88, 117–18; and migration to Altamaha River, 178; and migration to Saint Augustine, 179–80; origins of, 25; and Pocotaligo massacre, 1, 125; raided by Creek Indians, 269, 271; raided by South Carolinians, 182, 283–84; raids on Florida missions by, 44, 47, 60; raids on South Carolina by, 182, 277–78, 283; and relations with Creek Indians, 58, 120, 179, 183, 268, 276–77; and relations with Stuart's Town, 26–27; and relocation to Cuba and Mexico, 298; and residence at Fort San Marcos de Apalachee, 269; as slave hunters, 37, 107; and South Carolina government, 58–59, 124, 268; towns of,

59; trade abuse among, 99, 115–16; in Tuscarora War, 87–89; in Yamasee War, 124–27, 177–84

"Yamasee prince," 95

Yamasee War: casualties of Indians in, 138, 144–45, 178, 300; casualties of South Carolinians in, 126, 127–28, 137–38, 144, 167, 300; and colonial captives, 179, 208; comparison to Florida uprisings, 119; comparison to other Indian wars, 135, 304–5; and conspiracy myth, 10, 113, 123–24, 127, 306–7; and desertion, 145–46, 167; effects on imperial competition, 301; effects on Indian trade, 150–55; effects on settlement patterns, 300; effects on South Carolina economy, 149–50, 167; effects on South Carolina government, 146, 162–66; and Indian slavery, 117–18, 152; and inter-colonial relations, 155–62, 305; military tactics in, 144–45; outbreak of, 126–27; psychological impact of, 167–69, 175, 278, 287, 300, 309–10; reactions of British colonies to, 156–57; role of French Louisiana in, 129–30; role of Spanish Florida in, 130–31; South Carolina militia in, 143–45; South Carolina scout boats in, 145, 283, 286–87

Yemasee, The, 2, 299

Yfallaquisca, 126, 131

Yoa King, 179

Yonge, Francis, 165, 266

Yuchi Indians, 21, 100, 269